A Mirror to Life:
A HISTORY
OF WESTERN
THEATRE

A Mirror to Life:
A HISTORY OF WESTERN THEATRE

B. DONALD GROSE
University of Massachusetts-Boston

O. FRANKLIN KENWORTHY
*Indiana University-Purdue University
at Fort Wayne*

HOLT, RINEHART AND WINSTON
New York   Chicago   San Francisco   Philadelphia
Montreal   Toronto   London   Sydney
Tokyo   Mexico City   Rio de Janeiro   Madrid

Publisher: Susan Katz
Acquisitions Editor: Anne Boynton-Trigg
Project Editors: Melanie Miller and Biodun Iginla
Production Managers: Lula Als and Annette Mayeski
Design Supervisor: Robert Kopelman
Text and Cover Designer: Suzanne Bennett

Library of Congress Cataloging in Publication Data

Grose, B. Donald, 1943-
    A mirror to life.

    Bibliography: p.
    Includes index
        1. Theater—History. 2. Drama—History and criticism.
I. Kenworthy, O. Franklin. II. Title.
PN2101.G76   1984   792'.09   84-4646

ISBN 0-03-062146-1

Address correspondence to:
383 Madison Avenue
New York, N.Y. 10017
All rights reserved
Printed in the United States of America
Published simultaneously in Canada
5 6 7 8 016 9 8 7 6 5 4 3 2 1

CBS COLLEGE PUBLISHING
Holt, Rinehart and Winston
The Dryden Press
Saunders College Publishing

to Rosemary and Gay Ann

CONTENTS

x

Contents

PREFACE

"I say the stage is 'the Mirror of Nature'
and the actors are 'the Abstract, the brief
Chronicles of the Times'—and pray what
can a man of sense study better?"

Richard Sheridan, The Critic

And so indeed the theatre is a mirror to nature, a mirror to the life and times, the fools and follies of humanity. To study the history of the theatre is to examine the reflections in the mirror of the stage in an effort to make a connection with the original audience, a connection that allows a brief entry into another time and place in Western civilization. For the theatre, unlike any other art form, has always represented the largest collective expression of social consciousness at any particular period in history. To see the theatre as both a reflector and enforcer of social values is the guiding theme of this book, and it is the hope of its authors that it will assist the reader in discovering how the stage has been an intrinsic part of Western society, a mirror to the strutting players on the stage of history.

In the mirror of the stage, audiences saw themselves as they thought they were, as they wished they were, as they knew they were, or combinations of the three. It is the task of the theatre historian to examine these reflections from the past for what they tell of that culture and to interpret their significance for the present. From a study of the productions, actors, playscripts, audiences, and playhouses of a given period, it is possible to gain an important insight into what ordered, informed, and governed the social behavior of a period. To understand the popularity of a particular work on the stage is to begin to understand something of the cultural totality of the work's original audience members. The theatre, far from being an isolated art form, is truly a time machine to the past.

The object of any work of history should be to make intelligible, in their own terms, aspects of the past, and to show their importance to both the period in question and to the periods that came after. With this in mind, this book has been arranged to trace the major developments of and contributors to Western theatre in their cultural contexts with an eye to discovering how what happened did happen. As is necessary in a book covering such a large expanse of human history, exclusions abound among those who have contributed to the development of the theatre. The ordering of the material is in a general chronological pattern, but allusions to and amplification of key concepts throughout several chapters should assist in the formation of the overall frame of reference that is necessary for a humanistic understanding of the theatre.

We wish to acknowledge the help we have received in writing this book. Foremost is the immense obligation we owe to a vast array of theatre, literary, and historical scholars whose specialized studies have so greatly aided us in our work. Our grateful acknowledgments to those individuals, libraries, and special collections that aided us in acquiring illustrations: Stephen M. Archer, Paul M. Bailey, Søren Dyssegaard, Suzanne Embree, David Gillison, Dieter Kaisenberg, Louwrens Langevoort, Margareta Paul, Ruben Silver, Bob Taylor, Dorothy L. Swerdlove, the Danish Embassy, the Swedish Embassy, the National Museum of Fine Arts (Stockholm), the National Portrait Gallery, the Theatre Arts Library, Harry Ransom Humanities Research Center, the University of Texas at Austin, the New York Public Library, and the Theatre Collection of the Museum of the City of New York. To Elmer Denman and Kay Pylant our thanks for their assistance in photo and manuscript preparation, and a special thank you to our editor, Anne Boynton-Trigg, and her staff. Finally, we wish to thank our reviewers whose comments and observations kept the book on track: Wayne H. Claeren, Jacksonville State University; Roger Manvell, Boston University; Frank C. Mohler II, University of Virginia; Richard H. Palmer, College of William and Mary; and Louis E. Roberts, University of Massachusetts, Harbor Campus.

EDFU ●

PART I

A Mirror Conceived: THEATRICAL BEGINNINGS

INTRODUCTION

At its most basic level theatre history seeks to describe the theatre as it existed in each age and to show the changes that took place through the centuries. Yet the theatre is a complex institution, made up of several collaborative arts. Thus theatre history involves the study of the history of play writing, acting, and directing, as well as theatre architecture, scenography, stage machinery, props, lights, costumes, makeup, and the audience. These aspects will be reviewed not only in light of their artistic considerations, but also against their social context, since so much of the theatre is a reflection of the economic and intellectual climate in which it exists. For theatre history is a miniature view, a microcosm, of human history to be studied and enjoyed as a significant part of human existence.

There are many specific reasons for the study of theatre history. For the person who intends to make the theatre either a vocation or an active avocation, the reasons are most clear. Much of what goes into the practice of modern theatre has its roots in the past, and the modern portrayal of a role from antiquity or the creation of a modern setting along classical lines demands a certain knowledge of the period being presented. In addition to this direct transference of theatre history to the modern stage, today's theatre practitioner does little that is not rooted in the theatrical past. An appreciation and knowledge of these origins can contribute to an artistically sound modern production.

For the person who does not contemplate an active involvement in the theatre, the study of theatre history has other values. Because it is a microcosm of human experience, theatre history can provide insights into other areas of human activity. Economic, social, political, intellectual, and cultural aspects of life are all reflected in the mirror of the theatre, and such reflections grant a deeper understanding of various periods of human history. There is no other art form that so deeply portrays the totality of life around it and can show through its study a capsulated view of that life. The follies and fancies, the gore and glory of human adventure are all passing shapes in that mirror of life, the theatre.

1
THE EMERGENCE
OF THEATRE

It is unlikely that anyone will ever know just how the theatre emerged. Many theories are advanced, each rooted in a particular view of the relationship between humanity and the need for cultural expression. Yet from these various theories common themes emerge. Two will be examined here: the first is that theatre, in its most basic forms, seems to be an essential art, and second, that the origins of theatre lay in primeval religious rites.

Humanity and the Mimetic Influence

Some theories of the drama argue that the experience of theatre is not an essential one at all, yet an examination of the place of theatrical activity in the lives of most societies does not support this view. A few observations can be made from traditional, nonindustrial societies of today, but more fundamental conclusions can be drawn from the behavior of children (parallels to "primitive" tribes notwithstanding). Consider children's behavior. Without instruction, they seem to need to "act" or behave occasionally like something other than themselves and to know how to do it. No parent or peer forces this behavior; it is innate; hence, the influence of the mimetic in our lives. And the tools of the actor's craft are there also—as soon as the child is old enough, and occasionally before language is mastered, costumes and props are added in addition to makeup, so that the personification is complete. With the addition of these elements, it is only a short step to the formal actor's art, yet without identifying it as such. As we mature it becomes socially unacceptable for us to fulfill this basic need, so we must pay to have it fulfilled vicariously in the formal theatre; but that does not lessen or obviate the need. The human species continually tries to gain insights into its existence and to bring order into a disorderly world. To do this there is a need to engage in something larger than our individual existences, a need to re-create ourselves through something outside ourselves. Most often this is fulfilled as healthy fantasy, and here, too, the theatrical plays an important, indeed essential, role.

The Ritual Origin of Theatre

Parallel behavior can clearly be seen in observations of tribal societies and in what we surmise about ancient civilizations. As

3

Theatre in New Guinea. An actor playing the part of an old man with his bowstring.
(*Photograph by David Gillison*)

language became a human tool, early nomadic societies were still concerned with the needs of survival. Theatrical elements entered into the conveying of these needs among members of the group itself. To illustrate, imagine a cave dweller searching for food to ensure that the societal unit of which he is a member will continue to exist. He happens upon a small group of animals that he has successfully hunted before, notes the place, and returns home to inform others of his find so that they might all help in securing the food. Upon entering the dwelling, he puts on a dried skin from a previously killed animal, smears the exposed parts of his body with a mixture of earth and ash to approximate the animal's color, and dances around the central fire to convey to his colleagues a sense of "animalness." In time, the others understand that he has found more food, and they follow him to complete the kill. Upon returning home they all give thanks for the successful hunt. This dance-drama of rejoicing (or entreating if the kill was missed and they wished to ensure greater success next time) was done in some common meeting place with everyone participating. Support for this view can be seen in the cave paintings at Lascaux and the Volp River region. The illustration is fanciful, but it does provide an example of the close link between the basics of theatrical expression and life itself.

As nomadism gave way to a more stabilized way of life, the ritual dance-dramas moved from a concern over survival toward a deeper rooting in religion. By the time this occurred language had developed, and the rituals were more concerned with ensuring the health and continuance of the societal unit on a philosophical basis. In these rituals a supernatural force was identified and supplications were made for assistance. The seasonal cycles were not understood by these societies, so steps had to be taken to please the deities so that spring would follow winter and other aspects of the death-life cycle would be assured. Sacrifices and other rites were developed and built into ceremonies performed by special representatives, usually priests or shamans, who were believed to have special connections with the deities involved. Others in the social unit were less actively involved and served as spectators. Theatrical elements continued to be used, special people performing the ritual in special places. The basis for a true theatrical expression was established.

Theatre in New Guinea. An assistant adjusts the costume of a ''Janus'' figure during a performance.

(Photograph by David Gillison)

Theatre in New Guinea. A "Janus" figure with interlocking fingers.

(*Photograph by David Gillison*)

THEATRICAL BEGINNINGS: EGYPT AND MESOPOTAMIA

Examples of ritual drama exist from all parts of the world, but the earliest information about the presence of such drama comes from the countries of the Eastern Mediterranean, most notably Egypt. Egyptian religious myths follow the general life cycle of birth, death, and rebirth of its deities.

Egyptian Drama

The drama of Egypt was based on religious myths. In terms of its place in Egyptian life, the most important myth centered on the god Osiris and his struggle with Seth (sometimes spelled Set), his brother. Seth finally kills Osiris and buries parts of his body all over Egypt. Isis, the wife and sister of Osiris, travels the land gathering up her dismembered husband to have him revived by her uncle, Anubis, the god of mummification. A condition of this resurrection does not allow Osiris to remain on earth. Following his burial at a sacred precinct in Abydos, he travels to the underworld to become lord of the dead for eternity. The final part of the myth deals with Osiris's son, Horus, who avenges his father's death by defeating and killing Seth, thereby regaining the kingdom. For nearly two thousand years, until its extinction in 550 B.C., a commemorative ritual play was performed annually at Abydos. Alas, none of the text survives. There is a recorded account of the drama from a participant, Ikhernofret, who was actively involved with the Abydos Passion play around the middle of the nineteenth century B.C. Scholars are in disagreement about the accuracy and significance of the Ikhernofret hieroglyph, and are in similar disagreement over whether the celebration was indeed a ritual drama festival or the reinactment of a royal funeral.

One complete text of an Egyptian ritual play does exist, and from it can be deduced something of the scripts and presentations of ritual drama in Egypt. *The Triumph of Horus* is one of nine plays (the others are fragments only) that expand on the part of the Osiris myth dealing with Horus. Scholars are in disagreement about the importance and authenticity of the fragments, but the full text of *The Triumph of Horus* is able to stand as an authentic ritual play. In it the speakers are named at the beginning of speeches, stage directions appear throughout the play, the text is in a nonnarrative style, and the acts and scenes flow in sequential order, consistently developing the main theme of the play. Although these factors are not definitive in determining whether a work is a play, they are significant as far as ritual drama is concerned. This is not highly developed dramatic literature, but it is an excellent example of an early ritual play.

The play was performed annually at Edfu as part of the Festival of Victory from at least 1300 B.C. to the fall of Egypt's dominance around 400 B.C. The

Temple of Edfu.
(Courtesy of B. T. Batsford, Ltd.)

play was presented on each of the five days of the festival, beginning on the twenty-first day of the winter season's second month (around March 9–13). The festival itself commemorated the victory of Horus over Seth and the final triumph of Horus over a united Egypt. The play portrays a portion of the mythological happenings commemorated by the festival. The prologue offers praise for the festival and the triumph of Horus, and outlines the results of the whole play. There are five scenes in act 1, all dealing with the Harpoon Ritual. Horus is seen in two forms (presumably representing the kingdoms of Upper and Lower Egypt that emerged following the death of Osiris), each thrusting a harpoon into a hippopotamus representing Seth. This act ritually represents the battles between Seth and Horus and the ultimate defeat of Seth. In the two scenes of act 2, we see general rejoicing over the outcome of the events in act 1. Scene 1 is essentially a recitation by Isis over the glories of Horus's victories. Scene 2 deals with Horus's coronation on a ceremonial barge as king of Upper and Lower Egypt. Before he is crowned and embarks on the lake, he mimes the killing of the hippopotamus (Seth). The use of a chorus is unique here since it is divided into halves to antiphonally respond, presumably representing Upper and Lower Egypt. Act 3 deals with the final celebration of victory and, in scenes 1 and 3, two tellings of the dismemberment of the hippopotamus. Scene 2 is an interlude in which Horus mimes the harpooning of the hippopotamus again. A short epilogue concludes the play, with the reader, or chorus leader, declaring the final triumph over the enemies of Egypt. The health of the social unit has been assured and the purpose of the ritual drama served.

Egyptian Play Production

Information on the actual production of plays such as *The Triumph of Horus*, is, at best, fragmentary. Other than guidance from the text, the Ikhernofret hieroglyph, and scattered information about the Abydos Passion play, details are few. From the records that do exist and a great deal of speculation, a sense of Egyptian play production can be imagined. First, the plays were done at some common sacred site, usually a temple that was significant to the myth being presented. *The Triumph of Horus*, for example, was staged at the temple site of Edfu. The text suggests in direction as well as dialogue that the performance was to be staged around the Sacred Lake, located at the southeastern corner of the temple. If the play was really presented there, problems of access and visibility would be considerable. It may be, however, that a high degree of ritual symbolism existed, and that choral descriptions of being at the Sacred Lake are simply oral scene-painting for another site near the temple. Perhaps the play was presented outside the temple at the main gate, thus providing for good acoustics and visibility. If this were the case, the walls of the temple could have been used for a generalized scenic background and the actual kiosk around the lake could have served as an actor ready room. Other theories have advanced different places for the production's location. For our purposes it is of no great consequence as long as

Hieroglyphics for the The Triumph of Horus. *Depicted are Horus in the boat and the king on the bank.*

(Courtesy of B. T. Batsford, Ltd.)

we remember the need for the connection between the play and the sacredness of its playing space.

Other production elements are similarly hard to discern. It is highly likely that the principal actors were the religious leaders of the temple and that choruses were selected from the populace through some system now lost in history. Props would have been as realistic as possible, especially hand props, and real animals may have been used where needed. The problem of using real animals in *The Triumph of Horus*, however, would have been immense since numerous hippopotamuses are needed and they must be harpooned. Perhaps animal facsimiles were used in such cases. Whether any temporary scenic structures were used is a matter of conjecture. A temporary kiosk may have been erected for use as the hippopotamus hut, for example, but not many such structures were used given the Egyptian tradition of words as creators of illusion. Acting style must be surmised; likely it was formal, dignified, and physically beautiful, if the vase paintings and reliefs of the period are any indication. In order to carry to its audience, movement would have been stereotyped and exaggerated within its formal context. The speech would have been declamatory, in the tradition of priestly chants, and very precise, musical, and poetic. The makeup and masks used were exaggerated to carry to the audience, employing a great deal of ritual symbolism in addition to emphasizing realistic detail. Costumes were traditional for the role being played—basically white garments, full length, with richly colored accent pieces including jewelry and headdresses. Much use of music was made in these ritual dramas, basic string and wind instruments augmenting the extensive use of percussion.

A few words must be said about the audience. The plays they were seeing were ritual dramas, in which full participation was the norm. The stories were known, so a high degree of concentration on the plot was unnecessary. It is likely that audience participation, totally spontaneous and enthusiastic, often interrupted the presentation to the greater enjoyment of all. These plays were, after all, parts of great celebrations, and that spirit must have prevailed at the performances. In many ways the presentations of these ritual plays foreshadow the great productions of the Middle Ages in intent if not in scope. They were, indeed, a thing of and for the people.

Mesopotamian Theatre

Emerging about the same time as in Egypt, a series of cultures flourished in the Near East than can be collectively called Mesopotamia. Moving into dominance about five hundred years after Egypt, and quite different from it, the drama that developed here was ritualistic in content, dealing with the standard themes of birth, maturity, death, and rebirth, and their common connection with the seasonal or year-cycle theory. Beyond this general knowledge, it is difficult to be more definitive since all that is left of the dramatic ritual of these cultures are fragments of writing and carved reliefs of processions. These fragments and reliefs suggest that the oldest ritual plays of Mesopotamia dealt with the subject of the ''sacred marriage''—that is, the mythical union between the gods and humanity. The most common specific ritual drama involved a symbolic banquet for the sacred and human pair, Inanna, the fertility goddess, and Dumuzi, the royal shepherd. The fragments discovered thus far date from about 2700 b.c., and the drama was performed once a year, perhaps as part of a new year's festival, in every city that had a major temple.

Speculation from the various pieces of evidence leads to the general conclusion that the basic ritual performances were different from their Egyptian counterparts only in minor detail. Priests and priestesses still performed the major roles, and there was extensive use of music in the productions. But Mesopotamian reliefs suggest that ritual performances and processions may have been more staid and more heavily religious than those performed in Egypt. Certainly the costuming employed suggests movement patterns that were more ponderous and formal than the Egyptian. Gesture and general movement must have been more deliberate, given the additional weight of the costumes. In general, then, Mesopotamian ritual drama enjoyed a somber approach, no doubt suiting the culture and religion of the region and times.

FROM RITUAL TO FORMAL DRAMA

Most societies that developed a ritual drama traveled the route charted in this chapter, making changes in the pattern as their particular culture dictated. Some, like Egypt, never developed a fully indepen-

Theatre in New Guinea. A monster emerging from the forest.
(Photograph by David Gillison)

dent theatre, while others, such as Greece, did. The reasons for this selectivity will never be fully understood. It seems, however, that two special situations must occur for a fully independent theatre to develop. First, the society must arrive at a point where religion moves from a position of predominant concern to a less important place than the humans it serves. This movement is clearly a form of humanistic behavior, but until it happens the dramatic expression tied to ritual cannot move to a fully independent theatre servings humans in its own right. Second, some sense of a state or local consciousness must occur before drama can fully separate itself from ritual. There must be a pride in societal accomplishments that people wish to reflect in their arts, apart from major religious connotation. When these phenomena occur, a truly independent theatre can emerge. Happily, they did occur in Greece, and it is there that we shall trace the beginnings of the formal theatre.

SELECTED READINGS

Brown, Ivor J. C. *First Player: The Origin of Drama*. New York: William Morrow, 1928.
An early work that stresses the ritual beginnings of theatre and the importance mime plays in those beginnings.

Childe, Vere Gordon. *What Happened in History*. London: Penguin Books, 1954.
A general account of early human development and a good introduction to the subject.

Fairman, H. W. *The Triumph of Horus*. London: B. T. Batsford, 1974.
A detailed exploration of the drama in ancient Egypt with particular focus on the ritual play *The Triumph of Horus*, its background and production.

Gaster, Theodor H. *Thespis: Ritual, Myth and Drama in the Ancient Near East*. New York: Gordian Press, 1975.
A detailed examination of the emergence of drama in ritual magic and dramatized prayer.

Hans, James S. *The Play of the World*. Amherst: University of Massachusetts Press, 1981.
Although not dealing directly with the theatre, this theoretical approach to play is an attempt to define the cultural role of play in all human activities.

Huizinga, Johan. *Homo Ludens: A Study of the Play Element in Culture*. Boston: Beacon Press, 1950.
The classic study of the element of play and its importance in human existence. The emphasis here is on games and rituals.

Hunningher, Benjamin. *The Origin of the Theatre*. New York: Hill & Wang, 1961.
This standard work advances the theory that the origin of the modern theatre is in the medieval Church, and it traces similar ties between religion and theatrical origins in primitive and ancient societies.

Kirby, E. T. *Ur-Drama: The Origins of Theatre*. New York: New York University Press, 1975.
A unique exploration of the origins of drama based on the practice of shamanistic theatre and its influence on the drama of India, China, Japan, Greece, and Europe.

Montet, Pierre. *Eternal Egypt*. New York: Praeger, 1969.
A highly readable one-volume examination of Egyptian life.

ATHENS

PART II

A Mirror Emerges:
THE THEATRE OF THE GREEK AND HELLENISTIC WORLDS

Aretê, the Greek word for excellence, might serve as a key to our understanding of the peoples we collectively call the Greeks, although they called themselves Hellenes. They stressed excellence in body and mind, an excellence that was tested in competitions both physical and artistic. This constant striving produced a civilization whose accomplishments still cast long shadows into the late twentieth century. This civilization invented theatre as we know it.

A small mountainous peninsula, approximately the size of the state of Louisiana, with many excellent harbors but difficult inland travel, Greece

The Acropolis, Athens.
(Courtesy of Shmuel Ben Aharon Wahli)

did not offer a strong geographical base for the development of a centralized nation. What did develop on the peninsula was a small political unit, the *polis,* or city-state, organized around the most important town in an area. The city-states placed considerable responsibility on the individual in relation to civic and military affairs. The business of the city-state was the business of everyone. Although the citizens were often manipulated by politicians, many of these city-states provided ideal environments for intellectual development. The city-state of Athens provided the proper conditions for the birth of Western theatre. In Athens theatre thrived, prospered, and became a centerpiece in one of the greatest artistic cultures the world has yet known.

2
GREEK DRAMA

Much factual information about the Greek theatre is obscured by twenty-five hundred years of human activity. Numerous theories abound, but solid facts about origins, evolution, and practices are few. There are a few plays, some of them the greatest ever written; a few playhouses, all in ruin and most modified by later users; and a few historical records, contradictory in content and written long after the events described. All this should be kept in mind during a consideration of the world of Greek theatre.

TRAGEDY

Until recently it has been customary to trace the beginnings of tragedy to one of three preexisting sources: dithyramb, hero cults, or vegetation rites. The dithyramb was a processional song in honor of Dionysos, the god of wine, and it was sung by a large chorus arranged in a circle around the altar of the god. The Greek philosopher Aristotle, in his *Poetics*, states that tragedy originated with the dithyramb and was associated with the cult of Dionysos. Aristotle's account of the development of tragedy, although vague and brief, is the traditional version since it was written in the century following the composition of the major Greek tragedies. Yet Aristotle, too, lacked historical evidence; and he was not, in any case, writing a history of the Greek theatre but a treatise on poetry.

The hero cult theory places the beginning of tragedy in imitative performances given at the graves of heroes. These lamentations were later absorbed into existing rites of the cult of Dionysos and then evolved into tragedy. A third theory places the origins of tragedy in primitive vegetation rites that pitted the Black Man and the Fair Man of the Dionysos cult in ritualistic combat to ensure the victory of summer over winter. Anthropologists have found such rituals in cultures throughout the world; yet in ancient Greece there was an extra element that caused the creation of a complex theatrical form.

A recent theory on the development of the Greek theatre contends that anthropological parallels, in ancient Greece or elsewhere, are unimportant. Only in Athens did tragedy develop, and the development was not gradual from other forms but through major creative advancements by the dramatists Thespis and Aeschylus. This theory also holds that no solid evidence exists for connecting tragedy with Dionysos except its presentation at the City Dionysia, a festival developed for political, not religious, reasons. These points will be discussed in more detail in relation to the playwrights and the festivals in Athens.

Structure of Tragedy

Much less controversial is the structural form of Greek tragedy, which by the time of Aeschylus had developed a general pattern. The *prologos,* a brief scene or monologue that opens the play, is usually expository and establishes the dramatic situation. This section is followed by the *parodos,* the entrance of the chorus, which continues the exposition for another twenty to a few hundred lines. There then follows the main sections of play, which are presented in alternating *epeisoda* and *stasima.* The *epeisoda* are equivalent to the modern act, and in these the actors take the main line of action; the *stasima* are commentaries by the chorus between the *epeisoda.* The number of *epeisoda* and *stasima* vary from three to six, but five was the customary number. The climax of the play is usually before the last of the *stasima,* thus allowing the chorus to comment on the final resolution of the dramatic situation. The conclusion of the play, the *exodos,* allows for a final summation and exit of the chorus.

COMEDY

The origin of Greek comedy is as obscure as that of tragedy. There existed throughout the Greek-speaking areas the custom of dressing in grotesque costumes in the performance of religious ceremonies connected with fertility rites. Aristotle records the opinion that comedy grew out of these performances, called *komos.* A form of artistic unity was at some point given to the antics of these revelers, and tradition awards the honor to one Susaron, who is said to have "invented" comedy sometime around 570 B.C. Greek comedy is divided into three categories: Old Comedy, Middle Comedy, and New Comedy.

Although Old Comedy appeared in the fifth century B.C. in two distinct forms, Sicilian and Attic, the Sicilian form died out early and left the Attic type as the predominant form of Old Comedy. At first Old Comedy was only performed at the Lenaea, the minor local festival in Athens, but it was later included in the City Dionysia along with the performances of tragedies. The general subject matter of Old Comedy was current affairs, and it involved a great deal of invective directed at persons known to the audience.

Structure of Comedy

The structural form of the Old Comedy followed the general pattern of *prologue, parados, agon, parabasis, epeisoda,* and *exodos.* In the *prologue* the central character explains the situation and his plan of action, the "happy idea" that is usually wild and impractical. This is followed by the *parados*, the entry of the chorus, and the *agon*, in which the merits of the "happy idea" are debated in relation to the existing situation. The *parabasis* is a direct address to the audience by the chorus in which the views of the playwright are expressed, views that may have very little to do with the play. The *epeisoda*, a series of farcical scenes attempting to implement the "happy idea," are followed by the *exodos*, the conclusion of the play in some form of merrymaking. The chief surviving playwright from the Old Comedy period is Aristophanes, but other playwrights of the period include Kratinos, Krates, Pherekrates, and Eupolis. With the exception of Aristophanes, only fragments remain of the work of the Old Comedy playwrights.

Middle Comedy was composed in the period roughly covered by the years 404 to 321 B.C., and its development is connected to the altered political climate in Athens following the downfall of the city in the Peloponnesian War. Two of the last plays by Aristophanes, *Ecclesiazusae* and *Plutus*, are written in the Middle Comedy style. In Middle Comedy the chorus has a lesser role in the action, the *parabasis* is removed and with it most of the political comment, and the stories and character types begin to be somewhat uniform. Over fifty playwrights and over six hundred plays are associated with the Middle Comedy period, but the names are shadows and the scripts fragments.

New Comedy, which began to appear in the last quarter of the fourth century B.C., was the Greek comic form most copied by the Romans and the classical dramatic form most influential on later eras. In New Comedy can be seen the structure of the modern play, particularly the comedy of manners. The chorus remains only to sing or dance during pauses in the action, thus providing the arrangement for a five-act structure. The characters are drawn from contemporary Athens, and they fall into such stock character types as the old man, the young lover, the courtesan, and the parasite. The plays of New Comedy revolve around long-lost children, silly old men, frustrated lovers, and scheming servants. These plays have more in common with Molière than Aristophanes and, although the obscene language of the Old Comedy is gone, the moral tone of New Comedy is far below that of Old Comedy. New Comedy, the last frail blooming of Athenian theatre, reflects the cynicism of Athens in the decades after its fall from greatness. Menander is the only playwright from the period of whom we have any complete scripts, but other New Comedy playwrights include Diphilos, Antiphanes, and Philemon.

The Satyr Play

One additional form of comedy from the Greek theatre is the satyr play, traditionally said to have been first written by Pratinas around 500 B.C. Greek playwrights entered the dramatic competition at the City Dionysia with not one play but with a tetralogy consisting of three tragedies and a satyr play. The purpose of placing the satyr play, which is pure entertainment, at the end of the three tragedies is not known. The activities of the satyr play involved a mythic hero in some ludicrous situation connected with a chorus of creatures, half man and half beast, called satyrs. Only one complete satyr play is now extant, the *Cyclops* by Euripides, and there is no known connection between the satyr play and the development of either Greek comedy or tragedy. The satyr play is a true oddity of the Greek theatre and a bit of a mystery.

GREEK PLAYWRIGHTS

Little is known and even less survives of the work of Greek playwrights before Aeschylus. The name and person of Thespis, legendary founder of the thespian arts, are historically obscure. He is credited with winning the victory prize when tragedy was first performed at the City Dionysia (c. 534 B.C.), and Aristotle acknowledges him as the introducer of the spoken section of tragedy, in other words, the first actor. There are no historical records to indicate that any of his plays still existed in the fourth century B.C., so even to Aristotle he was something of a mythic figure. Yet all classical scholars acknowledge that Thespis, or someone like him, existed. It is probable that Thespis first successfully combined the epic hero from the Homeric tales with impersonation that stressed suffering and failure. This creative act, utilizing an actor and a chorus, brought the suffering of the hero into the present and allowed it to make a direct contact with an audience. This type of public performance permitted all Athenians to share a common emotional identification with the heroic spirit. The element of unification present in the audience during a performance was not lost on Peisistratus, the ruler of Athens at the end of the sixth century. He saw in this budding new creation called tragedy a way to educate and unite the various tribes and classes of Athens. To promote this goal, Peisistratus made the performance of tragedies the central focus of his new festival, the City Dionysia. In such a setting, theatrical productions grew into a showpiece of Athenian culture.

Early Playwrights

The earliest Greek playwright whose work survived for several hundred years was Phrynichus (fl. 511–474 B.C.). He wrote a number of plays, was admired for the beauty of his lyrics, and is credited as the first tragic playwright to introduce a female character. All that now remains of his work are a few fragments, which is more than we have of the work of two other early playwrights, Choerilus and Pratinas. Choerilus (fl. 523–468 B.C.), a contemporary of Aeschylus's, is the reputed author of 160 plays and the winner of thirteen victory prizes at the City Dionysia. The *Alope* is the only play by Choerilus known by name. Pratinas (fl. 500–470 B.C.) was a competitor with Aeschylus and Choerilus during at least one City Dionysia, and he is traditionally considered the first playwright to write satyr plays. The only long fragment extant from the fifty plays of Pratinas is a strong attack on the use of flute accompaniment in the theatre.

Aeschylus

It is with the plays of Aeschylus that we truly come to the fullness of the art of Greek tragedy. In the surviving plays of this playwright are found all the glories of the golden period of Greek culture, for Aeschylus was a true citizen of his age and a teacher to the peoples of Greece. Aeschylus (525–456 B.C.) was a member of a wealthy Athenian family, fought against the Persians at Marathon and Salamis, and was author of approximately ninety plays. Only seven of these plays have survived: *The Persians, Seven Against Thebes, The Suppliants,* a trilogy of plays called the *Oresteia,* and *Prometheus Bound.*

As a playwright, Aeschylus was a bold experimenter with the new artistic form of tragedy and was responsible for many developments. He increased the number of actors from one to two and possibly three, organized the episodes to move the action forward, increased the focus on tragic choice, placed strong emphasis on costuming and spectacular effects, and created a theological reinterpretation of the old myths.

It is significant that the oldest surviving Greek tragedy, *The Persians* (472 B.C.), was so closely related to the lives of its original audience. In this play the great Athenian victory over the Persian Empire at the Battle of Salamis, fought a mere eight years before the play's first production, was told to an audience

A 1965 production by the Greek Art Theatre of The Persians *by Aeschylus.*
(Courtesy of KaiDib Films International, Glendale, Calif.)

filled with veterans of the battle. The victory at Salamis was a turning point in Greek history, for it established Athenian leadership and started Athens down the path of imperialism. With this subject matter Aeschylus was dealing with living history, familiar to all in the theatre, so he gained his necessary sense of perspective by telling the story from the Persian view. The account of the battle occupies a large portion of the play as the audience is constantly reminded of the bravery of the Athenians. *The Persians* concludes with Xerxes returning in rags to his court, the vainglorious King of Kings brought low by freedom-loving Athenians. For the original audience the play was a glorious combination of pride, poetry, and patriotism.

The Persians is a play of triumph, and the tetralogy of which it was a part won the tragic competition for Aeschylus. But the play was also very much connected with Athenian political life at the time of its production. Even in this oldest extant Greek play the element of propaganda is present, for the script reflects the political intrigues of 472 B.C. as much as the naval battle of 480 B.C. In 472 B.C., Themistocles, who had commanded the Athenian fleet at the Battle of Salamis, was fighting for his political life in Athens. Aeschylus shows strong support for him in *The Persians* by demonstrating how much the people of Athens owe to his military skills. Although the play was well received, the enemies of Themistocles had him exiled the following year. *The Persians* was not the first tragedy to be used in the political battles of Athens. Four years earlier the playwright Phrynichus, a friend of Themistocles, wrote a tragedy about the Persian wars, *The Capture of Miletus*, yet the true tragedy was for the playwright. The subject matter of the play so depressed the audience that Phrynichus was assessed a large fine.

Aeschylus's support and admiration of Themistocles did not stop with the production of *The Persians*. *The Suppliants* is highly praiseworthy of the people of Argos for giving asylum and protection to those in need, and it was to Argos that Themistocles fled after he was exiled from Athens. The play's praise for Argos, which has no place in the mythic subject matter of the script, is clearly an expression of gratitude by the playwright to Argos for giving protection to his admired former military commander.

The *Oresteia* trilogy, which is the only surviving example of the connected tragic trilogy from Greek dramatic literature, is the most politically complex of the plays of Aeschylus. The trilogy, which is composed of the plays *Agamemnon*, *Libation-Bearers*, and *Eumenides*, has justice as its key concept, particularly justice expressed in the necessity of orderly legal proceedings. The Athenians were a people much given to litigation, a point of much humor in the comedies of Aristophanes. It was during the period of production of the *Oresteia* that many legal reforms were taking place in Athens, the most controversial being the Ephialtic Reforms of 462 B.C. These reforms were the beginnings of a new era of democracy in Athens, an era that allowed greater governmental participation of all citizens. The plays of the *Oresteia* trilogy are steeped in legal terminology, and in the final play the goddess Athena establishes the Areopagus, the Athenian high council. The legal reforms were stripping away many of the powers of the Areopagus, and this trilogy of plays is viewed by many scholars as an antireform statement by the playwright and a sign of Aeschylus's growing unhappiness with events in Athens.

In the last years of his life, Aeschylus went into voluntary exile from Athens, and during this period he wrote what is generally held to be his last play, *Prometheus Bound*. This play, which is highly experimental in its production demands, is a puzzle to scholars because it is so un-Aeschylean. Yet to claim that the play is not by Aeschylus is to deny a continued artistic growth for the playwright. *Prometheus Bound* is Aeschylus's strongest statement against tyranny. In the character of the chained Titan, Prometheus, Aeschylus condemns the evils of tyranny in terms that are later echoed in the philosophical writings of Plato and Aristotle. This play and the other surviving plays of Aeschylus speak of great majestic themes of divine justice, human dignity, and the burden of the freedom of choice, but they also reflect the playwright's never-ending concern about and interest in the contemporary affairs of Athens.

Sophocles

Sophocles (496–406 B.C.), the second of the major tragic playwrights of the Greek theatre, learned the techniques of tragedy from Aeschylus and was his artistic rival for a period of ten years. As has been noted, Aeschylus was not above using his plays to comment on events in Athenian society that were not to his liking. Such contemporary references are rare in the plays of Sophocles because he was closely aligned with those very individuals making the changes so displeasing to Aeschylus. Born into a wealthy family, Sophocles lived a nearly ideal existence. He was closely associated with the leaders of the Athenian empire, elected to important governmental posts, honored as a great poet, and buried as a hero.

Sophocles was the author of approximately 125 plays and the winner of twenty-four victories, the first in competition against Aeschylus in 469 B.C. Of this vast number of plays, only seven complete works are now extant: *Ajax*, *Antigone*, *Oedipus Tyrannus*, *Electra*, *Trachiniae*, *Philoctetes*, and *Oedipus Coloneus*. There is also a large fragment of a satyr play entitled *Trackers*. Based on the available plays and fragments, we can conclude that the work of Sophocles has several noteworthy characteristics: unity of plot, strong use of irony, conventional religious values, the importance of the character as a person, the pairing of characters of opposite qualities for purposes of development, and a lessening of the role of the chorus in the overall structure of the action. Aristotle, in the *Poetics*, credits Sophocles with the introduction of scene painting, discontinuation of the connected trilogy, and the increase in the size of the chorus from twelve to fifteen.

A strong commitment to conventionality is central in the extant plays of Sophocles. As a close friend to and a sometimes member of the small group of men who ruled Athens, treasurer of the wealth of the Athenian empire, and a general in the army, Sophocles had a strong personal link to the existing social order, and his plays reflect and defend this connection. *Ajax* both defends the reverence of a popular Homeric hero associated with Athens and illustrates the arrogance and mean-spirited nature of the Spartans, with whom the Athenians had an uneasy truce at the time of the play's original production. *Antigone* is one of the greatest treatments in dramatic literature of the moral problem of private versus public duty. Although there are numerous ironic twists in the story, the play is ultimately a plea for adherence to the laws of the state. This statement on law within a just social order came during a period in Sophocles' life when he was most involved in the running of the Athenian empire.

Oedipus Tyrannus, acclaimed by Aristotle as a near-perfect example of tragedy as an art form, was written during the early years of the Peloponnesian War. The play's opening description of plague-stricken Thebes must have been very moving for the audience in Athens, for during the second year of the war a plague in Athens killed nearly a third of the population. The stress of the war and the plague led to a breakdown in traditional beliefs and values in Athens, and these Sophocles upheld in his masterful unfolding of the battle of Oedipus against his fate. Sophocles again returned to the Oedipus legend in his last play, *Oedipus Coloneus*, which was produced after his death. In *Tyrannus* Sophocles shows the fall of Oedipus from greatness; in *Coloneus* he shows the old, blind Oedipus raised to supernatural greatness at his death. *Oedipus Coloneus* is a play about general recompense. It is both religious and patriotic, two characteristics that link Sophocles and Aeschylus. These elements are generally missing in the work of their contemporary, the last member of the great trio of Greek tragic playwrights, Euripides.

Euripides

Euripides (c. 484–406 B.C.), who saw the final plays of Aeschylus and was officially mourned by Sophocles, was the author of approximately ninety-two plays, of which eighteen are extant. Although he won only four victories at the festivals during his lifetime, he was a popular playwright with both the common people and the intellectuals of Athens. His lack of victories at the festivals may be attributable to official displeasure (Euripides was critical of Athens's leaders and their policies) and his innovations in music and poetic meter. Euripides was said to have been indifferent to theatrical success.

Based on the surviving scripts and still growing number of fragments, several major characteristics mark the plays of Euripides. They have realistic, nonheroic characters, use simple dialogue, and show a fascination with the passionate, irrational aspects of human nature. They also contain rhetorical debating between characters, make little use of the chorus, have a weak story construction and skeptical approach to traditional myths, and incorporate the familiar everyday things of life. Sophocles is reported to have said he portrayed men as they should be, but Euripides presented them as they are. In this Euripides was among a growing number of Greek writers, painters, sculptors, and philosophers who were making the human rather than the divine the focus of their work. The inquisitive and rhetorical aspects of the plays of Euripides reflect his association with such philosophers as Anaxagoras, Protagoras, and Socrates, and the changing subject matter of the plays is reflective of shifts in public opinion during the nearly thirty years of the Peloponnesian War.

Patriotic support for the war is seen in the praise given Athens in *Medea* and the *Heracleide*, and in the highly critical view of the Spartans in *Andromache*. *Andromache* also has an unflattering image of the god Apollo, whose oracle was pro-Spartan. The belief of Euripides and many of his fellow citizens in the war efforts of Athens was sorely tried with the Athenian capture and utter destruction of the citizens of the small island of Melos in 416 B.C. The "crime" of the Melians was their desire to remain neutral in the conflict between Athens and Sparta. The response of Euripides to this outrageous act was *The Trojan Women*, one of the greatest antiwar plays ever written.

Disheartened by the war and the political turmoil in Athens, Euripides turned to a new type of play during the final decade of his life. These final plays, which contain the seed of nineteenth-century melodrama, are clearly escapist in tone, filled with intrigue, romance, and happy endings. The romantic plays of this period, *Iphigenia in Tauris*, *Helena*, and *Ion*, were highly influential in the development of New Comedy.

In 408 B.C. Euripides left Athens for Macedonia at the invitation of King Archelaos, who was attempting to make his court a center of Hellenic culture. While resident at the court in Pella, Euripides wrote his greatest play, *The Bacchae*, which is the only extant Greek tragedy concerned with Dionysos. Euripides died in Macedonia in 406 B.C., and with his death the development of Greek tragedy as an artistic form came to an end. There were playwrights still working in Athens, such as Agathon and Theognis, but with the deaths of Sophocles and Euripides the creative flame of tragedy was extinguished.

Aristophanes

Nowhere in classical literature is there a better picture drawn of daily Athenian affairs than in the comedies of Aristophanes (c. 450–385 B.C.). The eleven surviving plays from the forty or so he wrote are populated with all classes from Athens and the Hellenistic world. While few are untouched by the barb of his humor, Aristophanes shows special dislike for politicians and a particular fondness for the average citizen, the little guy just trying to exist peacefully in a world filled with prejudice, war, ignorance, greed, and bad thinking. Aristophanes is perhaps the most moral and sympathetic of the Greek playwrights, yet he wrote some of the funniest and most obscene plays in the whole of dramatic literature.

In the lost play *The Babylonians*, produced at the City Dionysia in 426 B.C., the young Aristophanes concentrated his attack upon the person and policies of Kleon, the leader of the Athenian war party. For his boldness, Aristophanes was prosecuted by Kleon for making fun of Athenian institutions in front of foreigners. The politician's suit was apparently unsuccessful, since the playwright continued his attack against Kleon two years later in *The Knights*. In between these two plays was produced the earliest surviving script by Aristophanes, *The Acharians*. In this play the hero, unhappy with the conduct

Lysistrata *as presented by the Greek Art Theatre.*
(Courtesy of KaiDib Films International, Glendale, Calif.)

of the war with Sparta (an indirect dig at Kleon), negotiates his own private peace treaty. While this appeal for peace was close to being treasonous at the time, since the war still had general support from most of the population of Athens, it hit a chord of sympathy with the audience who also wished a return to the peaceful period before the war. For his efforts to delight his fellow citizen, and undermine Kleon's war policies, Aristophanes was awarded the first prize at the festival.

Kleon was killed in battle in 422 B.C., but after a brief period of peace the war with Sparta continued. The brief peace was celebrated by Aristophanes in the play *Peace*, but with the renewal of the Athenian military efforts, war became an ever-present theme in the plays of Aristophanes. In 411 B.C., the year *Lysistrata* was produced at the Lenaea, the war was going badly and Athens was also suffering from several violent leadership changes. The play concerns the revolt of the women of Greece against the war and their vow to go on strike against their men, refusing to engage in sex until a peace treaty is signed. Lysistrata, whose name means "she who disbands the army," and her allies are successful. The play is both a call for peace and a plea for Panhellenic unity, but neither goal was achieved. In the last year of the Peloponnesian War, Aristophanes presented another appeal to save Athens, in *The Frogs*. In this play, Dionysos goes to Hades to bring back a tragic playwright to teach the people of Athens. In the debate between Aeschylus and Euripides, the concerns

*A modern-dress production
of* Lysistrata *with June
Havoc in the title role.*

(Photograph by Fred Fehl, Hoblitzelle
Theatre Arts Library, Humanities
Research Center, University of Texas
at Austin)

of literature are connected with the troubles besetting contemporary Athens. In the end Aeschylus, the upholder of traditional values, is selected over Euripides, the exponent of clever thinking. Athens was defeated by Sparta and its allies in 404 B.C., and with Athens's fall from power fell the spirit that was central to Old Comedy and Aristophanes.

Menander

Writers from the classical period mention Euripides and Aristophanes as the inspirations for the plays of the New Comedy playwright Menander. Never having known Athens during its years of glory, Menander (342–292 B.C.) grew up and had his plays produced in an Athens that was scarcely more than a large provincial town governed by the Macedonians. Not only was Menander familiar with the earlier Greek playwrights, from both reading and viewing their works in production, but he was also of the first generation of playwrights schooled in the critical theories of dramatic literature. Aristotle returned to Athens in 335 B.C. under the sponsorship of his former student Alexander the Great and began writing and lecturing about numerous subjects, including dramatic theory. When Aristotle was

Aristophanes' The Birds *as presented at the University of Texas at Austin.*
(Courtesy of KaiDib Films International, Glendale, Calif.)

forced to flee Athens after the death of Alexander in 323 B.C., he was succeeded at the Lyceum by the philosopher-critic Theophrastus, the teacher of Menander.

The author of approximately one hundred plays, Menander is represented in our century by the remains of four scripts and many fragments. Two of the play scripts, *Arbitration* and *Dyscolus* (The Old Grouch), are complete enough to give some insight into Menander's style of writing and the characteristics of New Comedy. In Menander's work the chorus is no longer important. It is merely a group of performers who appear during pauses in the play, thus giving it a five-act structure. The characters in the plays are no longer known individuals, as in Aristophanes, but stock characters drawn from contemporary Athens. The scripts are concerned not with the fantastic or the mythic, but with the ordinary happenings of contemporary life. The comic costume of the Old Comedy has given way to contemporary dress in Menander's plays, and there is no attempt to be funny. These plays are about normal people in humorous situations, with the emphasis on the situation.

It can safely be said that Menander originated the modern play, for the type of play he wrote is still being written today. Menander was not a great playwright, and his debt to Euripides is considerable, yet he has been enormously influential. This influence is difficult to gauge owing to the small number of his extant plays, yet he was the model for Plautus and Terence, the two Roman playwrights most admired during the Renaissance. In Menander the modern theatre finds its strongest link to the theatre of the Greeks.

3
THEATRE ARCHITECTURE AND PRODUCTION IN THE GREEK AND HELLENISTIC WORLDS

Consistent with the origins of theatre, the physical places for theatre emerged where religious, harvest, or planting festivals were celebrated. These places proliferated throughout the Mediterranean world with the Hellenistic expansion of Greek culture under Alexander the Great. At the festivals, formal theatrical activity began.

FESTIVALS

At the inception of the festivals, religion, in its broadest sense, played a role. The dates for the Athenian festivals were not haphazardly chosen. The seasonal cycles, travel conditions, trade, and political considerations all played a part in their selection. Although the Greeks had many festivals, it was only at those centered on the god of fertility and wine, Dionysos, that drama evolved. Four separate festivals throughout the year involved Dionysos, and drama was presented at three of them. The principal festivals were the City Dionysia, presented in late March, and the Rural Dionysia, held in late December and likely used for some dramatic experimentation and actor training. Of less importance was the Lenaea, conducted in late January. Because of weather conditions that restricted attendance, it was probably the festival at which the most satirical plays was presented. After 443 B.C. the presentation of comedy was the basis for the Lenaea, although tragedies were added to this festival at a later date. There is no record of plays being presented at the fourth festival, the Anthesteria, held in late February. Some festivals were one- or two-day affairs, while others took the better part of a week to complete.

The City Dionysia, the major festival for the presentation of drama after 534 B.C., was one of the most complex. By about 500 B.C. it was a six- or a seven-day event with a major procession the first day, dithyrambic contests on the second, play-writing competition among the five comic poets on the third, and presentations of the plays of the three tragic poets selected for the festival on days four, five, and six. Performances ran from dawn to dusk. Judging of the play competition occurred on the seventh day, and prizes were awarded. The prizes usually consisted of a tripod, a crown of ivy, a bull, a goat, or a specified amount of wine or money. Originally prizes were only awarded to playwrights, but after 449 B.C. actors also competed for awards. After the defeat of Athens in the Peloponnesian War (404 B.C.), the festival was shortened by one day.

EVOLUTION OF THE PLAYHOUSE

The decision to design and locate a place for theatrical productions is based on many factors. Certainly one of the factors involved in locating the theatre structure used for the City Dionysia was the religious element in the festival. That undoubtedly led the planners to locate the Theatre of Dionysos in the sacred precinct of Dionysos. Other less lofty yet no doubt equally important considerations were more practical, such as wind direction for transmitting sound and travel access to ensure economic success.

The Theatre of Dionysos, Athens.
(Courtesy of Stephen M. Archer)

Earliest Forms

An essential element, indeed the most basic in creating a place for theatre, is a space for the presentation of the dramatic work. Lost in history is the record of the earliest development of the *orchestra*, the flat, usually circular playing space of the Greek theatre, but some general observations are possible. Probably because of the close connection between the harvest threshing areas and the dancing associated with early celebrations of harvest, the circular form for the *orchestra* emerged. For dramatic presentation the early *orchestra* could be located anywhere deemed appropriate, as influenced by religious considerations. Because these early presentations were done with no stage house or scenic background, the audience could sit entirely around the circle. In these early public theatre spaces, no need had yet been established for the advantages of hillside seating. Yet with the emergence of a rudimentary *skene*, initially a tent or hut, probably having a harvest storage function but used as a basic stage house, the production became directional with this structure as a background. Audience seating became localized around some 60 percent of the circle, and the naturally hilly terrain of Greece was utilized to improve seating for the audience. It is likely that at first the audience sat on the bare earth; later there was probably some sculpturing of

The proskenion *and* orchestra *at the Theatre of Dionysos.*
(Courtesy of Stephen M. Archer)

A model of the Theatre of Dionysos.
(Courtesy of the Clevelend State University's Theatre Arts Area)

the hill into earthen seats. This was followed by curved wooden bleacher-type seating and finally the arena-style stone seating extant in Greek theatres today. Even when stone seating became the norm in the fourth century B.C., Greek architecture used primarily a system for supporting its buildings that did not allow for efficient weight transferability, so tiered freestanding audience seating was not practical. Greek and Hellenistic theatres continued to use hillsides as the basic support for the *theatron* (auditorium).

Other elements of the physical theatre reinforced its religious origins. At the center of the *orchestra* was an altar, or *thymele*. Its approximate location can be seen in the floor stonework of the Theatre of Dionysos today. At Dionysos also was a temple, adjacent to the *skene*, but likely not very important to theatrical production.

Thus the Greek physical theatre emerged. Initially little more than a place for an audience to watch and participate in dance-dramas, the physical structure began to unfold as theatre practitioners needed new elements to convey the playwright's intent to an active audience.

Later Forms: The Fifth-Century Playhouse

Under Pericles, a fifth-century ruler noted for his concern for culture and architecture, the structure of the playhouse changed rapidly. Athenian play writing approached its zenith during this period and the structure responded in significant ways to what the playwrights needed. Always organic, growing from the dictates of the terrain, the weather, increased concern for audience comfort, and production visibility, many changes occurred. The *theatron* was given a steeper rise by moving the *orchestra* northward into the hillside. Because the playwrights were using a reduced chorus, the *orchestra* was similarly reduced in size from its original ninety feet in diameter to about sixty-five feet. During this century refinements were made in the wooden seating, and retaining walls were introduced for the channeling of water runoff down the hill. The addition of the *parodos*, the entrance paths or gates, focused attention on choral and actor entrances, and the *skene* was enlarged and took on more aspects of a complex structure that allowed a variety of entrances, exits, and performance levels.

Hellenistic Alterations

Most of the initial stonework on Greek theatres was completed in the fourth century B.C., and this structural concept spread throughout the Mediterranean world during the next hundred years. Many of the ruins extant today, although altered by second- and first-century-B.C. Roman modifications, were built during the Hellenistic expansion of the Greek empire. The Theatre of Dionysos in Athens experienced these same types of changes. Stone seating was installed, creating seventy-eight rows of seats that probably accommodated fifteen thousand to sixteen thousand people, although estimates range from fourteen to seventeen thousand. With seating

Theatre at Epidaurus prepared for use for a modern production of a classic Greek play.
(Courtesy of Stephen M. Archer)

Theatre at Epidaurus.
(Courtesy of Stephen M. Archer)

capacity for approximately half of the population of Athens, one can get a sense of the importance of the Theatre of Dionysos to the cultural life of the community.

Other changes occurred. In addition to the general stone seating, the seats of honor, which are in place today, were added during this period. The *skene*, now made of stone, continued to be expanded with *paraskenia*, side extensions, and a *proskenion*, an elaborate facade, added to the basic structure. As the art of acting continued to develop, so did the need for additional places from which to speak. It is likely that a second story, the *episkenion*, was added to the *skene* by the end of the fourth century B.C. As in the basic *skene* of the fifth century B.C., *thyromata* (doorways) were used for actor entrances and exits as well as to support scenic pieces and machinery. The *orchestra* continued to be a full circle, and the *theatron* was greater than a semicircle by several degrees. Examples of these features can be seen in the theatre ruins at Epidaurus, Eretria, Oropos, Delos, and Priene.

SCENERY, STAGE MACHINERY, AND SCENIC DEVICES

The extent to which the Greeks used anything resembling illusionistic scenery remains a matter of conjecture. Such scenery would have depicted actual scenes and locales as realistically as possible. The attempts at scenery that were made to support the production were, if not highly illusionistic, both symbolic and functional. Symbolically, the basic architectural facade of the *skene* was used to represent a variety of scenes. Although there is no general agreement on the exact nature of this usage, it seems likely that three portals were established in the basic *skene* and later in the *episkenion*. These portals were most likely used for royal entrances, entrances by deities, and for the general entrances of other speaking actors.

Functional scenic pieces were painted to suggest locale. The Greeks were highly interested in bright colors and vivid painting, and there is no reason to suspect that this concern did not translate into theatre practice as well. The *pinake*, a scenic panel that was roughly equivalent to the modern flat, was painted to suggest seascapes or landscapes and houses, and was hung between pillars in the *proskenion* colonnade. Record of the exact nature of the painting on the *pinakes* is lost, but the Roman architect Vitruvius, writing three centuries later, suggests three styles for the painted scenery. For the presentation of tragedy, he observes that stately homes are appropriate; for comedy, more common, or plain, homes are suggested; and for the presentation of satyr pieces, a rural landscape is to be used. These suggestions are offered in a time too distant from Aeschylus and Sophocles to be taken as gospel, but they provide some sense of the variety of Greek scene painting.

Scenic Devices

In addition to the placement of painted scenic panels in the *thyromata*, it is thought that they might also have been placed on

The parodos *at Epidaurus.*
(Courtesy of E. A. Nicholson)

The Theatre of the Greek and Hellenistic Worlds

periaktoi, devices for facilitating changes in the scene. The *periaktoi* were columnar rotating prisms mounted in an opening on a central pole so that one of the three sides would be flush to the opening when it was turned to face the audience. The three sides would have allowed for three scenes, with a one-third rotation accomplishing a scene change. The offstage sides could then have their *pinakes* replaced by those appropriate to later scenes in the play. Information about the *periaktoi* and their use is sketchy and does not apply until the development of the most elaborate wooden or earliest stone *skene*.

Other Greek stage devices dealt less with the display of scenery than with assisting the production in creating the specific effects in the playwright's stage directions. Chief among these were the *ekkyklema* and the *machina*. The *ekkyklema* is thought to have been a low rolling or sliding wagon stored behind a curtain or *pinake* and sent forward onto the *skene* floor at the place in a play where it was necessary to reveal the results of offstage action. It was a convention of the Greek theatre to have most violent action occur offstage. The decision to use violence onstage or offstage seems to have depended on the dramatist's desire for audience focus. When the victims of offstage violence needed to be seen, the *ekkyklema* was utilized. Another view of the *ekkyklema*'s form and function is that it was like a modern turntable, set in a *skene* opening and rotated at the appropriate time, revealing what was to be seen.

The *machina*, or machine, was a cranelike device used to raise or lower gods and other characters to and from the *skene* and *orchestra*. Another use was to support actors who had to remain aloft, such as those required to ride

The Great Theatre at the ancient city of Ephesus, near Izmir, Turkey.
(*Courtesy of KaiDib Films International, Glendale, Calif.*)

the backs of flying insects or animals. In use the *machina* actually functioned as a crane, located behind the *parodos*, with the ability to pick up or deposit actors offstage, even behind the *skene*, turn, and repeat the process onstage. Given the nonillusionistic nature of Greek production, it seems unlikely that there was high concern for masking or hiding the machine itself. The audience probably focused on the action.

Costumes, Masks, and Properties

Some aspects of Greek theatrical production were more illusionistic than the machinery and scenic elements mentioned above, and these were an integral part of the actor's presentation. Costumes reflected the general tone of Greek art in that they were quite colorful and decorative, usually reflecting the finest in dress for the social station of the character. The garments showed no concern for historical accuracy since little was needed, but they were conventionalized. Not only form but color was used symbolically, such as deep purples for royalty. The basic costume was the *chiton*, a flowing dresslike garment. On top of this was the *himation*, a cloak that was draped across the right shoulder. A shorter cloak worn over the left shoulder was the *chlamys*. The *peplos* was an outer garment worn by women characters. In comedy, the basic dress was a white tunic, the *exomis*. Actors for Old Comedy were grotesquely padded and wore large leather *phalluses*. On the actor's feet were boots called *kothurnoi*. While not quite the equivalent of the modern elevator shoe, this footwear did help to add height to the actor, a necessary aid to being seen at the back of the sizable auditoriums in use. Actors also wore *onkoi* (headdresses) that sat atop their masks and, along with the hairdressing, provided the proper finish to the entire costuming effect. Contemporary dress was worn in New Comedy.

Much of what is surmised about the masks worn by Greek actors come from a second-century-A.D. work entitled *Onomasticon* by the Roman grammarian Pollux. Although highly inaccurate, this source gives a sense of the importance of the mask to the actor's art. Masks, possibly invented by Thespis, were one of the main agents for creating stylized emotional effects. They were made generally of wood, cork, and plaster, covered with linen and painted in full color. By the late fifth century B.C., the mask covered the entire head, depicted the whole face full-front, and was considerably larger than the actor's head. Estimates vary, but some scholars believe that the Greek actor's height, in combination with the *kothurnoi*, mask, and *onkos*, might have reached seven feet. Certainly enough to be seen at the back of the house, but what about hearing the dialogue? The prevailing winds moving up the auditorium undoubtedly helped, and it has been speculated that the open mouth area of the mask served to amplify the actor's voice, like a cheerleader's megaphone. No hard evidence exists about this point, however, and it likely will remain a matter of speculation.

Although primarily discussing Roman New Comedy masks, Pollux indicates a greater variety of masks than might initially be imagined. An actor might change masks with his character's change of major mood or expression. Minor changes of mood could be handled by the actor using his mask in conjunction with his body position, vocal expression, and gesture. Nonetheless, some twenty-eight classes of masks existed in the four major categories of older men, young men, servants, and women. It is likely that members of a chorus or section of a chorus wore identical masks, except for the chorus leader. Since masks also existed for specific characters in specific plays, a tremendous quantity existed. Masks for comedies and satyr plays were more varied and exaggerated than those for tragedy.

Much that is advanced about the Greek use of properties is high speculation. The nonillusionistic, functional nature of the props can be generalized, but detailed specifics are lacking. Upon reading the plays, one can sense what was actually needed and what was left to the actor's art. Necessary props seem to include an altar as a place for refuge or to make a sacrifice, a tomb, sufficient furniture for sitting, and various vehicles to be used in conjunction with the *machina*, such as chariots. In addition to the *ekkyklema*, hand-carried litters were occasionally necessary. Hand props were probably more realistic in detail than set props, and included such items as torches and hand-held lamps to indicate nighttime since the plays were performed during the day. The props for tragedy were more symbolic than those used in comedy, and it is likely that those used in the satyr plays were quite realistic, numerous, and varied since much of the humor depended upon them.

ACTORS AND ACTING

The Chorus

Initially the chorus was the only performing element, and in the period before Aeschylus it numbered some fifty members. The early choral actors were amateur participants drawn from the five hundred to one thousand citizens who were actively involved in a festival. By the time of Aeschylus the chorus was reduced in size to twelve and then raised by Sophocles to fifteen. Euripides appears not to have altered the size of the chorus, but he certainly reduced its importance in his plays. The comic chorus consisted of twenty-four members, acting in unison or divided into two parts. As in other facets of Greek theatre, the chorus in comedy was much freer to act uninhibitedly than its counterpart in tragedy. The satyr chorus was the most raucous of all, often engaged in wild dancing and off-color humor.

The choral function in tragedy was somewhat different. The major choral entrance came just after the opening scene of the play, and the chorus was present throughout the action. The chorus members spoke by and to themselves at the end of each episode and served in the varied roles of prudent counselor to the protagonist, interested spectator, audience representative, and general facilitator and unifier of the play's action. Euripides and later dramatists of the second and first centuries B.C. reduced the importance of the chorus to little more than act break entertainment, a result of the rise in importance of dialogue and the individual speaking characters.

Rise of the Actor

Greek acting began to assume its place in theatre history with the emergence from the chorus of the first *hypocrite*, one who answers the chorus. This invention is generally credited to Thespis, who may have won first prize for it at the first City Dionysia. Thespis provided the model for a playwright to act in his own shows, rehearse the chorus, and attend to other production details, which became the norm for most of the sixth and fifth centuries B.C. By Aeschylus's time, a second speaking actor had been added so that real dialogue between characters was possible, and Aeschylus himself may have added a third speaking actor. The presentation of plays with three speaking actors not only allowed dialogue to occur, but also enabled a listener to overhear the dialogue and respond, a function previously assigned exclusively to the chorus. It has been noted that the chorus was in decline from the late fifth century B.C. onward, and the addition of these actors likely hastened its decline, no doubt to an increasingly appreciative audience.

As usual, comedy enjoyed more latitude. Three to six actors were often needed, and it's likely that the form of comic acting became increasingly broad and physical. As in tragedy, supernumeraries, those extras needed for crowd situations apart from the choral function, could speak a few lines and did not count as any of the three main actors. When not speaking, these actors may have functioned as stagehands. They wore no masks.

Earlier actors and chorus members were amateurs and were involved out of a sense of civic duty. By the late fifth century B.C., however, pay for principal performers was common, although few actors were in the occupation full time. During the fourth century B.C., acting rose in importance as a career, and specific actors attracted sizable audience followings. With the spread of the empire under Alexander, various victory festivals were added at which drama was presented, and this greatly assisted in making Greek acting and actors known and enjoyed over a large segment of the Mediterranean world. During the Hellenistic period, the actor's place in society was higher than at any other time in the history of the theatre. Actors were permitted freedoms not accorded to other citizens. They could visit hostile states to perform during times of war, they were granted immunity from military service, and their property was considered free from confiscation, should they run afoul of the law.

Acting Style

Little primary evidence exists regarding Greek acting style, yet the form of the theatre itself and what is generally accepted about theatre production can provide the basis for creating a consensus about the art of acting. The size of the auditoriums, ranging from a few thousand at Oropus to over twenty thousand at Ephesus, was responsible for the need to exaggerate the actor's height. In order to project to the rear of these auditoriums, a similarly exaggerated acting style was no doubt necessary. The body as a whole was used to convey the desired emotion. Gesture was broader and done more deliberately than today. With the mask providing whatever facial expression was necessary, expressiveness of face was not a factor in hiring and training actors, nor was the actor's personality an important factor. Acting in tragedy required the use of statuesque poses, and comic acting utilized more natural poses, yet both were highly stylized.

Vocally the Greek actor had to be a master in the art of speaking, and a great deal of speech training was required of those in the profession. A reading of the plays shows how closely the speeches parallel the principles of debate used in the Agora, providing further evidence of the need for oratorical training. In addition to speaking, the Greek actor also had to be able to sing or acclaim to music, for the plays reveal song-speech or song, particularly in the comedies. Actor training, then, no doubt included development of a strong resonant voice and much practice of musical scales. The three-actor limit on the production of Greek plays certainly necessitated that an actor play more than one part per play, given the number of speaking characters involved in many of the plays. Consequently, an actor needed a set of tonal and gesture qualities that could depict various emotional states, more than just the normal range needed for the portrayal of a single character. Above all, the Greek actor needed a natural plasticity for imitating and transmitting life in as many varieties as existed in the audience itself.

DEVELOPMENT OF
THE PROFESSIONAL THEATRE

Except for its choral beginnings, the method that developed for producing the Greek festival plays set a general pattern for the production of plays in the Western world. Since the festivals originated from religious sources, a member of the major religious order of Athens, and one of the city's nine principle magistrates, the *archon*, received applications from competing playwrights. The playwrights chosen to compete would each be provided a *choregos*, chosen by lot from the ranks of the wealthiest citizens of Athens, who would serve as the producer of the performance and pay most of the expenses of the play. In all, some fourteen *choregoi* per festival were selected, assuming one per play including the comedies. After 406 B.C., the costs of the long war between Athens and Sparta diminished the ranks of those able to serve as *choregoi*, and from that time cosponsorship, two *choregoi* per show, was permitted. Another party to the management function was the *architekton*, or lessee, of the theatre building. The function of this individual is clouded by inaccurate records and the passage of time, yet his function must closely parallel that of the modern theatre manager, the one responsible for minute house and production details and for operating the theatre at a profit.

Professional practices also began to appear in relation to audience control. By the mid–fifth century B.C., the use of an admission charge to buy tickets was

The Greek Theatre at the University of California at Berkeley.
(Courtesy of KaiDib Films International, Glendale, Calif.)

instituted under Pericles. For those who could not afford the price, Pericles is said to have created a policy of providing several hundred seats at no charge. Admission was general—that is, to an area of the *theatron* rather than to a reserved seat. A separate section may have existed for women, owing to the status of women in Athenian society. Performances, as the organization of the City Dionysia suggests, ran the entire day so that all of a single playwright's work could be seen in one sitting. "One sitting" must be taken loosely, for with wooden or stone bleacher seating, restlessness among the audience must have been the norm. The notion of a dispassionate public was quite foreign to the Athenian attender. Much eating and drinking and leaving the auditorium at will was common. Government officials were responsible for keeping order, and fines were imposed for improper behavior. It was not considered improper, however, to express opinions about the plays, actors, and playwrights by booing and cheering, throwing fruit and nuts, or leaving loudly in the middle of a scene. To the modern theatregoer this all seems strange, but one must remember that the plays were part of a week-long celebration, and the experience has no good modern parallel.

The profession of acting reached a zenith during the Hellenistic period. By the end of the fourth century B.C., professional actors had replaced amateurs in all facets of production, filling a demand created by the increased number of festivals. Not surprisingly, actor guilds formed to ensure equitable treatment for professional performers. The major guild, the Artists of Dionysos, was formed around 280 B.C. The Artists of Dionysos accepted anyone for membership who had a performance function at a festival, including playwrights. The guild maintained regional offices to handle local diversity and to be more responsive to the needs of its members. The strength of the guilds increased, so that by 133 B.C. there is record of fines being imposed for certain actor infractions such as missing rehearsals or extreme lateness for performances.

By the second century B.C., the Greek theatre was highly professionalized. This was achieved at the time the Greek world was falling under the control of the growing Roman Republic. Under the Romans the theatrical practices of the Greeks were either modified or forgotten, but a glorious period of world theatre was at an end.

RETROSPECT

The emergence of theatre as a formal art form occurred in Greece. More specifically, the two elements needed for theatrical activity to move from ritual to formal art occurred in Athens, namely, some sense of a state spirit and the movement of religion from a primary to a sophisticated concern. In Athens formal drama and theatrical practice were born. Why the city-state of Athens fostered the conditions for the birth of Western theatre may never be fully understood. Certainly the reasons are tied to politics since social and economic conditions are constant reflections in the mirror of the Athenian theatre. From the outset dramatic expression recognized that life has two broad facets, the tragic and the comic. The tragedy and comedy that emerged in Athens formalized these two concepts and established a standard of excellence that was to overshadow Western theatre for nearly two thousand years.

In theatre production, the essential elements of formal practice were also established in Greece. Needed was an area for the assembled audience to view the spectacle, a playing space for the chorus and basic character interaction, and an elevated area for the display of scenery and to emphasize certain elements of the action. Thus the basic spaces for the audience and presentation were defined; succeeding ages would refine and redefine them as their conventions required. Besides the specifics of the theatre structure, the basic tenets of theatre production were formed during the Hellenistic era. Acting and staging were initially defined, as were the basic notions of stage management, professionalism, and theatrical commercialism.

As in many other aspects of Western life, the theatre owes its formal foundations to the Greeks. In many elements of theatre practice, parallels to the theatrical quality established did not exist for several centuries. It truly was a fitting beginning for Western theatre. Later ages would alter and customize the practices laid down, but would rarely improve upon the basic fabric of theatre practice as defined by the Greeks.

Date	Greek History	Greek Theatre History	World History	World Theatre History
c. 1184 B.C.	Fall of Troy.		Period of the Judges in Israel. Twentieth Dynasty in Egypt.	Abydos "passion play" being performed in Egypt.
c. 1100 B.C.	Dorian invasion of Aegean area.		David, King of Israel.	
c. 800– 750 B.C.	Homer and Hesiod writing in Greece.			
594 B.C.	Solon's archonship in Athens.		Cyrus the Great establishes Persian empire.	
560–527 B.C.	Peisistratus is leader in Athens.	Thespis active as playwright and performer.		
534 B.C.		City Dionysia established by Peisistratus.		
525 B.C.		Aeschylus born.	Rome becomes a republic.	
c. 500 B.C.		Dramatic presentations moved to Precinct of Dionysos.	Celts arrive in Britain.	
496 B.C.		Sophocles born.		
490 B.C.	Battle of Marathon.		Xerxes I, King of Persia.	
487 B.C.		Comedy introduced into City Dionysia.		
484 B.C.		Euripides born. Aeschylus wins first victory at City Dionysia.		
480 B.C.	Battle of Salamis and Thermopylae.			
479 B.C.	Final defeat of Persians.			
472 B.C.		Aeschylus's *Persians*.		
469 B.C.	Socrates born.	Sophocles wins first victory over Aeschylus.		

Date	Greek History	Greek Theatre History	World History	World Theatre History
c. 465 B.C.		Orchestra built in Precinct of Dionysos.		
458 B.C.		Aeschylus's *Oresteia*.		
c. 450 B.C.		Aristophanes born.		
449 B.C.		Contest for tragic actors introduced.		
448 B.C.	Athenian empire established.			
442 B.C.		Contest for comic actors introduced.		
431–404 B.C.	Peloponnesian War.	Euripides' *Medea* (431 B.C.).		
429 B.C.	Plague in Athens.			
	Death of Pericles.	Sophocles' *Oedipus Tyrannus*.		
426 B.C.		Aristophanes' *Babylonians*.		
425 B.C.		*The Acharians*.		
c. 420 B.C.		Periclean Theatre built in Athens.		
416 B.C.	Athenian destruction of Melos.			
415 B.C.		Euripides' *Trojan Women*.		
406 B.C.		Deaths of Sophocles and Euripides.		
405 B.C.		Aristophanes' *The Frogs*.		
404 B.C.	Fall of Athens and end of the Peloponnesian War.			
		Period of Middle Comedy (c. 400–330 B.C.).		
399 B.C.	Socrates put to death.			

(Continued on page 46)

Date	Greek History	Greek Theatre History	World History	World Theatre History
396 B.C.	*Dialogues* of Plato.			
c. 385 B.C.	Plato's *Republic*. Theatre is oulawed in this utopian state.			
c. 380 B.C.		Death of Aristophanes.		
377 B.C.			Walls built around Rome.	
371 B.C.	Thebans defeat Spartans at Battle of Leuctra.			
c. 365 B.C.				Etruscan actors perform in Rome.
c. 350– 330 B.C.		Stone *skene* and auditorium built in Athens. Theatre built at Epidaurus.	Great Wall of China started.	
343 B.C.		Menander born.		
338 B.C.	Battle of Chaeronea. Macedonians become masters of Greece.			
336 B.C.	Alexander the Great begins his campaign of conquest.			
c. 330 B.C.		Aristotle's *Poetics*, first major theories of dramatic criticism.		
323 B.C.	Death of Alexander the Great.			
323–281 B.C.		Death of Menander (292 B.C.).	Wars among the generals of Alexander the Great.	
c. 280 B.C.		Formation of guilds for actors.		

Date	Greek History	Greek Theatre History	World History	World Theatre History
264–241 B.C.			First Punic War.	
			First public battles of gladiators in Rome (264 B.C.).	
c. 250 B.C.				Birth of Plautus.
c. 240 B.C.				Livius Andronicus translates Greek tragedies and comedies into Latin.
c. 235 B.C.				Tragedies of Gnaeus Naevius performed.
c. 220 B.C.				Ludi Romani established in Rome.
				Plautus, *Miles glorius* (205 B.C.).
219–201 B.C.			Second Punic War.	
218 B.C.			Hannibal crosses the Alps and invades Italy.	
202 B.C.			Defeat of Hannibal by Romans.	
190 B.C.				Birth of Terence.
186 B.C.				Cult of Bacchus (Dionysos) banned in Rome.
168 B.C.			Beginning of Roman domination of Western world.	

SELECTED READINGS

Arnott, Peter D. *Greek Scenic Conventions in the Fifth Century*. Oxford: Clarendon Press, 1962.
> An excellent brief introduction to production methods used in Athens.

Bieber, Margarete. *The History of the Greek and Roman Theatre*. 2nd ed. Princeton: Princeton University Press, 1961.
> A profusely illustrated history covering all aspects of classical theatre. Contains a highly useful glossary of ancient theatrical terms.

Bowra, C. M. *The Greek Experience*. London: Weidenfeld & Nicholson, 1957.
> Individual treatments of aspects of Greek culture such as religion, polis, art, and philosophy.

Cornford, Francis M. *The Origin of Attic Comedy*. New York: Anchor, 1961.
> In this work stress is placed on the irrational aspect of Greek thought with comedy seen as derivative of tragedy.

Ehrenberg, Victor. *The People of Aristophanes*. New York: Schocken, 1962.
> A sociological and historical account of the people of Athens as reflected in the plays. For evidence the author also draws upon playwrights other than Aristophanes. A very useful book.

Else, Gerald F. *The Origin and Early Form of Greek Tragedy*. New York: W. W. Norton, 1972.
> A detailed examination of the major theories on the origin of tragedy, and the presentation of a new and exciting approach to the origin and development of tragedy.

Graves, Robert. *The Greek Myths*. New York: G. Braziller, 1959.
> An excellent presentation of the essence of Greek mythology. A knowledge of mythology is a must for an understanding of the classical theatre.

McLeish, Kenneth. *The Theatre of Aristophanes*. New York: Taplinger, 1980.
> An examination of the plays from a production view, so it also touches on other aspects of Athenian theatre.

Pickard-Cambridge, A. W. *Dithyramb, Tragedy, and Comedy*. 2nd ed. Oxford: Clarendon Press, 1962.
> A standard and still useful study even if several points are under challenge from Else.

——————. *The Dramatic Festivals of Athens*. 2nd ed. Oxford: Clarendon Press, 1968.
> A major work of classical scholarship, this book is the most detailed available on the festivals, and it also contains very useful information on costuming, audience, actors, and the acting guilds.

Podlecki, Anthony J. *The Political Background of Aeschylean Tragedy*. Ann Arbor: University of Michigan Press, 1966.

A book that is indispensable to any attempt to gain an understanding of the relationship of Aeschylus to his society.

Robinson, Charles A. *Hellas: A Short History of Ancient Greece*. Boston: Beacon Press, 1962.
An excellent short history that covers all aspects of Greek civilization.

Sandbach, F. H. *The Comic Theatre of Greece and Rome*. New York: W. W. Norton, 1977.
A brief survey of comic forms and the major playwrights.

Walton, J. Michael. *Greek Theatre Practice*. Westport: Greenwood Press, 1980.
A fine treatment of the subject. If you have time to read only one book on Greek production methods, this should be it.

Webster, T. B. L. *An Introduction to Sophocles*. Oxford: Clarendon Press, 1936.
This work is a fine place to begin a detailed study of the craftsmanship of Sophocles.

——————. *The Tragedies of Euripides*. London: Methuen, 1967.
A major study that takes into consideration the extant plays, the fragments, and possible reconstruction of the lost plays.

ROME

ATHENS

PART III

Mirror Modifications:
THE ROMANS

The Romans, builders of the greatest cohesive empire of the classical world, had an inauspicious beginning in an agriculturally poor area on the Tiber River in central Italy. Yet in seven hundred years they became masters of the Mediterranean world, and part of their empire would endure until the middle of the fifteenth century. The contributions of the Romans in law, technology, architecture, and theatre still exert a powerful influence on modern civilization as it prepares for the twenty-first century.

A people not given to imaginative or speculative thinking, the Romans had a sense of duty, an urge for order, and a ruthlessness that made them dominate in Italy by the second century B.C. By the end of the third and last of the Punic Wars with Carthage, the Romans discovered themselves the major military power in the Mediterranean. "Some are born great, some achieve greatness, and some have greatness thrust upon them," notes Malvolio in Shakespeare's *Twelfth Night*. So it was with the Romans on their path to imperial glory: natural leaders who destroyed regional enemies to survive, only to discover the Western world was available for the taking.

Roman theatre was imitative; its inspirations and models were Greek. Theatre did not hold a position of respect in Roman society as it did in Greece. Laws and social conventions prevented Roman theatre from taking an active role in Roman life; as a result a vital link between a fledgling theatre and its public was denied. By the time Rome was in command of the Western world its theatrical fare was trivial. In the short span of less than two hundred years, Roman drama was created, briefly flourished, and then virtually disappeared. Yet the lesser Roman theatre has been more influential in the development of the Western stage than the greater Greek theatre. The direct line from modern theatre to the past runs not to Athens but to Rome.

4
ROMAN DRAMA

Origins of Roman Drama

Tradition assigns the birth of Roman drama to the year 240 B.C., yet earlier theatrical forms prepared the way for this literary nativity. The Italian origins of Roman drama are rooted in Etruscan dancing, the Greek *phlyakes* from southern Italy, the Fescennine verses, and the *fabula Atellana*. The Roman historian Livy noted the introduction of Etruscan dancers into Rome in 364 B.C. These dancers were highly popular, and their style was soon taken up by the young citizens of Rome, who incorporated into their dances improvised verses with accompanying gestures. The verses used were akin to the Fescennine verses, an improvised form closely associated with harvest festivals and weddings. At these times verses were exchanged between individuals in a contest of wits, and they were likely accompanied by gestures, thus providing a crude theatrical form.

The *fabula Atellana* was a short play with a long history of popularity in Roman theatre. These comic, semi-improvised plays of country life placed emphasis on the cunning and cheating of characters in a farcical situation. The most interesting aspect of the *Atellana* was its featuring of stock characters. Played by masked actors, these stock characters were four: Maccus, the stupid clown; Bucco, the greedy glutton; Pappus, the foolish old man; and Dossennus, the sly trickster. There are no surviving examples of the *Atellana*, but it is unlikely the plays were fully written out. Rather they developed out of a prearranged story line and relied on the actor's knowledge of the characteristics of his stock character. These popular Roman farces may well be the precursors of the *commedia dell'arte*, the popular plays of the Italian Renaissance.

The First Punic War (264–241 B.C.) sent the soldier-citizens of the Roman Republic into the Greek-dominated culture of southern Italy and Sicily for extended periods of time. There they were exposed to productions of Greek tragedies, comedies, and a type of farce, the *phlyakes*, that was unique to the area. The *phlyakes* were mimes that used travesties of mythology and daily life as their subject matter. They are shown in many vase paintings from the period, although the exact relationship between these paintings and actual stage productions is highly questionable. The stock characters and situations of the *phlyakes* were influential on the *Atellana* and the later Roman mimes.

Roman Festivals

The *ludi scenici* were the five major public festivals that included dramatic performances in their activities. They were the Ludi Romani, Ludi Florales, Ludi Plebei, Ludi Appolinares, and Ludi Megalensia. The number of festival days available for plays increased over the years: in 200 B.C. there were eleven; after 190 B.C. as many as seventeen; and by the reign of Augustus (27 B.C.–A.D. 14) the number had increased to forty-three. It is very difficult to state precisely the number of days available for play production in Rome because of the practice of *instauratio*, the repetition of an entire festival. All the festivals were connected to the state religion and officially offered up to a specific deity. An *instauratio* occurred when there was some impropriety in the observation. Since all aspects of the festival were official parts of the observation, opportunities for improprieties were numerous. Roman writers noted that if a dancer stopped at the wrong time or an actor forgot his lines, then the entire festival was deemed incorrectly performed. Additional performance days would be scheduled during the year for special events, such as state funerals, building dedications, and military triumphs.

Plays were not the only amusements provided during Roman festivals.

The Theatre of Herodes Atticus, Athens.
(Courtesy of Stephen M. Archer)

Chariot races, gladiatorial fights, beast fights, and rope dancers were among the other offerings, and often these events were staged at the same time as a dramatic production. In more than one prologue, the comic playwright Terence complains of losing his audience to a rival attraction. All the entertainments of the festivals were free to the people of Rome. The costs were paid by the state and by public officials who hoped to obtain votes in the next election. Popular plays helped win votes, but the plays of the festivals were not political since contemporary political affairs were forbidden as a subject in Roman drama.

DRAMA OF THE ROMAN REPUBLIC

The first written Latin comedy and tragedy were presented during the Ludi Romani in 240 B.C. The work of Livius Andronicus (c. 280–205 B.C.), they were translations from the Greek. Little survives from the plays of Andronicus, and even less factual information is available concerning his life. Although colorful stories exist about the Greek slave Andronicus who was later freed by his master, it is highly probable that Andronicus was an experienced actor-playwright who was brought to Rome to create a Roman version of Greek theatre.

Andronicus was the founder of Roman drama. His models were the Greek tragedies and the plays of Greek New Comedy, yet he was more than a mere translator. With his *fabula crepidata*, a tragedy based on Greek themes, and *fabula palliata*, a comedy in Greek dress, it was necessary for Andronicus to create a literary language for Latin, something that had not yet been done. A measure of Andronicus's success in this formidable task may be seen in the later honors he received. When the Roman Republic established a guild for poets, the *collegium poetarum*, the state recognized Andronicus as its leader.

Of the plays of Andronicus, all that remain are some fragments and the titles of three comedies and nine tragedies. Although his plays were dismissed as crude by later Roman writers, those writers owed a considerable debt to Andronicus. He was the founder and pioneer of Roman literature. Andronicus made many major achievements in Greek literature available to a non-Greek audience, he created metrical forms for Latin drama, and he set the pattern for Roman theatre for the next two hundred years.

The first native Roman playwright, Gnaeus Naevius (c. 270–201 B.C.), wrote both tragedies and comedies based on Greek originals. Yet unlike Andronicus, Naevius infused his plays with a strong Roman flavor that is apparent even in the few remaining fragments of his work. The known author of over forty plays, Naevius had his first production in 235 B.C. His originality and strong sense of patriotism led him to invent the Roman history play, the *fabula praetexta*. The *praetexta*, named after the toga worn by Roman magistrates, dealt with Roman heroes of history and legend. Unfortunately, the inability of Roman playwrights to work without Greek models and the sensitivity of the government to political subjects doomed this type of play to early extinction.

Naevius obviously had a marked preference for humor over history since over thirty of his known plays are comedies. As a writer of *fabula palliata*, he demonstrated a liveliness of line similar to the later work of Plautus. Even with his Greek settings, Naevius attempted to interject topical allusions into his plays. This practice led to political criticism appearing in the plays, and this led Naevius to jail. The ancient laws of Rome prescribed death for slander and a public beating for political allusions on stage. Powerful nobles had Naevius thrown into prison and later exiled. Naevius was a highly original playwright who attempted to make Roman drama reflect Roman life. His punishment placed a severe creative restraint upon later Roman playwrights.

Tragedy in the Roman Republic

Tragedy was very popular with theatre audiences in Rome. The plays of the three greatest tragic playwrights of the republic, Ennius, Pacuvius, and Accius, continued to be performed for two hundred years after their deaths. Such was the popularity of these plays that the entire audience would supply the proper line when an actor missed a cue. To a modern reader of the few fragments that remain, the plays seem pompous and highly rhetorical. Yet these were the very qualities that appealed to the Romans. With the works of these three playwrights, Roman tragic drama achieved its height.

Quintus Ennius (239–169 B.C.), who was strongly influenced by the plays of Euripides, brought a burst of Hellenistic enthusiasm into Roman drama. Ennius wrote at least twenty tragedies, yet only a few fragments are now extant. Judging by these, the most characteristic aspect of Ennius's work was a tendency to increase the rhetorical elements of the Greek originals. This particularly shows itself in an overemphasis on the emotional use of language. Overstatement was a general trait in Roman tragedy, the result of an attempt to create a noble-sounding diction. Ennius was not immune to this trait in his attempts to Romanize his Greek originals. His major contributions to the development of Roman drama were his innovations in meter and language.

Marcus Pacuvius (c. 220–130 B.C.) was Ennius's nephew and theatrical heir. Pacuvius was a painter in addition to being a playwright, and the time spent in this other artistic field may explain why he produced so few plays during a long lifetime. The titles of thirteen tragedies by this playwright are known, and from these plays fewer than four hundred lines have survived. He gained a reputation in antiquity as a scholarly writer. The available evidence illustrates a tendency in Pacuvius toward philosophical sentiments and reveals his considerable attention to the language of his plays. His tragedies remained popular for more than a century, which shows that the Romans enjoyed a serious play, but later audiences and readers found in them too much pathos and pedantry.

Lucius Accius (c. 170–86 B.C.) was the most prolific writer of tragedies in Roman drama, and his output of more than forty-five plays surpasses the combined efforts of both Ennius and Pacuvius. Accius was admired for the dignity of his style and his ability to express the Roman love of moral courage and heroism. Only seven hundred lines of fragments remain from the plays of

Accius, too few to gain a true sense of his skill as a dramatist. Later Roman writers praised his abilities, particularly the force and elevation of his language. While displaying the preference for violent stories common to all the Roman tragic playwrights, Accius's plays show a marked taste for the ghoulish.

Few new tragedies were written after the death of Accius, but tragic plays did not disappear from Roman theatre. Owing to the popularity of the old plays, tragedy remained on the stage in Rome for another hundred years. The decline in tragic play writing, and play writing in general, can be traced to the declining status of theatre at the end of the Roman Republic. The writing of plays for performance was not considered a worthy occupation. It was impossible to be associated with the theatre in the Augustan and post-Augustan eras and retain a respectable position in society. In the years following the reign of Augustus, the stage was dominated by the mime and the pantomime, and the only important tragic playwright after Accius was Seneca, who will be discussed later in this chapter.

Comedy in the Roman Republic

It is fortunate all the surviving examples of the *fabula palliata* from the Roman Republic are the works of two major Latin playwrights, Plautus and Terence. The *fabula palliata*, comedy in Greek dress, strived to retain the stories, stock characters, and settings of Greek New Comedy. The *palliata* is based on Greek originals, but the amount of dependence or deviation from the originals is conjectural since the Greek plays have not survived. The practice of *contaminato*, combining two or more Greek plays or their parts to get one Latin play, was very common. Roman comedies were composed of two elements: *diverbia*, the spoken scenes, and *cantica*, scenes recited or sung to musical accompaniment. Dialogue, song, and dance were all integrated into the action of the play. This interweaving of song and dialogue in Roman comedy makes it a far-distant cousin of the twentieth-century musical.

Plautus Titus Maccius Plautus (c. 254–184 B.C.) is the most outstanding playwright of Roman drama. Little is actually known of his life since the biographical evidence from antiquity is sparse and questionable. Accounts of early work in the theatre, before his career as a playwright, are believable since this would help explain his superb sense of comic effect and theatricality. How he learned Greek, gained his knowledge of New Comedy, and achieved his mastery of Latin remain a mystery. The plays are no mystery: they remain some of the greatest pieces of comic theatre in the world.

Roman writers give Plautus credit for writing as many as 130 plays during his career, but a more realistic figure is 48. Of these possible 48 plays, only 20 complete plays are extant, plus one hundred lines from a twenty-first. The best of these plays are generally considered to be *Amphitryon*, *The Pot of Gold*, *The Captives*, *The Twin Menaechmi*, *The Haunted House*, *The Rope*, *Pseudolus*, and *The Braggart Warrior*. All of the extant plays of Plautus appear to have been written during the last twenty-five years of his life.

Much of Plautus's work reflects the carelessness of the harried professional writer. Evidence from the Roman era suggests that comic play writing was a highly competitive field, so to be financially successful a playwright needed to be both a witty and a fast writer. In his hurry to produce plays for the theatrical marketplace, Plautus often neglected to connect various elements in his story or to successfully meld parts from his Greek originals into an artistic whole. The constant effort to provoke laughter in the ever-restless Roman audience resulted in the interjection of extraneous material into the action of the plays. Anachronisms abound in the scripts as actors, portraying Greek characters, drop out of character to tell jokes reflective of Roman life. Yet to fault Plautus for structural problems is to overlook his theatrical genius and the sheer energy and fun of his plays.

The comic elements in Plautus are numerous and varied: puns, satire, parody, backchat (repartee between audience and speaker), and pure slapstick are all part of the mixture. The mixture is served up in the colorful, colloquial language of the streets of Rome. Yet it is a glorious, living language that places its creator in the company of the masters of the comic stage: Aristophanes, Shakespeare, and Molière.

Terence The short life and meteoric career of Publius Terentius Afer (c. 195–159 B.C.) are cluttered with inconsistencies. The traditional account of his life holds that Terence was a Carthaginian by birth and brought as a slave to Rome, where he was educated and freed by his master, a Roman senator. He later became a close friend of some very important young Romans. His six plays were written and performed during the years 166–160 B.C., and during this period he was embroiled in an artistic controversy with other Roman playwrights. After 160 B.C. he left for Greece and never returned. Nearly all these events have been challenged and debated, and the truth is lost in the scholarly gossip of two thousand years.

Early manuscript depicting a scene from Terence's Adelphi.

All six of Terence's plays have survived. The plays—*The Woman of Andros, The Eunuch, The Self-Tormentor, Phormio, The Mother-in-Law*, and *The Brothers*—are based on Greek originals, four of them by Menander. Terence wrote for the same rowdy audience Plautus entertained thirty years earlier, but Terence was a more refined playwright, more Hellenistic in tone. Gone is the vulgarity, the broad humor, the anachronisms of Plautian comedy. In its place Terence substitutes subtle humor expressed in the language of the aristocratic culture of his friends. The madcap pace of Plautus is replaced by the slow, complex story structure of Terence. The dual story line with an interlocked final solution is a major contribution of Terence to Western theatre.

The prologues of Terence's plays reveal the intense rivalry that existed among playwrights in Rome. His friendships with the rich and influential created hostility and jealousy among other playwrights, and an effort was made to destroy his theatrical career. Four artistic charges were made against Terence: the mixing of Greek originals, plagiarism, assistance in composition from friends, and lack of content and strength in his plays. All the charges were answered in the prologues of his plays, some with more conviction than others. Time has vindicated Terence, and the names of his accusers are forgotten and their plays lost.

Influence of Plautus and Terence   Although Plautus and Terence worked from Greek originals, neither playwright can be accused of being merely a translator. The true originality of both was lightly covered with a Greek mantle. The twenty-six plays from these two dramatists represent the storehouses of humor, character, and situation from which comic theatre was drawn for two thousand years. Both playwrights continued to be read, if not produced, during the Roman Empire and the Middle Ages. During the Italian Renaissance the plays were read, performed, and used as models for early Italian comedies. Italian comedy, inspired by Plautus and Terence, influenced the development of comic drama in the rest of Europe. The Latin influence was always present as comic theatre grew and matured throughout Europe and the Americas. Plautus and Terence, in a thousand different guises, still continue to make us laugh.

Fabula Togata   About the time of Terence's death a new type of comedy, based on Roman life, appeared on the Roman stage. The *fabula togata*, comedy in Roman dress, found its themes in the lives of the lower classes in the city and country. The *togata* was also called *tabernaria*, after the name of the homes of the poor. The new *togata* and revivals of the older *palliata* were both popular on the Roman stage in the second century B.C.

Because of the more active role of women in Roman society, the *togata* represents family relationships in a more normal fashion than the earlier Roman comedies based on Greek originals. The courtesan and the slave girl were no longer the chief love interests in these plays, as the women of Rome were free to appear in public and manage their own affairs. The wily slave of Greek New Comedy disappeared since the Romans did not approve of a

Roman slave outwitting a Roman master. Although *togata* fragments do not enable the reconstruction of a complete story for any of the plays, it appears they centered on concerns about dowry questions, love affairs, marriage problems, and trickery. Three playwrights specialized in the writing of the *togata*: Titinius, Afranius, and Quinctius.

From Titinius, a contemporary of Terence and the inventor of the *togata*, there are fifteen titles and 180 lines. Of the works of Lucius Afranius, the most important writer of *togata*, there remain forty-four titles and over four hundred lines. Quinctius Atta, who was admired for his female characters, is represented by eleven titles and a mere twenty lines. After the death of Quinctius in 77 B.C., the *togata* declined in popularity on the stage.

Mime

Mime performances date back at least to the second century B.C. in Rome, and during the period of the empire the mime was the most popular form of theatrical entertainment. The Latin word *mimus* is from a Greek word meaning "to imitate," and "mime" refers to both the performer and the play. Mimes were so named because they were imitators of human affairs and, as such, took all things of heaven and earth as their subject matter. The common Latin term for the mime actor was *planipes*, "with bare feet," for the performer wore neither the slipper (*soccus*) of comedy nor the buskin (*cothurnus*) of tragedy.

The mime was mainly a nonliterary theatrical form. The action of the play was largely improvised on an announced theme or story, and it placed heavy emphasis on dance, gesture, and facial expression in addition to spoken lines. The subject was usually comic, and the performers, both men and women, appeared without masks. At the head of the mime company was the *archimimus*, the archmime, who was the master of the group. Mimes were not held in high social esteem, and Decimus Laberius, a Roman knight who wrote mimes, lost his social position when Julius Caesar forced him to perform as a mime. Yet the mime performers were often beloved by their public and were the friends of rulers. The mime Theodora married the emperor Justinian and ruled the Eastern Empire.

Obscenity, ritualistic satire, and adultery were three popular subject areas for mimes, and these subjects brought the mimes into conflict with the early Christian Church. Obscene gestures and dances, nudity, and simulated and sometimes actual copulation were not uncommon on the mime stage, and these activities gained the mime players their notoriety with the early Church fathers. Most scandalous to the early Christians were the mime plays based on the sacraments. A particular favorite with the mimes was the rite of baptism, for they and their audiences found the dunking of a person in a tub of water vastly amusing. Yet the early annals of the Church record the miraculous conversion of mime actors to Christianity during the performance of these plays. Saint Genesius, the patron saint of actors, was one such mime actor. Even after the triumph of Christianity in the empire and the fall of Rome, the mimes continued to amuse audiences in parts of the old empire.

DRAMA OF THE ROMAN EMPIRE

Throughout their vast empire the Romans built the-atres, but by the time these theatres were being constructed, the writing of drama for production had ceased. The performances presented in the grand theatres of the Roman world were mimes, pantomimes, and even gladiatorial battles. Roman sources suggest that the last new dramatic work written for the stage was for a victory celebration in 31 B.C. The tragedies of Seneca, the only extant Roman plays from the period, were written to be read, not performed.

Seneca

Lucius Annaeus Seneca (4 B.C.–A.D. 65) was the son of an important Roman lawyer and a member of an influential family. Although he was greatly attracted to philosophy, Seneca became a magistrate in the Roman government. His writing and eloquence drew the attention of the emperor Caligula, who out of jealousy would have had Seneca put to death except for rumors that the talented lawyer was already dying from natural causes. The rumors were false, but Seneca prudently turned from oratory to the safer fields of philosophy and literature.

Portrait bust of Seneca.

Prominent in the imperial court after the death of Caligula, Seneca was a favorite of Julia and Agrippina, the nieces of the emperor Claudius. Accused of intriguing with Julia, Seneca was exiled to Corsica for eight years. Recalled to Rome as tutor to the young Nero, he continued to guide his former pupil for five years after Nero became emperor in A.D. 54. Having fallen out of favor with the insane emperor, Seneca was implicated in a conspiracy in A.D. 65 and ordered by Nero to commit suicide.

Seneca was a poet, philosopher, lawyer, courtier, teacher, playwright, and multimillionaire. All of these elements of his life, with the exception of the last, enter into the style and content of his plays. Because of the low social status of the professional theatre, Seneca wrote his plays for private reading or recitation. They are vessels for conveying his philosophical thoughts, are highly rhetorical in style, and were not written with production in mind.

Of Seneca's nine tragedies, the most noteworthy are *Phaedra*, *Medea*, *The Trojan Women*, and *Oedipus*. All nine show his strong attraction to the plays of Euripides. This is not surprising since both playwrights have a strong interest in the irrational aspects of human nature. Seneca was far freer in working with his Greek models than earlier Roman tragic playwrights. He attempted to unify the story lines by eliminating minor characters and events and concentrating his attention on the major ones. He also introduced strong psychological motivation for his characters and subordinated the theological elements present in the Greek originals. Most unlike Greek drama is Seneca's stress on such supernatural elements as ghosts and soothsayers, his rhetoric for the sake of the sound of it, and his taste for the gruesome. These very elements appealed most to the later Renaissance playwrights who did not understand the subtle interplay of the original Greek scripts.

The structure of Seneca's plays is remarkably uniform. They are divided into five acts and the dialogue is terse. Seneca is fond of the use of *senteniae* in his plays: self-contained, pointed bits of wisdom such as "Successful and fortunate crime is called virtue" or "A good mind possesses a kingdom." The structure and dialogue form of Seneca's plays were much copied by later European playwrights, who found in these plays near-perfect models. Thus the plays of Seneca were to become the link between classical tragedy and the birth of modern tragic drama.

Influence of Seneca

It has been rightly said that the true memorial to Seneca is the tragic stage of England, France, and Italy. Without his plays the development of modern drama would have been significantly altered. Italian tragedy of the Renaissance was almost entirely Senecan in style. The early Italian playwrights considered Seneca far superior to the Greek playwrights, and they were particularly drawn to the gruesome elements in his plays. The French playwrights of the sixteenth and seventeenth centuries were fond of the Senecan rhetorical style since it provided a classical model for long lamentations on a tragic theme. An English translation of Seneca's plays was published in 1581, and in the following years his influence was intermixed with the popular Elizabethan theatre. Shakespeare, Jonson, and most of their contemporaries were strongly affected by Seneca's themes of revenge and murder, his ghosts, and his *sententiae*. The golden age of English tragedy has at its core the plays of Seneca.

Pantomime

Pantomime, a form of interpretative dance with script, was introduced into Rome in 22 B.C. The pantomime actors worked to musical and chanted accompaniment, and they silently related the action of the story through highly expressive gestures. The stories for the pantomimic plays were frequently taken from mythology and were often highly lascivious in presentation. The most talented pantomime actors had some fame among the general Roman public, but the fortunes of these performers were more closely tied to the imperial court than others in the Roman theatre. This involvement in the court and its intrigues led to many pantomime actors being banished or executed by the sometimes capricious emperors. The decline of the imperial court and the increasing power of the Church assured the eventual disappearance of the pantomime actor.

The Theatre and the Early Christian Church

As mentioned earlier, the rites of the early Christians were a popular butt of humor for the mimes, and the theatre was viewed by many early Christians as both pagan and evil. Both institutions used their

Wall painting from Pompeii showing the presentation of a mime.

Roman theatre at Sabratha, Libya.
(Courtesy of KaiDib Films International, Glendale, Calif.)

public forums, the pulpit and the stage, to present their point of view. The often uneasy relationship between Christianity and the theatre began in Rome and continues into the twentieth century.

For its first two hundred and fifty years, Christianity was tolerated and sometimes persecuted in the Roman Empire and exercised little influence in relation to the theatre. The most hostile early Christian campaign against the theatre was waged by Tertullian (c. 160–230), an early theologian whose *De spectaculis* (Of Spectacles) condemned the theatre, circus, and amphitheatre as places of idolatry and performers as creatures of the Devil. Early councils of the Church decreed that actors could not be received into the Christian community unless they gave up their profession, barred Christians from marrying actors, and threatened excommunication for any Christian who attended the theatre on a Sunday or holy day. In 392, Christianity was made the official religion of the Roman Empire, and the power of the Church began to grow.

Such was the popularity of theatrical entertainments in the Roman Empire that the Church, even working with the government, was unable to destroy the theatre. Laws were passed in an effort to curb the influence of actors: they were forbidden to wear gold or rich fabrics, to dress in ecclesiastical costumes on stage, or to be attended by slaves in public. Yet the concerns of the Church did not stop the majority of the Christian community from attending the theatre, which continued to be popular in the Eastern Roman Empire until the invasions of the Saracens in the seventh century. In the Western Roman Empire, what the Church could not remove, the invading barbarians destroyed. In 410, Rome

5
ROMAN THEATRE ARCHITECTURE AND PRODUCTION

The collaborative arts of theatre are rarely in equal balance at any one period in theatre history, and often the dominant art form gives a good indication of what was culturally important in a given period. During the Roman Republic, the period prior to 27 B.C., the emphasis of dramatic art was largely centered on elements other than the building and its scenery. During the empire period, the dominant art of the theatre gradually shifted to the structure and its stagecraft, and these totally dominated the other arts of the theatre in the final centuries before the Roman Empire collapsed.

EVOLUTION OF THE ROMAN PLAYHOUSE

As the Romans began to conquer various parts of the Hellenistic world, they pressed existing playhouses into their service with only minor modifications. These remodeled theatres ultimately helped to establish the formal structural pattern of the Roman playhouse.

Characteristics of the Greco-Roman Playhouse

Since the Greco-Roman playhouse was essentially a Greek theatre with Roman modifications, the tenets of the original playhouse still applied. The auditorium was larger than a semicircle even though the elaborated stage house of the Romans often touched the auditorium walls, thus making the entire structure seem like one architectural unit. The *orchestra* was similarly encroached upon by the expanded scene building. A key difference between the Greco-Roman and Roman theatres is in this encroachment, since the Greco-Roman modifications to the stage were simply built over the existing Hellenistic *orchestra*, creating the appearance of a semicircular form.

Several other changes to the Hellenistic theatre comprise the Greco-Roman structure. Although not all of them are seen in every theatre, enough are seen in sufficient variety that a consensus can be formed. The lowest row of seats was moved forward so that it abutted the circumference of the *orchestra*. The stage front received a major reconstruction to make it more elaborate and decorative, and this change contributed to the elaborate scenic facade known as the *scaena frons*, an important element in Roman theatres built after 55 B.C. The stage of the Greco-Roman theatre is lower and deeper than in the Hellenistic theatre; the depth ranged from twelve to twenty feet, and the height of the stage varied from approximately two to four feet. Since the Romans were most concerned with visual display, the *scaena frons* was more visible from the important seats in the front of the auditorium. The deepening of the stage ultimately allowed for expanded side wing (*versurae*) entrances, so necessary in staging the Roman drama. These changes were the major reforms to the playhouse begun by Roman modifiers. All were aimed at making the stage and its setting the dominant feature of the theatrical experience.

Characteristics of the Roman Playhouse

The stage and auditorium of the Greek playhouse had been separate parts of the general concept, and the entire arrangement had required a hillside to support the auditorium. With the development of the arch as a means of weight transference and better engineering on such problems as water runoff, the Roman playhouse was free from these restrictions. The most striking feature of the Roman playhouse was that it was a stand-alone structure, a single architectural unit, with no division between stage and auditorium. Where a Roman theatre is found built against a hillside, such as at Orange, France, it is a matter of choice, not necessity, and done to take advantage of natural conveniences. A single architectural structure does require greater accessibility for audience and performers. This was accomplished through the

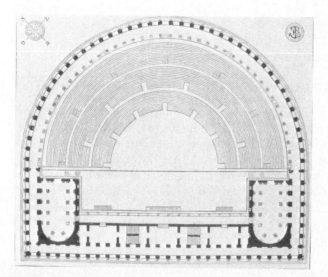

Plan for the Theatre of Marcellus, Rome.

vomitoria, vaulted tunnels that replaced the *parodoi* of the Hellenistic play-house. These passageways ran under parts of the seating and looked very much like the entranceways of a modern sports arena.

Other Roman changes in the auditorium reflect the concern with visual spectacle. The audience seating and the orchestra are both exactly 180 degrees, a true semicircle. The Roman architect Vitruvius, in his *De architectura* (15 B.C.), described precisely how to lay out these parts of the theatre, and it is clear that he not only prescribed correct procedure for future theatre architects, but also described what he had observed in previous theatre structures. The stage itself, the *pulpitum,* was higher and deeper than the Greco-Roman stage. Individual theatres varied, of course, but major theatres in large population centers had stages approximately five feet high and were deeper than twenty feet. The auditorium and stage house were of a uniform height, allowing for a three-story *scaena frons* of some twenty-plus feet per story to surround the *pulpitum.* The length of the *pulpitum* also varied widely, ranging from about one hundred feet to slightly in excess of the length of a modern football field. With this massiveness in the visual parts of the theatre, the other production elements were dwarfed and took on secondary importance. Over the stage was a coffered wooden roof that provided some protection from the sun and helped keep the focus of the audience on the *scaena frons.* Attached to a double row of wooden poles anchored in stone supports, an awning, called the *velium,* gave the Roman audience some

The Roman theatre at Arles.
(Courtesy of Ken Livingston)

The Romans

The Roman theatre at Orange.
(Courtesy of Ken Livingston)

protection from the sun. It did not cover the entire *orchestra* area because of problems with ventilation and lighting. The *scaena frons*, the most important visual element in the Roman theatre, grew in importance and dominance throughout the empire period as is seen clearly in the theatres built at Orange and at Aspendos and in the Theatre of Herodes Atticus in Athens. The major openings in the elaborate scenic facade replaced the singular stage openings in the Greek *skene*. The side wings were incorporated into the *scaena frons* as well, and they provided major entrance points for actor as well as dressing rooms and work spaces for scenery and properties. The *orchestra* had a low wall around it, no doubt to protect the audience from the activities there when the theatres were used for water spectacles or animal or gladiatorial contests.

Other parts of the Roman playhouse had more to do with performance than with the architectural unit itself. The use of a front curtain, or *auleum*, suggests concern for keeping some of the performance from audience sight until a specific time. The curtain was generally used only to begin and end the performance, and may have also been used to reveal special tableau scenes. Two theories exist about the workings of the *auleum*. One suggests that the curtain was stored in a trough at the front of the stage and raised on telescoping wooden poles to conceal a scene. The other theory, drawn from later theatrical practices during the empire period, suggests that the curtain was stored above the front of the stage and lowered on ropes, similar to its use today. A smaller back curtain, the *siparium*, was used for mimes and covered at least a portion

A drawing of a Roman theatre illustrating the use of the velium *to protect the audience.*

of the scenic facade. Located in the stage floor were a series of trapdoors that served the increasing need for spectacle in the Roman theatre.

Like the Greek theatre structure, the Roman playhouse did not come into existence until a century or two after the contributions of the major Roman playwrights. The nature of the Roman stage in their time is the subject of much conjecture. It probably was of the temporary wooden variety, assembled for each festival, and consisted of a simple flat playing space somewhat elevated above the ground. The audience sat or stood in front, and a plain back curtain, on which were represented the *thyromata* of the Hellenistic stage, provided access for the actors. When permanent theatres began to be built, they were often erected in some semisacred precinct, often in conjunction with a temple. The addition of a temple to the structure may have been necessary to placate certain politicians who thus felt more comfortable about allowing the theatre to be built at all. So it may have been with the Theatre of Pompey, the first permanent playhouse in Rome, which included a temple to Venus as part of its construction.

STAGE MACHINERY AND SCENIC DEVICES

Scenic Practice

Scenery in the Greek theatre had been used symbolically; that is, scenes depicted general types of settings rather than specific environments for each different play. Vitruvius's three scenes, one each for tragedy, comedy, and satyr plays, have been previously discussed, and these conventions continued. Since comedy was the mainstay of the Roman stage, the standard scene for it warrants further exploration. Roman comedies, including mime and pantomime, generally call for an outdoor street scene with at least three houses to line the street. The doors and windows of these houses

The Romans

need to be practical, capable of being used by an actor as if they were real. Certainly the staging is enhanced if all these elements are fully functional. There is disagreement about whether the openings in the *scaena frons* were routinely used or whether an elaborately painted *siparium* provided the locale and the needed entrances. Assuming the actual stage facade was used, enough entrances existed in the back wall alone to stage most of the comedies, and certainly enough existed if the *versurae* exits are included. The comedies include numerous devices in them that employ eavesdropping, mistaken identity, and robust physical activity. If the *scaena frons* were actually used, there were plenty of places extant among the niches and post-and-lintel facade pillars for these scenes to be played with comic plausibility. In Roman tragedy a single house is usually required. Likely all three main doors in the back wall were entrances to different parts of that house, with the *versurae* entrances leading to conventionalized places needed in the plays, or to buildings immediately adjacent to that of the major scene.

Machines and Devices

If Vitruvius is correct, the main method of changing scenery was with the *periaktoi*. The difference between the Hellenistic and

Supports for the velium poles in a Roman theatre.
(Courtesy of Ken Livingston)

Roman use of the device was one of degree rather than basic function. Likely Roman *periaktoi* were enlarged, both in individual size and in number, and were used about the stage. The increased size is the subject of speculation, yet it seems justified by the size of the *scaena frons* itself. If Vitruvius's suggestions for scene changes are to be believed, the *periaktoi* would have had to be of sufficient size to effect a visual change of such significance to be plausible. Placement of the *periaktoi* was most likely near the *versurae* since no conclusive evidence exists that they were fully integrated into the *scaena frons* itself.

Given the Roman penchant for spectacular scenic display, other scenic devices were probably widely used, although primary documentation is sketchy. The high walls forming the parameter of the theatre preclude effective use of machinery like the crane, and the extant plays do not suggest the use of such devices.

Costumes and Masks

If there is one area of theatrical production that shows a direct line between Greek practice and its Roman counterpart, it is the area of

A stone mask at the theatre at Ostia.

(Courtesy of Stephen M. Archer)

costumes and masks. Both aids to the actor were used as in the Hellenistic period, although there were variations in comedy and tragedy and more significant changes in mime and pantomime. In comedy the Roman *tunica*, a short-sleeved garment worn to the knee, formed the basic costume with a cloak, or *toga*, worn over it. Variations on this existed in the *togata* and the *palliata*. Tragic costumes varied the least from Greek models, the major difference being in the degree of stylization. All costume elements, including footwear, exaggerated the actor's height more than in the Greek theatre. Masks continue to be, in form and function, as described earlier.

In mime more significant changes occurred. The tunic remained the basic dress, but a hood (*ricinium*) and occasionally a patched jacket (*centunuculus*) were worn. These costume changes were primarily for characters from the lower strata of society or for specific character types. Following Greek principles, high-society characters continued to wear the finest in contemporary dress. Masks were usually not worn by mime actors since the form demanded a high level of realistic presentation.

Pantomime actors wore long *tunicae* and *togae* that were loosely fitted to allow for the active physical movement required in this dramatic form. Regarding the masks for pantomime, the basic form remained the whole-head mask with the mouth area closed. Ancient accounts refer to them as being more natural than regular masks. Given the demands of the presentation of Roman drama, these masks would likely have been the most natural of all Roman masks.

ACTORS AND ACTING

Roman actors (*histriones*) generally did not enjoy the high place in society that was accorded Greek actors, nor was the profession as respected. Since the acting profession included both slaves and freemen, its social standing tended to be low. Most Romans considered acting an occupation filled with slaves or former slaves. Whatever esteem the profession enjoyed was at its highest during the republic, for during the empire slave actors from conquered nations performed most acting functions on the Roman stage.

Acting Style

Like many other aspects of Roman theatre practice, acting drew heavily upon earlier Greek models. Tragedy and comedy were acted in a style very similar to their Greek counterparts; serious drama used more deliberate speech and movement patterns, and comedy utilized everyday speech combined with agility and flair in presentation. Gesture in all cases was enlarged to the size of Roman theatres.

It was in the new areas of mime and pantomime that most of the differences in Roman acting appeared. Since no masks were worn in the mime, there was an emphasis on the physical characteristics of the actor. Thus mime actors moved and spoke in a fairly natural style, with conventionalized patterns to enhance their physical characteristics. Pantomime required even more from the actor, since it was basically built upon individual efforts. Speech was of no consequence in pantomime, so the acting style was based entirely upon movement, which was highly athletic and dance-oriented. As with pantomime today, relatively restrained and understated gesture and movement were used to make a point. Versatility was part of the pantomime actor's art, since the portrayal of several characters in a single performance was necessary.

The Actors

Roman actors were either slave or free, depending upon the type of company and the specific art form. Although the tradition of male actors generally continued, female actors appeared in the mime. Highly talented freemen who chose to be actors could earn a considerable fortune from direct payment for services and indirect payment for special performances and favors. At the other end of the spectrum, slave actors could be punished or sold for turning in a bad performance.

The most famous actor of the Roman Republic was Quintus Roscius (c. 126 –62 B.C.). Although born a slave, he earned sufficient money through his acting to purchase his freedom. He was unusual for his time in acting both comedy and tragedy since an actor usually chose one only. Roscius's fame was so great that his name became synonymous with the term "actor" itself. Later in his career he founded a school for actors and public speakers, and one of its most famous students was Cicero, the great Roman senator. Other well-known actors in Roman history were Aesopus, a contemporary of Roscius, the playwright Livius Andronicus, and Publilius Pellio, who acted in many of the plays of Plautus.

Actor Training

The training of Roman actors did not differ significantly from that of Greek actors and centered on the technique of the craft. Oratory was studied as the proper way to speak on stage, particularly in tragedy. Comic speech, although more conversational, still demanded study in pronunciation and articulation to be heard by the rowdy Roman audience. Movement training was very like the training athletes and dancers received, for control of the body was a key element in all dramatic forms. Mime performers were recipients of special dance instruction, because of the nature of that art, as were practitioners of pantomime.

Actor Organization

Roman acting companies apparently had no direct restriction upon their size, which varied from four to six members in the basic troupe. With supernumeraries, these companies could be as large as sixty. As the Greek theatre had its *architekton*, so the Roman theatre had a similar functionary, the actor-manager (*dominus*). Much of what is known about the duties of the *dominus* comes from the prologues of Terence's plays. "Producer" is a good word for the actor-manager's function because he was responsible for hiring actors and other personnel, attending to the details of preparing the theatre, and generally overseeing the preparation of all other production details. Records indicate that the actor-manager had a financial interest in revivals of plays that he originally produced, and that occasionally he acquired property rights over the manuscripts.

No direct parallel to the Greek professional actors' union, the Artists of Dionysos, existed during the Roman Republic, but there was a loosely structured organization, the *collegium poetarum*. This organization of actors and poets was founded in 207 B.C., and its members were generally held in high esteem during the early years of the republic. It had no active life during the empire.

ROMAN PRODUCTION ORGANIZATION

As noted in Chapter 4, drama was introduced formally as an art of Roman life at the state festivals. The festivals were managed by magistrates, state-appointed men who, like their Greek counterpart the *choregoi*, contributed some of their own resources to the effort as a demonstration of public consciousness. The drama portion of any festival was left to the *dominus*, who was under contractural obligation to the magistrate. More than one company would perform during a festival, payment being made directly to the *dominus* for distribution to the company. Prizes, usually additional payment, were occasionally awarded, but these did not have the stature of the prizes awarded at the Greek festivals.

The Audience

Roman audience members were going to a festival, and a festive atmosphere prevailed in the playhouses. Although the plays were done as extended one-acts, no one felt compelled to sit and watch the entire performance. Vendors operated immediately outside the theatre building, so inattention to the play was probably heightened by indiscriminate exits from the theatre to obtain refreshments and attend to other personal needs. When paying attention, the Roman audience did not shrink from expressing its opinion, and acting troupes increasingly curried favor to enhance their prize money. To a large extent, the appreciation of the crowd determined who won the prizes.

In contrast to the Greek festivals, admission was free to all classes of Roman society. Although the prime *orchestra* seats were usually reserved for senators and other dignitaries, no apparent stratification of seating existed. One can only imagine the scramble that must have prevailed in the rush for seats.

Another reason for leaving the theatre while a play was in progress was to see another event of the festival, since circus-type entertainments were going on at the same time. In the prologue of Terence's *The Mother-in-Law*, the playwright complains that the current production is the third attempt at performance, the first two having been interrupted by such entertainments, and he entreats the audience to stay this time.

THE AMPHITHEATRE: ROMAN NONTHEATRICAL ENTERTAINMENT

The most popular nontheatrical entertainment was racing, and chariot races were chief among its forms. These events were held in a large oblong arena known as a *circus*. The largest ever constructed was the Circus Maximus in Rome, begun around 600 B.C. and eventually enlarged during the empire to hold 180,000 spectators. Laid out with an open end for starts and finishes, one turn, and a divided half-mile straightaway, twelve chariots could race simultaneously in the Circus Maximus. Its width was equivalent to the length of two football fields put end to end, and it contained a center island with appropriate statuary to divide the track. By the second century A.D., every provincial town of any size had its own *circus*. Other entertainments available at the *circus* were an assortment of the kinds

The amphitheatre at Pompeii.
(*Courtesy of KaiDib Films International, Glendale, Calif.*)

The Colosseum, Rome.
(Courtesy of KaiDib Films International, Glendale, Calif.)

presented today: juggling, rope acts, tumbling, trapeze shows, dancing, and assorted carnival acts.

Other than racing, the entertainments mentioned above were also done in amphitheatres, oval-shaped structures resembling the modern football stadium. Although they were present in many population centers, the most famous was the Flavian Amphitheatre, now named the Colosseum, built in A.D. 80. It held roughly fifty thousand spectators and had an arena area approximately two hundred by three hundred feet. The Colosseum is a late and highly developed amphitheatre. The basic form emerged around 46 B.C. and developed rapidly. Originally, amphitheatres were one or two stories high and had a simple dirt arena floor. By the time the Colosseum was built, amphitheatres could be three to four stories high, and the arena was a complex network of subterranean chambers beneath a trapped wooden floor covered with sand. The floor of the Colosseum chambers was some twenty feet below the arena floor, and the chambers themselves were used for animal storage, for gladiator dressing and ready rooms, and for retaining other production needs. Amphitheatre entertainments included contests between animals, between animals and armed men, between animals and unarmed victims, and between gladiators. Like actors, gladiators could be freemen or slaves. During the empire period, the Roman taste for carnage increased considerably. For the opening of the Colosseum, over one thousand animals were killed during the week-long celebration.

Interior of the Colosseum, Rome.
(Courtesy of KaiDib Films International, Glendale, Calif.)

The production of amphitheatre entertainments did involve some theatrical elements. Records indicate that when African animals were used to hunt each other, elaborate scenery was employed. The Colosseum floor was piled high with mounds of sand and dirt, and trees and shrubs were arranged so as to give the audience the illusion of African terrain. Stage machines were important in the operation of the amphitheatre. Animals were raised in cages from the under-floor chambers to the arena floor by means of winch-driven elevators or cranes operated by slaves. The tops of the cages would integrate with equal-sized traps in the arena floor so that the animals or men could make as natural an entrance as possible. Finally, amphitheatres were used for the staging of mock sea battles (*naumachiae*). Often done in sufficient scale to use slaves as sailor/actors, these battles usually commemorated some Roman sea triumph. The arena floor was flooded for the battle and then drained for regular use. The Romans were, after all, masters in the science and engineering of water movement.

THE END OF AN ERA

Neither theatrical nor nontheatrical entertainments were immune to the decay that affected the empire after the second century A.D. After the destruction of the Western Empire in 476, the new rulers of

The theatre at Leptis Magna, Libya.
(Courtesy of KaiDib Films International, Glendale, Calif.)

Rome kept organized theatre alive for a time, even rebuilding the Theatre of Pompey for performances in the sixth century. This effort, however, did not last. Although some Roman entertainment forms were retained in the Eastern Empire for several hundred years, the theatre structures and production practices of the Western Empire became dormant. They were not to be rediscovered until the early Italian Renaissance, at which time they infused new life into the theatre of Europe.

RETROSPECT

By the end of the second century B.C., Rome found itself the natural leader of the Western world. Although the Romans conquered or controlled the entire Mediterranean area, they did not assume the cultural leadership from the earlier Hellenistic era. Because of this, Roman drama and theatrical practice were highly imitative, more concerned with copying than with invention. Perhaps because this imitation did not yield innovative greatness, the theatre did not hold a respected position in Roman society. The dramatic culture that did grow and briefly flourish in Rome happened over the brief span of some two hundred years and was in rapid decline by the time of the empire.

Yet the modern theatre's debt to the past is owed not to Athens but to Rome. This is partly understandable in that Rome's achievements were closer in time to the Renaissance and hence were more readily accessible. The Roman love of building provided numerous examples of theatre structures to fire the imagination of Renaissance scholars and artists. Thus it is the Roman theatre building, albeit built on Greek models, that greatly influenced the architectural designs of Renaissance Europe, just as it was the New Comedy of Plautus and Terence that provided the model for Renaissance comedy. It was therefore to Rome that the first modern theatre practitioners looked for guidance on appropriate theatrical and dramatic practice. In few periods of history is the practice of theatre and drama more important to future ages than to its originators, but so it was with the mighty Romans.

Date	Roman History	Roman Theatre History	World History	World Theatre History
753 B.C.	Founding of Rome (traditional date).			
444 B.C.	Codification of Roman law.			
390 B.C.	Sack of Rome by the Gauls.			
364 B.C.		Etruscan dancers in Rome.		
323 B.C.			Death of Alexander the Great.	
292 B.C.				Death of Menander.
285 B.C.	Defeat of Gauls and Etruscans by Romans.			
c. 280 B.C.		Birth of Livius Andronicus.		
c. 270 B.C.		Birth of Gnaeus Naevius.		
264–241 B.C.	First Punic War.			
c. 254 B.C.		Birth of Plautus.		
240 B.C.		First comedy and tragedy presented at Ludi Romani.		
c. 239		Birth of Quintus Ennius.		
c. 220 B.C.		Birth of Pacuvius.		
218–201 B.C.	Second Punic War.	Comedies of Plautus being produced in Rome.		
c. 195 B.C.		Birth of Terence.		
168 B.C.	Beginning of Roman domination of Western world.			
166–161 B.C.		Comedies of Terence being produced in Rome.		

Date	Roman History	Roman Theatre History	World History	World Theatre History
149–146 B.C.	Third Punic War. Carthage is destroyed.			
148 B.C.	Macedonia a Roman province.			
146 B.C.	Africa a Roman province.			
129 B.C.	Province of Asia organized.			
82 B.C.	Sulla, dictator of Rome.			
73–71 B.C.	Revolt of the gladiators led by Spartacus.			
60 B.C.	Pompey, Caesar, and Crassus form First Triumvirate.			
58 B.C.	Subjugation of Gaul by Caesar.			
55 B.C.	Caesar invades Britain.			
48 B.C.				Destruction by fire of the great Library of Alexandria. Many Greek plays lost forever.
46–44 B.C.	Dictatorship of Julius Caesar.			
44 B.C.	Assassination of Caesar.			
43 B.C.	Anthony, Lepidus, and Octavian form Second Triumvirate.			
40 B.C.			Herod, King of Judea.	
30 B.C.	Death of Anthony and Cleopatra, and annexation of Egypt.			

(Continued on page 82)

Date	Roman History	Roman Theatre History	World History	World Theatre History
27 B.C.	End of the Roman Republic. Octavian named Princeps and Augustus.			
22 B.C.		Pantomimes introduced in Rome.		
27 B.C.–A.D. 14	Reign of Augustus.			Vitruvius, De architectura. 15 B.C.
A.D. 4		Birth of Seneca.		
c. 30			Death of Jesus. Beginning of Christianity in East.	
37–41	Reign of Caligula.			
41–54	Reign of Claudius.			
c. 42–67			Saint Peter, first pope.	
43			City of London founded.	
54–68	Reign of Nero.			
64	Great Fire in Rome.			
65	Conspiracy of Piso.	Seneca commits suicide.		
80		Flavian Amphitheatre built.		
161–180	Reign of Marcus Aurelius.			Tertullian, De spectaculis.
226			Rome establishes trade relations with China.	
313	Christians given freedom of religion.			
324–337	Reign of Constantine.	Public gladiatorial battles forbidden in Roman Empire.		

Date	Roman History	Roman Theatre History	World History	World Theatre History
380	All Roman subjects ordered to accept Christianity.			
395	Roman Empire separated into Western and Eastern empires.			
455	Vandals sack Rome.			
476	Romulus Augustulus, last emperor of Western Empire.			
548		Theodora, former mime, is crowned empress of Eastern Roman Empire.		
1453			Fall of Eastern Roman Empire to the Turks.	

SELECTED READINGS

Beare, William. *The Roman Stage: A Short History of the Latin Drama in the Time of the Republic*. 3rd ed. London: Methuen, 1964.
   The most readable and informative book available on the Roman theatre. All who would study or write about the drama of the Romans must consult this book.

Cary, Max, and H. H. Scullard. *A History of Rome Down to the Age of Constantine*. New York: Macmillan, 1975.
   A fine one-volume history of Rome with many illustrations, but hampered by the use of small type.

Duckworth, George E. *The Nature of Roman Comedy: A Study in Popular Entertainment*. Princeton: Princeton University Press, 1971.
   An extremely detailed and well-documented work on the theme, structure, and production of Roman comedy. Two chapters are devoted to the problems of Roman staging.

Hanson, John A. *Roman Theater-Temples*. Princeton: Princeton University Press, 1959.
   This work is concerned with the Roman theatre building but from the point of view of art and archaeology. One chapter is a detailed analysis of the Theatre of Pompey.

Nicoll, Allardyce. *Masks, Mimes and Miracles*. New York: Cooper Square Publishers, 1963.
   The first third of this useful but chatty book is a discussion of the Roman mime and its relation to earlier Greek and Roman theatrical forms.

Sinnigen, William, and Arthur E. R. Boak. *A History of Rome to* A.D. *565*. 6th ed. New York: Macmillan, 1977.
   A fine, well-balanced, highly readable history of Rome. This popular text has been around for a half-century.

COVENTRY

PARIS

LUCERNE

PART IV

Reflections of Heaven and Earth:
THE MEDIEVAL PERIOD

The medieval era, the period between 500 and 1500, still suffers from a bad press. Arnold Toynbee's image of the Middle Ages as a "vulture feeding on the carrion" of Roman civilization is a bit extreme, but it is representative of the attitude of some historians. A re-examination of the medieval era reveals that such a view is unacceptable. The commonly held opinion of the period is that of human endeavor in a long sleep between the nightfall of the glorious Roman Empire and the dawn of the enlightened Renaissance. The Roman Empire had been in a state of decay for four hundred years prior to its final collapse in the West, and the period after 1500, with its stifling neoclassicism, religious wars, and colonialism, is difficult to see as enlightened. The thousand years of human history covered by the Middle Ages was far from asleep. It teemed with activity as Western civilization sought to redefine itself.

The medieval period presents a definite break with the classical era. It was a period of growth during which there were major changes in the ways people thought, lived, and expressed themselves. In the Middle Ages, not the Renaissance, are to be found the roots of modern society. For nearly a thousand years the social order of Europe was a Christian one, united in a common concept of the divine and the place of human activities in divine history. Yet is was also a period of growing contradictions and tensions: Christian commonwealth versus national entities; Latin versus vernacular cultures; individual liberties versus institutional demands. The theatre of the medieval period reflected these contradictions and tensions between the demands of heaven and earth, the secular and the religious. Knowledge of classical theatre was not lost in the medieval world, but the theatre that emerged between 900 and 1500 was not indebted to earlier theatrical traditions. It was a new, dynamic theatre grounded in a common view of the world, an epic theatre that involved all members of its community. There was joy, exuberance, and a sense of innocence and sincerity in medieval theatre unknown in the classical and unheard of in the modern. It truly believed itself to be the stage of life.

6
DRAMA OF THE MEDIEVAL PERIOD

As the Church was the very center of life in medieval Europe, so it was also the center of medieval theatre. The medieval view of history was a continuum that began with the Creation, ended with the Last Judgment, and centered on the life and death of Christ. All human activities, in the medieval view, were merely shadowy events along the way to the Last Judgment. The Mass, a daily enactment of the life, ministry, Crucifixion, and Resurrection of Christ, was a theatrical presentation of this central point in the medieval world view.

DRAMA OF THE MEDIEVAL CHURCH

Allegorical interpretations of the Mass began to appear as early as the fifth century as an aid to worshipers who were unable to understand its historical and theological meanings. With an ever-increasing separation between the clergy and laity in terms of intellectual training, allegorical approaches to the meaning of the Mass became important. Amalarius, Bishop of Metz (c. 780–850), was the author of the *Liber officialis*, the most influential allegorical interpretation of the Mass produced in the medieval period.

The *Liber officialis* presents the Mass as an elaborate theatrical production with roles assigned to priests, deacons, and congregation. The priest, in addition to being celebrant, is also Christ and Old Testament High Priest; the congregation plays the roles of Hebrews, Gentiles, and Christians. Numerous roles were possible because of the desire for allegorical levels in the events of the Mass. This type of interpretation viewed the Church as a theatre and the order of the Mass as a structured play centered on the life of Christ, which reached its climax in the consecration of the Host. Thus the Mass was viewed not only as sacred drama, a presentation of the life, death, and Resurrection of Christ, but also as participatory theatre, an active drama that involved all present in its performance.

Even in the ninth century the allegorical approach to the Mass drew some opposition from Amalarius's fellow bishops, some of whom thought it encouraged "theatrical mannerisms and stage music." A twelfth-century French abbot complained that this dramatic style of Church liturgy "amazed the common people" but was proper "to the theatre, not the oratory." Yet this popular approach to the Mass continued well into the twentieth century, and it also prepared the way for further theatrical developments in the liturgy of the medieval Church.

Quem Quaeritis

The small piece of liturgical dialogue called *Quem quaeritis* has an importance in theatre history far greater than its brevity would suggest.

Quem quaeritis in sepulcho, O Christicole?
Ihesum Nazarenum cricifixum, O celicole.
Non est hic, surrexit sicut ipse dixit; ite nunciate quia surrexit.

Whom seek you in the tomb, O Christians?
Jesus of Nazareth the crucified, O heavenly one.
He is not here, he has risen as he said; go announce he has risen.

The *Quem quaeritis* dialogue is a dramatization of the key moment in history for the medieval world, the Resurrection. With the visit of the three Marys to the tomb and their discovery, the impact of the life of Christ is made manifest.

Numerous manuscripts of the *Quem quaeritis* survive from the tenth century, but there is no general agreement as to when or where the *Quem*

A twelfth-century German carving depicting the three Marys at the tomb.

quaeritis first appeared. The dialogue appears to have originally been part of a ceremony connected with the vigil Mass of the Saturday before Easter. It was later used in the Easter Mass and in other services connected with Easter. One of the most fully developed texts of the *Quem quaeritis* is found in the tenth-century *Regularis concordia* from Winchester, England. This text gives details of the costuming and role performance of the monks who will imitate the angel and the three Marys.

Not only did the dialogue provide ample opportunities for expansion (Peter and John racing to the tomb; one of the Marys buying perfume from a merchant), it also afforded a model for liturgical dialogues at other times of the Church year. The Nativity scene at Christmas ("Whom do you seek in the stable, O shepherds?") and the Wise Men of Epiphany ("Whom do you seek, O kings?") were soon added to the regular liturgical services. Although more elaborate religious and secular plays developed in the medieval era, these early liturgical plays continued to be performed for hundreds of years. The *Quem quaeritis* question-and-answer formula, combined with the allegorical aspects of the Mass, constitutes the spiritual center of medieval drama. These elements are never far from the surface no matter how complex the play.

LATIN DRAMAS OF THE MEDIEVAL PERIOD

Divine history is the primary focus of all medieval Latin plays whether or not they are directly connected with the liturgy of the Church. Plays dealing with events prior to the Resurrection were considered preparatory to this central point, and events following the Resurrection were either explanatory or related to the Last Judgment. Most of these plays were performed in the church or the churchyard, and the performers were members of the clergy. From the many examples of Latin plays from this period, a few will be briefly discussed to illustrate the variety and nature of these plays.

Fleury Play-Book

The Fleury Play-Book, a twelfth-century collection of ten plays from the monastery of Saint Benoit-sur-Loire, Fleury, France, is an excellent example of the expansion of the basic *Quem quaeritis* dialogue into a variety of Latin music-dramas designed for instructional purposes. In addition to an Easter play on the visit to the tomb and an Epiphany Magi play, the Play-Book contains four miracle plays relating to Saint Nicholas, and two New Testament plays on the conversion of Saint Paul and the raising of Lazarus.

Miracle plays are dramatizations of the life or legends associated with a particular saint. Those written in the vernacular were very popular during the late medieval period, but of Latin miracle plays only four are known, all concerned with Saint Nicholas and all recorded in the Fleury Play-Book. Typical of these miracle plays, either in Latin or the vernacular, is the *Tres filiae* (Three Daughters) from the Fleury plays. In this play, Saint Nicholas saves the three daughters of an impoverished father by providing dowries and husbands at the proper moment before disaster strikes. The play, in verse and set to music, was performed after evening prayers on Saint Nicholas Day, December 6.

The Fleury *Conversion of Saint Paul* is noteworthy for its production demands. The play requires four locations within the church, a bed, a wall, and a large basket in which Saint Paul is lowered during an escape scene. The script, with its technical and space demands, is a testament to the theatrical imagination of early medieval playwrights.

Hilarius

Since most of the playwrights of the medieval period are unknown, it is something of a pleasure to encounter the work of Hilarius (c. 1120–1160), one of few medieval Latin playwrights known by name. A former pupil of the great Abelard, Hilarius was a wandering scholar of French or English birth who wrote his plays around the middle of the twelfth century. Plays about Saint Nicholas, Lazarus, and Daniel, the Old Testament prophet, along with a couple of songs, a few poems, and a brief autobiography in verse constitute the known literary works of Hilarius.

The Saint Nicholas play is a retelling of one of the plays in the Fleury Playbook and rather dull, but the Lazarus play by Hilarius is both more theatrical and literary than its counterpart from Fleury. This play gains its freshness and emotional power from the use of French in the refrains. These passages in the vernacular must have been exciting to audience members with little or no Latin background, and they mark an early use of a language other than Latin in a church play.

The greatest dramatic achievement of Hilarius was in his third play, *Daniel*. This elaborate script is an enactment of certain events related in the Old Testament Book of Daniel: the feast of King Belshazzar, the mysterious handwriting on the wall, the destruction of Babylon, and Daniel in the lions' den. The versification and vocabulary of this play are far more advanced than those found in most medieval Latin scripts, and there is a major effort made to establish characterization in the dialogue. The staging of the play requires colorful costumes, elaborate props, a sizable battle, and writing to appear and disappear on a wall. This spectacular church play was most likely performed at the Christmas season during morning or evening prayers.

Ludus de Antichristo

One of the most fascinating Latin plays of the twelfth century is the *Ludus de antichristo* (Play of the Antichrist) from Tegernsee, Germany. This play appears to have had no connection with the Church year or liturgy., was most assuredly performed outside the church, and was a propaganda play for Emperor Frederick Barbarossa in his struggles against the pope and the kings of France and England. With a cast in excess of sixty, this play takes as its setting the entire known world of the twelfth century. In its enactment of the tale of the Antichrist, the play implies that Frederick

Barbarossa, Emperor of Germany, will be the last emperor of the East and West, and he will unite all the kingdoms of the world in preparation for the Second Coming. At the time of the composition of the play, Frederick was attempting to establish a centralized imperial government for the Holy Roman Empire. In this effort he was being opposed by forces all over Europe. The *Ludus de antichristo* is unique in it size and scope, its nonliturgical nature, use of traditional legends, and combining of current political events, German patriotism, and the medieval view of divine history.

Hrotsvitha

No brief survey of medieval Latin drama would be complete without mention of the plays of Hrotsvitha (c. 935–1000), Western theatre's first known female playwright. Hrotsvitha (also spelled Hroswitha or Roswitha) of Gandersheim was a well-educated canoness of the monastery of Gandersheim in north-central Germany. The monastery was founded by the royal family of Saxony, and the abbesses were selected from the royal family. Gerberga, the friend and abbess of Hrotsvitha, was the niece of the German emperor, Otto I. In such a setting Hrotsvitha was able to associate with the most educated people of her time.

Hrotsvitha, who referred to herself as "the strong voice of Gandersheim," was widely known for her writings and scholarship. The extant writings consist of a group of legends in verse, some contemporary history in verse, and seven plays. The plays—*Gallicanus I* and *II*, *Dulcitius*, *Calimachus*, *Abraham*, *Paphnutius*, and *Sapientia*—were written in praise of the virgin life and modeled on the plays of Terence. The plays are notable for their characterization and theatricality, as in *Dulcitius*, where a lustful governor, in hot pursuit of three lovely virgins, attempts to make love to pots and pans. These plays, with their skillful blending of the secular and the sacred, are remarkable achievements for the tenth century, and they appear to have been copied and widely circulated in central Germany. Although there is no direct evidence to establish the performance of these plays, the playwright's connections with the imperial court, her preface to the plays, and the structure of the plays themselves all strongly suggest they were intended for reading aloud and performance. Hrotsvitha's plays, particularly *Dulcitius*, may have been an important influence on another member of the Benedictine Order, Hildegard of Bingen (1098–1179), whose *Ordo virtutum* is the earliest known morality play.

VERNACULAR PLAYS OF THE MEDIEVAL PERIOD

Since the early part of the twentieth century it has been fashionable to describe the development of medieval theatre in an evolutionary manner: the seed of the *Quem quaeritis* develops into simple liturgical drama, grows in such size and secular elements that it is removed from the Church, at which point, under secular control and in the vernacular, it erupts into full flower only to wither under the brilliant heat of the Renaissance. Such an approach to the development of the medieval theatre is simple, tidy, and inaccurate. Plays in the vernacular developed not out of but contemporaneously with liturgical plays. During the period when Hilarius's *Daniel* and the Fleury *Conversion of Saint Paul* were being produced, vernacular plays, such as the Spanish *Auto de los Reyes Magos* or the Anglo-Norman *Adam*, were also being offered up to medieval audiences. These two theatrical traditions did not, of course, function in isolation of each other but rather freely borrowed of techniques. A fine example of this blending of the liturgical and the vernacular traditions is the twelfth-century French play *Le Mystère d'Adam*.

Le Mystère d'Adam

Written sometime between 1150 and 1175 by an unknown Anglo-Norman playwright, *Le Mystère d'Adam* is a delightful and remarkable play. A combination of numerous medieval elements, the play was obviously meant to entertain as much as to instruct. The three sections of the play deal with the story of Adam and Eve, the murder of Abel by Cain, and the procession of Old Testament prophets foretelling the coming of Christ. Three types of performers are required for this play: singers who are not involved in the action; actors portraying the Old Testament figures, who speak but do not sing; and actors portraying devils who run around and make a great deal of noise but do not have written lines of dialogue.

The text of the play is in French, but the commentaries to the actors and the detailed stage directions are in Latin. These stage directions are a rich source of information since they contain considerable indirect references to medieval theatrical production. For instance, the stage directions for the construction of Paradise suggest that sweet-smelling flowers and fruit trees be placed around the area, and in the section detailing the murder of Abel, directions are given for a pot of stage blood to be concealed on the person of Abel.

Although *Le Mystère d'Adam* is often praised for its artful dialogue (the seduction scene between the Devil and Eve is a small masterpiece), realism, and excellent characterizations, its most striking feature is its conceptualization. Using highly familiar material, the playwright retells these stories with remarkable insight into character and motivation. This play is not incorrectly considered one of the finest of the medieval era.

Vernacular Plays of Arras

The town of Arras, in northern France, was prosperous enough in the Middle Ages to support a resident group of poets, some of whom wrote plays. The earliest of the Arras playwrights was Jean Bodel (c. 1175–1210), who wrote his *Jeu de Saint Nicolas* around 1200. This play is the earliest known miracle play in the vernacular, and its characters and actions are taken from the everyday activities of Arras. The scenes of tavern life, which make up nearly half of the play, are highly entertaining but do little to advance

Saint Nicholas of Myra. A fifteenth-century devotional picture of this highly popular medieval saint.

the story of the play. They do, however, give a realistic picture of twelfth-century life and contribute greatly to making Bodel's Saint Nicholas play so much more theatrical than its Latin counterparts. The play, with its battles, miracles, rogues, saint, and Saracens, is rich in the slang and humor of the period and is a near-parody of the traditional saint's legend. There are few medieval scripts as exuberant as Bodel's *Saint Nicolas*.

The most famous of the poet-playwrights of Arras is Adam de la Halle (c. 1235–1288). Attached to the court of Robert, Count of Artois, Adam wrote two known plays during his career, *Jeu de la feuille* and *Jeu de Robin et Marion*. The *Jeu de la feuille* (Play of the Bower) is the most topical of all medieval play scripts. Writing to amuse his friends before leaving for an extended stay in Paris, Adam satirizes in this play the people and customs of Arras. Although essentially storyless, *Jeu de la feuille* is a series of sketches linked by characters. These characters include the playwright, his two close friends, his father, a monk, a fool, a physician, and a group of fairies. All the human characters are the objects of lampooning in this delightful slice of medieval life.

The script of *Jeu de Robin et Marion* relates the trials of the shepherdess Marion in warding off the attention of an overly friendly knight, and her devotion to Robin, her none-too-bright rustic lover. Because of its extensive use of songs and dances, this play is sometimes called the first French comic opera.

The Medieval Period

It is a theatrical treatment of traditional pastoral material, and like the pastoral lyrics, it presents a highly idealized picture of rural life. *Robin et Marion* is unique not only because it is the first utilization of pastoral material in a play script, but also because of Adam's effort to give these idealized shepherds and shepherdesses a touch of real life. The characters play actual games and sing well-known songs of the period, and they speak in the language of rural folk.

Feast of Corpus Christi

In 1264 Pope Urban IV instituted the Feast of Corpus Christi to be celebrated by the entire Church on the first Thursday after Trinity Sunday, a date falling sometime between the end of May and the end of June. This feast, established to honor the presence of Christ in the consecrated Host, provided an impetus for vigorous theatrical activity throughout Europe. Somehow (the dates and situations are unknown), theatrical presentations were incorporated into the Corpus Christi celebrations. These epic plays, actually a number of related plays but viewed as a single entity, presented divine history in the vernacular. These often massive offerings of community theatre, called *sacre rappresentazioni* in Italy, *autos sacramentales* in Spain, Passion or mystery plays in Germany and France, and Corpus Christi plays in England, are unique in Western theatre in their size, scope, variety, singleness of purpose, and level of audience involvement. The Corpus Christi play cycle from York, England, is an excellent example of the entire type.

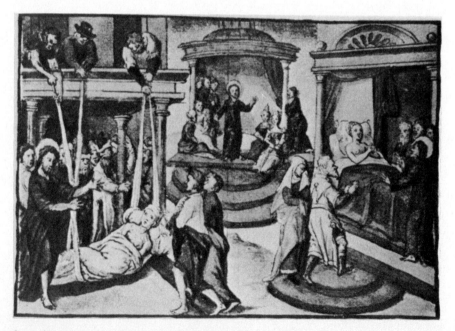

Scene from the manuscript of the Valenciennes Passion Play.

The York Play Cycle

There are four extant Corpus Christi cycles from England: York (48 plays), Chester (25 plays), Wakefield (32 plays), and the *Ludus coventriae* (42 plays). Parts of cycles exist from Beverley, Norwich, Newcastle-upon-Tyne, and other towns. The earliest references to the English cycle plays appear in the 1370s; the York cycle is known to have been in existence as early as 1376.

The cycle plays are the work of numerous playwrights, all unknown, and the plays were repeatedly revised during the existence of the cycles. The patchwork composition and revision of the cycles should not be understood to mean they lack unity, for such is not the case. The pieces fit together to form an artistic entity, a totality encompassing a variety of styles, meters, and tones, yet achieving wholeness through the frame of the subject matter. The four extant Corpus Christi cycles share a common structural pattern based on their subject matter, divine history from the Fall of the Angels to the Last Judgment.

The York cycle, the most extensive of the English cycles and requiring nearly fifteen hours for its performance, has forty-eight plays in its 1475 version. There are eleven plays based on Old Testament material, eight plays dealing with the Nativity, and nearly all the others are concerned with the life, death, and resurrection of Christ. The level of realism in the Crucifixion section of the York cycle is startling, so much so that twentieth-century productions at York have refrained from using it as written. Depicted are Christ and the four soldiers assigned to carry out the execution. The soldiers are very professional in their

A nineteenth-century lithograph of the Oberammergau Passion Play.

Scene from a passion play as shown in a woodcut by Albrecht Dürer.

approach, the first taking great satisfaction in a well-driven nail in Christ's right hand. At this point the soldiers discover mistakes were made in the construction of the cross; the holes for the left hand and the feet are too far out. The solution is to pull the arm and legs into the proper place with ropes. This the soldiers proceed to do, all the while commenting on what a hard job they have been given. Finished, they stand back and admire their work. While this Crucifixion scene may seem horrific by modern standards, it was intended to give the medieval audience a feel for an event usually considered in the abstract. Accustomed as they were to viewing public executions, the York Crucifixion scene forced the audience members to visualize and empathize with the pain and humiliation suffered by Christ.

The cycle plays, unlike the morality plays, did not urge people to change their way of life or be damned. Rather, they were a celebration of the salvation granted to all through the Passion and Resurrection of Christ. This salvation was the "good news" preached by the apostles and the Church, and it was an important element in the festive nature of the Corpus Christi celebration and its theatrical presentations. These plays represent the greatest achievements in English theatre during the Middle Ages.

The battle between England's Henry VIII and Pope Clement VII was destined to have a lasting effect on the cycles. Following Henry's excommunication and his establishment of the Church of England, those involved in the production of the cycle plays began to feel increased governmental interference as the scripts were challenged for their "popish" content. In 1548 the Feast of Corpus Christi was removed from the liturgical calendar of the Church of England. The last performance of the York cycle was in 1569, five years after the birth of William Shakespeare. Although small cycles continued to be performed in isolated parts of England until the early seventeenth century, the cycle plays ceased to be a major theatrical activity in England by the 1570s. In Europe, especially in those areas not involved in the Protestant Reformation, Corpus Christi plays were performed into the eighteenth century.

Morality Plays

The oldest known example of the morality play is Hildegard of Bingen's *Ordo virtutum* from the twelfth century. Hildegard's play is unique for its time since the morality play is really a product of the late Middle Ages, achieving its popularity in the fifteenth century. Morality plays are essentially sermons in theatrical form. The common thread in morality plays is the effort to persuade audience members to reform their lives and to consider their final rendezvous with death. The characters in a morality play

The Wheel of Fortune was a popular image in secular medieval drama.

differ from those in other forms of medieval drama. The morality characters are personifications of abstract qualities, such as Truth, Lust, Gluttony, Ignorance, or Good Deeds, or generalized personalities, such as King, Death, Priest, or Everyman.

A major difference between the morality play and other medieval dramatic forms is the importance of theme over story. The majority of medieval theatrical forms are built upon narrative, the retelling of some aspect of divine history. The important element in the morality play, as in the sermon, is the argument. The significance in this difference between the morality play and the other forms lies in the opportunities for development available to the morality play. The cycle plays, as an example, are ultimately confined to divine history. Although these plays could elaborate on the events surrounding Noah and the Flood, they could not change the given facts, as understood in the medieval view of history, that Noah must get into the ark and the Flood take place. The morality play, with its basis in argument, was not so restricted. It could begin with an argument about the condition of a particular human soul but, by using analogy, could move the argument on to national politics, the state of the world, and so on. There was no limit to the potential subject matter of a morality play. In its use of argument, the morality play paved the way for later developments in the drama.

Morality play scene of a man between his good and bad angels, with Death and the Devil looking on.

Although the potential for a variety of subject matter was available with the morality plays, the vast majority of these scripts dealt with the issues relating to human free will. Well-known English examples of the morality play are *The Pride of Life* (c. 1400), *The Castle of Perseverance* (c. 1440), and *Mankind* (c. 1471). Perhaps the most famous of all morality plays is *Everyman* (c. 1500), a translation of the Dutch *Elckerlijk*. A twentieth-century German version of this play, Hugo von Hofmannsthal's *Jedermann*, was staged in 1920 by Max Reinhardt at the Salzburg Festival, and the play was so successful that it has remained a permanent part of the annual festival. Of all the theatrical forms from the Middle Ages, only the morality play, because of its basis in argument, remains viable in the twentieth century.

The morality plays were the last true products of the medieval dramatic tradition. By the time *Everyman* was produced, the unique social and cultural aspects of the Middle Ages were already in vast disarray. The closed world of the medieval period, the mirror of heaven and earth, had been forever obscured by the rising clouds of nationalism, mercantilism, religious reform, and discovery. Theatre would also experience these changes. The shared theatrical traditions of the medieval era would give way and disappear. In their place theatre would begin to acquire nationalistic aspects, and the participatory nature of medieval production would disappear in the wake of professionalism and commercialism.

7

MEDIEVAL STAGING AND PRODUCTION

More than any other period in the history of the theatre, the Middle Ages is misunderstood. It is casually thought of as a drab period with little cultural excitement or achievement. While those thoughts might find some justification in the early Middle Ages, there is little to justify them from the tenth century on. The staging and production techniques that developed from the tenth to the sixteenth century reflect a growing concern for the finest in what makes theatre exciting. In terms of a total theatrical experience for both practitioners and spectators alike, the dramatic staging developed in the Middle Ages finds no peer in theatre history.

Before examining the rich heritage of this staging tradition in its specific forms, two characteristics, common to all medieval stage forms, should be understood. The first is that of theatre as a totally shared experience between player and spectator. There is no sense in the medieval theatre of separating the play and its playing space from the audience and its viewing space. Thus there is no notion of polarized areas for the presentation of these plays, as is generally found today. The second characteristic is built upon the first, and it is largely responsible for the effective fluidity of medieval staging. Although it exists by many names, we shall identify it here as the *mansion-platea* concept. A forerunner of the modern concept of simultaneous staging, *mansion-platea* staging utilizes a generalized playing area that becomes whatever the actor needs it to be. This *platea*, then, changes locale many times in the course of a play or plays, and is unencumbered by the specifics of detailed scenery. The other portion of this general staging concept, the *mansion* (Old French for "house"; sometimes the Latin *domus* is used interchangeably), is a scenic station providing the specific locale to be represented: heaven, hell, and so on. Whether these stations are singularly represented at a given time, as on the pageant wagons of England, or present together behind a large *platea*, as commonly done on the Continent, the staging concept is the same—they provide the actor and audience with appropriate suggestions of the scene being played. The staging traditions of the Middle Ages were rich and varied, developing over several centuries. All have, in varying degrees, some sense of these characteristics employed within the specifics of individual staging forms.

CHARACTERISTICS OF MEDIEVAL STAGE FORMS

The various staging forms of the Middle Ages realized the above characteristics in different specific ways. As noted in the previous chapter, the range of medieval drama covers both secular and religious forms and possesses a wide range of dramatic intent within each form.

Church Staging

The scope of medieval drama within the church varies from the *Quem quaeritis* to the more purely theatrical dramas of the thirteenth century, and the staging of these dramatic forms underwent a similar transition. The Marys who moved silently to take their places for the *Quem quaeritis* dialogue did so with the altar area of the church serving as their *mansion-platea*. By the time other Bible stories were dramatized, the entire

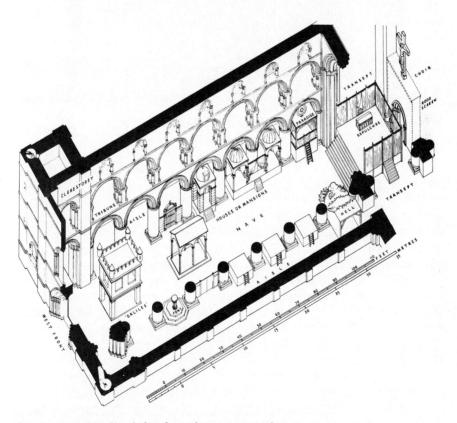

A reconstructed medieval church staging arrangement.

(*From Richard Leacroft,* The Development of the English Playhouse. *Used by permission of Cornell University Press.*)

A model set for a medieval church staging.
(Courtesy of the Cleveland State University's Theatre Arts Area.)

nave of the church was used for their presentation, with the *mansion* for each drama occupying a preset place against the interior pillars around the nave. Although the immediate floor area in front of each *mansion* took on the specific locality of that *mansion*, the general nave area served as the *platea* for all the stations. Originally done just for the attending faithful, the plays of the Nativity and Passion of Christ gradually increased in scope. The simple use of the *mansion* with its *platea* extension on the church floor became insufficient for proper viewing. From this time, probably in the tenth century, simple platform stages were employed for the *mansion* and much of the action. Several names are alternately assigned to these platforms, but the most common are *loci* or *sedes*. With these stages, the complexity of the medieval dramatic presentation began to increase. *Mansions* became more intricate, the interior church facade was increasingly used as an extension of the scenic stations, and the *loci* became larger. All this was happening as drama outside the church began to flourish. Some liturgical dramas were already being staged outdoors in the twelfth century. Others remained inside the church until the seventeenth century, and still others were staged in both places from the eleventh to the eighteenth centuries.

Outdoor Staging: Pageant Wagons and Mansion Stages

The outside staging of medieval theatre was presented through two basic forms: a rolling *mansion* or pageant wagon was the primary means of staging in Spain, the Low Countries, and England, while on the remainder of the Continent the town square *mansion* staging was primarily employed.

Definitive information about the pageant wagon is difficult to obtain, and opinions differ as to its form and use. There is general agreement that it was a wheeled cart or wagon that provided space for scenery and acting, and some theatre historians argue that more than one wagon was needed to stage the larger plays adequately. The wagons were pulled by horses, although there is evidence to suggest that some were pulled by hand. The size and shape of the wagons are difficult to ascertain since no pictures or detailed records are available. General accounts suggest that the wagons provided two or three playing levels, the major area being roughly six feet above the street. Thus it would be possible to have multiple playing surfaces in addition to the street *platea*. Heaven might be depicted on or near the roof area and hell below the main area. Other dimensions of the wagons are equally sketchy, but most likely

A reconstruction of a performance of a Corpus Christi play at Coventry.

(From Richard Leacroft, The Development of the English Playhouse. *Used by permission of Cornell University Press.)*

the wagons were ten to fifteen feet high, with a roof area capable of supporting simple stage machinery. There is no agreement on the width and length of the pageant wagons, but something on the order of ten feet wide and twenty feet long seems reasonable. Given that medieval streets were no more than thirty feet across, and the major building style included a second-story overhang, it would seem unlikely that wagons were bigger or taller than described.

Opinions vary as to the scope of the *platea* used in conjunction with the wagons. It may have been that a scaffold cart or simple scaffold stage against which the wagon would stop was all that was necessary. Possibly one or two wagons simply presented the *mansions* needed and the main *platea* was the street itself. The level of *mansion* embellishment is also unclear. There is agreement among historians that the lower level of the pageant wagon was curtained in order to serve as a prop storage and actor changing area when not in use. The roof area was the most ornate area because of its use as heaven or the place from which God spoke. Stage directions in the plays suggest high actor mobility and indicate that steps led from the main acting level to the street *platea*. Steps or ladders also allowed access to the upper acting level, and traps in the main acting level provided for level changes. It is doubtful that the full extent of the *mansion* embellishments on the English medieval pageant wagon will ever be fully known, but there is little reason to believe that these were solemn or visually austere productions. The festival atmosphere surrounding the production of these plays seems to preclude that view.

Regarding the use of the pageant wagons, the area of greatest disagreement lies in whether the plays were presented at set stops along the procession route or the procession went in parade fashion to a common area where the plays were then presented. Those who support the processional theory argue that preestablished stopping places were set and that each wagon in turn stopped there and presented its play. Through the course of the cycle plays, then, the audience could remain stationary while the various specific plays moved to them. This theory is plagued by serious logistical and time problems, but is plausible for some of the shorter and less complex cycles. The second theory, and the one that seems most plausible for the major towns and cycles, separates the procession from the presentation of the plays. The plays were still presented each on separate wagons, but the audience moved about the square or watched from the surrounding buildings. Likely both systems were in use. Whatever the actual case, and whatever its actual form, the pageant wagon was a vital part of the entertainment life of medieval society.

Town squares were central to the larger towns and cities of medieval Europe and England. Here a large crowd watching a single event could be supported, and the concept of simultaneous *mansion* staging emerged. This form of staging utilized all or many of the stations necessary for the various plays and set them around a single *platea*, which was usually the town square. Each *mansion* had its own *locus* that extended into the common *platea*. Usually the *mansion* and *locus* were elevated for visibility, and in some cases, as in Valenciennes, the *platea* was similarly elevated so that the movement from the *locus* to the *platea* was on the same plane. It is impossible to determine exactly

A model of the mansion-platea *staging used at Valenciennes, France.*
(Courtesy of the Cleveland State University's Theatre Arts Area.)

where the *locus* ended and the *platea* began. Suffice it to say that the actor defined these spaces and the audience had no trouble accepting or understanding these definitions. The conventions of the time clearly allowed the medieval audience to focus on the specific *mansion* and acting area in use and to put the others out of their mind. Thus we have the precursor of modern simultaneous

Modern mansion *staging in use at the Black Hills Passion Play in Spearfish, South Dakota.*

(Courtesy of the Institute of Outdoor Drama, University of North Carolina.)

staging—the elements needed are on stage together, and the dictates of the specific play or scene govern what is actually used at any specific time.

The staging form described above fits each medieval festival only in its most general context. With over one hundred towns staging their own plays, specificity varied widely. At Valenciennes, for example, the various stations are backing a common *platea* with heaven and hell represented at either end. A totally different approach was taken at Lucerne. Here, the open market served as the common *platea* with the individual stations set completely around the square, likely backing onto the facades of the surrounding buildings. Mons and Romans had their own variations.

Two questions remain pertaining to *mansion* staging. The first of these is size, and again a definitive answer is hard to find. Extant drawings are not to any scale. The size of the town and the scope of the plays no doubt influenced the size of the *mansion-platea* as a whole. The second question concerns the use of the stations themselves. Most likely the stations for the plays to be presented on a specific day were all set in place and were replaced by others as warranted. *Mansion* replacement occurred at night after the production day was ended or, if necessary, during breaks between plays. The importance and scope of these productions in the lives of medieval society were such that all needed to go well and according to plan.

Indoor Staging: Banquet Halls, University Stages, and Mummings

The stage of the early medieval actor was as transitory as the performance. The simple curtained platform of the mime artist served well. Later, in the large dwellings of feudal lords, these stages were incorporated into a unique implementation of the *mansion-platea* concept. A general sense of the flavor of this setting can be gleaned from Shakespeare's *Hamlet*, when the prince invites a group of strolling players into the castle to perform. The room often selected for secular medieval entertainments was the banquet hall, and the entertainment often followed a meal for the lord and his guest. Obviously the performance had to work around the banquet function. The traditional arrangement was likely one of tables around the sides and one end of the rectangular hall, with a raised dais at the end. The open center area thus created served as the *platea*, and the end without tables served as an area to erect a small, low stage. This end was usually the one with entrances to the kitchen area, and a curtain backing the small stage could serve to mask or hide actors coming and going into the hallway to the kitchen, and provide space for the changing of costumes and the storage of props.

Learning in the early Middle Ages was within the exclusive province of the Church, but as the Middle Ages progressed the responsibility for learning widened to include the growing concept of universities. At these centers of learning the study of Latin often involved the production of the plays of the Roman playwright Terence. The performance area used, known as a Terence stage, was a modification on the basic curtained platform stage. The *mansion*

A reconstruction of a banquet hall performance.

(*From Richard Leacroft,* The Development of the English Playhouse. *Used by permission of Cornell University Press.)*

backing the platform was a representation of a simple classical facade with three to four curtained openings, each usually indicating the house of one of the characters in the play. Since these productions were for educational reasons, they did not develop in complexity along with the street and town square staging.

Perhaps the most elementary use of the *mansion-platea* concept was employed by the mummers. The term "mummer" is a derivative of "mime" and commonly referred to one who put on a disguise and performed. Various plays exist, but two of the most famous and enduring are the plays of *Robin Hood* and *Saint George and the Dragon*. The stage for mummings was little more than a central space (*platea*) in whatever room an audience had assembled. Individual stations seem less important here; the entrances, exits, and other architectural features, such as a fireplace, were used as needed without specifically representing a scene. In *Saint George*, for example, Father Christmas enters the room and simply clears a space for the performance with his club. These plays and their mode of staging became tremendously popular with all social classes, and forms of mummers' plays are still staged in rural areas of England.

The Medieval Period

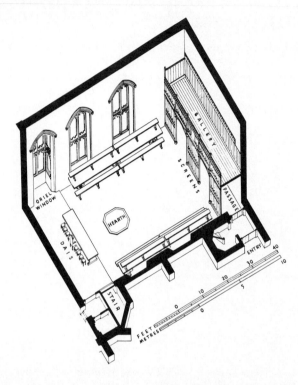

A reconstructed banquet hall staging arrangement.

(*From Richard Leacroft,* The Development of the English Playhouse. *Used by permission of Cornell University Press.*)

A late medieval royal banquet at the French court.

Tournaments, Royal Entries,
Street Fairs, and Pageants: Nontheatrical Contributions

Several medieval entertainments, while not classed specifically as theatre, contributed to the theatre of the Middle Ages owing to the development of theatrical elements within them. Tournaments were originally held as forms of medieval war games and made high use of emblems to identify competing families and royal houses. As they shifted to a popular sporting event, the use of emblems increased to make the events more colorful and visually exciting. Totally secular stations were used to represent particular towns and geographic landmarks. The techniques and emblematic ideas developed in these tournaments found their way into the theatrical mainstream of the late Middle Ages.

Although there is a specific meaning to the term "royal entry" that refers to the visits of royalty to a community, it is also used to indicate the various municipal processions and pageants enjoyed by medieval society. Originally these medieval events were little more than a parade or procession, but as the Middle Ages developed, actual plays were introduced. At first these plays were pantomimes of the themes of early liturgical drama, staged as tableaux. These living pictures were intended as compliments and thanks to the visitor for so

A depiction of a German tournament of the mid–sixteenth century.

honoring the town. Dialogue was later added as the tableaux changed to regular outdoor plays. The staging techniques of the outdoor theatre were employed, perhaps even utilizing some of the pageant wagons of the community.

SCENIC PRACTICE AND PRODUCTION DEVICES

Not only was the staging of the Middle Ages tremendously popular and diverse, but its specific production elements employed a high level of complexity and artistry. The medieval effort toward producing as realistic a framework for production as possible was so well done that some of the effects are the envy of today's theatre technicians.

Scenery

The types of scenery used in the Middle Ages can be classified into three general categories: symbolic, functional, and emblematic. The symbolic use of scenery occurs when architectural elements are employed as part of a scene to which they realistically do not belong. Thus the use of the elements of the interior church facade (pillars, crosses, altars, arches, steps, etc.) as extensions of the specific *mansion* near them was the symbolic use of those elements. Plays performed in town squares or banquet halls used these architectural features in a similar manner. Functional scenery is specifically built to represent a particular scene or locale. Emblematic scenery is built as an emblem to represent something, such as the large heaven emblem (depicting paradise) over the functional heaven at Valenciennes.

Although scenery had been used functionally in the Greek and Roman theatre, that usage attained a high degree of realistic specificity in the Middle Ages. Whether mobile or not, the stations suggested and were built for the specific depiction of a definitive scene. The heaven and hell stations were among the most common. Heaven was usually seen as an ornate place of tranquillity, often built on a higher level than the stations surrounding it. Hell, as a place of eternal torment, was often depicted as an austere tower with an iron gate or as an elaborate, fire-belching dragon's mouth. Light and fire were used in conjunction with these stations: torches helped to give heaven its aura, and smoke and fire issued from the hell-mouth along with cries from the damned. Other stations employed a similarly realistic approach in depicting scenes of Christ's Passion and in showing the required settings for other biblical stories. There is record of a single *mansion* being used to represent more than one scene, and occasionally more than one *mansion* was represented on a single pageant wagon. When these happened, the emblematic importance of medieval scenery came into play. Occasionally the change in scene was announced by posting the name of the new scene over the *mansion*, but more often some emblem was used on the *mansion* to suggest its change. These medieval equivalents of the modern logo or trademark clearly aided the understanding of a public that by and large could not read. The emblems of the barber pole and the three balls for a pawnshop are left from this tradition.

Production Machines and Devices

The scenery was enhanced by an equally elaborate system of production machinery and special effects, all designed for the most dramatic effect possible. Many of these scenic effects had their roots in the allegorical interpretations of the Mass. The embodiment of these interpretations in physical stage effects varied widely throughout Europe, France having the most elaborate, while Spain and England used more modest production elements. Chief among these elements were effects involving light. Among the important early light devices used in liturgical drama were star effects. Alternate names seem to be used depending on the manner in which the effect was presented. The *stella* was a lighted star effect either carried onstage, most likely on a pole, or drawn across the stage or nave on wires. In this manner it would be possible for the Wise Men to follow a star as they moved about the *platea*. The term *corona* applies to a type of lamp ringed with lights that was exclusively drawn on wires across the stage. These effects were practical, using actual fire in a controlled environment. Not only was fire an important stage effect, but fireworks also played an invaluable part in making these dramas highly realistic. Simple fireworks were carried as hand props for use as required, and larger fireworks, such as those to make the hell-mouth *mansion* as horrendous as possible, were mounted directly on stage. Animal sacrifices were common and were realistically staged, usually by burning a dummy animal on an altar. In one scene the reverse was seen—real fire does not consume the animal. Little wonder the medieval audience was in awe of these productions since they entertained and taught in a visually realistic way the miracles of the Bible.

Among the most important pieces of stage machinery were devices to raise and lower clouds, people, animals, and scenic displays. Likely hidden from the audience by a sky curtain, these machines were cranelike structures capable of various drop points among the stations and the *platea*. Medieval plays are filled with sky traffic—angels moving about, ascensions into heaven and lowerings into hell—and these machines, often disguised as clouds, could evoke a heightened sense of awe toward these happenings.

Other important devices include specific vehicles for stage-level travel around the *platea* and the stations. Ship effects were quite common and of three general types: fully practical ones that could be floated, wheeled ships for movable yet dry applications, as in a banquet hall; and prefabricated large-scale models to be assembled during production, such as Noah's ark. Still other machines assisted in producing effects without being effects in themselves. One example of this type of machine was the *trebuchet*, a vertical turntable device that allowed for quick substitution of a realistic dummy for a live actor in selected scenes of torture or mutilation.

The general use of dummies, or effigies, has been mentioned. In scenes that required executions, torture, and sacrifice, these were used instead of live performers. The plays call for a variety of such effects—many drawn from medieval life itself—and these were staged with as much realism as was possible. Devices of torture (racks, stakes, spikes, etc.) were shown in use on the dummies with surprisingly realistic effect. For burnings, the effigies were often loaded with parts of slaughtered animals to create a realistic sound and smell. Tortured human dummies would appropriately bleed as needed in scenes of mutilation, as well as reveal certain anatomical parts such as intestines (animal, of course) where disembowelments occurred.

The plays require occasionally instantaneous happenings of a mysterious nature. The raised stage floor had a variety of traps that allowed quick access to the space below. Thus appearances, disappearances, and substitutions could be quickly accomplished. Properties could also be quickly passed to actors as required, and set props could be exchanged as needed. Although these traps were not as elaborate as modern systems of traps, the developing technology foreshadows their continued development in the Renaissance and later centuries. In addition to the trapdoors, understage passages allowed actors who had "disappeared" to travel to another part of the stage and appear magically as the same character or another as the dictates of the production required.

In addition to the water needed in scenes of storms and tempests, supplied from the town square fountain, other aspects of such scenes were portrayed as well. For the sound needed, copper sheets were shaken (much as a thunder sheet is today) and large casks filled with stones were emptied into each other for the appropriate rolling effect. To augment thunder and storm effects, pots were struck and gun powder was exploded for lightning simulation.

Finally, music played an important part in creating the overall dramatic effect. Originating in the liturgy itself, the playing of instruments, singing, and dancing were used to provide bridges and accents at specific times throughout the production. In the larger pageants, over one hundred musicians ranging from choirboys to instrumentalists were employed, and were expected to entertain the audience before and after the presentations as well.

Production Aids for the Actor

In addition to the scenery and scenic devices that generally supported the medieval actor, the production elements of costuming, properties, and masks provided specific support. Costumes were largely contemporary, very similar to medieval street dress, with no attempt at historical accuracy. For the staging of nonliturgical plays, costumes from the Roman mime tradition were most often employed, and for the staging of both liturgical and nonliturgical plays, ecclesiastical garb served as needed. Minor characters wore clothing that reflected their social type and station. Principal characters, such as Christ, Mary, or Noah, wore costumes that were traditionally identified with their roles.

Properties used by the actors largely consisted of hand props, although set props were used where required. Records indicate that all properties were made as realistically as possible, and their use was consistent with their form. Whips and the crown of thorns, for example, were treated with animal blood so that, when they were used, the character would bleed as required. Still other props were built and used to fill very specific needs, such as the flaming sword of the archangel Michael.

Masks enjoyed limited use in medieval productions, principally in roles where actors were required to be totally separated from any sense of their own personality. Although the medieval audience would certainly recognize and make allowances for actors they knew, certain roles had to have more distance from the actor. Thus those playing God, the Devil, and similarly important figures used masks to heighten the continuity and ambiguity of their roles.

ACTORS AND THE ART OF ACTING

More is known about the organization of medieval actors and what was needed to prepare them for production than about the actors and their skills. This is mainly due to the complexities of the production and the individual anonymity that is characteristic of the medieval theatre.

Acting Style

Since the actor's personality was not a factor in casting medieval roles, other aspects emerged as primary considerations. Physical characteristics contributed to an acting style that was, at least, eclectic. Whether an actor moved with quickness or was extremely deliberate seemed to be a function of the role to be played and the actor's ability to play it, rather than any commonly held notion of acting style. Similarly, vocal variety was allowed, provided that the voice was of such quality as to be heard. Degrees of difference in vocal and visual presentation depended on the relative amount of comedy in the role as the motivating factor. If any commonality existed in the art of acting, it was in a presentational style that was devoted to being large enough to play to the crowd surrounding the *platea*. Stage directions in the plays indicate that character motivation and psychological development were not as important as in the modern theatre.

Actor Organization

Those who participated in the art of acting were known by a variety of names in the Middle Ages, yet two can be identified as generally defining the scope of the art. They include *mimi*, mime or comedy performers, and *histriones*, actors of serious drama. Those who participated in the great cycle plays throughout Europe were amateurs at their craft, although there is record of payment to principal players for the time taken away from work for rehearsal and performance. Players who made a meager living by performing regularly for compensation may be considered the precursors of the modern profession of acting. Many of the wandering scholars and clergy may have been particularly skilled as actors or play masters.

Extant records, most notably from Lucerne, provide a good indication of the process for acting in a pageant. Once the town council had assigned the trade guilds their specific responsibilities for preparing the plays, announcements of auditions were circulated. A potential actor could indicate what role or type of role was of interest, and be heard for the part. Casting was deeply rooted in tradition (playing the part the previous year was a major plus, unless it had been poorly done), and physical and vocal correctness were paramount factors. Following the auditions, a tentative cast was announced, and the potential actor had a set period of time to accept or reject the role. The size of these productions almost assured that every social class and station of townfolk would be involved, and so it was. Women did not generally act except in very specific and minor roles. Where the characteristics of females were needed, boy actors were commonly used.

The rehearsal period was quite short by modern standards. Two to four rehearsals were common for the smaller pageants. The length of rehearsal time and the number of rehearsals had more to do with simply getting through all the material rather than any sense of building quality. Although specific plays were done more than once, depending upon whether the entire production was stationary or movable, the production as a whole was presented as a single pageant. It was rehearsed as such, first in segments and finally as a single entity.

The actors were expected to take their work seriously and commit their physical and financial resources to it. Fines were imposed for drunkenness while rehearsing or for missing rehearsals. The performers were allowed food and drink during rehearsal and performance, and these were generally provided by the producing organization. Actors were generally responsible for their own costumes and simple props. Although multiple roles were possible, one ordinance required that no player act more than twice on the same day. Another financial impact on the actor was the requirement to pay for a substitute for a missed rehearsal. Overall the medieval actor gained in experience but not in the pocketbook.

MEDIEVAL THEATRICAL ORGANIZATION

Only one element of the complex structure of medieval theatrical production remains to be discussed, the general organization of the events. As in the other aspects of the medieval theatre, this organization followed a pattern that was almost as diverse as the number of towns participating.

Festival Organization

The term "festival" here is used in its largest sense to cover the theatrical events of the early Middle Ages as well as those emerging later, when the term more clearly applies. Initially, the Church was totally responsible for sponsoring the production of liturgical plays. As the Middle Ages progressed and the Church played a less active role in the productions, lay associations, most notably guilds and philanthropic societies, served as producers. These producing agents contracted with other individuals and groups to attend to the specifics of the festivals, including all technical aspects as well as the acting and stage management details. Everything was included, and what could not be bought or built was leased or rented. No production detail was left to chance. The town council or festival committee would agree in advance to the processional route to begin and end the festival, and would authorize places to stage the individual plays, either centrally or along the procession route. There is no single term that is commonly used to identify the person who was hired or recruited to fulfill the duties of stage manager, but "pageant master" probably is the most descriptive. Even when a committee provided general guidance, the day-to-day details of production were often assigned to one person who might work with a small group.

Festival Finances

At the outset of the Middle Ages the financing of a theatrical event was solely the responsibility of the Church, a town, or a feudal lord. The relative simplicity of early productions undoubtedly kept budgets in check, but as costs increased, more complex financial arrangements were necessary. On the Continent, Church funds were combined with municipal funds to raise the needed capital, and private gifts were often added to increase the available financial package. In England taxes were a common part of the financing of an event, a pageant tax being levied against participating guilds and their members. Actors would sometimes be compelled to contribute a fee based on the role to be played. A festival general admission fee was rare. Rather, special tickets for seating by social class were sold, priced according to ability to pay.

The Audience

In considering the nature of the medieval audience, the term "festival" in its most raucous sense captures the spirit that must have prevailed. Many productions of the Middle Ages were outdoor events, with all the attendant problems of crowd control and noise that a similar event today would entail. Eating and drinking throughout the plays were common, and there are records of fighting among spectators and the actors. The *mansion-platea* concept did little to protect against such occurrences. Even though spectators came and went at will throughout the festival, the length of the performance day did little to lessen tensions. In the longer, more complex festivals, performances began as early as 4:30 A.M. and ran as late as 6:00 P.M. or until dusk. All-day events with audiences in the thousands created significant problems in crowd control. The festival atmosphere could not be denied.

RETROSPECT

Like the totality of the Middle Ages itself, the medieval theatre was not a sleeping giant waiting for the glorious Renaissance to happen. As in other aspects of medieval life, the theatre, while somewhat knowledgeable about its classical heritage, chose to draw on the theatrical roots laid in earlier times, from the ritual drama tradition. The line from ritual theatre to the theatre of the Middle Ages is most clearly seen in the fact that, for nearly a thousand years, religion and the Church enjoyed a close working relationship with the theatre. To be sure, that relationship was tenuous as the Middle Ages drew to a close. Elements of the commercial and secular had permeated theatrical practice almost from the outset, yet the basic relationship did exist.

The medieval theatre, in writing as well as production, stood alone as good theatre. Medieval secular and religious plays, while reflecting the growing differences between the religious and the secular, still presented a common view of humanity and its place in the divine order of the universe. This fact was likely the reason for the strong continuity of the development of the cycle plays, for example, and the consistency of certain secular comedies. Except for selected elements of New Comedy, the secular comedies of the Middle Ages did not resort to classical models for their inspiration. Religious plays similarly did not grow from any sense of the classics, but rather grew from a free and unshakable belief in the medieval view of the world. Similarly, medieval staging reflected the proper way to depict all the wonders of creation through the various forms of the *mansion-platea* concept.

Finally, the theatre of the Middle Ages was a theatre of the total community. During few other times in human history has the theatre been so intrinsically tied to the basic social fabric of its age. Its popularity was all-encompassing, and it assumed a large place in the total order of God's universe. The Renaissance, for all its learning and enlightenment, could not boast of so vital a theatre.

Date	Historical Events in the Medieval Era	Theatrical Events in the Medieval Era
527–565	Justinian I, emperor of Eastern Roman Empire.	
570	Birth of Muhammad, founder of Islam.	
637	Jerusalem conquered by the Arabs.	
711	Arab conquests in Spain.	
732	Charles Martel defeats the Arabs at Battle of Tours and turns back their westward advance.	
771–814	Reign of Charlemagne.	
800	Charlemagne crowned first Holy Roman Emperor by Pope Leo III.	
841	Vikings invade Paris.	
846	Arabs sack Rome.	
930–950		Development of *Quem quaeritis* dialogue.
c. 970		*Regularis concordia* written.
980–1000		Plays of Hrotsvitha of Gandersheim.
1000	Vikings discover North America. Chinese invent gunpowder.	
1000–1150		Early liturgical dramas written and performed.
1066	Battle of Hastings and Norman conquest of England.	
1096–1099	First Crusade.	
1099	Crusaders conquer Jerusalem.	
1145–1147	Second Crusade.	
c. 1150		Hilarius's *Daniel*; Hildegard's *Ordo virtutum*; *Le Mystère d'Adam*.
1163	Construction of Nôtre Dame begins in Paris.	
c. 1165		*Ludus de antichristo.*
1170	Murder of Thomas à Becket at Canterbury.	
1187	Muslims retake Jerusalem.	
1189–1193	Third Crusade.	

Date	Historical Events in the Medieval Era	Theatrical Events in the Medieval Era
c. 1200		Jean Bodel's *Jeu de Saint Nicolas*.
1202–1204	Fourth Crusade.	
1215	King John of England signs Magna Carta.	
1265	Pope Urban IV establishes feast of Corpus Christi.	
1271–1295	Marco Polo travels to China.	
c. 1275–1285		Adam de la Halle's *Jeu de la feuille* and *Jeu de Robin et Marion*.
1347–1351	Black Death (bubonic plague) kills about 75 million people in Europe.	
1370s		Corpus Christi cycles established in England.
c. 1400		*Pride of Life*.
1415	English defeat French at Battle of Agincourt.	
1428	Joan of Arc directs French army against the English.	
c. 1440		*Castle of Perseverance*.
c. 1450	Invention of printing from movable type.	
1455	War of the Roses begins in England.	
	Gutenberg Bible printed.	
1485	Battle of Bosworth Field. Henry Tudor crowned Henry VII of England.	
1486		Vitruvius's *De architectura* published.
1492	Moors driven out of Spain. Columbus makes first voyage to the Americas.	
c. 1500		*Everyman*.
1564		Birth of William Shakespeare.

SELECTED READINGS

Axton, Richard. *European Drama of the Early Middle Ages*. Pittsburgh: University of Pittsburgh Press, 1975.
    This highly readable work deals with origins, selected plays in Latin and the vernacular, and the English cycle plays.

Chambers, E. K. *The Medieval Stage*. 2 vols. Oxford: Oxford University Press, 1903.
    The major work on the medieval theatre for nearly fifty years. Chambers's evolution-ary theory of the drama is now generally discredited, but this work is still important for the material collected and its influence on later scholars.

Frank, Grace. *The Medieval French Drama*. Oxford: Clarendon Press, 1954.
    The best account of the French medieval drama available in English.

Hardison, O. B. *Christian Rite and Christian Drama in the Middle Ages*. Baltimore: Johns Hopkins Press, 1965.
    An important collection of essays challenging the theories of Chambers and Young. This work was the beginning of recent reevaluation of the nature and development of medieval theatre.

Kahl, Stanley J. *Traditions of Medieval English Drama*. Pittsburgh: University of Pittsburgh Press, 1975.
    An interesting look at the English drama of the fifteenth and sixteenth centuries. The approach is by topic rather than play.

Nagler, A. M. *The Medieval Religious Stage*. New Haven: Yale University Press, 1976.
    This book takes a critical look at some of the commonly held theories of medieval staging and discusses them in light of current research. A well-documented approach to the subject.

Taylor, Henry O. *The Medieval Mind*. 2 vols. Cambridge, Mass.: Harvard University Press, 1962.
    A good, standard survey of medieval culture.

Tydeman, William. *The Theatre in the Middle Ages*. Cambridge: Cambridge University Press, 1978.
    Examines in detail the staging of medieval drama. Includes a glossary of medieval technical staging terms.

Wickham, Glynne. *Early English Stages: 1300 to 1660*. 2 vols. New York: Columbia University Press, 1959–1972.
    A wealth of information on things "theatrical" presented in Professor Wickham's unique style.

_____. *The Medieval Theatre*. New York: St. Martin's Press, 1974.
    A colorful and at times controversial account of medieval theatre. The author divides medieval theatre into three groups: theatres of worship, recreation, and commerce.

Woolf, Rosemary. *The English Mystery Plays*. Berkeley: University of California Press, 1972.

A discussion, by play type, of the four English Corpus Christi cycles. Students should find the background section very useful.

Young, Karl. *The Drama of the Medieval Church*. 2 vols. Oxford: Clarendon Press, 1933.

Although in the Chambers tradition, this work remains an extremely important collection and commentary on liturgical drama. Play scripts are given in the original Latin only.

VENICE

FLORENCE

PART V

Idealization of the Mirror:
THE ITALIAN
RENAISSANCE

The word "renaissance" means rebirth, and it is generally used to refer to an era of enthusiastic and vigorous activity in the arts and scholarship that took place from approximately 1400 to 1600. The Italian peninsula was the epicenter of the European Renaissance, and the Italian humanists provided the necessary models for change. The rest of Europe followed.

Renaissance humanism, a unique blending of classical and Christian thought, had as its ultimate goal the improvement of humanity. While elements of neopaganism did appear in the later stages of the Italian Renaissance, the humanistic scholars of the period were committed to fusing classical ethics into the Christian life. In this way the Renaissance essentially carried on the Christian didactic traditions of the Middle Ages.

The major contribution of the Italian Renaissance was not its break with things medieval, for such a break did not take place, but in its introduction of a new historical perspective. Out of this period came a new interest in history and a belief that change was important, that the past was significant in an understanding of the present. The modern historical consciousness is a product of the Italian Renaissance.

That the Renaissance began and flourished in Italy can be attributed to several factors. With the ruins of the Roman Empire all around them, the people of Italy held a pride in things classical throughout the medieval period. The scholasticism of the Middle Ages was centered in the universities of France, England, and Germany, whereas the universities of Italy were primarily associated with professional training in such areas as law and medicine. Thus when the new approaches to education expounded by the early humanists appeared, they met less resistance in the Italian universities. And finally, the Italian peninsula was generally free of the large-scale feudalism that developed in the rest of Europe.

Without the burden of large-scale feudalism, the small Italian city-states were essentially urban in outlook and the result was twofold: commercialism grew more rapidly in these city-states than elsewhere in Europe, and the citizens of the city-states, on all levels, had more interests in common. These were important factors for the arts because they made money and leisure available to a larger portion of the population than was possible in a feudal state. This made a shared theatre possible and encouraged the development of permanent playhouses.

One additional aspect of this period should be mentioned, since it resulted in the eventual decline of Italian influence in the cultural and political life of Europe. While a cultural transformation was taking place in Italy during the Renaissance, a political one was under way in the rest of Europe. By the end of the fifteenth century, the nations of modern Europe were emerging as unified states under strong monarchies. France, England, Spain, and the Hapsburg states were already beginning to engage in power struggles that would continue to rack the European continent until the middle of the twentieth century. These new unified nations would eventually produce armies and arts that would overwhelm and overshadow the small city-states of Italy. Yet for nearly two hundred years, all Europe would look to Italy for inspiration in literature, art, architecture, education, and theatre.

8 DRAMA OF THE ITALIAN RENAISSANCE

The foundations of the modern theatre are to be found in the Italian Renaissance. The plays of the Italian humanists went beyond the secular plays of the Middle Ages in presenting a new world view, a view that broke with the concept of divine history. Although designed for a small, cultured court audience in Italy, the *commedia erudita* soon was imitated throughout Europe. From these comedies and the classically inspired tragedies of Italy, playwrights began to develop new dramatic forms to replace the atrophying medieval traditions. From the Italian Renaissance emerged new types of drama and new critical theories to support them. The inspirations were scholarly and classical, but the productions were idealized reflections of a contemporary society.

COMEDY IN THE ITALIAN RENAISSANCE

Latin Humanistic Playwrights

The learned comedy of the Italian Renaissance, the *commedia erudita*, drew its inspiration from the classical Roman comedies of Terence and Plautus, but it developed within the traditions of the medieval drama in Italy. As the *commedia erudita* emerged in the fourteenth century, three medieval dramatic forms were in use throughout the Italian peninsula: the *sacre rappresentazioni*, peasant plays (*maggi*), and plays in Latin written by the early humanists. The *rappresentazioni* were religious plays in the vernacular, and the *maggi* were festival plays combining secular and sacred, history and fantasy, in an epic spectacle. The Latin comedies written by the Italian humanists truly prepared the way for the *commedia erudita*, for while they are medieval in form and spirit, they were written in an effort to re-create the comedy of Plautus and Terence.

Petrarch (1304–1374), the first great Italian humanist, is credited with the first modern attempt to write a classical comedy. His lost *Philologia* was written

Four scenes from a late-fifteenth-century edition of Terence that depict the Renaissance concept of Roman staging.

around 1330, but he suppressed it as youthful foolishness. The only extant fourteenth-century humanistic comedy is *Paulus* by Pier Paolo Vergerio. Other humanistic playwrights of this period are Sicco Polenton, Leon Battista Alberi, and Aeneas Sylvius Piccolomini, but the most representative of this group of early playwrights is Tito Livio dei Frulovisi (c. 1400–c. 1456).

A native of Ferrara, Frulovisi spent most of his stormy life in Venice and is credited with establishing the classical theatre there. The author of seven Latin comedies, he freely attacked social abuses in Italian society and satirized both character types and actual people. Although other humanists strongly criticized his Latin style, Frulovisi attempted to reproduce the language of the Roman theatre, and he greatly helped the Latin humanists move closer to the pattern of the classic theatre. The efforts of Frulovisi and other early humanistic playwrights produced no masterpieces, but their attempts to merge the elements of contemporary Italian life with the structure of Roman comedy prepared the way for the Italian language comedy called *commedia erudita*.

Commedia Erudita

Accessibility to the works of Plautus and Terence was greatly increased through the invention of printing. By the end of the fifteenth century, several editions with commentaries were available of both Roman playwrights, and the plays in Latin and in Italian translation were being presented throughout Italy. These theatrical productions were often affairs of state commanded by a ruling duke to entertain important guests. As such, these plain comedies from the Old Roman Republic were burdened with lavish scenic displays in the intermezzos placed between the acts. Intermezzos generally had little or nothing to do with the play being presented, but they did allow an opportunity for colorful displays, beautiful costumes, dancing, and music. Intermezzos continued to be a part of Italian theatre throughout the entire Renaissance.

Having learned the dramatic techniques of Roman playwrights through study and performance, the *commedia erudita*, comedy in Italian on Italian subjects but based on classical principles, was the next development by Italian humanistic playwrights. The typical learned comedy had a five-act structure, followed the classical pattern of exposition (*protasis*), complication (*epitasis*), and resolution (*catastrophe*), had a small cast, and followed the unities of time, place, and action. The basic structure of these plays was a result of the new critical theories that were emerging during the Italian Renaissance. These critical theories will be discussed later in this chapter. Although two examples of the new learned comedy appeared before 1508, Ludovico Ariosto's *La cassaria* (The Chest, 1508) is considered the true beginning of learned comedy.

A Florentine spectacle.

Ariosto

Ludovico Ariosto (1474–1553) was connected with the ducal court of Ferrara for his entire professional career and served as the superintendent of court spectacles. The author of five learned comedies, Ariosto displayed his best comic efforts in *I suppositi* (The Pretenders, 1509) and *La lena* (1528). The first major playwright of the learned comedy, Ariosto clearly demonstrates his artistic growth from the highly imitative nature of *La cassaria* to the originality of *La lena*. Particularly noteworthy in his plays is the portrayal of contemporary life in early-sixteenth-century Italy. In the early *La cassaria* the playwright uses the jargon of the Italian criminal underworld, comments on the Spanish troops stationed in the country, and criticizes judges and custom officials. The custom officials, who were a bane in the lives of traveling Italians because of the various independent dukedoms throughout the land, are again satirized in *I suppositi*. In this play, one of the characters fears the officials will flay him just to see if he has something hidden under his skin. In *La lena*, Ariosto's best comedy, the daily life of Ferrara is depicted and considerable satire and criticism are directed at the minor officials of the city.

Machiavelli

La mandragola (The Mandrake, 1520) by Niccolò Machiavelli is considered the best comedy written during the Italian Renaissance. Machiavelli (1496–1527), whose cynical book on statecraft, *Il principe*

Scene from a sixteenth-century Italian comedy.

(The Prince), shocked his contemporaries with its amoral approach to politics, applied the same philosophical view of humanity to the characters in his comedy.

Assuming a basic level of depravity in all humans, Machiavelli shows how individual desires can be manipulated by a clever person to achieve his own goals. Considering that all in the story are actively engaged to force a virtuous wife into an adulterous act, including the woman's husband, mother, and priest, the play would appear to be a tragedy rather than a comedy. Yet the craftsmanship of Machiavelli is such that the rogues are likable and the outcome of the play fortunate for all concerned. A masterpiece of construction and characterization, *La mandragola* merits more attention and production in the modern theatre.

Aretino

Pietro Aretino (1492–1556), called the "scourge of princes" because of his satiric writings, wrote five learned comedies. Satire is the focal point in these plays. The playwright is more interested in pointing out the corruption of Italian society than in writing tightly constructed plays. The papal court is under attack in *La cortigiana* (The Courtesan, 1526), the ducal court of Mantua in *Il marescalo* (The Marshal, 1526), and the world of the high-priced courtesan in *Talanta* (1534). Yet for all the cynical satire to be found in the plays of Aretino, his *Lo ipocrito* (The Hypocrite, 1542) contains romantic elements that represent a further development of the learned comedy away from its classical beginnings.

The comedies of Aretino lack the structural finesse of *La mandragola*, yet their very structural weaknesses illustrate a major change that was taking place in the learned comedies. He wished to show daily life in sixteenth-century Italy, and to do so he placed an emphasis on character sketches in his plays. These sketches were held together by the traditional five-act scheme, but what is foremost in these plays is artistic creativity unrestricted by classical rules. In utilizing this approach to play construction, Aretino established a foundation for the later popular theatre, the *commedia dell'arte*.

Beolco

The work of Angelo Beolco (1502–1542) represents a major link between the *commedia erudita* and *commedia dell'arte*. This actor-playwright, who was famous throughout Italy under the stage name Ruzzante, was the author of a dozen comedies, many of which combined the traditions of folk theatre with elements of the learned comedy. His plays feature peasant characters who often reappear in several plays. Beolco is truly fond of his peasants and strives to present them in a natural and sympathetic fashion. Beolco anticipates the theatre of the *commedia dell'arte* by allowing his actors opportunities to improvise, by establishing stock situations that are repeated in several plays, and by employing pantomime. Plays by Beolco that best illustrate this link with the *commedia dell'arte* are *Parlamento de Ruzzante* (Congress of Ruzzante, c. 1527) and *L'Anconitana* (The Girl of Ancona, 1522).

Influence of the Commedia Erudita Outside Italy

The Italian playwrights of the *commedia erudita* turned to Plautus and Terence to learn how to construct their comedies, but they were not chained to their classical models. Their rapid combination of the classical and the contemporary prepared the way for the development of comic theatre throughout Europe. When the French parliament outlawed the performance of mystery plays in 1548, French translations of Italian learned comedies appeared to fill the theatrical vacuum. By the end of the sixteenth century, the French had moved beyond their Italian models into a new type of French comedy that was a marriage of the *commedia erudita* and the *commedia dell'arte*. Spain, even with its strong native traditions in the theatre, was not immune to the influence of the *commedia erudita* since the comedy of intrigue introduced by Lope de Rueda was based on Italian models. The first English comedy in prose, George Gascoigne's *The Supposes* (1556), is a near-straight translation of Ariosto's *I suppositi*. Shakespeare, Ben Jonson, and George Chapman were among the many English playwrights who borrowed freely from the Italians. Playwrights in other countries learned classical dramatic structure from the comedies of the Italian Renaissance, found in them models for their own vernacular plays as they broke from medieval traditions, and discovered new characters, locations, and situations.

TRAGEDY IN THE ITALIAN RENAISSANCE

Eccerinus by Albertino Mussato is the earliest-known example of a tragedy written during the Italian Renaissance. This Latin play, written in 1315, is about actual events in Italy and is modeled on the plays of Seneca. All the tragedies written in Italy during the early Renaissance, whether in Italian or Latin, were modeled on Seneca. Only after the beginning of the sixteenth century, when translations of Sophocles, Euripides, and Aeschylus became widely available, was the authority of Seneca as the classical master of tragedy challenged. For a few decades a battle of words was waged, between those who favored the Greeks over Seneca, as to the form to follow in writing tragedies. With the emergence of Giambattista Giraldi Cinthio (1504–1573) in the middle of the sixteenth century as Italy's major tragic playwright, the battle was settled by merging Seneca with the so-called rules of Aristotle.

Giambattista Cinthio

Cinthio preferred the five-act structure of Roman tragedy because it allowed breaks between acts that could be used for intermezzos. Cinthio was not just writing for scholars; he had production in mind and knew how much Italian audiences enjoyed the color and music of the intermezzos. Cinthio did not limit the number of actors on stage to three but had a large number of speaking roles so, as he notes, the audience would not be bored seeing and hearing the same actors all the time. Cinthio retained the messenger and the soliloquy as highly useful devices, found nothing amiss in showing deaths on stage, and was very much in favor of scenic displays. For Cinthio, and the majority of the other Italian playwrights, the function of tragedy was to "induce wonder, pity, and horror," and he appeared to believe tragic drama had power to influence the audience to select virtue over vice.

Although the plays of Cinthio, Giangiorgio Trissino, Lodovico Dolce, Maffio Vehiero, and other tragic playwrights were influential in the development of modern tragedy, they have not fared well as pieces of dramatic literature. As a group they are lengthy, bloody, complicated, and generally boring to the modern reader. Cinthio's *Orbecche* (1541), the first Italian tragedy written and produced according to the new neoclassical rules, serves as a general example of this type of tragedy. Orbecche, the daughter of the King of Persia, is ordered by her father to marry the King of Parthia. This presents a problem since Orbecche has been secretly married for four years and has two sons. The king discovers his daughter's deception and pretends approval but plans revenge. His revenge is savage: he cuts off the hands of Orbecche's husband, forces him to watch as his sons are butchered, and then kills him. The king then presents the bodies to his daughter as a "wedding present"; she takes a knife out of one of the bodies, slays the king, removes his head and hands, then kills herself.

The play, when presented before the court at Ferrara, was very well received, an encore was required, and the printed edition went through nine printings in the next fifty years. *Orbecche* was the standard to match for sixteenth-century Italian tragedies and, for all of its indebtedness to Seneca's *Thyestes*, established a vogue for ghosts, violence, and moralizing. It helped spread the influence of Italian tragedy throughout Europe.

Influence of Italian Tragedy

The tragedies of the Italian Renaissance were saddled with the burdens of classical imitation and the newly established neoclassical rules. These burdens prevented the Italian theatre of the Renaissance from producing a major playwright whose work would stand the test of time, yet these very burdens were this theatre's contribution to the dramatic literature of other European nations. While France had rapidly taken possession of Italian comedy and made it her own, the adoption of Italian tragedy was much slower. What did impress the French was the regularity of Italian tragedy and its adherence to the neoclassical rules. These rules were taken up by the French, were further codified, and became the core of French dramaturgy. The English, from the time of Elizabeth I to the civil wars, were fascinated by the supposed wickedness of the Italians. Italy furnished the subject for nearly half of the tragedies written during the golden era of English theatre. These plays, many of which attempt to out-Seneca Seneca, show the strong influence of the complex stories of the Italian tragedies. Here the emphasis is on revenge, blood, lust, and cruelty, blended together in a highly intricate story. The results, in such plays as *The Duchess of Malfi*, *Othello*, and *'Tis Pity She's a Whore*, are tragedies far greater than their Italian models.

TRAGICOMEDY IN THE ITALIAN RENAISSANCE

Plautus, in the prologue to his *Amphitryon*, called his play a *tragicomoedia*, a tragicomedy, and from this single example the playwrights of the Italian Renaissance were able to justify their plays that were outside the rules for both tragedy and comedy. The Renaissance tragicomedy was anticipated by medieval theatrical traditions that mixed the tragic with the comic and the Terence-like plays of such playwrights as Hrotsvitha, but the first Renaissance play called a tragicomedy was *Fernandus Servatus*, written in 1494 by Carolus and Marcellinus Verardus.

As with tragedy and comedy, Giraldi Cinthio was active in the development of tragicomedy. Although he was not particularly happy with the term "tragicomedy," preferring instead "mixed tragedy," Cinthio always wrote with his audience in mind and composed several tragedies with happy endings. A major feature of these plays is romantic love, and this brings out another significant element in Cinthio's tragicomedies, the importance of women. There are important roles for women in classical drama, but those dramas in general reflect the inferior status of women in classical society. As Aristotle notes in the *Poetics*, "it is not appropriate in a female character to be manly or clever." Such was not the case in the society of the Italian Renaissance. Italian women of the upper classes were celebrated for their intelligence, artistic skills, and their abilities to function in the perilous realms of Italian diplomacy. This type of new Renaissance woman is portrayed in the tragicomedies.

Pastorals

Perhaps the most significant form of the tragicomedy is the pastoral. These plays, with their casts of shepherds, shepherdesses, and pagan deities frolicking in the mountains of Arcadia, were highly popular with aristocratic audiences. Torquato Tasso's *Aminta* (1573) and Giovanni Guarini's *Pastor Fido* (1590) are two of the most famous examples of the Renaissance pastoral tragicomedy.

Aminta is concerned with the love of the shepherd Aminta for the nymph Silva, and it takes five acts before the love is reciprocated. Tasso was Italy's greatest poet of the sixteenth century, and his play, which is an elaborate compliment to the court of Duke Alfonso of Ferrara, is filled with some of his most beautiful poetry. The work was very well received at Ferrara, performed throughout Italy, and printed many times. It, along with *Pastor Fido*, shaped the pastoral dramas of Italy, France, and Spain. Guarini's *Pastor Fido* lacks the poetic beauties of Tasso's play, but its merits established its author as the major

Characters from a pastoral drama.

authority on the tragicomedy. The story of *Pastor Fido* is extremely complex and defies any attempt at a brief description. Owing to the hostility of the Duke of Ferrara to Guarini, the play was not produced until 1596 even though it had been available in print since 1590. After the duke's death in 1598, *Pastor Fido* was widely produced and translated into all the major languages of Europe.

Influence of the Pastoral Outside Italy

In France the pastoral was advanced in the national theatre through the works of Alexandra Hardy and Jean Mairet. Hardy, instrumental in the development of so much of French dramatic literature, attempted to make the pastoral more stageworthy by including more action and fewer long speeches. Although his pastorals are much more than imitations of Tasso and Guarini, the narratives of these plays clearly show the influence of the Italians. Of the pastorals of Mairet, his *La sylvanire* (The Wood Nymph, 1630) is the culmination of this dramatic form in France. The preface of this play also continues the playwright's theories on the pastoral, which are taken directly from Guarini. The pastoral was short-lived in France and was absorbed into the developing French opera.

Portrait of Tasso as a young man.

Since the pastoral was directed to the taste of aristocratic audiences, it did not find a lasting place in the English theatre, which was largely a popular theatre. The pastorals of Samuel Daniel, John Fletcher, and Ben Jonson are all based on Italian models, but only Fletcher's *The Faithful Shepherdess* (1608) had any real success on the popular stage. Apparently English playwrights recognized the high artificiality of the pastoral, but they were still attracted to this Italian invention.

DRAMATIC THEORY IN THE ITALIAN RENAISSANCE

The Italian Renaissance produced the neoclassical rules of dramatic construction and criticism. These rules, a mixture of two parts Horace and Aristotle with one part creative invention, became a major force in European theatre for nearly three hundred years. The neoclassical rules were developed as standards for playwrights in their efforts to create distinguished plays in the classical tradition. Briefly stated, these rules are as follows. (1) A play should closely observe the unities of time, place, and action. That is, no more than twenty-four hours are needed for the events of the play, these events take place in a single location, such as the city of Rome, and there is only one story line. (2) A play should be written in verse. (3) A play should have a five-act structure. (4) Characters should speak in accordance to their station in life. (5) Each act should contain five or six scenes closely bound together. (6) No more than three major characters should be on stage at the same time. (7) No character should enter or leave without a reason.

These rules drew their inspirations from classical sources, but their dogmatic aspects were an invention of the Renaissance. Horace's *Ars poetica* was the major classical work of critical theory well known in the Middle Ages and the early Renaissance, since only an incomplete and bad translation of Aristotle's *Poetics* was available. All this changed in 1493 with the publication of a Latin translation of the *Poetics*. In 1536 the standard Latin and Greek texts of the *Poetics* were published. Aristotle's observations on the drama then became the focus of a great deal of scholarly interest. In the *Poetics* Aristotle does not set forth rules of composition; rather, he analyzes aspects of Greek dramaturgy in relation to a proposed aesthetic. The critics of the Italian Renaissance took these observations, combined them with elements of Horace and their own modifications, and produced the neoclassical rules. Foremost among these Renaissance critics were Giraldi Cinthio, Francesco Robertello, Julius Caesar Scaliger, and Lodovico Castelvetro.

Major Renaissance Critics

Giraldi Cinthio challenged and modified the rules as they conflicted with his efforts to please his audiences. He saw the main function of theatre as a moral one, to teach people good behavior. Cinthio disagreed with Aristotle in the preference for a single story line, since he had discovered that his audiences liked the complexity of at least two related stories. He was instrumental in the establishment of the rule of twenty-four hours.

Francesco Robertello (1516–1567) wrote the first major commentary on the *Poetics*, which he published in 1548. He believed the time lapse of the events of a play should be no more than twelve hours, since the characters must sleep, and that tragedy is superior to comedy. The preference for tragedy also reflected Robertello's emphasis on the rhetorical in drama, a view directly linked to Horace. Robertello's views are based on the idea that the audience of a play was an elite group who would be offended by the vulgarity of comedy. Although one of the leading Renaissance experts on Aristotle, Robertello often distorted the *Poetics* to put it into agreement with Horace.

Julius Caesar Scaliger (1484–1558) was one of the most influential of the Renaissance critics and chiefly responsible for spreading the theories of Aristotle in Europe during the sixteenth century. Scaliger developed a systematic theory of poetry and used Aristotle, often incorrectly, to fortify his own critical position.

Lodovico Castelvetro (1505–1571) wrote the first vernacular commentary on the *Poetics*, which was published in 1570. Castelvetro attempted to refute Aristotle and used him as an excuse to expound his own critical theories. To him belongs the dubious honor of first formulating the three unities of time, place, and action. In contrast to Robertello's ideal audience, Castelvetro assumed the audience was an ignorant multitude wanting only to be pleased. Thus it is the audience that is the direct cause for the rules since they lack poetic imagination.

These major critics and many lesser ones were generally concerned with dramatic theories, not with actual stage practices. But the end result of all these polemics on Aristotle and Horace was the creation of an artistic straitjacket that was placed on European theatre.

MUSICAL THEATRE OF THE ITALIAN RENAISSANCE

Opera is a true child of the Italian Renaissance. Tentative links can be made between this new form of musical theatre and the *sacre rappresentazioni* of the Middle Ages, but this new integration of music and drama was truly without a direct ancestry. The Italians, in an effort to re-create Greek drama, invented opera.

The initial interest in the *dramma in musica* came from the Camerata of

An intermezzo in La liberazione di Tirreno e d'Arnea *(1617) in a performance at the Uffizi Palace, Florence.*

Florence, a group of antiquarians who were determined to discover how Greek drama had been set to music. Their experiments resulted in the *recitativo*, a single vocal line freely sung in a declamatory style to a simple instrumental accompaniment. The goal of the *recitativo* was to capture dramatic language in a musical form. The first opera, *La Dafre* by Ottavio Rinuccini and Jacopo Peri, took place in Florence in 1597. This performance and later ones were given before distinguished audiences, who carried glowing reports of this new theatrical form to all parts of Italy and Europe. Opera had been born.

During its early history, the primary emphasis in opera was on the script and production, with music taking a lesser role. The importance of libretto and staging over music reflects their importance to sixteenth-century audiences. The intermezzos placed in the contemporary dramas of the Renaissance had instilled a taste for the sumptuous and spectacular in audiences. The desire to satisfy this audience demand resulted in more ingenuity on the part of designers and machine-makers than composers. The immediate result of this emphasis on production can be seen in pictures and drawings of the new permanent theatres built in Renaissance Italy, for in these new opera houses the spectacular is truly center stage.

At this early stage of its development, opera was fortunate to become an interest of a master musician with a flare for the dramatic. Claudio Monteverdi (1567–1643), a member of the court of Mantua, composed his first opera, *Orfeo*, in 1607, and even after nearly four hundred years this early work is still considered to have great appeal. With the work of Monteverdi the goals of the Camerata were achieved. Although early opera did not recapture the production styles of the ancient Greeks, it did successfully combine drama and music. As opera continued to develop, music would become the focus of the work, but this form of musical theatre would continue to be a powerful force in theatre architecture and technology for several hundred years. Opera began and continues to be theatre in the grand style of the Italian Renaissance.

COMMEDIA DELL'ARTE

The *commedia dell'arte* is a major contribution of the Italian Renaissance to the theatrical traditions of Western theatre. *Commedia dell'arte*—the term means "comedy of the [professional actors'] guild"—refers to a comedy that was essentially improvised around a written scenario by a company of stock characters. This unique theatrical form flourished in Italy in the mid–sixteenth century, spread throughout Europe in the seventeenth, and disappeared in the eighteenth. Theories on the origin of the *commedia dell'arte* attempt to connect it with the Atellan farces of the Romans, Asian mimes, and medieval clowns, but proofs are lacking. *Commedia dell'arte* appeared in the middle sixteenth century, perhaps as a result of the encounters of the skilled amateurs of the court *commedia erudita* and the professional actors of the intermezzos. The *commedia dell'arte* definitely reflects the mingling of the learned with the popular, the structured with the spontaneous. The result was a highly professional theatre that appealed to all classes.

Stock Characters

The dozen or so characters of the *commedia dell'arte*, most of whom wore half-masks and identifiable costumes, changed very little during the existence of this theatrical form. A typical *commedia* company would consist of Pantalone, Dottore (Doctor), Capitano (Captain), a young hero and an ingenue, two or more *zanni* (clowns), and assorted servants and tradespeople.

Pantalone is a major character in the plays of the *commedia*. One of the serious characters, Pantalone is a rich merchant who is often the obstacle to the young lovers. While sometimes thought of as a doddering old fool, the Pantalone of the surviving scripts and contemporary illustrations is a vigorous, middle-aged businessman, often with an eye for the ladies, who is not afraid to defend himself with sword or dagger. The characteristic costume is red tights and jacket, a round black hat, a long black gown, and black slippers. The mask is dark brown with a hooked nose, and this mask was complemented with a

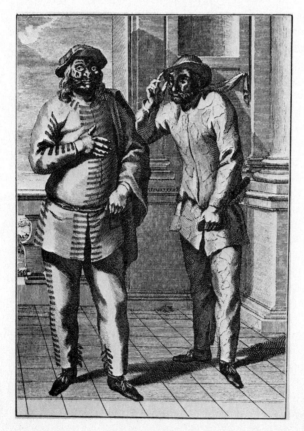

Brighella and Trivellino in a commedia dell'arte *scene.*

Capitano.

pointed beard. Pantalone is a Venetian and speaks in the dialect of Venice, even if the location of the play is in another city.

Dottore, the butt of much of the humor in the *commedia*, is the neighbor and sometimes friend of Pantalone. Dressed in black with short cloak, doctoral bonnet, and white ruff, he is generally a doctor of laws and speaks in the dialect of the city of Bologna. His brain is so fogged with useless knowledge that it is impossible for him to express himself logically or briefly. The mask for the Dottore has a large nose with cheek pads.

Capitano, the braggart soldier, is a Spaniard, the only non-Italian stock character in the *commedia*. Spanish troops of the Holy Roman Empire were stationed in parts of Italy throughout most of the Renaissance, but the native Italians did not consider them welcomed guests. Capitano is a fantastical character, given to bombastic speech and proclamations of his military prowess, but at heart a coward. The costume for this role is an extravagent military dress with a long cape, large sword, and hat with feathers. The mask for the Capitano has large, round eye holes and a long nose, but later *commedia* actors did not use a mask for this role. Capitano is a semiserious character, a suitor for the heroine's favors and often a victim of the tricks of the *zanni*.

Central to the story of most *commedia dell'arte* plays are the lovers. There are usually two pairs of lovers, the *innamorati*, and the concerns of Pantalone

Dottore.

and the activities of the *zanni* relate directly to them. The roles, played without masks, are most demanding on the actors. As ideal lovers, the performers need to be young and attractive in appearance, be very well versed in the latest fashions, and speak in the purest Tuscan, the dialect of grand Italian poetry. Many of the performers who excelled in these roles were educated to the highest standards of the period and were respected poets and dramatists.

The *zanni* are the best-known of the stock characters from the *commedia dell'arte*, particularly Arlecchino, Scapino, and Brighella. Arlecchino, or Harlequin, is considered the chief of the *zanni*. With his multicolored costume of patches, his black half-mask, and his wooden *batte*, or slapstick, Arlecchino is the character that most often comes to mind when *commedia dell'arte* is mentioned. This character excels at acrobatics and is somewhat amoral in his dealings with others. While often in service to one of the serious characters, Arlecchino generally spends his time looking after his own interests. Arlecchino's friend and fellow *zanno* is Scapino. Clad in white trousers, jacket, and cloak, all edged with green, Scapino is an intriguer, an inventor of plots and tricks, but of a kindly nature. The mask for this character is like Arlecchino's, and the illustrations for Scapino often show him playing a lute or guitar. The costume for Brighella is very similar to Scapino's, and he is also a musician, but there the similarity ends. Whereas Scapino is a kindly rascal, Brighella is cruel, cynical, and not averse to using the dagger he sometimes carries. The mask for this character is brutal, with a broad nose and sly eyes.

Commedia Companies

As mentioned before, the *commedia dell'arte* was essentially a theatre of improvisation built around an established scenario. The plays, because of the improvisation, have not survived, but collections of the scenarios were published. The most famous of these collections, Flaminio Scala's *Il Teatro delle favole rappresentative,* appeared in 1611. Such a collection provides a great deal of insight into the art of the *commedia dell'arte.*

The skills of some of the individual *commedia* actors were nearly legendary, but what is intriguing to the modern mind is the high level of ensemble playing

A Harlequin costume from the Italian Renaissance.
(Courtesy of Stephen M. Archer.)

the *commedia dell'arte* required. Not only must all of the players improvise their lines, but they were required to blend into the efforts of their fellow players and then to fine-tune the entire collective effort to the mood and taste of the audience. The burden on the actors for total improvising was lessened to some extent by memorized stock speeches and the *lazzi* of the *zanni*. The stock speech might be romantic poetry from one of the lovers, a variety of tirades by Pantalone, or humorous gobbledygook from Dottore. The *lazzi* were stock comic business used by Arlecchio and his fellows. Many of these *lazzi* were mimic or acrobatic, such as falling off a ladder or eating. These comic bits were rehearsed in advance and then inserted when needed. Some *lazzi* remained in use for generations.

The type of ensemble acting required by the *commedia dell'arte* was not possible under the normal acting conditions of the period. To develop the near-clairvoyance they needed for excellent *commedia dell'arte*, players formed into companies that remained together for decades. These organized companies began to appear in Italy in the middle of the sixteenth century. The most famous of the early companies was called I Gelosi (The Jealous Ones), and it was directed for much of its existence by the highly talented husband-and-wife team of Francesco and Isabella Andreini. Other famous companies were the Uniti, Confidenti, Accesi, and Fideli.

Although an artistic product of Italy, the *commedia dell'arte* was also performed outside the country. Yet the important Italian-language element of the *commedia*, particularly the dialect humor, was largely lost on most non-Italian audiences. Only in France did the *commedia* companies find a lasting audience for their efforts. In 1660 the Comédie Italienne was established in Paris. Except for a brief exile, this branch of the *commedia dell'arte* remained a

A medal depicting Isabella Andreini.

fixture of French theatre, slowly became more French than Italian, and was eventually absorbed into the Opéra Comique.

Influence of the Commedia dell'Arte

Since the *commedia dell'arte* is a theatrical form largely without written scripts, the tracing of its influence in countries outside Italy is difficult. The story matter of the *commedia* scenarios shares many common themes and devices with other sixteenth- and seventeenth-century comedies, but in most cases these can be traced back to Roman comedy. In England the language barrier was at its highest, and only the antics of the *commedia* players made a permanent impression. From the *commedia dell'arte* the English pantomimes were born, and from these harlequinades a debased form of the *commedia* retained a place in the English theatre into this century. In Spain only a very slight influence can be noted in the comedy of intrigue and in a couple of stock characters borrowed from the Italians. Eastern European countries, which were just emerging in the sixteenth century and lacked an established theatrical tradition, borrowed heavily from the *commedia dell'arte*.

In France are found the most direct links to the *commedia dell'arte*. Molière, whose acting company at one time shared a theatre with a company of *commedia* players, borrowed freely from Italians. Although his artistic genius made this material his own, his theatrical development would have taken a different direction without his association with the *commedia dell'arte*. Later French playwrights of the eighteenth century, Marivaux in particular, wrote some of their best scripts for the French *commedia* company. Although the spirit remains strongest in France and Italy, all modern Western theatre has been touched by the *commedia dell'arte* of the Italian Renaissance.

CONCLUSION

Springing from a desire to follow the models of the classical period and yet wishing to create art forms that would reflect the advancements of a new age, the Italian Renaissance blazed new artistic trails for Western culture. The comedies and tragedies of this era served as the foundation for the development of national theatres in most of Europe, and the critical tenets of neoclassicism controlled the structure of European dramaturgy until the nineteenth century. The society of Renaissance Italy was destroyed in the power struggles of postmedieval Europe, but the influence of its theatrical traditions is still an artistic force in the modern theatre.

9

RENAISSANCE THEATRE ARCHITECTURE AND STAGE PRACTICE

Emerging from the Middle Ages, the tradition of social-recreational entertainment became all-important to the rulers of Renaissance Italy. Pageants, parades, royal entries, and tournaments had sparked an insatiable desire for entertainments among those classes that had the leisure to enjoy them. This, coupled with the wealth that the merchant and ruling classes amassed, provided the financial basis for the arts patronage system that sponsored a great period of experimentation in theatre architecture and scenic practice. The rediscovery of Vitruvius's *De architectura* did more than provide some rules for the building of theatres and scenery; it also provided the justification for arts patronage. The emulation of Roman and Greek culture was the goal, the ultimate truth, of nearly every scientific and artistic inquiry of the period.

An important concept in Renaissance staging practice is verisimilitude. Verisimilitude is the attempt to bring the objective reality of nature to the stage, and for Renaissance practitioners it was nature as perceived by the classical world. Thus ceilings of some Renaissance theatres were painted to look like sky and clouds because the classical theatres were outdoors, and onstage objects were to look as lifelike as possible. All the aspects of verisimilitude were used to provide Renaissance audiences with the appearance of reality.

THE DEVELOPMENT OF PERSPECTIVE SCENERY

Next to the discovery of Vitruvius's work, perspective remains the most important development in the emergence of theatres and scenery during the Italian Renaissance. An understanding of its development is essential to an understanding of Italian scenic practice. Although the rapid advance of perspective scenery occurred between 1520 and 1590, its geometric mechanics were discovered earlier by the Florentine architect Filippo Brunelleschi (1377–1446). According to his rules, linear perspective was accomplished through a mathematically ordered system of receding planes that created a visual relationship among three-dimensional objects in a two-dimensional space. Following this initial description of perspective principles, many changes and clarifications occurred. The painter Massaccio (actually Tommaso Guidi, 1401–1428) perfected the illusion of atmospheric perspective, correctly noting that the appearance of objects was often affected by the atmosphere, getting hazy and somewhat bluish as the distance from the viewer increased. Most of these developments were simply parts of larger works on art and architecture, and it was left to Paolo Uccello (1397–1475), an excellent painter, to offer the first definitive work on perspective. Renaissance painters and architects of any note incorporated perspective into their basic styles, using it at first for nontheatrical purposes. An early use of perspective was to increase the size and scope of a patron's rooms by painting them so as to seem larger than they really were. This use can be seen in Renaissance structures extant today, and it is consistent with the concept of patron glorification. Among the

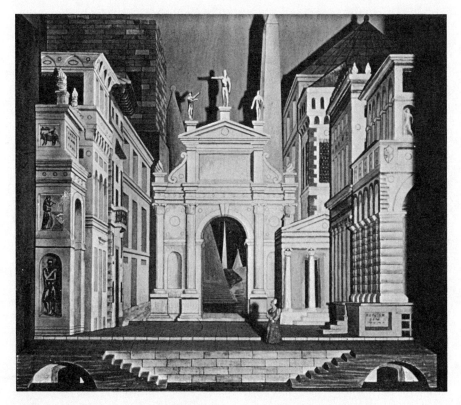

A model of Serlio's scene for tragedy.
(Courtesy of the Cleveland State University's Theatre Arts Area.)

masters of this practice was Baldassare Peruzzi (1431–1531). It is most likely he who first brought perspective painting into stage scenic design in Cardinal Bibbiena's 1513 production of *Caladria*.

Vitruvius's rediscovered work provided the basis for the form of the Renaissance theatre and its scenery. This Roman work was published in 1486 and soon became the scenic and stage bible for Italian stage practitioners. The impetus given to Renaissance designers generally came from statements that plays must have scenery and that scenery much change. Vitruvius noted that machinery for moving scenery and for creating stage effects was appropriate for the stage. Beyond these generalized brief comments, he described in detail guidelines for the proper types of scenery: "Tragic scenes are delineated with columns, pediments, statues, and other objects suited to kings; . . . comic scenes exhibit private dwellings with balconies and views representing rows of windows after the manner of ordinary dwellings; satyric scenes are decorated with trees, caverns, mountains, and other rustic objects delineated in landscape style." This simple statement provided Renaissance designers with the justification for the establishment of "proper" scenery for various kinds of plays, a system that was not totally broken for four hundred years.

Part of the support the court theatre gave to the development of perspective can be seen in the concept of patron glorification. A perspective setting is only truly in perspective when viewed from the center of the auditorium. In other places of the house the picture distorts. Knowing this, Renaissance scenic practitioners designed from the point of view of the patron's seat. Thus the perspective is perfect from that seat, and the patron is glorified by having his importance so affirmed.

The Evolution of Scene Design

Renaissance scene designers were, for the most part, also architects and painters. As architects, many of them wrote about the art and science of stage design in larger works on general architecture. So it was with Sebastiano Serlio (1475–1554), who, in his *Trattato di architettura* (Treatise on Architecture), wrote the first important work to combine both Vitruvian and Renaissance architectural principles. It was Book II, published in Paris in 1545, that contributed most to the development of theatres and scenery. Essentially a work on perspective and its application in the theatre, the final section of the work showed a keen understanding of Vitruvian principles as they were applied to the Renaissance stage. Serlio provided his observations on the correct classical form for use in both auditorium and stage. These observations, based on Vitruvian models, were widely copied during the Renaissance. Vitruvius called for an auditorium and an orchestra, for example, that were semicircular. In Renaissance practice, however, shows were produced in some part of the patron's palace, usually a large room on the second floor. Since most of these temporary theatres were constructed in a rectangular space, the seating became flattened at the back of the auditorium to allow for sufficient stage space. Serlio's drawing of the ground plan for a theatre did not

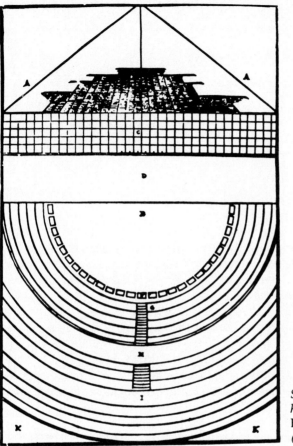

Serlio's ground plan for a hall stage, from the Second Book of Architecture *(1545).*

show this phenomenon, but, in order to have a sufficiently large auditorium, actual theatres were thus constructed to accommodate Serlian theory with actual practice. In larger rectangular halls the sides of the auditorium seating were elongated, thus creating a modified figure U. Moving toward the stage, Serlio provided space for the separation of playing space from seating space, which was occupied later by the proscenium. This separation of spaces is an important consideration in the development of later theatres, for it marks the end of the medieval tradition of a highly unified, open-ended presentation where audience and players mixed before a *mansion-platea*. Here began the increasing polarization of the audience and playing space, to be alternately seen as both the blessing and the curse of the modern theatre.

The stage itself was customized from Vitruvius's model to fulfill the Renaissance desire for verisimilitude and perspective scenery. After a flat space for the play's action was provided, the remaining stage floor was raked, that is, slanted up toward the back to aid in the perspective effect. The terms "upstage"

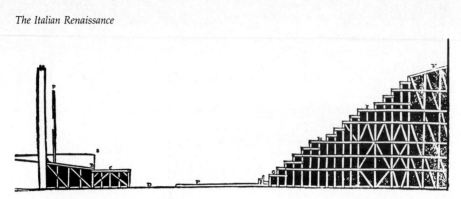

Serlio's cross-section of a hall stage.

and "downstage" originate from this practice, when to move to the back of the stage was literally to climb slightly. This space was filled with scenery to establish clearly the locale of the production, and the space was separated by receding pairs of wings, scenery on either side of the stage, that were appropriately decorated to establish that locale. Above each wing station was placed a decorated cloud and sky border, scenery above the stage, that covered the ceiling beams. At the back of the stage was a backdrop that ran across the length of the stage and finished the perspective. Although Serlio only mentions them, shutters, scenery providing the upstage view, were commonly used as the background, and they could part in the middle to reveal an inner stage. Occasionally these shutters parted to reveal an extension of the main

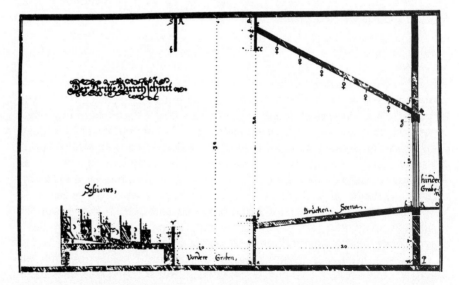

Furttenbach's cross-section of a theatre. Note the placement of the seats and the stage borders.

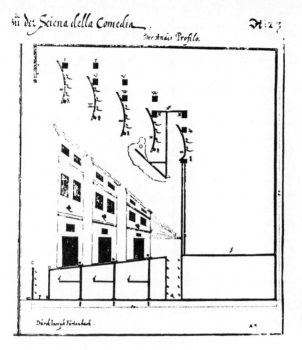

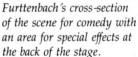

*Furttenbach's cross-section
of the scene for comedy with
an area for special effects at
the back of the stage.*

setting or a setting apart from the main set, usually an interior. The back shutters were painted to continue the general decoration of the side wings.

On the subject of the side wings themselves, Serlio is brief but explicit. They were to be two-sided, with a front face parallel to the audience and a perspective face that angled sharply upstage and slightly onstage. Known as the Serlian wing, this perspective device was the primary one used in Renaissance theatres for the balance of the sixteenth century. The Serlian wing provided the illusion of great depth and visually served perspective well, but it was difficult to change to another scene. The perspective face was angled at the top and bottom to provide the perspective needed, and with the three-dimensional decor used in the manner prescribed by Vitruvius, the wings were quite bulky. Serlio did not attempt to discuss methods of shifting his wings, for he was primarily concerned with artistically establishing Vitruvius's tragic, comic, and satyric scenes as guidelines for good practice. It was for others to grapple with reconciling the Serlian wing to Vitruvius's command to change the scenery.

No one grappled more with the problem of changing the Serlian wing than Nicola Sabbattini (1574–1654), an Italian architect and engineer. His *Practica di fabricar scene e machine ne'teatri* (Manual for Constructing Theatrical Scenes and Machines, 1638) became the standard handbook for staging practice in the seventeenth century. The work covered the entire spectrum of theatrical production, including directions for constructing a theatre within a patron's hall. Specific details were provided for both the auditorium and the

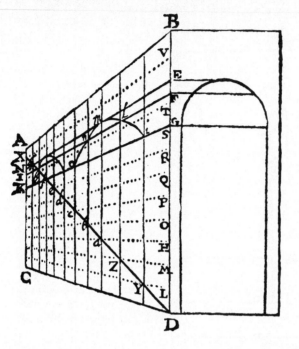

Sabbattini's method of laying out perspective arches on a Serlian wing.

stage, and the stage effects, scenery, lighting, and stage machinery necessary to achieve the required results were described. The *Practica* was composed of two books, the first dealing generally with theatre construction, scene painting, and lighting, and the second concerning the problems of moving scenery. Developing his ideas about perspective from his teacher, Guido Ubaldus (1540–1601), Sabbatini showed that he was aware of the importance of patron glorification in his concern for the location of the patron's seat in the theatre. He was similarly concerned about the location of the vanishing point for the perspective and the general floor plan for the scenery itself.

Perhaps the most important contribution of this book was the detailed shift from three-dimensionality on the Serlian wing to a high concern for painted detail in realizing the decor. Sabbattini was particularly concerned with the painting technique necessary to render, with highlight and shadow, balconies, doors, and windows with the same detail that Serlio had them built. Consistent with the concepts of Serlio, Sabbattini did not consider changing the scenery for the plays of the Italian Renaissance. He worked within the standard framework of the tragic, comic, and satyric scenes of Vitruvius, attempting only to heighten reality by detailed painting that increased depth.

In the second book Sabbattini addressed the problems of moving scenery, and that was primarily done in dealing with the scenic problems of the intermezzos. It was for the intermezzos that the bulk of Renaissance scenic machinery and devices for special effects were developed. Intermezzos were allegorical dramatic presentations performed between the acts of a regular play. Sabbattini spent considerable time in his second book discussing these

Scene changing by drawing a cloth across a Serlian wing.

(*From Richard Leacroft,* The Development of the English Playhouse. *Used by permission of Cornell University Press.*)

effects, with particular attention to the changing of scenes on the Serlian wing. He proposed several methods for accomplishing this task. First, each wing was covered by another scene that was stored at the offstage edge of the front face. At the appropriate time, it was pulled by two men across the front and perspective faces of the wing to be secured on the upstage edge. A second method required grooves or tracks in the stage floor for the perspective faces at each wing station, so that a set of wings hidden behind the set in use could be slid immediately upstage to create a change of scene. Finally, Sabbattini experimented with *periaktoi* for especially rapid and wonderful scene changes. *Periaktoi* were mounted on poles operated from under the stage floor. To change the scene, the poles were rotated 180 degrees to reveal a side on which was painted a different scene. Other scenic marvels about which Sabbattini wrote included enlarging and decreasing the stage space, destroying the entire scene (including by fire), and operating the back shutters.

That Sabbattini's work was the standard by which many seventeenth-century designers practiced their craft cannot be doubted, but in actuality he was neither innovative nor precise. He was a practical architect, oriented to the working rather than the theoretical stage, and this is revealed in his drawings and writings. He did not deal with the flat wing as a replacement for the Serlian wing, although the technology for this achievement had been explored by Guido Ubaldus in *Perspectivae libri sex* (Six Books of Perspective, 1600) some thirty-eight years before *Practica*. Yet Sabbattini used the flat wing in his back shutters, so the general concept must have been known to him. For all the inaccurate drawings and awkward use of language, *Practica* remained the definitive handbook on stage practice for the balance of its century.

Although Ubaldus is generally credited with the idea of using the flat wing as a side wing, it was probably Giovanni Aleotti (1546–1636) who first practically applied the principle at the Teatro degl'Intrepidi at Ferrara in 1606 and later at the Teatro Farnese at Parma. The flat wing was a tremendous innovation. It created the necessary illusion without requiring the same stage space as the

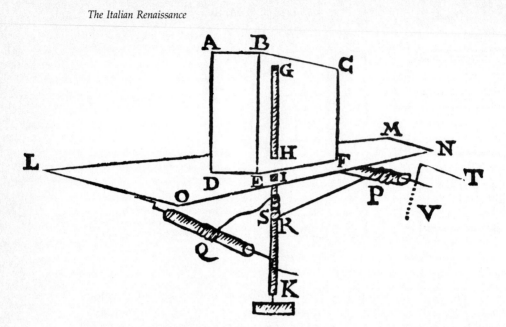

Sabbattini's periaktoi *method for changing the scene.*

Serlian wing, thus creating more onstage room for machines and people. It could be easily changed and stored, and its easier technological development went hand in hand with an increase in believable perspective painting. The device is still the mainstay for operatic scenery and for most modern exterior set masking. The modern theatre owes a large debt to the Renaissance for this development.

Undoubtedly the most innovative system for changing the flat wing was developed by Giacomo Torelli da Fano (1608–1678). His device, the *chariot-mat* (chariot and pole), became the rage of Europe shortly after its introduction. The system utilized a tall platform, supported scaffold-style on wheels in a track, that allowed movement onstage and offstage parallel to the proscenium plane. Two of these chariots were operational in the understage space below each wing station, thus allowing one to support the wing currently in view of the audience and the other to support the wing offstage, which could be changed to the wing of the next scene. The chariot supported a pole that extended through the stage floor onto which the actual flat wing was attached. The two chariots at each wing station were connected through a series of ropes and pulleys to a single central winch system so that all chariots could move at the same time. Thus the total stage picture could change exactly at the same time, to the wonder and amazement of all.

Torelli also contributed to the development of perspective, not so much as an innovator but certainly as a refiner of current practice. Although he concerned himself primarily with a single-vanishing-point perspective, he developed a drafting technique that was subtle and highly complicated. He did

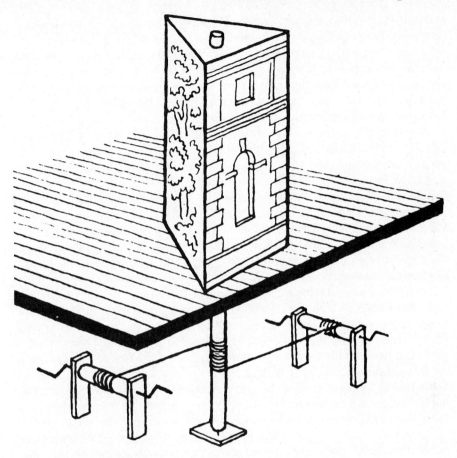

A reconstruction of the Sabbattini periaktoi.

(From Richard Leacroft, The Development of the English Playhouse. *Used by permission of Cornell University Press.)*

not use sharply rendered detail for set decoration, but rather blended his detail from upstage hazy atmospheric rendering to very heavily ornamented detail on the downstage wings. In addition, Torelli gave strong emphasis to onstage working special effects, such as fountains, that helped create the illusion of versimilitude and depth.

EVOLUTION OF THE PLAYHOUSE

As with the development of Renaissance scenery, the structure of the theatre itself originated in rediscovered classical writings and drawings. Vitruvius again is a key factor, for he had explored the form of the

The Italian Renaissance

classical theatre building and provided detailed instructions for its construction. Since the early theatres sponsored by various members of the secular and religious ruling classes were often built in their palaces, Vitruvius's concepts were slightly altered to fit those rectangular spaces. Nonetheless, it is from this period in history that the basic form of the modern theatre comes—a rectangular space, clearly divided between the area occupied by the production and the area inhabited by the audience.

We have already noted the contributions of Serlio in bringing Vitruvius's concepts to the Renaissance theatre architecture. Although theatres based on Serlio's work were built early in the sixteenth century (a theatre may have existed at Ferrara as early as 1532), the oldest remaining theatre employing Serlian principles exists at Vicenza. It is the Teatro Olimpico, built between 1580 and 1584. The structure was designed by the prominent architect Andrea Palladio (1518–1580), but he did not live to realize his design. His pupil, Vicenzo Scamozzi (1552–1616), finished the structure and probably altered the design to create a theatre distinct unto itself. The building was a realization of classical theatre concepts to the last detail. The orchestra and auditorium were slightly flattened semicircles, surrounded by copies of Greek statuary and a post-and-lintel facade. For acoustical purposes, the auditorium rose to the height of the stage facade, a Vitruvian principle. The stage was exactly copied from Vitruvius's description, complete with a Roman *pulpitum* and a *scaena frons*, but here the classical similarities end. Behind the facade (*scaena frons*) are five vistas, designed by Scamozzi, that are complete implementations of the Serlian wing concept. They set behind three openings in the main facade and are behind the acting area and the two openings in the side facade extensions. Each has a perspective street receding from the audience. The center view is actually three vistas—a main vista and two vistas immediately to the right and left of the central one. Except for actor entrances just downstage of the vistas, all action was in front of the facade so that the perspective was not ruined by not-to-scale actors in it. Consistent with Serlian principles, these scenes did not

Two views of the interior of the Teatro Olimpico.
(Courtesy of Stephen M. Archer.)

The central portal of the scenery at the Teatro Olimpico.
(Courtesy of Stephen M. Archer.)

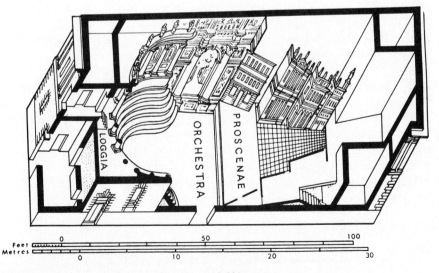

A reconstruction of the Teatro all'Antico at Sabbioneta.
(From Richard Leacroft, The Development of the English Playhouse. *Used by permission of Cornell University Press.)*

The Teatro all'Antico at Sabbioneta.
(Courtesy of KaiDib Films International, Glendale, Calif.)

change but provided a general setting for the staging of classical and Renaissance plays. Although the Teatro Olimpico is important because of its age, it did not establish a pattern for other theatres to follow. Other theatres used the classical principles upon which it was built, but none had permanent perspective vistas. This theatre did, however, establish classical theatre architectural principles in the Renaissance and deserves attention for that accomplishment.

In 1588 Scamozzi designed a smaller theatre, the Teatro all'Antico, at Sabbioneta. This theatre is more truly a model for Renaissance theatres in that it followed Serlio's prescriptions almost to the letter. There was no proscenium arch, although the first set of wings met the architecture of the auditorium in such a manner that a mild form of framing existed. The real importance of this theatre is that it was built as a unit unto itself, and it thereby shows the late Renaissance trend away from building theatres in ducal palaces and toward erecting theatres as separate buildings.

Development of the Proscenium

The earlier trend of building theatres in palaces did not die, however, and one such theatre became the true prototype of the modern theatre. It was the Teatro Farnese, designed and built by Giovanni Aleotti in 1619. In this theatre can be noted the first extant proscenium arch. A proscenium arch is an architectural unit that serves as a frame for the stage picture, much as a regular picture frame defines the picture shown therein. In the Renaissance the proscenium arch was the unifying device from which all lines for the perspective scenery were figured. Its origins were many: pictures frames, margin illustrations in medieval manuscripts, the architectural arch, and the stone framing of stained-glass windows all share elements with the proscenium arch. So the concept of some sort of framing device was not unknown, and only its specific application to indoor Renaissance theatres was to be developed.

Before its formalization, stage picture framing was suggested by the stage floor itself, which was raised according to classical guidelines and thus created a bottom to the picture frame. The first set of wings had the dual function of masking the offstage space and providing the locale, and the first border (usually a cloud) hid the machinery above to complete the frame. Consistent with this function, the proscenium arch at the Teatro Farnese had a formal masking device similar in style to the decoration of the stage facade itself. It complemented the decoration on the stage floor face, the first set of side wings, and the first border. This usage rapidly became the standard throughout Europe and set a pattern that is still in use today in traditional theatre structures.

The importance of the development of the proscenium can hardly be overstated. Not only did it establish the frame for the stage picture but it formally completed another notion of theatre practice extant in traditional theatres today—the polarization between the audience and actor. With the arrival of the proscenium arch, the practice of having the actors and their scenery at one end of the theatre and the audience at the other end was fully established.

Auditorium Changes

While the Teatro Farnese established the convention of the proscenium arch, it did little to advance the general U shape of the auditorium. As long as these structures were court-sponsored, there was no general need for architects to concern themselves unduly with auditorium development. It was the arrival of public theatres that provided the necessary changes in Renaissance theatre structure that would set the form for theatre architecture for the next three hundred years. Venice, the major republic in Italy, was the center of public theatre development. Although public theatres began to appear there as early as 1565, it was not until the public presentations of opera began in the seventeenth century that major innovations occurred. These were not the first changes in auditorium design—others of a minor nature can be noted in northern Europe—but they were significant ones and set the standard for auditorium construction. The first Venetian public opera house was the San Cassiano. Built in 1637, it had a five-balcony structure and an open pit area. Since it was a public theatre, all classes of society attended performances. Ticket prices were based on seating level. The lower two balconies were the most expensive and were used by the wealthier classes. The pit was reserved as seating and standing room for the poorer people, and the upper balconies were used by the middle class of Venice. As opera spread throughout Europe, so did this form of theatre. Box seats existed at the lower balcony levels, establishing the concept of pit, boxes in the prime balconies, and a gallery consisting of the upper balcony. Once established, the horseshoe-shaped auditorium became the dominant form for European theatres until the late nineteenth century.

STAGE MACHINERY AND SCENIC DEVICES

The Renaissance theatre, particularly with intermez-zos and opera, made extensive use of scene-changing devices. To fulfill the Renaissance thirst for verisimilitude, increasingly elaborate means for creating the illusion of reality on stage were developed. Most of these special effects were extensions of effects created or conceived in the Middle Ages, refined for the indoor stage. All were designed to bring a representation of the natural into the stage picture.

Stage Effects

Chief among the various effects were cloud ma-chines. Originally they were simple cumulus clouds that adorned the heavens, but practitioners like Sabbattini soon developed the machinery to provide horizontal and vertical movement. Most of the winches, ropes, and pulleys necessary for cloud movement were concealed by the proscenium, side wings, stage, and borders. Diagonal movement was soon possible as pulley and winch systems became more sophisticated and the main pulleys could float across stage roughly parallel to the path of the cloud. Sabbattini provided the ultimate

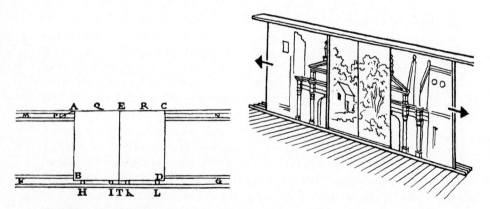

Sabbattini's grove method of operating the back shutter and a reconstructed Sabbattini back shutters parting to reveal another scene.

(From Richard Leacroft, The Development of the English Playhouse. *Used by permission of Cornell University Press.)*

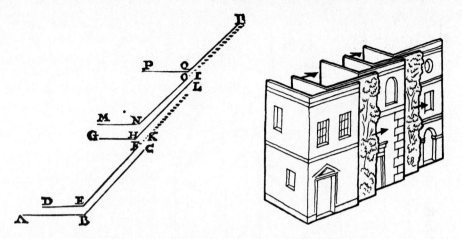

The nested wing, Sabbattini's second method of changing a scene and a reconstruction for changing Serlian wings according to the nested wing system.

(*From Richard Leacroft,* The Development of the English Playhouse. *Used by permission of Cornell University Press.*)

in cloud machinery, the expanding or triple cloud. Sabbattini's ultimate cloud was actually a collection of three clouds in tight formation to appear as one at the start of the effect. By a system that spread the clouds apart as they moved across the stage, the illusion of cloud expansion was created and verisimilitude served.

One distinct form of cloud effect, the glory, deserves special mention. This

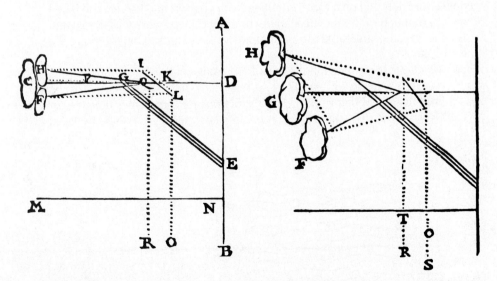

This Sabbattini cloud effect spreads into three parts and then collects into a single form as it rises.

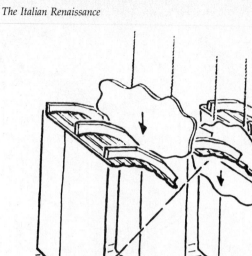

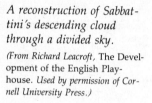

*A reconstruction of Sabbat-
tini's descending cloud
through a divided sky.*

(*From Richard Leacroft,* The Development of the English Playhouse. *Used by permission of Cornell University Press.)*

machine was an extremely large, multiple-cloud device complete with its own
lighting and, in the larger models, capable of descending with choruses of
actors. It was usually a centerstage effect located somewhat upstage. Up to fifty
people could descend on a glory, complete with chariots and horses, and when
it was used, much of the theatre's ability to rig and fly scenery was employed.
This effect created a great sense of admiration, awe, and wonder among the
audience.

Sea effects closely rivaled the mechanical clouds on the Renaissance stage.
These involved a variety of sea items, such as ships, but the common element
was the sea itself. Sabbattini provided instructions for three types of wave, or
sea, machines. The first employed a large cloth alternately pulled and released

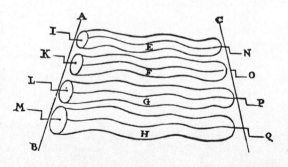

*Sabbattini's cylinder method
of showing a sea.*

by ropes to approximate the pitching and tossing of the sea. Another used wood slats to create the wave forms, with a cloth covering them to provide the illusion of the complete sea. But the most far-reaching effect utilized wave-formed cylinders, set wing to wing across the stage and turned by stagehands rotating crank handles behind each set of wings. Thus, each receding wing station was provided with a wave cylinder so that a sense of the entire sea was achieved. By altering the movement pattern of the various cylinders, different states of sea excitement were possible. Later, other practitioners created even more violent wave forms for greater variety.

Ship machines, varying from distant images to models that could carry several people, moved between the wave cylinders. Mounted on carts that were hidden from audience view by the waves, the ship moved across the stage just upstage of any given wave machine. The ship effect was mounted on the cart so that it appeared above the wave, as if riding on the wave. The cart was then pulled across the stage while the wave machine was rotating, and to provide the final illusion the ship could tilt back and forth on a central pivot in the cart to give the proper "pitching" effect.

Monsters inhabiting the sea were also shown. One of the most common monster effects utilized a triangular cartlike device that moved across the stage in a similar fashion to the ship cart. Along the diagonal of the device the cut-out

Furttenbach's ship machine. The cutout ship could pitch in its support cart as the cart rolled between the waves.

Furttenbach's whale. Like the ship machine, this device could move in its tracks as it was wheeled between the waves.

monster moved so that the effect was one of riding the waves as the monster crossed the stage.

All sorts of flying machines graced the Renaissance stage. Chariots, monsters, and other animals, some capable of carrying actors, could appear from any wing or border and travel the same paths as the cloud machines. Much of the rigging necessary for these effects was driven from behind the side wings since the notion of a large space above the stage for elaborate flying systems had not yet developed. But the desire for flying machinery to support effects and scene changes was insatiable. This was a major factor in the change from curved borders to flat borders since this allowed more room for flying apparatus.

Other objects also enjoyed audience fascination. From the understage trees, rocks, and mountains rose and sank through trapdoors in the stage floor. Actors could appear and disappear with these effects. In their most elegant state, mountains could rise to stage level, open to reveal internal effects and actors, close once the actors took other stage positions, and retreat to their original position. Similarly, machines using water for fountains and waterfalls were very popular. Taking their form from the central fountains of medieval towns, these effects worked through a system of piping from the understage space. Animal machines existed that could move mechanically about the stage. Birds suspended on wires could fly across the stage, and large animals, operated much like puppets from under the stage floor, could roam about. Again, medieval tradition is important here.

LIGHTING

The move to permanent indoor theatres during the Renaissance created new problems in illumination. From the solutions to these problems were born the theory and practice of theatrical lighting. Two types of illumination were possible during the Renaissance, candles and oil lamps. The typical approach was to use candles in large chandeliers to light the auditorium, and oil lamps in various forms to brighten the stage wings and borders. The candles used for auditorium lighting needed to be of sufficient size to last through the entire production, and the chandeliers in which they were placed were built to provide some protection for the audience against dripping wax. Onstage the acting area downstage of the scenic display was lit by the "float," the forerunner of the modern footlight. This device was a long trough of oil wherein wicks mounted in corks were floated and lit to give a broad band of light. The primary use was in front of the acting area or upstage for the inner stage. The wings and borders were illuminated by individual oil lamps in sufficient number to make the onstage lighting brighter than the auditorium lighting. For the side wings these oil lamps were placed on "wing ladders," shelved open boxes attached to the pole or supporting device of each wing. The downstage wings were illuminated from the float lighting or the light from the auditorium chandeliers. Floats were occasionally used in a similar fashion among the borders but the more common practice was to have horizontal "wing ladders" there. Where more light was needed, the lamps could be tipped toward the upstage wing or border, and crude reflectors made of mica were placed on the side of the lamp away from the scenery to be lit.

Special Effects

Lighting played an important part in the creation of special effects. Fire, either consuming a specific object or the whole set, was achieved by igniting powdered resin or sulfur as it was thrown onstage through doorways and windows or between the wings. Lightning was achieved by passing a flash-shaped scenic piece covered with reflective tinsel and mica across the stage. This was lit by the border ladders or by a light ring around the flash. Coupled with this were thunder effects achieved by rattling metal sheets or by rolling square-wheeled carts across the backstage areas. Perhaps the most ingenious device for thunder was offered by Sabbattini when he placed a stair-stepped device in a rectangular box and ran cannonballs down the steps. The steps were designed so that the rise was less and the steps were closer together at the end of the run to achieve a realistic pealing effect.

Major Lighting Theories

Beyond the general practice of lighting described above, some designers theorized about its use. Of major importance among these was Leone de Somi (1527–1592). His *Dialoghi in materia di rappresenta-*

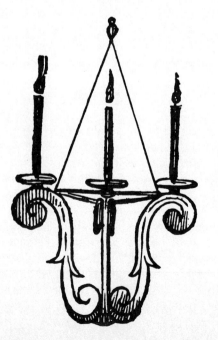

Two examples of auditorium lamps taken from Sabbattini's Practica, *book 1.*

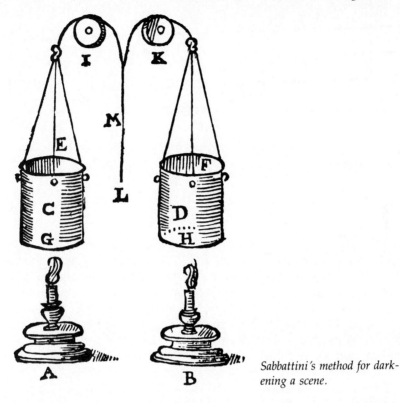

Sabbattini's method for darkening a scene.

zioni sceniche (Dialogues on Stage Affairs, c. 1565) offered some insight into the proper use of lighting for the theatre. Early in the fourth dialogue, he argued for brighter light on the stage than in the auditorium and stated that comedy should enjoy a higher level of illumination than tragedy.

Clearly the most practical or applied theoretician of stage lighting practice in the Renaissance was Josef Furttenbach (1591–1667). Furttenbach, a German who practiced primarily in his native land, gained his ideas and training from the Italian Renaissance. His work in Italy and Germany provided the basis for three books on civil and recreational architecture. In the third, a collection of sixteen treatises call *Mannhaffter Kunstspiegel* (The Noble Mirror of Art, 1663), he set forth ideas about the practice of stage lighting that are still primary in modern theory. Furttenbach is concerned, in a treatise on perspective scenery, with providing a description of the various lighting instruments to be used in the various stage positions and with getting more light on the production. Starting with a simple plain reflector behind the lamp flame, his drawings indicated that when a checked pattern was put on the reflector, the light was better spread over the surface of the scenery to be lit. He also discovered that side reflectors added to the back reflector helped focus the light specifically where he wanted it and helped keep light from unwanted areas. In addition to lighting, he gave his own views on the uses of the inner stage and the design and construction of stage machinery. Furttenbach was a major contributor to the spread and advancement of Italian stage practice.

The Italian Renaissance

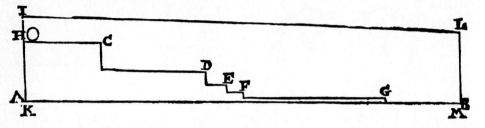

Sabbattini's thunder roll in which stone balls were rolled down the steps to create the needed sound effect.

CONCLUSION

The Italian Renaissance scenes and machines now seem crude attempts to create the illusion of reality on stage. But to the extent that these were the initial attempts in what would be a centuries-long search for verisimilitude in the theatre, they are worthy of serious consideration. Later centuries would largely refine and build upon the principles discovered during the Italian Renaissance. The architectural and technical developments of the Italian theatre established models and standards that were to govern Western theatre until the twentieth century. For sheer awe, wonder, and glory, it was a truly remarkable era.

RETROSPECT

In many ways the foundations of the modern age were set in the Italian Renaissance. Emerging from the Middle Ages, the philosophical basis for the Renaissance was characterized by the debate between worldly and spiritual values. This debate fueled the scientific, artistic, and technological advances of the Renaissance, and these advances were instrumental in establishing a new foundation for Western theatre.

Consistent with the general spirit of the Renaissance, both art and architecture sought to express truth through verisimilitude, the capturing of objective reality in the artist's medium. The development of perspective provided the framework for verisimilitude in art, and in turn, the design and construction of theatres and scenery. Consistent with the emphasis on arts in the Renaissance, the dominant artists in the theatre were the architect and scene designer (often the same person fulfilled both functions). The work of these individuals, motivated by the search for verisimilitude and the concept of patron glorification, provided the basis for modern theatre structure and production practices. The basic form for the playhouse emerged in the works of Serlio, Palladio, Scamozzi, Aleotti, and the various designers of the Venetian opera houses. From the opera houses came the shape and parts of the modern theatre building, that unique combination of pit, boxes, and galleries. In addition, the development of the proscenium arch clearly framed the stage picture and separated the production space from the audience space. Behind the proscenium, detailed illusionistic scenes and machines brought verisimilitude to Italians thirsty for the image of objective reality on stage. Since these theatres were indoors, lighting became important, and its importance resulted in the development of lighting theories and practices that still play a role in the theatre today.

In addition to theatre architecture and scenography, several unique forms of theatre emerged during the Italian Renaissance. Intermezzos grew to be an allegorical, mythically based dramatic presentation performed by both professional and amateur actors between acts of classical or humanistic plays. They were a major influence in the development of opera and ballet. The *commedia dell'arte*, the professional actors' theatre of comic improvisation, arose from wandering bands of players to occupy a major place in European theatrical entertainment for over two hundred years. Its influence extended well beyond its active life, clearly shaping the writings of some of the world's major playwrights. Opera, invented in an attempt to recapture the essence of Greek theatre, became Italy's greatest contribution to world theatre and still preserves, even in the late twentieth century, a taste of the visual glory of the Renaissance.

The Italian Renaissance was least strong in dramatic literature. Except for *Mandragola*, the plays of this period would be difficult to perform before a modern theatre audience. Yet these comedies and tragedies had a tremendous influence on the development of theatrical literature throughout Europe, and the principles of neoclassicism would shape the work of playwrights well into the nineteenth century. Thus the Italian Renaissance provided the basis for modern theatre practice in all areas of theatrical endeavor, from its relatively weak dramatic literature to its strong architecture, scenery, and scenic machines. Truly, in all aspects of human endeavor, including the theatre, the Italian Renaissance began the modern age.

Date	Italian History	Italian Theatre History	World History	World Theatre History
1238				Birth of Adam de la Halle.
1239	Frederick II excommunicated by Pope Gregory IX.		Mongols conquer Russia.	
	Papal States invaded by Frederick.			
1241			Mongols conquer Poland, Serbia, and Albania.	
1244			Christians lose Jerusalem.	
1249			Oxford University founded.	
1250	Death of Frederick II.			
1258			Mongols invade China.	
1264	Venetian fleet defeats the Genoese fleet.			
1295	Marco Polo returns to Italy from China.			
1304		Petrarch born.		
1314			Scots defeat the English at Battle of Bannockburn.	
1315		Mussato's *Eccerinus*.		
1316	Pope moves residence to Avignon, France.			
1328	Gonzagas establish their rule in Mantua.			
c. 1330		Petrarch's *Philologia*.		

(Continued on page 172)

Date	Italian History	Italian Theatre History	World History	World Theatre History
1337			Start of Hundred Years' War between England and France.	
1338	University of Pisa founded.			
1346			Battle of Crecy, first use of cannon in battle.	
1349			Plague begins to spread in Europe.	
1369	Venice stops Hungarian invasion.			
1370s				Corpus Christi cycles start.
1381			Peasants revolt in England.	
1396	Study of Greek literature begins in Florence.			
1400	Medici rule begins in Florence.			
1412		Brunelleschi's *Rules of Perspective*.	Birth of Joan of Arc.	
1415			Battle of Agincourt.	
1435		Alberti's *Della pittura*.		
1449	Birth of Lorenzo de'Medici.			
	Birth of Leonardo da Vinci.			
1453			Fall of Constantinople to Turks.	
1455			Beginning of the War of the Roses in England.	
1463–79	War between Venince and Turks.			

Date	Italian History	Italian Theatre History	World History	World Theatre History
1469		Birth of Niccolò Machiavelli.		Birth of Juan del Encina.
1470				Birth of Gil Vicente.
1474		Birth of Ariosto.	First book in English published by Caxton.	
1475	Birth of Cesare Borgia.			
1483			Birth of Martin Luther.	
1485			Battle of Bosworth Field, beginning of Tudor dynasty.	
1486		De architectura published.		
1492		Birth of Aretino.	Spain united as single kingdom.	
			First voyage of Columbus to New World.	
1493			Pope divides New World between Spain and Portugal.	
1494				Birth of Hans Sachs.
1495			English Parliament passes law against strolling actors.	
1498			Vasco da Gama sails to India.	
1499	French take Milan and Genoa.			Rojas's Celestina.
1500	Lodovico Sforz, Duke of Milan, taken by the French.		Columbus returns to Spain in chains.	
1502		Birth of Beolco.		Plays of Vicente given for royal family of Portugal.

(Continued on page 174)

Date	Italian History	Italian Theatre History	World History	World Theatre History
1504		Birth of Cinthio.		Birth of Nicholas Udall.
1507	Death of Cesare Borgia.			
1509		Ariosto's *Cassaria*.	Henry VIII begins reign.	
1512	French driven out of Italy.			
1514			Ponce de Leon discovers Florida.	
1517			Luther posts his protests at Whittenberg. Start of Protestant Reformation.	
1520			Pope Leo X excommunicates Luther.	
1521			Aztec empire destroyed.	
1527	Rome sacked by troops of Emperor Charles V. Emperor in control of Italy. Influence of Italy in politics falls into decline.			
1530	Republic of Florence.		Religious wars in Switzerland between Protestants and Catholics.	
1533			Henry VIII excommunicated. Birth of future Elizabeth I of England.	
1536		Latin and Greek text of *Poetics* published.		
1538		Birth of Guarini.		
1541		Girladi's *Orbecche*.		
1544		Birth of Tasso.		

Date	Italian History	Italian Theatre History	World History	World Theatre History
1545		Serlio's *Architettura* published.	Council of Trent begins. Start of Counter-Reformation.	
c. 1550		*Commedia dell'arte* appears.		
1553				Sach's *Tristan und Isolde*.
1558			Elizabeth I begins reign.	Births of Robert Greene, Thomas Kyd, and George Peele.
1560	Catherine de'Medici, Regent of France.			
1561		Scaliger's *Poetics*.		
1562				Birth of Lope de Vega.
1564				Birth of Shakespeare and Christopher Marlowe.
1568				First public theatre in Spain.
1569	Cosimo de'Medici, Grand Duke of Tuscany.			
1570		Castelvetro's *Poetics*.		
1571	Turks defeated at Battle of Lepanto.			
1573		Tasso's *Aminta*.		
1576				Burbage opens The Theatre in London.
1579			Dutch declare independence from Spain.	
1585		Teatro Olimpico opens.		Shakespeare arrives in London.

(Continued on page 176)

Date	Italian History	Italian Theatre History	World History	World Theatre History
1588			Destruction of the "invincible" Armada.	Marlowe's *Doctor Faustus*.
1590		Guarini's *Pastor Fido*.		
1596				Blackfriars Theatre opens.
1597		*La dafre*, first opera.		
1600	Henry IV of France marries Maria de'Medici.			Shakespeare's *Hamlet*. Birth of Calderón.
1603			Death of Elizabeth I.	
1606				Births of Corneille and William Davenant.
1607			Jamestown, Va., founded.	
1608		Monteverdi's *Orfeo*.		Fletcher's *Faithful Shepherdess*.
1610	Maria de'Medici, Regent of France.		Henry IV assassinated.	Jonson's *Alchemist*.
1614				Webster's *Duchess of Malfi*.
1616	War between Venice and Austria.			
1622			Richelieu begins his rule of Louis XIII's France.	
1625			Reign of Charles I of England begins.	
1634				First performance of the Oberammergau Passion Play.
1635				Calderón's *La vida es sueño*.
1637		San Cassiano opens in Venice.		

Date	Italian History	Italian Theatre History	World History	World Theatre History
1638		Sabbatini's *Practica* published.		
1642			Start of the English Civil War.	English theatres closed by order of Parliament.
1643				Molière founds Illustre Théâtre in Paris.
1649			Charles I is beheaded.	

SELECTED READINGS

Berenson, Bernhard. *Italian Painters of the Renaissance*. London: Phaidon Press, 1957.
A general study of Italian Renaissance art for those who need a good, detailed introduction.

Bush, Douglas. *The Renaissance and English Humanism*. Toronto: University of Toronto Press, 1939.
The first two lectures in this book, "Modern Theories of the Renaissance" and "Continental Humanism," are most useful for an understanding of the period.

Ducharte, Pierre Louis. *The Italian Comedy* R. T. Weaver, trans. New York: Dover Publications, 1966.
A classic study of the *commedia dell'arte*.

Hay, Denys. *The Italian Renaissance in Its Historical Background*. Cambridge: Cambridge University Press, 1961.
A highly useful collection of essays on aspects of the Renaissance.

Herrick, Marvin T. *Comic Theory in the Sixteenth Century*. Urbana: University of Illinois Press, 1950.
The late Professor Herrick was one of the foremost specialists on the drama of the Italian Renaissance. This work and the others by him listed below are indispensable to a study of Renaissance theatre.

_____. *Italian Comedy in the Renaissance*. Urbana: University of Illinois Press, 1960.

_____. *Italian Tragedy in the Renaissance*. Urbana: University of Illinois Press, 1965.

_____. *Tragicomedy*. Urbana: University of Illinois Press, 1962.

Hewitt, Barnard, ed. *The Renaissance Stage*. Coral Gables: University of Miami Press, 1958.
This work contains English translations of important documents written by Serlio, Sabbattini, and Furttenbach along with illustrations from their works.

Nicoll, Allardyce. *Masks, Mimes, and Miracles: Studies in the Popular Theatre*. New York: Cooper Square, 1963.
The third section of this book deals with the *commedia dell'arte* and contains a great deal of information on the characters and famous companies. The appendix is a list of the names of the characters and the principal actors.

_____. *The World of Harlequin: A Critical Study of the Commedia dell'Arte*. Cambridge: Cambridge University Press, 1963.
A study of the creative force of the *commedia* during its existence. Contains good coverage on the major masks and their performers with many illustrations.

Potter, G. R., ed. *The Cambridge Modern History*. Vol. 1: *The Renaissance, 1493–1520*. Cambridge: Cambridge University Press, 1957.
The best one-volume treatment of European history for the Renaissance period.

Radcliff-Umstead, Douglas. *The Birth of Modern Comedy in Renaissance Italy*. Chicago: University of Chicago Press, 1969.

This work provides a fine background and examination of Renaissance comedy. It should be read along with Herrick.

Scala, Flaminio. *Scenarios of the Commedia dell'Arte: Flamino Scala's "Il Teatro delle favole rappresentative."* Henry F. Salerno, trans. New York: New York University Press, 1967.

This translation of *commedia* scenarios is useful in any attempt to understand the art of the actors of the *commedia*.

Sypher, Wylie. *Four Stages of Renaissance Style*. Garden City, N.Y.: Anchor Books, 1955.

A thought-provoking examination of literature and art from the Renaissance through the Baroque period.

Weinberg, Bernard. *A History of Literary Criticism in the Italian Renaissance*. 2 vols. Chicago: University of Chicago Press, 1961.

An exhaustive study of the subject.

LONDON

PART VI

Diverse Reflections:
ENGLAND DURING THE REIGN OF THE TUDORS AND STUARTS

From 1485 to 1700 English society moved from the medieval to the modern world. In 1485 Henry VII, an absolute monarch, began the task of building a centralized government and creating a national identity. In 1700 William III, a constitutional monarch, presided over a unified nation well on its way to establishing the greatest commercial and military empire the world has yet known. These 215 years encompassed political and religious turmoil of an unprecedented scale, voyages of discovery into the unknown, both geographical and scientific, increasing individual liberties and responsibilities, and the greatest and worst periods of the English theatre.

Throughout most of this period the English theatre maintained a close connection with the English crown, serving as a mirror for magistrates if they would but look. "All representations," noted Ben Jonson, "especially those of this nature, public spectacles, either have been or ought to be mirrors of man's life." During the reign of the Tudors, the royal theatrical mirror also reflected the aspirations of the English people, their dreams of new worlds, and their fears of old problems. With the Stuarts, the stage began to reflect a more narrow view and closely followed courtly fashion. The total self-regard of the early Stuart kings resulted in civil war, regicide, and the closing of the theatres. The early Restoration theatre was a creature of the court, which was itself highly theatrical, and during this period it is difficult to discover which had more reality, the court or the stage. As the seventeenth century drew to a close, the English theatre had lost its link with the court, was under attack by religious reformers, and was without an audience. The age of Shakespeare and Jonson seemed but a dim memory.

10
ELIZABETHAN AND STUART DRAMA

The reign of Henry VII (1485–1509) brought a return of stability to England after years of intermittent warfare over the kingdom. The beginning of the Tudor dynasty also introduced a new direction in English theatre away from the religious elements of the medieval stage. The Tudor interlude represented a definite break from the medieval theatre, for these theatrical pieces moved from religious abstraction to secular topicality, from unknown to known playwrights. The origin of the term "interlude" is unclear, for it had been applied in earlier periods to various dramatic forms. To theatre historians it means a short play of the Tudor period that was performed indoors by a small cast. Of the numerous writers of interludes, three have been selected to represent the scope and ultimate direction of this dramatic form.

PLAYWRIGHTS OF THE TUDOR INTERLUDE

Henry Medwell

Henry Medwell (c. 1462–c. 1502), chaplain to John Cardinal Morton, Archbishop of Canterbury and Lord Chancellor of England, was the author of the earliest-known purely secular play written in English. This early interlude, entitled *Fulgens and Lucrece*, was only discovered in 1919. It was first performed at Lambeth Palace on Christmas 1497 as an entertainment for ambassadors from Flanders and Spain. This interlude, although in the tradition of the medieval debate, is much concerned with a contemporary English issue, the question of birthright versus ability.

Lucrece, a Roman heiress, is wooed by two suitors: Publius, an aristocrat given to excesses of idleness, and Gaius, lowborn but now prominent because of his administrative abilities. The heiress selects the commoner over the noble as her husband. In the court of Henry VII there existed a group of commoners who had risen to importance because of their learning and administrative abilities. These talented English humanists were regarded with suspicion and contempt by members of the established noble families of England. *Fulgens and Lucrece* places this competition between the old order and the new in a theatrical form.

Medwell, as well as his master the Lord Chancellor, was among the new men of the court, so it is not surprising that the bulk of the satire in the play is directed against the nobles. The edge of this satire against the old noble families, members of whom were surely present when the play was first presented, is blunted by the introduction of a low-comedy substory involving two servants. These two characters come out of the audience, discuss the play to be presented, and then shove their way into the story as servants for Publius and Gaius. This use of the servants both defuses any possible offense to the nobles and introduces a new dramatic device, a substory that parodies a main story.

John Heywood

A member of the household of Sir Thomas More, John Heywood (c. 1497–c. 1580), the attributed author of at least seven plays, is considered the finest writer of Tudor interludes. These plays—*Witty and Witless*; *Gentleness and Nobility*; *John-John, Tib, and Sir John*; *Love*; *The Pardoner and the Friar*; *The Four P's*; and *Weather*—all share similar characteristics. The plays contain lively action, and they show the most natural use of entrances, exits, and stage business yet seen in English theatre. The dialogue is witty, sometimes obscene, with frequent use of double entrendres and tongue-twisting word play.

The Four P's is the best example of Heywood's efforts as a playwright. In this debate between a palmer, pardoner, apothecary, and pedlar, the approach might appear to be merely farcical, yet the issues are current to the English people of the early 1520s. The Reformation was under way in Europe, and many in England were calling for radical reforms in the Church. Heywood satirizes the religious charlatans of his play, but he also pleads that the Church be allowed to reform itself from within and that discord, both civil and religious, be avoided.

The Four P's reflects Heywood's faith in the ability of young Henry VIII to guide his ship of state skillfully in the rising seas of religious turmoil. Such optimism was misplaced in Henry. As the king began his long battle with the pope and the Church of Rome, the interlude was pressed into service as a propaganda vehicle in the growing religious controversy in England.

John Bale

Henry VIII broke with Rome in 1532 and declared himself Supreme Head of the Church in England. Henry's lord chancellor during this period was Thomas Cromwell, a zealous reformer for Protestantism. Under the sometimes protection of Cromwell, John Bale (1495–1563) wrote a number of strongly propagandistic interludes supporting the Protestant reformers. During the years 1538 and 1539 Bale organized a company of players and, under government sponsorship, took his plays on the road.

Of the approximately twenty-one plays written by Bale, five are extant: *God's Promises, John the Baptist, The Temptation of our Lord, Three Laws*, and

King John. All are alike in their support of king, country, and Protestantism. Since they were commissioned by either Cromwell or his assistants, they reflect government policies in relation to such things as monasteries, church liturgy, unmarried priests, and doctrinal issues. Interestingly, Bale even condemned "popish plays" in *King John*, evidently because they are propaganda. In 1540 government policies were reversed, Cromwell was executed, Henry VIII withdrew his support from propaganda plays, and Bale fled from England.

The excesses of the propaganda interludes greatly assisted in the destruction of the interlude as a dramatic form in Tudor England. It had been created as a courtly entertainment for an aristocratic audience. With the steady increase of political and religious elements in its contents, humor, and gaiety disappeared from the interlude. Yet in its debased form, as a vehicle for polemics, the interlude continued to be popular until the end of the reign of Queen Elizabeth I.

ELIZABETHAN COMIC PLAYWRIGHTS

Nicholas Udall

The plays of Plautus and Terence were an important part of medieval and Renaissance education as models for conversational Latin. The performance of the plays of these Latin playwrights for educational purposes also resulted in their influencing the development of early English comedy. This educational process resulted in the production of *Ralph Roister Doister* (c. 1553), the "first regular English comedy." This play was the creation of Nicholas Udall (c. 1505–1556), headmaster of Eton and master of the King's Grammar School, Westminster Abbey.

Although *Ralph Roister Doister* is modeled on Terence, has a five-act structure, and closely observes the unities of time and place, it is totally English in spirit. The play is a depiction of middle-class life in London. Ralph Roister Doister and Merrygreek, his parasite, are English transformations of the Roman braggart soldier and parasite, but the principal character of the play, Dame Christian Custance, is solely English. The play is essentially a battle of the sexes, and Dame Christian was, no doubt, intended as a dramatic complement to Queen Mary. While Roister Doister and his household depict comic confusion and disorder, Dame Christian and her household are orderly, sane, and forebearing. The play ends on a note of reconciliation, something sorely needed during the troubled years of Queen Mary's reign.

William Stevenson

Gammer Gurton's Needle (c. 1553), which vies with *Roister Doister* for the title of "first regular English comedy," is believed to be the work of William Stevenson (c. 1521–1575). This five-act play about the loss of a needle was written for a university audience, and it attempts to depict rural life in sixteenth-century England, at least as seen from the university. Although this farce is as classical in structure as *Roister Doister*, its characters and situations show no traces of Roman comedy. The tone of the play is condescending, a playful view of colorful rustics for the amusement of an educated audience. Yet even in his condescension, the playwright created several amusing characters and a script that can still provide entertainment to a modern audience.

John Lyly

In 1576, the year James Burbage opened the first public theatre in London, there came down from Oxford an elegant young man determined to win his way to fortune with his pen. John Lyly (1554–1606) first captured the attention of fashionable London with his prose works, *Euphues* and *Euphues and His England*. The highly mannered, rhetorical style of these narratives, called euphuism, gave free rein to the Elizabethan love of verbal play. Lyly incorporated into his plays his euphuistic style, which is characterized by duplication of sound patterns, elaborate comparisons, rhetorical questions, and carefully balanced structure.

Scorning the public theatre, Lyly tailored his plays for a royal audience and the talents of "Her Majesty's children," the boy actors of the Chapel and Saint Paul's. His seven plays—*Campaspe* (1584), *Sapho and Phao* (1584), *Gallathea* (1588), *Endimion* (1588), *Midas* (1589), *Mother Bombie* (1590), and *The Woman in the Moon* (1590)—are all romantic comedies, filled with fantasy, gentleness, and stately language. The popularity of these plays is reflective of the transitional stage of Elizabethan society. Cut off from the chivalric traditions of the reign of Henry VII by the violent final years of Henry VIII, the men who surrounded Elizabeth and kept her on her throne were rough survivors, great men not long removed from farm and hamlet. In the plays of Lyly they discovered that English could be as elegant and artificial as the languages of the courts of Italy, France, and Spain.

With the plays of Lyly a new dramatic type appears in England, the courtly play written especially to flatter. Perhaps from a desire to strengthen her position indirectly, Queen Elizabeth encouraged this type of dramatic production as a means to gain royal favor. Thus a courtier would commission a play to present his plea and manage to have it staged at court or while Elizabeth was on one of her numerous "progresses" to various noble houses. At this form of royal flattery Lyly was a master, not only for his patron, the Earl of Oxford, but also for himself since he greatly desired the position of Queen's Master of Revels. His most elaborate compliment play was *Endimion*, performed before the queen on February 2, 1588. The play is also the last major example of this dramatic genre. When the court and country turned to preparing for the great battle with Spain, the devotional drama to Elizabeth went into decline. With that decline went Lyly, a victim of changing tastes in theatre and the appearance of far greater playwrights.

The University Wits

At the end of the 1570s a group of young men, sometimes referred to collectively as the University Wits, arrived in London from Oxford and Cambridge and attempted to support themselves as professional writers. These young scholars, Thomas Nashe, Robert Greene, Thomas Lodge, and George Peele, found the public theatres in constant need of new plays, a need their empty purses and stomachs compelled them to try to fill. Most of their efforts were little better than hack work, but occasionally their plays were noteworthy for poetry or experimentation not far removed from the later masterpieces of Marlowe, Shakespeare, and Jonson. The brief careers of two of these University Wits provide examples of the precarious life of the Elizabethan playwright.

George Peele From 1581 until his death, George Peele (1556–1596) earned his livelihood as a writer of plays, pageants, and poetry. His first play, *The Arraignment of Paris*, was presented before the queen by the Children of the Chapel in the early 1580s. Based on the classical story of the selection by Paris, the Trojan prince, of the most beautiful of the Greek goddesses, the play is experimental in style and is the first known English effort to fit poetic meter to character and subject. The play was apparently not a success with Queen Elizabeth. At fifty the queen may have found the elaborate personal compliment at the end of the play too much even for her well-known vanity.

Peele's second theatrical venture, *The Battle of Alcazar* (c. 1593), was built around a popular contemporary figure, Thomas Stukeley, who died heroically in Morocco fighting for the King of Portugal. The play incorporates the public's strong anti-Spanish feelings with the revenge motif from Thomas Kyd's popular *The Spanish Tragedy*. Ridiculed by later Elizabethan playwrights, the play is far from good theatre, but it does reveal the nationalistic fervor current in London in the post-Armada years.

Of the five extant plays definitely known to be by George Peele, *The Old Wives Tale* (c. 1593) is clearly the most remarkable. This fairy-tale adventure, which may be an indirect satire on the popular romantic comedies of the period, has a dreamlike structure that might be claimed as a forerunner of modern expressionism.

Peele's last two plays also reveal his continued experimentation with existing theatrical forms. *David and Bethsabe* (c. 1594) is the most developed of his plays, showing advancements in story unification and containing some of his best poetry. *Edward I* (c. 1596) was Peele's most popular play with Elizabethan audiences, being presented at least fourteen times in the public theatres. In this play he made one of the first uses on the Elizabethan stage of telescoping time, a technique later put to excellent use by William Shakespeare.

Peele is to be remembered not as an excellent dramatist, for he was not, but for his experimentations in play writing and his imagination. Of the pre-Shakespearean playwrights, he was the most lyrical in his poetry and the most versatile in working with the existing forms of popular theatre.

Robert Greene The most colorful, and perhaps most disreputable, of the University Wits was Robert Greene (1558–1592), who by 1586 was well known in London as a writer of prose romances. Drawn to the possible financial rewards of writing for the stage by his ever-pressing debts, Greene began to cast his romances into dramatic form in the late 1580s. His six plays—*Alphonsus* (1587), *Friar Bacon and Friar Bungay* (1589), *A Looking Glass* (1590), *Orlando Furioso* (1591), *James IV* (1591), and *George A Greene* (1592)—were all written with haste and carelessness, but the comedy *Friar Bacon and Friar Bungay* is among the best of the period.

Friar Bacon and Friar Bungay is a fantastic mixture of magic, romance, and patriotism that amply illustrates Greene's skill in juggling stories for maximum complexity and enjoyment. Of central interest are the magical powers of Friar Bacon and the love of Margaret, a commoner, for Lacy, Earl of Lincoln. Included are a duel of magic between Bacon and a German magician, visits of the Emperor of Germany and the King of Castile, and a royal wedding. In this theatrical potpourri, Margaret and Bacon manifest the virtues and experience the successes that were the dreams of the working-class Londoner. For such magic they made their way to the public theatres at Bankside.

ELIZABETHAN TRAGIC PLAYWRIGHTS

As with comedy, the major influence in the development of English tragedy was Roman, in particular the plays of Seneca. The first performance of a Senecan play in England was in 1551, and the first English translations of his plays began to appear in 1559. During the next ten years the shade of the Roman statesman-philosopher haunted the dramatic efforts of budding English playwrights. The first regular English tragedy, *Gorboduc; or the Tragedy of Ferrex and Porrex* (1561) managed to combine Seneca with English elements.

Thomas Norton and Thomas Sackville

Gorboduc, the work of two lawyers, Thomas Norton (1532–1584) and Thomas Sackville (1536–1608), was presented before Queen Elizabeth at Whitehall on January 18, 1562. This sensationalistic story is about a legendary English king, Gorboduc, who divides his kingdom between his two sons with tragic results. This first English tragedy had strong contemporary overtones, which is not surprising considering that its authors were both lawyers and members of Parliament.

Norton is believed to have written the first three acts and Sackville the final two. Both wrote in blank verse, its first use in English dramatic literature. Both shared a common fear, indirectly expressed in the play, that Elizabeth would fail to name a successor during her lifetime and the nation would face possible anarchy at her death. Not only did the play comment on the problem of the royal succession, but it also touched on the question of royal authority and parliamentary power. The play ends with two very long speeches strongly praising a parliamentary government. Although the play may seem dull to the modern reader because of the long political speeches (it was, after all, written by lawyers for lawyers), it got English tragedy off to a good start. Unfortunately it was a premature start. It would be another twenty years before tragedy was firmly established on the Elizabethan stage.

Thomas Kyd

The Spanish Tragedy (c. 1585) was the most popular play of the Elizabethan era, holding the stage well into the early 1600s and being published in a least ten editions. No author is listed for the play in any of the printed versions, so were it not for a brief mention of the author and the play by Thomas Heywood in his *The Apology for Actors* (1612), Thomas Kyd's claim to fame would have been lost.

Kyd (1558–1594) was a native Londoner, son of a scrivener and graduate of the Merchant Taylor's School, who began writing for the public theatres in the early 1580s. *The Spanish Tragedy* is the only play that can be assigned to him with certainty, although he is generally credited with writing *Soliman and Perseda*, a translation of Garnier's *Cornelie*, and an early version of *Hamlet* (now lost), which may have been used by Shakespeare. *The Spanish Tragedy* merits attention, not only because of its vast popularity, but for its successful adaptation of the Senecan tragedy to English tastes.

The play, written in passable blank verse, concerns the revenge of Hieron-imo, the Knight-Marshal of Spain, for the murder of his son, and includes eight onstage murders or suicides, a public hanging, the biting off of a man's tongue, and a general slaughter for the conclusion. All this in a story so complex that at two points there is a play-within-a-play-within-a-play being watched by the audience at the play. The Elizabethans loved it.

Kyd was only a fair poet, but his true dramatic gifts were in story management and character analysis. From Seneca he borrowed ghosts, the revenge theme, and the use of declamation and soliloquy. To this he added a contemporary setting and events, a highly involved story, numerous strange characters, and a large amount of stage business. Kyd, who managed to get himself involved in the nefarious, nontheatrical affairs of Christopher Marlowe, died in poverty and neglect, but his play continued to thrill theatre audiences for many years after his death.

Christopher Marlowe

By the mid-1580s the Elizabethan theatre was estab-lishing itself as both high entertainment and sophisticated art form. With the work of Lyly, Kyd, and the University Wits, significant advances had been made in versification, structure, and language. What was lacking was a joining of these advances with a rare poetic talent and wide-ranging imagination. With the appearance of Christopher Marlowe (1564–1593), the golden age of the English theatre was announced with a brilliant flash. Before being murdered in his twenty-ninth year, he created some of the greatest characters and wrote some of the finest lines in English dramatic literature.

Christopher Marlowe's Doctor Faustus *as presented by the Royal Shakespeare Company.* (*Courtesy of KaiDib Films International, Glendale, Calif.*)

The son of a Canterbury shoemaker, Marlowe was born a few months before Shakespeare, yet he is considered Shakespeare's predecessor rather than his contemporary since his career came to a violent end just as Shakespeare's was beginning. A scholarship student at Cambridge, Marlowe received both B.A. and M.A. degrees from the university. Between degrees he apparently served the government in some secret capacity, perhaps as a spy, and he continued to have a shadowy connection with the government. Shortly before his death, he was staying with Sir Thomas Walsingham, Queen Elizabeth's spymaster. On May 30, 1593, while in the company of a well-known spy, Marlowe was stabbed to death, perhaps assassinated, in a tavern fight.

Marlowe's first play, *Dido, Queen of Carthage* (c. 1586), was performed by the Children of the Chapel. His second play, *Tamburlaine, Part One*, was probably written before he left Cambridge in 1587. This play came into the hands of Edward Alleyn, the leading actor of the Lord Admiral's Men. The role of Tamburlaine and Alleyn were a perfect match, a second play was requested, and Marlowe began to produce powerful, poetic scripts featuring a superhuman character. In rapid succession came *Tamburlaine the Great, Part Two*, *The Jew of Malta*, and *Doctor Faustus*, all with overreaching protagonists: Tamburlaine after world conquest, Barabas the Jew after power and wealth, and Faustus after knowledge. His other plays, also written in the period between 1587 and 1593, are *The Massacre at Paris* and *Edward II*.

Marlowe brought near-perfect dramatic blank verse, a strong sense of romanticism, and a sure feel for dramatic value to the English stage. In the short period of six years, he took the London stage to maturity. He taught the English theatre more about theatricality than any other playwright except Shakespeare.

WILLIAM SHAKESPEARE

The dramatic works of William Shakespeare (1564–1616) are the towering achievement of the Elizabethan period. He has been acknowledged by many as the greatest playwright in the history of theatre, and there are few who would deny the claim. With the exception of the King James Bible, no writings in English have been as influential or as much quoted as those of Shakespeare. Again excepting the Bible, no body of literature has been as closely studied as the plays of Shakespeare. The complexity of the plays and the vastness of the available scholarship makes a brief discussion of this playwright nearly impossible. The following comments provide only an overview of Shakespeare's career and his place in the English theatre.

William Shakespeare was born in Stratford-on-Avon, Warwickshire, a rural area closely associated with events in the War of the Roses and peopled by the

William Shakespeare.

rustics, tradesmen, and gentry who would later fill his plays with life. Educated at the excellent Stratford Grammar School, he may have continued his education with a brief stay at Oxford. Married in 1582, Shakespeare remained in the Stratford area until near the end of the decade. When he arrived in London, how and why he entered the theatre are unknown, but by 1592 Shakespeare was known as an actor and playwright with friends in high places at court. By 1595 he was a shareholder in the Lord Chamberlain's Men, and four years later one of the seven partners involved in the construction of the Globe. His apparently ample earnings from his theatrical ventures allowed him to make numerous investments in property in both Stratford and London. In 1610 he retired to Stratford, but he did not entirely sever his connections with the London theatre. Before his death at age fifty-two, he collaborated on two or more plays for his old company.

In the period from approximately 1590 to 1613, Shakespeare contributed at least thirty-six plays to the theatre. Sixteen plays were published during his lifetime, the editions after 1598 stressing his name on the title page in such a manner as to suggest that it helped sales. In 1623, seven years after his death, two of Shakespeare's friends and fellow actors, John Heminge and Henry Condell, were responsible for the publication of the first collection of his plays, the famous First Folio edition. This large volume is the only source for eighteen of Shakespeare's plays and is perhaps the most important single volume ever published in English.

The assassination scene in a 1968 production of Julius Caesar *by the Royal Shakespeare Company.*

(Courtesy by KaiDib Fims International, Glendale, Calif.)

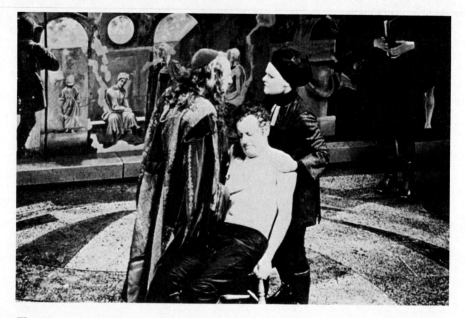

The Merchant of Venice, *Royal Shakespeare Company.*
(Courtesy of KaiDib Films International, Glendale, Calif.)

Shakespeare's early plays show him as both learning his craft and writing to please the London audiences. Thus there is a good deal of imitation in the early works. *Titus Andronicus* is a bloody revenge play in the fashion of *The Spanish Tragedy*, although he followed the Senecan style more closely than Kyd. *The Comedy of Errors* is Plautus doubled, and *Love's Labor's Lost* is clearly influenced by Lyly. These and other early scripts illustrate Shakespeare's desire to learn, to adapt, to fashion plays like those in vogue. The most numerous of his early plays are the histories, for the simple reason that history plays were very popular in the 1590s. In these plays he shows the strong influence of Christopher Marlowe on his writing.

By the late 1590s Shakespeare had achieved some fame as a playwright, and some scholars note this period of his career as showing signs of this fame in his high rate of productivity and lessened creativity. Yet to this period belong the great "happy" comedies (*Much Ado about Nothing, As You Like It, Twelfth Night*), *Julius Caesar, Henry V*, and *Hamlet. Hamlet*, in the minds of many *the* play of the English theatre, is perhaps the purest example of a play as cultural artifact. An artistic touchstone, such as the Mona Lisa or Beethoven's Fifth Symphony, *Hamlet* is familiar even to those who have never read or seen it. The play itself marks the beginning of Shakespeare's mature period as a playwright and was reflective of the uncertainty in English society near the time of the death of Queen Elizabeth.

With the accession of James I to the throne in 1603, the good fortune of Shakespeare and his company improved as they were taken under the

Sir Alec Guinness as Macbeth in a Royal Court Theatre production.
(Courtesy of KaiDib Films International, Glendale, Calif.)

protection of the sovereign and called the King's Men. In this period of his career, when he was a favorite of both the court and the public, Shakespeare wrote his most troubled plays, the so-called dark comedies and his great studies in evil, *Othello, King Lear*, and *Macbeth*. The complex analyses of human motivation that mark these plays comes to an end with *Timon of Athens*, perhaps because the playwright suffered a physical breakdown at this time. The final plays, *Cymbeline, The Winter's Tale*, and *The Tempest*, are· technically dazzling, a grandmaster's farewell performance, but they lack the dramatic power or poetry of an *Othello*. With them came to an end the most awesome creative career in dramatic literature.

STUART PLAYWRIGHTS

The period from 1603 to 1649 was a troubled one for England, a period that ended with the execution of a king. During this era, ushered in with the crowning of James I and ending with the beheading of Charles I, the fortunes of the English theatre were closely linked to those of the royal family. James I became the patron of Shakespeare's company, and by 1613 all of the officially recognized acting companies in London were attached to the royal family. This association was one of the principal reasons why there was a significant change in the plays of the Stuart period and why the Puritan opposition to the theatre grew to such a high level of hostility. During the reign of the Stuarts, the broad, common base of the Elizabethan theatre disappeared as it became a pastime of gentry. This shift in emphasis was to prove the undoing of the English theatre.

Thomas Heywood

With his career of over forty years and his "hand or at least a main finger" in over two hundred and twenty plays, Thomas Heywood (c. 1570–1641) successfully made the transition from the Elizabethan to the Stuart theatre, and his surviving plays reflect the shifts in theatrical tastes.

Heywood spent most of his professional life as the principal playwright for the Earl of Worcester's Men, later known as the Queen's Men. This company was the least distinguished of those in London and drew upon the laboring classes for its audiences. The newly risen Protestant work ethic is pronounced in most of the extant plays of Heywood, reflecting the attitudes of his audiences. *The Four Prentices of London* (1592), one of the earliest of his extant plays, is a story of four sons of the Earl of Boulogne who are apprenticed to different trades. This romantic mixture of adventure, history, and London commercial life is ridiculed in Francis Beaumont's *The Knight of the Burning Pestle* (1607), but Heywood's play was popular with Londoners and Beaumont's was not. Heywood was sensitive to the attitudes of the working classes, Beaumont to those of the court. This sensitivity kept Heywood in his profession longer than most of his contemporaries.

Heywood's plays may be classed as classical, historical, and romantic, and all three categories are infused with strong elements of local color, domestic life, and humanity. His classical plays (*The Golden Age, The Silver Age, The Brazen Age, The Iron Age*) are stories from classical mythology and were an attempt to expose the London middle class to Greek culture, "to unlock the casket long time shut, of which none but the learned keep the key." Heywood also wrote three plays with Roman settings, including one adaptation of a play by Plautus. The history plays overlap some of the same areas as Shakespeare's history plays and even include some of the same characters. Heywood's two plays about Queen Elizabeth are sentimental tributes to the late queen and her more humble subjects. His history plays differ from Shakespeare's in that he portrays the life of the common citizen, whereas Shakespeare concentrates on the tragedy of the great. The romances touch on recent history, particularly the adventures of England's merchant class, and in plays such as *Fair Maid of the West* (1630), *Fortune by Land and Sea* (1607), and *The Four Prentices*, much is said and shown of the superiority of English men and women. To Heywood's audience it was a delightful affirmation of an obvious truth.

Ben Jonson

Counting among his patrons some of the wealthiest nobles of the land, Ben Jonson (1572–1637) was for a period the court poet and most famous writer in England. Bricklayer, soldier, actor, and scholar, the complicated and choleric Jonson had a career that encompassed both a near-hanging for killing a fellow actor and a near-knighthood for pleasing King James I.

Jonson began his association with the theatre around 1594 as a strolling actor, and his first efforts at play writing, *The Isle of Dogs*, landed him in jail because of its biting satire. His first successful play was *Every Man in His Humour* (1598), performed by the Lord Chamberlain's Men with Shakespeare in the cast. The action of the play, although set in Italy, is a satire on the insincerities of contemporary London society. This success was followed with a sequel, *Every Man Out of His Humour* (1599), another satire in which a number of eccentric characters are knocked out of their particular "humour" or affectation.

These plays were followed by *Cynthia Revels* (1600), performed by the Chapel Boys. It was the closing comments in this play that involved Jonson in the so-called War of the Theatres, which was really a verbal battle among London's dramatists. In several plays the practicing playwrights of London ridicule each other, their styles, and even their audiences. Jonson's contribution to this "warfare" was *Poetaster* (1601). From Thomas Dekker's *Satiromastix, or the Untrussing of the Humorous Poet* (1601), another of the "war" plays, a great deal can be learned about how Jonson was viewed by his peers.

Jonson's two Roman plays, *Sejanus* (1603) and *Catiline* (1611), were presented by the King's Men at the Globe, but they were not well received. Unlike Shakespeare with *Julius Caesar* and *Anthony and Cleopatra*, Jonson selected historical characters and events unknown to the average Londoner and failed to concentrate his focus. The resulting plays are dull and untheatrical.

Volpone (1606), *The Silent Woman* (1609), and *The Alchemist* (1610) are considered Jonson's masterpieces for the theatre, and rightfully so. *Volpone, or the Fox* is that rare thing in dramatic literature, a comedy that continually skirts the borders of tragedy but never crosses over. Jonson's control of his material is excellent, particularly in regard to the substory of the Would-Bes, which gave his audience a desired dual story line and allowed the playwright to counterpoint the doings of Volpone and his parasite, Mosca. Jonson considered *Volpone* one of his best literary efforts and an excellent example of the high moral purpose of theatre. Modern audiences find it a fascinating study in debased cunning.

Epicoene, or The Silent Woman is one of Jonson's lightest plays, nearly a farce, and very unlike the darkly comic *Volpone*. Concerned with the marriage of a wealthy curmudgeon who has an acute dislike of noise, the play's surprise ending was said to have left the first audience silent. Unfortunately, the play caused displeasure at the court. Lady Arabella Stuart, cousin to King James, saw something of herself in the cast of characters and caused the play to be suppressed.

After his misfortune with *The Silent Woman*, Jonson returned to his successful greed theme for his next play, *The Alchemist*. Set in contemporary London, the play uses the plague outbreak of 1610 to provide the atmosphere and opportunity for a trio of likable rogues. Neither as harsh as *Volpone* nor as

A production of Jonson's Volpone *at Carnegie-Mellon University.*
(Courtesy of KaiDib Films International, Glendale, Calif.)

moralistic, *The Alchemist* sparkles as a gem of design and characterization. Of Jonson's plays, it is the one most often presented to modern audiences.

The last twenty years of Jonson's career include several noteworthy plays, *Bartholomew Fair* (1614), *The Devil Is an Ass* (1616), and *The Staple of News* (1626), but nothing of the same artistry as the three masterpieces. Ill health and a falling out of favor at court clouded Jonson's last years, yet he retained his preeminent position among English writers. He died in 1637 and was buried with much honor in Westminster Abbey. He is the foremost satiric playwright of the English stage and second only to Shakespeare among the playwrights of his period. He well deserves the epitaph on his grave: "O rare Ben Jonson."

Beaumont and Fletcher

The career of Francis Beaumont (c. 1584–1616) was surely one of the most tranquil of the Stuart period. A minor aristocrat educated at Oxford and the law courts, Beaumont was one of the "Sons of Ben," friends and admirers of Ben Jonson, and he wrote his first play, *The Woman-Hater*, in 1607. This comedy is a somewhat sentimental tale, yet in the style of Jonson, about generally pleasant people.

Beaumont is the first of a new type of dramatist of the Stuart era, playwrights from aristocratic or well-to-do families who identify with the court and not the commons. Beaumont's second play, *The Knight of the Burning Pestle* (1607), reflects a cavalier disdain for the middle-class citizens of London. Although not

José Ferrer in a 1948 New York production of Jonson's The Alchemist.

(Photograph by Fred Fehl, Hoblitzelle Theatre Arts Library, Humanities Research Center, University of Texas at Austin.)

a success at the time, the play is one of the greatest English burlesques, poking gentle fun at the tastes and social attitudes of its intended audience.

Sometime before 1610, Beaumont began collaborating with John Fletcher (1579–1625) in what was to be one of the most famous partnerships in the English theatre. In all, the Beaumont and Fletcher efforts were to produce over fifty plays before Beaumont married an heiress in 1613 and retired from the theatre. The bulk of the collaborative work was contributed by Fletcher who, as the son of a bishop and another Son of Ben, was also of the new group of playwrights.

The Maid's Tragedy (1608), *Philaster* (1609), and *A King and No King* (1611) are generally considered the best examples of the plays attributed to Beaumont and Fletcher. These are free-flowing plays, set in distant lands, where young, romantic nobles are called upon to set things right. They are not unlike some of the late plays of Shakespeare. Following the marriage and departure of Beaumont, Fletcher found a new partner in William Shakespeare. Together they produced *King Henry VIII, Two Noble Kinsman*, and possibly *Cardenio*.

In 1613 Fletcher was selected to succeed Shakespeare as the company playwright at the Globe. He continued to write for the King's Men, often at the rate of three or four plays a year, until his death from the plague in 1625. Most of the plays written during these twelve years are standard theatrical wares of the period, but *Rule a Wife and Have a Wife* (1624), *The Wild-Goose Chase* (1621), and *The Island Princess* (1621) should be noted as slightly better than the rest. During this period of high productivity, Fletcher collaborated with several other playwrights. Collaboration was a very common and successful business arrangement during the Stuart era, a necessary one to fill the ever-changing repertories of the professional acting companies. Among those who worked most with Fletcher during this period was Philip Massinger, one of the finest technicians of the English drama.

Philip Massinger

The position of company playwright passed to Philip Massinger (1583–1640) upon the death of Fletcher in 1625. By this time Massinger, through his collaborations with Fletcher and his work for other companies, had established himself as a reliable and accomplished playwright. The author of approximately forty plays, he is now chiefly remembered for only two, *The City Madam* (1630) and *A New Way to Pay Old Debts* (1622). Yet his other plays deserve some attention before a discussion of these two major dramas.

An interest in religious issues, rare on the Stuart stage, is noted in several of Massinger's plays. In the popular *The Virgin-Martyr* (c. 1620), which he wrote with Thomas Dekker, the subject is the persecution of the Christians during the reign of the Roman emperor Diocletian. *The Renegado* (1624) features a Jesuit priest as the central manipulator for good, a surprising element since the Jesuit Order was highly in disfavor in Protestant England. Religious elements also figure prominently in *The Maid of Honour* (c. 1627), in which the heroine ends the play by becoming a nun.

Massinger also touched on sensitive political issues in his plays, often to the displeasure of those in authority. Charles I demanded changes in speeches given to the King of Spain in *The King and the Subject* (1638), and *The Bondsman* (1623) contains thinly veiled allusions to court favorites, particularly George Villiers, first Duke of Buckingham and intimate friend of James I. The duke again figures in *The Great Duke of Florence* (1627), written shortly before Buckingham's assassination in 1628.

Contemporary themes highlight Massinger's two finest plays, *A New Way to Pay Old Debts* and *The City Madam*. The central character in *A New Way*, the archvillain Sir Giles Overreach, was modeled on Sir Giles Mompesson, an extortioner and a friend of the Duke of Buckingham's. Overreach is the Stuart version of Al Capone, but his power is broken through the tricks of his own nephew, whom he had earlier cheated. The role of Overreach was a great favorite with nineteenth-century actors, particularly Edmund Kean, whose performance "was so intense that women in the audience shrieked with terror and Lord Byron was seized with a convulsive fit." It was mainly due to the character of Overreach that *A New Way to Pay Old Debts* remained an active play until the end of the last century.

The City Madam also features a supervillain in the person of Luke Frugal, who, once he believes he has become a wealthy heir, turns into such a monster that he is willing to ship his sisters-in-law off to the American colonies to be given to the Indians. In this play, Massinger's satire is turned against the greed of London merchants and their ambitious and pretentious wives. To the end of his career, Massinger remained a somewhat didactic playwright with a strong moral view in his work. With this in mind, we can see that he was the last of a line of playwrights that reached back to Marlowe.

Many of Massinger's contemporaries during the reign of Charles I worked a darker, more cynical aspect of their society, one devoid of morals or ethics. Early appearances of this element in Stuart playwrights are visible in the work of John Webster (1580–1638), whose *The White Devil* (c. 1611) and *The Duchess of Malfi* (1613) are remarkable studies in terror and unmitigated evil. John Ford (1586–c. 1655) carried on Webster's work with his pathological studies of love and honor in a debased society. Greatly influenced by Robert Burton's *Anatomy of Melancholy* (1621), a collection of essays on human dissatisfaction, Ford's major plays are studies of good but weak people destroyed by their psychoses. In *The Broken Heart* (c. 1629), *'Tis Pity She's a Whore* (c. 1628), and *Love's Sacrifice* (c. 1626), he undertakes a near-clinical investigation of erotic frustrations. It is almost as if Ford, in probing the unhealthy state of his characters, was also attempting to cast light on an English society that was growing increasingly divided and frustrated.

John Webster's The Duchess of Malfi *as performed by the Royal Shakespeare Company.*
(Courtesy of KaiDib Films International, Glendale, Calif.)

CLOSING OF THE THEATRES

The breakdown of the common audience bond that marked the Elizabethan theatre occurred gradually during the rule of the first two Stuart kings. During the reign of James I, angry apprentices tried on several occasions to destroy one or more of the public theatres. During the reign of Charles I, merchants complained of the coaches of theatregoers blocking streets, the indoor theatres became more the domain of the wealthy, courtly circle, and fewer of the better playwrights provided plays for the open-air theatres. Increasingly, the playwrights identified themselves with the monarchy as the gentleman-dramatist became a permanent fixture of the London theatre. Support for the theatre was lacking from the middle-class citizens of London by the mid-1630s. When the civil war drew the king and his court from the city in 1642, the actors and playwrights found themselves without an audience. The official closing of the theatres was almost anticlimatic.

On September 2, 1642, the House of Commons passed a motion forbidding the staging of plays "while these sad Causes and set Times of Humiliation do continue." This closing of the London theatres in 1642 is often noted as a victory for the antitheatre Puritan forces. This is an overstatement. While there was Puritan opposition to the theatres, the real reason behind the action was most likely the war. There were precedents in other brief closings during plagues and times of national crisis. The ordinances of 1647 against the staging of plays, however, were put through by the Puritans, who were now in control of Parliament. These ordinances state that plays are not for Christians. The change in tone also indicates a change in the rules. The English theatre was forced to go underground until 1660. The 1642 closing brought to an end the golden age of English theatre, a period of less than eighty years whose level of creativity has its only parallel in the fifth century B.C. in Athens.

11

EVOLUTION OF THE ENGLISH PLAYHOUSE AND THEATRICAL PRACTICE

There is a certain lack of neatness in attempting to discuss definitively the nature of the theatre of the English Renaissance. Owing to the complexity of the various aspects of theatrical activity and the tremendous interchangeability among methods and forms of theatre production, clear handles for the grasping of concepts are not readily available. The staging of one specific play by a specific company at a public theatre, for example, was totally different from the staging that same company would employ for the same play when done at court. Although cross-fertilization did occur, it is best to separate the basic components of English Renaissance staging, if only to understand the basic elements that were mixed in common practice.

PLAYHOUSE DEVELOPMENT

In their most basic forms, there were three distinct types of English Renaissance playhouses—the public theatres, the private ones, and the theatres built for court entertainments. All had their roots in the English medieval tradition. The public theatres found their basic form in the outdoor *mansion-platea* concept of the Middle Ages, where the audience and production mixed freely in a nonpolarized common space. On the other hand, the court theatres grew directly from the banquet hall tradition, employing illusionistic staging practice and separating the audience and production spaces at either ends of the hall. The private theatres, so named because of the clientele they drew rather than from any sense of formal exclusivity, seemed to be an amalgamation of the other forms. Like the court theatres, they were indoors, yet there is no suggestion that illusionistic production techniques were used until well into the seventeenth century. Rather, the free-flowing rapidity of public playhouse staging was dominant. It is a credit to the genius of the theatre practitioners of the period that productions could flow easily from one form of playhouse to another.

The Public Playhouses

Beyond these general roots of the English public playhouse at least three specific traditions contributed to its development. The first of these was the medieval inn and its common area, the innyard. The medieval inn had always been a center for local social-recreational entertainment. In the late Middle Ages, innkeepers often contracted with players for the presentation of plays to entertain their guests and thus enhance their business. The innyard was a logical place for these presentations in that it provided an excellent view from all inn rooms (which formed a U around it) and allowed controlled entrance to the yard itself. Thus a company of players could easily move its portable stage into the innyard and set it up against the wall opposite the inn entrance. The innyard became a natural *platea* for the performance of the play in addition to serving as standing and sitting room for the audience. Most inns were three-story structures, and the viewing places from the doors, windows, and balconies of the rooms on the upper floors were excellent. It is very likely that the three-story gallery structure of the English Renaissance public playhouse had a direct precursor in the inns of England.

The second specific root of the public playhouse was the portable stage. Continuing from its medieval origins, it was little more than wooden planks laid on top of supporting devices, such as barrels or sawhorses, and backed by curtained entrances. Behind the curtained entrance wall an area existed for the changing of props and costumes. When placed against the inn wall, the stage extended into the innyard to create the three-dimensional acting area the public playhouse would formalize in its structure.

Finally, the medieval pageant wagon must be counted as a precursor of the English public playhouse. To review, it was a curtained wagon on which and against which the plays were performed. One of its functions was to reveal, by a quick parting of the curtains enclosing it, a scene totally apart from the scene then being played. Thus a new scene, new characters, and a new situation were "discovered" by the audience. This "discovery" function was important to English Renaissance drama, and its utilization as a staging technique was undoubtedly incorporated into the stage facade of the public playhouse.

From these forms the public playhouses of England emerged. The first, built by James Burbage (c. 1530–1597) in 1576, was called the Theatre (not a term commonly used then to identify playhouses). Eight additional public playhouses were built around London during the reign of the Tudors and Stuarts, most of them appearing before 1605. In the order of their construction they were, in addition to the Theatre, the Curtain, Newington Butts, the Rose, the Swan, the Globe, the Fortune, the Red Bull, and the Hope. Most experienced remodeling changes during their active lives, and two, the Fortune and the Red Bull, survived the Commonwealth. Two appear to have had temporary stages so that other entertainments, such as bearbaiting, could supplement theatrical

A view of Elizabethan London with the Globe marked as number 38.

activity. Few successful plays were given at the Hope during its four-year life span, while others, like Shakespeare's Globe and Philip Henslowe and Edward Alleyn's Fortune, prospered throughout the period from their inceptions in 1599 and 1600 respectively. Largely for political and religious reasons, the playhouses were not permitted to operate within London itself. Thus they were built either in the suburbs to the north and east of the city or just south of the Thames River, in a residential and recreational area known as Bankside.

Primary evidence about the exact form of the public playhouse is virtually nonexistent. All that survives is a drawing of the Swan by a Dutchman, Johannes de Witt (actually a sketch made by a friend from the original, now lost), and two building contracts, one for the Hope and one for the Fortune. The Fortune contract refers to a lost drawing, so details are vague. Although it is clear that there was no uniform design among the public playhouses, some common elements can be cited. The shape of the structure itself was rectangular, round, or octagonal, with three-tiered roofed galleries surrounding an open yard or pit area. The galleries probably had bench-type seating set in three or four rows, with a corridor behind allowing passage among the various sections and levels of the galleries. The lower gallery of at least one playhouse was divided into private boxes, no doubt sold at a special price. Extending into

The stage of the Red Bull playhouse.

the pit area was a stage platform built four to six feet above the yard floor and protruding approximately halfway across the yard. At the Fortune, for example, it extended some twenty-seven feet into a fifty-five-foot yard. The stage was erected against one wall of the rectangular playhouses, or against one-fifth to one-quarter of the wall space in the octagonal or round ones. The Fortune figures are a good guide to overall dimensions. The playhouses were approximately eighty feet across, and fifty to sixty feet were devoted to the yard. Estimates of their capacity range from 1,500 to 3,000, with a realistic maximum of about 2,500. Construction technique was wattle-and-daub, a woven wooded network filled with a plasterlike substance, set against precut and notched timbers that provided the structural support. The look thus created was one of standard Tudor architecture, and the playhouses, although large, probably looked quite at home in the residential areas where they were built.

Against the wall from which the stage emanated, a "tiring house," or stage facade, was constructed instead of the usual galleries. The tiring house is a unique feature. Taller than the galleries, this combination of dressing rooms, storage, access to entrances and exits, and the various levels of entrances and exits themselves provided for an organic flow to the staging so necessary in successfully executing the plays. The flow of scenes in the plays, and the pace at which they were presented, did not show an interest in or allow for the detailed illusionistic scenery of the Italians. Rather, the tiring house and stage were a marvelous extension of the medieval *mansion-platea* concept in that the parts of the playing spaces became whatever the actor suggested they were. A new location was indicated either by an announcement from an actor or by a signboard.

The tiring house itself was composed of three levels, one at the level of each gallery. At the stage level, at least two doors allowed direct and quick access to the stage. The de Witt sketch shows no more than this at the Swan, but from the plays done at the Globe, the Rose, and the Fortune, it is clear from the stage directions that more places for action existed at this first level. Exactly what was there has been the subject of much conjecture and historical inquiry, but probably there was some sort of curtained area, set either in the tiring house or in the area that jutted out from the facade like a curtained wheelless pageant wagon or scaffold. Whatever the form, it was used for "discovery" scenes or

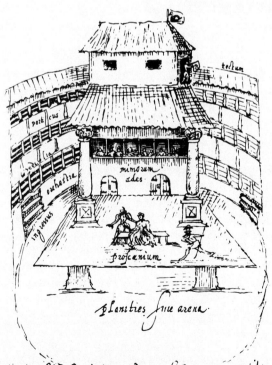

The interior of the Swan as drawn by de Witt, a Dutchman who was visiting London in 1596.

A reconstruction of the interior of the Swan Theatre based on the de Witt drawing.

(From Richard Leacroft, The Development of the English Playhouse. *Used by permission of Cornell University Press.)*

actions where a quick and fairly complete change of scene was required. Some supporters of the scaffold theory suggest that the device may have been temporary so as to accommodate large crowd scenes. Whether it was permanent or not, it is very likely that once the "discovery" was made, the actors moved forward to play the scene on the large stage proper.

At the second level there was additional acting space. The Swan drawing shows a gallery there, but the plays done at the Swan did not require a second story. At the Globe, half the plays staged there required such, and most likely this was either an acting area on the roof of the first-level extension or an additional recess into the facade at the second level. Also at the second level were windows and balconies that allowed other scenes to be played from these parts of the tiring house. From one of these second-level openings, for example, Juliet would have overheard Romeo professing his love below. At the third level was a small recess in the facade that probably accommodated the musicians necessary to provide the large quantity of background music called for in the scripts. Another use suggested for this space was for the entrance of deity-type characters, those from the spirit world, and certain very high-placed rulers.

The stage platform utilized a number of other features in addition to the tiring house. Above most of the stage area was a roof, painted to look like, and called, the "heavens." This ceiling was supported by columns that were painted to look like marble, if de Witt's description of the Swan is accurate:

A reconstructed Elizabethan playhouse at the Shakespeare Festival, Ashland, Oreg.
(Courtesy of KaiDib Films International, Glendale, Calif.)

"[the roof is] supported by wooden columns painted in such excellent imitation of marble that it is able to deceive even the most observant." The roof was on the same plane as the thatched roofs of the galleries, by some estimates approximately thirty-two feet high. In the roof were several traps that allowed descents of equipment and actors to the stage platform below. The machinery for this was located immediately above the roof in a series of workrooms called the "huts." Traps also existed in the stage floor that allowed entrances and exits to and from "hell." The number of traps leading from the understage space, the cellarage, to the stage floor is disputed; estimates range from two or three to as many as five. Whatever the actual number, it is likely that the traps were located in various places about the stage, with a fairly large trap somewhere near the center of the stage platform.

The Private Playhouses

The term "private" in regard to the English private playhouses is a misnomer, for these theatres were open to the public. The clientele was somewhat different from the public playhouses owing to the increased admission price, which was often six times as high, and the fact that more sophisticated plays were offered. Perhaps the term arose because these playhouses were located within the city limits proper on land owned originally by various monastic orders. The private playhouses were different in some respects from the public ones. These indoor theatres were partially polarized; that is, audience and players were somewhat separated, in that the audience was assembled along the lines of Italian models with floor and gallery seating,

England During the Reign of the Tudors and Stuarts

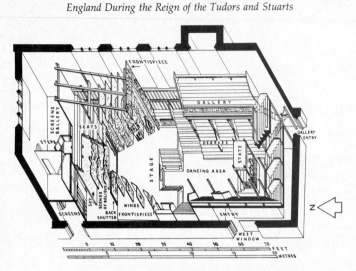

A reconstruction of a Tudor hall arranged for a performance.

(From Richard Leacroft, The Development of the English Playhouse. *Used by permission of Cornell University Press.)*

yet without a proscenium arch and front curtain. The stage resembled the structure of the tiring house of the public playhouses, with the platform extending from side wall to side wall and only a little, about 30 percent, into the total length of the hall. The basic relationship between stage and audience area probably originated in the form of medieval banquet hall staging, certainly

A reconstruction of a performance in a Tudor hall.

(From Richard Leacroft, The Development of the English Playhouse. *Used by permission of Cornell University Press.)*

in the notion of the dramatic use of an indoor rectangular room. The individual boxes were arranged in galleries as in the public playhouses, and the pit was completely filled with bench seating. From the records of the best-known of the private theatres, the Second Blackfriars, detailed information about the size and shape of this type of theatre can be gleaned. Built in 1596 by James Burbage, the theatre was 101 feet long and 46 feet wide, with a working ceiling height of some 50 feet. The stage was raised three to four feet and, with the tiring house, occupied about one-third of the entire length. Beside the Second Blackfriars six other private theatres were built in London between 1576 and the general closing of all theatres in 1642. Initially these structures were used for dramatic presentation by the children's companies until 1610. Thereafter the theatres became the winter playhouses for the major adult companies that operated in the public theatres during the summer months. Because of the higher admission price and therefore the potential for greater profit, the use of the private playhouses by the adult companies increased throughout the period before the Commonwealth.

The Court Theatres

As distinguished here from the private theatres, the court theatres were those playing spaces built in royal residences primarily for

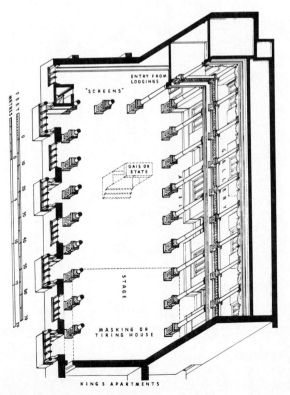

A reconstruction of the Banqueting Hall, Whitehall, c. 1606.

(From Richard Leacroft, The Development of the English Playhouse. *Used by permission of Cornell University Press.)*

the staging of masques and other nonpublic entertainments for an invited audience. Although these theatres, typical of the general practices of the time, employed professional players from the public playhouses to stage the more conventional fare, the distinct significance of these theatres was that in them the introduction of Italian Renaissance stagecraft in England occurred. The theatres in other respects differed little from the private theatres. But in the important aspect of presenting illusionistic scenery, these theatres were the most polarized of the English playhouses in that they most distinctly separated playing space from audience space.

The most famous of the court theatres and the one where most of the court masques were staged was the Banqueting House at Whitehall Palace. Essentially a large rectangular room of some 120 by 53 feet, it was originally built in 1581. Surviving a fire in 1619, it was rebuilt in 1622 and served as the principal space for masques until Charles I built a new masking room there in 1637. The auditorium was clearly distinct from the playing space, separated by a proscenium arch. The stage itself occupied some forty feet of the fifty-three-foot width of the room, with the depth taking approximately one-quarter to one-third of the length of the hall, depending upon which reconstruction is considered.

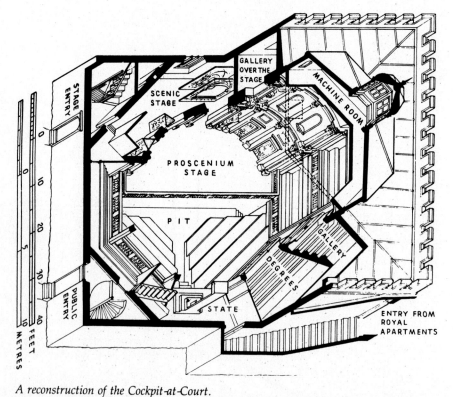

A reconstruction of the Cockpit-at-Court.

(From Richard Leacroft, The Development of the English Playhouse. *Used by permission of Cornell University Press.)*

The rectangular form was by no means the only shape for the court theatres. Another, the Cockpit-at-Court, was an octagon located within a square space. Built by the stage and scene designer Inigo Jones in 1630, this theatre closely followed the Italian school of theatre design advanced by Palladio. Jones's drawings exhibit none of the "discovery" spaces of the public and private theatres. The theatre was approximately sixty feet across, with a semicircular stage along three sides of the octagon, taking up about a third of the interior space. Pit and gallery seating was available in the remainder of the theatre.

STAGE MACHINERY AND SCENIC PRACTICE

It was said earlier that the total practice of theatre during the English Renaissance was extremely diverse. Certainly this is true when the staging practices at all playhouses are considered. Much of what is known about English Renaissance staging is based generally on the notion that what was used depended upon where the production was to take place rather than on any preset idea about the type of playhouse in which the production was presented. What simply existed at any given playhouse was more the determinant of the staging than the fact that the production had recently been completed elsewhere. Because of this variety and diversity, it is difficult to establish clear notions of exact staging at each type of theatre. Given the amount of theatrical activity, primary sources of information are sparse. The records of the Office of the Master of Revels, the licenses of plays and playhouses, the diary and other papers of manager and producer Philip Henslow (?–1616), and the directions and dialogue in the plays themselves are about all that exist.

Scenery and Properties

Although specific conclusions are hard to draw, common generalized concepts can be determined. First, the connection between the scenic practice of the English Renaissance and the Middle Ages seems clear. That the stage platform itself served as a *platea* has already been established, and whatever scenic units were used most likely paralleled medieval *mansions* in the public and private theatres. The court theatres, as noted, most closely paralleled Italian illusionistic scenic practices. Second, while the scenery of the court theatres was based heavily on illusionistic practice, that is, concerned with the creation of an environment apart from the theatre space itself, the public and private theatres were clearly nonillusionistic. They were concerned with the creation of a locale that, while suggestive of a place apart from the theatre, clearly recognized and acknowledged that its life was part of the theatre itself. Third, this nonillusionistic suggestion in the public and private theatres was accomplished through vocal and visual means. Throughout the plays, constant references to place are made, and presumably these, along with the visual suggestion of selected set pieces, were enough to establish setting. English Renaissance theatre practice was based on commercial pragmatism and was not encumbered by theoretical inconsistencies.

From the sources available can be gleaned the types of set pieces and properties that helped create the setting on the English Renaissance stage. Standard items supplied by the Master of Revels's Office or kept by the theatres for use included necessary furniture (tables, chairs, bed) for the staging of various interiors, floor coverings and curtains, appropriate furnishings for palaces and churches, natural scenes (rocks, trees, bushes, caves), and necessary prison and funeral equipment (biers, coffins, stocks). This list is by no means exhaustive but should give some sense of the scope of the standard items used to set the scene. It is likely that large pieces, once set, remained onstage throughout the scene or play and that smaller pieces were revealed through the specific playhouse's "discovery" mechanism. Small items were handed directly to the actors by assistants, possibly wearing a neutral mask to indicate a state of nonpresence, or were brought onstage by the actors themselves upon their regular entrances. A comparison of early and late plays confirms the notion that the interest in scenic embellishment increased throughout the period. But in no case did the entertainments of the public and private theatres approach the detailed scenic spectacle of the court theatres. Items were added as needed given the stock on hand. Only rarely was there a sense of acquiring props and set pieces for a particular play, and a piece originally used for a certain play would likely find its way into another. In regard to properties, the medieval tradition continued. There was much use of noise and fire. At Blackfriars, for example, a cannon was fired at the conclusion of *Hamlet*.

Costumes and Makeup

Because of its proximity to the audience, costuming was probably the most fully realized of the visual elements of the English Renaissance stage. Continuing in the medieval tradition, most costumes were similar to contemporary dress for the social station of the character. Color symbolism was important. Although no attempt at full historical accuracy was attempted, some stock notions of period costuming began to emerge before 1642. Chief among these notions were costumes that suggested antiquity, such as classical Greek and Roman; special costumes for allegorical or mythological characters, including gods and ghosts; costumes for distinct characters and character types like Falstaff and Shylock; and costumes for nationalities other than English. There was no perceived inconsistency in mixing these costumes with the English contemporary garments worn by the leading characters. Both actors and audience alike were quite comfortable with this mix, as there were similar blendings of set pieces and props. Henslowe's and other accounts indicate that the costumes were carefully made. Each company likely owned a considerable stock and kept replenishing it from specially constructed or purchased clothing, and from royal favor, the patron either donating the clothing or purchasing it for the company. More money was invested in costuming than any other production element. The age was extremely clothes-conscious, and the productions reflected this fact. Makeup also began to come into its own during this period. Already used in selected areas, such as a medieval devil's face, it became more widespread and generally replaced the mask as a method of creating a character.

Music and Dance

Like other elements of English Renaissance theatre practice, music and dancing continued in the traditions started in the Middle Ages. The use of these elements was prolific by both boy and adult companies and in all types of playhouses. The plays indicate the number of times musical flourishes precede and follow certain types of action—battle scenes and royal entries, for example. Dance, particularly the jig, and music often began and concluded the afternoon's entertainment. In the private and court theatres, these production elements were more sophisticated than in the public theatres, but their importance remained every bit as strong.

THEATRE ORGANIZATION

In all aspects of theatrical life, commercialism prevailed. Thus the practice of theatre had a business orientation from the outset. The builders of London's playhouses were motivated by the desire for financial gain rather than the wish to create great houses of culture. The owners, a combination usually of the actors in the company who had invested in the theatre and others not connected with the productions, were responsible for rent, upkeep, and hiring and supervision of all house personnel. Income was derived from renting the facility for other activities, from the sale of concessions and souvenirs, and from admissions. Admissions were of two general types, yard receipts and gallery income, the hired actors receiving the yard money and the owners and shareholder actors dividing the gallery cash. Usually the shareholders and other owners divided the expenditures and profits; the hired actors and other personnel were simply paid weekly for services rendered with no opportunity to share in the profits. Occasionally the builder or other sponsor could advance cash for a future share of the take from all sources of income.

Those who wanted to produce a play in or around London had the Master of Revels's Office to deal with first. Beginning in 1574, it was there that the necessary licensing of the dramatic work and place of presentation was arranged. Payment for the proper license was one day's gross or a set single payment of two pounds per play. If a new work was to be licensed, the office took on a censorship function, looking particularly for attacks on the court. If corrections had to be made, the single payment for the license was higher, presumably for the extra work done by the office. Another function of the Master of Revels was to supply the scenery and props for all appearances before the court, whether professional or not.

Playwrights did not fare as well as other theatre practitioners. No royalty system yet protected them in even a minimal way, and most plays were sold outright by the playwright. The payments varied considerably. The average playwright probably earned about twelve shillings per week for a full-time effort, considerably more than the average skilled tradesman of the period. Often, for financial reasons, playwrights maintained close working relationships with the various companies, sometimes becoming shareholders in the company. Shakespeare enjoyed such a relationship.

Audience Considerations

Policies effecting the English audience were similarly along commercial lines. By any standard prices were cheap and were designed to attract as large an audience as possible. The base price charged in the public theatres was a penny, which was about the cost of a draft beer in one of London's taprooms. This price was charged for space in the pit and probably allowed about four square feet of standing room if the area was filled to capacity. The amount charged for other sections of the theatre increased in penny increments for the public galleries and the gentlemen's rooms or boxes, respectively. Still this was quite a bargain. No other entertainment, except for bearbaiting, was as inexpensive, and since it was the major form of amusement, all strata of society attended. No doubt this created occasional rowdiness, but to assume disorder throughout would be a mistake. Large crowds in relatively confined spaces for long periods of time will behave in ways that are less than genteel, and this was exacerbated by the presence of criminals, cutpurses, and prostitutes regularly working the crowd. The practice of allowing those who cared to pay enough to sit on the stage itself did not help quiet the audience. The prices in the public theatres naturally stratified the audience according to social class; lower classes controlled the pit, the middle class occupied the public galleries, and the aristocracy frequented the private rooms. All who attended fully expected to participate actively in the afternoon's entertainment.

In the private theatres, prices during the seventeenth century were set at one shilling for the pit benches and half a crown for the boxes at the side of the stage, about six to ten times more expensive than the public theatres. These prices remained fairly standard throughout the period. At all times, however, special deals could be arranged with the right people and for the right price. Moneymaking was a major motivator of English theatre practice before 1642.

Whether the playhouses operated at capacity is subject to much speculation. If Henslowe is correct, the average crowd seldom got above 50 percent of capacity except for special events and play openings, where higher than normal prices were charged. Assuming that is correct, and given the average performance week of six days after James I outlawed Sunday performances, probably some 15 to 20 percent of the area's population attended the theatre. With the higher prices charged at the private theatres, it is no wonder that more and more performances were done there even though they commonly held only five hundred to a thousand spectators; more money was to be made. There is some evidence that audiences followed a favorite company or companies from theatre to theatre rather than showing any loyalty to a particular playhouse or type of playhouse. Thus all classes of audience existed everywhere, except for those who could only afford the public pit.

As noted, plays were performed six days per week, and they usually began around 2:00 P.M. Travel home was not advisable after nightfall, especially during the winter season, when shorter days prevailed. Bad weather could cancel a performance, and plays were not given on religious holidays and during special civic situations, such as a siege of the plague. The common practice that emerged was to perform at a public theatre during the summer months and seek the interior comfort of a private theatre during the winter. Shakespeare's King's Men, for example, performed at the Globe in the summer and at Blackfriars the remainder of the year.

Certainly any theatre that is rooted in commercialism depends on advertising to help sell its product, and the companies of the English Renaissance were no exception. Although literacy had not increased significantly from the late Middle Ages, handbills and posters were common forms of advertising during the seventeenth century. No doubt they made considerable use of emblematic art in conveying their messages to the populace. Written material was also included. The actors announced future events from the stage as a teaser for the audience to return. In the medieval tradition, preplay processions to announce the forthcoming production were common when the companies were on tour. Finally, as in many stadiums today, a flag was flown over the "huts" on the days that a play was to be performed. Since these playhouses towered over the residential structures around them, English theatregoers simply had to look toward the playhouse of their choice to see if an entertainment was scheduled. The decision to attend might have been that spontaneous. There was, after all, no advanced ticket reservation system or box office as we know it today.

ACTING, ACTORS, AND COMPANY ORGANIZATION

In the public and private theatres of the English Renaissance, the actor and the playwright were the dominant artists in production collaboration. The actor was of primary concern to audience and fellow artist alike.

Acting Style

Little is known about the style of acting that was employed by the actors of the period. Firsthand comments have not survived, and scholars are divided on the extent to which the acting approached any sense of the realistic. But judging from the plays, including select bits such as Hamlet's advice to the players, some common traits may have existed. Given the proximity between player and audience and the lack of quiet in the playhouses during performances, no doubt the acting style was enlarged by today's standards. The delivery of dialogue probably was somewhat oratorical to get above the din and quite rapid to keep the action moving. Indeed, Shakespeare's "two hours' traffic" of a play on the stage may have been close to the norm. Since there was essentially no pause between acts, it is likely that the general delivery of lines was similarly paced. Much of the actor's physical delivery was based on gesture and rather broad movement, no doubt influenced by mime and the *commedia dell'arte*. Like the delivery of dialogue, movement was undoubtedly rapid to sustain the pace of the show. Whereas movement had been generally suited to the type of character portrayed, English actors probably brought distinct movement to individual characterizations, a clear shift toward the more realistic.

Actors

England had no shortage of actors. Given the number of playhouses and companies, actors emerged and disappeared with a regularity that made continued popularity and a regular audience following difficult to maintain. The profession was not considered all that honorable, probably because of its long association with the seamier side of life. It did, however, provide those engaged full-time in it a decent living financially, and a few of those who excelled are known. The first well-known actor of this time was Edward Alleyn (1566–1626), who is credited with significantly raising the art of acting in England. One account describes him as having "a pleasant voice, a good figure and a fine presence," but it is difficult to assess that statement in light of unknown norms. By 1583 he was already a respected member of the Earl of Worcester's Men. In 1592 he became Philip Henslowe's son-in-law and thereby part owner (and ultimately sole proprietor) of a number of Henslowe's operations. He was a principal player at the Rose from 1594 to 1597 and at the Fortune from 1599 until his retirement from acting in 1604.

Alleyn's most serious rival in acting artistry was Richard Burbage (c. 1567–1619). He originated many of Shakespeare's major roles, including Hamlet, King Lear, and Othello. His career began early, probably in 1584 with the Admiral's Men at his father's playhouse, the Theatre. Although comments about his style are virtually unknown, his name became synonymous with the finest in acting.

In addition to actors who portrayed principal characters, there were those who specialized in a variety of types of roles. Indeed, within any company, the type of role played was protected by common agreement so that a given actor had the right to portray all characters of that type for the terms of the agreement. Among the most popular of these characters were the clowns, and the foremost among actors who so specialized was William Kempe (?–1603). Kempe was known for his jigs, bawdy song-and-dance afterpieces to most Elizabethan theatre productions, and for such roles as Dogberry in *Much Ado about Nothing*. Active in Denmark before coming to London, his reputation

Edward Alleyn.

came with him, and he became one of the founding shareholder actors of the Lord Chamberlain's Men in 1594. He stayed with the company for six years. Thereafter he traveled between England and the Continent for the balance of his career.

Obviously these are but a few of the actors who made a living at their trade in Tudor and Stuart England. At the average rate for shareholders of five to ten shillings per week, the pay was roughly twice that of a skilled worker in a standard trade. Hired actors probably earned at about the same rate as a skilled tradesman. To be fair, these were London salaries. When on tour the rate of pay was approximately half the London rate, and the boys in the children's

Richard Burbage.

companies were paid less. Yet even for these, acting in the live theatre was a living. The same cannot be said for the profession today.

Acting Company Organization

The growth of acting companies during Tudor and Stuart England was intrinsically tied to politics. Indeed, the whole growth of theatre during this period came about, in large measure, because it was treated as the special plaything of the court, and this attitude even extended to the regulations affecting the public playhouses. At several points during her reign, Elizabeth I enacted legislation that further restricted the scope of theatre practice, drawing it more and more under court control. In 1572, for example, an "Acte for the Punishment of Vagabondes" was significant in that it provided professional protection for sponsored companies and increased royal participation that lasted until 1642. The act restricted the movement of strolling players and made others legitimate by requiring that each company had to receive authorization from or be sponsored by a nobleman at the rank of baron or higher. In certain cases, two judicial officials could sponsor a troupe, but in no case could those of lesser rank support a group of players, as had been past practice. Thus, increased stability was guaranteed for those companies that were licensed, no doubt a factor that spurred the building of the first public playhouse some four years later.

When the Stuart dynasty came to the throne in 1603, further consolidations of theatre were enacted. James I took away the right of noblemen to sponsor troupes, and until 1642 only the royal family could license companies. Although restrictive, that action had one positive result. Under royal sponsorship, theatrical activity could take place within the city limits of London, thus allowing for the building of more theatres and the establishment of a few more companies. King James also outlawed the operation of companies outside London, the net result being that provincial theatre ceased to exist except for the occasional tours of London-based companies. In all things theatrical, activity emanated from London.

The Adult Companies

Adult acting companies were organized with two classes of performers: shareholder actors and hired actors. The shareholder actors were, with other owners, the decision makers of the company and its playhouse, in obvious conjunction with the patron. As such, they shared in the expenditures and profits of their joint venture, being paid from the money that was left over after all expenditures were settled. The hired actors, on the other hand, were paid a set fee weekly for the period of their contract, usually two years. Company size varied from eight to twelve shareholders, with a like number of hired actors. While this was the norm, other variations existed owing to the demands of the play and the playhouse. When on tour during the forced closing of theatrical activity in London, which occurred from time to time because of plagues or religious or political disputes, the companies operated at half size, largely because provincial theatres were temporary and could not accommodate large casts. In those cases, the doubling of roles was a necessity.

Although roles were sometimes double-cast, only rarely did an actor play the same part for more than two days running, given the repertory system in common use. The bill was changed daily, and a new play was added every two weeks. Since there were performances in both the public and private theatres, a great number of plays were needed. Plays already in the repertory remained there so long as the audience taste for them persisted; once that taste waned, the play was revised or retired to be seen at another time. Seldom did an actor play the same part more than twice a week in this system, and because actors were hired to perform set types of parts for the entire season, there was probably more emphasis on the memorization of lines than on the development of individual characterizations. To help protect the play's owner, actors used "sides," a listing by acts and scenes of their individual lines and their cue lines only. The entire play, which was issued by the Master of Revels as a promptbook in a single copy, was thereby somewhat protected from too wide a distribution, there being no copyright law. Protection was minimal, however, because plays were quickly memorized and printed elsewhere under other names.

A new play was rehearsed only a few times before its presentation, so it is no wonder that there was so much focus on memorization and that the prompter was an important part of the production. To the extent that someone conducted the rehearsals as a director does today, that responsibility was probably shared between the playwright and the prompter. Thus, the prompter's responsibilities included running performances and providing the numerous lists of backstage details for the production. Above all he was responsible for making sure the actors and the technical aspects of the show were ready. In all, his responsibilities were akin to those of the modern stage manager.

The adult company had boy actors apprenticed to it. This apprentice system worked like others in the skilled trades, each boy being assigned to a responsible master who was paid by the company for the boy's service. The boys played the roles of younger women in the plays, female actors not being allowed on the English stage before 1660. Older women were played by adult men whose line or possession of parts included those types of roles.

Throughout the period of the Tudors and the Stuarts, companies came and went. Similarly, actors moved from one company to another, depending upon economic and professional gain. The Earl of Leicester licensed the first troupe of any note in 1574, and as long as James Burbage was associated with it, it maintained a position of dominance. After the plague of 1592–93, two troupes dominated the English stage: The Lord Admiral's Men, under the direction of Edward Alleyn and Philip Henslowe, and the Lord Chamberlain's Men, directed by the Burbages and the acting shareholders, Shakespeare among them. All in all, there were some half-dozen adult companies operating in London during most of the seventeenth century. They earned extra money and protection by playing command performances at court. For example, Charles I commissioned some twenty-five such productions each year.

The Boy Companies

In addition to the adult troupes, boy companies flourished during the late sixteenth and early seventeenth centuries. Beginning as extensions of school programs, they were composed entirely of choirboys based in churches whose masters sought to enhance the educational process by having the boys present plays. The educational nature of this venture was quickly influenced by commercialism, however, and the masters soon charged admission. In the late sixteenth century, the professionalism of the boy companies had risen to such a degree that they posed serious competition to the adult companies. The two most respected companies were the Children of the Chapel, operating from the Chapel Royal, and the company known as Paul's Boys, based at Saint Paul's Cathedral. Their repertory was compiled from the same adult dramas that the adult companies performed, and a few authors even wrote especially for them. They operated in the indoor private theatres until those playhouses were taken over by the adult companies in the early days of the seventeenth century. Because of their rivalry with the adult companies and their constant running afoul of local authorities, they gradually declined in number so that by 1608 only one company was left. After 1610 they were gone, their members either working with the adult companies or simply grown and active in other professions.

STUART COURT MASQUES

Along with all that has been described thus far, an active court theatre, quite different in focus and intent, existed. The notion of theatrical activity at court was nothing new, and court theatre probably emerged from the royal entries and banquet hall staging of the Middle Ages. Both Henry VII and Henry VIII had companies of actors primarily for performance at holiday events in the early sixteenth century. Part of Elizabeth's

A Knight of Apollo, a costumed masquer from a Stuart masque of 1607.

reforms after 1588 were to strengthen the court theatre through infusions of legal edicts, financial assistance, and a general attitude that greatly favored it. At first, presentations at court were largely transplants from the public playhouses. James I, for example, at various Christmas celebrations in 1612, had some thirty plays presented at court.

While the practice of importing plays from other sectors of the English theatre continued under the Stuarts, clearly the major form of court entertainment was the masque. Essentially like the intermezzo in that it was a spectacular musical dance-drama, the form was particularly popular with Henry VIII and James I, much less so with Elizabeth I. Although visually beautiful, the masque does not rate as great literature. The texts are simplistic and the characters fairly one-dimensional mythological or allegorical beings. Everything is given the most superficial treatment possible, and that is a bit surprising considering the stature of some of the playwrights that wrote masques. For example, Ben Jonson (1572–1637) wrote eight, most notable among them *The Masque of Blackness* (1605), *The Masque of Queens* (1609), *Oberon, the Fairey Prince* (1611), and *The Masque of Beauty* (1608). Another writer of masques was William Davenant (1606–1668). Writing in the style of Jonson, Davenant worked closely with Inigo Jones in staging them. Most of his masques were staged during the decade before the Commonwealth, when he enjoyed tremendous popularity, having succeeded Jonson in 1638 to the post later known as poet laureate. His best-known masque was *Salmacida Spolia* (1640). His association with Jones was important not only for the advancement of court masques but also for its artistic link to the theatre of the Restoration.

Inigo Jones

The masques are valuable because they were the vehicle through which the principles of Italian Renaissance stagecraft were introduced in England. The man most responsible for that introduction was Inigo Jones (1573–1652). An English architect and artist, Jones studied in Italy and became very familiar with the principles of illusionistic perspective scenery, particularly as practiced by Serlio. After some refining of the techniques in Denmark, Jones returned to England and took control of producing the masques through his assignment to the household of Prince Henry. He probably had a major design function in all of the masques produced between 1605 and 1613, the first being Jonson's *Masque of Blackness*. His rise to a position of dominance led to ill feeling among the masque playwrights. Although Jones won a much-celebrated dispute with Jonson during the reign of Charles I, the victory was short-lived. During the Commonwealth, he fell out of favor and died in obscurity and poverty.

Jones's contributions nonetheless remain significant. In staging masques, he experimented with Italian Renaissance practice in an attempt to find what would work best in England. In so doing he not only assured the implantation of those ideas into English staging practice, but finished the transition from medieval stagecraft forms to the Italian illusionistic perspective scenery and scenic methods. Along with his scenic achievements, he established the concept of the proscenium arch in England and began experimenting with a workable system for moving scenery. This was the one area where the Italian ideas underwent the most change, for English theatres, even at court, did not have adequate cellars for the housing of the understage equipment commonly used in Italy. By 1640 Jones had devised the system of grooves on and above the stage floor for moving flat wings onstage and offstage that would become the standard of English stage practice for the next 250 years.

Like most other practicing artists, Jones's style developed throughout his career. His early masques made heavy use of the Serlian wing, and it was only after 1634 that the flat wing emerged in his designs. His experiments with *periaktoi* and back shutters emerged as early as 1606, with the back shutters parting to reveal other scenes after 1608. By the time of the Commonwealth, Jones has introduced most of the illusionistic stage practices of the Italians to England. And the principles introduced would last, for it was his principal student, John Webb, who, in conjunction with Davenant, would fully realize these practices in the theatre of the Restoration.

CONCLUSION

The theatrical style of the great public and private theatres of the Tudors and Stuarts, in their own time clearly more at the core of theatrical activity than the masques, would disappear forever during the Puritan-dominated Commonwealth. England during the Restoration would join the rest of Europe in fostering the concept of illusionistic stage practice and in the continuing chase for verisimilitude.

12

THE COMMONWEALTH AND THE RESTORATION

THEATRE DURING THE COMMONWEALTH (1642–1660)

Theatrical activities did not cease in London after September 2, 1642, when the playhouses were closed by order of Parliament, but they did take on a distinctly furtive air. Many actors, including those of the King's Men of Blackfriars and the Globe, left the stage and took up arms in the service of King Charles I. Actors who chose to remain uninvolved in the civil war continued to perform in the playhouses in defiance of the law. Their performances were occasionally interrupted by raiding soldiers who stopped the play, chased off the audience, and took the costumes.

By 1647, however, the actors considered the ban on playing a dead letter and openly performed at the Fortune, Salisbury Court, the Red Bull, and the Cockpit. Such bold defiance of the will of Parliament did not go unanswered. On October 22, 1647, Parliament passed new measures against the theatre, this time imposing imprisonment on any actor caught practicing his profession. This was followed by an additional ordinance that allowed the confiscation of box office receipts, the fining of members of the audience, and the destruction of the playhouse. These new laws created considerable hardships for the actors and their audiences, but plays continued to be performed.

After the execution of Charles I in 1649, the soldiers dismantled the interiors of the Fortune, Cockpit, and Salisbury Court theatres. The Red Bull somehow managed to survive as a theatre and offered employment for a few actors, but the wrecking of the other playhouses forced many actors to seek occupations outside the theatre. Although the Cockpit and Salisbury Court theatres were again fitted out as playhouses during the Commonwealth, actors worked in fear of raids and prison. Two elements necessary for good professional theatre, trained actors and audiences, were nearly extinguished in England during the Commonwealth.

Playhouses of the Commonwealth

Constructed during the first years of the reign of James I, the Red Bull was an open-air public playhouse built along typical Elizabethan lines. Even before the closing of the theatres by Parliament, the Red Bull had a reputation for spectacular staging of plays that catered to the tastes of London's less discerning audience members. During the period of the Commonwealth, this playhouse specialized in presenting jigs, dances, rope walkers, and drolls, which were scenes or abridged versions of popular plays. Although the Red Bull was raided several times in the 1650s, it managed to escape demolition by the soldiers of Parliament. In use briefly after the return of Charles II, the theatre was an early victim of the newly restructured English theatre. By 1663 it could be said of the Red Bull that "there are no tenants in it but old spiders."

In 1617 Christopher Beeston established an acting company at the Cockpit, a newly constructed playhouse on Drury Lane near the Inns of Court and the

Tickets of admission for London theatres. Number 1 is for the Red Bull.

Whitehall palace. In use during most of the period before 1642, this private theatre was the site of numerous illegal performances during the Commonwealth. On March 24, 1649, the interior of the Cockpit was destroyed by government troops. Refitted as a playhouse in 1651 by Beeston's son, William, it was the site of a 1656 performance of Sir William Davenant's *The Siege of Rhodes*. In 1660, before the imposition of the monopoly on theatrical performances, the Cockpit was home to a company of actors headed by John Rhodes. During the month of October 1660, this playhouse served a newly formed acting company, His Majesty's Comedians, which was under the joint direction of William Davenant and Thomas Killigrew. Following the establishment of separate companies by Davenant and Killigrew and their relocation in new playhouses, the Cockpit fell into disuse by the mid-1660s.

Another of the illegal theatres of the Commonwealth period was the Salisbury Court playhouse. This small, private playhouse was constructed in 1629 as the home for the Children of the Revels and the Salisbury Court players. Wrecked by soldiers in 1649, the playhouse apparently saw little use in the 1650s. Refitted as a theatre in 1660, it was used by Davenant's company while his new theatre was being built. The Salisbury Court was destroyed in 1666 during the Great London Fire.

The last Commonwealth playhouse to be considered is the most unusual one, a tennis court. An indoor tennis court, with its oblong shape and good, natural lighting from high side windows, was easily converted into a temporary theatre. This type of conversion was common in Europe by the middle of the seventeenth century. Gibbons's Tennis Court, on Vere Street near Lincoln's Inn Fields, was opened for the health and recreation of "persons of quality" in 1634. The first recorded use of this tennis court as a theatre was in March 1653, when a play by Thomas Killigrew was raided by the soldiers. In 1656 William Davenant used the tennis court for one of his entertainments. Killigrew returned to Gibbons's in 1660 with his new King's Company, renovated the structure into a permanent theatre, and opened the first Theatre Royal. This new theatre was professed by one contemporary to be "the finest playhouse, I believe, that ever was in England." Three years later the King's Company moved to a new theatre, and Gibbons's Tennis Court, by then known as the Vere Street Theatre, fell into disuse.

Sir William Davenant and the Commonwealth Theatre

A court poet and playwright, Sir William Davenant (1606–1668) was involved with the English theatre for nearly forty years and strongly influenced its direction in the period after 1660. The godson of William Shakespeare, Davenant had written ten plays and five masques before the closing of the theatres in 1642. His services to King Charles I during the civil war earned him a knighthood, exile in France, and imprisonment in the Tower of London for two years.

Upon his release from prison in 1652, Davenant set about trying to legally produce theatrical ventures in Commonwealth London. In this he was success-

Sir William Davenant.

ful and presented before a paying audience *The First Day's Entertainment* at *Rutland House* in May 1656. This performance, which consisted of songs, instrumental music, and declamations, was presented in a small, temporary theatre in Davenant's home, Rutland House. It was followed in September by his play *The Siege of Rhodes*. This work, often called the first English opera, recalled the masques of the prewar court. In the cast of the play, in the role of Lanthe, was Mrs. Edward Coleman, who was the first woman to appear on the English stage.

These semiprivate performances met with no opposition from the government, and Davenant received permission to present his next work in a professional playhouse. *The Cruelty of the Spaniards in Peru* was presented at the Cockpit in July 1658. Since England was at war with Spain at the time, Davenant's play was something of a propaganda piece for the government, which may help explain why he was permitted to stage the work. The large stage of the Cockpit allowed Davenant to employ a number of stage machines for scenic effects, thus paving the way for the introduction of Continental stagecraft after 1660. Davenant was to play a major role in ensuring that the proscenium arch stage, perspective scenery, and stage machines were dominant features of the Restoration stage.

Davenant's last theatrical offering before the Restoration was *The History of*

Sir Francis Drake. This Cockpit production in late 1658 drew complaints from hard-core Puritans, but it was not closed. In 1659 Davenant was arrested for his possible involvement in a conspiracy against the government, but he was only imprisoned for a brief period. In March 1660 he went to France to renew his contacts with the English court in exile. Upon the return of Charles II to England, Davenant, along with Thomas Killigrew, was granted the monopoly on theatrical performances in London. He then set about continuing the work he had begun at Rutland House and the Cockpit.

RESTORATION DRAMA

The plays written in England after 1660 were markedly different from those produced before 1642. Prior to the closing of the theatres by Parliament, a sizable number of playhouses offered a variety of theatrical fare to a large segment of the population of London. When the theatres were reestablished with the return of Charles II, there were two playhouses providing plays to a small, select audience. During the nearly twenty years the playhouses of London were officially closed, an entire generation lost the theatre habit. When the theatres legally reopened, they were under the control of two personal friends of the king, and attendance at a play became the pastime for courtiers, would-be courtiers, and their hangers-on. This close connection between court and stage would be the dominant influence on the English theatre until the end of the seventeenth century.

Charles II took an active interest in the theatre (and in actresses) throughout his reign. His circle of close friends included several courtier-playwrights, he suggested topics for plays and made suggestions for improving existing ones, and he enjoyed discussing literary theory. His selection of Davenant and Killigrew to control the London stage ensured that the royal standard in things theatrical would be upheld.

Since the court of Charles II in the 1660s was young, gallant, witty, and somewhat amoral, the dramas presented for its amusement reflected these elements. This was particularly true in the comedies of manners, for which this period is best known, and in the heroic tragedies. These two types of plays clearly illustrate what Restoration playwrights considered was their major improvement over earlier playwrights, the refinement of language.

Restoration Tragedy

The heroic play is the major form of tragedy on the Restoration stage, a dramatic form unique to this period. A blending of the French heroic romances and the Italian neoclassical epics of the sixteenth century, the heroic play places great emphasis on valor, love, virtue, and honor. The fact that these elements are almost entirely missing in Restoration comedy establishes the Restoration heroic play as its antithesis. Both forms were appreciated by Restoration audiences, who saw themselves as witty and

Two scenes from Elkanah Settle's Empress of Morocco.

wicked in the comedies and noble and eloquent in the heroic plays. They were willing to accept both views.

Invented and named by William Davenant, whose *The Siege of Rhodes* is the first primitive example, the heroic play was intended to inspire admiration in the beholder. This goal was to be attained through the use of a heightened style of language and action, music, and spectacular scenic effects. The heroic play was set in an exotic location, featured characters of high rank and higher virtue, and was written in rhymed couplets. This type of play was tailor-made for the artistic needs of the Restoration stage. With its use of the rhymed heroic verse, called by John Dryden "the last perfection of Art," it was set apart from the plays of earlier periods. The need for large-scale scenic effects in the plays fit the requirements of the new playhouses of the Restoration.

The first heroic play performed during the Restoration was *The Indian Queen* (1664) by John Dryden and Sir Robert Howard. Dryden went on to write the best of the heroic plays of the period, including such works as *Aureng-Zebe* (1675) and *The Conquest of Granada* (1670–71). Other authors of several heroic plays are John Crowne, Elkanah Settle, and Nathaniel Lee. Heroic plays and their playwrights are the objects of satire in the Duke of Buckingham's *The Rehearsal* (1671), but the attack did not lessen the popularity of the form. The heroic play remained on the stage until early in the eighteenth century, at which point it was replaced by pathetic tragedy.

Restoration Comedy

The comedy of manners so dominates most commentaries on the drama of the Restoration that the other forms of comedy presented on the English stage from 1660 to 1700 are nearly forgotten. The comedy of manners had two periods of popularity during the seventeenth century, 1668–1676 and 1691–1700. In between and during these two periods other forms of comedy, from the intrigue plays of Aphra Behn to the Jonsonian humor plays of Thomas Shadwell, appeared.

The comedy of manners, so called because its comic elements are found in the highly ordered social pattern and hierarchy of the period, is peopled by a set of stock characters: the rake, who is the hero, the fop, the country gentleman, the male bawd, angry ex-mistresses, and witty young women. These characters exist in an amoral society governed by decorum, where what is humorous is what violates social protocol. In these plays the story line is multiple, the tone cynical, the repartee sharp.

Colley Cibber, a Restoration actor famous for playing fop roles.

The first period of the comedy of manners includes George Etherege's *She Would If She Could* (1668) and *The Man of Mode* (1676) and William Wycherley's *The Country Wife* (1675). The second period of manners plays contains George Farquhar's *The Constant Couple* (1699), John Vanbrugh's *The Relapse* (1696), and William Congreve's *The Way of the World* (1700). Condemned in the eighteenth and nineteenth centuries for its flagrant sexuality and cynical view of the world, the Restoration comedy of manners has come back into fashion and production only in the last sixty years.

MAJOR PLAYWRIGHTS OF THE RESTORATION

John Dryden

The major poet and playwright of the Restoration era, John Dryden (1631–1700), turned to the theatre to make money. From 1663 to 1680, Dryden wrote twenty-one plays for the London stage. His early efforts

John Dryden.

were in the heroic play, whose meter, the closed rhymed couplet, was his favorite verse form. *The Indian Queen* (1664) a joint effort of Dryden and his brother-in-law, Sir Robert Howard, was followed the next year with Dryden's sequel, *The Indian Emperor*. His *Tyrannic Love* (1669) features the villain of the piece as the leading character and is the first of Dryden's heroic plays with heightened diction and rants, the eloquent tirades unique to the heroic play. His most elaborate heroic play is the two-part, ten-act *The Conquest of Granada* (1670–71), whose hero, Almanzor, is the most flamboyant of a class of heroes not noted for their modesty.

All for Love (1677), Dryden's retelling of the tragic affair of Anthony and Cleopatra, offers an excellent example of the changes in tragedy from the Elizabethan period to the Restoration. In Shakespeare's version of the story, the emphasis is on the individual and the telling involves many locations and several years. Dryden focuses on decision making and confines the action of the play to a single day. Although lacking the emotional power of Shakespeare's play, *All for Love* is the best tragedy of the Restoration period.

Dryden appears to have been uncomfortable with comedy, and he often stated he wrote them solely for their financial rewards. In his comedies he followed audience demands and tried his hand at most of the forms of the period. *The Wild Gallant* (1663), *Secret Love* (1667), and *Marriage à la Mode* (1671) are comedies of manners, *An Evening's Love* (1668) is a farce, and *The Rival Ladies* (1664) is an intrigue with a double story line. Dryden's comedies are not equal to some of the best work of his contemporaries, but because of his versatility and his complete mastery of the heroic play, he is the most significant playwright of the Restoration period.

George Etherege

The first comedy written by Sir George Etherege (c. 1635–1691), *The Comical Revenge, or Love in a Tub* (1664), had a great success, but its multiple stories, multiple prose and verse styles, and numerous characters who are in and out of disguise would weary a modern audience. In 1668 Etherege made his first venture into satire with *She Would If She Could*, a comic depiction of intrigues among the idle rich of London society. The dialogue is fast and witty, and the attitude of the playwright is carefully detached.

The Man of Mode, or Sir Fopling Flutter (1676), the third and final play by Sir George Etherege, is one of the few masterpieces of Restoration drama. Its hero, Dorimant, is, according to one of Etherege's contemporaries, "an admirable picture of a courtier in the court of King Charles the Second." The original audience, filled with Charles's courtiers, accepted this picture. Dorimant is a vain, inconsiderate, unethical young gallant. He is surrounded by fools, victims, and potential victims. The play is a picture of a world in disorder, held together by pretense and social ritual. The portrait is satiric, and the audience members were not supposed to identify with the hero but were to laugh at the ridiculous nature of his existence. Etherege's ability to satirize his contemporar-

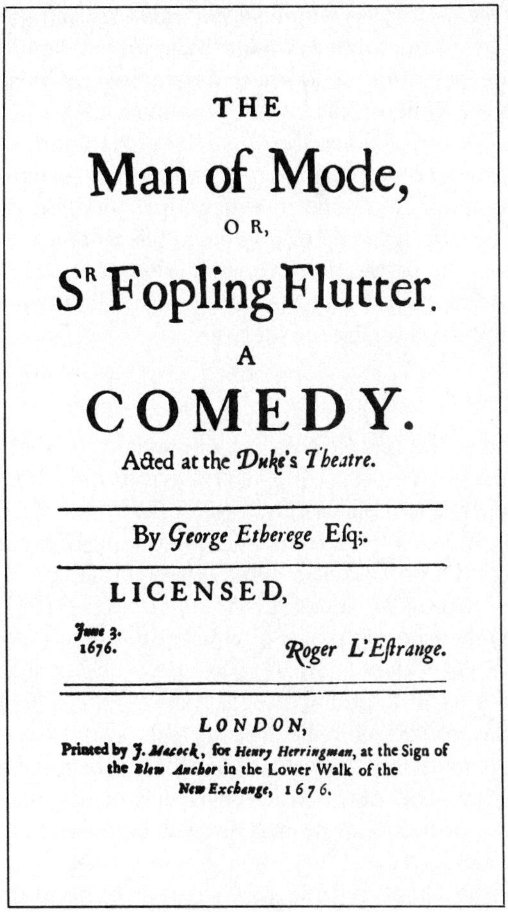

THE

Man of Mode,

O R,

Sr Fopling Flutter.

A

COMEDY.

Acted at the *Duke's* Theatre.

By *George Etherege* Esq;.

LICENSED,

June 3.
1676.   *Roger L'Estrange.*

LONDON,
Printed by *J. Macock*, for *Henry Herringman*, at the Sign of
the *Blew Anchor* in the Lower Walk of the
New Exchange, 1 6 7 6.

Playbill for The Man of
Mode.

ies in a manner both agreeable and instructive is a mark of his excellent talents
as a playwright.

William Wycherley

William Wycherley (1641–1716), like Etherege a
member of the Stuart court circle, wrote four plays in five years and then, at the
age of thirty-five, lost interest in the theatre. All four of Wycherley's comedies
are based on the hypocrisy of certain segments of Restoration society. To a
certain degree they must have reflected the playwright's own disgust, for the
tone of satire in the plays grows progressively more bitter.

Love in a Wood (1671) is a series of intrigues involving a group of characters
in search of sex and money. *The Gentleman Dancing-Master* (1672) is
Wycherley's weakest play, perhaps because it is his least scornful. This artistic
failure was more than corrected in his next effort, *The Country Wife* (1675).

This play, along with Congreve's *The Way of the World*, is the most frequently revived play of the Restoration in the modern theatre. The major situations of the play revolve around the activities of Horner, whom several husbands mistakingly believe to be in a condition "as bad as an eunuch."

An idealistic strain in *The Country Wife*, in the character of Harcourt, has led some critics to believe this excellent comedy of manners signals a significant change of taste in the Restoration. A change in Wycherley's attitude is most obvious in his last play, *The Plain Dealer* (1676), whose title character is the antithesis of the typical hero of Restoration comedy. This play, obviously influenced by Molière's *Le Misanthrope* and the numerous malcontents from Elizabethan drama, is extreme in its attack on society.

Nathaniel Lee

One of the few Restoration playwrights to specialize in one dramatic form, Nathaniel Lee (c. 1649–1692) wrote only tragedies during his brief career as a professional playwright. Producing a total of thirteen plays, including two collaborations with Dryden, Lee based most of his scripts on Greek or Roman figures and emphasized conflicts involving love.

His first three plays, *The Tragedy of Nero* (1674), *Sophonisba* (1675), and *Gloriana* (1676), were all rhymed heroic plays. Giving up the heroic couplet form in his next play, *The Rival Queens* (1677), Lee wrote one of his most successful plays. In *Mithridates* (1678), perhaps Lee's best play, he reflects the movement of the heroic play to the pathetic tragedy that was to rule the eighteenth-century stage. In *Lucius Junius Brutus* (1680), Lee got involved in the political issues of the day. The play, which was viewed by many as celebrating the concept of a constitutional monarchy, was banned after three performances.

After writing *Constantine the Great* in 1683, Lee's career came to an end when he suffered a mental breakdown and was confined in Bedlam, a London insane asylum. His plays are filled with highly fanciful flights of imagination and some remarkably good poetry. The emotional level of the plays is high, the set speeches are pyrotechnic, and the action is swift and violent. Small wonder Lee was a favorite with the actors of the period.

Thomas Shadwell

Thomas Shadwell (c. 1642–1692) wrote eighteen plays in the course of his career in the English theatre. A professed disciple of Ben Jonson, Shadwell was opposed to the comedy of manners. In the preface to his first play, *The Sullen Lovers* (1668), he renounced the silliness of witty repartee, the clichés of love and honor, and fashionable lovers, and declared his aim to follow the example of Jonson. For all his praise of Jonson, Shadwell adapted five of his early plays from Molière and used material from his plays for two more. The strongest Jonsonian elements in Shadwell's plays are a narrow moralistic tone and eccentric characters.

Shadwell's first success, *The Sullen Lovers*, is a satire on John Dryden's in-laws, the Howards, and contains serious young lovers who are in favor of marriage. This is in obvious contrast to the gay couple of the comedy of manners. *The Virtuoso* (1676), Shadwell's best comedy, directs its satiric blows at would-be scientists and their experiments, while *The Squire of Alsatia* (1688) is a comedy about London gangsters that includes a great deal of underworld slang. His last play, *The Volunteers* (1692), might be considered an early example of nineteenth-century melodrama because of its use of dramatic stereotypes.

Shadwell's reputation since the Restoration has suffered from the picture Dryden drew of him in the biting satiric poem "Mac Flecknoe," the result of a long feud between the two playwrights. He deserves better. Although his plays are flawed by coarseness and tedious dialogue, he had a keen eye for the contemporary scene. In his plays we find fine character sketches and some of the best depictions of Restoration life, but little artistic grace.

William Congreve

The most dazzling technician of the Restoration playwrights was William Congreve (1670–1729), whose last play closed out the seventeenth century. All five of Congreve's plays were produced before he turned thirty. The first, *The Old Bachelor* (1693), sparkles with wit, was a great success and illustrates the playwright's command of dialogue. His second play, *The Double Dealer* (1693), was not well received, perhaps because its bitter

Scene from a production of William Congreve's Love for Love *at the Asolo State Theatre, Sarasota, Fla.*

(Courtesy of KaiDib Films International, Glendale, Calif.)

satire made it more of a tragicomedy than a comedy of manners. *Love for Love* (1695) was for nearly a hundred years Congreve's most popular play. The control of the dialogue in this play is masterful and unique in Restoration drama in that it is individually tailored for each character.

In 1697 Congreve wrote his only tragedy, *The Mourning Bride*, and then turned his attention to defending himself against the attacks of Jeremy Collier. During the last decades of the seventeenth century, the hostile criticism of the London stage increased as the direct involvement of the court with the theatre lessened. In 1698 this criticism came to a head in the publication of Jeremy Collier's *A Short View of the Immorality and Profaneness of the English Stage*. Collier, an Anglican clergyman, strongly objected to the use of profanity on stage, deplored the unfavorable depiction of clergymen in the drama, and charged that the comedies encouraged immorality. He was particularly critical of Congreve's plays. The controversy started by Collier lasted well into the eighteenth century and had some effect in hastening the changes that were already under way in the English drama.

Congreve's last play, *The Way of the World* (1700), is one of the most sophisticated and brilliant comedies in the English language. The work is serious, witty, and complex, and it can safely stand as the culminating play of the Restoration stage. In the writing of witty conversation, Congreve's only rivals in the English-language theatre are Oscar Wilde and Noël Coward.

THEATRE COMPANIES OF THE RESTORATION

By 1663 Thomas Killigrew and William Davenant had formed two acting companies based on their royal patents of monopoly (Killigrew's King's Company and Davenant's Duke's Company), removed all their illegal competition, and settled down to controlling the London stage. The patentees or their assistants selected plays, hired actors, and assigned roles. They and their successors were the dominant force in the life of the English theatre in the seventeenth and eighteenth centuries. In addition to the near-absolute power of the patentees, there were government controls. The Lord Chamberlain held authority over the theatre, and on occasion the individual holding this post meddled in the internal affairs of the theatrical world. The Master of Revels was in charge of licensing and censuring all plays to be produced. Such were the outside forces that controlled the lives of actors during the Restoration.

The Acting Companies

The King's Company was formed in 1660 by Thomas Killigrew (1612–1683), a courtier and playwright. The company was built around a group of veteran actors who had been giving semilegal performances at the Red Bull playhouse. This group was led by Michael Mohun, an actor

Nell Gwyn in Sir Patient Fancy.

favored by Charles II, and included Edward Kynaston and Charles Hart. Nell Gwyn began her acting career in the King's Company and left the company in 1670 to become the king's mistress. The King's Company began at the Vere Street Theatre but in 1663 moved to its new home, the first Theatre Royal, Bridges Street. Thomas Killigrew remained in charge of the company until 1677, when his mismanagement forced his son, Charles, to take control.

The Duke's Company, named after the king's brother, the Duke of York and the future James II, was under the personal management of Davenant from 1660 until his death in 1668. At that time control passed to his widow and sons, and the company was directed by Thomas Betterton and Henry Harris. The leading man of the company was Thomas Betterton (c. 1635–1710), the outstanding actor of the Restoration period. Elizabeth Barry, the first great English actress, was also a member of this company. The Duke's Company started at Salisbury Court Playhouse while Lisle's Tennis Court, Lincoln's Inn Fields, was being remodeled. In 1671 they moved to the new Duke's Theatre, Dorset Garden.

In 1682 the King's Company was in such sorry financial shape, owing to bad management, that it was forced to merge with the Duke's Company. This new company, under the direction of Thomas Betterton and William Smith, was called the United Company. Working out of Drury Lane, this company

Thomas Betterton.

presented the only theatrical productions in London for the next dozen years. Disagreements between the new holders of the patents, businessmen named Christopher Rich and Thomas Skipwith, and the leading actors of the United Company resulted in the formation of a new group. After receiving permission in 1694 from the Lord Chamberlain, Betterton, Elizabeth Barry, Anne Bracegirdle, Cave Underhill, and several others among the better actors of the United Company established a new company, the Seceded Company, which continued in existence for the next ten years.

Acting on the Restoration Stage

The English theatre of the Restoration and eighteenth century was dominated by the actor. In the early years of the Restoration, when the theatre was closely associated with the court, theatrical performers were courtly toys. Yet for all its association with royalty, the status of the acting profession was very low in the seventeenth century. Sir Ralph Verney wrote in 1660 that "players and fiddlers are treated with ignominy by our laws." Professional freedom was restricted, since it was difficult for an actor to receive permission to change companies. There were even cases of actors being arrested when they tried to leave London to perform in another city.

Anne Bracegirdle.

Yet for all its restrictions, low status, and, sometimes, physical dangers, people from all areas of English society were attracted to acting as a career. In 1660 there were some professional actors who had performed in the pre-Commonwealth theatre. Most of the new performers, however, learned their trade in the Nurseries, the training schools established in connection with the two acting companies, or as apprentices. These young actors were admitted to one of the two companies for a payless three-to-six-month probationary period, and they were expected to learn their skills by copying senior players. Performance was strongly governed by tradition in the seventeenth and eighteenth centuries, and success in a role was best guaranteed by following as closely as possible the style and interpretation of an acknowledged master.

The style of acting on the Restoration stage was natural. Everyday behavior in the period was much more formal and ritualistic than it is in the late twentieth century, and it was governed by a rigid social standard and a strong sense of decorum. This everyday behavior was transported to the stage and then heightened to some degree so as to be theatrical. Comic acting was modeled on the behavior of ladies and gentlemen of the court, and it demanded a high degree of grace and elegance to capture the highly artificial manners of the courtiers. The heroic plays, being more rhetorical than the comedies, required a very formal approach. The major speeches were delivered in a patterned cadence directly to the audience from the stage apron, and there was little or no attempt to relate to other characters on stage. Physical gestures were very limited and highly stylized, but facial expression was important because of the smallness of the Restoration playhouses.

Performances were scheduled daily during the Restoration except Sundays and holidays, October to June, and occasional performances through the week during the summer months. Curtain time was between three and four o'clock in the afternoon and performances ran from three to four hours. By the turn of the century curtain time had been moved ahead to six or six-thirty.

The audience expected the performers to be excellent in their roles, and management expected, in addition, versatility, the ability to sing and dance, and a good memory. The presentation of a number of plays a week required the actors to stay prepared in a number of roles and to be constantly learning new ones. The repertory system of the period made extreme demands on the actors, but audiences were none too forgiving of bad performances. Often their expression of displeasure with a play or actor grew so hostile that the completion of the performance was impossible. The life of an actor on the Restoration stage was not one to envy.

THE RESTORATION PLAYHOUSE

When Charles II returned to England in 1660, much of the cultural life to which he had become accustomed in Paris came with him. The theatre practice he knew was heavily rooted in the transplanted Italian illusionistic staging, both in the form of the theatre building itself and in the scenic practices. Yet it ought not to be assumed that the practice of theatre during the Restoration was totally transplanted from Europe. Such was not the case. The playhouse itself was rooted in the pre-Restoration court theatre of the early seventeenth century. Continuing the traditions established by Inigo Jones, the Restoration playhouse was a unique blend of refined court theatres, European theatre models, and a smattering of elements from the Tudor and early Stuart public playhouses. Although it is hard to establish an absolute norm for the Restoration playhouse because of variations in individual theatres, some common features can be observed.

General Elements

The playhouse of the Restoration period was divided basically into the two main sections of the pre-Commonwealth theatre: a stage divided by a proscenium arch for the display of illusionistic production techniques and an auditorium on the other side of the proscenium. The auditorium was divided into the classic pit, boxes, and upper and lower galleries examined in Chapter 11. The size and shape of the auditorium came from the pattern set by the Commonwealth and early Restoration tennis courts, providing the rectangular form for the theatre that would last into the late nineteenth century. The work of Inigo Jones and Christopher Wren (1631–1723) clearly shows the influence of European models on the architectural facade of the Restoration playhouse.

Wren first influenced playhouse architecture with his unique classical domed roofing system over the Sheldonian Theatre in Oxford. His influence spread when, in 1661, Charles II appointed him to the important post of assistant surveyor-general. In this position Wren had a hand in the architectural planning of the major theatres built in London before 1700. His style was primarily influenced by the European Renaissance, for Wren had traveled to France in the mid-1660s and was impressed by the art and architecture he saw there.

Although the link to the European Renaissance was strong, the Restoration playhouse was not totally dependent upon Continental models for its basic form. The stage behind the proscenium arch was raked and equipped with the machinery to handle Renaissance illusionistic perspective scenery, but extending from the proscenium into the auditorium was an extensive forestage primarily used for acting. Doors in the proscenium gave access to the forestage. Before 1700 at least two sets of proscenium doors on each side of the arch were common, although shortly after the beginning of the eighteenth century many theatres reduced the number to one door per side, a standard that would last for a hundred years. Balconies were occasionally located above the doors and were used either as small second-story acting levels or for the seating of special patrons. All these elements came from the public and private playhouses of pre-Commonwealth England and were Restoration extensions of the tiring house and the platform of the Elizabethan stage.

An important departure from European models also existed in the Restoration method of shifting scenery. European theatres used systems such as the *chariot-mat*, an elaborate below-stage wagon and wing mounting system. But English playhouses lacked large, usable understage spaces. Generally built on a smaller scale than Continental playhouses, these theatres used a flat wing system with grooves in the stage floor and immediately overhead, supported from the side walls. The grooves allowed a flat wing to slide far enough onstage to create the proper illusion and yet be far enough offstage to be masked by the proscenium arch. With at least two pairs of grooves at each wing station, scene changes would be accomplished with minimum disruption to the flow of the production. The top grooves, which provided an upper track to guide the wing along the same path as the floor grooves, were hinged about halfway along the run on stage so that the wings could easily by changed by operating ropes from the stage floor that raised and lowered the section of the upper grooves off the stage.

Specific Playhouses

In addition to the playhouses extant from the pre-Commonwealth era and the tennis courts, several new theatres were built during the Restoration. As with pre-Commonwealth playhouses, official details

Samuel Pepys.

are sketchy about the specifics of the Restoration playhouses, but thanks to an English diarist who had a passion for the theatre, unofficial details abound. Samuel Pepys (1633–1703) was secretary of the Navy Office and an ardent playgoer. He has provided rich details about the world of early Restoration theatre. His diary is a carefully kept notebook of his impressions of the plays, the actors, stage conditions, and audience behavior he observed. Having many friends in the theatre, he also filled the diary with tidbits of theatrical gossip that help create a general, and likely accurate, picture of the Restoration stage. Of the playhouses he discussed, only a few will be examined here.

Although several playhouses bore the name Drury Lane, the initial one was the first Theatre Royal, Bridges Street. Contracted for in 1661, it opened in May 1663. Only 112 feet long, it was small for a Restoration theatre. In Pepys's description, the theatre had a sloping pit up from the stage, a tier of boxes along the outer edge of the pit, a second tier or middle gallery segmented into boxes, and an open upper gallery. The stage was equipped with the standard traps and flying equipment necessary for the proper display of Renaissance illusionistic scenery. Lighting in the auditorium was from candles and a cupola in the ceiling, which, according to Pepys, occasionally allowed rain to drip onto the spectators. In January 1671, fire destroyed the playhouse.

Among the major playhouses built during the Restoration was the Duke's

Duke's Theatre, Dorset Garden.

Theatre, Dorset Garden. Sir Christopher Wren designed the structure. Thanks to notes made by one François Brunet, who visited the theatre in 1676, more details are known about Dorset Garden than many theatres. Completed in 1671, the theatre was in the traditional rectangular shape, 140 feet long and 57 feet wide. The pit sloped slightly upward toward the boxes and galleries. The lower tier of boxes numbered seven, with each seating some twenty patrons. The middle gallery was similarly divided, but the upper gallery was open, or undivided, with traditional bench seating. Although it is difficult to assess the capacity of the upper gallery, it is clear that the boxes could accommodate 280 patrons. Allowing for the pit benches and the upper gallery, the total seating capacity was five hundred to six hundred, typical for a Restoration theatre. The stage at Dorset Garden extended approximately thirty-five feet into the length of the theatre, thus occupying some 25 percent of the structure, common for theatres built during this time. Initially the home of the Duke's Company, after 1682 it was used by the United Company for operas and works requiring larger spectacle. Over the years it fell increasingly into disuse, and it was torn down in 1709.

Probably the most famous and enduring playhouse of the Restoration period

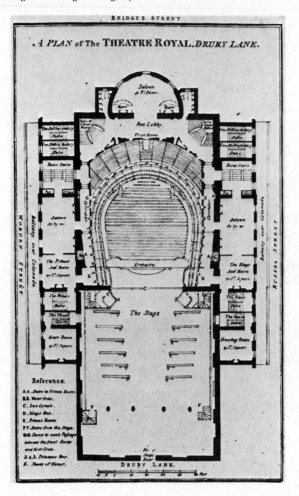

Floor plan for the Theatre Royal, Drury Lane.

was the second Theatre Royal, Drury Lane. It opened in March 1674 and had almost the exact dimensions of Dorset Garden, 140 feet by 59 feet, but was more intimate in atmosphere and had less elaborate stage equipment. Its auditorium configuration was traditional, with the pit sloping up toward the boxes and galleries. There were two galleries, the lower one divided into boxes and the upper one with two rows of backless benches, like those used in the pit. The stage projected some thirty-four feet into the length of the hall, roughly divided in half by the proscenium arch, thus separating the forestage acting area from the upstage scenic display area. Although the proscenium was not heavily adorned, it did have two sets of proscenium doors on each side of the stage with balconies over them. The capacity of Drury Lane is difficult to estimate because of the unknown numbers of people who could be crowded onto an open bench. But if box office receipts are any valid guide, it is likely the

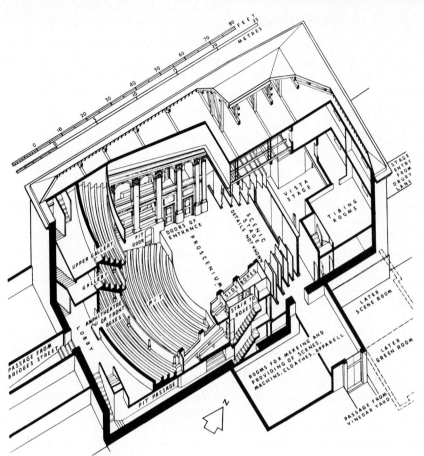

A reconstruction for the Theatre Royal, Drury Lane, c. 1674.

(From Richard Leacroft, The Development of the English Playhouse. *Used by permission of Cornell University Press.)*

theatre held some 650 spectators. The King's Company and the United Company both used Drury Lane, and this theatre survived well into the eighteenth century.

When Thomas Betterton and other actors broke with the United Company to form their own group in 1695, they needed a theatre. Lisle's Tennis Court at Lincoln's Inn Fields had not been used for some time, and the company obtained a permit to modify Davenant's old theatre within the walls of that structure. Small even by Restoration standards and poorly equipped for Renaissance spectacle, the theatre, known as Lincoln's Inn Fields, opened in April 1695 and was called by its detractors "Betterton's Booth." Nonetheless, Betterton's company operated there successfully into the eighteenth century.

The Audience

The playhouses of the Restoration served a rather specific clientele. Certainly the royal patronage of Charles II set the tone, and most of those who attended were more than likely connected with the court. Pepys refers many times to attendance at various theatres of the king and queen, various dukes and duchesses, the royal mistresses, and others of high rank. In addition to the court attenders, Pepys' diary also establishes proof that government bureaucrats (Pepys among them) and those employed in the professions were avid attenders. Between 1689 and 1715, the English government grew at a faster rate than at any previous time in English history. Thus employees of the Admiralty, the War Office, the Treasury, and scores of minor bureaucrats regularly attended. Other classes of English society, notably members of the business community and other "ordinary citizens," as Pepys often disparagingly called them, hardly attended at all. Primarily for political and religious reasons, the audience for Restoration theatre was not the active cross-section of the populace that had enjoyed the great variety of theatre available during the age of Shakespeare. The plays often expressed a certain satirical contempt for these citizens, and it is not surprising that they did not attend.

Pricing may have also been a factor in the nonattendance of certain elements of English society. Unlike the bargain rate charged by the public playhouses during Elizabeth's reign, basic pricing during the Restoration reflected the royal clientele's ability to pay. Bench seats in the pit were half the price of the boxes and twice that of the first and upper galleries. This pricing structure forced the general English working classes to seek their entertainments elsewhere, even if they had been disposed to attend. With a population base of about 575,000 in London by 1700, it is estimated that not more than 2 percent attended the Restoration theatre.

From most accounts of the time, it seems clear that although ability and willingness to pay were the actual determinants of where one sat, societal norms also played a part. Royalty, and those connected with it, typically occupied the first-level boxes. Younger, upwardly mobile junior bureaucrats were the principal users of the pit, while their superiors and the professionals occupied the middle gallery. The upper gallery was occupied by court servants and the few common people who did occasionally attend. Male and female patrons freely mixed in all parts of the house since there was no stratification according to sex. In all, the Restoration theatre commonly played to those about whom the plays were written.

RESTORATION PRODUCTION PRACTICE

Scenic and stage practice in the Restoration differed little from that established at the court theatres of pre-Commonwealth England.

Indeed, after 1660 there was essentially no difference between English practice and that of Italy and France except for scale, and this lasted until the nineteenth century.

Scenery and Scenic Practice

The principles established by Inigo Jones became common practice during the Restoration, both in design and implementation. Thus wings, back shutters, borders, and occasionally roll drops became the norm. No other theatre practitioner was more responsible for this phenomenon than Sir William Davenant and his scene painter, John Webb (1611–1672). Webb was Inigo Jones's son-in-law and pupil, and was hired by Davenant to be his chief designer and painter of scenery on an occasional basis. This relationship began with *The Siege of Rhodes*. Throughout his career Webb specialized in painterly landscapes based on actual scenes in and around London, and this preference seemed to distinguish him from other designers who were more inclined toward French scenic models. Although it was common practice to create new scenery and scenic effects for the premiere season at a theatre, that scenery was considered part of the stock owned by the company and as such found high reuse in other productions. Stock scenes needed for the presentation of Restoration plays included standard interiors and exteriors of the living places of the aristocracy and the well-to-do, temples, tombs, streets, prisons, gardens, and a variety of London gates and walls that were known to the audience. The aim was to capture locale rather than suggest any specific environment.

The practice of shifting scenes or changing scenery likewise differed little from Italian, French, and pre-Commonwealth court practice. As noted, the major difference that did exist was the absence in England of any understage shifting devices such as the *chariot-mat*. The groove system provided the basic method for changing scenery, and this was operated in full view of the audience. At each wing station, sets of grooves were operated by scenekeepers, the Restoration equivalent of the modern stagehand. They were responsible for changing the scenery by sliding the appropriate wings on and off the stage at the signal, a whistle from the stage manager. Common practice dictated that the wing of a preceding scene would be pulled off to reveal the wing of the succeeding scene behind. Thus the wing for the next scene could be set in place while another scene was playing, and the actual change could be quite rapid with only one wing to move per station when the whistle sounded. Probably eight to twelve scenekeepers were required per play. The front curtain was used only to begin and end the play, being drawn after the prologue and closed before the epilogue. What masking might have hidden the setting up or changing of scenery was left to the back shutter, which parted in the middle to reveal a different scene behind it. For the special effects that were occasionally needed, traps in the stage floor and limited flying machinery of the Italian order were in common usage, built and operated by machinists.

Indeed, from the Restoration until the beginning of the nineteenth century, illusionistic staging practice was the order of the day.

Properties, Costumes, and Lighting

Apart from scenery and scenic practice, information is sketchy about the other elements of theatre production. In most cases it appears that practices established in pre-Commonwealth England continued.

Extensive hand props and actor use-oriented small set pieces were predominant. Larger props and major pieces of furniture were usually set with a scene behind the back shutters and were brought forward by servants once the shutters had parted. The inventory of available properties provided for the needs of all types of plays and situations. Like scenery, props were not specific to a particular play and were part of the production stock of the theatre. Pepys gives us a little information about that stock. During the plague of 1665–66, he loosely inventoried the properties of the darkened Bridges Street Theatre, finding there the usual assortment of eating hardware, furniture, and "here a wooden-leg, there a ruff, here a hobby-horse, there a crown." Indeed, the other prop inventories indicated much devotion to eating and drinking, and it is likely that real food and drink were consumed on stage. These items were consistent with those in daily use in the real world. From other records it appears likely that the care of properties was entrusted to the scenekeepers, one of whom perhaps served primarily in that capacity, much as a properties master would today.

More is known about costumes. The common practice was contemporary dress for principal characters, seen in the finest light possible. Also continued was the practice of specialty costumes, such as for classical and Eastern characters. Women wore the finest garments available. The Restoration continued the practice of dividing the responsibility for securing the costumes between the management and the individual actor. More personal items, such as gloves and hats, were the actor's responsibility, while the more generalized costume fell within the province of the manager. Occasionally the company's patron or the Crown supplied funds to the management for the purchase of special costumes, particularly if a court production was involved. For these productions, the more elaborate the costume the better.

Lighting practice varied little from that employed in the Elizabethan court theatres. Candles provided the main source of illumination both in the auditorium and on the stage. The major change seems to have been that wax, rather than tallow, candles were in common use. These were more expensive than the older type and subject to less dripping and smoking, which no doubt benefited patron and production alike. No attempt was made to darken the house while the production was in progress, for there was no good means to achieve this effect. Conversely it was common practice to put out some of the onstage candles for scenes that required a darkened stage, but how and when they were relit again is not clear. It can only be speculated that some of the scenekeepers had this responsibility while the wings were being changed.

THEATRICAL FINANCING

Financial arrangements regarding theatre practice grew more out of necessity than philosophy. The theatre structures left from the Commonwealth did not permit adequate production of Restoration plays requiring increased spectacle. The patent companies thus found themselves immediately in need of money to construct new theatres more suited to the production demands of the times. Such was certainly the case with Dorset Garden and Bridges Street. The usual arrangement for the construction of a new theatre involved the shareholders of an acting company and a number of outside individuals. Someone representing the shareholders would negotiate with the owner of a piece of land for a lease to the property, the rent charged to be paid from the weekly income once production started. The actual construction was financed through the selling of shares to the acting company shareholders and others who might want a financial interest in the venture. At the same time, the acting company would agree to operate the proposed theatre and to pay the building sharers a set fee for each actual day of operation. The price of the building shares varied depending upon the sharers' confidence in the perceived prosperity of the acting company. This form of financing held until the nineteenth century.

While the rent for the lease on the land where a theatre was located was paid on an annual basis, the other expenditures were not. An "acting day," a normal day of operation, became the norm in the late seventeenth century, and this was quite fair to the acting company. Forced closing for an extended period could bankrupt a company; thus, suspending debts when not in operation was a decided advantage. When in operation, the patent company made money. Although they seldom operated at more than 50 percent of capacity, ticket prices were sufficiently high and revenues from ancillary services like concessions guaranteed success. The United Company, for example, over ten seasons from 1682 to 1692 grossed fifty pounds an acting day, about one hundred times the average salary of a single skilled tradesman, for a season of some two hundred performances. Since admission prices went up for openings and special events, revenues twice that amount were possible. Other sources of income were from "after-money" charges, the practice of charging partial admission to those who came late or just wanted to see an act or two, usually applied after the third act, and for forfeits and fines assigned to the company, all of which went into the general fund. Fines had existed since medieval times and were regularized as standard practice during the pre-Commonwealth period, so the concept was not new. However, an actor could lose sizable income. Failure to accept a part assigned, for example, cost a week's salary, as did taking properties from the playhouse without permission.

We can only approximate the standard of living that actor income would buy. Obviously sharers faired better than the hirelings, who were paid per-service actors and thus were not part of the basic company, and the scenekeepers and other nonacting personnel. Salaries were computed weekly, and a principal actor such as Mrs. Barry earned fifty shillings weekly in 1694.

England During the Reign of the Tudors and Stuarts

This was an average salary for a skilled tradesman. In addition to the weekly salary, at least one benefit performance a year was held for sharers. The practice became standard in the 1680s for principal performers. Lesser actors and key nonacting personnel enjoyed group benefits. This was an important addition to the weekly salary and was used by some managers to induce actors to remain with a company.

Advertising

Emerging from the pre-Commonwealth period, four methods of advertising a play were standard, and they have close parallels in today's theatre. The most valuable, then and now, was word of mouth. A good recommendation from a friend who had no vested interest in the production carried much weight in the decision to attend. Another method, the vocal announcement of coming events at the end of an acting day, certainly kept regular attenders informed. Two printed means of advertising existed: one was the posting of playbills at set places where people congregated, and the other was the spreading of handbills to those gathered at various places. Promotional schemes also existed, such as distributing complimentary tickets, at times by throwing them into a passing carriage. In these ways, along with the uncontrollable talk and theatrical gossip about events and happenings, the theatre of the Restoration advertised itself, albeit to a select clientele.

CONCLUSION

Theatregoers, as noted, were largely those in court favor. During the reign of William and Mary, the patronage decreased, and the brilliant and proud theatre of the Restoration gradually lost its sparkle as English theatre moved into the eighteenth century, to be dominated by the Puritans and the emerging middle class.

RETROSPECT

Emerging from the Middle Ages, England began its theatrical Renaissance slowly. While the medieval theatre had been a fairly steady and singular progression of theatre practice for over a thousand years, the English Renaissance saw a tremendous diversification of the practice with the forces of Renaissance progress, commercialism, and court government embracing theatre as its own. The theatre of this age was a curious mix of medieval tradition, Italian staging concepts, commercial entertainment, and court plaything. The writers and theatre practitioners of England showed their mastery of and ability to work in this mixed theatrical milieu by moving freely among the theatrical forms of their time—public performances before a large segment of London's population, private performances in indoor theatres to a slightly different clientele, and court performances. The variety of this expression was tremendous, for it ranged from the free, open, nonpolarized staging of the public theatres to the polarized, illusionistic theatre of the English court.

This diverse theatre was tied to commercial success in the public and private playhouses, and to currying favor through the court entertainments. The increasing influence of the court in theatrical politics can be seen throughout the period. As relationships between Parliament and the Crown grew more strained, the gulf between the theatre and its public audience widened. Yet a classic bind existed: while court favors were necessary for the theatre to exist creatively, financially, and politically in an increasingly hostile environment, that very favor was a major reason for the increasing hostility. This stressful situation ended with the closing of the theatres in 1642.

Following an eighteen-year hiatus from legal, formal practice—illegal theatrical activity did occur—the theatre officially resumed with the restoration of the English throne in 1660. A brilliant drama emerged under this court's patronage, albeit a drama that seemed to satirize as well as compliment the aristocracy. The staging practice for these dramas was totally within the framework of Italian illusionistic perspective scenery in indoor theatres behind a proscenium arch, although deference was paid to the past through the use of an extensive forestage upon which all the action was presented. Although a brilliant theatre, it held the seeds of its own destruction, planted through court patronage prior to the Restoration, and they grew rapidly after 1660. Virtually no one not connected in some way with the court attended the theatre, and the attacks from church pulpits became increasingly intense. Because of these attacks, coupled with a new relationship emerging between the court and the

England During the Reign of the Tudors and Stuarts

commercial classes, the political and economic pursestrings were soon held by those who demanded that the theatre meet their own terms of morality and decency. Thus, by 1700, the stage was set for the values of the middle class to be represented in the drama of England, and that practice was the major focus of English theatre for the balance of the eighteenth century.

Date	English History	English Theatre History	World History	World Theatre History
1485	Battle of Bosworth Field. Henry Tudor defeats Richard III. Henry VII crowned, beginning of Tudor dynasty.			
1491	Future Henry VIII born.			
1492			Columbus sails to the New World.	Aretino born.
1497		Medwell's *Fulgens and Lucrece.*	Vasco da Gama sails around Cape Horn.	
1509	Reign of Henry VIII begins.			Ariosto's *Cassaria.*
1520	Henry named Defender of the Faith by Pope.	Interludes of John Heywood.		
1533	Henry breaks with Rome. Birth of future Queen Elizabeth I.			
1535	Sir Thomas Moore executed.			
1537	Future Edward VI born.			
1538		Propaganda interludes of John Bale.	The name "America" used for first time in Europe.	Birth of Guarini.
1547	Death of Henry VIII. Edward VI begins reign.			*Commedia dell'arte* appears in Italy.
1553	Death of Edward. Queen Mary begins reign.	Udall's *Ralph Roister Doister.*		Sach's *Tristan und Isolde.*
1558	Death of Mary. Queen Elizabeth begins reign.	Births of R. Greene, T. Lodge, G. Peele.		
1561	O'Neill's rebellion in Ireland.	Sackville and Norton's *Gorboduc.*		Scaliger's *Poetics* published.

(Continued on page 254)

Date	English History	English Theatre History	World History	World Theatre History
1562			Start of the religious wars in France.	
1564		Shakespeare and Marlowe born.		
1565	Future James I born.		St. Augustine, Florida, founded.	
1576		Burbage builds the Theatre.		Death of Hans Sach.
1577	Drake begins voyage around the world.	The Curtain built.		
1583		Queen's Men established.	William of Orange ruler of the Netherlands.	Renwart Cysat directs the Lucerne Passion Play.
1587	Execution of Mary, Queen of Scots. Pope calls for a crusade against England.	Kyd's *Spanish Tragedy*. Marlowe's *Tamburlaine*.		Spanish Church condemns theatre.
1588	Battle of Spanish Armada.	Lyly's *Endimion*.	Duke and Cardinal of Guise assassinated in France.	Theatre in Sabbionetta built by Scamozzi.
1589	Greene's *Friar Bacon*.		Henry III of France assassinated.	
1592	Plague in London.	Plague closes theatres for nearly two years. Deaths of Greene and Kyd.		English actors perform in Germany.
1595	Drake dies in West Indies. Spain invades Cornwall.	Shakespeare's *Richard II* and *Romeo and Juliet*.		
1599	Birth of Oliver Cromwell, future Lord Protector of England.	The Globe theatre built. War of the theatres. Jonson's *Every Man Out of His Humour*.		
1601	Essex's revolt and execution.	*Hamlet*. Death of T. Nashe.		

Date	English History	English Theatre History	World History	World Theatre History
1603	Death of Elizabeth. James I crowned, beginning of Stuart dynasty.	Lord Chamberlain's Men become King's Men.	Champlain explores St. Lawrence River in North America.	
1605	Gunpowder Plot and arrest of Guy Fawkes.	Red Bull playhouse built. *King Lear.* Jonson's *Masque of Blackness.*		
1607		Beaumont and Fletcher's *Knight of the Burning Pestle.*	Jamestown, Va., founded.	
1613		Globe burns. Shakespeare retires from theatre.	Romanov dynasty established in Russia.	
1616		Death of Shakespeare. Jonson's *Works* published.	Richelieu made French secy. of state.	
1625	Death of James I. Charles I begins reign.	Massinger's *New Way to Pay Old Debts.*	Wallenstein appointed head of imperial armies.	
1630	Birth of future Charles II.	Theatres closed for seven months because of plague.	Boston, Mass., founded.	
1642	Civil war begins.	Parliament closes theatres.		
1647	King seized by army.	Players return to London and perform illegally. New orders passed against theatres.		
1649	Execution of Charles I. Commonwealth established.	Interiors of Fortune, Cockpit, Salisbury theatres destroyed.		
1653	Cromwell expels Parliament and establishes Protectorate.			George Jolly's English actors in Germany.
1656		Davenant's *Seige of Rhodes.*		

(Continued on page 256)

Date	English History	English Theatre History	World History	World Theatre History
1658	Death of Cromwell.	Davenant stages performances at the Cockpit.		Molière arrives in Paris.
1660	Charles II returns. Monarchy re-established.	Davenant and Killigrew granted theatre patents, establishment of theatre monopoly. First professional actresses appear on English stage.		
1663		Opening of Theatre Royal.	Turks declare war on Holy Roman Empire.	
1666	Great London Fire.		France and England at war.	Molière's Le Misanthrope.
1668		Death of Davenant. Elizabeth Barry begins career.		Death of Molière.
1674		Drury Lane Theatre opened.		
1677		Dryden's All for Love.		Racine's Phèdre.
1680				Comédie Française founded.
1682		United Company established.	LaSalle claims Mississippi Valley for France.	
1685	Death of Charles II. James II crowned.			
1688	James II flees England. The "Glorious Revolution."		Beginning of the War of the League of Augsburg.	
1689	Beginning of reign of William and Mary.		France declares war on England. Peter the Great, Tsar of Russia.	

Date	English History	English Theatre History	World History	World Theatre History
1690	Battle of the Boyne, forces of ex-king James II defeated.			
1695		Betterton and other actors leave the United Company to form their own company.		
1700	Succession of English throne to be passed to Elector of Hanover, future George I.	Congreve's *The Way of the World*.		

SELECTED READINGS

Avery, Emmett L., and Arthur H. Scouten. *The London Stage, 1660–1700: A Critical Introduction*. Carbondale: Southern Illinois University Press, 1968.
  This is a reprinting of the critical introduction to the respective volumes of the eleven-volume work.

Barroll, J. Leeds, Alexander Leggatt, Richard Hosley, and Alvin Kernan. *The Revels History of Drama in English*. Vol. 3, 1576–1613. London: Methuen, 1975.
  A good introduction to the late Elizabethan period, although the section on the plays and playwrights is, unfortunately, weakened by its stylish approach to the subject. The bibliography includes an excellent brief section on Shakespeare.

Bentley, G. E. *The Jacobean and Caroline Stage*. 7 vols. Oxford: Oxford University Press, 1941–1968.
  The major sourcebook for information relating to the plays, playwrights, acting companies, and playhouses of the period.

Bevington, David. *Tudor Drama and Politics: A Critical Approach to Topical Meaning*. Cambridge, Mass.: Harvard University Press, 1968.
  An exhaustive study of the political elements in plays of the Tudor period, from Henry VII to the death of Elizabeth.

Boas, Frederick S. *An Introduction to Tudor Drama*. Oxford: Oxford University Press, 1933. *An Introduction to Stuart Drama*. Oxford: Oxford University Press, 1946.
  These two works provide an excellent starting point for a more detailed study of the major playwrights.

Bradbrook, M. C. *The Rise of the Common Player*. Cambridge, Mass.: Harvard University Press, 1962.
  This work traces the development of acting as a profession and discusses the actor's changing social standing.

Campbell, Lily Bess. *Scenes and Machines on the English Stage during the Renaissance*. Cambridge: Cambridge University Press, 1923; New York: Barnes and Noble, 1960.
  A near-classic work on the evolution of staging during the English Renaissance. Detailed and well documented.

Chambers, E. K. *The Elizabethan Stage*. 4 vols. Oxford: Oxford University Press, 1923.
  This work is considered the standard reference source on theatrical matters for the Elizabethan era. Some of the scholarship has been called into question since its publication, but it remains a highly valuable guide.

Edwards, Philip, G. E. Bentley, Kathleen McLuskie, and Lois Potter. *The Revels History of Drama in English*. Vol. 4, 1613–1660. London: Methuen, 1981.
  An outstanding one-volume introduction to the Jacobean and Caroline stage.

Gurr, Andrew. *The Shakespearean Stage 1574–1642*. Cambridge: Cambridge University Press, 1970.

An extremely well-documented, detailed, and readable work on the staging and theatrical organization of the English Renaissance theatre.

Hotson, Leslie. *The Commonwealth and Restoration Stage*. Cambridge, Mass.: Harvard University Press, 1928.
This work still remains the major source of information on theatrical activities during the Commonwealth, and it contains highly detailed information on the acting companies of the Restoration.

Joseph, Bertram. *Elizabethan Acting*. London: Oxford University Press, 1964.
One of the few detailed theoretical analyses of acting in pre-Restoration England.

Loftis, John, Richard Southern, Marion Jones, and A. H. Scouten. *The Revels History of Drama in English*. Vol. 5, 1660–1750. London: Methuen, 1976.
An excellent one-volume treatment that touches on all aspects and includes an excellent bibliography.

McAfee, Helen F., ed. *Pepys on the Restoration Stage*. New York: B. Blom, 1964.
During the first nine years of the Restoration, Samuel Pepys made a point of attending the theatre as often as he could. His observations, recorded in his diary, are a primary source of information on the Restoration stage. They are also delightfully amusing to read. This work is a selection from the diaries on things theatrical.

Southern, Richard. *Changeable Scenery: Its Origins and Development in the British Theatre*. London: Faber & Faber, 1952.
The standard work on the development of scenery and scenic devices in England during the seventeenth and eighteenth centuries.

Wickham, Glynne. *Early English Stages 1300–1600*. 2 vols. New York: Columbia University Press, 1959 and 1962.
One of the most detailed examinations of the development of drama and staging in England during the Middle Ages and the Renaissance.

Wilson, Frank P. *The English Drama 1485–1585*. New York: Oxford University Press, 1969.
Although the emphasis here is on drama as literature, this work is an excellent account of early Tudor drama with particular attention paid to the political and religious aspects.

Wright, Louis B. *Middle-Class Culture in Elizabethan England*. Chapel Hill: University of North Carolina Press, 1935.
This work investigates all aspects of middle-class society of the period, includes a chapter on drama, and provides considerable insight into attitudes of theatre audiences.

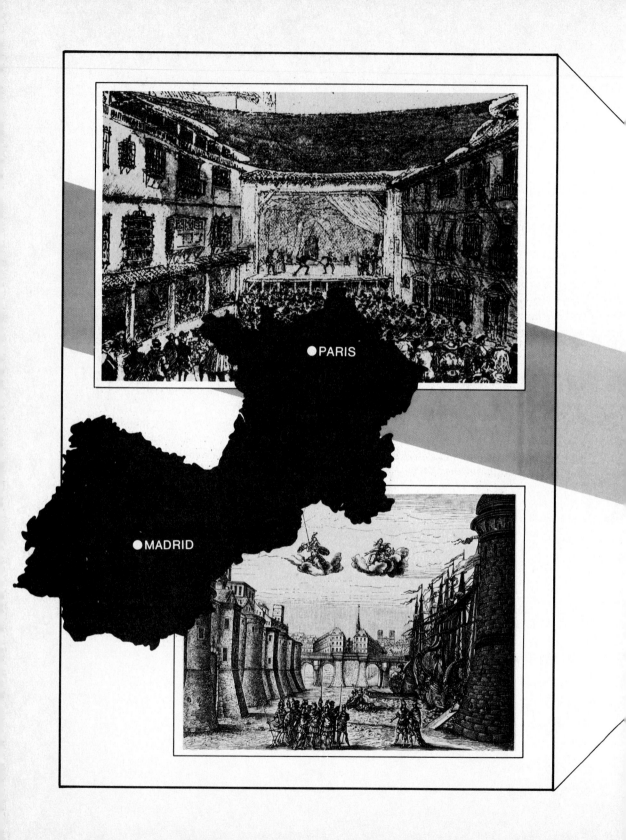

PARIS

MADRID

PART VII

Reflections of Honor and Glory: SPAIN AND FRANCE BEFORE THE EIGHTEENTH CENTURY

The first two areas of Europe to develop into powerful national entities were Spain and France. By the middle of the sixteenth century, Spain had rapidly risen to a position of dominance on the Continent. When Philip II began his reign in 1556, Spain controlled large sections of Italy, the Netherlands, parts of France, the Philippines, parts of North and South America, and all of Central America. The nation had a large, efficient army and navy, huge amounts of silver and gold from the Americas, and a royal court whose splendor dazzled all visitors. In less than 150 years Spain and its empire were in ruin and decay, helpless against destroying forces inside and outside the country.

France moved into the power position left in Europe by the collapse of Spain. The France of Louis XIV, who reigned from 1643 to 1715, set the social, cultural, and political standards for Europe during the second half of the seventeenth century. Such a collection of artists, authors, and architects at one court had not occurred since the reign of Augustus Caesar. This period in French history is considered by many historians the apex of modern European civilization.

Both Spain and France developed national theatres during the sixteenth and seventeenth centuries that radiated their glory and power. The contributions of these national theatres are now part of the cultural heritage of world civilization.

13

THE SPANISH THEATRE OF THE GOLDEN AGE (1500–1700)

The theatre of the Golden Age is unique in European theatre because Spain is unique among the nations of Europe. At the end of the fifteenth century the area of Spain occupied by the Moors in the eighth century was finally reconquered. In the same year the Moors were defeated, 1492, Spain began the exploration, conquest, and exploitation of vast areas of the Americas. By the middle of the sixteenth century, when other nations in Europe were attempting to survive the disunity of religious strife and warfare, Spain had an empire spread over the world. The pride, wealth, and economic disasters brought about by this empire combined with strong feudal traditions to create a society unlike any other in Europe. The Spanish theatre of the sixteenth and seventeenth centuries reflects this fantastic mixture of pride and piety, honor and horror, stateliness and squalor. It was a national theatre so outstanding in its vitality and originality that it is called the *Siglo de Oro*, the Golden Age.

SPANISH DRAMA OF THE GOLDEN AGE

Forms of the Spanish Drama

The *comedia* and the *auto sacramental* are the two major dramatic forms of sixteenth- and seventeenth-century Spain. The *comedia* is unique to Spain, a dramatic form that may be tragic, comic, tragicomic, or any combination. All plays are *comedias* and no distinction is made as to comedy or tragedy. Although the first Spanish *comedias* were written in 1517, they did not achieve their final form until after 1580. The *comedia* has three acts and is in verse. The verse is generally in an eight-syllable line, a short meter that tends to increase pace. This is important because the *comedias* are primarily plays of action and theme, not characterization. The major themes of the *comedias* are honor, love, and religion.

Spanish society and drama of the Golden Age were driven by a nearly fanatical code of honor. Governing all relationships, the concept of personal honor was of foremost importance. If one's honor came into conflict with the demands of love or religion, honor must be defended at all costs. Yet the code was a social one, and the public knowledge of a loss of honor was considered worse than the affront itself. Such a rigid social code presented tremendous dramatic possibilities, so it is no wonder that aspects of honor figure prominently in most *comedias*. The *comedias* are highly reflective of their society and were written with acceptable social standards always in mind. They support the class structure, the Church, marriage, and the monarchy. They consistently reject and condemn forms of rebellion against conventionality. Since the *comedias* were highly popular with all levels of society in Spain, they were a powerful influence in reinforcing and maintaining the status quo in Spanish society.

The *auto sacramental* as a dramatic form grew out of the medieval Corpus Christi pageants. As a one-act allegorical play, the *auto* came into being in the sixteenth century and continued to be performed in Spain until late into the eighteenth century. The subject range of the *autos* could be religious, historic, or legendary, but the plays always concluded with a discovery and display of the Eucharist. The greatest period of creativity for the writing of *autos* was from 1650 to 1680.

Autos were performed outside on movable carts (*carros*). Three carts in a row were used for the *auto*. The two end carts were towerlike structures that housed stage machinery for the production. All three carts were pulled into alignment with a temporary stage. This arrangement allowed the *autos* far greater opportunity for visual effects than was available in the *corrales*, the open-air public theatres. *Auto sacramentales* were considered staged theology, sermons in verse, and they neatly captured the religious intensity that is so much a part of the Golden Age.

EARLY SPANISH PLAYS

Although there was considerable contact between Spain and Italy in the early sixteenth century, the classically inspired efforts of the Italian humanists did not take root in Spain as they did in France. As in England, the Spanish drama grew out of medieval traditions. The tenets of neoclassicism were known and discussed in Spain during the Golden Age, but they never had a significant influence on the Spanish theatre before 1700.

Juan del Encina

The first Spanish playwright to show the influences of the Renaissance was Juan del Encina (c. 1469–c. 1530), who is traditionally called the father of Spanish drama. Encina's early plays, called *églogas*, were short pastorals performed at the court of the Duke of Alba in the 1490s. Although pastorals, these little plays were medieval in character and showed no Italian influence. The Italian touch is noticeable in Encina's work after he arrived in Rome in 1499 to serve the Spanish pope, Alexander VI. The three eclogues written by him while in Rome contain classical conventions, pagan gods, and a strong flavor of the Italian Renaissance. The plays have dramatic tension, and the characters are carefully individualized by different types of speech. For his peasants he invented a comic dialect called *sayagués* that became a convention of Spanish drama. Spanish drama had its beginnings in these pastorals written by Encina.

Torres Naharro

In 1517 the publication of *Propalladia* provided Spain with a collection of plays and its first major statement on dramatic theory. The collection was the work of Bartolomé de Torres Naharro (c. 1485–c. 1524), who spent much of his adult life as a member of the large Spanish colony in Rome. He divided his nine plays into *comedias a noticia* (plays of observation) and *comedias a fantasia* (plays of invention). These plays are the first *comedias* written with a sense of dramatic structure in terms of exposition, development, and climax. Torres Naharro was also the first Spanish playwright to attempt the use of contemporary customs to depict realistic characters on stage. Thus it is in his plays that the *pundonor*, the point of honor, first appears in the Spanish drama. His dramatic theories are heavily influenced by Horace and not important to the development of Spanish drama. But what is important is their illustration of a preconceived structural form for the Spanish stage and the concept of the *comedia a fantasia*. This concept was a break with the classical drama since it stressed a presentation of life with no attempt to interpret or explain. Through his plays Torres Naharro advanced Spanish drama and moved it away from the developing drama of Italy.

Gil Vicente

Acknowledged by many as the most gifted playwright in Europe before Shakespeare, Gil Vicente (c. 1465–c. 1536) was a member of the bilingual Royal Court of Portugal. Forty-four of his plays are extant: sixteen in Portuguese, eleven in Spanish, and seventeen in a mixture of the two languages. The plays fall into five groups: pastorals, moralities, farces, allegories, and romances. The pastorals were in the style of Encina, but the remainder of the plays show Vicente's experimenting with the development of new dramatic types out of existing medieval forms and court entertainments. Foremost of these plays is a trilogy of boat (*barca*) plays—*Auto da barca do inferno* (1517), *Auto da barca do purgatorio* (1518), *Auto da barca da gloria* (1519)—which depict boatloads of souls on the way to heaven, purgatory, or hell. These plays contain a good deal of social satire and observation on sixteenth-century life. Vicente's masterpiece is considered to be the *Auto da sibila Casandra* (Casandra the Sibyl, 1513), an outstanding Christmas play and one of the most humorous dramas of the Golden Age. Although somewhat geographically isolated at the Portuguese court, Vicente's mastery of stage technique, fine verse, outstanding use of language, and character study represented a significant contribution to the development of Spanish drama.

Lope de Rueda

The plays of Encina, Torres Naharro, and Vicente were written for private performance before the courts and households of their patrons. But the early sixteenth century saw the development of a commercial theatre in Spain, a public theatre that required the services of professional playwrights. The first major author of plays for the public theatres was Lope de Rueda (c. 1507–1565). Rueda was both a playwright and one of the first actor-managers (*autor de comedias*) in Spain, so his play-writing skills were employed to furnish material for his own company of actors. Since he was writing for a noncourt audience, there are elements of the careless and crude

Lope de Rueda.

along with the comic and colorful in his plays. Rueda's four extant plays are based on Italian models and have little merit. His major contribution to the Spanish stage was his *pasos*, short farces intended to be placed in the longer *comedias*. Of the more than forty *pasos* written by him, twenty-four have survived. As an actor, Rueda is said to have excelled in playing comic peasant characters in the *pasos*. He was in the vanguard of playwrights working for the public stage as theatres and acting companies began to appear throughout Spain. The rapid growth of the commercial theatre produced a flood of *comedias* to meet audience demands for new plays. By the 1590s the dramatic output in Spain exceeded that of the other European countries combined.

MAJOR PLAYWRIGHTS OF THE GOLDEN AGE

Lope de Vega

Lope de Vega Carpio (1562–1635), whose highly colorful life furnished him with much material for his *comedias*, is the most important playwright of the Golden Age and the most prolific author in the history of the theatre. During a career crowded with many love affairs, two marriages, imprisonments, military service, exile, and the priesthood, he managed to write over eight hundred plays, of which approximately half survive. Although this level of dramatic output is staggering to consider, it is small compared with the number attributed to him at the time of his death— eighteen hundred *comedias* and over four hundred *autos*. In addition to his works for the theatre, Lope also wrote a large amount of poetry, essays, and novels. Small wonder his contemporary, Miguel de Cervantes, called him *monstruo de naturaleza*, a prodigy of nature.

Such an enormous number of plays defies examination in a brief review of the Golden Age; what follows is an assessment of Lope's major contributions to the Spanish theatre. Simply put, his plays are the basis of a national theatre. Even if there were no other playwrights from the Golden Age, Spanish drama as represented by Lope's plays would still rival that of England and France. His theories on drama are found in *Arte nuevo de hacer comedias en este tiempo* (New Art of Playwriting in Modern Times, 1609), and they stress his belief that theatre should give pleasure and be true to life. His plays obviously gave a great deal of pleasure. Such was his fame with the public that a common expression to denote the excellence of anything was *"Es de Lope"* (It's a Lope).

Lope was primarily responsible for establishing the form for the *comedia*. He reduced the five-act form, did away with prologues, integrated *pasos*, songs, and dance interludes into the play's structure so as to heighten suspense by slowing down the naturally rapid development of the story. He strongly reinforced the metaphysical structure of the *comedia* through grounding his plays in a concept of natural harmony in human society, a harmony that reflected the Church's belief in the divine harmony of the universe. This view of

Lope de Vega.

natural harmony as divine harmony reflected is most important in such plays as *Fuente ovejuna* (The Sheep Well, c. 1618), *El mejor alcalde el Rey* (The King's Justice Is Best, c. 1621) and *Peribañez y el comendador de Ocaña* (Peribañez and the Commander of Ocaña, c. 1606).

Although Lope wrote some elaborate entertainments for the court and made contributions to the *auto* form at an early stage of its development, he will forever be remembered as the master dramatist of the *corrales*. In his *comedias* he captured the warmth, nobility, and basic integrity of Spanish culture. To see or read these *comedias* is to partake of life in Spain in the Golden Age.

Having consolidated the form of the *comedia* and made it extremely popular through his writings, Lope indirectly spawned an entire generation of playwrights. Most of them were hacks who produced plays vastly inferior to Lope's. Rising above the level of this dramatic fodder for the ever-demanding *corrales* was the work of Luis Vélez de Guevara (1579–1644) and Juan Ruiz de Alarcón y Mendoza (c. 1581–1639), who was also the first significant playwright to be born in the Americas. But by far the most important of the disciples of Lope de Vega was Tirso de Molina.

Tirso de Molina

Gabriel Téllez (c. 1581–1648), a friar in the Order of Mercy, wrote approximately four hundred plays under the pen name of Tirso de Molina. Of this large number of plays from Tirso, second only to Lope in productivity, a questionable eighty-six survive. A brilliant playwright, he served as a bridge between the spontaneity of Lope and the complexity of Calderón. In the development of the Spanish drama, his importance is only slightly less than that of Lope or Calderón.

Tirso constructed his plays with more care than Lope, and he began the movement toward featuring a central character in the *comedia* rather than a group of characters of equal importance. His plays are more witty, sensual, and satiric than Lope's, and these elements caused him to fall into disfavor with both the government and his religious order. He must also be given credit for the increased emphasis he placed on female characters, characters who were fully prepared to take a very active role in their male-dominated society. Such strong characters clearly illustrate Tirso's interest in the psychological aspects of his plays.

Tirso is best known as the author of two masterpieces of the Spanish theatre, *El burlador de Sevilla* (The Rogue of Seville, c. 1625) and *El condenado por*

Gabriel Téllez (Tirso de Molina).

desconfiado (The Man Damned for Lack of Faith, c. 1624). *El burlado*, the first major theatrical treatment of the legend of Don Juan, and *El condenado* are profoundly moral plays that focus on such topics as free will, evil, repentance, and divine mercy. These plays take abstract theological issues and transform them into exciting theatre that comments on the human condition. They also point out a significant difference between Lope and Tirso. In Lope there is a note of balance at the end of his plays, a sense that the harmony of society has been reestablished and will prevail. With Tirso there is a strong feeling of disharmony, of a culture out of balance and in danger of damnation for lack of faith. This difference reflects Spanish society at a time when it was trying to adjust to its increasingly minor role in European affairs.

Calderón de la Barca

The last major playwright of the Spanish Golden Age was Pedro Calderón de la Barca (1600–1681), the author of over one hundred *comedias* and seventy *autos*. He was the official court playwright of Philip IV and wrote most of his *comedias* for the Coliseo, the royal theatre. His most famous *autos*—and he was the master of this dramatic form—were written after his ordination into the priesthood in 1651.

Calderón.

The *comedias* of Calderón are distinguished from those of Lope de Vega by the obvious care that was taken in their composition. They are characterized by their literary artificiality, striking imagery, and high intellectual level. Although he utilized many of the same themes as Lope, Calderón is much more didactic in his *comedia*. The rhetorical nature of these plays produced a slower pace, and the long monologues are reminiscent of the later neoclassical French theatre. In Calderón is rarely found the realistic touches of Tirso or the common characters of Lope. The *comedias* of Calderón were the most formal and aristocratic written in the Golden Age.

His finest religious play is *El mágico prodigioso* (The Prodigious Magician, 1637), a *Faust*-like story in which the Devil is unable to fulfill his part of a bargain. His two best-known plays outside Spain are *La vida es sueño* (Life Is a Dream, 1635) and *El alcalde de Zalamea* (The Mayor of Zalamea, c. 1640). *La vida*, which he wrote first as a *comedia* and later reworked as an *auto*, is a play of regeneration, of human progress from disillusionment to enlightenment. *El alcalde*, an honor play in the tradition of Lope's *Peribañez*, is remarkable for the richness of its characterizations and its view on the traditional code of honor.

From 1649 until his death, Calderón wrote most of the *autos* performed in Madrid at the Feast of Corpus Christi. His two best-known *autos* are *El gran teatro del mundo* (The Great Theatre of the World, 1649) and *La vida es sueño* (1673). The didactic approach he used in his *comedias* was ideal for *autos*, and his fondness for imagery fitted perfectly with this highly allegorical form. The *autos* of Calderón continued to be produced in Spain until late in the eighteenth century.

Of the playwrights of the Golden Age, Calderón had the greatest influence outside of Spain. Several of his plays were translated and staged in France and England in the late seventeenth century, but he and the entire *Siglo de Oro* era of the theatre were forgotten in Spain and Europe during the next century. With the nineteenth century would come a rediscovery of this glorious period.

ACTORS AND ACTING
OF THE GOLDEN AGE

In addition to the contributions of the authors of Spanish Renaissance plays, actors captured the fancies of Golden Age audiences. It was a phenomenal period for actors and the art of acting. The names of over two thousand are known, and although their social status was not terribly high, their average annual income was above that of the common worker. Because of the close link between the Church and the theatre, there was greater religious and civil tolerance for the profession and its participants than existed in either England or France. In the Spanish Golden Age, it was possible to go about the job of acting without the fear that someone was going to run you out of town, or worse.

Acting Style

Little is known about the acting style of the Golden Age, but the demands of the plays and the physical elements of the stage provide the bases for fairly accurate speculation. Most likely, acting was rooted in the athletic, rapid physical delivery of the *comedia* and demanded a musical approach to the vocal expression. Pure, clean tone in singing and speaking was desired, and the integration of vocal and physical action needed to be vivacious. Only the plays of Calderón and his followers suggest a style bearing a resemblance to the staid, poised, deliberate acting style of classical tragedy.

A consideration of the standard bill of fare for the public theatres gives a sense of the acting style demanded. An afternoon's entertainment opened with the musicians, often assisted by singing and dancing actors. The *loa* (prologue) followed this musical opening, the audience was complimented, and the actors outlined the story of the *comedia* to be presented. Next the various *jornadas* (acts or episodes) were presented, and between each came one of the *pasos* or *entremeses* (brief farce interludes) that heavily depended upon broad acting to hold audience interest. After the final *jornada*, a *fin de festa* was performed, a lively dance that concluded the afternoon's activities. With so much reliance on dance, singing, and movement, the predominant style of acting in Renaissance Spain was no doubt very active.

Actors

With so many actors active in the theatre of the Golden Age, only a small sampling can be covered here—a coverage that is at best superficial, since so little is known concerning individual performers. Probably the finest actor in the Golden Age was Damien Arias de Penafiel (fl. 1617–1643). He possessed the attributes of a clear, resonant voice and a lively physical delivery that attracted much audience attention. The most famous actress of her time was Jusepa Vaca (fl. 1602–1634). No doubt she had a style and attributes like Arias's, but because of society's preconceived notions about actresses and government regulations limiting their performance possibilities, less is known about her. Cosme Perez (c. 1585–1673) was considered the outstanding comic actor of the Golden Age, and it is likely that his style was the most similar to that of the *commedia* actor of Italy.

Company Organization and Regulation

As the seventeenth century developed, most major cities had at least one company of professional actors, generally assigned on the basis of one company per theatre. Small population centers and those without permanent theatres got their professional entertainment from touring companies. When a company toured, an allowance was provided to actors for food, lodging, and distance in addition to the regular compensation.

Unlike the companies of England and France, where a mix existed in each company between share and salaried members, Spain's usual practice was to keep the membership to a single type depending upon the company. Thus, two types of companies existed: one was the *companias de parte* (share member troupes), and the other consisted of salaried members working for an *auto de comedias* (actor-manager). Company size varied considerably. Most sixteenth- and seventeenth-century Spanish plays require at least eight players, assuming the usual doubling of roles. Before 1610 the average company size was somewhere between eight and sixteen. Later in the seventeenth century the upper limit rose to about twenty members in the larger companies, which performed a general repertory in excess of sixty plays. Members of both sexes were in the troupes, women having been first licensed to appear on the stage in 1587. In most companies men slightly outnumbered women, consistent with the character demands of most plays. Each company included at least a leading man and leading lady, known as the *primer galan* and the *primera dama*. In addition to these there were at least two *graciosos* (comedians) and two *barbas* (older character actors). Apprentices were used in minor roles as needed.

The process of presenting a play involved political elements. In order to license a play for production, the *autor de comedias* was required, sometimes in conjunction with the *arrendadores* (the lessees who ran the theatres), to present a special performance for religious and civic officials. If no censorship problems stemmed from the performance, and with the understanding that the company might be called at any time for a court performance of the play, it was licensed. Each play was licensed to a specific company wishing to perform it; the license did not imply that the company had received performance permission in perpetuity. It was further understood that a portion of the admission prices was to go to charity, with both the *arrendador* and the *autor* making contributions from their separate admission incomes. These contributions assisted in the general acceptance of the theatre by both Church and Crown.

Politics also affected the actors directly. Regulations governing women on the stage were particularly harsh. By 1600 the royal council had decreed that actresses could only appear on stage if male family members were in their companies, and that they could not appear in male dress. Another costuming restriction came in 1653, when actresses were forbidden to wear certain types of clothing considered risqué, including hoop skirts and dresses shorter than floor length.

As in England and France, the Spanish actor had considerable professional expenses against what was generally good income. Costume costs were the responsibility of the actor, although some received an allowance to help with this expense. With a developed taste for elaborate costuming, Spanish audiences demanded brilliant costuming during the Golden Age. An actor could spend 25 percent of all income for stage dress, an expense freely borne since onstage success partially depended on it. Share members had the normal expenses associated with that type of membership, and the daily receipts were divided after these were deducted. Salaried company members were paid the contractual amount for each performance on the same daily basis.

The theatrical season was roughly tied to the liturgical calendar. Companies were formed during Lent, performances began at Easter, and the season lasted until the following Lent. Breaks in the season occurred during the summer, for state occasions, health emergencies, and war periods. Following the tradition of the Middle Ages, performances were allowed only on religious holidays and Sundays until the 1580s, when weekday performances were permitted. During the seventeenth century performances were held every day of the week except Saturday. Performances began in the early afternoon, usually around two or three o'clock. Failure to end the performance before dusk resulted in a heavy fine assessed to the company. The bill was changed every two to three days depending upon public acceptance as seen through continued good admissions, and a long run before 1700 was no more than a week.

The social station and professional standing of acting received a major boost when, in 1631, actors were allowed to form a trade guild. Known as the Cofradía de la Novena, it served as the clearinghouse for most theatrical employment in the seventeenth century, with actors traveling to Madrid to secure acting assignments even in the provinces. The Cofradía still operates and serves as a major union for all theatrical positions.

THE PLAYHOUSE OF THE GOLDEN AGE

During the last twenty years of the sixteenth century, Spain established theatres in major population and cultural centers. The *corrales* (municipal public courtyard theatres) appeared as unique theatrical forms built for unique purposes and gradually increased in number, quality, and equipment for performer and audience throughout the period before 1700. The open-air playhouses established at this time were to remain the principal playhouses of Spain until the middle of the eighteenth century, when they began to be replaced with enclosed theatres based on Italian design.

Origins of the Corral

In 1565 a charitable organization was formed known as the Cofradía de la Pasión y Sangre de Jesucristo. Its mission was to care for the poor, and its primary means of doing so was to run a hospital. In order to raise funds for the hospital, the city of Madrid granted the Pasión y Sangre permission to sponsor the production of plays in the courtyards of its own property. The yards are technically known as *corrales*, but the term is commonly applied to the theatre structures erected there. So successful was this venture that the society leased other yards throughout Madrid and sponsored productions in them. But the Pasión y Sangre was not the only society so operating. The Cofradía de la Soledad de Nuestra Señora had also been sponsoring plays for charitable purposes, and in 1574 the two organizations, working with the city, agreed to share the profits from all performances. Thus combined the societies worked with a *commedia dell'arte* troupe in the city, led by Alberto Ganassa, to build a stage and audience seating in the Corral

Spain and France Before the Eighteenth Century

de la Pacheca, which had held temporary facilities for staging plays. Soon others were built. In 1579 the Corral de la Cruz was built, and shortly thereafter, in 1583, the Corral del Príncipe was erected. These two permanent theatres replaced the Corral de la Pacheca, and they remained the municipal public theatres of Madrid throughout the seventeenth century.

Basic Concepts and Parts of the Corrales

The size and shape of a *corral* was dictated by the dimensions of the courtyard in which it was built. Since most courtyards were open rectangular areas between rows of houses, the *corrales* were similarly shaped and open to the elements. Only parts of the stage and some of the side and back seating were covered, usually with an awning or a simple tiled roof. Consistent with other European outdoor theatres, there was no proscenium arch or front curtain.

Although no two *corrales* were exactly the same, their basic parts were quite similar. Central to all of them was the *patio* (the yard floor or pit), a benchless open area immediately in front of the stage where the *mosqueteros* (male commoners) had to stand. Around the *patio* were the *gradas* (tiered platforms), set at two levels along the courtyard sides. These were primarily used by the middle classes and were supplied with *bancos* (benches) for audience seating. *Aposentos* (boxes) were erected above the *gradas*, on an upper gallery that surrounded all sides of the *corral* at that level. The *aposentos* were formed

A nineteenth-century reconstruction of the Corral del Príncipe.

essentially by the exterior walls and windows of the rows of houses, and in many cases, entrance to them was through the houses against which they rested. At the back of the *corral* was the *alojería*, or *frutería* (the *corral* bar), from which food and drink were served during the performances, and above it was the *cazuela* (stewpot), a gallery especially reserved for women, who were, by common practice and lease agreement, generally segregated from the men of the *patio*. Above the *cazuela* was a gallery for city officials, and above that the *terlulia*, a separate gallery for the clergy.

Some of the form of the *corrales* came directly from the common theatrical business practice of the time. There were two main entrances at the back of the *corral*, usually to either side of the *alojería*, segregated according to sex. At each entrance two admission collectors were present, one to receive the regular admission to the theatre and the other to receive the charitable contribution for the Cofradías. Inside, an additional admission was charged for the *grada* and *aposento* areas. Some owners of the houses backing the *aposentos* leased these boxes by the year to a single set of patrons.

The Corral Stage

At the front end of the *corral* was a stage. It was a large wooden platform divided into three areas: an apron extension into the *patio* used for the acting; a midstage area used for special effects and some acting; and the *foro*, or backstage area, separated from the midstage by a curtain. The *foro* was the main area for scenic display and for scenes of "discovery." In addition to these areas, the stage facade included the *aposentos* of the gallery above the stage proper, with ramps and ladders from the stage floor to these auxiliary playing areas. To either side of the *foro* were curtained doorways to the offstage *vertuarios* (actor dressing rooms), from which actors made their entrances. The basic platform in most large city *corrales* was twenty-five to thirty feet wide and twenty-five to twenty-nine feet deep, with the apron extending about five feet into the *patio*. The height above the *patio* floor on the stage platform can only be estimated, but given the extensive use of understage space for special effects, something on the order of five to six feet must have been common. Directions in the plays indicate that much of the midstage and the *foro* was trapped for access to the understage area, given the special effects required. Action could occur on several levels of the stage, thus creating a production style similar to that of Elizabethan England.

Scenery and Stage Machinery

Like the general staging, the scenery of the *corrales* was similar to that of Elizabethan England. An actor's word or action could establish locale. If the curtain between the *foro* and the midstage did not serve as the backdrop for a scene, and it often did, then it was opened to reveal another scenic drop, usually a generalized landscape garden or a city street complete with windows and doors. The roof area was equipped with machinery for flying effects and actors to the stage, consistent with Italian practice.

Although the practice of painted scenery increased after the middle of the seventeenth century, full illusionistic perspective painting was never a major factor in *corral* scenery.

Costume Practice

In costuming there was no attempt at historical accuracy, but some attention was paid to certain types, particularly classic characters and Eastern types. These were costumed in stereotypical dress, consistent with preconceived notions about the country and period. The face was costumed mostly by masks, similar to the partial face masks of the *commedia dell'arte*. Although these masks had been used in the Spanish medieval theatre, they continued as standard practice into the seventeenth century.

Court Performances

Spain did not have formal court acting companies. Whenever theatrical entertainments were desired at court, the professional companies were hired. Indeed, the players were virtually ordered to perform, although there was more than adequate compensation. These theatrical events were done in fairly simple palace theatres, not much more elaborately than medieval banquet hall staging in earlier centuries.

Court entertainments reached their zenith under Philip IV (reigned 1621–1665). Not only were there more court performances during his reign than ever before, but he also fostered an increasing awareness of Italian illusionistic scenery. He imported the Italian designer Cosme Lotti (?–1643) to stage most plays at court. In 1633 Lotti was instrumental in making the new Buen Retiro palace the primary place for court entertainments. In 1640 Lotti built the Coliseo, a permanent form of the *corral*, albeit with proscenium arch, in the Buen Retiro and staged a combination of plays from the public theatres along with a number of theatrical works that required full Italian scenery, machinery, and special effects. The Coliseo was equipped for flat wing scenery, operating in grooves. In addition, Lotti staged many productions on the palace grounds. The staging was elaborate; for Calderón's *El major encanta amor* (The Witchcraft of Love, 1635), he built a stage on the lake in Retiro Park. His outdoor productions included masques and tournaments using multiple stages and massive special effects. His death in 1643 brought to an end the most active period of court theatricals.

After a brief respite, court theatricals resumed. In 1652 Italian designer Baccio del Bianco staged entertainments in the full illusionistic manner of his country. Following Philip's death in 1665, Spain's first native scene designer, Jose Caudi, staged court entertainments until the death of Carlos II in 1700. After that the court theatre, which had been partially responsible for the decline of public entertainments by siphoning off its talent, found itself in rapid decline.

DECLINE OF THE SPANISH THEATRE

By the 1630s the center of Spanish theatre production and play writing was Madrid. There was located the court theatre, which set the standard for the country, there the playwrights lived, the plays were published, and the actors' guild had its headquarters. The fortunes of the Spanish theatre were by this time wedded to the fortunes of the capital and the country. By the middle of the seventeenth century, Madrid was a center of misfortune.

As Spain's prestige and power fell in the theatre of world politics, so its dramatic theatre began to lose its vigor and spontaneity. Written for performance in the *corrales*, the great plays of the Golden Age projected the vitality of the Spanish spirit. These plays revealed a strong trust in God's ultimate mercy but also proudly proclaimed a willingness to dare. By midcentury the court theatre was rapidly retreating into a world of fantasy, placing great emphasis on big spectacles as if to hide from the political realities of a ruined empire. In 1700 Philip V, the grandson of Louis XIV of France, was named heir to the Spanish throne following the death of the childless Carlos II. After the turmoil of the War of the Spanish Succession, which saw once-mighty Spain helpless before invading armies, the Spanish theatre of the eighteenth century became a poor imitation of the French theatre. The glorious theatre of the Golden Age, so unlike the neoclassical theatre of the eighteenth century, would remain forgotten for over a hundred years.

14
THE FRENCH
THEATRE BEFORE
1700

Medieval theatrical traditions remained strong in France until near the middle of the sixteenth century. La Confrérie de la Passion, the society of amateur actors licensed in 1402 to present mystery plays in Paris, was still offering medieval plays in the 1540s. The humanistic reforms of the Italian Renaissance were slow to take root in France because of the political instability that plagued the country throughout most of the sixteenth century. Francis I, who reigned from 1515 to 1547, made an effort to introduce and patronize the new humanistic arts, but most of his energies were expended in a costly and bloody rivalry with his fellow ruler, Charles V, King of Spain and Holy Roman Emperor. From 1559 until 1589, France was ruled by four kings and was beset with religious wars. The country was more the subject of a tragedy than the place for its development.

FRENCH DRAMA OF THE SIXTEENTH CENTURY

The first concentrated attempts to move French theatre out of its medieval forms came from the efforts of a group of poets collectively called the Pléiade. The poets of the Pléiade sought to establish a new French literature based on Greek, Roman, and Italian models. Joachim du Bellay, an early spokesman for the group, called on French poets to write tragedies and comedies instead of farces and moralities. In 1549 Pierre de Ronsard, the finest poet of the Pléiade, translated and had performed Aristophanes' *Plutus*. But the honors for writing the first comedy and tragedy of the French Renaissance belong to another member of the Pléiade, Etienne Jodelle (1532–1573).

Etienne Jodelle

Jodelle's only tragedy, *Cléopâtre captive*, and comedy, *Eugène*, were both performed in 1552. *Cléopâtre*, played before Henri II

Etienne Jodelle.

and his court, is a five-act play concerning the fate of Cleopatra after the death of Mark Antony. It is closely modeled on Seneca and focuses on the misery of the heroine. Although there is a confrontation in the third act between Cleopatra and Octavian, this first French tragedy lacks the conflict of wills and the mental anguish that are to be the hallmarks of later French tragedy. Jodelle's comedy, *Eugène*, is little more than a medieval farce in classical dress, although it is an advance over the medieval form in that it is a complete play rather than a single scene. These plays represent the early efforts of a young playwright working at new dramatic forms in French. Yet because of his vanity, court intrigue, and the harsh realities of sixteenth-century France, Jodelle made no other contributions to the development of French drama.

Robert Garnier

Following the success of Jodelle's plays, several new playwrights tried their skill at creating plays in the new classical style. Jacques Grévin was the author of two comedies and a tragedy, *La Mort de Cesar* (The Death of Caesar, 1560), which contains touches of the glorious rhetorical style found in the plays of Corneille in the next century. Jean de la Taille's *Saul le Furieux* (Saul the Impetuous, 1562) is remarkable for the unsubdued spirit of the hero as he struggles against the will of God. When this play appeared in

Robert Garnier.

print in 1572, it was prefaced by a treatise on tragedy, *De l'art de la tragedie* (On the Art of Tragedy), the first commentary by a French playwright on the neoclassical unities. Yet the plays of Grévin, Taille, and other playwrights of the sixteenth century are overshadowed by the work of Robert Garnier (1535–1590).

The author of seven tragedies, Garnier is the most original and important of the playwrights of the early French Renaissance. His first play, *Porcie* (1568), is strongly Senecan in structure and no major improvement over Jodelle. *Hippolyte* (1573), his second play, shows increased skills in character development. *Les Juives* (The Jews, 1580), considered his best play, is a biblical tragedy with considerable pathos and dramatic force. Garnier was a gifted poet whose plays have style, lyrical power, and individualized characters. A collected edition of his plays was first published in 1585 and went through over forty editions before 1619. Several of his plays were reworked by later French playwrights, and his *Cornélie* was translated into an English version by Thomas Kyd.

Dramatic Forms

By the end of the sixteenth century, tragedy, comedy, pastoral, and tragicomedy were all being written by those playwrights attempting to produce a national dramatic literature for France. Tragedy received the most attention, the best efforts being produced by Garnier. Comedy did not fare well in the French Renaissance. From the beginning French comedy of the sixteenth century was strongly influenced by the medieval farce, and this element remains noticeable in French comedy into the twentieth century.

Greek, Roman, and Italian models of comedy were available to French playwrights, but they seemed unable to write interesting imitations or create originals. An important inhibitor of the development of national comedy in France was the presence and great popularity of visiting *commedia dell'arte* companies from Italy. Thus it is not surprising that the best-known comic playwright of the period, Pierre de Larivey (c. 1540–1619), made his reputation from adaptations of Italian plays.

The first pastoral of the French Renaissance was *Les Ombres* (The Shadows) by Nicolas Filleul, which was presented before Charles IX in 1566. Translations of Spanish and Italian pastorals in the early 1580s created an interest in this dramatic form. Nicolas de Montreux wrote three pastorals between 1585 and 1597, but the true vogue for this type of play came during the first decade of the next century. The slowness of this form to gain popularity among the French nobles may in part have been due to the unstable conditions in the nation. No

A ballet at the Petit Bourbon, c. 1581.

doubt it was difficult for French nobles to pretend to be innocent shepherds in a peaceful land when they were so busy slaughtering each other in the religious wars of the period.

Tragicomedy was introduced into the French theatre with Garnier's *Brada-mante* (1582). Yet it was changing theatrical conditions in the last decade of the sixteenth and the first decade of the seventeenth century, along with the skills of Alexandre Hardy, that finally made tragicomedy popular on the French stage. Performance is necessary for the development of any significant drama, and production possibilities were difficult for new plays in the French Renaissance. This factor alone must be considered a major reason for the slow development of the French theatre.

The playwrights of this period had little knowledge of stage production, and few ever saw their plays performed in a theatre by professional actors. Theatres were virtually nonexistent in sixteenth-century France, and the few profession-al actors available were involved with the production of farces and mystery plays. Nor would they have understood what these playwrights were trying to present. The play scripts of the French Renaissance received their productions in the halls of academia and the homes of nobles. They were presented by amateurs to audiences eager to see a French classical play, no matter how badly written or performed. Such conditions were not conducive to the development of a strong national theatre.

FRENCH DRAMA, 1600–1630

The civil and religious conflicts that had plagued France for half a century were brought under control during the reign of Henri IV (1589–1610). Effecting a degree of religious tolerance with the Edict of Nantes (1598), and with it decreasing the possibilities of a renewal of the civil wars, Henri turned his attention and energies to rebuilding the economic and political structures of France. By the time of his assassination in 1610, Henri IV had returned France to a nearly stable condition. This stability was more or less maintained after 1610, and it presented a social and cultural climate far more favorable to the development of French theatre than had been available during the previous fifty years.

Alexandre Hardy

The first professional playwright of the French theatre was Alexandre Hardy (c. 1575–c. 1632), who may have written seven hundred plays in his career. Hardy, who only claimed six hundred plays, was for most of his professional life a *poète à gages*, an author hired by an acting company to write a fixed number of plays over a limited time period. These plays became the property of the company and could not be printed without the actors' permission, which was infrequently given. These conditions of employment explain both Hardy's high rate of composition and the small number of his plays, fewer than forty, that are extant.

Hardy was, to a large degree, a hack playwright whose place in theatre history rests primarily on the huge number of plays he wrote rather than on his significant contributions to French dramatic literature. But credit should be given to him for some advances over sixteenth-century dramaturgy. As a result of his connection with professional actors working before a paying public, Hardy developed a strong feeling for the theatrical, and he produced plays that were much more playable than anything written earlier for the stage. As a result, his plays were very popular during his lifetime. In tragedy he removed the chorus, increased the number of characters, and unified the action presented to the audience. Hardy established the popularity of tragicomedy on the French stage by introducing a romantic story line, characters from various social classes, some comedy, and a happy ending.

Hardy is the most important of the playwrights of France in the period before 1625. Although aware of the dramatic theories of neoclassicism, he used and abused the rules in his plays to make them successful with various classes of French society. He did a great service to the development of French theatre with his attempts to reconcile the demands of theatrical performance with theory and make theatre a popular art form.

Richelieu and French Theatre

Late in his career, Hardy was attacked by younger playwrights for his language, style, technique, and deviation from the rules of neoclassicism. The reason behind these attacks was a reform that was taking place in the French theatre. A major force behind this reform was Cardinal Richelieu. Armand-Jean de Plessis Cardinal Richelieu (1585–1642), son of the grand provost of France, was a bishop at twenty-two, chief minister and second most powerful man in France at thirty-nine, and one of Europe's greatest statesmen. He was also one of the great patrons of the theatre. France became the major political power on the Continent and French theatre entered its greatest era because of the policies of Richelieu.

Richelieu's chief form of relaxation from running France was to involve himself in things theatrical: he built theatres; encouraged, advised, and subsidized playwrights; wrote plays; had laws passed regulating production; and greatly influenced public taste. While making France into a great nation, he selected the theatre to reflect this new grandeur. This special treatment of the theatre was to continue after his death in the policies of Louis XIV.

Richelieu was much taken with the critical theories of neoclassicism, and he saw to it that the newly established Académie Française, the national French Academy he formed in 1634, was encouraged to support the neoclassical rules and oppose irregular literary innovations. The type of drama championed by Richelieu, promulgated by the Academy, and written by most of the playwrights of the period placed great stress on credibility (*vraisemblance*) and taste (*bienséance*) in the dramatic illusion to be presented on the stage.

Credibility and taste are achieved in French neoclassical drama through a highly rhetorical language. The primary focus of these plays was not so much the presentation of a story as the detailed illumination of a subject. In comparison with Elizabethan drama, physical action is minimal in seventeenth-century French plays. The emphasis is on mental action, on the characters thinking and reflecting their way through a situation. This rational approach to life situations found its intellectual center in the work of the French philosopher René Descartes (1596–1650), from whose famous dictum "*Cogito, ergo sum*" (I think, therefore I am) a new form of philosophical inquiry was launched. In the French theatre the *cogito* was joined with the neoclassical rules and, surrounded by some of the finest French poetry ever written, produced the greatest period of French dramatic literature.

FRENCH DRAMA OF
THE CLASSICAL PERIOD, 1630–1680

The drama of seventeenth-century France is dominated by a trio of playwrights of outstanding genius: Corneille, Molière, and Racine. The plays of these three writers receive most of the attention in discussions of this period, although there were other contemporary playwrights who were considered their rivals, if not their equals. The majority of these playwrights have now been forgotten, even in France. But it should be remembered that all playwrights of the period, from the greatest to the forgotten, found writing for the stage an inadequate way to earn a living. Fame, if any, was fleeting and fortune always seemed to escape their grasp. Hardy, for his vast output of plays, died in near-poverty, Corneille was always on the outlook for patrons, and Racine gave up writing for the stage to pursue a career at court. It would not be until the nineteenth century that a French playwright, even a highly popular one, would be able to find great financial rewards writing for the stage.

Pierre Corneille

Achieving considerable success and public attention with his first play, the comedy *Mélite* (1629), Pierre Corneille (1606–1684) was to write an additional thirty-one plays for the stage before his permanent retirement in 1674. In a professional life that stretched across most of the seventeenth century, Corneille became the first outstanding French playwright and the first to be appreciated outside of France. His theatrical career can be divided into three periods.

The first period of Corneille's career, from 1629 to 1635, was one of experimentation as the playwright, following the favorable reception of *Mélite*, wrote a tragedy, five comedies, and a tragicomedy. The early comedies are remarkable for their rejection of typical Renaissance comic types and their attempt to capture the society of seventeenth-century Paris. During this period Corneille was one of the *cinq auteurs* (five authors) selected by Cardinal Richelieu to write plays in collaboration. Several of the plays from this first

Pierre Corneille.

period show the growing skills of a fine dramatic talent, and the comedies did much to return this drama form to popular favor among more sophisticated audience members. Yet these plays were overshadowed by the power, popularity, and controversy of Corneille's next play.

Le Cid (1637) ushered in the second, and greatest, period in Corneille's career and is a milestone in the development of French drama. The play is the first masterpiece of the French theatre. Based on the Spanish play *Las Mocedades del Cid*, the play is a tragicomedy (as it was first titled by the author) of honor, duels, war, revenge, and love. Yet in shifting the focus from the outer world of action to the inner world of mental anguish, this tragedy (as it was later titled by its author) introduced a basic conflict of French drama, passion versus reason, and the resolution of this conflict through a dramatic assertion of will. The characters in a tragedy of Corneille are not helpless victims of fate. They are individuals who attempt to understand and then control their destinies. Beginning with Corneille and continuing into the present century, French tragedy places the dramatic emphasis on the need of characters to understand what befalls them.

The controversy that grew out of the production of *Le Cid* was a product of the vanity of its author and the jealousy of his rivals. Corneille's chief rivals in Paris were Jean Mairet and Georges de Scudéry. They and others were jealous of the play's success, and a few months after the first production of *Le Cid*, Corneille published a poem, "Excuse à Ariste," which pointed out that he owed his success only to himself and that he was second to no dramatist in France. Such arrogance could not go unanswered, and thus erupted the famous quarrel over *Le Cid*. The main points of the quarrel were that the play violated the "rules," that it was stolen from the Spanish, and that the subject matter was worthless. After charges and countercharges flew back and forth for a few months, Cardinal Richelieu, in an effort to clear the air, had the matter referred to the French Academy. The Academy's opinion was that the play did violate *vraisemblance* on several points. Corneille, his feelings hurt, withdrew from the theatre to reconsider his art.

He returned in three years, determined to please both the scholars and the shopkeepers, and in a short period produced four plays that established tragedy as the most popular dramatic form in seventeenth-century France. *Horace*, *Cinna*, *Polyeucte*, and *Pompée* show Corneille at the heights of his powers as a mature playwright. Nine plays later, in 1652, he experienced his first major failure with *Pertharite*. This play marked the end of the second period in Corneille's career, and after its production he retired from the stage for seven years.

Returning to the theatre in 1659 with a version of the Oedipus story, Corneille then produced ten more plays during the next fifteen years. While some of these scripts showed signs of the power of his middle period, a few were near-embarrassments, and two were complete failures. He was losing his hold on the audience of Paris, who were shifting their attention to a new, young writer of tragedies, Racine. In 1670 both wrote a tragedy on the same subject, and Corneille's was judged the much inferior. Following the dismal failure of *Suréna* in 1674, he withdrew forever from the French theatre.

Corneille wrote in an age when intellect and will power were in ascendence over passion and brute force. The forces of intellect and will are important elements in his plays, and his tragic heroes and heroines depict fine stylish grandeur and high ethical standards. His theatrical vision was of an ordered and rational society, yet is was heroic in a far truer sense than that of Dryden. The quality of the plays is uneven, going from the sublime to the shoddy, and Corneille was obviously uncomfortable working within the restrictions of the neoclassical form. Yet even while hampered by the highly structured bonds of neoclassicism, he soared to great dramatic heights. Corneille ranks as one of the world's great playwrights, and his best plays will continue to be performed as long as French is a living language.

Molière

Jean-Baptiste Poquelin (1622–1673), who will forever be remembered by his stage name, Molière, was to assume his father's position as royal upholsterer. As preparation for such a highly respected role in French society, young Poquelin received an excellent education at the Collège de Clermont. Yet at the age of twenty-one he gave up his secure place in society and became an actor. The French king lost an upholsterer, but the world gained Molière, one of the finest actors in the history of the French theatre and one of the greatest comic playwrights in the history of the world.

Molière's first theatrical venture, an acting company called Illustre Théâtre, had a very brief life in Paris before collapsing into bankruptcy. Reorganizing themselves, the actors set off for the provinces of France, where they performed and perfected their skills from 1645 to 1658. The experienced actors returned to Paris and, at the invitation of the brother of Louis XIV, performed before the young king and his court on October 24, 1658. The tragedy they offered was not well received, but the comic afterpiece, *Le Docteur amoureux* (The Amorous Doctor), greatly pleased the king. The short comedy had been written by Molière. With the support of Louis XIV, Molière and his company remained in Paris. The king granted them a theatre, the Petit Bourbon, which they shared with a *commedia dell'arte* troupe. During the next fifteen years, Molière would amuse, scandalize, and instruct the French court and the citizens of Paris.

Molière rapidly established his acting company in the esteem of Paris theatregoers and himself as the leading comic playwright in the country. Yet his sharp eye and wit won him enemies as well as admirers. The one-act *Les*

Two portraits of Molière.

Précieuses ridicules (The Affected Ladies, 1659) offended certain female members of the upper class because it mocked their affectations, and *Les Fâcheux* (The Bores, 1661) did the same for equally silly young men. But Molière found himself involved in his first major theatrical uproar with his *L'Ecole des femmes* (The School for Wives, 1662), which was attacked on literary and moral grounds. The quarrel over this play nearly equaled the literary battle over *Le Cid*. Molière defended himself in two plays, *La critique de L'École des Femmes* and *L'Impromptu de Versailles*, both written in 1663 and the latter commissioned by Louis XIV. These plays are literary criticism in dramatic form. They both presented Molière's views on the theatre and ridiculed his attackers. *L'Impromptu* is particularly enlightening to theatre students because of the information it provides on acting and actors at the Hôtel de Bourgogne.

In 1664 Molière presented his *Tartuffe* to the king during an entertainment at Versailles. With this play about a man deceived through hypocrisy, he found himself engaged in the greatest conflict of his professional life. Opposed to additional presentations of the play were arrayed some of the most powerful people of France. So strong was the opposition that the king prohibited any public performances. Molière had not intended to attack religion or religious zealots. The play contained some of the best characters he had yet created and was an excellent depiction of a seventeenth-century household in turmoil. But he had misjudged the religious temper of the time and the intense animosity of his enemies. It would take him four years to get the ban lifted from the play.

Molière's next effort, written in haste to replace the banned *Tartuffe*, was *Don Juan* (1665), which also got him in trouble because of the atheistic remarks of the title character. With *Le Misanthrope* (1666), he wrote his most cynical and brilliant comedy, one that constantly touches on the borders of tragedy. Intellectual skepticism abounds in this study of the totally honest man who calls into question the standards of contemporary society. Molière was to write fifteen more plays after *Le Misanthrope*, but never again was he to produce a work of such depth. The play is generally considered his masterpiece. On February 17, 1673, during the third performance of his last play, *Le Malade imaginaire* (The Would-Be Invalid), Molière suffered a severe hemorrhage while performing the title role. He finished the performance, but died later that day.

Louis XIV is said to have asked the literary critic Boileau whose work, of all the French playwrights of the era, had most graced his reign. Boileau is reported to have replied with no hesitation, "Molière." During his lifetime, Molière raised comedy to the level of tragedy on the French stage and showed that comedy was fully capable of exploring and exposing the human condition. In his presentation of characters he was a grand observer of the human condition. And the human condition, as Molière was so very aware, is the greatest comedy of all.

Racine

Early in this century an English critic remarked that the English had always loved Molière and detested Racine. Although "detest" is too strong a word, the plays of Racine remain a difficulty for the non-French because the cool, concise brilliance of the writing evaporates in translation. He is the most classical of the great trio of seventeenth-century French playwrights and the most inaccessible.

Jean Racine (1639–1699) wrote a total of twelve plays, all tragedies except for his only comedy, *Les Plaideurs* (The Litigants, 1668). His first play, *La Thébaïde* (The Theban, 1664), was produced by Molière and his company at the Palais Royal. Although this play was indifferently received, Molière encouraged the young playwright, befriended him, and agreed to stage his second play, *Alexandre* (1665). Racine, unhappy with Molière's production, took the play away from him and gave it to a rival company. To add injury to insult, he also persuaded one of Molière's leading actresses, Mlle du Parc, to leave and join the rival company. Molière never again spoke to his former friend.

Andromaque (1667), Racine's third play, established him as a major tragic playwright. Its tragic intensity, focused on the decisions of a single person, caused many of his contemporaries to liken Racine's dramatic skills to those of the great Corneille. In 1669 Racine openly challenged his older rival by writing a play set in ancient Rome, an exclusive territory of Corneille's. *Britannicus* (1669) clearly demonstrated Racine's structural skills and his ability to work comfortably within the neoclassical rules. Yet many found the play's retelling of the deeds of the emperor Nero *noire et horrible* (dark and shocking), and did not approve of its psychological approaches to evil.

With *Bérénice* (1670) Racine built a five-act tragedy around six words from the Roman historian Suetonius. The play is a technical marvel and a masterpiece of dramatic invention: void of violence, high in human interest, simple yet deeply emotional in its presentation. As the play was judged far superior to Corneille's on the same subject, Racine found himself proclaimed the greatest living tragic playwright. After writing three plays during the next four years—*Bajezet* (1672), *Mithridate* (1673), and *Iphigénie* (1674)—he brought his dramatic career to its culmination with *Phèdre* (1677). This play has been called the pinnacle of classicism because of its successful harmonizing of Greek, Christian, and French civilizations. The title role is perhaps the greatest part ever written for an actress.

Racine was a haughty and irritable man who made many enemies during his rapid rise to fame. An elaborate plot was conceived to destroy Racine by sabotaging the success of *Phèdre*. The Duchess de Bouillion commissioned another play on the same subject and purchased most of the seats for six nights at both theatres. While a highly inferior play was being played to full houses and great applause, *Phèdre*, one of the great masterpieces of the French theatre, was performed to empty seats. Racine withdrew from the theatre and became the historiographer to the king. Twelve years later he wrote *Esther* (1689) and *Athalie* (1691) for the schoolgirls of Saint-Cyr. Both plays contain beauty and power, but neither was given a public performance until nearly twenty years after Racine's death. He would have no more bitterness, no more controversy.

The comparison of Corneille and Racine has been a favorite French pastime since the seventeenth century. Racine built upon the dramatic structure

Spain and France Before the Eighteenth Century

provided for him by Corneille. They are alike in their observance of the neoclassical rules, although what was a hindrance to Corneille was an enhancing framework to Racine. Both playwrights concentrated on exposition of characters in mental and spiritual conflicts, but while the will is all-powerful in Corneille the characters of Racine vacillate and seem to lose control. The grandeur of Corneille gives way to humanity and reality in Racine, who increased the believability of his characters by his simple but highly polished style. As one French critic noted, in summing up a comparison of the two playwrights, Corneille portrayed people as they would wish to be, whereas Racine portrayed them as they are.

ACTORS AND ACTING

As in other aspects of the French theatre before 1700, the profession of acting moved from the relatively amateur status of the Middle Ages to a well-developed, fully professional practice by the end of the seventeenth century. This shift included changes in acting styles, in the organization of acting companies, and in the social station of actors as respected professionals.

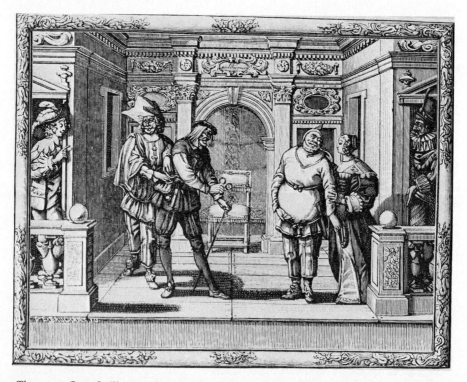

The actors Gros-Guillaume, Gaultier Garguille, and Turlupin in performance at the Hôtel de Bourgogne.

Acting Styles

Emerging from its medieval roots, the predominant style of acting in France was little different from that of the Middle Ages elsewhere. The style had developed from classic rhetoric, and the name "classical" is best applied to it. It involved speech that resembled declamation in basic delivery, and used physical action that was poised, staid, and larger than life. Gesture and facial expression were important. Physical delivery was not integrated with the dialogue and could come before or after the lines surrounding it were delivered. This oratorical style, not thought of as artificial at all in the centuries before the seventeenth, was the major acting mode throughout Continental Europe.

Beginning in the 1630s, however, some disenchantment with the classical style began to enter the thoughts of those who desired to bring some heightened reality to their craft. The times seemed to them to demand a reappraisal of the art of acting, consistent with the Renaissance reexamination of the classics generally. Thus the natural style emerged, a style that concentrated on portraying more emotion than the classical. Consistent with this approach, the natural style relied on more normal vocal delivery and a closely related physical presentation in intensity and timing. Although the greater freedom of the natural style allowed more emotional content to be expressed, it should not be assumed that the style was by any means realistic in the modern sense of the term. During the eighteenth century, the natural style would gradually rise in popularity to become the dominant acting style throughout Europe and in England.

Actors

Before there were permanent theatre companies in Paris, touring companies played the city and the provinces. It is from these companies that the first actors of any substance emerged. The first actor of note in Paris was Valleran LeComte (fl. 1590–1613), who also served as manager of his own company. Little is known of his acting, but presumably he was equally adroit in farce comedy and in tragedy. Most likely his style was classical. In addition to acting, he distinguished himself as the first major theatre manager of the French Renaissance. In his company, Les Comediens du Roi (The King's Players), was Agnan Sarat, a respected comedian, and Maria Venier, the first French actress known by name. His principal author was Alexandre Hardy, and his company operated at the Hôtel de Bourgogne, at that time the only permanent playhouse in the city. Much of the respectability the professional theatre earned in Paris during the early years of the seventeenth century came through his efforts.

The first major actor of the natural style was Bellerose (Pierre le Messier, 1592–1670). He was the leading actor of the company that took permanent residence at the Hôtel de Bourgogne. Although he practiced the natural style equally well in comedy and tragedy, it still was foreign to most critics, who found Bellerose too sentimental and quiet. Nonetheless, he was significant in establishing French classical tragedy and in raising the art of acting above the broad style of the farce players.

The chief rival to Bellerose was Montdory (Guillaume des Gelleberts, 1594–1651). He was an actor of the classical school, specializing in tragedy. Although his acting was declamatory, he was an acknowledged master of his art and may have been the first French tragic actor never to have had an apprenticeship in farce. Unfortunately, he became somewhat of a pawn in the artistic struggle between Louis XIII and Richelieu, the king favoring Bellerose and the King's Players, while Richelieu favored Montdory. In 1634 he founded, with Charles LeNoir, a company that performed at the Théâtre du Marais, in rivalry to the Hôtel de Bourgogne. He was forced to retire from the stage prematurely because of a loss of voice during a performance before Richelieu. His departure from the Paris theatre scene brought to an end the career of a fine actor and an acute theatrical businessman and company manager.

Montfleury (Zacharie Jacob, c. 1600–1667) was second to Bellerose at the Hôtel de Bourgogne. He was considered a fine tragic actor, although he did not have a lean appearance and his classical style accentuated a loud and pompous delivery. Molière and his friends did not care for the man or his style, and he was a principal target of some satire in Molière's *L'Impromptu de Versailles* (1663). Edmond Rostand, in his play *Cyrano de Bergerac* (1898), retells the story, supposedly true, of Molière's friend Cyrano ordering Montfleury from the stage. An active playwright as well as an actor, Montfleury wrote a number of comedies and farces, but the plays did not have staying power. He was nonetheless a major force in the acting and writing of plays for the Hôtel de Bourgogne.

The natural acting counterpart to Montfleury was Floridor (Josias de Soulas, Sieur de Primefosse, 1608–1672). He acted initially at the Théâtre du Marais, but switched to the Hôtel de Bourgogne around 1643. His style was in marked contrast to Montfleury's and was described as quiet and authoritarian. He was so respected, even by rival companies, that Molière did not attack him in *L'Impromptu*. After Bellerose, he was the leading actor at the Hôtel de Bourgogne until an illness forced his retirement from the stage in 1671.

Molière (Jean-Baptiste Poquelin, 1622–1673) has already been discussed as a playwright, but he must be considered as an actor as well. Indeed, he is considered by most critics to be the outstanding comic actor of the French Renaissance. An excellent mimic, Molière's farce acting was probably influenced by the style of the *commedia dell'arte*. His small stature and slight speech impediment did not allow much of a career as a tragedian, a fact that he himself recognized. His acting was physically oriented, possessing a high degree of agility and rapid grace. He is rightly credited with raising French comedy to the level of French tragedy through his writing and acting.

With the formation of the Comédie Française, which was ordered by Louis XIV in 1680, the major acting company of the late seventeenth century was created. Both acting styles of that century were represented in that company; the chief practitioner of the classical style was Mlle Champmesle (Marie Desmares, 1642–1698) and of the natural style, Michel Baron (1653–1729). Mlle Champmesle was the leading tragic actress of the company and played opposite Baron, who was the leading tragedian. The conflict in styles among acting partners indicates the high level of coexistence that was acceptable to French audiences. Mlle Champmesle was extremely beautiful, vocally and physically, and she played scenes of passion and tenderness with equal aplomb. Although pleasant to listen to, her vocal delivery was somewhat like a rhythmic musical chant. She had no rival up to the time of her death.

Michel Baron had no peer in tragedy on the French stage at end of the seventeenth century. Working primarily at the Hôtel de Bourgogne and the Comédie Française, he was known for a stage presence that included meaningful gesture, a fine voice, and an intelligent and quick response to stage situations. He also brought dedication and much attention to detail to his acting. He was highly regarded as an individual and, as such, largely raised the status of actors by his personal and professional example. Like many other actors of his time, he wrote several comedies and saw them produced in the 1680s. Baron retired from the stage in 1691, presumably to pursue other interests, but he returned to the stage in the eighteenth century and worked at the Comédie Française from 1720 until his death. During that time he instituted a number of reforms affecting the art and organization of acting, including the guiding of the early careers of several major actors and actresses of the eighteenth century. At the time of his death, he was probably the most respected actor on the French stage.

Michel Baron.

Acting Companies

The history of acting companies in seventeenth-century France was intrinsically tied to the evolution of the theatre structures in which they operated. For purpose of identification, then, they will be considered in light of where they were housed. Before the beginning of the seventeenth century, no permanent acting companies existed in Paris. What professional theatre did exist was presented by traveling troupes either at the Hôtel de Bourgogne or at the *jeux de paume*, the French tennis courts. With the founding of the Troupe Royale (also known as Les Grands Comédiens) in 1629, Paris had its first permanent company of actors. The company was installed in the Hôtel de Bourgogne and operated there until 1680. The second company to become a permanent fixture in Paris was the Théâtre du Marais company, operating in its own theatre of the same name. This company retained that theatre until both it and the Hôtel company ceased existence in 1673, the actors being assigned duties in other companies. Molière's company found a home at the Palais Royal and commenced operation in 1661, but they had to share the theatre with Italians (a *commedia* troupe) in order to make the operation fiscally sound. When Molière's company left the Palais Royal in 1673, the Opéra company took over and successfully operated the theatre until 1763. Molière's company first merged to form the Théâtre Guénégaud company and then merged with Les Grands Comédiens to form the Comédie Française in 1680. The Italians formed the Théâtre Italien and moved to the Hôtel de Bourgogne until their expulsion from Paris in 1697.

By 1700 only two troupes provided the entire spectrum of dramatic art in Paris. Shows demanding heavy spectacle were done by the Opéra company primarily for court audiences at the Palais Royal, and more regular dramatic fare was presented by the Comédie Française at its own theatre. The other companies were victims of court politics, economics, or actor defections to still other companies, all common practices of French Renaissance theatre.

Company Organization

The basic organization of the French acting company developed throughout the seventeenth century and did not differ radically from similar companies in England and Europe. The typical company by century's end was divided into two types of actors. At the Comédie Française they were known as *sociétaires*, the share members of the company who had a policy-making role in the organization in addition to their acting duties, and *pensionnaires*, the salaried members of the company who were specifically contracted to perform onstage and offstage duties, usually for two or three years. Apprentices served with this latter group in a variety of capacities. In the early part of the seventeenth century, most companies, including Valleran's, were composed of eight to twelve share members plus as many hired members and apprentices as were needed to act the repertory and conduct the front of the house and backstage business. By the late 1600s the company size had increased to approximately double that of the early companies. At the Comédie

Française, for example, there were twenty-seven share members. The shares were set by contract with the government and were not necessarily equal to the number of share members in the company. Thus it was quite possible for the actor-manager of the company to receive two shares (as was common practice) and for less important share members to receive as little as a one-eighth share. Often an actor who was new to the company would start at a half or three-quarter share, to be raised once an initial period with the company was served.

Developed during the seventeenth century was a unique pension system for shareholders. After twenty years' service—a *sociétaire* was not allowed to quit a share membership without a heavy financial penalty—the full share member could receive a retirement allowance. This pension was paid by the actor or small group of actors who took over the share and probably amounted to around 25 percent of their yearly income. Actors of considerable note could also sell their shares at retirement, and this sum, sometimes as high as half a year's income, had to be paid by the share receivers in addition to the pension.

Share members participated in policy matters of the company in addition to acting. After 1607 women were included in the companies, and those who were share members participated fully in the affairs of the company. Although exact responsibilities varied somewhat from company to company, general duties for share members included the setting of business policies, admitting new members, assigning roles, and deciding on the repertory. The share members were financially responsible for hiring salaried actors and other production personnel, the scenery, costumes of a special nature not assumed by the individual actors who wore them, properties, other production and box office expenses, the purchase of plays from an author, and the rental fees and taxes necessary to pay for the theatre. Even for theatres that did not have a rental charge, such as the Palais Royal, the actors were responsible for maintenance.

In spite of these heavy drains on an actor's income, most share members earned more than a living wage. Obviously, yearly incomes varied depending on the success of the company at the box office. Incomes closer to that of the average Parisian worker were more common during the early years of the seventeenth century. By century's end share members in companies enjoying royal patronage had income figures that were well above the average income of the French worker.

Income Sources

Income to offset the rental and other expenses came from several sources. The major source was admissions. By the second half of the seventeenth century, fifteen sous was the standard admission price to the *parterre* of most Paris theatres, and admission to the premiere boxes was half a louis. These prices were not cheap—fifteen sous was approximately a day's wage for a nonskilled laborer in Paris. And the prices were usually doubled for performances of a new play, or for one with heavy production expenses, such as a "machine" play.

Other income sources were available to the companies. Performances at the homes of wealthy patrons and at court were done for a set fee, paid either by the patron or by the government if done at court. In an age of increasing court favor, the royal subsidies became increasingly important. The various troupes also depended on peripheral sales to supplement their main activity. Concessions were commonly sold, and occasionally items like librettos for "machine" plays.

THEATRE ARCHITECTURE AND SCENIC PRACTICE

At the close of the sixteenth century there was only one permanent theatre in the city of Paris, the Hôtel de Bourgogne. During the course of the seventeenth century, four additional theatres were built by and for the permanent companies that were established in Paris. In the order in which all five were built they were: the Hôtel de Bourgogne (built in 1548 and lasting until 1782), the Théâtre du Marais (1634–1673), the Palais Royal (1642–1763), the Théâtre Guénégaud (1673–1689), and the Comédie Française (1689–1770). All of these theatres were somewhat different in shape and size, yet the basic structures had some common elements. Scholars of the evolution of theatre architecture and scenic practice are particularly indebted to a work entitled *La mémoire du Mahelot, Laurent et d'autres décorateurs de L'Hôtel de Bourgogne et de la Comédie Française au XVIIe siècle*. The details about the theatres and their staging practices, compiled between 1678 and 1686 from the notices of principal designers Mahelot and Laurent, provide the type of primary information that allows detailed and accurate historical analysis.

Basic Elements of the French Theatre

The basic shape for most French Renaissance theatre is the rectangle, divided into the basic parts for audience and stage established during the Italian Renaissance. The stage, usually behind a proscenium, raked upward toward the back. The floor immediately in front of the proscenium or the stage was flat and was open the entire length of the auditorium. Known as the *parterre*, or pit, this area had no seats but occasionally held unconnected chairs or stools. Most of the time, however, the audience simply stood, no doubt adding to the lack of decorum in that part of the auditorium. Along the sides of the auditorium flanking the *parterre* were rows of boxes (*loges*). Early in the seventeenth century two tiers of boxes were common, but by the end of the 1600s three tiers were the standard. Boxes filled all tiers—none was open as in England—and an ordinary box held eight people. At the back of the *parterre* was a raised platform called the *amphithéâtre*. Benches were placed throughout this area for audience seating, but because of the extreme distance from the stage this was the least-used section of the auditorium. In the 1680s, *balcons* were first employed in French theatres. These were extensions to the box tiers over the front portion of the stage where spectators occasionally sat. This use of seating over the stage was likely the forerunner of the eighteenth-century proscenium box, a device that would be standard in theatre architecture until the beginning of the twentieth century. There is no evidence of a front curtain to commence or conclude a play until about midcentury. The first such use was for Richelieu's production of *Mirame* in the early 1640s.

The Jeu de Paume

It has been noted that the early companies in Paris had to use either the Hôtel de Bourgogne or one of the numerous *jeux de paume* for their productions. The *jeu de paume* (literally the game of tennis, but in common usage meaning the place where the game was played, the tennis court) was a common site for theatrical production, used throughout the century. When the Comédie Française moved from its first home in 1689, it remodeled the Etoile tennis court for its productions, and this structure served as its theatre well into the eighteenth century. All tennis courts were rectangular, the average size about thirty by ninety feet. No doubt this rectangular form guided the design of sixteenth- and seventeenth-century theatres. The floor was flat and open with a gallery for spectators on one side and a row of windows on the other. All that had to be done to convert these indoor halls to usable theatres was to put in a platform at one end and extend the gallery around the hall. Indeed, some tennis courts had temporary stage platforms so that both sport and theatrical uses could be made of them.

Specific Theatres

Clearly the most illustrious playhouse of the French theatre before 1700 was the Hôtel de Bourgogne (*hôtel* means a public building, not a hotel). Built near the middle of the sixteenth century, it outlasted all theatres built during the seventeenth century and had on its stage most of the outstanding actors of its time. Initially it was the home of the Confrérie de la Passion and was Paris's only permanent theatre until 1634. All touring companies played either there or at a tennis court, and in either case they owed the Confrérie a fee since the brotherhood had a monopoly on all theatre practice in the capital until the middle of the seventeenth century. Partially because its inception is somewhat lost in history, some details, like the actual size of the theatre, are not available. Records suggest, however, that the interior dimensions of the Hôtel were some 40 by 105 feet, not extremely large when compared with its seventeenth-century counterparts. The first-floor pit was traditional, and the theatre had three galleries with boxes. The upper back gallery, like an *amphithéâtre*, was open for bench seating. The stage was raised some five feet above the pit floor and was approximately twenty-five feet wide by thirty-five feet deep. The theatre had no proscenium and was not used for productions requiring heavy illusionistic scenery. Most productions at the Hôtel were staged in essentially medieval fashion, with stations, until the 1630s.

A brief look at the history of the Hôtel gives an insight into the progress of French theatre as it moved toward 1700. From 1548 to 1577, the theatre was leased to the Enfants Sans-Souci troupe, a group of farce players. The Confrérie rented the theatre to various touring groups from 1577 to 1599, when Valleran's Comédiens du Roi occupied the theatre. There was no serious rival to the supremacy of the Hôtel until the Théâtre du Marais was built in 1634. Until 1680, less medieval, contemporary productions were seen at the Hôtel. Various designers attempted to solve the problems of the small stage by adapting different Italian scenic methods, but nothing was tremendously successful. When the Comédie Française was formed in 1680, the Théâtre Italien took over the Hôtel until it was expelled in 1697. For the balance of the seventeenth century, the theatre was dark, to be awakened in 1716 when *commedia* returned to Paris. The movement of theatre practice in and out of the Hôtel is reflective of Paris theatre itself.

Although the Hôtel de Bourgogne was not equipped for heavy illusionistic scenery, other Paris theatres were. The most distinguished of these, in terms of the acting companies housed therein, was the Palais Royal. Originally built by Richelieu as the Palais Cardinal in 1641, it had a stage much larger than the Hôtel and one that was more appropriate for illusionistic scenery. The stage

A chariot-mat *system for scene changes based on a Torelli design.*

was fifty-nine feet wide and forty-six feet deep, and the auditorium was the same width and only some twenty feet longer. The theatre had a proscenium, and the stage was equipped for flat wing scenery. In 1642 it was remodeled by Torelli and equipped with the *chariot-mat* system. From that time on it was used primarily for court shows, although in 1660 it was given to Molière's company. Upon the death of Molière, Jean-Baptiste Lully (1632–1687) operated his Opéra troupe there until his death. More than any other man in Paris during the seventeenth century, Lully was responsible for the development of opera and for introducing Italian staging methods in his productions. In 1679, the Opéra company rebuilt and reequipped the theatre for even more elaborate opera productions, establishing the model for full-perspective illusionistic scenery in France.

Two other Parisian theatres that deserve mention are the Petit Bourbon and the Salle des Machines. Both greatly furthered the development of illusionistic scenery in Paris, and both were essentially royal theatres. The Petit Bourbon was originally opened in 1577 by the Gelosi troupe, a famous *commedia* company of the sixteenth century. From 1578 to 1645 many traveling troupes used the theatre primarily for the staging of court entertainments. In 1645, however, Cardinal Mazarin, the hand-picked successor to Cardinal Richelieu, brought Torelli to Paris to stage *Orpheus and Euridice*. The theatre was not suitable for the Italian illusionistic scenery that was required, so Torelli enlarged the stage and installed a complete *chariot-mat* system for changing the scenery. The court entertainments done there included various "machine" plays, operalike productions, yet with spoken dialogue, done for the display of scenic spectacle. Although not really important in their own right, these plays provided the foundations for the rich traditions of French ballet and opera and significantly contributed to the development of these art forms.

Next to Torelli, the Italian scene designed Gaspare Vigarani (1586–1663) was most important to the development of perspective illusionistic scenery in Paris during the seventeenth century. He was responsible for the most significant implantation of Italian scenic norms in France, primarily through his work at the Salle des Machines. Opened in 1661, the theatre was 52 by 232 feet, with 140 feet of its length devoted to stage depth. By any measure, the effects at the Salle des Machines were gigantic—whole choruses could be raised and lowered to and from the stage floor, and great fountains actually flowed in upstage spaces. The theatre more than justified its name—the "room of scenic machines." Thus among its various theatres Paris audiences could find the entire spectrum of dramatic fare—from the simplified, almost medieval staging of the Hôtel to the fully illusionistic practices of the Salle des Machines. Their tastes could accommodate it all.

Scenery

Before the seventeenth century French staging and scenic practices were essentially medieval. Various court festivals, including elaborate royal entries and tournaments, were commonplace. In the 1560s, for example, Catherine de'Medici (1519–1589) began a progress, an extended royal entry, that lasted two years. Even in the public theatre sector, medieval scenic practices prevailed. At the Hôtel the Confrérie routinely rented sets, props, and costumes that were in the tradition of the Middle Ages. Before the late 1630s, *décor simultane* was the norm. This was the practice of using generalized *mansion* staging to suggest all the scenic stations needed. Productions at court in the 1620s began to introduce the idea of Italian perspective scenery and production techniques in Paris, although the provinces continued to rely on medieval production techniques.

Seventeenth-Century Design

Beginning in the 1640s, the contributions of Torelli and Vigarani, along with the rule of unity of place, slowly but successfully implanted the notion of full illusionistic scenery and machinery on the French stage. Particularly Vigarani, working with his son Carlo (1623–1713), established the norm for late seventeenth-century scenic practice: the belief in the unity of place virtually required a static, single setting, and verisimilitude demanded a tremendously dynamic system of scenic machinery and special effects. This norm would hold for French scenic practice throughout most of the eighteenth century. By the end of the seventeenth century, another father-and-son designer team, Jean Berain *père* (1637–1711) and Jean Berain *fils* (1678–1726), brought the full baroque aesthetic of illusionistic scenery and machinery

Scene from a performance at the theatre at Versailles, c. 1685.

to Paris, primarily through their work at the Salle des Machines. By 1700 the stage and scenic practices that would govern the French stage for the next hundred years could be seen at the new home of the Comédie Française. The stage, equipped for flat wings and shutters, was six feet above the pit floor and was forty-one feet wide by fifty-four feet deep. Two static sets were commonly used at the theatre: for tragedy a neutral palace and for comedy a simple room with several doors. Thus, although Italianate illusionistic perspective scenery was firmly in place by century's end, a clear move toward some simplicity was established for nonopera and ballet-type productions.

Costumes

Before 1700 the medieval tradition of actor-supplied general-use contemporary costumes continued. Except for specific types of costumes that the company supplied, such as classical dress, Indian, or Oriental costumes, individual actors paid for their costumes themselves and were expected to maintain them. After 1680 records indicate that this expense could take some 25 percent of their income, but the practice was so common that few actors felt ill-used by it.

THE AUDIENCE

The French audience was drawn from many walks of life. In the first two decades of the seventeenth century few of the aristocracy attended the theatre, so it was mostly a plebeian audience similar to that in attendance at medieval theatricals. By the third decade the more educated and cultured sectors of the middle class were predominant in the general audience. The middle classes soon controlled the *parterre* and from there exercised great control over the financial and artistic success of a play. From the age of Louis XIII to the end of the century, another shift occurred. While the middle class was still well represented, there was a resurgence in the aristocratic sector of the audience. By the time of Louis XIV, however, the aristocratic nature of the public audience had lessened considerably and the lower classes were gone, no doubt because of the increased price of admission.

The capacities of the theatres in the capital varied widely. It is doubtful that the Hôtel de Bourgogne seated more than one thousand; the larger hall in the Palais Royal seated between three and four thousand. Rarely were the theatres filled. Attendance probably never got much above 50 percent except for the opening of new plays or illusionistic spectacles. Specific figures were much lower. In 1682–83, for example, the Comédie performed 352 times, to an average attendance of 440 per performance. In a hall that seated 2,000, that was 22 percent of capacity. It remains to speculation whether the prices kept the audience away or whether the lack of audience response resulted in higher prices. Whatever the case, it is clear that most Parisians did not participate in the theatrical life of their city.

Given that attendance, it is somewhat surprising to realize that the Comédie Française gave performances every day of the week. This was not generally the case in the early decades of the seventeenth century. Initially, only two performances per week were given, usually starting in the early afternoon, around three o'clock. By midcentury the usual starting time was around 5:00 P.M., with three performances a week as the standard, usually on Sundays, Tuesdays, and Fridays. New plays were commonly opened on Fridays, with full-length plays performed as a single bill. Daily rotation of the bill was the norm for a large company, such as the Comédie Française, which had some seventy plays in its repertory.

The audience in Paris before 1700 was by no means genteel. With the *parterre* attenders standing or roaming about, complete attention was not paid to the play. Little wonder that the declamatory acting style carried the day, and that the presence of spectators on the stage was a concern for author and actor alike.

THE END OF AN ERA

As Louis XIV and his court became the model for all the lesser courts of Europe in the seventeenth century, so was the French

A double glory is seen in this scene from a French production of the late 1680s.

theatre the standard for all other theatres. In drama, production, and acting the French were imitated throughout Europe. Yet by the end of the seventeenth century the French theatre had lost its vitality and was in decline. Racine represented the perfection of the French classical theatre, and he had no worthy successors. The Comédie Française would carry on the traditions of this glorious era into the eighteenth century, but they would eventually become so bound up in their sense of history as to help spark the romantic revolt in France in the nineteenth century. Although the ideals of neoclassicism dominated European theatre for three hundred years, its finest moments were in France between 1660 and 1700.

RETROSPECT

The neighboring countries of Spain and France followed paths out of their respective Middle Ages and into the Renaissance that were at the same time parallel and distinct. Both became national powers before all the countries in Europe. Both experienced a rapid rise to power, but by 1700 France was the greatest national power on the Continent. Both nations made substantial contributions to the development of Western theatre.

Culturally, the contribution of these two powers to world civilization and theatre closely followed the development of their national politics. Because both countries developed large population and governmental centers, Madrid and Paris served as reflections of the theatrical practice in their respective countries. Both countries had a strong medieval tradition that influenced the popular theatre from the twelfth through the middle of the seventeenth century, most clearly seen in the *corrales* of Spain and the Hôtel de Bourgogne in France. This tradition was in conflict with the growing scope of court entertainments and the rather complete acceptance by the royalty of Italian illusionistic staging practices. Acting companies continued to serve both the public and the court theatres throughout the period before 1700. The special patronage of the court and the acceptance of Italian Renaissance stagecraft influenced the public theatre practice by the beginning of the eighteenth century. The ideals of neoclassicism were present in the dramatic literature of both countries, but only in France did they become the guiding artistic standard for playwrights.

Spanish and French staging and stagecraft in the late seventeenth century followed a similar path. Spain and the rest of Europe followed France's lead in bringing Italian illusionistic theatre practice fully to the stage. With the exception of a few important designers and theatre architects, France was concerned with significant changes to the principles already established rather than initial innovation and fundamental reform. After 1700 the artistic vigor of the Spanish and French stages lessened. Theatrically, the century immediately ahead for these countries would be shallow indeed.

Date	Spanish and French History	Spanish and French Theatre History	World History	World Theatre History
1500		Encina's pastorals performed in Rome. Vicente's plays performed at Portuguese court.		
1509	War between Spain and France.		Henry VIII begins reign.	Ariosto's *Cassaria*.
1515	Francis I begins reign in France.			
1516	Charles V begins reign in Spain.			
1517		Torres Naharro's *Propalladia*.		
1518		Vicente's *Barco do purgatorio*.		
1519–1522	Cortés conquers Mexico.		Magellan first to sail around the world.	
1520			Luther declared a heretic.	
1522			Turks capture Rhodes.	
1527	Future Philip II born.		Rome sacked by Spanish army.	
1530	Charles V crowned Holy Roman Emperor.		Cardinal Wolsey of England dies.	
1532–1534	Pizzarro conquers Peru.			
1533			Birth of future Queen Elizabeth of England.	
1541			Turks conquer Hungary.	Giraldi's *Orbeeche*.
1545				Serlio's *Architettura* published.
1547	Death of Francis I.		Death of Henry VIII.	
1548		Hôtel de Bourgogne built.		

(Continued on page 306)

Date	Spanish and French History	Spanish and French Theatre History	World History	World Theatre History
1552		Jodelle's *Cléopâtre*.		
1553				Udall's *Ralph Roister Doister*.
1554	Philip II marries Queen Mary of England.			
1556	Philip II begins reign.			
1557	National bankruptcies in Spain and France.			
1558	Mary, Queen of Scots, marries Francis II.		Queen Elizabeth of England begins reign.	
1559	Death of Henry II.			
1560	Death of Francis II.	J. Grévin's *Mort de Cesar*.		
1561				Sackville and Norton's *Gorboduc*.
1562	Religious wars in France.	Birth of Lope de Vega.	Beginning of slave trade in Americas.	
1563	Assassination of Duke of Guise.	Confrérie de la Passion formed.		
1567	Duke of Alba begins reign of terror in Netherlands.		Abdication of Mary, Queen of Scots.	
1571	Battle of Lepanto.			
1572	St. Bartholomew Massacre.	Taille's *L'Art de la tragedie*.	Sir Francis Drake attacks Spanish ports in Americas.	
1574	Death of Charles IX of France.	First permanent *corral* built in Madrid.	Turks take Tunis from Spain.	
1576				The Theatre built in London.
1577		Petit Bourbon built.		

Date	Spanish and French History	Spanish and French Theatre History	World History	World Theatre History
1580	Philip II adds Portugal to his empire.	Garnier's *Les Juives*.		
1585			Teatro Olimpico opens.	
1586	War of the three Henrys in France.			
1587		Women allowed to appear on the Spanish stage.		Kyd's *Spanish Tragedy*.
1588	Defeat of Spanish Armada.		Boris Godunov, regent of Russia.	
1589	Assassination of Henri III.			
1590	Henri IV begins reign.			
1590		A. Hardy active as professional playwright.		
1595	War between Spain and France.			
1598	Death of Philip II. Edict of Nantes.	Le Comte's acting company settles in Paris.	Boris Godunov, Tsar of Russia.	
1599				The Globe built in London.
1600		Birth of Calderón.		
1601				Shakespeare's *Hamlet*.
1602	Spanish army lands in Ireland.			
1603			Death of Queen Elizabeth I.	
1606		Birth of Corneille.		
1608				Monteverdi's *Orfeo*.
1610	Assassination of Henri IV. Louis XIII begins reign.			

(Continued on page 308)

Date	Spanish and French History	Spanish and French Theatre History	World History	World Theatre History
1616	Cardinal Richelieu becomes French secretary of state.			Death of Shakespeare.
1618		Lope's *Fuente Ove-juna*.	Start of Thirty Years' War.	
1620			Mayflower sails for America.	
1621	Death of Philip III.			
1622		Birth of Molière.		
1624	War between France and England.			
1625		Tirso's *El burlado*.	Death of James I of England.	
1629		Troupe Royale established.		
1631		Formation of Spanish actors' guild.		
1634		Théâtre de Marais built.	Assassination of Wallenstein.	
1635		Death of Lope de Vega. Calderón's *La vida es sueño*.		
1637		Corneille's *Le Cid*.		
1640	Portugal gains independence from Spain.	Corneille's *Horace*. Coliseo, Spanish palace theatre, built.		
1642	Death of Richelieu.		English Civil War begins.	London theatres closed.
1643	Death of Louis XIII.			
1645		Torelli arrives in Paris.		
1648	French civil wars begin.			

Date	Spanish and French History	Spanish and French Theatre History	World History	World Theatre History
1649		Calderón's *Gran teatro del mundo*.	Charles I beheaded.	
1653	End of French civil wars.		Cromwell becomes Lord Protector of England.	
1656				Davenant's *Siege of Rhodes*.
1658		Molière's company acts before Louis XIV.		
1660			Monarchy restored in England.	
1661	Louis XIV begins personal rule of France.			
1662	Construction begins on Palace of Versailles.			
1664		*Tartuffe* controversy begins. Racine's first play produced.		
1665	Death of Philip IV.			
1666		Molière's *Le Misanthrope*.		
1667	Louis XIV begins wars of conquest in Europe.	Racine's *Andromaque*.		
1673	French expedition against Ceylon.	Death of Moliére.		
1677		Racine's *Phèdre*.		Dryden's *All for Love*.
1680		Formation of Comédie Française.		
1681		Death of Calderón.		
1682	LaSalle claims Mississippi Valley for France.			

(Continued on page 310)

Date	Spanish and French History	Spanish and French Theatre History	World History	World Theatre History
1688			James II flees England.	
1694	English navy shells French ports.			
1698	First Partition Treaty divides up Spanish possessions in Europe.			
1699		Death of Racine.		
1700	Death of Carlos II. Spanish throne goes to grandson of Louis XIV.			

SELECTED READINGS

Brereton, Geoffrey. *French Comic Drama from the Sixteenth to the Eighteenth Century*. London: Methuen, 1977.
>   A highly useful study of French comedy up to the time of the French Revolution.

_____. *French Tragic Drama in the Sixteenth and Seventeenth Centuries*. London: Methuen, 1973.
>   This fine treatment of the development of French tragedy up to Racine is a companion volume to the title above.

Gossip, C. J. *An Introduction to French Classical Tragedy*. Totowa: Barnes & Noble, 1981.
>   This study of the various elements of French classical tragedy fits nicely with Lough's background study listed below.

Jeffery, Brian. *French Renaissance Comedy 1552–1630*. Oxford: Oxford University Press, 1969.
>   A detailed study that includes material on plays, production details, and dramatic conventions.

Lancaster, Henry Carrington. *A History of French Dramatic Literature in the Seventeenth Century*. 9 vols. Baltimore: Johns Hopkins Press, 1929–1942.
>   The most exhaustive study available, in French or English, of the plays of the seventeenth century.

Lough, John. *Seventeenth-Century Drama: The Background*. Oxford: Oxford University Press, 1979.
>   A brief but excellent introduction to the period.

_____. *Paris Theatre Audiences in the Seventeenth and Eighteenth Centuries*. Oxford: Oxford University Press, 1957.
>   A study of the audiences and theatre operations in Paris from approximately 1600 to 1800.

Moore, Will G. *The Classical Drama of France*. Oxford: Oxford University Press, 1971.
>   An interesting investigation into the nature of the classic period of French theatre. A very useful study for those without the time to use Lancaster.

Shergold, N. D. *A History of the Spanish Stage*. Oxford: Oxford University Press, 1967.
>   The single most important English language source on the Spanish stage, this book traces the development from the medieval to the end of the seventeenth century. The emphasis here is on production rather than play writing.

Wiley, W. L. *The Early Public Theatre in France*. Cambridge, Mass.: Harvard University Press, 1960.
>   An interesting study of actors, performance conditions, theatres, and audiences from the 1580s to 1630.

Wilson, Edward M., and Duncan Moir. *A Literary History of Spain: The Golden Age Drama 1492–1700*. London: Ernest Benn, 1971.

More detailed than the next title, this fine single-volume treatment places more emphasis on the lesser playwrights of the era. Contains a very useful bibliography.

Wilson, Margaret. *Spanish Drama of the Golden Age*. Oxford: Pergamon Press, 1969.

An excellent starting point for anyone wishing to gain a basic background in the Golden Age drama.

LONDON

PARIS

PART VIII

The Gilded Mirror:
THE EIGHTEENTH CENTURY

Depending on the country involved, the eighteenth century has been called the Age of Reason, Age of Elegance, Age of the Enlightenment, or some other age with the name of some literary figure or ruler filling in the phrase. Attempts to label an entire century are often misleading, yet there is a great temptation to consider the eighteenth the century of neoclassicism. In that century the concepts of neoclassicism were applied to many of the cultural and social aspects of life. There was a rage throughout Europe for order, and neoclassicism supplied the rules for that ordering.

Neoclassicism was itself a reaction to the excesses of the Renaissance. It suggested limits for the human potential, which the writers of the Renaissance believed to be unlimited, and it played down individuality and emphasized collective endeavors. This in itself may help explain why the century is noted for developments in the production aspects of theatre rather than in dramaturgy. The cultural and social ideals of the time stressed logic, restraint, and proper form. Yet by midcentury these ideas were being strongly assailed by a new philosophical primitivism that hailed the natural man in opposition to the social man, by the forces of the industrial revolution, and by the aspirations of the rising middle class.

Throughout the century wars among the European nations troubled the quest for order. The domination of France, the center of neoclassicism and of things cultural and political, was repeatedly challenged. In the last quarter of the eighteenth century, open rebellion flared in the American War for Independence, the German *Sturm und Drang*, and the French Revolution. A century that had striven for order and reason ended in revolution, bloodshed, and terror.

15
EIGHTEENTH-CENTURY DRAMA

The drama of the eighteenth century was in a state of stagnation and decay. It was a century of great actors and inferior playwrights. With the exception of the Scandinavian countries and Germany, the age was so closely bound by the traditions of neoclassicism and overshadowed by the creative excellences of previous centuries that it was unable to produce a major playwright or significant new direction in dramaturgy. Throughout Europe the social fabric was disintegrating and the century was to end in revolutionary turmoil. So, too, with Europe's cultural mirror, the theatre.

FRENCH DRAMA IN THE EIGHTEENTH CENTURY

The dramatic masterpieces of Corneille, Molière, and Racine dominated the eighteenth century as they had the seventeenth. Plays by new playwrights were produced, but they were considerably inferior to the better offerings of the previous century. The climate for the reception of theatre cooled in the eighteenth century, partly because of the growing popularity of opera and the loss of royal favor. In the final decade of his long reign, Louis XIV ceased attending theatrical performances. He also saw that new controls were placed on the theatre, and by 1710 a formal censorship office had been established for both the production and publication of plays. These controls remained in place during the succeeding reign of Louis XV (1715–1774).

Eighteenth-century France, although the cultural and social center of Europe, was more cynical and materialistic than the France of Molière. The long wars at the end of the reign of Louis XIV had undermined the economy and made financial corruption rampant on all levels of society. Crooked tax officials and financiers began to appear in large numbers in the comedies of the period, and lawyers replaced physicians as a principal butt of theatrical humor. Tragedy continued to be the darling of the aristocrats, and many of the plays written in this century had social preferment rather than artistic achievement as their goal. Yet the French still regarded the theatre, even in this cynical age, as a didactic instrument to be used to educate as well as delight. This was especially true with the new dramatic form born in the eighteenth century, the *drame bourgeois*.

A creation of the philosopher Denis Diderot (1713–1784), the *drame bourgeois* was to fit between tragedy and comedy. Its subject matter was to be a serious discussion of the problems of middle-class (bourgeois) life. Although Diderot's own two attempts at *drame*—*Le Fils naturel* (The Illegitimate Son, 1757) and *Le Père de famille* (The Father of the Family, 1758)—are feeble plays, his concept for a new dramatic form filled a need in the eighteenth-century theatre. The comedy of the period made no attempt to depict the middle class accurately but merely ridiculed its supposed vices. Tragedy, with its emphasis on decorum and aristocratic honor, was becoming irrelevant to the middle class. This new and powerful group of French citizens had gained wealth through hard work and shrewd business practices. With an ethos centered on the family unit, an interest in stability, and a fear of radical innovations, the bourgeoisie looked in vain for a sympathic portrait of their class on the stage. They found it in the *drames*. In the next century the drama of the bourgeoisie would dominate European theatre.

Voltaire

The major dramatist of eighteenth-century France was François-Marie Arouet, who, following the success of his first tragedy in 1718, changed his name to Voltaire (1694–1778). One of the outstanding men of letters of the eighteenth century, Voltaire wrote for the theatre from 1718 until his death in 1778. His twenty-seven tragedies represent slightly over half of his total dramatic output, and they are much superior to his attempts at comedy.

His first play, *Oedipe* (Oedipus, 1718), was an enormous success, being presented thirty times in two months and earning Voltaire more money than had ever before been paid to a playwright for a single script. The play was based on Sophocles and modeled on Corneille, and the fine verse was favorably compared to Racine's. The play earned the young author an honored place in the French theatrical establishment, one he managed to retain for sixty years. He wrote several other plays in the style of the seventeenth-century French masters, and then in 1726 he left for thirty months' residency in England. There he learned the language, read widely in English literature, and attended the theatre. This exposure to the more physically active English theatre had a lasting effect on his own work.

On returning to France, Voltaire sought to combine what he considered the best elements of the French and English stage. His innovations, particularly in relation to settings and costumes, excited his audiences. *Zaïre*, written in 1732, was his first play to show the results of his visit to England. Voltaire's move to include more physical action and scenic display in his plays met with the approval of the French audience. By 1750 he had introduced ghosts, period-type costumes, and onstage death scenes to the neoclassical French theatre. In 1760, when the stage itself had finally been cleared of spectators (thus ending a

A statue of Voltaire.

French tradition that had lasted since 1636), he was able to give full rein to his predilection for spectacle in such plays as *Tancriède* (1760) and *Olympie* (1763). His innovations were copied and enlarged upon by less talented playwrights, which caused a troubled Voltaire to write, "I wanted to insert some life into the theatre by adding more action, and now all we have are action and pantomime. There is nothing sacred enough to be safe from abuse."

Voltaire was one of the strongest defenders of the neoclassical tradition in the French theatre, yet through his innovations in staging, subject matter, and the use of local color, he was a major contributor to the destruction of that tradition. A transitional playwright, working from seventeenth-century models, he prepared the way for the nineteenth-century romantics, who would reject his dramatic theories. He was not a great playwright or a great poet, but his plays managed to hold the respect and attention of audiences for nearly one hundred years and are among the best of the eighteenth-century French stage.

Marivaux

In an age of cynicism and classicism, Pierre Carlet de Chamblain de Marivaux (1688–1763) created plays noted for their originality, optimism, and gaiety. Between 1720 and 1746 the majority of Marivaux's plays were produced by the Théâtre Italien, the resident *commedia dell'arte* company in Paris. His comedies of love, which are totally at odds with the classical comedies of Molière, are light, fantastic pieces that deal with the psychological aspects of courtship. They are unique in French dramatic literature, and for over two hundred years they have been the subject of praise and condemnation.

Arlequin poli par l'amour (Harlequin Refined by Love, 1720) was Marivaux's first success and established the general pattern for his following plays. Since it was written for the Théâtre Italien, it was not bound by the rules of neoclassicism. Fantasy abounds, and the writing, in a style later to be called *marivaudage*, was elegant and precious. His characters speak and act in a manner reflective of the grace and artificiality of the eighteenth-century drawing room. In his best plays, such as *La Surprise de l'amour* (The Surprise of Love, 1722), *La Double inconstance* (1723), *Le Jeu de l'amour et du hasard* (The Game of Love and Chance, 1730) and *L'Epreuve* (The Test, 1740), he builds on the psychological complexities of awakening love, *l'amour naissant*. In his examinations of the inner struggle of lovers, Marivaux accomplished for comedy what Racine did for tragedy.

Because of the delicacy and precision of the language of his plays, Marivaux had little influence outside France. As with Racine, the plays are difficult to translate and contain subtleties of language only appreciated by native speakers. In France his reputation has varied with changes in acting style, this

Pierre Marivaux.

due to the fact that his plays are unsuitable to a declamatory approach. Today he is considered one of the greatest French dramatists and placed by many critics immediately behind Corneille, Molière, and Racine on the honor roll of the French theatre.

Beaumarchais

The final eighteenth-century French playwright of note was Pierre-Augustin Caron de Beaumarchais (1732–1799), whose two major comedies, *Le Barbier de Séville* (The Barber of Seville, 1775) and *Le Mariage de Figaro* (The Marriage of Figaro, 1784), are noteworthy for their reflection of French society on the eve of the Revolution. The remarkable career of Beaumarchais included being a clockmaker, music master to the daughters of Louis XV, secret diplomat for two French kings, gunrunner for the insurgent North American colonies, intrigant in the courts of France and Spain, and founder of the Society of Authors.

Both *Barbier* and *Mariage* are indebted to earlier playwrights, particularly Molière and Marivaux, but their level of social criticism is unique for plays produced in the late eighteenth century. Greed, corruption, and apathy had so completely permeated the upper structures of French society that the country was at a near standstill. Change was necessary, but the monarchy was no longer capable of activating change. Revolution was in the air. Beaumarchais's plays praised egalitarianism and condemned the existing class system, with its economic exploitation of the lower class. They are excellent examples of comedy used to protest social abuses. The plays served as foundations for operas by Paisiello, Mozart, and Rossini. In five years the entire society depicted in *Le Mariage de Figaro* would be destroyed in the fury of the French Revolution. The Revolution would also change the direction of the French theatre in the next century.

ENGLISH DRAMA IN THE EIGHTEENTH CENTURY

The theatre of eighteenth-century England is noted for its outstanding performers and hack playwrights. During this century the drama was in such a state of artistic decline that its remembered contributions amount to three comedies, one early melodrama, and a ballad opera. The major English playwright of the century was the newly rediscovered William Shakespeare. At the beginning of the century the stage was still under the cloud of the Jeremy Collier attack in *A Short View of the Immorality and Profaneness of the English Stage* (1698), and many of the newly formed societies for the reformation of manners openly campaigned for a moral and inspirational theatre. Such was the moralizing trend during this period that the actor, playwright, and theatre manager David Garrick suggested that steeples be placed on the playhouses.

The theatre monopoly had broken down in the early eighteenth century, and playgoers had a selection of four companies in London in the 1730s. But this situation was soon to change. The bite of the political satire in such plays as Henry Fielding's *The Tragedy of Tragedies* (1730), *Pasquin* (1736), and *The Historical Register of 1736* (1736) and the anonymous *The Golden Rump* brought down the wrath of Prime Minister Robert Walpole. Attracting the attention of Walpole to the London theatrical scene resulted in the Licensing Act of 1737, which reestablished Drury Lane and Covent Garden as London's two official theatres and subjected all new plays to a rigorous censorship. The censorship and the reduction in the number of available theatres, combined with the religious and moralizing temper of the times, greatly contributed to the paltry state of English drama in the eighteenth century.

John Gay

One of the few bright events in eighteenth-century English stage history was the production of John Gay's *The Beggar's Opera* (1727). Gay (1685–1732) followed a suggestion from his friend Jonathan Swift that a Newgate pastoral "might make an odd pretty sort of thing." Newgate was London's principal jail, and Gay wrote a ballad-opera about characters from the city's criminal population. The play was presented by John Rich at Lincoln's Inn Fields and ran for more than sixty performances over two successive theatrical seasons. As a wit of the period noted, the play made Rich

A portrait sketch of John Gay and a playbill for The Beggar's Opera.

gay and Gay rich. It started a vogue for ballad-operas that lasted until the middle of the century.

Gay is credited with inventing the ballad-opera, a play of a topical nature with numerous songs containing new lyrics set to well-known melodies. This presented a fine opportunity for double irony, since the familiar melody could be suggesting one thing to the audience and the new lyrics just its opposite. The collection of rogues in *The Beggar's Opera* was both a satire and a parody of London society in the 1720s: the thieves and prostitutes represented the aristocracy, and the prison warden and the fence the middle class. The double irony used in the songs was also present in the dialogue, with characters saying one thing and implying another. Although the play appeared to be light-hearted, there was serious social criticism just under the surface. The play has been successfully revived in this century, and it is the basis for Bertolt Brecht's *Die Dreigroschenoper* (The Threepenny Opera, 1928). The social satire was not lost on the audiences in the 1720s, and the play's sequel, *Polly* (1729), was banned by the Walpole government.

George Lillo

While *The Beggar's Opera* was a popular play that spawned a host of imitations, another highly popular play of the period was actually a hundred years ahead of its time. *The London Merchant, or The History of George Barnwell* (1731), a precursor of nineteenth-century melodrama, was successfully performed throughout the century, yet it produced no contemporary imitations. The author, George Lillo (1693–1739), was unique in managing to write a middle-class tragedy expressive of middle-class beliefs.

The play tells the tale of a young businessman who falls under the spell of a prostitute, steals for her, and eventually murders his kindly uncle. For his crime he and his harlot are executed. The play centers on commercial life and uses dialogue not unlike the speech of its first audience members. It was the only eighteenth-century English play to have an impact outside the country. It was translated into several languages, praised by Diderot in France, and used as a model by Gotthold Lessing for his *Miss Sara Samson* (1755), a play that started German domestic drama. For all of its melodramatic nonsense, intensified good and evil, and last-minute repentance, *George Barnwell*, as it was usually billed, was the most influential English play written in the eighteenth century.

Goldsmith and Sheridan

Oliver Goldsmith and Richard Sheridan are the only eighteenth-century English playwrights now represented in the standard theatrical repertoire. *She Stoops to Conquer*, by Oliver Goldsmith (1730–1774), was produced at Covent Garden in 1773 and was hailed, then as now, as a comic gem. Dr. Samuel Johnson, a friend of the playwright's, rightly noted that the script fulfilled the chief purpose of comedy, to make people laugh. In the year the play was produced, Goldsmith published an essay comparing sentimental

A production of Oliver Goldsmith's She Stoops to Conquer *at the Abbey Theatre, Dublin.*

(Courtesy of KaiDib Films International, Glendale, Calif.)

and laughing comedy. He remarked, in relation to the moralizing tone of the English stage, that genuine humor appeared "to be departing from the stage, and it will soon happen that our comic players will have nothing left for it but a fine coat and a song. It depends upon the audience whether they will drive those poor merry creatures from the stage, or sit at a play as gloomy as at the tabernacle." Goldsmith's script, which relates the adventures that follow when a private home is mistaken for an inn, is reminiscent of the best of Restoration comedy but lacks its artificiality and brittle quality. It is a delightful comedy and still fulfills its original purpose to make people laugh.

Richard Brinsley Sheridan (1751–1816), playwright, politician, and theatre manager, wrote several plays but is now remembered for only two, *The Rivals* (1775) and *The School for Scandal* (1777). *The Rivals* was Sheridan's first play and shows signs of hasty construction. Nevertheless it is a charming comedy, and the character of Mrs. Malaprop, with her "nice derangement of epitaphs," is an immortal creation in the annals of comedy. *The School for Scandal* is the finest English play of the eighteenth century, and its merits alone place Sheridan in the top rank of English comic dramatists. The command of language and the stagecraft of the play is brilliant. Few today would disagree with Sir Henry Irving's observation that Sheridan brought the comedy of manners to its highest perfection. *The School for Scandal* is unquestionably a sparkling moment in a dull century of English drama.

Two of the greatest actors of the twentieth century, Sir John Gielgud and Sir Ralph Richardson, in a scene from Richard Sheridan's The School for Scandal.

(Photograph by Fred Fehl, Hoblitzelle Theatre Arts Library, Humanities Research Center, University of Texas at Austin.)

DRAMA IN SPAIN AND ITALY IN THE EIGHTEENTH CENTURY

Spain

The drama of eighteenth-century Spain was of poor quality, the result of an apparent lack of original talent and a century-long battle between neoclassicists and traditionalists. Although the traditional theatres of the Golden Age drama were replaced in the eighteenth century with Italian-style playhouses, the plays and the style of production remained products of the seventeenth century. The accession of Philip V to the Spanish throne in 1700 brought in a strong tide of French influences in many areas, but the popular theatre remained untouched. During the reigns of Philip V and Ferdinand VI (1700–1759), the court turned its attention to Italian opera, critics called for plays to be written in the French neoclassic style, and actors and inferior playwrights continued to mine the exhausted traditions of an earlier century.

Neoclassical Conflicts In the middle of the eighteenth century, just at a time when the dramatic treasures of the Golden Age were receiving some admiration outside Spain, a concerted effort was made in Spain to introduce French neoclassicism. An Academy of Good Taste was founded in Madrid in 1749, and a major critical battle erupted over the merits and faults of Spanish drama. The neoclassicists sought to reform the stage and to correct or revive the old plays. In this battle the neoclassicists found an ally in the Church, where many ecclesiastics were calling for a total ban on the Golden Age theatre. During the century theatres were forced to close for long periods of time in some parts of Spain, comedies about religious subjects were banned by the king, and, in 1765, the *autos sacramentales* were suppressed by royal decree. Yet for all their efforts to get traditional plays removed from the theatres and replaced by new neoclassical scripts, the neoclassicists made very little progress until late in the century. Two major obstacles in their path were their lack of a good playwright and Ramón de la Cruz.

Ramón de la Cruz In midcentury Madrid, at the time the reformers were attempting to get their new plays staged, the theatres of the city were under the indirect control of Ramón de la Cruz (1731–1794), a writer of highly popular *sainetes*. These one-act sketches developed out of the tradition of the sixteenth-century comic *paso* and centered on observations of scenes and characters of urban life. With their lively, colloquial dialogue and realistic depiction of city life, *sainetes* have remained a popular dramatic form in Spain. Cruz's *sainetes* were so popular with audiences that he controlled the direction of the public theatres in Madrid.

Cruz also used his *sainetes* to ridicule the goals of the neoclassicists, thus helping to sustain a negative attitude toward the new drama in the minds of audience members. Yet new plays finally did get a hearing in Spain, not so much on their own merits as on the bankruptcy of the old plays. By the latter part of the eighteenth century, the Golden Age plays were losing their appeal because they no longer reflected Spanish life. The first of the neoclassical plays to receive favorable receptions were Tomas de Iriarte's *El señorito mimado* (The Pampered Youth, 1788), *La señorita mal criada* (The Ill-bred Miss, 1788), and Leandro Fernandez de Moratin's *El viejo y la niña* (The Old Man and the Young Girl, 1790). The majority of the new plays presented on the Spanish stage in the late eighteenth century were either translations of French plays or Golden Age plays reworked to conform to the tastes of the neoclassicists. The neoclassicists were finally establishing themselves in the Spanish theatre at the beginning of the nineteenth century when the entire country was thrown into upheaval by the invasion of the armies of Napoleonic France. Development in the Spanish theatre came to a halt as the country became an international battle zone.

Italy

Italian opera continued to be the dominating influence in eighteenth-century Italy, as it had been in the previous century. By the middle of the seventeenth century, the *libretti* of opera had nearly ceased to be of dramatic interest as the focus shifted to star soloists and spectacular staging.

Magnificent theatres were built in all parts of Italy to showcase the beauties of the opera, but Italian drama was neglected and ignored. The theatrical needs of the Italian people appeared to be met by the opera, which appealed to all social levels, and the traditional *commedia dell'arte*. The *commedia* had grown stale since the sixteenth century and increasingly relied on memorized speeches. Nevertheless, it retained its popularity throughout Italy.

Although Venice in the eighteenth century was coming to the end of its thousand years of existence as a republic, it was still the theatrical capital of Italy. All seven of its beautiful theatres staged productions during a season lasting from early October to Ash Wednesday. *Commedia dell'arte* was the principal fare, but in the 1740s Italian comedy took a new direction with the appearance of Carlo Goldoni.

Carlo Goldoni   For nearly half his life Carlo Goldoni (1707–1793) played at being both a lawyer and a playwright. All this changed in 1748, when he signed a contract with one of the acting companies in Venice and devoted himself totally to the theatre. He hoped to reform Italian comedy away from the *commedia*, but, as it was difficult to wean the actors and audiences away from the traditional, Goldoni was forced to compromise. The over 150 plays by Goldoni may be divided into three groups: *commedia* types with masked characters; comedies in Italian with unmasked characters; and comedies written entirely in the Venetian dialect.

Carlo Goldoni.

Carlo Gozzi.

The best plays of the first group include *Il servitore di due padroni* (The Servant of Two Masters, 1745), *La famiglia dell'antiquario* (The Antiquarian's Family, 1750), *Il bugiardo* (The Liar, 1750), and *Il teatro comico* (The Comic Theatre, 1750), a play-within-a-play and an expression of Goldoni's theories on comedy and acting. The second group contains *La locandiera* (The Mistress of the Inn, 1752), one of his masterpieces, and *Gl'Innamorati* (The Lovers, 1759). The plays in this group are often compared to the work of Molière, and they contain the strongest social criticism to be found in Goldoni. The best comedies are in the last group, those written in the Venetian dialect. In such plays as *I pettegolezzi delle donne* (The Gossip of Women, 1751), *La casa nova* (The New House, 1760), and *Le baruffe chiozzotte* (Scuffles at Chioggia, 1762), his realism in depicting the lives of the common people of Venice is remarkable and innovative. In these plays many characters are used, and their dialogue is crisp and overlapping. Here are the sounds of eighteenth-century Venice captured as if on a recording.

In 1761 Goldoni left Venice for Paris to write French comedies for the Italian actors of the Théâtre Italien. In 1776, his career as a dramatist at an end, he became a tutor in Italian to the children of Louis XVI. He died in Paris in 1793. He was the most admired Italian playwright of the eighteenth century and still remains one of the true masters of the Italian theatre.

Carlo Gozzi   Angered by Goldoni's attempts to re-form the *commedia*, Carlo Gozzi (1720–1806), a Venetian noble, wrote a new play for the old form and unintentionally launched his own brief career as a playwright. The 1761 production of *L'Amore delle tre melarane* (The Love of Three Oranges) was Gozzi's attempt to illustrate that people will attend any type of theatre if it promises to be novel. The play was in the *commedia* style and contained a caricature of Goldoni in the character of the magician Celio. The success of this play prompted Gozzi to write nine more in the same vein, all *fiabe*, fantastic plays. The best-known of these are *Turandot* (1762) and *L'Augellino belverde* (The Pretty Little Green Bird, 1764). The novelty of this type play did not last beyond 1765. The *fiabe* of Gozzi were admired outside Italy, particularly in Germany where the early romantics were greatly attracted to the mix of the serious and the fantastic. *Turandot* and *Tre melarane* were turned into operas in the twentieth century, and some of Gozzi's scripts have been successfully produced in the last fifty years. They hold great potential for innovative direction and design.

Vittorio Alfieri   The only significant eighteenth-cen-tury Italian tragic playwright was Vittorio Alfieri (1749–1803), who wrote over a dozen tragedies and a few comedies during his theatrical career. Although his tragedies held the stage in Italy for over a century, he is now remembered only for *Saul* (1782) and *Mirra* (1784), two dramatic studies of mental torment and anguish. Unlike many tragic playwrights of the century, Alfieri expended little effort on the settings of his plays and instead concentrated his energies on depicting the inner struggles of his major characters. His style is severely simple and completely neoclassic. With his death in 1803, the spirit of creativity in Italian drama disappeared for over fifty years.

DRAMA IN SCANDINAVIA

Although slower in development, the theatre in Scandinavia followed the same pattern established throughout Europe. Thus it was that the eighteenth century in Scandinavia was a period of awakening nationalistic theatre rather than the theatrical ebb that existed in most European countries. Throughout the seventeenth century and the early decades of the eighteenth, professional theatre in Scandinavia was provided by visiting acting companies from France and Germany and occasionally from England. But changes were under way in the early eighteenth century. In 1722 the first permanent national playhouse in Scandinavia was constructed in Copenhagen, and that same year marked the beginning of a national theatre with the premiere of *Den politiske kandestøber* (The Political Tinker) by Ludvig Holberg.

Ludvig Holberg

A philosopher, historian, and university professor, Ludvig Holberg (1684–1754) wrote a total of thirty-three plays during his brief career as a playwright. He created a native-language theatre for Denmark and was the most significant playwright in Scandinavia in the eighteenth century. Combining elements of Plautus, Molière, and the *commedia dell'arte*, Holberg created an original drama that, for the first time, placed Danish and Norwegian characters upon the stage.

During the first eighteen months of the national theatre in Copenhagen, Holberg provided it with fifteen new comedies. The majority of his plays he called comedies of character. These plays, like Molière's, focus on one character who is exposed to ridicule. Holberg predates Goldsmith in being a champion of laughing comedy, but at the same time he retained the classical principle that a comedy should both please and instruct. The best of his plays are *Den politiske kandestøber* (1722), *Erasmus Montanus* (1725), and *Jeppe paa bjerget* (Jeppe on the Hill, 1723). Translated and produced in Germany and admired in France, Holberg was Scandinavia's first playwright of international stature.

With the accession of Christian VI as King of Denmark and Norway in 1738, the theatres were closed and plays were officially forbidden. But the movement for a national drama found a new home in Sweden. There, in 1737, a new vernacular theatre was opened in Stockholm. Unfortunately, Sweden produced no Holberg to give its native theatre plays worth attending, and public indifference nearly killed it. It took a king, as playwright, to give it new life and purpose.

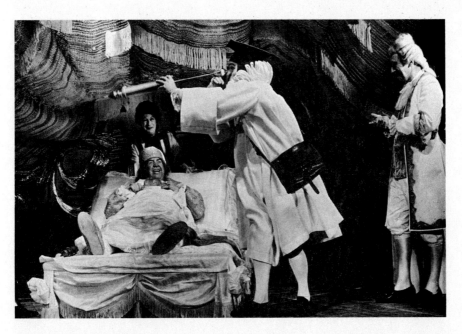

A scene from a 1979 production of Ludvig Holberg's Jeppe on the Hill *at the Danish Royal Theatre, Copenhagen.*

(Photograph by Rigmor Mydtskov, used courtesy of the Royal Danish Embassy and the Danish Royal Theatre.)

Gustav III

In the 1770s theatre had a new burst of creativity in Scandinavia: the newly established Danish national theatre became the Royal Danish Theatre; efforts were made in Norway, still a Danish possession, to establish a native company of actors; and Swedish sparkled under the close attention of Gustav III, who frequently exercised his passion for acting and play writing during his reign (1771–1792). The king desired plays that would glorify Swedish history, and when no plays were forthcoming, he provided them. In 1783 the court theatre at Gripsholm produced six plays, all written by Gustav III. Although the plays of Gustav are not major contributions to world drama, they did anticipate the popular historical melodramas of the nineteenth century and helped establish a favorable climate for the further development of Swedish theatre. In 1788 the Royal Swedish Dramatic Theatre began its long history. Gustav III's direct involvement with the theatre came to an end on March 16, 1792, when he was assassinated in his private box at the Royal Opera House. No doubt Gustav III would have approved had he known his own life and assassination would be the subject of theatrical works by Scribe, Verdi, and Strindberg. Even in death he continued to assist his great passion, the theatre.

A design by Louis Desprez for the first act of Queen Christina *(1785), a play planned by Gustav III.*

(Courtesy of the National Museum of Fine Arts, Stockholm.)

DRAMA IN EIGHTEENTH-CENTURY GERMANY

There is little remarkable in the German drama of the seventeenth century. The work of Andreas Gryphius (1616–1664), who was Germany's major dramatist of the period, was only staged sporadically owing to the lack of permanent playhouses in the country. In the second half of the century translations and adaptations of French dramas and opera dominated the German stage. At the beginning of the eighteenth century, the German theatre was in need of reform, revival, and new plays. Johann Christoph Gottsched was prepared to supply all three.

J. C. Gottsched

The first playwright to attempt to reform the German stage along the lines of French neoclassicism was Johann Christoph Gottsched (1700–1766). With a repertoire consisting mainly of his own translations of seventeenth-century French plays, Gottsched had the good fortune to form a working arrangement with a company of professional performers headed by Caroline Neuber, Germany's first major actress. With Neuber's aid he presented to German audiences the best of French neoclassicism. Yet Gottsched's attempts at reform were doomed from the start because of a lack of audience interest and the unwillingness of German actors to totally give up the old farces. In 1740 the tensions created by Gottsched's arrogant demands for reform and Neuber's need to please paying audiences resulted in a breakdown of their relationship. Regardless of its unhappy conclusion, the Gottsched-Neuber collaboration was an important turning point in the development of the German theatre.

Lessing

Gotthold Ephraim Lessing (1729–1781) arrived in Leipzig to attend the university just a few years after the Gottsched-Neuber break. Gottsched was still a powerful force in the literary circles of the city, but the young Lessing spent his free time with actors rather than reformers. His first play, a comedy entitled *Der junge Gelehrte* (The Young Scholar, 1748), was produced by Caroline Neuber's company. After its production Lessing committed himself to a career as a playwright and literary critic. His first major play appeared seven years later and established him as the founder of modern German drama.

Miss Sara Sampson (1755) broke with the attempts to establish a German neoclassical drama. The influences for the play came from England, not France. This middle-class domestic tragedy owes a great deal to George Lillo's *The London Merchant* and the English novels of Samuel Richardson. As a tragedy it broke with tradition by being written in prose, and its dialogue is natural, if still somewhat within traditional tragic conventions. The play was a success at its premiere and in later productions.

In his critical writing Lessing defended Shakespeare against the charges of "irregularity" made against him by the neoclassicists, and he introduced the concept of the writer as original creator rather than artistic imitator. This concept would become a major principle with the writers of the later romantic movement. In 1767 he gave the German stage *Minna von Barnhelm*, the first masterpiece of German comedy. In the same year he began publishing his *Hamburgische Dramaturgie* (Hamburg Dramaturgy), written as a result of his appointment as official critic of the newly established National Theatre of Hamburg. The *Dramaturgie* is important for its statements on Lessing's views on the possibilities and needs of a German national drama.

Lessing's last play, *Nathan der Weise* (Nathan the Wise, 1779), was not produced until 1801, twenty years after his death. This plea for religious tolerance has held a place in the German repertoire ever since. Lessing's influence outside Germany was small, and his plays are rarely performed outside that country. Within Germany, Lessing is an important figure, and he is generally credited with founding modern German literature and criticism.

Sturm und Drang

In the 1770s a major literary movement in Germany, collectively called *Sturm und Drang* (Storm and Stress), changed the focus of German drama. It was also a powerful influence on the entire romantic movement that overwhelmed the decaying citadel of neoclassicism at the end of the eighteenth century and the beginning of the nineteenth. *Sturm und Drang* was a literary epoch, lasting approximately twenty years, that encompassed a number of different literary groups in Germany. The term *Sturm und Drang* comes from the title of a play by Friedrich Klinger (1752–1831), whose dramatic works were highly characteristic of the entire *Sturm und Drang*. These poets, critics, novelists, and playwrights were protesting against the rigidity of neoclassicism and were demanding total artistic freedom for the literary creator.

As a group these young writers professed a fondness for folklore, medieval atmospheres, and the wildness of nature. They hailed individual genius and believed the artist should not be restricted by rigid social, political, or religious traditions. The strong emphasis placed on emotion over reason by these writers resulted in their being called irrational and irresponsible by their elders. With the *Sturm und Drang* writers a revolt was under way, and the political revolutions of the period served to increase their ardor.

The dramas of the *Sturm und Drang* best reflect the concerns of these young champions of change and their yearnings for freedom. In these plays the hero, who is usually a highly superior individual, is depicted as in total conflict with the society in which he lives. In structure the plays show a near-contempt for the rules of neoclassicism, and the dialogue is strongly idiomatic, although somewhat self-important. The two finest young playwrights of the *Sturm und Drang* were Schiller and Goethe.

Schiller

The son of an army surgeon and likewise trained as a physician, Johann Christoph Friedrich von Schiller (1759-1805) abandoned his medical career after the success of his first play, *Die Räuber* (The Robbers, 1781). This play, about the hostility between two brothers, condemns society as evil and praises the rebellious, natural man. It met with a riotous success on its opening night, even though the cautious manager of the theatre at Mannheim insisted on script changes to remove what he considered offensive lines and characters. Even with its considerable flaws, *Die Räuber* is one of the finest *Sturm und Drang* plays.

In 1783 Schiller was appointed the resident playwright at the Mannheim Theatre and assigned to write three plays during the next year. Schiller wrote only two additional plays in the *Sturm und Drang* style, then moved on to a transitional period in his career. From this period came *Don Carlos*, a historical drama first presented in 1787, and one that illustrated the playwright's shift of emphasis from heroic rebellion to larger humanitarian issues.

After a hiatus of twelve years spent in research, writing, and teaching at the University of Jena, Schiller issued one of his major achievements, a trilogy of

Friedrich Schiller.

plays on the great seventeenth-century German general, Wallenstein. This trilogy (*Wallenstein's Camp*, *The Piccolomini*, and *Wallenstein's Death*) has its greatest appeal to a German audience because it depicts the struggles of the country during the Thirty Years' War, but the theatrical power and fine lyric poetry in these three plays place them in the company of Shakespeare's best history plays.

By the time the Wallenstein trilogy was completed, Schiller was living in Weimar and working in collaboration with his fellow playwright, Goethe. The entire trilogy was presented for the first time at the new Weimar State Theatre, which was under Goethe's direction. Before his early death in 1805 from tuberculosis, Schiller wrote four additional plays: *Maria Stuart* (1800), *Die Jungfrau von Orleans* (The Maid of Orleans, 1801), *Die Braut von Messina* (The Bride of Messina, 1803), and *Wilhelm Tell* (1804). All four are considered masterpieces of the German theatre. They serve as a magnificent bridge from the eighteenth to the nineteenth century, and they have earned their author the title of Germany's greatest playwright.

Goethe

Looming as a colossus over all of Germany literature, Johann Wolfgang von Goethe (1749–1832) is one of the outstanding geniuses of world literature. Acquiring an early interest in the stage from the gift of a

Johann Wolfgang von Goethe.

puppet theatre received when he was four, he began to write plays at a young age. His first serious attempts at writing for the professional stage were during his student years at Leipzig University. In 1773 he wrote *Götz von Berlichingen*, the first German play composed in a Shakespearean manner and the first important drama of the *Sturm und Drang*. This story of an honorable robber baron made extensive use of the common vernacular, coarse expressions, and fine poetic rhetoric. It was highly influential in setting the tone of the *Sturm und Drang* and remains one of Goethe's most popular plays.

His next two plays were *Clavigo* (1774) and *Stella* (1775), and they were his last efforts in the *Sturm und Drang* mood. In 1775 Goethe was invited to assume a position in the court of the Dukedom of Saxon-Weimar. By 1779 he was a privy councillor to the duke, and in 1782 he was granted a rank of nobility and appointed minister of finance. His duties included the responsibility for the Court Amateur Theatre (1775–1783) and the professional company at the Court Theatre (1791–1817). Several of his plays were produced at the Amateur Theatre, but of these only the prose version of *Iphigenie auf Tauris* (Iphigenia in Tauris, 1779) is a major work. In 1786 Goethe went to Italy for two years, and the visit caused him to reflect at length on classicism.

In 1788 Goethe returned to Germany and in that same year formed his friendship with Schiller. Appointed artistic director of the Court Theatre in 1791, Goethe made major innovations in acting and directing. In addition to directing the theatre, he also provided it with scripts.

Goethe's theatrical masterpiece, *Faust*, parts 1 and 2, belongs to the nineteenth century, although he started work on it in 1773. This huge work, composed of over twelve thousand lines, is four times the length of *Hamlet*. Although the work has been successfully staged in its entirety, it is truly too vast for the ordinary stage. It is a work of theatrical genius, but its concept and spiritual panorama place it beyond comparison with other plays. *Faust*, like its creator, outgrew the bounds of ordinary theatre. It is unique, a new type of theatrical experience that is yet to be fully realized on the stage. The work had a strong influence on the English romantic poets and Henrik Ibsen.

The Influence of Schiller and Goethe

In their plays Schiller and Goethe show a willingness to experiment with the laws of art as given by the eighteenth-century proponents of neoclassicism. Although both these young rebels of the *Sturm und Drang* returned to a form of classical theatre, their plays broke the eighteenth-century theatre away from the stale traditions of the past. Yet they also contributed to a new appreciation of the dramatic masters of earlier eras and set the stage for the experimentations, excesses, and revisions of the nineteenth century.

16

EIGHTEENTH-CENTURY THEATRE ARCHITECTURE AND PRODUCTION PRACTICES

The eighteenth century was a relatively impoverished period for dramatic literature in Europe. It was, however, tremendously exciting in terms of the technical perfection that the theatre achieved. While this was primarily seen in terms of innovations in scene design and moving scenery, the physical form of the theatre also underwent major changes.

PLAYHOUSE EVOLUTION

Playhouses in the eighteenth century were generally of two types: those operated through public admission and those built for the private use of royalty. The companies and their managers who operated public theatres were faced with rising costs as the demand for illusionistic scenery and machines increased. In order to fill houses two choices existed: raise prices or increase seating capacity. Most theatres catering to the public underwent significant changes in design to accommodate more seating and to permit better sight lines and acoustics. London's Drury Lane, for example, seated around 650 patrons in 1700; by the end of the eighteenth century it could accommodate some 2,300. The court theatres, primarily concerned with the gratification of a single patron, experienced fewer changes. They were, after all, concerned with the sight lines from one place in the auditorium, usually a royal box at the back of the house. But for both types of playhouses, the century was one of change.

Basic Design Concepts

The standard rectangular, or straight-sided, auditorium generally fell from favor as the major seating configuration during the eighteenth century. While it continued to be present in theatres built in earlier times, few new theatres utilized the shape, and most of those were houses for opera or for court entertainments. The London Opera House, built in 1763, and the Drottningholm Theatre in Sweden, built in 1766, serve as two of the few examples of the continuation of this auditorium shape.

Two other shapes were far more common. The first of these, the horseshoe shape, provided better sight lines to all but those in the boxes near the proscenium. For many who chose to sit there, however, being seen was about as important as seeing. The horseshoe shape also allowed for extra space in the pit, a popular standing and sitting area, thus potentially increasing revenues. French and Italian theatres largely utilized this shape, notably the Teatro Nove in Milan, the Teatro Filarmonica in Verona, the Paris Opera House, and the Comédie Française. The second shape to gain widespread popularity in the eighteenth century was the ovoid, or bell shape. This shape allowed slightly better sight lines from the front boxes to the stage, but less space was available in the pit, and the back boxes and galleries were a little pinched. This shape was common throughout Europe. Notable examples include the Teatro San Carlo in Naples, the Berlin Opera House, Margrave's Opera House in Bayreuth, Sadlers Wells in London, and the Teatro alla Scala in Milan.

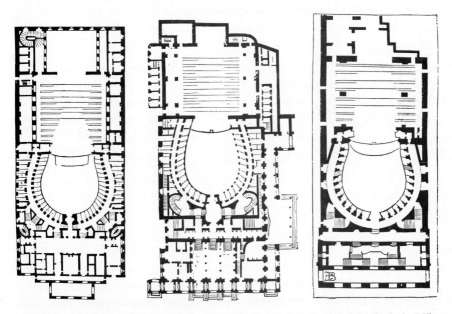

Examples of the bell and horseshoe-shaped auditoriums: (left to right) *La Scala in Milan, Carlo Felice in Genoa, San Carlo in Naples.*

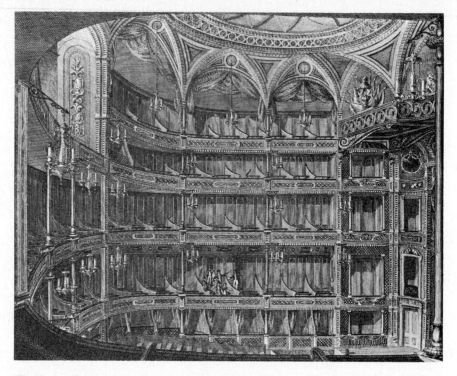

The Theatre Royal, Drury Lane, at the end of the eighteenth century. Note the balcony compartments and the proscenium doors and boxes.

The basic parts of the auditorium remain the same as they were during the seventeenth century, that is, pit, boxes, and galleries. Three galleries became standard during the eighteenth century, although occasionally five were used. Yet it was the pit that experienced the biggest change with the gradual introduction of bench seating in that area throughout the eighteenth century. Some of the countries of northern Europe resisted the change from a standing pit, but it was inevitable. Primarily a move to quiet the audience, the addition of benches in the pit was part of a general trend toward the modernization of the experience of theatre that could not be denied. By the end of the eighteenth century, virtually all European theatres had converted to or been built with pit seating.

The Stage

The stage experienced significant changes as well, similarly motivated by the increasing demand for spectacular scenery and effects. By the end of the seventeenth century, the concept of doorways in the proscenium arch leading onto a rather large stage apron thrust into the auditorium was commonplace in England. This trend continued throughout the first half of the eighteenth century, fueled largely by the necessity to separate the actor from the scenic space. As scenic developments became efficient and refined, the actor began to move upstage toward the scenic display and began the process of becoming one with it. As this process began toward the second half of the eighteenth century, the large apron began to shrink and the double set of proscenium doors became a single door consistent with the decreased depth of the proscenium arch itself. The countries on the Continent were far less affected by these changes than was England. The theatres there utilized a shorter apron and proscenium boxes rather than the doors (the actors thus entering primarily from the first set of wings) that were typical of all court theatres and many opera houses. Yet by century's end, most stages in Europe and England were united in a small apron, proscenium boxes or one set of doors, a flat stage floor, and more space devoted to scenery. For theatres whose stages did not utilize the extended apron, the space was divided into two parts by an act curtain separating scenic space from acting space.

Another important change after 1760 was the gradual rejection of the practice of seating audience members on the stage. The stage was first cleared in France in 1759 for a production of Jean-Baptiste Chateaubrum's *Les Troyennes*, where the share members hired thirty soldiers to appear on stage as supernumeraries and crowd-clearers at the same time. David Garrick cleared the stage of the Drury Lane in 1762, and most other countries rapidly followed before the end of the decade.

Regency Theatre, London, during a late-eighteenth-century performance of Othello.

A contemporary photograph of the Théâtre de la Monnaie in Brussels.
(Photograph by Jean-Pierre Stevens, used courtesy of the Belgian National Opera.)

By century's end, another device was common on most European stages, and that was a downstage center protruberance from the stage floor known as the prompter's box. Essentially a hole in the stage floor hidden from audience view by a boxed shield, the box provided the prompter, whose duties more closely paralleled those of the modern stage manager, a working vantage point for the successful discharge of his duties. He could conduct the performance without being a part of it. All these changes suggest an undeniable trend toward distinguishing the stage space from the auditorium space, and they looked toward the nineteenth-century concept of the fourth wall.

The European triumph of the neoclassic ideal on staging was, by century's end, complete. In the 1740s both of the major Spanish playhouses, the Teatro del Principe and the Teatro de la Cruz, were rebuilt along classic Italian lines, becoming indoor, proscenium arch theatres. In Munich, Germany, the Residenztheater (1771) was constructed along Italian principles, as was the Théâtre de la Monnaie in Brussels (1700) and the Nieuwe Schouwburg in Amsterdam (1664). The Renaissance idea of theatrical verisimilitude was, by the end of the eighteenth century, close to fruition.

SCENIC PRACTICE AND STAGE MACHINERY

The centuries before the eighteenth had gradually but firmly convinced audiences that verisimilitude was best served by ever-increasing scenery and stage effects, both in complexity and scope. Thus throughout the eighteenth century, scenery became larger and more intricate, machines for special effects became more impressive and complex, the concept of perspective underwent a fundamental change, and the very notion of a designer's responsibility was reexamined. All of the changes were, like the changes in playhouse construction, oriented toward achieving greater reality in theatrical presentation.

Scene Design Concepts

In the aesthetics of scene design, the eighteenth century was the age of the baroque and the foreshadowing of the romantic. The baroque was characterized by a heavy emphasis on diagonal and curved lines rather than on the straight horizontal and vertical lines of the Renaissance. There was far more concern with the creation of mood through the use of painted highlight and shadow. Thus the old concepts of Serlio and Sabbattini gave way to those of a new generation of scene designers.

The most fundamental change to scene design came primarily through the contributions of one family of scene designers. Working during the hundred years from the 1680s to the 1780s, the Bibiena family created theatrical designs for the finest houses and patrons in Europe. This age was, after all, governed by a conspicuous consumption that caused the wealthy and prestigious to flatter themselves by ostentatious patronage of the arts. And the arts, particularly scene design, responded and grew accordingly. One of the major changes in scene design that this patronage fostered was an alteration in the basic concept of a single eye point perspective itself. Before the 1680s perspective scenery had been oriented to an extension of the scale of the auditorium. The proscenium arch governed the size of the downstage wings, and all the scenery upstage logically extended into the stage space toward a single vanishing point. This concept, which had reigned supreme for nearly two hundred years, was broken by Ferdinando Bibiena (1657–1743) through his stage design work for the Hapsburgs in Vienna. One of eight famous scene designers, each a generation apart, Ferdinando formally presented his ideas in his book *Architettura civilis* (Civil Architecture, 1711). This book became the standard volume

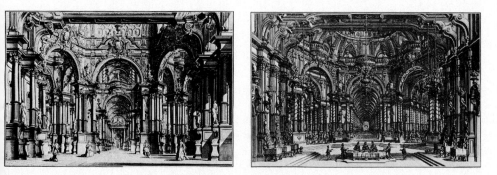

Two Bibiena-designed sets from a production given for the Prince Elector of Saxony.
(From G. Bibiena, Architectural and Perspective Designs, *Dover Publications, 1964.)*

The Eighteenth Century

A Bibiena-designed set for wing and drop staging.
(From G. Bibiena, Architectural and Perspective Designs, *Dover Publications, 1964.*)

on stage practice for the balance of the eighteenth century. The primary concept in the book, *scena per angolo* (angled or corner perspective scenery), considerably changed the accepted view of perspective onstage. Basically, *scena per angolo* presented a setting that did not confine itself to the stage space or to the size of the proscenium. The view provided was that of a corner of a great room that extended into the auditorium itself, culminating in some unseen corner that provided clear focus on the patronage box or seat. Thus only a portion of the scenic idea was seen through the proscenium, and the magic of the baroque was affirmed. This style of scene design was the specialty of the Bibiena family. True to the family's stature, when Ferdinando went blind, his son Giuseppe (1696–1756), who had worked with him for a number of years, was appointed Austrian court decorator.

Other Designers

The Bibienas were not the only contributors to the development of scene design in the eighteenth century. Among others, Filippo Juvarra (1676–1736) made significant contributions. Working primarily for his patron, Cardinal Pietro Ottoboni (1667–1740), Juvarra used his own version of *scena per angolo* to create elaborate opera scenery. In addition, he designed and constructed a small theatre for the cardinal in his Palazzo della Cancelleria. His principal theatre work was done between 1708 and 1714, after which he was involved in civic and church architecture. In France the leading native scene designer of the eighteenth century was Jean-Nicolas Servandoni (1695–1766). His settings were reminiscent of the simpler neoclassicism of the seventeenth century, although his work at the Salle des Machines at the Tuileries employed considerable movement of special effects. Another designer who blended *scena per angolo* technique with the growing concern for atmospheric highlight and shadow was Gian Battista Piranesi (1720–1778). He specialized in the addition of mood to his settings, purposefully depicting some details unclearly. His fascination was with prisons and scenes from antiquity rendered in a ruined state. He was a significant contributor to the neoclassic revival and clearly foreshadowed the romantic movement.

England had remained fairly free from the baroque and by the middle of the eighteenth century was moving toward an emphasis on the romantic, particularly the landscape garden and other natural landscapes. The chief exponent of this style was Philippe Jacques de Loutherboug (1740–1812). Hired to design scenery at Drury Lane in 1771, he pioneered the use of atmospheric illusion, particularly fanciful notions of volcanos, fire effects, sun- and moonlight, and glory-type cloud effects. He was concerned with the realistic portrayal of weather-related sound effects, especially sounds for storms. Although he was criticized for his overly vivid colors, he paved the way for natural scenic effects. He experimented with practical scenery, that is, scenery that an actor could actively use, but those experiments were premature for the taste of the times. Primarily through his work with Garrick at Drury Lane, Loutherbourg is known for his re-creations of specific real settings in and around London. Finally, he was the first designer to concern himself with the coordination of all technical aspects of production, thereby foreshadowing modern organic unity as applied to all aspects of stage design.

Another scenic practitioner in London was William Capon (1757–1827). Working at Drury Lane in 1791, Capon was the first major designer in London to concern himself with scenery that was historically accurate. Because of his antiquarianism, his settings were extremely large and cumbersome to move. Nonetheless, he enjoyed tremendous popularity into the early nineteenth century. Following his Drury Lane years he worked at Covent Garden, where his settings were used for years following his retirement. He provided an important link to the fully historically accurate scenery of the nineteenth century.

The styles of these men clearly show the trend in scenery throughout the eighteenth century. As the century began the baroque aesthetic held full sway, but by midcentury a simpler style had emerged. This was slowly supplanted by growing romantic notions touched with flickers of historical accuracy by century's end.

Stage Machinery

Although the eighteenth century was a great period of scene painting, it was also a period of significant innovations in theatrical machinery. Much attention was paid to the movement of scenery and the creation of special effects, and France set the standard for emulation through-out Europe. The specific machinery used was not conceptually new, but was refined in sophistication and size. Chief among these devices was the *chariot-mat*. Originally developed by Torelli, this scene-changing machine continued to allow simultaneous shifts of all wings. The changes it underwent in the eighteenth century allowed more even and rapid scene changes. The increased fluidity by which the large flats moved on and off the stage was, no doubt, impressive.

Another system for moving scenery, less common than the *chariot-mat*, was the *cassette-ame*. The *cassette* was an understage hollow groove (also called a *slote*), and the *ame* was a wooden chock that traveled in the *cassette* and rose through a slit in the stage floor at each wing station. The *ame* would travel up the *cassette*, thus revealing the wing for all to see in one burst of energy and noise. These changes were done in full view of the audience and were undoubtedly part of the magic of the theatre in the eighteenth century.

These two systems were complemented by methods for moving other elements of the scenic display. Borders existed at each wing station, as they had in centuries past, but in the eighteenth century there was an increasing interest in changing them more often. This was in keeping with the increasing consciousness that verisimilitude was best served by creating scenery that was more specific to each play and scene. Thus new scenery was designed and built more often as the production of new plays increased. Borders, therefore, had to change, and this was accomplished by securing them to battens located in the above-stage space. Stagehands raised and lowered the borders as needed, working from the pinrails. In addition, machinery continued to be developed to support specific effects. Actors were flown in by machines that allowed diagonal descent (not unlike that used for earlier cloud effects), wave motion descent, and a descent path that followed an arc. Similarly, set pieces such as pageant wagons or *carros*, clouds, glory effects, and even mountains descended to the stage. Working water machines allowed for practical waterfalls, and boats rode elaborate wave machines. None of this was new since it had emerged during the Renaissance. What was new was the concern for the movement of these set pieces and the implementation of that movement by means of large stage effects and supporting machinery.

All over Europe, French models were copied. Germany was probably the most complete copy as each prince aspired to the theatrical glory of the French court. The terms were different—*Kulissenwagon-Kulissenbaum* for *chariot-mat* for example—but the practice was the same. In the Scandinavian countries, French techniques were commonly used but on a somewhat smaller scale. Thus theatres like Gripsholm and Drottningholm were fully illusionistic playhouses, yet cut down in scale. England, as usual, had its own modifications to fit its unique circumstances. The wing and groove system introduced in the late sixteenth century prevailed as the major system for changing English scenery. For the most part, the flats were moved by hand, although by the end of the century some experiments in mechanization were tried. A trolley system was implemented that allowed the flats to be transported on low wheeled guides, tied together so that one flat went on stage as the flat from the preceding

Note in these two photographs of the Gripsholm Court Theatre the flat wings, which have been painted to achieve an exterior perspective.

(Courtesy of the National Museum of Fine Arts, Stockholm.)

scene went off, not unlike a simplified version of the *chariot-mat*. London theatres did not have adequate basements for great understage effects. The high water table probably precluded the construction of elaborate basements. Thus the use of overstage space rapidly developed in England during the eighteenth century for the placement of machinery from which special effects were generated. During the nineteenth century, flying machinery would rapidly overtake elaborate understage machinery as the main method of shifting scenery. Except for opera, the *chariot-mat* and the *cassette-ame*, like the baroque aesthetic itself, would collapse under their own weight.

While existing sets from Gripsholm and Drottningholm confirm that wings and backdrops were the traditional way in which scenes were depicted, they also suggest a rising concern for creating an environment in which the actor could work rather than simply stand in front of a painted set. As the pictures from those theatres illustrate, the painting on each wing realistically suggests a retreating wall to the next wing. Similarly, the borders suggest a single sense of ceiling. From this point it has a rather small yet significant step to the fully three-dimensional or box set of the early nineteenth century. Indeed, evidence suggests that practical doors were occasionally used between wings in the late eighteenth century, and through these, the actors made upstage entrances. Thus in terms of design concept and practical implementation, the box setting was on its way.

Costuming

For most of the eighteenth century, as in the centuries preceding it, historical accuracy in costuming was not a major factor. But by the end of the century some designers and actors began to show at least a

A contemporary production of Scarlatti's L'honesta negli amori *at the Drottningholm Court Theatre. Note the prompter's box and traditional wing scenery.*
(Courtesy of the National Museum of Fine Arts, Stockholm.)

passing concern about the historical accuracy of their stage dress. No doubt this was fueled by the rising interest in science and the tenets of antiquarianism, which demanded that some attention be paid to the accuracy of the stage picture. Part of the problem full historical accuracy had in gaining a foothold was that the practice of costuming was dictated by public taste and convention. In addition, costume practice was essentially in the hands of the actors, who depended upon public acceptance for their survival. To be sure, Beaumarchais described the clothing his characters should wear, and actress Mlle Clairon appeared with bare arms in a Voltaire piece, but the old practices of contemporary dress with a few character types done in stereotyped costume was the norm. After the 1770s some sense of historical accuracy was noted in the costuming practices of most European countries. It appeared side by side with the older conventions, however, which indicates that it was in its novelty stage until the nineteenth century. For most of the eighteenth century, costume practice differed little from that of the seventeenth century.

Lighting

As in the other technical aspects of eighteenth-century theatre, the practice of lighting experienced few inventions yet many refinements on older ideas. Footlights and wing ladders were in common use

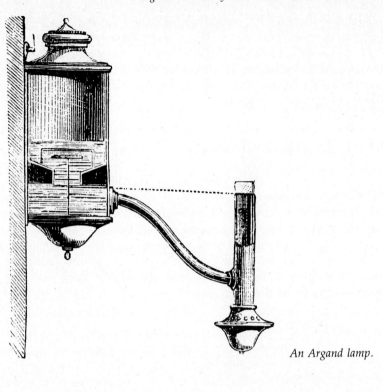

An Argand lamp.

throughout the century, as were border floats and auditorium candle chandeliers. Alterations to these basic approaches to stage lighting included considerable experimentation with reflectors to shield the light from the audience and
to focus it more directly and with more efficiency on the scenery. Thus at Drury
Lane shields were constructed and placed so that footlight spill was kept from
the audience's eyes. Similar devices were placed on the downstage side of
wing ladder oil lamps to help focus more light on the upstage flats. Reasons for
this were two: the extra brilliance that the reflected light created onstage
helped draw attention to the stage and away from the large auditorium
chandeliers, and notions of increased verisimilitude required that the lighting
devices be concealed from the audience.

A major invention that affected stage lighting in the eighteenth century was
the Argand lamp. In the 1780s Aime Argand, a Swiss chemist, invented an oil
lamp with a hollow cylindrical wick that allowed air to mix directly with the
center of the flame. Thus a brighter flame was possible. One of Argand's
assistants later made the important discovery that the problem of flickering
could be controlled if the flame burned within a glass tube, thus controlling air
flow. The glass chimney was born, and the resulting steady flame was a
tremendous boon to stage lighting. For the first time a steady light could
illuminate the actors and scenery, and a major source of audience distraction
was eliminated. With this invention, oil lamps, primarily using whale or plant
oil, rapidly replaced candles for onstage lighting, although the candle chande-

lier remained the standard for auditorium lighting for the balance of the century. As had been the practice in the sixteenth and seventeenth centuries, the auditorium was still lit in conjunction with the stage. Whatever focus the stage enjoyed was created by adding extra light, both through sharpened focus or increased quantity of lamps. There was no attempt to darken the house until the middle of the nineteenth century.

ACTORS AND ACTING

As in the seventeenth century, the stage of the eighteenth century presented audiences with a variety of specific styles, depending on the form of drama being presented and the individual styles of the various actors. Opera required the most traditional style, while some of the newer plays demanded emphasis on the rising natural style. It remained a century, however, where no single sense of verisimilitude in acting was commonly agreed upon. Both the classic and the natural styles coexisted, sometimes concurrently on the same stage.

Acting Style

The two major styles that had come forward in the seventeenth century continued to dominate the stage of the 1700s, but after the middle of the eighteenth century the natural style became dominant. There was considerable variety within the natural style as it came to the fore. It varied from a fairly high degree of emotional energy portrayed in an exaggerated manner to a somewhat more restrained approach, bordering on real life actions and intensities. In no case, however, was this "real" in terms of realistic acting today, for it lacked the psychological introspection and restraint of modern acting. Actors would commonly enter and immediately go downstage center to deliver their lines, facing full front. Although the declamatory chant of the classic actor was no longer in use after the middle of the century, varieties in vocal performance ranged from forced conversational speaking to clearly pointed and accentuated emotional delivery. But the seeds of modern realism in acting were sown in the eighteenth century as acting began to be taken seriously as an art form to be formally studied and practiced.

Actors

Nowhere does the simultaneous conflict and coexistence of the classic and natural styles find greater champions than in England with James Quin and David Garrick. James Quin (1693–1766) was a leading tragedian. Rather set in his ways, he was the major exponent of the classic style in the eighteenth century. His acting was described as declamation, and his insistence upon preserving the old even affected his choice of costume. He was nonetheless a man of great talent who championed his style with integrity. By the time of his retirement in 1751, the tide was against his style. His rival,

A woodcut depicting James Quin in the role of Coriolanus.

David Garrick (1717–1779), ranks among the greatest English actors. He was more responsible for the movement of acting toward the natural than any performer of his day. Not only did he significantly reform acting, but these reforms were in connection with his long management of Drury Lane. Equally adept at comedy and tragedy, Garrick brought an emotional energy to the stage hitherto unknown, particularly in such roles as Lear. The energy and emotional power of his characterizations transcended an awkward physical stature not normally suited to tragedy. In terms of the totality of his career, he was the most significant theatrical force on the eighteenth-century English stage.

In style, other English actors fell somewhere between Quin and Garrick. Charles Macklin (1699–1797), an Irish actor, probably employed a natural style, certainly if his characterization of Shylock is any measure. His playing of Shylock in a dignified tragic manner was considerably different from the low comedy status that had been assigned to the part. This represented a significant break from the past in an age where roles and stage business were handed down from actor to actor for exact copying. Late in his career, he founded an acting school and thereby contributed most significantly to the art of acting in his century. Anne Oldfield (1683–1730) was considered the finest actress of her time after the premature retirement of Anne Bracegirdle (c. 1663–1748) in

A painting of David Garrick as Macbeth and Mrs. Pritchand as Lady Macbeth.

1707. Oldfield was competent in both tragedy and comedy, but she greatly preferred comedy and specialized in those parts. Possessing an excellent figure and fine voice, she played with "majesty and power" in creating her characters. As an indication of her stature, she was the first actress to be accorded the honor of burial in Westminster Abbey. John Philip Kemble (1757–1823) was one of a family of fine actors. His style, often called the "teapot" school of acting from the position the actor assumed with one hand on his hip and the other extended, had a quiet, stately, formal approach to acting. Normally that would make him a classic actor, but the lack of declamation puts him more toward the center of the style continuum. He specialized in tragedy and played most parts with an intensity of feeling. Occasional comments about his deficiencies include references to a harsh voice and stiff gestures and movement. He managed Drury Lane for a time before his retirement and instituted a number of reforms that made him a significant figure in advancing the profession of acting. Another member of the Kemble family, Mrs. Sarah Siddons (1755–1831), was the greatest actress of tragedy on the English stage during the late eighteenth and early nineteenth centuries. The sister of John Philip Kemble, she rose to prominence after 1782 and dominated the stage with her tragic and heroic roles. A woman of beauty, dignity, intelligence, and good judgment, with a rich voice and well-executed gestures, she brought these characteristics to her playing. Words such as

A woodcut of Charles Macklin as Shylock.

A portrait of Sarah Siddons by Thomas Gainsborough.

The Eighteenth Century

"tender" and "noble" were used to describe her acting, and the critic William Hazlitt said upon her retirement in 1815, "Who shall make tragedy stand once more with its feet upon the earth, and its head above the stars, weeping tears and blood?" Such was the aura around the woman some have called England's finest tragic actress.

In France the same dichotomy of style existed, and an examination of a few actors will illustrate the point. Mlle Marie-Françoise Dumesnil (1713–1803) was a natural actress of the first order. She excelled in passionate roles and had a wide range of characters she could play within the tragic heroine genre. She survived the French Revolution and was able to pass on some of her knowledge to a younger generation of actors, thus somewhat influencing the early-nineteenth-century French stage. She was not interested in reforms. Mlle Claire-Josèphe-Hippolyte Léris Clairon (1723–1803) was, however, reform-conscious. She excelled in tragedy in the same parts that were the specialty of Dumesnil, but her range was more limited. Her voice was said to have surpassed her rival's in beauty, and she paid far more attention to character history in the study of her parts. She brought a determination and a fervor to her acting that made her a favorite of Voltaire. Throughout her career she moved more toward the natural style, and her deep voice was perfect for it. The leading French actor of his time was Henri-Louis Lekain (1729–1778). Beginning his career as an apprentice at the Comédie Française, he was noticed and encouraged in his early years by Voltaire. Although small, not very

Mlle Clairon in the title role of Medea.

Henri-Louis Lekain.

handsome, and possessing a harsh voice, Lekain was able to transcend these attributes by careful study and great energy in portraying his roles. He was a natural actor in the fine sense of discipline he brought to his craft, being called on occasion the Garrick of France. And like Garrick, he was a reformer, working toward more accuracy in costuming than had been known.

France also contributed significantly to the study and theory of acting, primarily through the works of one man, Denis Diderot (1713–1784). Fueled by a passionate interest in the theatre, Diderot, through his many writings, argued for the establishment of the bourgeois drama so rooted in the middle-class audiences of the eighteenth century. His *Paradoxe sur le comédien* (Paradox of Acting, completed 1778, first published 1830) first posed the still current and largely unanswerable question of whether acting is primarily driven by internal, emotional forces or external techniques. Further, he notes that while the actor must appear more ''real'' in portraying a believable role, that effort is essentially a stage, or conventionalized, reality. In other works, he argued for greater unity in production, especially between the playwright and the actor, and for greater reality in every aspect of the theatre. A tremendous influence on Gotthold Lessing, he was a profound theoretician about the theatre who greatly affected the rise of realism in the nineteenth century.

Germany began to be actor-conscious as its national conscience rose and its theatre became prominent. Frederika Carolina (Caroline) Neuber (1697–1760), with Johann Gottsched, brought German theatre out of the age of buffoonery and low farce that had plagued it. Although her acting was not great in itself— her tragedy was said to be pompous and her comedy affected, suggesting a classic style—her work in the training of actors and her insistence on discipline and order in preparing a production were sufficient contributions. Her high-spiritedness and, after a time, her unwillingness to compromise constantly hurt her financial success. She occasionally offended partner and patron alike, and she died in poverty. She is, however, the starting point of modern German acting.

The work of Neuber began the change in German taste to a more subtle, restrained, natural style of acting. One of the finest exponents of this style was Konrad Ekhof (1720–1778). His acting was supple and restrained, and he brought dignity and grace to the German stage. He approached his art seriously and founded in 1753 an acting school that focused on teaching the natural style to its students. His style developed into a technique that was equally at home in tragicomic and pathetic roles and, with his controlled yet flexible voice and expressive gestures, he paved the way for the acting of F. L. Schröder. Besides his acting, he generally concerned himself with raising the standards of his profession in other ways, such as starting the Actors' Benevolent Fund, an early pension system. More than any other man in Germany, Ekhof raised the entire profession of acting and the status of theatre to a place of dignity and respect.

This legacy was passed on to a man who became the most famous German actor in the eighteenth century, Friedrich Ludwig Schröder (1744–1816). Originating over seven hundred roles, Schröder learned serious acting from Ekhof at the Hamburg National Theatre, the first noncommercial theatre in Germany. He is best known for bringing Shakespeare to the German people and for managing companies that concentrated on detailed acting, discipline, and teamwork. His personal acting and his work with his ensembles laid the groundwork for subtle and refined playing in Germany. He escaped the financial fate of Neuber and retired a wealthy and respected man, honored for his contributions to the German stage. The emergence of the strong German national theatre, notably the Gotha Court Theatre (1775) and the theatre at Mannheim (1779) owe much to Schröder's contributions.

The men and women cited above contributed significantly to the maturity of European acting and its organization during the eighteenth century. It was truly a coming of age as the groundwork for serious national theatres was laid, and the detailed discipline in the art and craft of acting that the nineteenth century would depend upon for its advancements was set in place.

Acting Organization

The organization of acting companies and theatres during the eighteenth century varied considerably in detail, yet all organizational changes were moving generally in the same direction. For the most part companies increased in size, the productions were more carefully prepared, and more attention was paid to the business end of the theatre. As in other aspects of the theatre, the basis for the modern practice of the art was being established.

Theatre companies of the eighteenth century were considerably larger than their seventeenth-century counterparts. The standard size in England was eighty, and the Comédie Française and the Théâtre Italien had about fifty and seventy members, respectively. The theatrical season ran from mid-November to mid-May in most countries, with daily performances common by the end of the century. In 1766 London enjoyed its first summer season of the post-Commonwealth era, and by 1800 year-round performances were the norm. The playing time gradually shifted later, moving to around 6:30 P.M. by the end of the century. The standard evening at the theatre included one regular play and a short comic afterpiece to conclude. Nonstandard performances included the presentation of several short pieces and the addition of dancing, acrobatics, and fireworks.

The actor's role in the company varied little from earlier times. The share members continued to exert much of the control over the affairs of the company, and in France the salaried members were formally admitted to policy-making status by the end of the century. Casting continued by mutual agreement, although the actor-manager had more to say about assigning roles and selecting repertory than in the seventeenth century. Each established member of the acting company had a "line of parts," a concept that assigned each actor similar types of roles for all the plays done in a given season. Four distinct "lines" existed by the end of the eighteenth century. They were primary parts, including romantic or heroic leading roles; secondary parts, including low comedy leads; tertiary parts, including walking gentlemen; and utility roles. In terms of prestige, importance, and financial return, an actor aspired to as high a line as was possible and could change lines throughout a career, although the usual practice was to remain in the originally assigned line for life. And an actor only advanced to line status after an appropriate apprenticeship in sub-line roles and other duties. The concept of line of parts differs slightly from possession of parts, in which the actor would "possess" the right to play a certain role for as long as he or she remained with the company. The foreshadowing of modern typecasting became well entrenched, and actors often claimed their "possession" rights when they were unable to artistically carry their assigned roles.

Actor compensation remained much the same as it had been with the notable exception of the "benefit" concept in the early part of the century and the straight salary concept of the late 1700s. Here practices in different countries, and in sections of countries, varied widely. London, for example, went on a salary-only scheme in the last half of the eighteenth century, while the provinces continued with the old sharing system. In France *sociétaires* kept their hold on the theatrical pursestrings by including private box rental in their private income domain, ensuring themselves salaries some fifteen times higher than *pensionnaires*. Whether salary or share was the basic method of payment, most eighteenth-century actors enjoyed an occasional "benefit" performance.

This scheme allowed each individual actor who qualified, in rotation, to receive the net receipts from at least one performance a year. While actors occasionally lost money on their benefit because of the evening's expenses, most made out well since patrons were willing to pay an extra amount for their favorite performer.

Authors also fared better in the eighteenth century. Individual systems varied from country to country, but generally in France one-ninth to one-seventh of the receipts for a long play and one-eighteenth to one-twelfth for a short play prevailed. In England the net of every third performance was considered just compensation. As further protection, English authors enjoyed a fourteen-year copyright that could be renewed and sold, reverting to the author at its expiration. In France Beaumarchais founded the Bureau Dramatique in 1777, a society of authors that provided additional protection for French playwrights against unfair practices on the part of actors or theatre owners. Clearly, concern for the authors' rights was finally emerging. In 1791 the National Assembly of France passed a royalty payment law that allowed an author rights to a play until five years after death, with the provision that a fee could be collected for each performance.

Box office provisions also stabilized in the eighteenth century. Prices

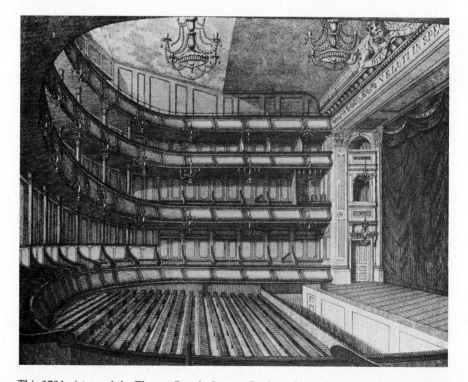

This 1794 picture of the Theatre Royal, Covent Garden, shows the standard stage, proscenium, pit, and balcony features of the period.

gradually rose throughout the 1700s. The concept of charging half price after the regular play started continued owing to its popularity. No concept of reserved seating yet existed, although tickets were sold some hours in advance of the performance. A seat occupied was a seat taken, and scuffles often ensued over who had the right to sit where. Plays were advertised as in the past, with the notable exception that newspapers, now in existence, were used for performance advertisements.

From all of these developments came a notion of theatre production that was increasingly professional in business practice, acting technique, and company organization. Ideas not considered before, but pivotal to the foundations of modern theatre practice, emerged in the eighteenth century. It was, in all respects, a proper precursor to the theatrical energy of the 1800s.

RETROSPECT

More than anything else the eighteenth century tried to be a century of order. That sense of order transcended any active concern with the basic fabric of society that was being controlled. Thus the major dramatic tenets of neoclassicism were more concerned with form than with substance, leading to a dearth of good dramatic writing until the Germans revived European play writing at the end of the century. Similarly, the theatres and staging practices of the eighteenth century were essentially modifications of those developed in the seventeenth. Responding to the need for larger audiences, auditorium size greatly increased. This need was in part created by the declining level of court patronage of the theatre and the increase in theatrical support from the rising middle class.

The economic, political, and social control of Europe was beginning to shift to the middle class throughout the eighteenth century, and that change was reflected in the theatre. Middle-class morals and tastes were reflected in the plays of the eighteenth century, most notably the French *drame bourgeois*. In staging, the insatiable craving for spectacular reality was catered to in every aspect of production. Acting continued its movement toward more realistic portrayal by fully embracing the natural style. Stages and machinery moved toward greater verisimilitude, although differences between England (proscenium doors, extended forestage, stage grooves) and the Continent (proscenium boxes, narrow forestage, *chariot-mat*) continued. Scenery was larger than stage spaces had formerly allowed through *scena per angolo*, and the generalized locales thus represented changed to individualized and picturesque locations. Historical accuracy in costuming began to be taken seriously through the experiments of such actors as Macklin, Garrick, Lekain, and Clairon. Stage lighting, both in theory and practice, moved toward reality through more atmospheric illumination of the stage.

The whole of the eighteenth century, then, was marked by an increase in the professionalism of theatrical practice. Serious discussions of the art of acting, stagecraft, and scenic and theatre design emerged, consistent with the rise of national theatres and increased commercial practices. Old stigmas against the profession were gradually removed, either by law or by common practice. The theatre became ready for the explosion of romanticism and the heightened realistic staging of the nineteenth century.

The seeds for the cultural revolution of the 1800s were clearly planted in the final years of the eighteenth century. Cultural and actual revolution was in the air as the old order neared collapse. The values of the middle class were to be affirmed, and the theatre would cater absolutely to those tastes in the nineteenth century.

Date	European History	European Theatre History
1700	Swedish armies defeat Russian armies at Narva.	Anne Oldfield begins career on English stage.
1701–1714	War of the Spanish Succession puts France at war with most of Europe.	
1702		Censorship office established in France.
1704	English defeat French at Battle of Blenheim.	
1714	Reign of George I of England begins.	
1715	Death of Louis XIV of France.	
1718	New Orleans founded.	Voltaire's *Oedipe*.
1720	Royal Bank of France goes bankrupt.	
1721	Sir Robert Walpole appointed English prime minister.	
1723		Holdberg's *Jeppe paa bjerget*.
1725	Death of Peter the Great of Russia.	
1727	Death of George I of England.	Gay's *The Beggar's Opera*.
1730		Marivaux's *Le Jeu de l'amour et du hasard*.
1731		Lillo's *The London Merchant*.
1736		Fielding's *Pasquin*.
1737		Licensing Act passed in England.
1739		Gottsched-Neuber reforms in Germany.
1741		David Garrick's debut as professional actor.
1742	Walpole resigns as prime minister.	
1748		Danish Royal Theatre opens.
1749		Lekain begins career on French stage.
1750		Goldoni's *Il bugiardo*.
1752		Hallam acting company leaves England for North America.
1753	France goes bankrupt.	
1755		Lessing's *Miss Sara Sampson*.
1756	War between England and France.	

(Continued on page 360)

Date	European History	European Theatre History
1758		Diderot's *Le Père de famille.*
1759		Spectators cleared from French stage.
1760	Death of George II of England. France loses Canada to England.	Goldoni's *La casa nova.*
1762		Gozzi's *Turandot.*
1763	End of Seven Years' War between England and France.	Spectators cleared from English stage.
1765	English Parliament passes Stamp Act for duties on American colonies.	*Autos sacramentales* banned in Spain.
1766		Second Drottningholm Theatre opens.
1767		Lessing's *Hamburgische Dramaturgie.*
1770	English troops fire on citizens of Boston.	*Sturm und Drang* in Germany.
1771	Gustave III begins reign in Sweden.	Loutherbourg begins scenic work in London.
1773	Boston Tea Party.	Goethe's *Götz von Berlichigen.* Goldsmith's *She Stoops to Conquer.*
1774	Louis XVI begins reign.	
1775	Battle of Bunker Hill. Start of the War of American Independence (–1781).	Beaumarchais's *Le Barbier de Séville.* Sheridan's *The Rivals.*
1776	U.S. Declaration of Independence.	Garrick retires from the stage.
1777		Sheridan's *The School for Scandal.*
1778	France and England at war. France signs treaty with warring American colonies.	Teatro alla Scala opens.
1781		Schiller's *Die Räuber.*
1782		Alfieri's *Saul.*
1783	England recognizes the independence of U.S.A.	
1784		Beaumarchais's *Le Mariage de Figaro.*
1788	Washington sworn in as first U.S. president.	Royal Dramatic Theatre established in Stockholm.

360

(Continued on page 361)

Date	European History	European Theatre History
1788		Goethe appointed director of Weimar Court Theatre.
1789	French Revolution begins.	
1792	First French Republic established. Gustav III of Sweden assassinated.	Teatro La Fenice in Venice opened.
1793	Louis XVI executed. Reign of Terror begins in Paris.	
1795	The Directory formed in Paris.	
1789		Pixérécourt's *Victor*.
1799	Napoleon Bonaparte named First Consul, virtual ruler of France.	

SELECTED READINGS

Baur-Heinhold, M. *Baroque Theatre*. New York: McGraw-Hill, 1967.
An excellent pictorial history of seventeenth- and eighteenth-century theatre and stage practices.

Brereton, Geoffrey. *French Comic Drama from the Sixteenth to the Eighteenth Century*. London: Methuen, 1977.
Previously cited.

Bruford, Walter H. *Theatre, Drama and Audience in Goethe's Germany*. London: Routledge & Kegan Paul, 1950.
A very useful study of the social background of eighteenth-century Germany.

Cook, John A. *Neo-classic Drama in Spain*. Dallas: Southern Methodist University Press, 1959.
A detailed analysis of the critical conflicts that troubled the Spanish theatre of the eighteenth century.

Lancaster, Henry C. *French Tragedy in the Time of Louis XV and Voltaire, 1715–1774*. 2 vols. Baltimore: Johns Hopkins Press, 1950.
A highly detailed study built upon the author's earlier investigation of the seventeenth-century French drama.

Marker, Frederick J., and Lise-Lone Marker. *The Scandinavian Theatre: A Short History*. Totowa: Rowman & Littlefield, 1975.
An excellent and highly readable history that helps the student to understand the important part Scandinavia plays in world theatre.

Price, Cecil. *Theatre in the Age of Garrick*. Totowa: Rowman & Littlefield, 1973.
The emphasis here is on production, acting, and audience. A fine work for the beginning student who might be overwhelmed with the amount of material available on eighteenth-century England.

Prudhoe, John. *The Theatre of Goethe and Schiller*. Oxford: Basil Blackwell, 1973.
The first chapter is a highly useful discussion of the origins of the professional theatre in Germany. In addition to examinations of the plays of Schiller and Goethe, the book has two helpful chapters on the Weimar theatre.

Southern, Richard. *Changeable Scenery: Its Origins and Development in the British Theatre*. London: Faber & Faber, 1952.
Previously cited.

Reed, T. J. *The Classical Centre: Goethe and Weimar, 1775–1832*. London: Croom Helm, 1980.
An excellent work for the student wishing additional information on Goethe and German literature of the eighteenth century.

BERLIN

PARIS

LONDON

PART IX

A Mirror for the Masses:
THE EARLY NINETEENTH CENTURY

The French Revolution shattered the social and cultural framework of Europe. For twenty-six years, from 1789 until 1815, France continued to be the center of attention for a troubled group of nations. Out of the terror and confusion of the Revolution there rose to power one of the most remarkable men in human history, Napoleon Bonaparte. In 1785 he was a sublieutenant in the French army; in 1793 a general; in 1799 first consul; in 1804 Emperor of France; and by 1808 master of all of Europe. Throughout the Continent Napoleon spread the spirit of the Revolution, which curtailed the traditional powers of the aristocracy and the Church while increasing the influence and economic power of the middle class. Although Napoleon fell from power in 1815, the middle class continued its upward movement. By the middle of the nineteenth century, it held the dominant position in European society.

In addition to warfare on an unprecedented scale, the first half of the nineteenth century witnessed the spread of the industrial revolution in Europe. Starting in England in the late eighteenth century, it moved next to the Low Countries and, by the 1830s, into France. Industrialization brought with it incredible wealth for a few, increased agricultural and commercial goods for some, and appalling poverty and working conditions for many. The need for abundant and cheap labor for the developing industrial factories was met by displaced agricultural workers and a population explosion in the 1820s. By the end of the century these large masses of unskilled laborers would become a force for change. But in the first half of the century they sought relief from the bleak conditions of their lives in the melodrama. In the theatre of the early nineteenth century, if nowhere else, good triumphed and virtue was rewarded.

17
EARLY-NINETEENTH-CENTURY DRAMA

In the nineteenth century a major shift took place in the direction and perception of the role of theatre in society. Since the Greeks and Romans the theatre had been considered to serve two functions, to teach and to delight. Although the didactic functions of theatre were often overshadowed by the element of amusement, they remained an important consideration for many gifted playwrights. These dramatists considered entertainment the job of tumblers and court fools while their work was the serious business of instructing society. In the nineteenth century instruction dropped to the wayside as theatre became the major commercial entertainment source for Europe, England, and the United States. The need to provide amusements for large audiences, composed of all elements of society, resulted in significant theatrical developments. The nineteenth would also be the last century in which the theatre would serve as a major cultural and social force in Western civilization.

NEOCLASSICISM AND THE ROMANTICS

The German *Sturm und Drang* era was the first true manifestation of a literary movement, called romanticism, that swept over Europe during the first three decades of the nineteenth century. Although both Goethe and Schiller returned to classical forms in their mature years, their youthful works, particularly Goethe's *Götz von Berlichingen* and his novel *Die Leiden des Jungen Werther* (The Sorrows of Young Werther) and Schiller's *The Robbers*, sent a shock wave of artistic rebellion through Europe. While many of the battles of the romantics against neoclassicism were fought in the theatre, the contributions of the romantic movement to the stage were more spectacular than lasting.

The word "romantic" means so many things that of itself it means nothing. For our purposes it will mean the artistic revolt against the principles of neoclassicism, a revolt that stressed sensibility, feeling, individuality, spontaneity, and a fondness for the primitive and natural. Although romanticism is thought of as a literary movement, it was closely connected with the institutional and personal changes that took place in Europe between 1789 and 1850. Romanticism was, at heart, a populist movement since the major differences between romanticism and neoclassicism were social and political. A significant reason why romanticism did not develop in the theatre was that its populist nature struck at commercialism and the middle class, the major pillars of the nineteenth-century stage.

The two groups of romantics that developed in Germany following the *Sturm und Drang* era, the *Frühromantik* (early romantics) and the *Hochromantik* (high romantics), produced no significant playwrights. The essays on the drama written by A. W. Schlegel, a member of the early group, had a major influence in the development of romanticism in France, but they did not help romantic drama gain a foothold in the German theatre. Since neoclassicism was not as strong a tradition in Germany as in other countries in Europe, the German romantic movement soon found itself faced with a rebellion from a group known as Das Junge Deutschland (the Young Germany). This group believed the romantics were out of touch with reality and that literature should have political goals.

In England the romantics were diffused and never banded together in an organized movement. The major romantics were poets, and their few efforts at play writing, such as Shelley's *The Cenci*, were unactable. These poets lacked any knowledge of the theatre and were unwilling to learn. Melodrama was king in England at the time, and the few romantic plays that were well received, such as Byron's *Werner* (1830), made their mark because of their high melodramatic content. English play writing during the first half of the nineteenth century was sorely lacking in originality and was only partly English, since 50 percent of the plays produced between 1800 and 1850 were taken from French originals.

In Spain and Italy, romanticism was imported from France and, as in England, was principally poetic in expression. In Italy the romantics were actively involved in the struggle for a united, independent Italian state. Because of the political involvement of the romantics and strong classical traditions, romanticism never became a major literary movement in Italy. In Spain romanticism appeared on the stage in the form of translated French plays. There was irony in this, since the French romantics found much to admire in the Spanish drama of the Golden Age.

France was the theatrical center of romanticism in Europe in the early nineteenth century. Madame de Staël, a friend of A. W. Schlegel's and a champion of German literature, popularized the romantic movement in France in the years immediately after the fall of Napoleon. Yet it remained for Victor Hugo to give the *mouvement romantique* popular expression, and he moved the literary battles into the theatre, both figuratively and actually. The stormy production of Hugo's *Hernani* at the Comédie Française in 1830 was considered a major victory of the French romantics over the neoclassical traditionalists. Yet it was a short-lived victory. By the mid-1840s romanticism as a literary movement had peaked and was in rapid decline in France and the rest of Europe.

MELODRAMA

No other theatrical genre suffers the degree of bad press that is imposed on melodrama. The term itself is nearly synonymous with bad theatre and hammy acting. The pejorative connotations of the term in the twentieth century are not justified and are misleading. Melodrama dominated the stages of Europe, England, and the United States for over a century. It is represented by tens of thousands of plays that were performed before millions of people, and it clearly merits serious attention.

Development

Although the structural roots of melodrama can be found in the plays of Euripides, melodrama as a distinct dramatic genre appeared in eighteenth-century France and developed in the cultural vacuum created by the Revolution. In 1770 the philosopher Jean Jacques Rousseau wrote *Pygmalion*, a *scène lyrique* in which dialogue and music were heard alternately. The novelty of the form caught on and was imitated by others in the 1770s. To distinguish this type of music play from opera, the term *mélodrame* was applied. By the time of the Revolution, the term meant a play in which dialogue was spoken against a musical background. The new genre rapidly became the rage on the Boulevard du Temple in Paris, the city's entertainment center. Here were to be found jugglers, rope walkers, animal shows, and theatrical enterprises that nibbled away at the edges of the official monopoly of the Comédie Française.

In the mid–1790s, following the Revolution, those who were attempting to govern France thought that plays recalling or portraying the old regime should no longer be given. As the vast majority of French plays written before 1789 reflected the life or social codes of the French aristocracy, theatre owners found themselves with few available plays to produce. This lack of plays came at a time when playhouses were popping up all over Paris—in 1792 there were over two hundred theatres. The new melodrama met the demand for new plays, and the structure of this new genre filled a psychological need for the people of Paris. For several years following 1789, nearly every citizen of France had been involved in the bloody chaos of creating a new social order. Daily life during the Reign of Terror was on a heightened level beyond anything the theatre could provide. But the spectacle, the emotionalism, the clear-cut issues of right and wrong, of life and death, that were the fare of the Revolution for the average French citizen found their theatrical counterpart in the developing rituals of the melodrama. As stability returned to France, melodrama was there to provide excitement and adventure.

The Nature of Melodrama

Melodrama presents the human experience in a simplified and idealized manner. The hero or heroine has an undivided personality and is not required to deal with the inner struggles that are characteristic of tragedy. The battles of melodrama are all external, thus making this dramatic genre highly dependent on forces beyond the control of the protagonist. This dependency gives melodrama its uniqueness and makes it a drama of near-total action or reaction. It is a world of black or white, good or evil, win or lose, but not one of psychological or philosophical reflection. It is an extremely violent world, yet one that always ends in triumph and joy. It is the world as we would like it to be, with clear choices, definite villains, and always a happy ending for the deserving.

The melodramatic formula requires that character stereotypes be placed within a rigid moral code and stirred briskly with adversity. The three principal character types are the hero, heroine, and villain. They are supported by a comic man, comic woman, and at least one elderly man or woman. The ritualistic nature of melodrama requires that there be very little variation in these character stereotypes. This is necessary so the audience will quickly know the cast of characters and not be bored with relation-defining exposition. Nothing should stand in the way of the action, not even plausibility.

The hero is, as a rule, young, handsome, brave, athletic, and none too bright. He is totally devoted to the heroine, who is either his wife or sweetheart, but he spends much of his time getting out of troubles arranged for him by the villain. The heroine is the center of interest in the melodrama. The pitiful victim of the unwanted attention of the villain, the heroine spends the entire play

A stock poster for William W. Pratt's Ten Nights in a Bar-room *(1858), a popular temperance melodrama.*

fleeing from one indignation into another. Since the hero is seldom available, the heroine receives some assistance from the comic man. But she mainly manages to survive to the final curtain through her own perseverance. The villain is the force of the melodrama; he makes things happen. Two varieties of villains often appear, the black and the white. The white is the associate villain, cowardly, comic, and incompetent; he is dominated by the black villain when paired in a play. The black villain is a determined force of evil whose major weakness is overconfidence. He seldom repents or survives.

Throughout the nineteenth century, music remained an important element in melodrama. This tradition has survived into this century in film, where music is still used to heighten a scene or set a mood. The scripts of melodrama contain numerous music cues for effect, ("threatening music") or mood ("plaintive and descriptive music"), or to bring characters on or off. There is also considerable use of single chords to highlight dialogue: "Revenge! (chord) Revenge! (chord) Revenge! (chord-thunder)."

Acting in Melodrama

The acting of melodramas was highly stylized and involved the active participation of actor and audience. Both knew how a role was to be played, how a line was to be delivered, and deviation from the prescribed ritual was not permitted. One of the major reasons the majority of the melodramas are not now producible is not so much that they are bad scripts as that the participatory ritual has been lost.

Movement, gestures, and speech received strong emphasis within established patterns. The patterns grew out of the declamatory acting styles of the previous century combined with pantomimic gestures made necessary by the huge theatres of the early nineteenth century. Although somewhat idealized, the frozen attitudes and gestures of nineteenth-century theatrical posters and photographs capture the ritualistic nature of these acting patterns. Acting manuals of the period give careful instructions on how to assume these ritualized attitudes, such as the following for an actor depicting pride: "The proud man, thrusting one hand into his bosom, carries it as high as he is able, and places the elbow of the other arm a-kimbo; his head is thrown a little backwards; his turned-out feet are at a distance from each other; he rests on one leg, while the other is thrown before it with extended dignity." Such stylized gestures may still be seen in early silent films, many of which were produced totally in the traditions of the nineteenth-century melodrama.

Speech was the most distinctive element in melodramatic acting. Melodramatic speech evolved out of eighteenth-century stage speech patterns. These patterns stressed an elevated manner of delivery that often had little relation to the meaning of the line of dialogue. From this tradition the speech of melodrama developed special rhythms and peculiar pronunciations. There was a tendency to pronounce every syllable and to insert unnatural rhythmic pauses. In the 1850s, Charles Dickens recorded this trait in the following transcription of a line of dialogue from a play: "I ster-ruck him down and fel-ed in er-orror! . . . I have liveder as a beggar—a roadersider vaigerant, but no ker-rime since then has stained these hands!'' Speech distortion of this type gradually disappeared by the 1880s as melodrama itself changed to serve more sophisticated audiences.

THE WELL-MADE PLAY

While one aspect of the melodrama continued to provide thrills and spectacles into the second decade of the present century, another developed in the early nineteenth century into a theatre that catered to the middle class. A major element in this development was the invention of the well-made play. The well-made play (*la pièce bien faite*) was the creation of Eugène Scribe (1791–1861), the most successful playwright of the first half of the nineteenth century.

Scribe began his career as a writer of *vaudevilles*. The term has a long history that ended with the American and English entertainment form ultimately destroyed by radio and television. In nineteenth-century France it meant light, farcical comedies with song and dance. As it was necessary to hold an audience's complete attention to please it completely, Scribe developed a play-writing formula to ensure that the audience would be expectant from

Eugène Scribe.

beginning to end. Starting to put his formula to work in the early 1820s, Scribe, alone and with collaborators, produced approximately five hundred plays and opera libretti before the end of his career.

The formula for *la pièce bien faite* was applied by Scribe and his followers to all theatrical forms, but in all its guises certain features are distinguishable: (1) The story revolves around a secret known to the audience but not to the major characters until it is revealed in a climactic scene. (2) Since the script usually begins at the conclusion of a long story, the audience receives a large dose of expository dialogue at the start. (3) Tension is increased through the course of the play by a carefully arranged pattern of entrances, exits, and revelations. (4) The good and bad turns of fortune for the protagonist create an emotional rhythm for the play. (5) The major crisis of the script is rapidly followed by the climax, which occurs in a *scène à faire* (obligatory scene). (6) The denouement of the play is completely understandable and leaves no unsolved puzzles for the audience. (7) The overall pattern of the play is repeated in each act so that the acts become structural miniatures of the whole.

The well-made play, as it was polished and perfected by later playwrights, became the structural foundation for the mainline commercial theatre of the late nineteenth and twentieth centuries. It is fitted out for the needs of the middle class: it is topical, nonmetaphysical, nonchallenging, self-assuring, and highly playable. The major theatrical rebellions of the last hundred years have been directed against the well-made play and the middle-class audience it represents. Yet the formula remains, still under attack, but still providing a means for popular theatre.

SIGNIFICANT PLAYWRIGHTS OF THE EARLY NINETEENTH CENTURY

Pixérécourt

Credit for developing the melodrama into a highly popular dramatic form belongs to Guilbert de Pixérécourt (1773–1844), whose *Coelina, ou L'Enfant du mystère* (Coelina, or the Child of Mystery, 1800) is generally acknowledged to be first true melodrama. Pixérécourt, who was called by his contemporaries the Corneille of Melodrama, wrote, alone or in collaboration, over 120 plays. These plays were extremely popular in France, and many of them were translated into English, Dutch, and German. This master of the early melodrama declared he wrote "for people who cannot read," and his plays did cater to the tastes of the unlettered masses who were moving into the major cities of Europe. His plays set the tone for melodrama in France and England for several decades. Thomas Holcroft's *The Child of Mystery: A Melo-drama* (1801), England's first produced melodrama, was an adaptation of Pixérécourt's *Coelina*.

*Guilbert de Pixérécourt,
whose* Coelina *is considered
the first true melodrama.*

Kleist and Kotzebue

The career of Germany's first significant playwright of the nineteenth century, Heinrich von Kleist (1777–1811), was cut short by suicide, but he wrote several plays remarkable for their realism and innovations. *Der zerbrochene Krug* (The Broken Jug, 1808) is one of the finest German comedies and a delightful picture of provincial town life. The best of his seven plays is *Prinz Friedrich von Homburg* (The Prince of Homburg, 1810), a psychological drama based on a historical incident. Filled with dramatic reversals and masterfully paced, the play probes the mind of a hero condemned for his heroism. For all their power, Kleist's plays were not appreciated during his lifetime. Instead, German audiences much preferred the plays of the prolific August von Kotzebue (1761–1819). Kotzebue, who for a brief period was the most popular playwright in Europe, wrote over two hundred plays. Translated and performed in every nation in Europe, his plays, such as *Menschenhass und Reue* (The Stranger, or Misanthrophy and Repentance, 1789) or *Die Spanier in Peru* (Pizarro, or the Spaniard in Peru, 1795), were notable for their pathos, action, and scenic effects. They appealed to audiences who were growing fond of the new melodrama. Melodramatic playwrights mined the plays of Kotzebue for decades.

Dumas

Now chiefly remembered as a novelist, Alexandre Dumas *père* (1802–1870) was a highly popular playwright in the third and fourth decades of the nineteenth century. His first play, *Henri III et sa cour* (Henry III and His Court, 1829) was a significant triumph for the romantics when it was produced. While totally disregarding the neoclassical rules, this historical drama had great box office appeal. *La Tour de Nesle* (The Tower of Nesle, 1832), a historical play set in fourteenth-century France, was his most famous play. *La Tour* ran for nearly eight hundred performances, making it the most popular romantic drama of the century. A tale of lust, murder, incest, and adultery, the play illustrated the propensity of the romantics for pure melodrama and their willingness to allow the popular appeal of the genre to assist their cause.

Much less the rebel than others in the romantic movement, Dumas wrote for fame and fortune and stayed alert to changes in popular taste. The rapid pace and sheer theatricality of his plays influenced other French playwrights of the nineteenth century. Yet his characters lack universal qualities and are trapped in the style of the period. Because an appreciation of this high theatrical style is lacking in the twentieth century, the plays of Alexandre Dumas *père* have not been revived.

Victor Hugo

In 1827 theatre audiences in Paris were presented with the opportunity to see a company of English actors present four tragedies by William Shakespeare. While Shakespeare's plays had been available in French translation for many years, this was the first chance most Parisians had to see them in performance. Among those most dazzled by Shakespeare's powerful scripts and the energetic style of English acting was the young poet Victor Hugo (1802–1885). Committed to reforming the French stage and destined to lead the French romantic movement, Hugo issued that same year the movement's manifesto in the preface to his unactable play, *Cromwell*.

In the *Preface to Cromwell*, Hugo praised drama as the greatest form of artistic expression, condemned the restraints of neoclassicism, and urged full artistic freedom. When he announced that "the object of modern art is not beauty but life," he struck at the heart of the French theatrical tradition. The preface did not improve the play, which was not performed, but in 1829 he got his opportunity to illustrate his beliefs when the Comédie Française accepted his *Hernani* for production.

The selection committee of the Comédie Française decided upon Hugo's play in an effort to dampen the growing clamor of the romantics. They believed that in producing *Hernani*, they would clearly show "how far the human mind can go astray when it is freed of every rule and of all decorum." What they got was a riot. Alerted that the partisans of neoclassicism intended to hiss the play from the stage, Hugo arranged for a large number of his young friends and supporters to be in the theatre for the first performance on February 25, 1830.

A portrait of Victor Hugo at the age of twenty.

A contemporary news drawing depicting the fighting at the first performance of Hernani *in 1830.*

With the opening lines of the play the verbal and physical battles between the romantics and the neoclassicists erupted, and they continued for months. In the end, the victory was with the romantics. During the next thirteen years Hugo wrote seven more plays, but by the early 1840s the French romantic movement had run its course. Hugo turned to politics and writing novels, and left theatrical reforms to others. The reforms that took place in the next two decades were commercial, not artistic, as the Scribean well-made play set about its task of amusement.

CONCLUSION

Melodramatic and romantic dramas dominated the stage during the first half of the nineteenth century. Both stressed the sensational and the spectacular, shared a simplistic level of dramatic conflict, and equally emphasized physical action. But at the center of each form there was a major difference, for melodrama was social and romantic drama was antisocial. Melodrama reflected a belief in the ultimate triumph of good and in a kindly Providence guiding the affairs of humanity. The romantic dramatists viewed the world as cruel and the noble hero as victim. In romantic drama the hero was a rebel who declared his independence from an evil society. In melodrama society was beneficent, the social order good, and only an occasional individual, who broke the rules, was evil. Thus melodrama's role of enforcing the existing social organization, and reflecting the rightness of that social organization, ensured its existence into the second half of the nineteenth century. Romantic drama, on the other hand, was, like the melodramatic villain, fated for an early demise.

18
EARLY-NINETEENTH-CENTURY THEATRE ARCHITECTURE AND PRODUCTION PRACTICE

The early nineteenth century had one major goal toward which most of its theatre architecture and production practice strove—heightened verisimilitude. Architectural and staging changes reflected the public's desire to have reality on stage, and that concept of reality was fueled by two philosophies that fired the imaginations of Europe as the nineteenth century began. The first, antiquarianism, was a growing interest in the study of antiquities or old relics and times. The common notion was that these older societies possessed a greater "truth" than modern times, and current society could benefit from a detailed study of their lives. This study was to be accomplished through a second philosophy, scientism, which held that the method of the natural scientist in discovering truths and acquiring knowledge should be used in all areas of human inquiry, including the humanities and the social sciences. Those embracing scientism believed that only through such methods of inquiry could "truth," including stage "truth," be discovered. These concepts, combined with early-nineteenth-century technology, began to bring the complete placement of objective reality as "truth" to the stage.

PLAYHOUSE CONSTRUCTION

The industrialization of western Europe during the first half of the nineteenth century caused a large migration of workers to the major cities. Accordingly the nature of the theatre audience shifted. Primarily a middle-class audience at the end of the eighteenth century, the theatregoing public gradually shifted to a mass audience by the middle of the nineteenth century.

The Auditorium

The theatre building, particularly the auditorium, responded to accommodate the new and larger audience. Auditorium size increased dramatically. Playhouses commonly seated several thousand by midcentury. Drury Lane, for example, seated well over thirty-six hundred after the renovations of 1812. In concept the design of the early nineteenth-century playhouses followed the general patterns set forth in the late eighteenth century. The bell- and the horseshoe-shaped auditorium became more common, while the U-shaped house declined to a point of near-extinction by the end of the nineteenth century. By the beginning of the nineteenth century the main floor area had been converted to permanent seating, but the floor area was still flat, and this hindered audibility and adequate sight lines. During the first half of the nineteenth century the floor area was gradually inclined toward the rear of the auditorium, and the bench seats near the stage front were converted to conventional seating. This trend, fully realized by the end of the nineteenth century, greatly aided audience comfort. The pit, boxes, and galleries remained the basic parts of the auditorium, although the gallery area underwent a slight change during the first fifty years of the century. Then the galleries began to resemble undivided balconies that followed the general

The Royal Cobourg Theatre, Surrey, in 1818, showing the traditional parts of the early-nineteenth-century theatre.

sweep of the box seats around the house. As balconies were stacked to accommodate larger lower-class audiences, the first row of the upper balcony was set slightly farther away from the stage than the first balcony row below it. Audibility and sight lines were somewhat enhanced by this change, although this was little more than a novelty until the late nineteenth century.

A major alteration that occurred during the early nineteenth century was the gradual increase in the attention paid to the lobby. This change was clearly seen in the major opera houses of Europe, and although it influenced provincial and nonopera theatres less, it was a growing concern in every town that considered building a civic theatre. Audience flow to and from the auditorium was eased, and the columns and porticoes that adorned the lobbies were magnificent. Cities vied with one another for the grandest of theatre edifices, and one measure of this competition was in the complexity and beauty of the lobby space. Improvements were also made in air handling and heating.

The Stage

Consistent with the increasing polarization of the basic parts of the playhouse, the English forestage gradually shrank to the size of Continental aprons, and the concept of proscenium doors similarly lessened.

Backstage at the Royal Theatre, Leicester, showing the upper and lower grooves and the upstage trap.

(From Richard Leacroft, The Development of the English Playhouse. *Used by permission of Cornell University Press.)*

Although theatres continued to have large proscenium boxes, they began to disappear in smaller theatres in favor of the solid proscenium commonly found by the end of the nineteenth century. The size of the stage and its equipment, located fully behind the proscenium, lent itself well to the spectacular staging of the day and would accommodate well the rise of realistic staging in the late 1800s.

Consistent with the demands of spectacular staging, the stage floor area became larger and more elaborately trapped. Upstage a large trap, known as the bridge or opera trap, allowed a sizable portion of the floor to be raised or lowered, bringing large set pieces or groups of actors to and from the stage floor. Several traps were developed for specific plays or scenes. The Corsican or ghost trap was originally developed by Dion Boucicault for the Princess Theatre production of *The Corsican Brothers* in 1852. Other specialty traps included the star trap, the bristle trap, and the vampire trap. Noisy and crude by today's technological standards, these traps fascinated and amazed early-nineteenth-century audiences.

An early nineteenth-century trap in operation.

Building Methods

The early nineteenth century witnessed the most significant change in the building techniques for playhouses since the Renaissance. The old post and wood-joist, brick, and stone method for theatre construction that had served for four hundred years was gradually replaced by the technology of iron and steel. Accordingly, some early nineteenth-century theatres, such as the Théâtre Français (1808), were built with wrought-iron framing in the roof areas, balanced so that comparatively thin walls could be used externally. The old wooden stairways, interior beams, and partitions were replaced with stone vaulting, hollow tile, and flagstone. This trend toward greater use of structural, nonflammable building materials spread rapidly through Europe and England. In 1811, for example, the Theatre Royal in Plymouth replaced its structural timbers with cast-iron supports.

Hundreds of new playhouses sprang up after the Napoleonic Wars, many as physical evidence of a city's growing wealth and civic pride. Major theatres included the Schauspielhaus in Berlin, the Teatro Carlo Felice in Genoa, the Alexandrinsky in Saint Petersburg, the Hoftheater in Dresden, and the Opera Real in Madrid. This listing illustrates the widespread acceptance of the new theatre technology.

STAGE MACHINERY AND SCENIC PRACTICE

Scene Design

Early-nineteenth-century scenic design concepts followed the growing trend toward the antiquarianism of William Capon and other eighteenth-century designers. Picturesque specific locales, done for new plays rather than pulled from stock, became the order of the day. And those locales were designed on an asymmetrical basis during the early years of the nineteenth century, a rather important change from the symmetrical settings of the eighteenth century. For the first time the extensive use of large three-dimensional set pieces placed stage right or left brought an exciting new aesthetic to the design of scenery. Most scenery during the early nineteenth century utilized the wing and drop method of staging, with three-dimensional pieces within the basic scenic framework as needed. By the end of the first third of the nineteenth century, however, audiences became disenchanted with the illusion of an interior that did not actually show walls, doors, and windows as they existed in real life. An increase in verisimilitude was demanded from stage practitioners, consistent with the increased interest in objective reality in literature and art. In response to this demand from the theatre's paying audience, the precursor of the modern box set was born.

The Box Set

The exact evolution of the box set (so named for its shape's resemblance to a shoe box with one side removed) may never be known. Most certainly the idea for such a device emerged in the eighteenth

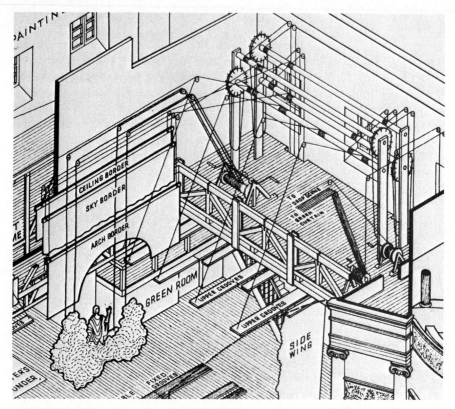

The prompt side fly gallery and machinery at the Theatre Royal, Plymouth, in 1811.

(*From Richard Leacroft,* The Development of the English Playhouse. *Used by permission of Cornell University Press.*)

century when actual doors and windows were placed between sets of wings and used by the actors. It was a simple matter to proceed from that to the addition of angled or raked walls to the practical door and window units, from whence the concept of the box set emerged. Such devices can be noted in Italy before 1810 and in Berlin in the 1820s. By the late 1830s the device was no mere novelty. Although it would not be in common use until the 1870s, it was in use in the major theatres of Europe, England, and America.

Early use of the box set coupled it with flat wing and drop sets, and much of the realistic detail of set dressings during the first two decades of the nineteenth century was still painted on the raked walls of the set. One of the first managers to employ the box set and to furnish it with realistic dressings was Mme Vestris (Lucia Elizabetta Vestris, 1797–1856). It is probable that the common form of the box set—that is, three walls running from one side of the proscenium to the other—was covered with a ceiling. Mme Vestris covered her floors with real rugs, had working hardware on the doors and windows, and furnished the stage with real bookcases and furniture. Most of these developments occurred

The Royal Olympic Theatre, where the first function box sets were used by Mme Vestris in the early 1830s.

at the Olympic Theatre, London, and it is likely that the first fully functional box set emerged there in 1832. From that point, its use spread rapidly.

The box set was not without its problems. At first shifting had to be done by hand as individual portions of walls were run on and off by individual stagehands. This was slower than the automatic systems of wing and drop changes, and may have been less impressive to the audience because of the time it took to change the scene. The early side walls were supported by the side wings, but as the convention of using them in concert diminished, another means of wall support was found. That means, the stage brace, provided a method of quickly setting a stage wall in an upright position and allowed for its equally quick removal. An early use, perhaps the first, of this device was at Booth's Theatre in New York in 1869.

Designers

Although the stage brace created greater popularity for the box set in the last half of the nineteenth century, the painted detail of the wing and drop set persisted during the early decades of the century. The demand for scene painters was still high. In England the traditions of Capon and Loutherbourg were maintained by the design family of John Henderson Grieve (1770–1845). Working in the theatrical mainstream of London, Grieve and his two sons, Thomas (1799–1882) and William (1800–1844), designed and painted the scenery for various managements at Covent Garden and Drury Lane. All three painted in the antiquarian style of the day, but their work was considered so superior in its beauty and brilliance that their names were prominently displayed on the programs. William Grieve may well have been the first scene designer in modern times to command a curtain call. Other designers of the period prospered as well. Clarkson Stanfield (1793–1867) specialized in landscapes, and William Telbin (1813–1873) worked for Charles Kean at the Princess's Theatre and under Macready at Drury Lane. Telbin and his son, William Lewis (1846–1931), were excellent at antiquarian painting and often included costume design in their overall concepts.

The leading French designer of antiquarianism was Pierre-Luc-Charles Ciceri (1782–1868). He opened a scenic studio in Paris in 1823 because of the heavy demand for his work, and he employed several designers to work on various portions of the same production. He worked for several theatres in Paris, and his notion of an independent scenic studio apart from the scene shops of the individual theatres was to establish a trend. Ciceri's use of color and his detailed historical ruins and local settings set the pattern for French scenery throughout most of the nineteenth century.

The Panorama

One of the most fascinating machines to invade the theatre in the early nineteenth century was the panorama. Invented in 1787 by Robert Barker, it was developed for stage use by Louis-Jacques Daguerre (1787–1851). In stage application it was a large scene painted on a continuous piece of cloth that was rolled on one upright spool, or roller, crossed the upstage area in full view of the audience, and was attached to another spool, opposite its starting point. As the view rolled from one spool to the other, everything that was painted on it moved by the audience in one continuous scene. Initially a device used by itself, it was eventually used as a backdrop in regular stage productions by the end of the century, and contributed in large measure to the elimination of upstage wings and borders.

Costume

The trend toward historical accuracy in costuming continued during the first half of the nineteenth century. There were five general periods appropriate for different costumes: the classical era, the medieval, and the sixteenth, seventeenth, and eighteenth centuries. Much time was spent researching the dress of each period, and although the conclusions were often wrong, the taste for accurate dress was satisfied. The term "accurate" must be viewed against the scientism of the day, for it is hardly interchangeable with "realistic" as we know it. Often the vague notions of historical accuracy fostered by a Talma or a Charles Kean would be broken by contemporary nineteenth-century dress in the same production. John Robinson Planché (1796–1880) brought antiquarian costuming to new heights by requiring that each role in Covent Garden's 1823 production of *King John* be historically accurate. Planché articulated such reforms in his work *British Costume* (1834), a book that was the standard work on the subject throughout much of the nineteenth century. But reforms were accepted slowly, and were not fully accepted until the last few decades of the nineteenth century. The trend, however, was clear—costuming would shortly dress the stage in truly accurate style according to each specific period.

GAS AND ELECTRIC LIGHTING

Few changes have been as important to the development of the physical theatre as the introduction of gas and electric lighting. Emerging during the first half of the nineteenth century, the developments in gas lighting and electricity fostered greater flexibility and artistry in stage illumination and significantly quieted the audience by allowing for a darkened house.

Developments in Gas Lighting

Although lighting the stage with gas had been demonstrated by F. A. Winsor at the Lyceum Theatre in London in 1803, no practical application was attempted until the late 1810s. This was due primarily to the fact that no central supply of gas yet existed. Theatres had to generate their own supply, which was an expensive and time-consuming process. Nonetheless, England and the United States led the way in pioneering gas lighting with its introduction at the Chestnut Street Theatre in Philadelphia in 1816, and at Covent Garden and Drury Lane in 1817. Other countries followed suit in the 1820s, but it was not until the 1840s that the supply problems were solved and gas stage and auditorium lighting became common.

Although it did not alter the theory of stage lighting in any substantial way, gas had tremendous advantages over oil and candle lamps. Since no trimming of wicks was involved, the number of light sources (in this case, burners) increased dramatically. Gas wing ladders emerged, as did gas battens among the borders and gas floats for footlights. Gas lines were run to every conceivable location, the net result being a greatly increased brilliance on the stage. Gas also allowed for relatively successful dimming of the stage, an important aspect in creating the moods of the antiquarians. By the 1840s elaborate gas dimmer boards, called gas tables, were installed on the stage manager's or prompt side of the stage, and generalized control from a single point was possible.

Gas lighting had disadvantages. Most contemporary accounts from critics, audience, and actors alike comment on the fumes and intense heat. The burners were open-flamed devices and the potential for fire was an ever-present danger. Changes after 1850 would decrease these dangers and problems, but for most of its stage life gas lighting was not totally free from these concerns. Even the brilliance was at times a disadvantage. As one critic in 1826 noted, "The disposition of the lamps at present is such that no shadow whatever can be presented to the audience, everything upon the stage and in the audience part [of the house] is a glare of undistinguished lights, painful to the eye."

The Limelight

Some degree of success was achieved in directional lighting when Thomas Drummond invented the limelight (sometimes called the Drummond light) in 1816. Drummond brought two gases together, hydrogen and oxygen, and the ignited mixture heated a calcium core to a glow. The light given off was brilliant, yet was steadier and more mellow than burner flames. Reflectors and lenses were soon developed for the limelight, and attempts were made to use it as a spotlight. A main use was for lighting the backgrounds of sets, for its relatively soft and atmospheric qualities suited that purpose well. It was also used in footlights, but the undue emphasis on ankles and the fact that someone had to keep the flame and the core properly aligned did not foster great use in that application. Its most common use was as a followspot.

Electricity

Electricity did not make an impact in the theatre until Thomas Edison provided the first practical incandescent lamp in 1879, but some activity in electric lighting before 1850 can be noted. Sir Humphrey Davy

An early carbon arc lamp.

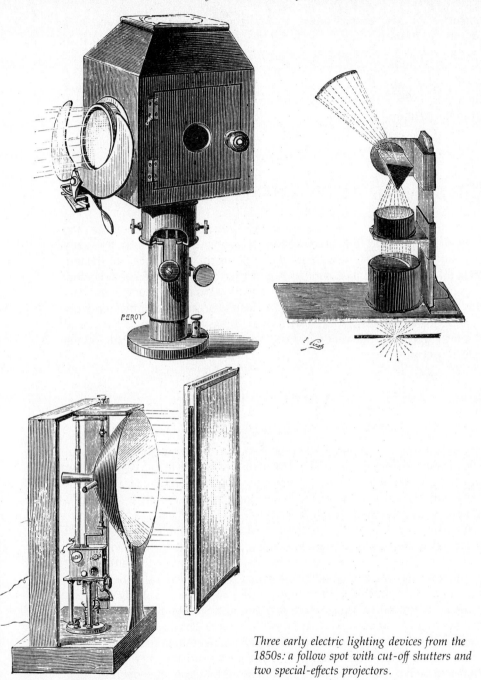

Three early electric lighting devices from the 1850s: a follow spot with cut-off shutters and two special-effects projectors.

had invented the carbon arc lamp in 1808, but wide acceptance of the instrument was not practical because users had to generate their own power. By the 1840s, however, larger theatres in the major metropolitan centers were able to generate their own electricity, and the arc lamp gained some acceptance. As Davy demonstrated, an arc light is made possible by attaching a carbon rod to each side of a potential electric current. The rods are placed sufficiently close together so that when the current is restored, it completes its path by leaping from one rod to the other, thus creating an intense light, much like controlled lightning. A series of these arc lights was installed as spotlights at the Opéra in Paris in 1846, but common usage of the device occurred much later in the century.

ACTORS AND ACTING STYLES

The various acting styles, the great number and variety of actors, and the organization of acting companies in the early nineteenth century continued to set the patterns for the practice of theatre. During this period romantic acting emerged, fired by the worship of individual and eccentric genius, but natural acting remained the mainstream. Significant changes occurred in the basic fabric of acting organization, the repertory system, as the theatre began to move from art to business. These philosophical and practical changes would find full realization in the last half of the nineteenth century.

Acting Style

In the early years of the nineteenth century the classic acting style of Kemble, although still practiced, was dying out. By midcentury it would have no serious practitioners. The natural style was to carry the day, but even it would experience subtle yet significant changes. In the late eighteenth century and the early years of the nineteenth, the natural style still had a modicum of classical grace. With the triumph of romanticism and melodrama, however, some of the glorification of individual emotional feeling from those forms invaded the natural acting style. The romantic style emerged in the first half of the nineteenth century, and by midcentury its place in theatre history was assured. The art and practice of acting were fueled by a heightened emotionalism that allowed greater improvisation and variety in body positions and vocal expression on stage. From this period, for example, come the first references to an actor's speaking with his back to the audience, an unheard-of practice in the previous century. But some older conventions continued. Upon entering, actors traditionally moved downstage toward the center cluster of footlights to deliver their lines. Having completed that task, they often stepped aside to within an arm's length of other actors to allow access to this traditional speaking place. Realistic acting, as we know it, was obviously a long way off. Since the classic, natural, and romantic styles appeared occasionally onstage together, acting style in the early nineteenth century was somewhat eclectic.

Early-Nineteenth-Century Theatre Architecture and Production Practice

Actors

Natural and romantic actors far outnumbered classic actors. Each country had its leading exponent, but the best-known as a pure romantic was England's Edmund Kean (1787–1833). From a romantic point of view, Kean's life was hard to separate from his acting since both were full of emotional excesses. Specializing in byplay, Kean relied less on his voice, which was harsh, than on the power of his physical delivery. He traveled about the stage with a "murderous frenzy" and was not above such stage devices as dropping to his knees or crawling about the stage. His Shylock was seen as "a swarthy fiend with a huge butcher's knife in his grasp and blood-lust in his eyes," and Macbeth was played with such "heart-rending" power that "on coming to himself after the murder, his voice clung to his throat at the sight of his bloody hands." England also provided the finest example of natural acting in William Charles Macready (1793–1873). One of the finest tragedians of all time, he combined some of the classical grace of Kemble with some of the emotional power of Kean. It was his lot during his career to be seen as the rival to someone—first Kean himself, followed by the American Edwin Forrest. Although respected as an actor and responsible for a number of reforms that

EDMUND KEAN.

A contemporary drawing of Edmund Kean as Hamlet.

William Charles Macready
in the title role of Sheridan
Knowles's Virginius *(1820).*

benefited his profession, he constantly disparaged it and alienated himself from some fellow actors and managers alike. Nonetheless, he was a cultured man, and this attribute showed in his acting, which was described as graceful yet powerful. In many ways, he was the leading exponent of early-nineteenth-century mainstream acting.

France also had natural and romantic actors of major stature. François-Joseph Talma (1763–1826) played mostly neoclassical roles in a romantic style that was not as emotionally driven as Kean's. He was concerned with the detailed study of a role before presentation and insisted upon antiquarian accuracy in his costuming. Talma played, to mixed audience reaction, a Brutus with bare arms and legs. Mlle Mars (Anne-Françoise Boutet, 1779–1847) was a natural actor of comedy and the leading comic actress of her period. She was tremendously popular, in part because of her lovely voice and fine physical appearance. If Kean had an equal in France, it was Frédérick (Antoine-Louis-Prosper Lemaître, 1800–1876). Said to be the most versatile actor of his day, he frequently broke the "line of parts" convention and brought innovative interpretations to a variety of roles. His acting style was described as filled with "passionate outbursts," and he was able to please critics and the masses alike. Throughout his career he blended study and application with innovation and inspiration onstage. Finally, Rachel (Elisa Félix, 1821–1858) contributed

François-Joseph Talma.

significantly to the development of romantic acting in France by bringing her special brand of excitement to the Comédie Française. Her repertory consisted mostly of classical plays, but she played them with acidity, rage, and lust. She had an intensity and power unequalled in her time.

Actors in Germany followed a similar yet more restrained path. The state of German acting had been well established in the late eighteenth century by August Wilhelm Iffland (1759–1814). In 1779 he had joined the Mannheim State Theatre, and his work there contributed significantly to nineteenth-century German acting. His concentration on gesture and facial expression was superb, and his playing of sentimental roles was seen as a major factor in moving Germany toward romantic acting. Following in the footsteps of Iffland, the finest romantic actor in early-nineteenth-century Germany was Ludwig Devrient (1784–1832). He played classical and romantic roles equally well, but owing to "possession of parts" conflicts he was relegated to comic roles for most of his short career. His style was described as passionate and versatile. He was an actor of fiery temperament who played with much inspiration and little discipline.

Frédérick as the character Robert Macaire in L'Auberge des adrets *(1823).*

Russia, like Germany, had a theatrical emergence in the eighteenth century that brought forth a few good actors and set the pattern for the nineteenth century. One of the first of these was Ivan Afanasyevich Dmitrevsky (1733–1821). Equally gifted in comedy and tragedy, he was an exponent of the natural style. Like Schröder in Germany, he was heavily involved in the evolution of the state theatres and insisted on careful preparation in all phases of production. His contributions to Russian theatre include those of an actor, theatre administrator, and writer. He was a major force in bringing French refinements in acting and staging to the Russian theatre. Another major contributor to acting and the development of the Russian professional stage was Feodor Grigoryevich Volkov (1729–1763). He received his training as an actor at Cadet College with Dmitrevsky. Little is known about his style, but most likely it was natural. He became the leading actor of the first Russian professional theatrical company, largely funded by those who would be responsible for the overthrow of Peter III and the ascendency of Catherine the Great. Volkov's theatre thus flourished. The first truly great Russian actor was Mikhail Shchepkin (1788–1863). Shchepkin was a serf and began his career in a serf troupe. An extremely well disciplined romantic actor, he strove for the natural in all aspects of his art. In addition to his acting contributions, he modified the approach his company

Ludwig Devrient.

used in the preparation of a play. Shchepkin insisted on reading the play before casting and served as a de facto "director" by assisting other actors with their characterizations.

Company Organization

During the early nineteenth century there occurred changes in the organization of theatre that pointed the way to the late-century shift to commercialism as the driving force in theatrical decisions. Most of the changes were fueled by the demands of the increasingly mass audience or were in response to theatre managers' perception of those demands. Although the repertory system continued to be the dominant scheme for the presentation of plays, long runs of a single play on consecutive nights emerged. One hundred consecutive performances can be noted from time to time, no doubt responding to popular demand and box office potential.

The tradition of the leading performers of a troupe contracting for a season or longer was placed under great stress as star actors began the practice of hiring out for a single role to individual theatres on a touring basis. This shift from repertory ensemble to starring performers happened because it made money for the actor and the theatre. In addition, the advances in transportation in the 1850s provided better travel arrangements for more profitable star tours. This led to rather mediocre resident companies as the better-known actors weakened entire troupes by their comings and goings. Rachel, for example, could fill the Comédie Française when she played there, but her frequent absences for star tours left the resident company on perilous financial ground.

The general organization of sharing companies declined during the first half of the nineteenth century. Managers, responding to the fiscal pressures of box office survival and the changing opinions of the mass audience, hired actors on contract to give themselves more flexibility. Coupled with this was the gradual deterioration of the "line of parts" concept as the idea of star tours rose. None of these changes sounded the death knell of the resident repertory system of producing theatre in the early nineteenth century, but they did serve as precursors to the massive changes that would be in place by 1900.

Reforms and Reformers

The concern for business in the theatre did not mean that all art was forsaken. A number of reforms had artistic merit, but they, too, were fueled by tailoring a product to popular demand. For artistic and box office reasons, theatrical seasons were lengthened and the variety and length of an evening's fare was increased. By midcentury year-round performances were commonplace and every night of the week could be used. Performances usually lasted five to six hours, starting at 7:00 P.M. The theatre was expected to supply a full evening's entertainment. Artistic effort was heightened by a rising competitiveness among various theatres as official sanctions were either replaced or lifted. In England, for example, the Theatre Regulations Act of 1843 finally allowed competition to flourish in London, which had not been the case since 1660.

Several theatre managers actively fostered reforms. In Germany, Ludwig Tieck (1773–1853) pressed for romantic acting set against a simple, open stage. In his practice as a manager, he strove to reduce the pictorial antiquarianism of the time, and he was partially successful in his own country. Karl Immermann (1796–1840) did not share Tieck's enthusiasm for romantic acting, but he did work to integrate all production aspects into an organic whole under his guidance. Directing, as a distinct theatrical function, did not exist until the last decades of the nineteenth century, but Immermann and Mme Vestris came close. So did William Charles Macready, who actually attempted to set the acting in his plays so that the entire stage picture would fit into the general scheme of historical accuracy he insisted upon in scenery and costuming. He also insisted upon a detailed and organized rehearsal period (ten rehearsals were common) that required all actors, including supernumeraries, to get into their roles early by acting at rehearsal and not to "save themselves for performance." Charles Kean (1811–1868), manager of the Princess' Theatre at midcentury, set the standard in historical antiquarianism for the rest of the nineteenth century. Months were spent in preparation for his Shakespearean revivals to ensure that they were historically correct in every detail. Elaborate program notes were issued giving the background research for each artistic decision, all approved by him. In this attention to the totality of his productions, he was a forerunner of the modern director.

Finally, the playwright was not forgotten. In France, for example, the Society of Dramatic Authors was formed in 1829, ensuring, for the first time, decent compensation for playwrights. Authors were assured a royalty for each performance of their plays, which usually amounted to 10 to 15 percent of the gross receipts. Coupled with this was a pension fund for authors, so some degree of financial stability was added to the profession.

CONCLUSION

The first half of the nineteenth century witnessed the emergence of significant changes to the theory and practice of theatre that were to be fully realized by the end of the century. All were in response to theatre's increasing role as the major provider of entertainment to the masses, a role that required an increasing awareness of artistic "truth" for the time and the fiscal sensibilities to ensure its success.

RETROSPECT

The changes that occurred in dramatic literature and theatre practice during the first half of the nineteenth century were precursors to the rapid change that would so radically alter the practice of theatre in the late 1800s. Most of these changes were prompted by basic shifts in the power structure of European society itself. In the post-Napoleonic years the middle class rose to a position of political and economic dominance from which it would not retreat. The pursestrings of Europe were increasingly controlled by the expanded middle class, and theatre changed to accommodate its tastes as well as those of the people who were flocking to the urban centers seeking work. This new, largely uneducated mass audience found in melodrama a temporary haven from the harsh realities of the industrial revolution. Not concerned with the gray compromise areas of human existence, melodrama portrayed a world that was black and white, where good was ultimately rewarded and vice finally punished. Another dramatic genre, the well-made play, similarly emerged and catered to middle-class tastes. Based on a writing formula that ensured an expectant audience, the well-made play was not concerned with psychological or philosophical development. It reassured the middle class that its morals and mores were correct and was written with staging values clearly in mind.

Both these and other dramatic forms were staged in theatres that catered to the mass audience's demand for more sensational, spectacular staging. Antiquarianism carried the day as scenery and costuming gradually moved from the generalized locale of the neoclassicists to the specificity and individuality of the romantics. The larger stage spaces housing this specificity applied a host of nineteenth-century theatre devices to eighteenth-century scenic theories and machinery, with the resultant increase in scope and complexity of traps and flying systems. Scenic exteriors continued to be staged in the traditional wing and drop manner, while interiors utilized the increasingly popular box set. Lighting devices experienced the most fundamental changes since the Renaissance with the realization of gas and the emergence of electricity. For the first time significant focus was achieved by dimming and brightening the stage.

Change also came to the basic fabric of theatrical organization. To accommodate the varied tastes of the mass audience, going to the theatre had to be a complete event with the main piece or play only one of the evening's offerings. Five hours of entertainment were not uncommon as theatre assumed its role of providing all types of performances to the masses. The old repertory system was challenged by longer consecutive runs of single plays, usually headed by star actors who joined the resident companies for the leading roles. When finished, these star performers traveled to other cities and companies to repeat the roles or play others in the same "line." This weakened the resident companies significantly but reflected the movement of theatre from a focus on art to that of a business investment.

The move toward the mass audience and theatre's response to that movement was set during the first half of the nineteenth century. Solutions to the problems and concerns would increase exponentially in the last half of the nineteenth century as theatre found itself nearing its long-time goal of verisimilitude. At the same time it would begin to question the validity of that long-time goal in the final decades of the nineteenth century.

Date	European History	European Theatre History
1799	Napoleon appointed First Consul of France.	
1800	France purchases Louisiana from Spain.	Pixérécourt's *Coelina*.
1803	France sells Louisiana to U.S.A.	
1804	Napoleon proclaimed Emperor of France.	
1805–1815	Napoleonic wars in Europe.	
1805	British defeat French in naval battles at Trafalgar; Napoleon declared King of Italy.	Death of Schiller.
1807	British fleet shells Copenhagen.	
1808	France invades Spain.	Covent Garden burns.
1809	War between France and Austria. Napoleon annexes Papal States and takes Pope prisoner.	Ludwig Devrient begins acting career.
1810		Kleist's *Prinz Friedrich von Homburg*.
1812	France invades Russia. Moscow burned by French. French army loses 300,000 in retreat from Russia. War declared between Britian and U.S.A.	From Russia, Napoleon issues the Moscow Decree, which reorganized the Comédie Française along lines still followed.
1813	France invaded by allied armies.	
1814	Paris captured by allied armies; Napoleon sent to Elba. Louis XVIII declared King of France.	Edmund Kean's debut at Drury Lane.
1815	Napoleon returns to France. Louis XVIII flees. Battle of Waterloo. Napoleon exiled to St. Helena.	
1816		Macready's debut at Covent Garden.
1817		Gas lighting used at Drury Lane and Covent Garden.
1818	Allied armies finally leave France.	
1819		Kotzebue assassinated by member of Young Germany movement.
1820	Beginning of reign of George IV of England.	
1822–1828	War for Independence in Greece.	

Date	European History	European Theatre History
1822	Famine in Ireland.	Gas lighting at Paris Opéra.
1823		Charles Kemble's staging of *King John*.
1824	Beginning of reign of Charles X of France.	
1827		English actors in Paris. Hugo's *Preface to Cromwell*.
1829		Dumas's *Henri III*.
1830	Paris riots. Charles X abdicates and Louis-Phillippe is proclaimed King of France.	Hugo's *Hernani*. Vestris begins management of Olympic Theatre.
1832		Death of Goethe. Dumas's *La Tour*.
1833		Death of Edmund Kean. Passage of Copyright Act in England.
1834–1839	Civil war in Spain.	
1836		Scribe elected to French Academy.
1837	Queen Victoria begins reign in England.	
1838	Riots in England.	Rachel appears at Comédie Française.
1841		Macready takes over management of Drury Lane.
1843		Theatre monopoly ends in England.
1845–1848	Great Famine in Ireland.	
1846		Electricity used at Paris Opéra.
1848	Riots in Paris. Louis-Philippe abdicates and the Second Republic is proclaimed. Revolts in Central Europe. Louis Napoleon elected President of France.	
1849		Ibsen completes his first play, *Catiline*.
1852	Louis Napoleon, as Napolean III, declared Emperor of France.	

SELECTED READINGS

Booth, Michael R. *English Melodrama*. London: Herbert Jenkins, 1965.
   A very useful and highly readable account of the melodrama. Note should be made of the section on melodramatic acting, a topic on which it is difficult to find information.

_____. *Hiss the Villain: Six English and American Melodramas*. New York: Arno Press, 1977.
   The introduction to this selection of melodramas is very useful for anyone without the time to read Booth's study listed above.

Brown, Frederick. *Theatre and Revolution: The Culture of the French Stage*. New York: Viking, 1980.
   Although this work is mainly concerned with twentieth-century France, the first three chapters are very useful for an understanding of the revolutionary background of melodrama.

Carlson, Marvin A. *The French Stage in the Nineteenth Century*. Metuchen, N.J.: Scarecrow Press, 1973.
   A general survey of French theatre and production practices.

_____. *The German Stage in the Nineteenth Century*. Metuchen, N.J.: Scarecrow Press, 1972.
   A companion study to the title above, but with more discussion of the plays of the period.

_____. *The Italian Stage from Goldoni to D'Annunzio*. Jefferson, N.C.: McFarland, 1981.
   This study is helpful for understanding the political problems that hampered the Italian drama of the nineteenth century.

Downer, Alan S. "Players and the Painted Stage: Nineteenth-Century Acting." *PMLA* 61(1946): 522–76.
   The best single source of information on the subject.

Driver, Tom F. *Romantic Quest and Modern Query: A History of the Modern Theatre*. New York: Delacorte Press, 1970.
   This work includes an interesting discussion of aspects of romanticism and a chapter on the well-made play.

Heilman, Robert B. *Tragedy and Melodrama: Versions of Experience*. Seattle: University of Washington Press, 1968.
   An informative examination of the two genres and their complementary elements. Makes a very strong case for melodrama as a broad dramatic form.

Hewitt, Barnard. *History of the Theatre from 1800 to the Present*. New York: Random House, 1970.
   A brief, clear examination of the development of the modern theatre.

Rahill, Frank. *The World of Melodrama*. University Park: Pennsylvania State University Press, 1967.

An interesting look at English, American, and French melodrama. Contains an excellent bibliography.

Smith, James L. *Melodrama*. London: Methuen, 1973.

A brief (less than eighty pages) study that will correct any impressions that all melodramas are bad plays.

Valency, Maurice. *The Flower and the Castle: An Introduction to Modern Drama*. New York: Macmillan, 1963.

Although chiefly concerned with Ibsen and Strindberg, the first part of this excellent work contains highly useful information on European drama in the first half of the nineteenth century.

Watson, Ernest B. *Sheridan to Robertson: A Study of the Nineteenth-Century London Stage*. Cambridge, Mass.: Harvard University Press, 1926.

A general summary of production practices in London during the first two-thirds of the nineteenth century.

OSLO

MOSCOW

PART X

The Mirror Reflects Itself:
THE LATE NINETEENTH CENTURY

During the second half of the industrial revolution, the years between 1870 and 1914, significant advances were made in nearly all fields of human endeavor. It was, however, a period chiefly identified with the continuous growth of industrialism. During these years the linking of pure science with technology began to produce major inventions and improvements. The steam turbine provided electricity as an abundant new source of power, and the invention of the internal combustion engine resulted in the birth of the automobile and airplane.

The nations of Europe used their technological superiority to dominate other parts of the world and at the same time to export their wealth and populations into underdeveloped areas. During the period 1870 to 1900 over twenty-one million people emigrated from Europe, and they took with them European technology and culture. For those who remained in Europe, especially those who had been exploited during the earlier stages of the industrial revolution, there were increased opportunities to have a say in the direction of their lives. This period witnessed a steady growth of unionism in Europe, and the unions were both militant and political. In the areas of political governance there were even greater changes. During the years after 1870, national governments began their development into comprehensive regulators of society, and the result was large-scale projects in public health and education. The outcome was an improved quality of life for all. The improvement in living conditions was also assisted by one of the longest periods of peace in European history.

The European stage from 1870 to 1914 reflected these major social changes. Technology was fully utilized in the construction of new and better theatres, and electricity brought a new era to theatrical production. The playwrights of dramatic realism attempted to incorporate the new discoveries in psychology and sociology in their work, and their concerns for social reform and the problems of spiritual isolation appear often in the scripts of the period. Yet there remained over the entire period a feeling for the joy of life. It was *La Belle Epoque*, the beautiful epoch, an era of theatricality both on and off the stage.

19

THE RISE OF REALISM

The second half of the nineteenth century witnessed many advances and discoveries in the areas of the sciences, technologies, and the arts. During this period, the theatre grew into a large, commercial entertainment industry that catered primarily to the tastes of the prosperous middle class. The demands for entertainment opposed a growing call to use the theatre as a tool for social criticism. The result of this tension was the emergence of two types of professional theatre in the last quarter of the century, the commercial theatre and the art theatre. Both theatres were faced with the challenge of realism.

REALISM IN DRAMA

Early Development

Realism, like most literary movements of the nineteenth and twentieth centuries, had its beginnings in France. Theatrical realism was both a reaction against the excesses of romanticism and a natural development of the well-made play. The first steps toward theatrical realism in France were in the social drama and the thesis play (*pièce à thèse*), which built upon the topicality of the well-made play formula.

Both the social drama and the thesis play were based on the conventions and prejudices of middle-class society. They implied that the concerns of the middle class with family, money, business, and social position were among life's most serious problems. These plays brought into the theatre the furniture, dress, manners, and conversation of the members of the audience, and they attempted to depict a life that was familiar and natural to the spectators.

Emile Augier (1820–1889) and Alexandre Dumas *fils* (1824–1895) were two of the foremost playwrights in France in the 1860s and 1870s, and both helped to establish the great popularity of the social drama. Dumas *fils* (son of the romantic playwright and novelist Alexandre Dumas *père*) set the standard for social drama with his *La Dame aux camélias* (The Lady of the Camellias, 1852), which presented a picture of contemporary Parisian life. Augier's *Le Gendre de M. Poirer* (M. Poirer's Son-in-Law, 1854) depicted the uncomfortable marriage alliance of middle-class money and aristocratic poverty and the tension between the two social classes. These plays stressed topics of contemporary society, and they were presented in a relaxed, quiet manner so as to suggest that the audience was watching an actual event unfold before them. Still written according to the formula of the well-made play, these scripts' emphasis remains on the story rather than the characters, but they do suggest a far greater sense of reality than the plays of earlier eras.

By the end of the decade of the 1860s, Dumas was attempting to move the social drama in a new direction with the thesis play, which presented and offered a solution to a particular social problem. In such plays as *Le Fils naturel* (The Natural Son, 1858), *La Princesse Georges* (Princess Georges, 1871), and *La Femme de Claude* (Claude's Wife, 1873), he dealt with illegitimacy, adultery, and divorce. A major difference between the social drama and the thesis play, as developed by Dumas and later playwrights, was the relationship to the audience. Whereas the social play contained an implied, and often explicit, affirmation of middle-class standards, the thesis play contained an attack on some accepted social standards that the playwright viewed as unjust, such as the stigma attached to illegitimate children. This element of direct social criticism would become increasingly important in the theatre as the realistic movement emerged. Since this criticism often resulted in alienation of the audience, with its negative effect on the box office, realism on the nineteenth-century stage was generally presented in the art and not the commercial theatre.

Nontheatrical Influences on Realism

Several forces outside the theatre played an important role in the development of realism on the stage. In the early 1820s the positivist philosophy of Auguste Comte began to have an impact on the intellectual community of France. By the mid-1850s, following the completion of Comte's two major works, *Course of Positive Philosophy* and *System of Positive Philosophy*, the claim was being put forth that positivism was the replacement of theology in contemporary society. Positivism stressed a rigorous empirical and scientific approach to modern life and emphasized verifiability and cause and effect relationships. Science was viewed in the nineteenth century as capable of reforming the sorry conditions of the world. Theatre, to be more scientific, would need to present reality, not fantasy, on the stage.

Charles Darwin's *Origin of the Species* (1859), with its evolutionary theory based on natural selection, and *The Descent of Man* (1871), which placed humans in the evolutionary chain, challenged the traditional views of creation. Darwin's theories of survival of the fittest and adaptation to environment were converted by social thinkers into social Darwinism. This view held that the idea of survival of the fittest also applied to business, government, and all forms of human relations. Increased importance was placed on the belief that people are creatures of their environment and that surroundings form or reinforce character.

In the last quarter of the nineteenth century, the new science of psychology began to question traditional views of behavior and the concepts of guilt and sin. The increasing awareness of the complex workings of the unconscious mind opened new possibilities on the reasons for human actions. Sigmund Freud, an Austrian physician, established the foundations of psychoanalysis and opened the way for the reconstruction of troubled personalities. These new discoveries presented playwrights and novelists with vast areas of character motivation and gave new dramatic dimensions to the old questions of good and evil.

This period in the nineteenth century was also one of political turmoil as the mass of underprivileged workers began to find their voice and call for reform. The Chartist movement in England agitated for worker rights in the 1840s, and the socialists in Paris staged an uprising in 1848. Movements were started in most European countries to improve working conditions in factories, shorten the work week, improve slum housing, and remove children from the labor force. Often the call was not for reform but for revolution. Karl Marx published *the Communist Manifesto* in 1848, and in 1867 appeared his *Capital*, the classic work of Marxist theory. The evils of the industrial revolution were now appearing in the form of an angry and growing workers' movement. Many of the concerns of reformers found expression in the thesis play, where the *raisonneur*, the character spokesman for the playwright, addressed the complaints to an audience containing factory owners and slum landlords.

Realism in the Theatre

Theatrical realism emerged in the 1870s as a natural development of the technical reality of stage presentations (box set, improved lighting, real food) and an interest in applying to the theatre the new theories in science and psychology. The leaders of the realist movement took the social and thesis plays to task for their politeness and conventionality. Foremost among the new realists was Emile Zola (1840–1902). The preface to his play *Thérèse Raquin* (1873) expressed his belief that it was possible to discover natural laws of human conduct, laws based on heredity, environment, and social forces. These laws could be discovered by the playwright in the same way that the scientist discovered laws of the natural world. Zola called his approach naturalism. In the late nineteenth century, the terms "realism" and "naturalism" were used interchangeably to describe theatrical productions that endeavored to create the appearance of real life on stage without flattery or sentimentality. Naturalism, as attempted by Zola and his followers, developed into an extreme form of realism in which theatricality disappeared in the quest for accurate observation and reproduction of detail. In such an environment the art of the theatre ceased to exist. Naturalism in the theatre disappeared before the end of the century, but realism became the principal approach of modern drama.

Two concerns of the early realists in the theatre were the problem of art in a scientific age and the relationship of imagination and truth. How was an imaginative creation, such as a play, to be justified in a world governed by scientific laws? The naturalists responded by declaring that theatre would apply the techniques of science, yet in the process they lost the theatrical. And even the naturalists were controlled by creativity in their choice of subjects, creation of environments, and use of dialogue. In the end the realists acknowledged the manipulative aspects of their art, but they strived to cover their theatrical framework with the appearance of reality. Thus imagination was made to serve truth. With realism came greater emphasis on character and less stress on story development. Audiences found their interest directed to the reactions of characters to environmental and social forces as the nineteenth-century theatre moved from a storybook to a laboratory of human studies.

ACTING

Acting Style

With the retirement of William Charles Macready from the stage in 1851, the last star of the classic acting tradition was extinguished. During the next two decades acting styles would change in reaction to forces both in and out of the theatre. Technical innovations in the theatre, production changes that emphasized accuracy of detail, and the near-dominance of the well-made play all called for more subtlety in acting than had been required in earlier periods. In these acting reforms, the French set the example.

The well-made play, as opposed to the high histrionics of the romantic play, required elegance, a somewhat natural form of delivery, and interactive stage byplay among the actors. There was a stress on quietness, stage business, and a lack of force. When Charles Fechter (1824–1879), a well-known French actor, made his London debut in 1860–61 as Hamlet, he astonished British audiences with his disregard for all the traditional points and poses of the role. His portrayal of the Dane as a quiet, troubled gentleman drew audiences to the production for five months and made the Fechter "reforms" a topic of considerable discussion among London theatregoers. While most were in favor of this new style of acting, one contemporary critic noted that the details of daily life were not consistent with tragedy, that "lounging on tables and lolling against chairs," in an effort to convey reality, was unnatural in tragedy. Although this argument is still heard today in relation to modern approaches to the classics, the early French style of realistic acting began to be incorporated into theatrical production throughout Britain, Europe, and the United States.

Social Position of Actors

If the style of acting in the 1860s was becoming more genteel, so, too, were the actors, particularly in Britain. The acting profession in Europe had largely lost most of the stigmas attached to it during earlier eras, but during the first half of the nineteenth century British actors were still held in low esteem. This began to change after 1860 when actors with strong middle-class backgrounds started to enter the profession. Many of these new recruits to the stage got their first taste of theatrical life from performing in amateur productions in college or the military. These actors, educated and often with private incomes from their families, easily moved about in influential social circles and helped bestow on the profession a dignified demeanor. This changing social role of the actor was taking place at the same time that acting techniques and plays were requiring a more refined approach; thus the two complemented each other. By 1880 the gentleman actor was a commonplace in Britain, and in 1895 the profession received its first knighthood.

Working Conditions and Training

Although the social position of the actor had greatly improved by the 1890s, working conditions remained dangerous and training haphazard. Exploitation was the rule rather than the exception in the over-crowded acting profession, yet only major stars were able to complain about the conditions of employment. Owners were willing to spend huge sums of money to beautify the auditoriums of their theatres, but were most reluctant to spend any money to improve conditions backstage. Behind the curtain it was dirty, damp, and drafty, with few dressing rooms and even fewer toilets. The ventilation was generally poor and the gas lighting stifling and sometimes deadly. The open flames of the gas jets on more than one occasion ignited the long gown and petticoats of a dancer or actress. Such conditions and risks would continue to trouble the profession until the actors' unions of the present century began to force changes on theatre owners.

Actor training in the second half of the nineteenth century underwent a change because of the decline of the repertory company and the rise of the long run. Touring companies from major cities reduced the need for a large resident company in a provincial theatre. This reduced the number of positions available for actors and the opportunity to learn a large number of roles and gain experience. The long run kept a few experienced actors employed, but offered few chances for the beginner to learn the profession. Formal schools or conservatories were available for actor training in most European countries, but in Britain there were no schools or agreed-upon theories of acting. A Royal Dramatic College was established in 1859, only to go bankrupt in less than twenty years. The topic of a national training school continued to be discussed during the rest of the century, but only in 1904 was the Royal Academy of Dramatic Arts finally and firmly established. Before that time, actor training in Britain was an individual affair obtained from a retired actor, in an amateur theatre club, or from one of the expensive training companies established to provide services to stage-struck members of the middle class.

MAJOR ACTORS

The late nineteenth century is considered the last great era of the actor. Thereafter, although exceptional performers would appear, the focus of the stage would be on the director or the play itself. A few actors in the last decades of the century established international reputations and, thanks to improved transportation, mass-circulation newspapers, and the familiarity of the well-made play formula, were able to mount highly visible and profitable tours.

Sarah Bernhardt

The first true international stage star to capture the hearts and pocketbooks of audiences in Britain, Europe, Australia, North and South America, and North Africa was Sarah Bernhardt (1845–1923). She made her debut at the Comédie Française in 1862, and ten years later, because of her remarkable voice, attractiveness, and mastery of acting, she was considered the finest actress in France. She was shortly to become the best-known actress in the Western world. Bernhardt first performed outside France in 1879, when the Comédie Française performed in London. The attention she received from the press and theatregoers convinced her that future success, fame, and fortune would be greater as an independent performer and not as a contract player.

Breaking with the Comédie Française, Bernhardt arranged to tour the United States in 1880 with her own company. Performing in French in plays by Dumas

Sarah Bernhardt.

fils and Victorian Sardou, she toured fifty-one cities in six months and was an enormous success. For the next thirty years, Bernhardt divided her time between being an actor-manager in Paris and performing on tour. By the 1890s critics began to complain about her "old fashion" plays and her increasingly mechanical approach to acting. Achieving fame in formula plays often written to showcase her somewhat melodramatic acting style, the "Divine Sarah" was at odds with the more realistic plays and acting styles that began to appear by the turn of the century. It was of small concern. The legend of Bernhardt continued to fill theatres wherever she toured, and in France she was considered a national treasure beyond criticism.

Henry Irving

Sir Henry Irving (1838–1905) once remarked to Ellen Terry, his long-time leading lady, that "for an actor who can't walk, can't talk, and has no face to speak of, I've done pretty well." Well indeed, for in 1895 he became the first British actor to be knighted for services to his profession. Born John Henry Brodribb, he took the stage name Irving when he began his career in 1856. After ten years of acting in provincial theatres, where he performed

Henry Irving and Ellen Terry in a scene from W. W. Wills's Olivia, *which Irving revived at the Lyceum in 1885.*

over six hundred roles, Irving finally achieved success and notice in London in the mid-1860s. In 1871 he created a sensation at the Lyceum Theatre with his deeply psychological portrayal of the murderer Mathias in *The Bells*. The performance made Irving a star, and in 1878, after taking on the lease of the Lyceum, he became the managing director of his own theatre company. In the next two decades he made the Lyceum Britain's temple of the theatrical arts.

Throughout his career Irving was criticized for his thin legs, strange walk, high nasal voice, peculiar manner of pronouncing vowels, and general lack of power. Yet he possessed an eloquent face and eyes that transfixed audiences, and he had a unique ability to visually present a character in such a manner as to cover his own physical weaknesses.

While Irving had several notable successes in classical roles in his career, such as Hamlet, Iago, and Shylock, his major acting triumphs were in inferior plays that stressed his gifts for the mysterious or sinister. He was at heart a romantic actor and was unwilling to yield to Ellen Terry's requests that he try an Ibsen play. That was a shame, for it appears Irving would have made a very interesting John Gabriel Borkman or a Master Solness, self-possessed men much like himself. Eight times Irving took his company to the United States and each trip was a great success. He was hailed by many as the greatest actor who had ever lived. Yet throughout his career there was always a strong voice of derision about his abilities. In the early 1880s Irving was offered a knighthood, but he refused it because of the jealousy it would have created among his fellow actors. In 1895, when he was considered by all in the profession as their leading figure, he accepted the honor of the knighthood. Sir Henry Irving died in 1905, a few hours after finishing a performance, and was buried with honors in the Poet's Corner of Westminster Abbey.

Eleanora Duse

Born the child of poor traveling actors, Eleanora Duse (1858–1924) literally spent her entire life on the stage. She was born on the road and she died on the road, and in between this small Italian actress showed the theatrical world a new level of performance. By the time she was twenty, she had established a solid reputation as a major actress in Europe. On her second trip to London, in 1875, she and Bernhardt appeared in the same role at different theatres and offered audiences an opportunity to compare their different acting styles. The champions of the traditional, such as critic Clement Scott, preferred Bernhardt, while the reformers, such as critic George Bernard Shaw, highly praised Duse.

While performing the same repertory, the two actresses were nearly opposites. Duse avoided publicity and reporters, and she professed a great dislike of the theatre. But unlike William Charles Macready, another great actor who disliked the stage, Duse was drawn to the theatre as a near-religious experience. This mystical view of the theatre was a strong element in her acting, and she had the ability to share it with her audiences. She did not use stage makeup and was able to blush or turn pale on cue. She was noted for the

Eleanora Duse.

softness of her delivery, her sparse but eloquent gestures, and the great naturalness of her performance. As one contemporary critic observed, "She creates out of life itself an art which no one before her had ever imagined: not realism, not a copy, but the thing itself." Although some critics accused her of lack of technique, of just playing the moment, she was a highly disciplined artist and totally in control of her performance. This, in the words of the great American actress Eva Le Gallienne, made Duse the greatest exponent of the actual "art of acting" in her time.

DIRECTING

Acting styles, ensemble playing, realism, and the demands of increasingly technical productions necessitated that one individual be in total control. During the second half of the nineteenth century, the *regisseur*, or director, became an indispensable element in stage productions. The roots of modern directing can be traced back to Goethe's work with the Weimar State Theatre, but it achieved its first successes in another part of Germany, at the Court Theatre in Saxe-Meiningen.

Meiningen Court Theatre

At the Court Theatre of Georg II, Duke of Saxe-Meiningen, the inability to hire major performers was turned into a theatrical triumph. Georg II came to the throne of his small dukedom in 1866 and immediately began to indulge his passion for theatre. The theatre was under the direct control of the duke, but a director was hired to carry out his plans. The theatre began its major developments in 1873 when Ludwig Chronegk (1837–1891) was appointed director. The duke stressed the authenticity and beauty of the company's costumes and sets, but Chronegk dealt with the acting problems. Without first-rate actors to carry the company, he turned his attention to ensemble playing. Here his abilities as a director made the large crowd scenes compensate for second-rate performers. Years later, when the company was performing in Moscow, Constantin Stanislavsky noted that the director used a large court scene to such good effect that the audience didn't notice the "cheap acting" of the leading actress, who used "the worst stage methods, rolling her eyes and giving vent to vocal fireworks."

Discipline was the key to the success of the Meiningen company. As the personal acting company of the duke and without the pressures for commercial success, plays were rehearsed until the duke was satisfied. Rehearsals were in

Duke Georg II

the evening, after the duke had completed his state business, and often lasted past midnight. Actors were required to act, not just walk through their lines, at all rehearsals and great attention was paid to the use of stage properties. All members of the company were used in all productions. Actors unwilling to perform walk-on parts in mob scenes were dismissed. All movements in the large scenes were individually choreographed and rehearsed in small groups. When all these parts were put together, they presented a highly remarkable ensemble effect.

Georg II insisted on the highest level of historical accuracy in his productions. Costumes and sets were carefully researched, and the reproductions produced for the stage were the most detailed yet seen on the European stage. Armor and furniture were custom-built of the original materials, and actors were forbidden to make adjustments in their costumes. The accuracy and detail of the sets and costumes greatly impressed audiences, but the duke's director, Chronegk, once grumbled, "I brought them [the audience] Shakespeare, Schiller, and Molière, and they are interested in the furniture."

The Meiningen company gave its first performance outside its home theatre in 1874 in Berlin. The visit was so successful that the original stay of four weeks was extended to six. After two return engagements in Berlin in 1875 and 1876, the company expanded its touring schedule. During the next fourteen years, the company performed in the major cities of most of the countries of Europe except France and Italy. During this period it was the most admired theatrical company in Europe. Both the ensemble techniques and the power of the director were widely copied. The work of Chronegk was particularly influential on the later work of Otto Brahm and Constantin Stanislavsky. Directors for the commercial stage had not the time, money, or legal power of Georg II, but the Meiningen Court Theatre's manner of presentation set a standard of excellence that many tried to follow.

The Bancrofts and the Prince of Wales's Theatre

In 1864 Marie Wilton (1839–1921), a young actress who had been on the professional stage since childhood, borrowed money from her brother-in-law and leased a small and somewhat shabby theatre in London. After elegant remodeling and with a new name, the Prince of Wales's, the theatre opened to modest success in 1865. Wilton was soon joined in the management of the theatre by her future husband, Sidney "Squire" Bancroft (1841–1926). Together with their house playwright, T. W. Robertson (1829–1871), they were to establish new production standards for the British theatre.

The plays of T. W. Robertson are more remarkable for their elaborate directions for actors and designers than for their dramatic content. But these light, domestic comedies were perfectly suited to the desires of the Bancrofts, who were trying to entice London's wealthier citizens back to the theatre. They succeeded nicely and were able to retire, wealthy themselves, in 1885. The first Robertson play, *Society* (1865), established the playwright and the Bancrofts and made the Prince of Wales's theatre a gathering place for

Sir Sidney Bancroft.

London's high society. *Society* and Robertson's next five plays (*Ours, Caste, Play, School, M.P.*) remained in the repertory of the company until the Bancrofts' retirement.

The Bancrofts introduced modern scenic effects to British audiences and forever changed the way they would view the stage picture. Although Mme Vestris, with whom Robertson had worked as a young man, had given British audiences walls, carpets, and doors in her sets, the Bancrofts placed their well-rehearsed actors in sets that re-created the world of Victorian society. In addition to their early use of realism in stage decors, the Bancrofts were responsible for a number of other innovations in the British theatre: good salaries and working conditions for their actors, presentation of a single play as the sole entertainment for the evening, popularization of the matinee, permanent removal of the pit, and touring companies of their popular productions. The Bancrofts, through their play selection, high quality of production, and the comfort and beauty of their theatres (the Prince of Wales's, 1865–1879, and the Haymarket, 1879–1885), reintroduced the middle and upper classes of

London to the theatre and greatly helped to improve the status of the stage in Britain. For their efforts, Squire Bancroft was knighted in 1897.

Henry Irving

As a director Irving was in total control of every aspect of the production, but he paid particular attention to technical problems. Ellen Terry, who performed with him for over twenty years, recounted that as they neared the opening night of a production of *Hamlet* and she expressed to Irving her concerns about their scenes together, he remarked, "We shall be all right, but we are not going to run the risk of being bottled up by a gas-man or a fiddler." The sheer size of some of Irving's productions at the Lyceum required a dogged sense of detail: his 1899 production of *Robespierre* had a cast of 355 and a backstage staff of 284. Like Chronegk, Irving was a master director of crowd scenes. Yet unlike the Meiningen Court Theatre, Irving did not use crowd scenes to cover weak actors. The Lyceum had a star, Henry Irving, and scenes were directed to focus attention on him. He presented a production as a total, unified picture, and at its center was Henry Irving.

Irving began the first rehearsal for a new production by reading the entire script aloud to the assembled cast and giving an interpretation of all roles. That was how the roles were to be done. He worked his casts arduously to achieve in their performances the interpretation he gave them at the first rehearsal. The details he exacted from his actors he also got from the technical staff. Plays were carefully researched, and sets and costumes constructed with close attention to historical accuracy. He had the old wing and groove arrangement removed from the Lyceum stage and used three-dimensional sets. These elaborate sets required Irving to rehearse his stagehands as much as his actors. As a director and performer, he paid great attention to lighting as an important element in the total production. He gave British audiences the most unified productions they had yet seen. The plays presented by Irving, with the exception of Shakespeare's, were second-rate, but after his years at the Lyceum, the British theatre was ready for the new drama of the twentieth century.

THE INDEPENDENT THEATRE MOVEMENT

During the last half of the nineteenth century, the movement toward realism was unmistakable but slow. Realistic reforms in acting and staging remained out of the theatrical mainstream for the balance of the century. Midcentury experiments were conducted and reforms introduced, but what was needed to ensure the triumph of realism was a single major thrust at the heart of European theatrical conservatism. That thrust came with the Independent Theatre Movement.

The Independent, or Free, Theatre Movement varied slightly in detail from country to country, although it had a common goal and objective. The movement sought to foster realistic writing and production practices in Europe, and in that sense it was a reaction against the pictorial antiquarianism that dominated the nineteenth-century European stage. To do so was no easy task. The theatrical mainstream was carefully controlled by established theatres, laws, and censoring bodies that did not allow major competition. From these controls and from the movement's response to them came the movement's name. The theatre that the realists desired to practice could flourish only if it was free and independent from mainstream constraints. Thus, by supporting themselves primarily through subscriptions rather than individual ticket sales, these theatres could organize in a way that allowed them to be essentially private theatrical societies. Open to members only, they were free and independent from the various forms of censorship that would have otherwise plagued them. In addition, the movement's leaders would be free from the antiquarian production methods that they felt were stifling the European theatre. Thus liberated, the movement was able to pursue the art of the theatre as it wished. By century's end all four major countries in Europe—France, Germany, England, and Russia—had established an organization of the Independent Theatre Movement, thus ensuring the triumph of realism. The first country in which the movement flourished was, as in so many other nineteenth-century areas, France.

France

The French Independent Theatre Movement was founded by André Antoine (1858–1943), a most unlikely candidate for such a position of honor. Antoine had been active in amateur productions and had occasionally performed as a supernumerary with professional companies, but that was the extent of his involvement with the theatre. While employed as a clerk by the Paris Gas Company, he became interested in producing the realistic plays then emerging in Europe, particularly the works of Zola. The amateur group he had occasionally worked with had no such interest, so in 1887 Antoine established his own theatre, the Théâtre Libre (Free Theatre). The success of the venture was meteoric. Absolutely the right idea at the right time, the Théâtre Libre not only was enthusiastically embraced by the new playwrights, including Zola himself, but was reviewed by major critics before its first season ended. Antoine's future as a theatrical producer was thus assured, and he devoted himself full-time to that cause until his retirement in 1914.

The Théâtre Libre was important not only for the drama it produced, but for the style of production as well. Everything was based on realism to such an extent that detailed environment, rather than locale, was the norm. Actors performed at the curtain line facing upstage as though there were no audience, and the furniture was often arranged along the curtain line with backs to the audience. This was the practice of the "fourth wall" convention in the extreme. Like the playwrights of realism, Antoine believed in the importance of environment as the proper setting for his plays. He demanded ensemble,

A set from Antoine's 1891 production of Ibsen's **The Wild Duck** *at the Théâtre Libre.*

natural acting from his actors, and absolute reality in the other aspects of his productions.

Antoine's initial venture at the Théâtre Libre lasted only a few years. By the second season, he had introduced non-French dramatists to Parisian audiences by presenting selected works of Tolstoy and Ibsen. In 1890 he directed and performed in Ibsen's *Ghosts*. More than anyone, Antoine was responsible for the acceptance of Ibsen and his drama in France. But his style of production was expensive, and the theatre never prospered financially. As the popularity of the type of drama he established began to enter the theatrical mainstream, he faced a new problem: his actors and writers left the Théâtre Libre to work for major companies. By 1894 the Théâtre Libre had become a financial failure. Nonetheless it was of immeasurable artistic importance, not only in France but throughout Europe as others formed similar organizations and championed the tenets of realism.

The remainder of Antoine's career reflected his earlier zeal as a realist, although to a lesser extent. In 1897 he took control of the Théâtre des Menus-Plaisirs, renamed it the Théâtre Antoine, and produced realistic plays from a variety of young playwrights. From 1906 until his retirement, Antoine served as director of the state-supported Odéon, where he sought to revive the French classics and Shakespeare. By producing these plays as authentic period pieces, he brought a sense of realism to the concepts of theatrical convention and historical accuracy. Thus Antoine's contribution to French theatre was across the entire spectrum of dramatic literature. No other European producer was more influential.

Germany

The German theatre had been touched by the realistic movement, but censorship had kept any concerted efforts from reaching the stage. As in France, an unlikely champion appeared to bring focus to the cause of presenting objective reality in the theatre. German drama critic Otto Brahm (1856–1912) had been concerned about the state of the German stage, particularly its archaic mode of acting. He had established a journal, *Die Freie Bühne* (The Free Stage), in which he had argued for reforms. In 1889 Brahm was elected president of a similarly committed theatrical enterprise in Berlin that took the same name, the Freie Bühne. Unlike the Théâtre Libre, the Freie Bühne had a formal organizational structure and from the outset was a professional theatre organization. In order to use professional actors, who had to be retrained in the new realistic style, Brahm's company only performed in the afternoon since most of the players were otherwise employed for evening performances. Because it was a private stage society, the Freie Bühne provided a professional forum for the new realistic plays not allowed presentation in the German theatrical mainstream. Its opening production was *Ghosts*, and by 1890 all the major realistic playwrights had enjoyed a presentation at the Freie Bühne. The major German playwright introduced there was Gerhart Hauptmann (1862–1946). His works, showing humans as victims of an environment over which they have no control, were among the theatre's major efforts.

By 1894 Brahm, who had always wanted the theatrical mainstream to reflect the tenets of realism, realized that the time was right for such a move and affiliated his Freie Bühne with the Deutsches Theatre, a larger and well-established company. Brahm was named director of the new amalgamation, and the group specialized in the production of new and older realistic plays.

Other theatrical ventures picked up on the success of the Freie Bühne. The most successful of these was the Freie Volksbühne (Free People's Theatre), organized in Berlin in 1890 for the express purpose of raising the cultural tastes of the working class. Performing matinees on Sundays, it was limited to season subscribers who were assigned seats by lot. The theatre brought realism to the working class at affordable prices, and it was no doubt responsible for assisting the trend toward theatregoing among the German working class that is still current today.

England

In many ways England was further behind in recognizing the new realism than much of the Continent. Certainly the early works of Henry Jones and Arthur Wing Pinero did introduce realism to the British stage, but it was not until Ibsen was readily available in translation and production that the need for an English Independent Theatre Movement was felt. And as in Germany, it was a drama critic who led the way.

J. T. Grein (1862–1935) was a Dutch-born British playwright and drama critic who spent his early career writing commentary on the contemporary English stage for the *Dutch Art Chronicle*. He became fascinated with the work

A photograph of J. T. Grein taken during the period when he established the Independent Theatre in London.

of Antoine and, seeing a need in the British theatre for a similar effort, founded the Independent Theatre of London in 1891. The Independent Theatre was a subscription house, and it followed the model of the Freie Bühne by cooperating with the principal London theatres through Sunday matinee performances. Its opening production was Ibsen's *Ghosts*, but the reception was not as enthusiastic as the one that had met Continental efforts. Slowly, however, the Independent Theatre made England aware of the rising tide of realism.

Primarily, the Independent Theatre produced translations of Continental plays, for little in the new genre was being written in England. In 1892, however, George Bernard Shaw's *Widower's Houses* was produced, and Shaw's career was established. The Independent Theatre continued to produce plays until 1897, although the actual production mounting was left to practitioners hired by the organization. By that time succeeding groups had taken up the cause of realism. The foremost of these was the Incorporated Stage Society, founded, with Grein's assistance, in 1899 to produce contemporary plays. This organization did much to foster the career of Shaw.

Russia

Near the end of the nineteenth century, the Russian theatre was primarily bound by the theatrical conventions it had developed during the closing years of the eighteenth century. A few dramatists, such as Turgenev, had introduced elements of realism to Russian audiences, but it was not until the Meiningen Court Theatre toured the major cities in the 1880s that Russians realized how far behind they were in theatrical productions. Minor experiments were conducted in the late 1880s and early 1890s, but it was not until 1898, when Constantin Stanislavsky (1863–1938) and Vladimir Nemiro-vich-Danchenko (1858–1943) formed the Moscow Art Theatre, that realism had a focal point in Russia.

Among the theatrical organizations of the Independent Theatre Movement, the Moscow Art Theatre reigned supreme. Unlike the Freie Bühne and the Independent Theatre, it not only was a producing organization but concerned itself with mounting the productions as well. And unlike the Théâtre Libre, it concentrated on developing realistic production aspects rather than simply relying on the realistic production of otherwise censored plays. It also had a different organizational structure. In essence it was a sharing company, a group composed of amateur and professional actors drawn from two prominent dramatic groups, the Society for Art and Literature and the Philharmonic Society. Although it was a cooperative venture, its members were not expected to participate in the expenses to the extent that members of older sharing companies had. The finances were supported by subscription sales and contributions of rich patrons from the Russian intelligentsia.

The Moscow Art Theatre opened with a production of Tolstoy's *Tsar Feodor Ivanovich*, which received much acclaim for the realistic production methods employed. It was not until its fifth production, however, that success would come to stay, and that was achieved through the introduction of Anton Chekhov (1860–1904) to Moscow audiences. Largely because of the approach to acting upon which Stanislavsky insisted, the production of *The Sea Gull* was a huge success, and Chekhov went on to write three additional plays—*Uncle Vanya*, *The Three Sisters*, and *The Cherry Orchard*—for the Moscow Art Theatre.

Without doubt the artistic center of the Moscow Art Theatre was Stanis-lavsky's approach to acting and production. Stanislavsky insisted on extensive rehearsal periods, including careful research into the play and its actual setting. This approach was required of every member of the company, and it laid the groundwork for the approach to acting generally known as the Stanislavsky System. The System divided the actor's job into parts and demanded analysis of each part in order to realistically and efficiently portray a believable character to an audience. It will be discussed in detail in a later chapter.

As the twentieth century began, the Moscow Art Theatre was preeminent in Russia. In 1902 it built its own theatre, more than doubled the size of its company, and standardized its repertory to include up to five new plays a year in addition to its revivals. It championed the works of a new playwright, Maxim

Gorky (1868–1936), whose dramas about the Russian proletariat would stand him and the Moscow Art Theatre in good stead long after the Revolution.

CONCLUSION

Thus did realism come to the fore in Western theatre and drama. It was, like most theatrical movements, a product of its time. It reflected the current philosophical and scientific thought of the day, in which environment was clearly seen as more important than other factors in charting the course of human affairs. The stage achieved through this movement the ultimate verisimilitude—objective reality was reproduced as truth in the theatre. This long-time goal of the theatre had been reached, and the twentieth century would refine it, modify it, and, true to theatrical inquiry, question whether it was worth the search at all.

20
THE REALISTIC PLAYWRIGHTS

The Independent Theatre Movement did a great deal to make the work of the early dramatic realists available to the public. But of equal or greater importance in the development and acceptance of realism in the theatre was the printed play script. Before the last quarter of the nineteenth century, contemporary plays were generally available only for viewing on the stage. The lack of printed play scripts hampered the spread of innovations in play writing in Europe. With the improvement of national and international copyright protection in the nineteenth century, playwrights were able to exercise some control over the presentation of their plays. The availability of printed plays allowed playwrights to gain increased financial rewards and reach a much wider audience than they could within the walls of the playhouse. The popular success of the printed form of *Brand* (1866) gave Ibsen both financial security and an international reputation. For the next thirty years, he made it a point to have his newest play arrive in the bookshops during the Christmas season.

Ibsen's example was not lost on other successful playwrights. The four creative masters of the early years of the modern drama, Ibsen, Strindberg, Shaw, and Chekhov, were as closely involved with book publishers during their careers as with theatre managers. The dramatic realists were greatly influenced by realistic novelists, and the plays were written in a prose style much akin to the contemporary novel. Many of these plays were written to be seen and read, and this may account for their lack of verbal color and imagery. Part of the later reaction against realism in the theatre was an attempt to separate the stage from the novel. Theatre as an art of sound and sight was to become an important issue in the twentieth century.

MAJOR PLAYWRIGHTS

Henrik Ibsen

Henrik Ibsen (1828–1906) looms on the creative peaks of nineteenth-century dramatic literature as some dark, forbidding mountain troll from his native Norway. He was both the culmination of

Henrik Ibsen in 1874.

nineteenth-century dramaturgy and the starting point for twentieth-century play writing. The period since his death has been too brief for an accurate assessment of his place in the pantheon of great playwrights, but it appears he was less influential in the development of the modern stage than his two contempories, Chekhov and Strindberg. Yet he remains unique, without artistic offspring, and his twenty-five plays stand unchallenged as an acknowledged master achievement in dramatic creativity.

Born in Skien, Norway, Ibsen was the eldest of five children of a well-to-do merchant. His father's business failed when Ibsen was eight, and the family suffered economic hardships. When his formal education ended in his early teens, Ibsen worked for a druggist and prepared to enter the university. In 1849, at the age of twenty-one, he wrote his first play, *Catiline*. Refused for production, the play was privately printed in 1850. When Ibsen arrived in Christiania (now Oslo) in 1850 to take his university exam, he brought with him another script, which he revised and submitted to the Christiania Theatre. The successful presentation of this one-act poetic drama, *Kjempehøjen* (The Warrior's Barrow, 1850), launched Ibsen's theatrical career.

During the next fourteen years, Ibsen wrote seven plays, served as playwright in residence and stage manager at the Bergen Theatre, and was artistic director of the Norwegian Theatre in Christiania. His plays of this period are based on Norwegian history and folk material, and they reflect Ibsen's intellectual involvement in Norway's struggle for independence from Sweden. In 1864, disillusioned by the sham of Scandinavian unity in the face of German military power and troubled by his own artistic drives, Ibsen left his native Norway for twenty-seven years of self-imposed exile. He returned to Norway in 1891 as an honored and respected man of letters. He died in Oslo in 1906 after a long illness.

During most of the fifty years of his career, Ibsen was continuously experimenting with dramatic form. The early, pre-exile plays were romantic dramas with a strong nationalistic bent. The numerous productions from French well-made plays that Ibsen supervised in Bergen and Christiania impressed upon him the Scribean techniques and the ways to maintain audience tension and expectation. His skills with the Scribean formula are evident in the early *Fru Inger til Østraat* (Lady Inger of Ostrat, 1855), and he shows complete mastery in the later social plays.

Brand (1866), Ibsen's first success after he left Norway, was a complete break with the well-made play. This rarely staged verse drama created a sensation in northern Europe when it was published, and it established a vast reading public for the plays of Ibsen. The play's hero, the rebel pastor Brand, has an uncompromising ideal of "all or nothing," and he zealously tries to impose his views on all he meets. Brand has great courage, but his lack of compassion and compromise bring destruction. *Peer Gynt* (1867), Ibsen's next large-scale verse drama, has at its center a man who is all compromise. Without a life purpose, Peer spends his years in empty adventures. He is saved from the mysterious Button Molder, who would melt his soul down into nothingness, only by the love of his old sweetheart, Solveig. After one more large work, the historical play *Kejser og Galilaer* (*Emperor and Galilean*, 1873), Ibsen returned to the form of the well-made play, but with a level of intensity and artistic purpose that startled theatregoers throughout Europe.

The plays Ibsen wrote during the period 1875 to 1890 represent one of the most sustained high levels of creativity in the history of the theatre. These plays (*Pillars of Society, A Doll House, Ghosts, An Enemy of the People, The Wild Duck, Rosmersholm, The Lady from the Sea, Hedda Gabler*) are the works most commonly associated with Ibsen. They are the foundation stones of his international reputation, yet they represent less than a third of his total dramatic output. They also reflect his continuous growth as a dramatist.

Samfundets støtter (Pillars of Society, 1877) and *En folkefiende* (An Enemy of the People, 1882) are not far removed from the earlier thesis plays of Dumas *fils*, and they center on the corruption just under the surface in sections of middle-class society. The issues in these two plays are not complex moral ones, and the questions of right and wrong are easily answered. Their strengths are in Ibsen's characterizations and handling of the story. In *Et dukkehjem* (A Doll House, 1879) and *Gengangere* (Ghosts, 1881), Ibsen housed explosive issues in nearly flawless well-made plays. They became Ibsen's most controversial works.

When Nora slammed the door in the final act of *A Doll House* and went out to find herself in the world, leaving behind home, husband, and children, the reverberations from that slam were felt throughout Europe. Voices were raised everywhere that no woman would willingly abandon her home and children. For its German production, Ibsen was required to alter the ending of the play so that Nora would remain with her family. Although the play was hailed, then as now, as a call for women's rights in a male-dominated society, Ibsen disavowed this interpretation. It is a play of strong moral issues and individual behavior centered on the accepted conventions of the middle class. Nora and her husband are both victims of these conventions, but the resolution of their difficulties remains on the far side of the slammed door.

Gengangere (Ghosts, 1881) was written as a reply to those critics of *A Doll House* who insisted that Nora remain in her home and attend to her duties as decreed by social convention. Mrs. Alving's return to her family is the first in a series of bad choices, all made in the name of social propriety. The play is very tightly written, an excellent example of the best use of the well-made play formula, and reveals Ibsen's mastery of the retrospective technique of exposition. Rather than reveal all the necessary details from the past at one point early in the first act, Ibsen brings them out at critical moments throughout the play,

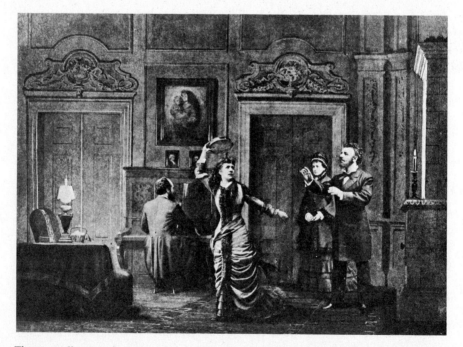

The tarantella scene from Act II of the Danish premiere of A Doll House *at the Royal Theatre, Copenhagen, 1879. Shown are Betty Hennings as Nora and Emil Poulsen as Helmer.*

(Courtesy of the Royal Theatre Archives and Library, Copenhagen)

thus increasing tension and giving a more natural narrative flow to the script. Since the play alludes to venereal disease, adultery, and near-incest, it encountered production problems in the commercial theatre, and most of its early presentations were in connection with the Independent Theatre Movement. The hostile reactions to *Ghosts* caused Ibsen's angry dramatic reply, *En folkefiende* (An Enemy of the People, 1882). This play shows a righteous individual at odds with an outraged majority, and it ends on the note that "the strongest man in the world is the one who stands most alone."

In the last decade of the century, Ibsen relinquished his self-chosen role of the man who stands most alone, and returned to Norway. During this last period of his career, he wrote a group of plays that moved beyond the confines of realism. These plays are more philosophically motivated and psychologically complex than anything Ibsen had written earlier. Through these plays recur the themes of death, love, self-sacrifice, and the role of the creative person in society. The most successful of these plays, in terms of merging philosophy with theatre, is *Bygmester Solness* (The Master Builder, 1892). The dramatic technique is a fascinating combination of folklore narrative ("Let me tell you a story"), retrospection, and dreams. Over the entire play hovers the specter of madness. Master Solness is led to his death by the mysterious Hilde, but it is a

A scene from the 1951 New York production of The Wild Duck *with Maurice Evans as Hjalmar, Mildred Dunnock as Gina, and Diana Lynn as Hedvig.*

(Photograph by Fred Fehl, Hoblitzelle Theatre Arts Library, Humanities Research Center, University of Texas at Austin)

death he willingly and eagerly accepts, an artist's death as a direct result of his art.

Ibsen's last play, *Naar vi døde vaagner* (When We Dead Awake, 1899), like his early poetic drama, *Brand*, ends with an avalanche of snow. Perhaps impossible to stage successfully, *When We Dead Awake* was intended by Ibsen to be the epilogue on his fifty years in the theatre. Still searching at age seventy-one, he planned to move on in new directions in a different artistic form, but he was prevented by a paralyzing stroke and death. He brought theatrical realism to great artistic heights. At the end of his career he realized that the theatre and the human race were about to begin a new journey. This journey would abandon the comforting details of realism and traverse the dark workings of the mind and the absurdities of twentieth-century existence. It would be a journey into a world of lunacy, a theatrical world first entered by August Strindberg.

August Strindberg

A megalomaniac and a genius, August Strindberg (1849–1912) was an extremely neurotic individual who through his entire adult life drifted in and out of madness. One of the most important creative forces in the establishment of modern drama, Strindberg's voluminous output includes poems, novels, short stories, essays, scientific articles, and a huge amount of autobiographical material. Life was a great, searing pain to this tormented Swede, and he found his release in writing. While it is usually misleading to draw connections between writers' private lives and their work, with Strindberg it is difficult to separate the two.

Born the son of a steamship agent and his former housekeeper and mistress, Strindberg had a troubled childhood. His university career was marked by failure, though he proved himself gifted in languages. His first plays were written in 1869, and he had his first production in 1870. His first recognition as a successful writer came in 1879 with the novel *Roda rummet* (The Red Room), and his first dramatic success occurred with *Mäster Olaf* (1881). For the next thirty years, Strindberg would be driven by his own private devils through brief bouts with fame, poverty, and insanity, three violent marriages, and incredible periods of productivity. He died in 1912 in Stockholm, his tempestous duel with life finally over.

The approximately seventy plays by Strindberg may be roughly divided into three groups: historical, realistic, and experimental. He wrote in all of these groups throughout most of his career. In all three groups certain themes that were obsessive with Strindberg reoccur: the battle of the sexes, the use of suggestive powers, the trials of the superior man, and the struggle with God. These themes were drawn from the playwright's own life, for he was never far removed from the characters in his plays. The historical dramas were written at two periods in Strindberg's career, before 1883 and after 1894, and they provide Sweden with a cycle of plays comparable to Shakespeare's English history plays. These plays cover Swedish history from the thirteenth to the early nineteenth century, and they are rich in social and cultural elements and

August Strindberg.

abound with fascinating characters. Strindberg believed that even though he was writing historical drama, it was the inner human struggle rather than the historical event that held the interest. Outstanding among these plays is the Vasa trilogy, consisting of *Mäster Olof*, *Gustav Vasa* (1899), and *Erik XIV* (1899).

The realistic plays of Strindberg were a result of his being influenced by the French naturalists, particularly Emile Zola. During the 1880s, he wrote seven plays in what he understood to be the naturalist manner. Of these plays two, *Fadren* (The Father, 1887) and *Fröken Julie* (Miss Julie, 1888), are regarded as masterpieces of the modern theatre. *The Father*, which depicts a husband totally destroyed by his wife, reflected the playwright's own marriage problems and concern about what he thought was an international conspiracy of women to enslave men and reestablish a prehistoric matriarchical order. Strindberg believed Ibsen's *A Doll House* was part of this conspiracy. The play is superbly constructed and has a strong emotional impact on an audience.

Miss Julie is Strindberg's best-known play, and its famous preface is one of

In this scene from a 1949 New York production of The Father, *Raymond Massey portrays the Captain and Grace Kelly, in her first Broadway role, portrays the daughter.*
(*Photograph by Fred Fehl, Hoblitzelle Theatre Arts Library, Humanities Research Center, University of Texas at Austin*)

the major documents in the history of stage realism. The preface was written for the premiere of the play, which was given at the Théâtre Libre in 1893. This story of the seduction and destruction of an unmarried noblewoman by her father's valet was perfectly in keeping with the objective observation technique of the naturalists. Factors of chance, heredity, and environment are carefully introduced by the playwright so that both of the principal characters appear victims of their social classes.

Strindberg's experimental plays were written in the period following his most serious mental breakdown, a time referred to as the Inferno crisis. These plays were unlike anything that had been written previously for the European theatre, and they were to be highly influential on later expressionistic and surrealistic writers. These dream plays combined dreamlike perceptions and aspects of reality in an attempt to show the theatregoer the total complexity of a character. In the Damascus trilogy, *Till Damaskus* I, II, and III (To Damascus I and II, 1898; III, 1901), Strindberg sought to express his struggles with God and his newly found religious peace. The structural arrangement of these plays departed radically from traditional drama, and audience members could no longer assume that character motivations would be logical or predictable. Of Strindberg's experimental plays, two of the most remarkable are *Ett drömspel* (A Dream Play, 1901) and *Spöksonaten* (The Ghost Sonata, 1907).

Of *A Dream Play* the playwright wrote that it was a "conglomeration out of a dream in which, however, there is a definite logic. Everything nonsensical becomes believable. Human beings appear at several points and are sketched, sketches flow together, the same person splits into several persons only to flow into one again." Leaving realism far behind, *A Dream Play* is a series of imagistic experiences in a spatial frame. As one modern critic noted, it "is the most exasperating and also the most impressive piece of dramatic writing of our time." *A Ghost Sonata* was written for Strindberg's Intimate Theatre, a small theatre in Stockholm that from 1907 to 1910 was devoted to producing his plays. This extremely complex play is a study in madness and, although it proceeds in the fashion of a realistic script, nothing is what is appears. It is this mixture of the insane and the real that makes the play unique and a definite forerunner of the later surrealists.

In the years since his death Strindberg's reputation has grown steadily, and it may be that future generations will acclaim him the greatest playwright of the modern era. Over sixty years ago, the American playwright Eugene O'Neill said, "Strindberg still remains among the most modern of the moderns, the greatest interpreter in the theatre of the characteristic spiritual conflicts which constitute the drama, the life-blood of our lives today." Strindberg remains a challenge to the theatre, even in the postmodern era.

George Bernard Shaw

The person of George Bernard Shaw (1856–1950) stands as a formidable barrier to his plays. For over half a century, he was a professional curmudgeon who used not only his plays but their success as an opportunity to expound his views on nearly everything. Shaw the playwright made an important contribution to modern drama, but Shaw the personality had a tendency to obscure this contribution. A strong Puritan streak in Shaw caused him to dislike the theatre, and for him, his role as playwright was justified only by his use of the stage as a pulpit. He is accounted a major playwright because, in spite of himself, some of his sermons are fine theatre.

Born in Dublin, Ireland, into genteel, middle-class poverty, Shaw's formal education ended when he was fifteen. After a brief career in a real estate office, he went to London in 1876 to become famous. Fame was to come very slowly, and in the meanwhile Shaw became involved in politics, tried his hand at journalism, and lived off his relatives. From 1888 to 1894 he was a music critic for two London newspapers. In 1895 he was appointed drama critic for the London *Saturday Review*, and for the next three years he wrote witty and invigorating reviews of the stage and opinions on the state of drama in England. His first play, *Widower's Houses*, was produced by J. T. Grein in 1892 as one of the early offerings of the Independent Theatre. His first commercial success was in 1894 with *Arms and the Man*, and during the next ten years he established himself as one of England's major new playwrights. Although Shaw wrote over fifty plays during his career, his most significant work, with the exception of *Saint Joan*, was written before 1918. Shaw was awarded the Nobel Prize in

George Bernard Shaw.

Literature in 1925, wrote his last play in 1947 at the age of ninety-one, and died three years later.

Shaw believed great theatre was a theatre of ideas, not action. He thought Ibsen had made a significant advance in drama when he had Nora and Helmer discuss their problems at the end of *A Doll House*. This was the type of play he felt the theatre needed, plays of intelligent characters for intelligent audiences. To make this type of play, Shaw borrowed the familiar dramatic structure of the commercial theatre and added his discussion. This creative use of the familiar form was one of Shaw's contributions to the modern stage. His emphasis on discussion moved the focus of the play away from the actors to the intellectual content of the script. The play and not the player was the important thing to Shaw. In his adaptation of the well-made play to his own purposes, Shaw developed a mastery of the anticlimax, so much so that it became a Shavian hallmark.

The important discussions in the better Shaw plays are not mere set pieces arranged by the playwright to express his views; rather they grow out of the action of the characters. Shaw, following the lead of Ibsen, introduced into his scripts active characters who make things happen rather than have things

A scene from a Hunter College production of Arms and the Man.
(Courtesy of KaiDib Films International, Glendale, Calif.)

happen to them. The characters do the unexpected, at least unexpected to audiences familiar with the traditional pattern of the well-made play. These unexpected moments are often connected to a Shavian anticlimax. *Arms and the Man* (1894) was the earliest Shaw script to fully utilize his manipulation of audience expectations, active characters, and anticlimaxes. Although the script is nearly a hundred years old, Shaw's structural tricks still charm and delight.

Shaw's major plays—*Arms and the Man, Mrs. Warren's Profession* (1894), *Candida* (1895), *Caesar and Cleopatra* (1898), *Man and Superman* (1903), *Major Barbara* (1905), *Pygmalion* (1912), *Heartbreak House* (1919), *Saint Joan* (1923)—reflect a Victorian belief in progress, a conviction that humanity will learn, improve, and make a better world. A cynical note is sounded in *Heartbreak House*, which Shaw wrote during the destruction of the First World War, and in *Saint Joan* it appears it will be a long time before the world is ready for the pure of heart. But the bitter cynicism that enveloped the theatre after 1918 was not a part of Shaw's world. Crusading socialist though he might be, he never really left that twilight period known as the Edwardian era. The sinister side of life did not really interest Shaw. As the world grew sinister in the twentieth century, his plays became less engaging. Yet his early works remained to dazzle, as fables from an intellectual world that should have been.

Anton Chekhov

The fame of Anton Chekhov (1860–1904) in modern drama rests on only four plays. Yet these four masterpieces of dramatic literature are so beautiful, so inventively crafted, and so touching that their creator is considered one of the greatest playwrights of the theatre. The plays themselves represent the perfection of nineteenth-century dramatic realism.

Chekhov was born in southern Russia, the grandson of a serf who had purchased his freedom. Chekhov arrived in Moscow in 1879 to enter medical school, and the following year, to earn money, he began his career as a writer of short stories. He received his medical degree in 1884 and began to practice medicine, but the money from his writing remained an important financial support for his family. By the late 1880s Chekhov had gained a considerable reputation as a writer of short pieces, and it was also during this period that his first unsuccessful efforts at play writing were produced.

Chekhov's first major play, *The Sea Gull*, was produced in Saint Petersburg in 1896. Since the cast and director of the production either did not understand or were not sympathetic to the innovations in the structure of the play, it was a failure. Humiliated by the reception given his play, Chekhov vowed to abandon the theatre forever. Persuaded by his friend Vladimir Nemirovich-Danchenko to allow the newly formed Moscow Art Theatre (MAT) to mount a production of *The Sea Gull*, Chekhov was in 1898 rewarded with a resounding artistic triumph. His aims in play writing and the artistic goals of the MAT were a perfect match. For the next six years, until his death from tuberculosis, Chekhov wrote for the MAT. It was the most successful pairing of playwright with acting company in the history of the theatre.

Chekhov's last four plays were highly innovative in their demands on both performers and audiences. These plays, although extremely objective in nature, are works of indirect action with the emotional preoccupations of the characters taking the central focus. There is an emotional web connecting the characters, and the audience is invited to become a part of the web. The emotions involved are not the strong, violent ones that burst forth in melodrama. Rather they are the subtle aches of everyday existence, feelings of regret, frustration, nostalgia, and disillusionment. The care needed to project and balance these all-important emotional levels makes these plays difficult to perform, yet when done well they are extremely effective.

Certain elements are unique to the plays of Chekhov and greatly assist in giving them their quiet power. All-important is the decentralization of the cast. These plays require impeccable ensemble acting because the playwright avoided traditional heroes and villains. No one character stands out, and even minor characters are given traits to make them memorable. All the characters are presented in the first act and remain in the play through the final act. The characters are generally known to each other, and this strengthens the emotional foundation of the script. These characters reside in a single location, and the majority are from the same social class, the gentry. Although the cast is a closed group in a single location, disruptions in the form of arrivals and departures are key elements in these plays. These disruptions give the plays their structural framework and create principal moments of emotional anguish and resolution.

The Sea Gull (1896) is, in a way, a preparatory work and reveals Chekhov's experimentations in arriving at the structure that was to form the next three plays. In this play the emotional web is not firmly established, and Chekhov relied on conventional nineteenth-century stage dialogue to carry the play. It alone of his masterpieces is somewhat autobiographical, dealing with artistic people rather than the gentry and based on events known to the playwright. The type of symbolism seen in the use of the sea gull was not used again by Chekhov. Several other experiments in the play were dropped by the playwright when he began work on his next play. *The Sea Gull* is a beautiful play, but it lacks the emotional power of Chekhov's next three scripts.

Uncle Vanya (1897) contains all the elements of the fully developed Chekhovian play. Here the emotion of frustration completely permeates the actions of the major characters. The play was the result of a complete reworking of an earlier work, *The Wood Demon* (1889), and a comparison of *Vanya* to the earlier script gives an impressive lesson in the changes Chekhov made in nineteenth-century play construction. The earlier script is a traditional play of action, but its reconstruction resulted in a play of emotion. With its construction a new type of drama was born. Here there are no heroes, only victims of self-delusion.

"Vsyo dyelayetsya nye ponashemu" (Nothing ever happens as we'd like it

A scene from a 1928 production of **The Cherry Orchard** *with Alla Nazimova as Madame Ranevsky.*

(*Courtesy of the Theatre Collection of the Museum of the City of New York*)

to), Olga's comment from act 4 of *Three Sisters* (1901), neatly sums up the contents of the play. In this play of disappointed hopes and expectations, Chekhov made a number of refinements in his dramatic technique. The dialogue of the play is considerably less formal than in *Vanya*, and there is a significant use of disconnected group dialogue that actually creates a single flow of thought for the audience. The play has the most decentralized cast of all the plays, ten characters of roughly equal importance, and the emotional level is skillfully varied through all four acts. The note of cynicism on which the play ends is very profound, the world-weary view of a dying playwright.

Chekhov's health was badly deteriorated when he began work on *The Cherry Orchard* in 1903. It was to be his last play. Events in Russian history after the premiere of the play in 1904 have had a tendency to color the reception of it. The loss of the family estate and the destruction of the nonproductive orchard have been linked with the revolutionary events of 1905 and 1917. There is an awareness on the part of the play's characters of the world beyond the estate, but it is pointless to try to see the play as a forewarning of the Russian Revolution. Chekhov was a superb dramatist, not a fortuneteller.

Chekhov and Stanislavsky strongly disagreed about the nature of the play. Chekhov described it as a comedy, but Stanislavsky considered it a tragedy and so staged it. The tragic interpretation of the script has prevailed in this century. But if the play is seen as a parody of the melodramatic "mortgage" play, then its elements of comedy are apparent. The play is the simplest of Chekhov's masterpieces in terms of story development. Everyone's fate is linked to the sale of the estate. And with its sale, all go their separate ways. The emotional web is broken and the play is over.

OTHER REALISTIC DRAMATISTS

Ibsen, Strindberg, Shaw, and Chekhov have been duly recognized during the last half century as the major founding playwrights of modern drama. Their contributions to the theatre are now considered seminal, and many of their plays will remain in the performance repertory of the world stage. These dramatic masters did not work in isolation but were part of a large, highly productive community of writers for the stage. Often their innovative creations were ignored in favor of what we now consider inferior plays. Since they were part of a larger dramatic community, it is useful to consider briefly a few of the other nineteenth-century playwrights who were once considered artistic equals or betters of Ibsen, Strindberg, Shaw, and Chekhov.

Bjørnstjerne Bjørnson

Along with Ibsen and Strindberg, Bjørnstjerne Bjørnson (1832–1910) was responsible for bringing world attention to Scandinavian drama, and for many years his reputation overshadowed both of his famous contemporaries. A novelist, poet, playwright, and politician, Bjørnson, unlike his sometimes friend Ibsen, had a joyfully active life. A national hero in Norway by his middle years, Bjørnson attracted attention with his first play, *Mellem slagene* (Between the Battles, 1857), and was considered a major playwright from that date until his death. Although his early work was in folk and historical drama, he is best remembered for his realistic plays such as *De nygifle* (The Newly Married, 1865), *En fallit* (A Bankruptcy, 1875), and *En handske* (A Gauntlet, 1883). In 1903 he was awarded the Nobel Prize for Literature, the first playwright to receive this honor.

Gerhart Hauptmann

In Germany the work of the Freie Bühne brought before the public in 1889 the first play by Gerhart Hauptmann (1862–1946). With this production of *Vor Sonnenaufgang* (Before Sunrise), the Zola school of realism was established on the German stage, and its playwright became nationally known. Hauptmann followed this first success with several other well-received plays, and in 1893 he produced what is regarded as his masterpiece, *Die Weber* (The Weavers). This huge, sprawling work, based on the revolt of the Silesian weavers in 1844, is a play with a collective hero, the weavers, and it foreshadowed the later German epic theatre. Hauptmann moved away from realism in 1896 with his symbolic play *Die versunkene Glocke* (The Sunken Bell). His plays of the twentieth century varied in type between symbolism, realism, and verse historical dramas. He was awarded the Nobel Prize for Literature in 1912, but his last years were darkened by the criticism he received for failing to leave Nazi Germany as so many other German artists and intellectuals had done.

Becque and Brieux

Two of the leading exponents of the type of theatre championed in France by Zola were Henri Becque (1837–1899) and Eugène Brieux (1858–1932). In the plays of Becque, the stress is on characters and the use of natural language. Troubled with financial worries all his life, Becque emphasized in his plays the corrupting powers of money. Becque is best known for two plays, *Les Corbeaux* (The Vulture, 1882), which is about the destruction of a once-happy family, and *La Parisienne* (The Woman of Paris, 1885), which concerns a woman who uses sex to advance her husband's career. Brieux was a great favorite of George Bernard Shaw's, and he shared with Shaw a tendency to preach to his audiences. His first play was produced by Antoine at the Théâtre Libre in 1890. Brieux's plays continued the crusades first started in the thesis plays of Dumas *fils*. The best representatives of his approach to this type of theatre are *Les Trois Filles de M. Dupont* (The Three Daughters of M. Dupont, 1897), *La Robe rouge* (The Red Robe, 1900), and *Les Avaries* (Damaged Goods, 1902).

Galsworthy and Pinero

John Galsworthy (1867–1933) and Arthur Wing Pinero (1855–1934) were two contemporaries of Shaw's who followed his example with discussion plays. Pinero, author of over fifty plays, established himself as a dramatist with highly popular farces such as *The Magistrate* (1885), *The School Mistress* (1886), and *Dandy Dick* (1893). In the 1890s he began to write plays that brought social criticism to the commercial English stage. Of these plays, *The Second Mrs. Tanqueray* (1893), *Trelawny of the "Wells"* (1898), and *Mid-Channel* (1909) are the best known. *Trelawny*, a play about the theatre, concerns itself with the changing tastes of the English stage. Pinero was knighted in 1909 for his contributions to English drama. Galsworthy is now chiefly remembered as a novelist, but in the years before World War I, he achieved considerable distinction in the commercial theatre with his plays protesting injustice in English society. Of the twenty-eight plays that he wrote for the stage, three early works, *The Silver Box* (1906), *Strife* (1909), and *Justice* (1910), best represent his skills and commitment to social reforms.

CONCLUSION

By the late 1890s realism was acceptable on the commercial stage and was slowly moving into a position of dominance, a position it continues to hold. Yet even as early as the 1890s there were reactions against realism by those who believed it to be restrictive and unimaginative. In his last plays Ibsen moved away from realism; Strindberg's dream plays called into question the very nature of reality; and Chekhov, with his exploration of unspoken emotions, was attempting to move realism in a new direction. By 1912, with the exception of Shaw, the creative giants of realism were dead. Many said that the new art form, the motion picture, was the ultimate expression of realism and that the theatre should go in a new direction. In the years before and after World War I, the proponents of the various theatricalisms—expressionism, symbolism, futurism, surrealism—would all claim to be the new direction. These conflicting claims and the continued viability of realism in the commercial theatre would greatly contribute to the tension and confusion that mark the twentieth-century theatre.

21

LATE-NINETEENTH-CENTURY THEATRE ARCHITECTURE AND PRODUCTION PRACTICES

Most of the changes in theatre architecture and production practices made during the last half of the nineteenth century were motivated by the same force that influenced similar changes during the century's earlier decades. Basically these were alterations to suit the increasing taste for realism in the mass audience and to accommodate increased visibility, audibility, and comfort.

PLAYHOUSE EVOLUTION

The Auditorium

Throughout the final decades of the nineteenth century, changes in playhouse form and structure came gradually and were simply modifications of the basic, well-established form. The auditorium continued to be large to accommodate the increasing mass audience, and more attention was paid to audience comfort in an attempt, largely successful, to attract bigger and more diverse crowds to the theatre. Although permanent seating had been common in the pit or orchestra area of the house from the early days of the nineteenth century, the floor had remained flat. To enhance sight lines, a slight rake up from the proscenium to the back of the auditorium was employed in the more advanced theatres in the 1860s, and this feature was commonplace by the 1890s. The notion of a raked house is, of course, a standard feature of the modern theatre.

Above the house floor, the arrangement of boxes and balconies was still in a bell or horseshoe shape, with galleries at the rear of the auditorium. The major

The Late Nineteenth Century

Modified nineteenth-century seating in the Théâtre de la Monnaie.
(Photograph by Jean-Pierre Stevens, used courtesy of the Belgian National Opera)

change in this part of the house during the last decades of the nineteenth century was the gradual elimination of private, partitioned boxes in favor of open balcony seating. Boxes were still part of the proscenium and initial balcony decor, but audience use of them was declining by century's end. It was still important for some patrons to be seen in the theatre, but this concern was rapidly being transcended by the desire to see the production adequately and the changing nature of the audience. Rather than social class, price became the prime factor in seating selection.

One final change in the seating on the auditorium floor had emerged by midcentury and was in common usage by the 1890s. To ease audience flow in and out of the rows of house floor seats, a center aisle was added to allow a reasonable number of people access to their seats from two directions. Fueling this change was a slight concern for audience flow in the event of an emergency, although the center-aisle concept did remove seats traditionally known as the best in the house. But that concern lessened with the advent of realistic three-dimensional scenery, and the center aisle allowed for less space between rows since fewer people had to climb over each other to reach their assigned seats. This, in turn, allowed more rows of seats, thus creating larger capacities and more gross revenue potential. The center-aisle concept remained popular into the early twentieth century, when staggered, continental seating with more space between rows would render it unnecessary. Even the theatrical alterations to Covent Garden and Drury Lane, in 1901 and 1902 respectively, included the addition of center aisles. Two of the best earlier examples of this convention, however, are Daly's Theatre in New York City in 1879 and the Volkstheatre in Worms in 1887.

The Stage

The typical late-nineteenth-century stage was designed to display the two- and three-dimensional scenery that could create the illusion of realistic life on the stage. The proscenium became the absolute divider between stage and auditorium with the triumph of realism in the final decades of the 1800s. By century's end no really usable stage apron remained. And the stage became in essence a machine equipped for the display of three-dimensional realism. Not only was the stage a machine for the display of this scenery, but in keeping with its role as a "picture frame" for realism with the fourth wall of that environment removed, none of the machinery was shown to the audience. Accordingly, elaborate offstage, understage, and overhead apparatus continued to be developed along the same lines as that in the first half of the nineteenth century. The major difference in the last half of the century was the increased use of available science and technology to enhance

The proscenium of the Théâtre de la Monnaie, Brussels. Built in 1700, this theatre is still in active use.

(Photograph by Jean-Pierre Stevens, used courtesy of the Belgian National Opera)

the stage as a machine. New machine technology rapidly replaced the older, simpler technology of the late eighteenth and early nineteenth centuries.

Nowhere is this more evident than in the changes that occurred in the stage floor itself. The relatively simple traps of earlier times gave way to a series of stage traps across the length and depth of the onstage floor area to such an extent that at the larger opera houses the entire stage was trapped. At the Budapest Opera House (1881) and the Halle Theatre in Germany (1883), for example, large metal traps operated by hydraulic lifts could not only move vertically, as in earlier models, but could achieve ascent and descent angles depending upon how high the hydraulic pistons were raised. Some larger traps were capable of sending up smaller traps within themselves. In this arrangement, known as the Asphaleian system of floor control, virtually every plane and configuration was possible. From here it was only a short step to using the entire stage as a single lifting device, and although not common, it was accomplished. When the remodeled Madison Square Theatre opened in New York in 1880, Steele MacKaye introduced the concept of the entire stage as an elevator operating on three levels—the normal floor level behind the proscenium, in the basement below, and in the flies above. In this way, entire sets could be changed while another scene was in progress. Realism was served to the fullest measure by this arrangement.

In addition to the elevator stage, other whole stage renovations were developed in the late nineteenth century for shifting large, three-dimensional, realistic set pieces. Germany led the way in the development of these devices, and undoubtedly its most important contribution was the revolving stage. Developed by Karl Lautenschlager (1843–1906) at the Residenz Theatre in Munich in 1896, the entire stage was constructed as a single turntable, usually with three settings in place on it at a single time. The scene was changed by revolving the stage to the appropriate setting, which neatly fit between the sides of the proscenium arch. With one-third of the turntable in use at any given time, the remaining two-thirds were available backstage for whatever set changes were necessary. Because of its ease of operation, the revolving stage was widely adopted throughout Europe by the end of the nineteenth century.

Variations on either the elevator or revolving stage quickly followed. One such development was the introduction of low wagons or platforms located offstage. These were loaded with the appropriate scenery and run onstage in tracks. Usually one wagon per side was sufficient and was large enough to accommodate a full stage setting. Occasionally smaller wagons were used for portions of sets or more intimate scenes. Another system combined the basics of the elevator stage with small wagons, using either or both to achieve the desired shift of scenery. All theses were driven by increasingly complex machinery as technological changes allowed. The stage was, indeed, a machine.

In addition to the trapped stage floor and the understage machinery needed to support it, the basic grid system above the stage was refined as well. The basic system of counterweighted lines that allowed an individual great control in moving large pieces of scenery to and from the stage floor was still the norm,

The prompter's box, located at center stage at the foot-lights.

but fly spaces became larger and more elaborately mechanized. In the larger theatres it was not uncommon for the flies to be two and one-half times the height of the proscenium arch, allowing large pieces of scenery to be raised well out of the sight lines of the front rows of the audience. Elaborate winch systems and line and pulley schemes allowed the lowering of three-dimensional scenery and angled walls from above the proscenium. At the rear of the flies in most sizable late-nineteenth-century theatres was a bridge (usually a steel frame) capable of supporting the large upstage scenery required for the production or for the preparation, usually painting, of such scenery.

Offstage, late-nineteenth-century versions of the *chariot-mat* and the wing and groove system continued to enjoy some usage, particularly for exterior scenes and for selected opera productions. Where three-dimensional scenery was emphasized, stage grooves and slots were closed to make a smooth, even floor. There was also an increase in available offstage space. To store in the wings the large amounts of scenery required for many productions, up to one and one-half times the width of the proscenium opening was needed on each side of the opening.

Although upstage wings and borders continued to be used, there was a growing concern that this system did not adequately support realism. Accord-

A view from backstage showing the large pieces of scenery that were often used to meet the demands of spectacular realism.

ingly, what is commonly referred to as the cyclorama received considerable attention. A transplanted Italian working in Germany, Mariano Fortuny (1871–1949), developed a lighting system that utilized another of his ideas, the *Kuppelhorizont*, or plaster sky dome. This domed cyclorama was permanently installed on the stage floor as far upstage as possible, and curved toward the audience at the top and sides. Thus it gave the feeling of great depth and space, but somewhat restricted the upstage entrances and work areas. A more useful form of the sky dome, the *Rundhorizont*, was developed, and it surrounded the stage space without such restriction. The flat cyclorama continued to be used, but it required the standard masking of wings and borders, and was employed in those theatres where space or economic conditions precluded use of the others.

The technology of the last half of the nineteenth century, in addition to artistic considerations, fostered major changes in the theatre. When Henry Bessemer developed the first practical converter to make steel from pig iron in 1856, the steel age was ushered in and theatre construction benefited considerably. Greater spans were possible with fewer upright supports, and the sectioned stage floor and lattice grid floor were soon so constructed. In addition to this versatility, the fireproofing advantages of steel over wooden traps and grid floors were tremendous. Fire had been a major problem in theatres since the Renaissance. At first, fire control was the responsibility of the theatre owner, but as dependence on the mass audience rather than private patrons increased there was a growing insistence on better fire control measures. Responding to this demand, the late nineteenth century was a period of active governmental regulation for fire safety measures. Uniform fire codes were yet a long time off, but at least the consciousness of governmental responsibility in that area had been raised. As in the past, the house for theatre—auditorium and stage—benefited greatly from scientific and techno-logical changes developed for purposes other than the creation of illusion.

Innovators and Innovations

The last half of the nineteenth century was filled with theatrical pioneers, but three who deserve special attention here, because of their contributions and their influence on others, are Richard Wagner, Hubert von Herkomer, and E. W. Godwin. Each contributed significantly to the unification of the arts within theatrical contexts and stands as a worthy precursor to the major theorists covered later in this chapter, Adolphe Appia and Edward Gordon Craig.

Richard Wagner (1813–1883) fundamentally changed the way music, drama, and theatrical production were integrated during the last half of the nineteenth century. A German composer, he wrote and produced opera throughout much of his career. Wagner's experimentation stemmed from his belief that music alone should not be the end of opera. He desired that all musical and theatrical elements be united in an organic whole oriented to a single artistic goal. Believing that the orchestra was at the core of this artistic unity, Wagner built his own theatre, the Festspielhaus, in Bayreuth, Germany, in 1876. The theatre featured egalitarian seating in a wedge-shaped oval auditorium constructed with a steep rake that forced attention toward the stage. Wagner believed that the audience must be able to concentrate on the stage picture, so he constructed a second proscenium arch to enhance that effort. Between the prosceniums, and below sight level, was his orchestra, whose music served to unite spectacle and spectator by enveloping all in the *mystischer Abgrund* (mystic gulf). The stage was quite deep, 118 feet, and provided for the most elaborate pictorial realism to be displayed. Although tremendously innovative, the theatre did have drawbacks. Wagner eliminated the balconies and seated everyone (over 1,600) on the main floor, which hurt adequate visibility since the back seats were considerably distant from the stage. The wedge shape did not allow for good sight lines to the upstage areas except from those seats along the center line of the auditorium. But the notion of a steep rake to the auditorium greatly influenced early-twentieth-century theatres, as did Wagner's concept of artistic unity. His operatic compositions

The Late Nineteenth Century

alone place him with such masters as Mozart and Verdi; his work in staging them places him in a class by himself.

Far less well known was a theorist and production practitioner in England who, like Wagner, was concerned about artistic unity. Hubert von Herkomer (1849–1914) was primarily a visual artist who had a deep interest in the unification of the arts and in aesthetic experimentation. In 1883 he founded the Herkomer School at his home in Bushey, and there for the next twenty-one years he conducted classes and experiments in the unification of the visual arts with music and theatre. As part of these exercises, an annual dramatic experimentation was conducted known as the "pictorial-musical" plays. As the title suggests, the plays were vehicles for uniting music and the visual arts, but they cannot stand by any measure as great drama. The experiments were attended by such notables as Henry Irving, Ellen Terry, and her son, Edward Gordon Craig. There can be little doubt that these experiments influenced the young Craig. Professor Herkomer was also interested in the structure of the theatre and in 1892 demonstrated his concept for a contracting proscenium. Demonstrated through a scale model, the machine allowed the sides and the top of the proscenium arch to move toward the center of the opening, thus closing the opening to a smaller scale when that suited the production. Although not widely accepted in its own time because of its limited practical use, the concept does serve as a precursor of the twentieth-century notion of the false proscenium, which allows small scenes to be done in a scale more fitting the actors. A problem with large, late-nineteenth-century theatres was

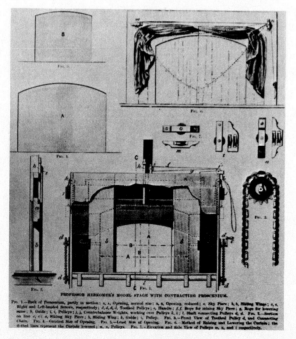

A drawing of Herkomer's contracting proscenium stage model.

(From Magazine of Art, *1892)*

that an intimate scene was often done in a scale that suited the proscenium rather than the other production elements. Thus Herkomer's experiments remain important more for their connection with the twentieth century than their practical reality in the final decades of the nineteenth.

Another theatre designer who contributed to the spirit of innovation in the last half of the nineteenth century was the architect E. W. Godwin (1833–1886). Godwin, who was the father of Edward Gordon Craig, was primarily interested in the relationship between archaeology and the theatre, and he insisted upon that connection in the productions he supervised. Shakespeare was approached in that fashion, and for a production of *Helena in Troas*, he constructed a Greek theatre inside Hengler's Circus in 1886. He was a prolific writer on the place of archaeology in the theatre and, between 1874 and 1875, published some thirty-two articles on the subject "The Architecture and Costumes of Shakespeare's Plays" in *The British Architect*. In regard to that important unification between the art of the theatre and a major branch of science, and their impact on the early twentieth century, Godwin was an important pioneer.

SCENERY

During the last half of the nineteenth century, realism emerged as the dominant style in the theatre. This was true for the technical arts of the theatre as well, and by the last few decades of the 1800s scenery had

A view of a late-nineteenth-century scene shop.

basically developed along two distinct lines. Interior scenes were represented through box settings complete with ceilings, and exterior settings employed various three-dimensional pieces against a painted backdrop or cyclorama. Thus late nineteenth-century scenery was a blend of the two-dimensional painterly antiquarianism of the early 1800s and the three-dimensionality of the environmental realism of the later decades. All settings strove to create a realistic environment in which the audience witnessed the psychological development of the characters.

While the move toward realism was undeniable as seen through the Independent Theatre Movement, there arose concurrent with it a reaction against its tenets. Although the reaction will be covered in detail under the New Stagecraft section of this chapter, a general introduction to it is in order here. As the realistic movement was given its first concerted push by the Théâtre Libre, so the first concerted reaction against the movement occurred in Paris shortly after Antoine's theatre opened. In 1891 a group of artists and writers, headed by Paul Fort, opened the Théâtre d'Art in direct reaction to the work of the Théâtre Libre. This group, to be known as the symbolists, felt that the exact copying of nature on stage was not art in that it stifled the "higher" artistic goals of free imagination. Within this framework, the proper role of scenery was not to describe accurately but to elicit an emotional, or felt, response. Objective reality was considered far less important than the display of subjective reality. The appropriate scenic rendering of a tree, for example, was not to show the external reality of a tree but rather the internal essence of a tree. Thus scenery was simplified and stylized toward the impressionistic, and all notions of illusionistic perspective were abandoned, particularly the use of a backdrop or painted cyclorama.

All of these movements were growing concurrently, and by the end of the nineteenth century three styles of scenery were common throughout Europe. Clearly the most prevalent was two-dimensional painterly realism, seen primarily through ballet and opera. Three-dimensional realism was the hallmark of the Independent Theatre Movement, and it was used with painted scenery in other mainstream theatrical productions. Finally, the departures of the symbolists from realism emerged in the last decade of the nineteenth century, and these became a significant first break from the norm in the early years of the 1900s. From that period on, verisimilitude in scenery was to be questioned seriously.

GAS AND ELECTRIC LIGHTING

During the decades after 1850, gas lighting in the theatre became a fine art. Elaborate gas dimmer boards allowed centralized control of all auditorium and stage lighting, gas fixtures burned cleaner and brighter, and gas wing ladders and gas battens amply lit the sides and top of the stage, respectively. Gas footlights blazed away, and the whole effect was one of brilliant visibility. This was a welcome change from the state of affairs at the start of the century, when adequate visibility was a major problem. And the

Backstage in the nineteenth century. Note the gas border lights and the use of flat supports by the crew.

steady, brilliant light possible after the development of the gas mantle finally solved the problem of flickering that the Argand lamp had initially addressed. Never before had visibility been greater.

There were those, however, who were concerned that the brilliance in stage lighting was too much technology and not enough art. As late as 1892, one critic still complained: "Modern [gas] stage lighting is opposed to the exhibition of facial expression. There is such a flood of light, and the face is so bathed in effulgence, from above to below, that there is no relief. There are no shadows." Theatre practitioners were not unaware of this criticism, and some took action. Chief among these was Henry Irving, who, through his work at the Lyceum, achieved some success in mood lighting for the general acting area and a great deal of artistry in lighting background surfaces and special effects. He was the first practitioner to consistently darken the auditorium for the entire production. Known to take his gas apparatus with him on tour, Irving constantly experimented with different sources, colors, and directions of various lighting effects. He was probably the most significant developer of the artistic use of gas lighting in the theatre, and this use of lighting made a particular impression on a young actor in his company, Edward Gordon Craig.

Electricity

The use of electric light in the theatre was not new to the last half of the nineteenth century. Arc lights had been introduced at the Paris Opéra in 1846 and, along with limelights, were used for special effects and crude followspotting into the last quarter of the century. The arc remained basically unworkable as a general source of illumination until Paul Jablochkov developed the self-regulating carbon rod lamp that bears his name, the Jablochkov candle. The first full use of the candle was at the Paris Hippodrome in 1878. Although this development provided a steadier flame needing much less individual attention, it was noisy and did not lend itself well to lighting scenes of quiet intensity, as was increasingly demanded by psychological realism.

Clearly the outstanding lighting invention of the late nineteenth century was the development in 1879 of the first practical electric incandescent lamp by Thomas A. Edison. Almost immediately theatres became fascinated with the possibilities of Edison's invention and, despite the difficulties in generating their own electricity, experimented with it in nonstage areas like stairs and entrances. The first stage use of the electric lamp was at the Savoy Theatre for the premier production of Gilbert and Sullivan's *Patience* in 1881. Steele MacKaye used electric lamps in 1885 at the New Lyceum Theatre in New York City, and they were installed at the Paris Opéra in 1886. By the 1890s, having solved the electric generating problems, most theatres had converted to electric lamps. And a tremendous boon it was. Electric lamps were safer to use, operated more economically, and produced a more even, brighter, and higher-quality light than before. Still, the initial use was for general brilliance, but, as with gas, artistic reforms were not far behind.

Innovators

The electric lamp allowed control of intensity and direction as never achieved before. With the ascendancy of the spotlight, complete with lens and reflector, footlights and other flood-type lighting diminished rapidly. Spotlights, especially when used from the house or auditorium position, gave the illusion of depth that the Renaissance theorists had sought. A detailed discussion of the contributions of David Belasco is found in a later chapter, but his early experiments in the 1880s and 1890s with frontal area lighting and his concern for the subtle realistic lighting of background surfaces and special effects were noteworthy. In Europe, however, the basis for modern stage lighting theory and practice was being laid by a Swiss practitioner, Adolphe Appia.

The contributions of Adolphe Appia (1862–1928) to the design of stage lighting stemmed initially from his work with Wagnerian opera, and his publication, in 1895, of *La Mise en scene du drame Wagnerien* (The Staging of Wagnerian Music-Drama). Another work, *Die Musik und die Inscenierung* (Music and Staging, 1899), expanded his theories and provided a total working aesthetic for scenery as well as lighting. Basically, Appia believed that theatre production should focus on the actor. Since the actor was three-dimensional, the scenery and the lighting should also be three-dimensional. As for lighting (scenery will be discussed in the section on the New Stagecraft), Appia believed that the flat, bright, essentially two-dimensional lighting commonly

An Appia designed set for Paul Claudel's The Tidings Brought to Mary *(1910).*

used was counterproductive to this aesthetic. Lighting in nature was, after all, three-dimensional in that it was shadow-producing, and stage lighting must follow suit. With directional, variable-intensity lighting, the actor's form could be most successfully revealed in that the shadow produced would emphasize three-dimensionality. Appia argued that light was to a theatrical production what Wagner's music was to opera—the great unifier of the entire artistic enterprise. Beyond these aesthetic considerations, Appia discussed the use of arc lamps as excellent actor emphasizers and described the placement of other instruments to achieve mood, color balance, and directional mobility. His lighting concepts were at once symbolist and realistic, and he must be considered the father of modern stage lighting design and practice.

Mariano Fortuny has already been mentioned in connection with the development of the *Kuppelhorizont*, but that development was fueled by his interest in and experiments with stage lighting effects. Fortuny believed that light on the stage should be the same as that found in nature, which was chiefly reflected light from the earth's atmosphere and physical colors. Thus stage light should be reflected light. This was achieved by employing the *Kuppelhorizont* as a giant reflector, using silk against it to reflect the light onto the stage. Direct light, as found in the direct light of the sun, occupied a place of secondary importance to Fortuny, but it was certainly acceptable in highlighting movement on stage. Although not directly applicable to most lighting situations, Fortuny's system did give the concept of indirect light to the aesthetics of modern stage lighting. Most of his experiments were conducted in Germany after 1902.

APPIA, CRAIG, AND THE NEW STAGECRAFT

The term "New Stagecraft" is applied to the production portion of the first major revolt from realism as it emerged in the late nineteenth and early twentieth centuries. Heavily rooted in the dramatic ideas of the symbolists, the New Stagecraft sought to affirm that verisimilitude, or the presentation of objective reality as truth in the theatre, was not an appropriate artistic goal. Rather, the dramatic essence for scenery and the other production elements was to focus on the internal, or spiritual, truth of the play and its character using symbolic parts of the whole to express the whole. The movement believed that all art exists in symbols, and through the use of them true art is restored to the theatre because the artist is making a thing stand for something larger than itself, the parts reflecting the organic whole. The purpose of the setting, then, is to capture and enhance the mood of the play. It does this by focusing attention on the action, and by remaining unobtrusive to the action, which, according to New Stagecraft practitioners, visual realism had

A model of a set by Adolphe Appia.
(Courtesy of Cleveland State University's Theatre Arts Area)

not done. The overall appeal of New Stagecraft scenography was to the emotions rather than to scientific objectivism. The two men most responsible for the introduction of New Stagecraft ideals and their gradual acceptance into mainstream theatre production were Adolphe Appia and Edward Gordon Craig.

Adolphe Appia (1862–1928) has already been discussed in connection with his theories of lighting, and they are indeed a part of this stagecraft. But he theorized about the entire production process as well, and all these elements must be considered to appreciate his view of the New Stagecraft. Appia found a great aesthetic contradiction between the flat, two-dimensional scenery of his day and the inherent three-dimensionality of the actor. In order to emphasize the actor, he believed that a nonillusionistic yet three-dimensional setting was necessary to reveal form and movement. This combination of actor and scenery was to be unified by the lighting, which, by being directional and shadow-producing, would emphasize the human form. The setting was to be formal and simple, as the eighteen designs in *Die Musik* suggest, bringing out the more important aspects of the production. Consistent with New Stagecraft ideals, Appia believed that, in the true art of the theatre, stating less was indeed saying more.

Edward Gordon Craig (1872–1966) worked totally apart from Appia, but also significantly contributed to the development of the New Stagecraft. Craig's basic aesthetic for the theatre is found in his writing, primarily *The Art of the*

Appia sacred forest scene for Wagner's Parzifal.

Edward Gordon Craig at his studio in Florence, Italy.

A model of an abstract set by Edward Gordon Craig.
(Courtesy of Cleveland State University's Theatre Arts Area)

Theatre, published in 1905. In many ways, he was more abstract than Appia in his use of symbolism as the proper aesthetic for the theatre and was less compromising with the realities of actual stage production. His basic system for an appropriate setting for most plays was an elaborate series of tall screens that could be arranged in a variety of ways to suggest the essences of the locales needed, and provide the steps, levels, and entrances necessary for the actor's use. In his absolute insistence upon avoiding pictorial or realistic elements, Craig alienated many producers, some of whom were not in total disagreement with his ideas. In addition to his views on the visual side of theatre production, he saw contemporary production practice as archaic and the cause of the sorry state of the theatre as he found it. Craig desired production unity with no single collaborative artist dominant over any other save the single individual responsible for the entire production. If possible this one individual should be a superartist, at once producer, director, author, and technical practitioner. In this vein, he articulated his concept of the *Übermarionnette*, a superpuppet replacement for the actor, willing to do the superartist's bidding without question and essentially devoid of the ego of the international stars that Craig so despised. While this last part of his philosophy was viewed as outrageous, Craig's superartist concept was in line with the rising figure of the superproducer, or *régisseur*.

Craig's practical work in the theatre was less influential than his writing about it. His most famous production experience was in designing *Hamlet* for

Scene from Craig's 1926 production of Ibsen's The Pretenders *at the Royal Theatre, Copenhagen.*

(*Courtesy of the Royal Theatre Archives and Library, Copenhagen*)

the Moscow Art Theatre in 1912, which was not an unqualified success. But through his writing, he advanced the cause of the New Stagecraft and symbolism with a flair that few attained. His periodical, *The Mask*, issued between 1908 and 1929, continued to advance his ideas. When he died in 1966, he was the acknowledged dean of theatrical theorists.

Many of the points raised by Appia and Craig did not find their way into the theatrical mainstream as articulated, but they did serve a useful function in keeping that mainstream more artistically honest. And they paved the way for a new consensus aesthetic—realism blended with its departures, often working together—that is the hallmark of modern eclectic theatre practice.

In addition to the contributions of Appia and Craig, the entire New Stagecraft movement was significant to the development of the modern aesthetic of theatre. It provided the first major break from realism and fostered the first serious examination of the role of the visual arts in theatre practice in more than two hundred years. In the many forms it took, to be examined in detail in Chapter 24, it forced the "theatrical" back into the theatre and gave impetus to the notion that the theatre had a higher visual calling than the photographic duplication of stage realism. In particular, it would influence not only the commercial theatre but the little theatre and amateur theatre movements as well. In the early twentieth century, it would be the single most important factor in the development of modern scene design and technology.

RETROSPECT

With the dawn of the nineteenth century, the stage was set for the final rejection of the aristocratic ideals that had governed society since the Renaissance. Since the middle class now controlled the pocketbooks and hence the culture of Western society, drama and theatre production reflected the standards, tastes, and mores of this new power group. After a tenuous start in the early decades of the nineteenth century, a style emerged that reflected these factors—realism. By the last half of the 1800s, realism was the dominant aesthetic in the theatre.

Realism prevailed in all aspects of theatrical endeavor. In drama, Ibsen, Chekhov, Strindberg, and Shaw paved the way for a written theatre of the people, and production methods followed suit. The ensemble work of the Duke of Saxe-Meiningen and the Independent Theatre Movement provided new concepts of artistic unity on the stage, refining production realism more sharply. In design and technical staging, the late nineteenth century continued the trend established in the first half of the 1800s. Work essentially continued on advancing the design and practicability of stage devices conceived in the previous century. New modes of power allowed traditional stage machinery and lighting to function more smoothly and efficiently, refining what had previously been discovered. And in the area of stage design, the two-dimensional painterly realism of the first half of the nineteenth century gave way in the 1880s to three-dimensional structural realism. This was achieved through the work of MacKaye, Beerbohm-Tree, Belasco, Daly, Boucicault, Irving, and the creative genius of those in the Independent Theatre Movement.

No sooner had the achievement of verisimilitude through realism been accomplished than the break from it began. In drama, realism came to be perceived as only the surface truth in human affairs. The form had its limitations in that it could be "real" only to a point; ultimately theatre, and all art, must be more. The reformers sought to define dramatic truth not as objective reality in the theatre, but as subjective, internal reality, heavily based on Freudian psychology. In staging, the New Stagecraft, headed by Appia and Craig, questioned similar values and goals. Scene and lighting design turned similarly inward, searching for a higher concept of art in the theatre through subjective theatricality.

Thus, as the twentieth century began, the art of the theatre was in a state of flux. Realism still held sway, but it was seriously challenged as the goal and proper aesthetic of the theatre. The early twentieth century would be characterized by an ever-increasing array of "isms"—expressionism, symbolism, futurism, surrealism—each claiming to be the new truth for the theatre. These directions would, in turn, rise rapidly as pure styles, then be assimilated into the theatrical mainstream. The reformers of the theatre in the early twentieth century would reconsider its basic reason for being, and return its aesthetic to that goal established so long ago—that of providing an artistic experience, through highly theatrical means, with the actor and the audience sharing a common playing space. Alternative theatre architecture and staging, seen through the rejection of the proscenium arch, would lead to some exciting theatrical experiments. At the same time, this would lead to a confusion of theatrical styles and the final emergence of the late-twentieth-century aesthetic of the theatre—the embracing of no particular style at all.

Date	European and U.S. History	European Theatre History
1850	College of Science and Technology established in London.	
1851	Coup d'état of Louis Napoleon in France. Great Exhibition held in Crystal Palace, London.	Macready's farewell performance.
1852	Napoleon III, Emperor of France.	
1853–1856	Crimean War.	Birth of G. B. Shaw. (1856)
1857	The Great Mutiny in India.	
1858	Transatlantic cable completed between Britain and U.S.A.	Dumas fils, The Natural Son.
1859	Construction of the Suez Canal begins.	
1860	First practical internal combustion engine built.	Birth of Chekhov.
1861	Victor Emmanuel II declared king of united Italy.	Death of Eugène Scribe. Fechter performs Hamlet in London.
1862		Sarah Bernhardt's debut as actress.
1863	Construction begins on London subway system.	
1864	War between Denmark and Prussia. Invention of pasteurization.	Ibsen leaves Norway.
1865	First attempt at antiseptic surgery.	Bancrofts at Prince of Wales's.
1866		Ibsen's Brand.
1867	Prussia establishes state mail service.	
1869	Opening of Suez Canal.	
1870	Franco-Prussian War. Fall of Napoleon III and establishment of Third French Republic.	
1871	William I of Prussia proclaimed emperor of united Germany.	Henry Irving performs in The Bells.
1873	Remington typewriters introduced.	
1874		Meiningen company in Berlin.
1875	Britain enacts Public Health Law.	
1876	Bell invents telephone. Elementary education made compulsory in England.	
1877	Edison invents the phonograph.	

(Continued on page 460)

Date	European and U.S. History	European Theatre History
1878	Electric street lighting first used in London.	Irving becomes manager of Lyceum Theatre.
1879	Birth of Albert Einstein.	Ibsen's *A Doll House*. Zola's *Thérèse Raquin*.
1880	First practical electric light bulb invented.	
1881	Boers defeat British and establish Transvaal Republic.	Ibsen's *Ghosts*. Meiningen company in London. Savoy theatre lit completely by electricity.
1882	Early work in psychoanalysis begins in Vienna.	Becque's *The Vultures*.
1884	Practical steam turbine engine invented. Universal male suffrage in Britain.	
1885		Gilbert and Sullivan's *The Mikado*.
1887	Celebration of Queen Victoria's Golden Jubilee. International Copyright Act.	Founding of Théâtre Libre. Strindberg's *The Father*.
1889		Freie Bühne founded. Théâtre Libre visits London.
1892	Invention of diesel engine.	Ibsen's *The Master Builder*. Hauptmann's *The Weavers*. Shaw's *Widower's Houses*.
1893	Four-wheel cars built by Ford and Benz.	
1894	Beginning of the Dreyfus affair in France.	Shaw's *Arms and the Man*.
1895	Marconi invents radio telegraphy. Motion picture camera invented.	Irving knighted. Duse and Bernhardt both perform in London.
1896		Chekhov's *The Sea Gull*.
1898	War between Spain and U.S.A. First Zeppelin airship built.	Moscow Art Theatre founded.
1899	Boer War.	Ibsen's *When We Dead Awake*. Appia's *Music and Staging* published.
1901	Death of Queen Victoria.	Chekhov's *Three Sisters*.
1903	Successful powered flight by Wright Brothers.	
1904	Russia badly defeated by Japan in Russo-Japanese War.	Abbey Theatre opens in Dublin.

(Continued on page 461)

Date	European and U.S. History	European Theatre History
1905	General strike in Russia. Einstein formulates theory of relativity.	Death of Sir Henry Irving. British Actors Union established. E. G. Craig publishes *The Art of the Theatre*.
1906	First radio broadcast in U.S.A.	Death of Ibsen.
1907		Strindberg's *A Dream Play*.
1908		E. G. Craig begins to publish *The Mask*. Strindberg's *Ghost Sonata*.
1909	Henry Ford builds first Model T.	
1911	Suffragist riots in London.	
1912	First Balkan War.	Craig and Stanislavski produce *Hamlet* at MAT. Death of Strindberg.
1913	Principle of jet propulsion discovered.	Copeau establishes Théâtre du Vieux-Columbier.
1914	World War I begins.	Meyerhold opens Studio in Moscow.

SELECTED READINGS

Antoine, Andre. *Memories of the Théâtre Libre*. Translated by Marvin Carlson. Coral Gables: University of Miami Press, 1964.
   Excellent account of the aims and accomplishments of the first of the independent theatres by its founder.

Appia, Adolphe. *The Work of the Living Art: A Theory of the Theatre*. Coral Gables: University of Miami Press, 1960.
   Appia's view of stagecraft and the role lighting plays in it.

Baker, Michael. *The Rise of the Victorian Actor*. London: Rowman & Littlefield, 1978.
   An interesting study of various aspects of life in the professional theatre from approximately 1830 to 1890.

Brockett, Oscar G., and Robert R. Findlay. *Century of Innovation: A History of European and American Theatre and Drama Since 1870*. Englewood Cliffs, N.J.: Prentice-Hall, 1973.
   A well-documented and illustrated history of the modern era.

Brustein, Robert. *The Theatre of Revolt*. Boston: Atlantic–Little, Brown, 1964.
   A stimulating and argumentative book with chapters on Ibsen, Strindberg, Shaw, and Chekhov.

Carlson, Marvin A. *The French Stage in the Nineteenth Century*. Metuchen, N.J.: Scarecrow Press, 1972.
   Previously cited.

Craig, Edward Gordon. *On the Art of the Theatre*. New York: Theatre Arts Books, 1957.
   An account by Craig of his theories with emphasis on mood, simplicity, and aesthetic control of the theatre.

Donaldson, Frances. *The Actors-Managers*. Chicago: Regnery, 1970.
   A good survey of the leading actor-managers of the English stage during the Victorian and Edwardian eras.

Gorelik, Mordecai. *New Theatres for Old*. New York: E. P. Dutton, 1962.
   A study of theatrical style from realism to the mid–twentieth century.

Irving, Laurence. *Henry Irving: The Actor and His World*. New York: Macmillan, 1952.
   Of the many biographies of Irving, this one written by his grandson is perhaps the best.

Johnson, Walter. *August Strindberg*. Boston: Twayne, 1976.
   An excellent study of Strindberg's creative career by a noted Strindberg scholar and translator.

Le Gallienne, Eva. *The Mystic in the Theatre: Eleanora Duse*. London: The Bodley Head, 1966.
   A highly readable study of Duse by one of the great actresses of the American stage.

Osborne, John. *The Naturalist Drama in Germany*. Manchester: Manchester University Press, 1971.
> A detailed study of the subject with considerable attention paid to the works of Hauptmann.

Pitcher, Harvey. *The Chekhov Play: A New Interpretation*. New York: Barnes & Noble, 1973.
> An excellent study of the nature of the Chekhovian play and the four major plays.

Richardson, Joanna. *Sarah Bernhardt*. London: Max Reinhardt, 1959.
> A good, concise biography of a very colorful life.

Rowell, George. *Theatre in the Age of Irving*. London: Rowman & Littlefield, 1981.
> A very readable work that touches on Irving's theatre and the other theatrical ventures available in London during the last two decades of the century.

_____. *The Victorian Theatre*. Oxford: Clarendon Press, 1956.
> A fine introductory study of the nineteenth-century English theatre.

Stein, Jack M. *Richard Wagner and the Synthesis of the Arts*. Detroit: Wayne State University Press, 1960.
> A detailed discussion of Wagner's musical and staging ideas.

Stokes, John. *Resistible Theatres*. New York: Harper & Row, 1972.
> An intriguing study of British noncommercial theatre practice in the last quarter of the nineteenth century.

Valency, Maurice. *The Cart and the Trumpet: The Plays of George Bernard Shaw*. New York: Oxford University Press, 1973.
> This is one of the best books on Shaw and his place in the English theatre.

_____. *The Flower and the Castle*. New York: Macmillian, 1963.
> Previously cited.

Volbach, Walther. *Adolphe Appia: Prophet of the Modern Theatre*. Middletown, Conn.: Wesleyan University Press, 1968.
> A detailed discussion of Appia's design concepts.

Waxman, S. M. *Antoine and the Théâtre Libre*. Cambridge, Mass.: Harvard University Press, 1926.
> A still-useful study of Antoine's theory and practice.

NEW YORK

PART XI

New World Reflections:
THEATRE IN THE UNITED STATES TO WORLD WAR I

By the middle of the seventeenth century, the great American adventure was well under way. Although many European nationalities were involved in the settlement of North America, the predominant cultural influence was the Anglo-Saxon heritage from England. This English heritage would shape and direct the development of the United States until the twentieth century.

The first half of the nineteenth century was an arrogant, blustering period for the young American republic. Americans shocked foreign visitors with their egalitarianism, materialism, and anti-intellectualism. Following the War of 1812, often called America's second war of independence, the nation's aspirations were largely confined to its continental destiny, a widely held belief that the future of the United States was to govern the entire North America continent. This philosophical stance was anti-European, and it expressed itself in a desire to keep the United States free from foreign alliances, a foreign policy position the nation was to hold until World War II. Yet part of the bluster of United States chauvinism was the result of a national inferiority complex in the face of established European cultural traditions. This national uncertainty repeatedly expressed itself in calls for American artists, writers, and actors, and then their rejection in favor of Europeans. But the cultural indirection in the United States was also the result of regional fragmentation caused by the sheer size and ever-expanding nature of the nation.

The Civil War tore through the social and cultural fabric of the nation. It was a destroyer of lives, property, and an entire social structure, but it was ultimately a unifier of the nation. The postwar boom made the United States the largest industrial and agricultural producer in the world by the end of the nineteenth century. A major element in the nation's economic growth was the vast improvement in national transportation and communication systems. The first transcontinental railroad was completed in

1869, and by 1887 over 33,000 communities had access to regular train service. The electric telegraph was patented in 1840 and was in widespread use by the time of the Civil War. The next advance in electric communication came in 1876 with the invention of the telephone. Long-distance telephone service was introduced in 1884, and by 1900 nearly a million and a half telephones were in use in the United States. These improvements in transporation and communication helped remove the strains of the war by giving the country a sense of economic and national unity.

The enormous economic growth of the post–Civil War years also provided an ideal climate for large-scale political corruption, financial manipulation, and human exploitation. Business leaders used their wealth and power to control state and federal politics, financial trusts restricted output and maintained high prices for goods while destroying competitors, and the accelerating pace of industrial technology demanded more of workers for less pay. These excesses gave birth to the labor movement and an organized reform movement, and both held goals to regulate government and industry. Major reforms were enacted during the first decade of the twentieth century, but additional industrial and governmental changes would wait until after World War I.

Since the Revolutionary War, Americans had taken great pride in their unique "system," as they called it, and considered their form of government a model for the peoples of the world. This idealism was still present at the time of U.S. entry into World War I. President Wilson called the war a "People's War, a war for freedom and justice and self-government amongst all the nation's of the world, a war to make the world safe for the peoples who live upon it." American leaders had been interested in world power since the nation's victory in the Spanish-American War, but in most respects the United States was a very provincial nation in 1914. World War I and its aftermath was to change that, and it formed a coming-of-age period for the nation.

The years after the war were also to be a maturation period for the American theatre. Since the Revolution it had developed along with the nation, reflecting its pride and problems. Yet it had remained an isolated theatre that produced few artists and playwrights of major significance. All that was to change by the middle of the twentieth century.

22
THEATRE IN THE UNITED STATES TO THE CIVIL WAR

COLONIAL THEATRE

Professional theatre got under way in the American colonies in the fall of 1749 when a small company of actors, managed by Walter Murray and Thomas Kean, appeared in a refitted warehouse in Philadelphia. The lot of the professional actor in the colonies was a hard one since many settlements were founded by religious groups strongly opposed to theatrical activities. Religious leaders thought dramatic productions a poor way to prepare for the burdens of life, and they had few kind words to say about the "vagabond profession." Formal opposition to the development of theatre often took the form of local laws forbidding the performance of any plays. Under such conditions the Murray-Kean company worked for twenty years, but its efforts fade from the historical record with the arrival of the Hallams.

The Hallam Family

When enforcement of the Licensing Act closed his London theatre, William Hallam became interested in the American colonies. Enlisting himself as London agent, Hallam organized a pioneer theatre company around his brother and sister-in-law, Mr. and Mrs. Lewis Hallam, and their three children. In May 1752 the five Hallams plus ten additional players set sail aboard the *Charming Sally*. Arriving in Virginia in June, the Hallam company made straight for Williamsburg. Upon receiving permission from the royal governor, the company presented its first play in the colonies, *The Merchant of Venice*, on September 15, 1752, "before a numerous and polite audience." Such was the success of the Hallams in Williamsburg that they remained until the following June, performing plays from the typical repertory of the period.

Although it took the Hallams three months to obtain permission to perform in New York, they began a highly successful seven-month engagement there in the fall of 1753. Moving to Philadelphia, the Hallams again overcame local opposition to their performing and delighted the citizens until the company departed in June. In the fall the actors were in Charleston, and in January 1755 they departed for Jamaica. There Lewis Hallam died.

Before falling victim to yellow fever, Lewis Hallam merged his company with one already on the island. For three years this new company performed in the West Indies before appreciative audiences of British and Danish planters and merchants. In 1758, when the company returned to the mainland, it was under the management of David Douglas (c. 1720–1786). From 1758 until the time of the American Revolution, Douglas's "American Company of Comedians" was the major theatrical force in the colonies. The political climate of the revolutionary period was not favorable to the spread of theatre, so David Douglas and his actors embarked for Jamaica in 1775 to wait out the war.

The Colonial Playhouse

Before the 1760s, amateur and professional actors in the colonies used temporary stages housed in converted warehouses. One exception was in Williamsburg, Virginia, where the first playhouse in the colonies was constructed in 1716. This structure was first used in the spring of 1718 and remained in sporadic use until 1745. The first concerted efforts at playhouse construction in America were instigated by David Douglas. Starting with the Douglas company's first North American tour in 1758, its enterprising manager, concerned about the future development of his company, construct-

The interior of the John Street Theatre, which David Douglas opened in New York in 1767.

(Courtesy of KaiDib Films International, Glendale, Calif.)

ed playhouses in nearly every city in which it performed. The Southwark and John Street theatres are two examples of Douglas's pre-Revolutionary structures.

Built in 1766, the Southwark Theatre had the typical pit, box, and gallery arrangement of the period. The view of the stage, which was illuminated by open oil lamps, was obscured for many in the audience by the large wooden pillars that supported the roof and the upper tier. The Southwark was the first theatre built in America with a view toward permanency, and it remained in use as a theatre until 1821.

The John Street Theatre in New York was Douglas's second major structure. Opened in 1767, this frame building contained the usual pit and gallery along with a double tier of boxes. In an effort to cater to wealthier New Yorkers, Douglas had a covered passageway connected to the building to protect those arriving in carriages from inclement weather. The John Street Theatre remained New York's major playhouse until the construction of the Park Theatre in 1798.

Douglas attempted to acquire the best scenery available for his new theatres by having it constructed in London. Since the illumination from candles and oil lamps was so poor, scenic detail was secondary to bright, bold colors. Scenes were painted on fabric, and in typical eighteenth-century English fashion, the shutters parted in the middle and moved to the sides on grooves.

Play Writing in the Colonies

Credit for writing the first play in North America must be given either to a Spanish captain for a 1598 *comedia* or to Marc Lescarbot for *Le Théâtre de Neptune en la Nouvelle-France* (1606). William Darby's *Ye Bare and Ye Cubb* (1665) is the earliest recorded English-language effort in play writing in the New World. The first English play script printed in the colonies was *Androboros*, written in 1714 by Robert Hunter, the royal governor of New York and New Jersey. There are a few other examples of American play writing before the 1750s, but it was the arrival of professional actors in the colonies that provided the opportunity for an increase in the quantity, if not the quality, of native play writing.

The first play written by an American colonial to be performed by professional actors was *The Prince of Partha* by Thomas Godfrey. This five-act verse tragedy was performed only once by the Douglas company, on April 24, 1767, at the Southwark Theatre, and is now only a historical footnote. Other early American efforts include Thomas Forrest's *The Disappointment* (1767) and Robert Rogers' *Ponteach; or, The Savages of America* (1766), which was the first play script by a colonial to be published in London.

The revolutionary period witnessed an increase in play writing, most of it of high propagandistic but low theatrical merit. These scripts were not truly intended for the stage but were to be read by various political factions in the colonies. Hugh Henry Brackenridge's *The Battle of Bunkers-Hill* (1776) and *The Death of General Montgomery* (1777) are highly patriotic, while the anonymous farce *The Battle of Brooklyn* (1776) is an antirevolutionary attack on the courage and morals of the American leadership. The revolutionary period produced other similar dramatic efforts, but the true flowering of American play writing came after the war.

THEATRE AND THE NEW REPUBLIC

Professional actors returned to the United States shortly after the end of the war, and by 1785 the Old American Company, under the director of Lewis Hallam, Jr., and John Henry, was in full control of the theatrical scene. But the new nation was growing rapidly and the increases in potential audience members created competition in the theatre. Most of the new theatre companies grew out of the membership of the Old American Company. The first major actor to leave the Old American Company was Thomas Wignell, the company's leading comedian and the favorite actor of President Washington.

Wignell joined with Alexander Reinagle in 1791 to establish the Chestnut Street Theatre in Philadelphia. When this new theatre opened in 1794, it presented the best English actors yet seen in the United States. Although this company included such talents as Eliza Kemble Whitlock, Anne Burton Merry, and William Warren, its most impressive member was Thomas A. Cooper (1776–1849). An outstanding exponent of the acting style popularized in England by Sarah Siddons and John Philip Kemble, Cooper had a major impact on the development of American acting.

Hallam and Henry, in an effort to combat the success of the Chestnut Street company, also recruited in England. Their efforts brought to America the celebrated tragedienne Mrs. Melmoth, Joseph Jefferson I, and John Hodgkinson, who soon eclipsed John Henry as the leading actor of the Old American Company. By 1794 Hodgkinson had replaced Henry as comanager of the company, and in 1796 William Dunlap was added to the management team. By the end of the century the hostilities within the old American Company had left Dunlap as sole manager, with Thomas A. Cooper, late of the Chestnut Street Theatre, as his leading actor.

New Theatres in a New Nation

Increasing population and a growing demand for entertainment resulted in the removal of most antitheatre laws in major cities and towns by the mid-1790s, and this aided the rapid establishment of playhouses and acting companies. Between 1791 and 1798 new theatres opened in New Orleans, Newport, Boston, Baltimore, New York, and Washington, D.C. Typical of the theatre architecture of this period was the Park Theatre in New York City.

At its opening in January 1798, the Park Theatre was considered one of the most substantial buildings in the city. The three-story structure, framed by seven arched doorways, could seat an audience of two thousand in its spacious interior. Although still adhering to the pit, box, and gallery arrangement, the pit was unusually large, with three rows of boxes. Much was made of the size of the stage in comparison with the old John Street Theatre, and the scenery was accounted the most elegant ever seen in America. Although often beset with financial difficulties, the Park enjoyed fifty years of operation, and from 1815 to 1840 it was considered the nation's most prestigious playhouse.

Frontier Theatre

As towns and villages began to appear beyond the Appalachian Mountains, groups of strolling players were attracted to these new population centers. Noble Luke Usher, the Drake family, Sol Smith, the Chapman family, Noah M. Ludlow, and James H. Caldwell were all closely associated with frontier theatre in the decades before the Civil War. In 1814 Noble Usher recruited a company in Albany, New York, led by Samuel Drake, to perform in his father's playhouses in Kentucky. In addition to six Drakes, the other actors were Noah M. Ludlow and Frances Denny. Traveling by horseback, wagon, flatboat, and foot, the Drake company arrived in 1815. Within two years an established theatrical circuit was developed in Kentucky by Drake. In 1817 Noah Ludlow formed his own company and went off to conquer new theatrical frontiers in Nashville, Natchez, and St. Louis. Ludlow (1795–1886) and his sometimes partner Sol Smith (1801–1869) both wrote fascinating narratives of their careers in the theatre.

James H. Caldwell (1793–1863), an experienced English actor, brought a company of actors from Virginia to New Orleans in 1820. From that date until the mid-1830s, Caldwell dominated theatre in the Mississippi Valley. When Caldwell's Camp Street Theatre opened in 1824, it was the first building west of the Alleghenies to be equipped with gas lighting. In 1833 Caldwell surpassed the Camp Street structure with his St. Charles Theatre. This playhouse, with its seating for four thousand, was said to be equaled in elegance only by two or three European opera houses. In addition to his activities in New Orleans, Caldwell was involved in theatre operations in Natchez, Nashville, Cincinnati, Louisville, and St. Louis. When Caldwell left theatre management, he could look back over a highly productive period during which he established quality theatre in the Mississippi Valley.

America's major rivers were the principal routes of transportation before the Civil War, and the opportunities afforded by river travel were realized by an enterprising English theatre family, the Chapmans. America's first showboat, the *Floating Theatre*, was launched in Pittsburgh by the Chapmans in the summer of 1831. The theatre was built on the frame of a flatboat, one hundred feet long and sixteen feet wide, and it was equipped with a small stage in the stern, a pit in the middle, and a gallery in the bow.

The *Floating Theatre* drifted down the Ohio and Mississippi rivers, and the Chapmans gave performances at every river landing where an audience was likely. At New Orleans the boat was sold, the family returned to Pittsburgh, another boat was built, and the process started again. With the acquisition of

The Centennial Showboat of the University of Minnesota.
(Courtesy of KaiDib Films International, Glendale, Calif.)

their first steamboat in 1836, the Chapmans were able to move up and down the rivers at will. The success of the Chapmans was noted by others, and in the years before the Civil War numerous small showboats plied their theatrical wares on the rivers of the United States. The showboat was to remain an active element in U.S. theatre until the twentieth century, and its way of life has been immortalized in the classic musical *Show Boat*.

By the time of the American Civil War, actors had penetrated all the civilized and not too civilized areas of the United States. Playhouses, from the elegance of the St. Charles to the canvas functionalism of the Eagle Theatre in the California gold fields, were appearing throughout the nation. Thanks to the efforts of America's theatrical pioneers, visiting star performers of the nineteenth century were able to perform before audiences who had some knowledge of the world of theatre.

Foreign Stars

The first major English star to visit the United States was George Frederick Cooke (1756–1812). Persuaded by Thomas A. Cooper and William Dunlap, managers of the Park Theatre, Cooke made his first American appearances in 1810 in New York, Philadelphia, and Boston. Cooke, whose style of acting was more emotional and forceful than that of any actor in the States, was popular with audiences. He introduced the visiting star system to America, and astute theatre managers were quick to pick up on this new profitable venture.

From a Drawing in the possession of Tho.ˢ Harris Esq.ʳ

George Frederick Cooke.

Stephen Price, of the Park Theatre management, was most impressed with the box office potential of foreign stars, and he became a major recruiter of English stars. Edmund Kean was signed up by Price for American tours in 1820 and 1825, and William Charles Macready in 1826. Macready was to make two additional trips to the United States, in 1843 and in 1848. The last tour of this leading English actor found him unwillingly engaged in an artistic rivalry with the United States's leading actor, Edwin Forrest. This theatrical duel culminated in the Astor Place riot, which is discussed later. Other major imported stars during this period included Charles Mathews, Junius Brutus Booth, Fanny Kemble, and Mme Vestris.

American Actors

The first American-born actor to perform professionally was most likely Samuel Greville, a Princeton dropout who appeared with the Douglas company in 1767. Until the second decade of the nineteenth century, Greville's successors were forced to play second fiddle to the English actors who dominated the American theatre. Yet in resident companies throughout the nation young native-born players were learning their craft. By the 1820s some of these actors were ready to challenge the English control of the American stage. In the forefront of these performers was Edwin Forrest, America's first native-born star.

Edwin Forrest (1806–1872) made his professional stage debut at the Walnut Street Theatre in Philadelphia at the age of fourteen. For the next six years he performed with various resident companies. These apprentice years allowed him to act with such major stars as Junius Brutus Booth, Thomas A. Cooper, and Edmund Kean. Forrest's strong physique and powerful voice led him to develop a heroic, muscular style of acting that seemed to embody the energy and strength of the young United States. In the summer of 1826, he made a triumphant New York debut at the Park as Othello. The following year Forrest became a star.

Although he was often accused of ranting in his roles, Forrest was a studied performer who strove for realistic details. He was most popular in bold, heroic roles that emphasized his physical and vocal powers. In an effort to find roles of this type, Forrest began a series of play-writing contests in 1828. The first prize-winning play was John A. Stone's *Metamora*, and the play remained in Forrest's repertory for the rest of his career. Forrest gave a total of twenty thousand

Edwin Forrest in the role of Metamora.

(Courtesy of the National Portrait Gallery, Smithsonian Institution, Washington, D.C.)

dollars in prizes for play scripts, and these contests did much to assist the cause of native play writing.

The long career of Edwin Forrest was marred by two scandals, his protracted divorce and the Astor Place riot. The riot, which was the worst in the history of the American theatre, left thirty-one people dead and nearly fifty wounded. It grew out of a quarrel between Forrest and William Charles Macready, but it took on nationalistic aspects among the working-class fans of Forrest and the aristocratic fans of Macready. The riot took place on May 10, 1849, outside New York's Astor Place Opera House, when a mob of over ten thousand attempted to prevent Macready from performing. The infantry was called to prevent the total destruction of the opera house, and Macready barely escaped alive. The 1851 divorce action between Edwin and Catherine Forrest was one of the most notorious trials of nineteenth-century America, and Forrest continued to appeal the court's decision for the next eighteen years. Both the riot and the divorce cost Forrest some of his popularity. Yet he remained for a vast number of his fellow citizens the living embodiment of the ideal of the American actor.

Charlotte Cushman (1816–1876) was a contemporary of Edwin Forrest, and her professional career covers nearly the same time period. Cushman made her stage debut as a singer but soon ruined her voice by overtaxing it. Turning to acting, she served in various resident companies for two years before being named the leading lady of the Park Theatre company in 1843. She had the

GREAT RIOT AT THE ASTOR PLACE OPERA HOUSE, NEW YORK

The Astor Place riot.

(Courtesy of KaiDib Films International, Glendale, Calif.)

Charlotte Cushman.
(Courtesy of the National Portrait
Gallery, Smithsonian Institution,
Washington, D.C.)

opportunity to act with Macready during his first tour of the United States, and he was impressed by her raw talent. Following the urging of Macready to work in England to improve her skills, Cushman left the United States in 1844. For the next five years she worked her way to theatrical prominence in England. She returned to America in 1849 as a star, and she remained the leading American tragic actress until her retirement in 1875.

With her height, broad shoulders, and husky voice, Charlotte Cushman specialized in strong female roles and in male roles such as Romeo and Hamlet. Along with the physical and emotional power she brought to a role, Cushman was also an excellent elocutionist with a great vocal range. The American critic William Winter summed up her style when he noted, "No woman in the theatre of this period shows the inspirational fire, the opulent intellect, the dominant character and abounding genius that were virtorious and imperial in Charlotte Cushman."

Ira Aldridge (1807–1867), the first great black actor of the English-speaking theatre, was born in New York but achieved his fame in England and Europe. Aldridge may have gained some acting experience at Brown's African Theatre in New York in the early 1820s, but, because of prejudicial conditions, he immigrated to England in 1825 and never returned to his native land. During the next four decades, Aldridge built a highly successful career in England and

*Ira Aldridge in the role of
Aaron in* Titus Androni-
cus.
*(Courtesy of KaiDib Films
International, Glendale, Calif.)*

Europe. His fine physique and deep voice were employed in an acting style
that combined the techniques of Kemble and Kean.

The major portion of the career of Edwin Booth (1833–1893) occurs after
the Civil War, but by the early 1860s Booth had developed into a major
independent star. Booth was the fourth son of actor Junius Brutus Booth, and in
his early teens he served as keeper and valet to his half-mad father and
occasionally played minor roles. With the death of his father in 1852, Booth
began his acting apprenticeship in California. By the time he made his 1856
debut in the East, Booth was an established star. During the prime years of his
career, Booth was considered America's finest tragic actor, and he has been
acclaimed by many as the finest actor America has ever produced.

The important elements in Booth's acting style were his consistency,
thought, and lack of mannerisms. His gift was a near-perfect combination of
mind, body, and voice. Booth's life was plagued with personal tragedies—the
early death of his first wife, his brother's assassination of Lincoln, the insanity of
his second wife, and financial difficulties—yet through it all he continued to
perfect his art. At his death his home at 16 Gramercy Park, New York, was

A portrait of Edwin Booth in the role of Iago.
(Courtesy of the National Portrait Gallery, Smithsonian Institution, Washington, D.C.)

bequeathed to the Players Club, and it stands today as a memorial to this great nineteenth-century American actor.

Forrest, Cushman, Aldridge, and Booth were major stars in a century filled with an extraordinary amount of acting talent in the United States. Other significant performers of the pre–Civil War period were James H. Hackett, James E. Murdoch, Anna Cora Mowatt, Edward Davenport, and William Burton. The period from the 1850s to the turn of the century was truly the golden age of American acting.

POPULAR ENTERTAINMENT

Theatre in nineteenth-century America included not only the glories of Edwin Booth's Hamlet but also the high jinks of P. T. Barnum's American Museum. In the early part of the nineteenth century, minstrelsy, burlesque, and vaudeville were most often a part of a theatrical evening along with a full-length play. Specialization of performers and development of audience tastes caused these forms to evolve into distinctive entertainments with their own theatres and traditions. Minstrelsy is discussed here, burlesque and vaudeville in the following chapter.

Minstrelsy

The minstrel show was the most popular form of mass entertainment in America in the middle decades of the nineteenth century. Although white actors had previously "blacked up" and sung songs associated with the slave culture in America, the first professional blackface performer was Thomas D. Rice (1808–1861). Rice introduced his highly popular dance and song "Jim Crow" in 1830, and by 1833 he was putting together "Ethiopian Operas." From these early beginnings evolved the minstrel show.

In 1843 Don Emmett and the Virginia Minstrels began to offer a self-sufficient musical and comedy entertainment set within a two-act frame. In blackface and dressed in striped shirts, white trousers, and blue swallowtail coats, Emmett and his group set the pattern for pre–Civil War minstrelsy. In the 1850s Edwin Christy and the Christy Minstrels, the most famous of the nineteenth-century groups, developed the traditional three-part form of the minstrel show. During the first part, the performers sat in a semicircle with the interlocutor in the center and the endmen, Mr. Tambo and Mr. Bones, at either end. This section consisted of comic banter and group songs, and it concluded with a "walkaround," an upbeat number featuring the entire company. The second third of the show, the "olio," was a collection of variety acts performed

A stageful of audience members "jumping Jim Crow" along with Thomas D. Rice at the Bowery Theatre, New York, in 1833.

(Courtesy of KaiDib Films International, Glendale, Calif.)

before a drop curtain. The final third was a one-act skit of a highly improvisational nature that was usually a takeoff on some popular play or event of the day.

Minstrel shows continued in popularity until the turn of the century, and blackface performers continued as a tradition in American entertainment until the 1950s. The minstrel show was nearly exclusive in its use of white male performers. Women never successfully broke into minstrelsy, and the few successful minstrel companies composed of blacks were forced to adhere to the traditional model, complete with blacking up with burnt cork. The minstrel show was uniquely American in its origins, and it has an important relationship to the development of vaudeville, burlesque, and the American musical. It is not coincidental that this entertainment form developed at a time in the nation when the question of human slavery was a major moral and political issue. The minstrel show presented slavery and the black in a nonthreatening manner, and it did much to offset the moral condemnations of the Abolitionists. The stereotypes of the minstrel show lodged in the culture, and they continue to plague black Americans long after the demise of the happy, singing "darky" of minstrelsy.

P. T. Barnum

Phineas Taylor Barnum (1810–1891), the father of American show business, was born in rural Connecticut, and from 1825 to 1834 he learned the ways of the Yankee trader in the grocery business. Barnum

P. T. Barnum and his American Museum.
(*Courtesy of KaiDib Films International, Glendale, Calif.*)

scored his first success in show business in 1836 by promoting the exhibition of the supposed 161-year-old nurse of George Washington. Purchasing Scuddler's American Museum in New York in 1841, Barnum replaced Scuddler's name with his own and embarked on his career as America's foremost master of humbug. He invented the "media event" for the American tour of singer Jenny Lind, and he perfected this publicity technique in his promotion of the dwarf General Tom Thumb. Master promoter, producer, theatre owner, and con man, P. T. Barnum's legacy to the American theatre was his championship of inexpensive entertainment for the masses.

U.S. PLAYWRIGHTS

William Shakespeare remained the most popular playwright in the United States from the time of the Revolution until after the Civil War. Conditions in the United States during this period were not favorable to native playwrights, and this was attributable to several factors: (1) lack of need existed since the absence of an international copyright law meant foreign plays could be had for free; (2) the central position of the actor meant scripts had to be tailored to meet the actor's audience-pleasing expectations; (3) little or no reward was available for playwrights either in fame or money; (4) there was little encouragement since many audience members and theatre managers appeared to believe the terms "American play script" and "second-rate" were synonymous. Yet even under these adverse conditions, some plays of note were produced. They deserve attention as efforts at reflecting the newly emerging American character upon the stage.

Royall Tyler

The Contrast, produced in 1787 at the John Street Theatre, is the first comedy written by an American to be professionally staged in the new nation. Its author, Royall Tyler (1757–1826), was a major in the Continental Army and later become chief justice of the Vermont Supreme Court. Although the author of other plays, essays, and a novel, Tyler is chiefly remembered for this one comedy. *The Contrast* was favorably received in the major cities of the East, mainly because it was a fine reflection of the manners, tastes, and social attitudes of Americans in the 1780s. The play's hero, Colonel Manly, is a patriotic, plain-speaking American who is contrasted with an Europeanized American fop. The story of the play, which owes a heavy debt to Sheridan, is not the script's strong point. It pleased its audiences because of the author's clever caricatures of postrevolutionary American society.

William Dunlap

With his claim of fifty-three original or adapted play scripts, William Dunlap (1766–1839) was the nation's first professional playwright. His management position at the Park Theatre provided a ready outlet for his play-writing abilities, and Dunlap had the intelligence to provide the theatre public with the type of plays it desired. Patriotism reigns supreme in such Dunlap scripts as *Huzza for the Constitution, Darby's Return,* and *The Glory of Columbia—Her Yeomanry.* Sensing the growing audience demand for sentiment and heroic melodrama, Dunlap adapted and introduced to Americans the plays of Augustus von Kotzebue, the popular German playwright. In addition to his work in the theatre, Dunlap was a painter, teacher, and author of the first *History of the American Theatre* (1832).

Other Playwrights

In the United States, as in England and Europe, the melodrama dominated the nineteenth-century stage. With its emphasis on clearly visible issues of good and evil, its stereotypes, morality, and elevation of the common man, melodrama was increasingly popular with the large, less sophisticated audiences that filled the huge playhouses. U.S. playwrights, actors, and theatre managers gauged this preference for the melodramatic and tailored their products accordingly.

Mordecai M. Noah (1785–1851) wrote one of the most popular American plays of the first half of the nineteenth century, *She Would Be a Soldier, or The Plains of Chippewa.* First produced in 1819, this play held the stage until after the Civil War with its winning combination of spunky patriotism, romance, ridicule of England, bravery, and one noble Indian. Noah's other nationalistic offerings include *The Siege of Tripoli* (1820), *Marion* (1821), and *The Siege of Yorktown* (1824). John Howard Payne (1791–1852), the author of over sixty plays, had the strongest reputation of any U.S. playwright in the first half of the nineteenth century, but he wrote most of his plays for the English theatre. After a brief career as a child actor, Payne sailed to England in 1813 and remained there for nearly twenty years. Best remembered of his plays are *Brutus* (1818), which he wrote for Edmund Kean, and the comedy *Charles the Second* (1824), on which he collaborated with Washington Irving.

The city of Philadelphia produced such a significant number of early playwrights that they are collectively known as the Philadelphia school. In addition to Mordecai Noah, some of the other notable playwrights from this school are Robert Montgomery Bird, James Nelson Barker, and John Augustus Stone.

A versatile man of letters, Robert Montgomery Bird (1806–1854) introduced a strong element of romanticism into American drama. The winner of four of Edwin Forrest's drama prizes, Bird is best remembered for *The Gladiator* (1831) and *The Broker of Bogota* (1834). Highly disappointed in his financial dealings with Forrest, Bird renounced the theatre and turned to other activities. James Nelson Barker (1784–1858) was the author of eleven plays and a series of critical articles on the state of American drama before 1820. Barker's *The Indian Princess* (1808) was the first Indian play to be presented in the United States. John Augustus Stone (1800–1834), the author of ten plays, is now remembered mainly as the author of *Metamora* (1828), the first Forrest prize play and one of the most popular plays of the nineteenth century.

Native Character Drama

Patriotic fervor and glorification of the common man, so much a part of U.S. politics in the decades before the Civil War, were reflected on the stage in popular distinctive American characters. The Indian, Yankee, and frontiersman embodied traits audience members identified as representative of American culture. Playwrights of the nineteenth century built scripts around these characters and several actors specialized in their portrayal.

The Indian character was introduced to the American theatre in Barker's *The Indian Princess* (1808), which was the first of many dramatizations of the story of Pocahontas. Edwin Forrest's portrayal of Metamora gave the nineteenth-century theatre its most noble savage and started a vogue for Indian heroes that lasted for nearly twenty years. The Indian character appeared in three basic forms on the American stage: virgin princess, such as Pocahontas; noble savage, such as Metamora; and red devil, the treacherous enemy of the white settlers. These three forms of the nineteenth-century Indian are still the most frequently seen on the stage, in film, and on television.

The defender of the frontier against the "red devils," and the paragon of American rugged individualism, was the frontiersman. Novelist James Fenimore Cooper established the literary frontiersman with his Natty Bumpo character in *The Last of the Mohicans* and *The Prairie*. Playwrights were soon attempting to put this character on the stage. Although there were several stage adaptations of Cooper's novels, the first major frontier character was Colonel Nimrod Wildfire in James Kirke Pauling's *The Lion of the West* (1831). The character of Wildfire, "half horse, half alligator, and a touch of the earthquake," was written for actor James Hackett, who played the part with great success. Other popular plays featuring the frontiersman were Louisa H. Medina's *Nick of the Woods* (1838), Mordecai Noah's *The Frontier Maid* (1840), and W. R. Derr's *Kit Carson* (1850). Although introduced in the period before the Civil War, the frontiersman character was highly popular in the 1870s and 1880s. During these decades such real frontiersmen as Buffalo Bill Cody performed in scripts built around their dime-novel reputations.

The Yankee character evolved slowly on the American stage, but its first noteworthy appearance was in the role of Jonathan in Royall Tyler's *The Contrast*. In the character of the Yankee, playwrights were able to express the strong sentiments of nationalism and democracy beloved of early-nineteenth-century audiences. Usually a good-hearted New England rustic, the Yankee was an outspoken opponent of aristocratic sham and city ways. The Yankee appeared in such popular plays as *The Forest Rose* (1825), *Sam Patch* (1836), *The People's Lawyer* (1839), and *The Yankee Peddler* (1841). Actors who specialized in Yankee roles were George Handel "Yankee" Hill, Dan Marble, James H. Hackett, and Joshua S. Silsbee.

In addition to the black characters of the minstrel shows, dramatists of the nineteenth century incorporated a black character into their pictures of American life. With few exceptions, the black character was never a principal character because playwrights could not visualize blacks in any role higher than servant. The nineteenth-century stage black was either comic or sentimental. As with the Indian character, the stereotypic molds formed in the nineteenth century for blacks are still present in modern society.

Uncle Tom's Cabin

Uncle Tom's Cabin, a novel by Harriet Beecher Stowe, was published in 1852, and within the year it sold over 300,000 copies in the United States and over a million copies in England. The book became the biggest international best-seller of the nineteenth century and a very important theatrical property. So popular were the adaptations of this novel that few theatrical careers in the nineteenth century were not touched by *Uncle Tom's Cabin*. Twelve different stage versions of *Uncle Tom's Cabin* appeared in print before 1900, and in the years before the Civil War the play was a staple in the repertory of nearly all resident theatre companies in the United States. In the late 1870s "Tom shows" became common as traveling shows as the play continued to rise in popularity during the next twenty years. As the United States entered the twentieth century, nearly five hundred Tom companies were performing throughout the nation. *Uncle Tom's Cabin* was the most popular play of the nineteenth century and one of the most staged productions in the history of Western theatre.

A scene from William A. Brady's 1901 production of Uncle Tom's Cabin.
(Courtesy of the Theatre Collection of the Museum of the City of New York)

CONCLUSION

From 1752 to 1865 the U.S. theatre grew from infancy to early adolescence. Like the human child, the early theatre was largely imitative with flashes of rebellion. English theatre practices and English actors dominated the U.S. theatre well into the nineteenth century. By the time of the Civil War, however, the nation had produced a few actors of international renown, and its playwrights were beginning to answer Walt Whitman's plea for American plays for American audiences using American actors. Playhouses had been constructed in nearly all the settled sections of the country, and two uniquely American theatrical innovations, the minstrel show and the showboat, had been produced. In the national maturing that took place in the aftermath of the Civil War, the theatre would take its place of prominence among the American arts.

23
THEATRE IN THE UNITED STATES FROM THE END OF THE CIVIL WAR THROUGH WORLD WAR I

The boom period following the Civil War was driven by tremendous diversity and energy. To serve similar theatrical tastes and needs, nineteenth-century theatre practitioners were equally diverse and energetic.

THE PLAYHOUSE

In the staging of legitimate plays, the type of production Americans desired to see was one that moved closer to theatrical realism. The theatre structures developed following the Civil War, then, needed to be those that were able to present the detailed reproduction of actuality on the stage.

To handle the demand for theatrical production, more theatres were built in every populated section of the country. Major technological innovations became commonplace in theatres by the start of the twentieth century. Beginning with such innovative theatres as Booth's Theatre in New York City, these playhouses, by the turn of the century, had no apron and no proscenium doors. Elaborate machinery was developed to move the scenic display. The stage grooves were gradually replaced by innovations such as the stage brace, which could support the three-dimensional sets needed for realistic plays. The relationship between the stage and the auditorium appeared, by the beginning of the twentieth century, as it exists in proscenium theatres today—a stage house framed by a proscenium arch, a small pit, and house seats composed of gallery, boxes, and main floor seating.

Lighting for the stage also continued to develop consistent with the tenets of realism. Gas had replaced oil and candle lighting by 1850, and with it came increased versatility and mechanical control. By 1870 border lights had replaced wing lighting as the mainstay of theatrical lighting, and such innovations as the limelight illustrated creative ways to take advantage of gas lighting. Following the development of the first practical incandescent electric lamp by Thomas Edison in 1879, electricity rapidly replaced gas as the major source of power for stage lighting. By the start of the twentieth century, the development of individual spotlights allowed for the establishment of the lighting technology in common use today.

The Movement toward Realism

The theatrical innovations of Edwin Booth (1833–1893), Augustin Daly (1838–1899), Steele MacKaye (1842–1894), and David Belasco (1854–1931) set the pace for the movement of theatre practice toward realism in the late nineteenth century.

Booth's Theatre, New York.
(Courtesy of KaiDib Films International, Glendale, Calif.)

When Booth's Theatre opened in New York City in 1869, it revealed a number of innovations for the movement and support of scenery. The concept of a raked stage was abandoned by Booth, as were the notions of a stage apron and proscenium doors. Although wings were still used to create the scenic illusion, there were no grooves for their movement. Hydraulic lifts in the stage floor and several elevators were used to raise and lower pieces of scenery and set props, and an elaborate fly system above the stage allowed other pieces of scenery to be lifted out of the audience's line of sight.

Augustin Daly is important to the development of the theatre not only because of his theatre structures—the Fifth Avenue Theatre (1869), Daly's Theatre, New York (1879), and Daly's Theatre, London (1893)—but because he insisted on absolute control of every aspect of his productions. Daly was probably the most important figure since the Duke of Saxe-Meiningen in establishing the position and authority of the director. With him the producer-director began to be the major figure in the American theatre. Not only did Daly insist upon and provide realistic special effects with his productions, but he also insisted on training and coaching his own actors. With John Drew II (1853–1927), Ada Rehan (1860–1916), James Lewis (1840–1896), and Mrs. G. H. Gilbert (1822–1904), it is likely that Daly had the finest acting ensemble in the country.

If Booth's Theatre revealed what technical innovations could mean to

Steele MacKaye's elevator stage at the Madison Square Theatre, 1880.

realistic theatre production, then the Madison Square Theatre of J. Steele MacKaye, which opened in 1880, was a technological masterpiece. The theatre was equipped with a double stage, one above the other, so that when one set was completely in view of the audience, the other stage could be fitted with the subsequent set. In his lifetime MacKaye produced many theatrical innovations, including a project for the Chicago World's Fair of 1893 and the establishment of the first professional acting school in New York.

The most flamboyant of the producer-directors of the early twentieth century was David Belasco. The most successful proponent of spectacular realism, Belasco was known for his attention to technical details. Perhaps his most enduring contribution was in the area of stage lighting. For his production of *Madame Butterfly* (1900), Belasco treated his audience to a seventeen-minute fade from evening to dawn, and hung spotlights from the balcony rail position to give to his actors increased three-dimensionality. Because his dedication to realism required that the proscenium must be absolute as the frame for his plays, footlights were eliminated from his productions.

Like Daly, Belasco insisted upon the control of every aspect of the production. Consequently he became a leading "starmaker," casting unknown

David Belasco.

(Courtesy of the National Portrait Gallery, Smithsonian Institution, Washington, D.C.)

A scene from the first act of Belasco's The Girl of the Golden West *(1905).*
(Courtesy of the Theatre Collection of the Museum of the City of New York)

actors and working with them until their stardom created more independence than the somewhat dictatorial director could allow. Belasco continued to be a major force in the theatre until his death in 1931.

The Departure from Realism

The American theatre generally paid little attention to European staging innovation in the late nineteenth and early twentieth centuries, and it emerged from its cultural cocoon only after the First World War. This awareness came about through the various nonprofessional and educational theatre groups that were emerging in the early twentieth century. The major commercial theatres of New York could not afford the financial risk of experimentation, so they clung to the mainstream of realism for their plays. The little theatre movement and educational theatre were primarily responsible for advancing the case of the New Stagecraft in America. Built along the pattern of the European Independent Theatre Movement, the little theatre movement used volunteers for all aspects of production and was dependent upon gifts and subscriptions for financial support. By 1920 this group of theatres had done much to pave the way for the acceptance of new stagecraft production methods in the United States.

That is not to say that the commercial theatre was not aware of New

Stagecraft techniques and trends. But it was the smaller, often regionally based companies and producers that provided visibility for these techniques. Notable among the early-twentieth-century efforts in this regard were the Little Theatre of Winthrop Ames and the contributions of Joseph Urban at the Boston Opera Company. Perhaps the most significant single event was the 1915 New York Stage Society production of *The Man Who Married a Dumb Wife*. The scene designs for the production were by Robert Edmond Jones (1887–1954), and they are considered to be the first expression of New Stagecraft techniques in the United States. In addition to the groups already mentioned, other production groups like the Provincetown Players, the Theatre Guild, and the Washington Square Players provided the framework for the gradual acceptance of the new European techniques into the theatrical mainstream of the United States by 1930.

ACTORS AND THE TRAVELING SHOW

Like the playhouse, acting and acting styles experienced profound changes in the late nineteenth and early twentieth centuries. American acting significantly matured during this period as well. Recognition of American actors abroad, which had begun before 1850 with Edwin Forrest, Charlotte Cushman, and Anna Cora Mowatt, increased considerably after the Civil War. By the end of the century American actors were pleasing European audiences as well as their own.

Acting styles after the Civil War were basically a continued modification and evolution of the more realistic elements that had existed in American acting before the outbreak of hostilities. Such performers as Minnie Maddern Fiske (1865–1932), Maude Adams (1872–1953), Lionel Barrymore (1878–1954), and Ethel Barrymore (1870–1959) all moved American acting to a new emphasis on the intellect rather than on emotionalism. Among these, Fiske, one of the leading actresses of her day, was a chief exponent of realistic drama, particularly in her championing of the production of Ibsen in the United States. Because her productions emphasized strong ensemble playing and her own acting style incorporated logical motivation, she made significant contributions to the development of twentieth-century American acting and directing.

The Organization of Acting

The most profound changes in the organizational system of the American theatre occurred in the structure of acting companies and in the marketing of these companies throughout the United States. Before 1870 the number of resident companies actually increased throughout the nation, but their greater dependence on the traveling star was already sounding the death knell for the resident repertory actors. A number of notable theatre managers, such as Augustin Daly, Laura Keene, and William Burton, tried to counter the effect of the star system by maintaining resident companies, but the die was cast.

Theatre in the United States to World War I

Maude Adams.

The traveling star and touring company were not the only innovations in the late nineteenth century that served to undermine the resident repertory company. Another and perhaps more damaging charge was the notion of the long run. As long as the repertory system was flourishing, no play was given more than a dozen times consecutively in any particular season, and then it was placed in the repertory with other plays to be alternated throughout the season. Obviously any increase in the length of the run of any play would lead to a decrease in the number of plays presented in any one season. By the 1890s repertory theatre had come to mean the presentation of a series of plays given for relatively long runs. This was a logical extension of a theatre practice developed after 1870, the combination company. This full company, including star performers, toured without the need of a resident company as backup support. The effect of this practice was devastating to the resident repertory company. Of the fifty permanent companies in 1870, none remained after 1900.

Another change that greatly affected the actor's position in the United States in the late nineteenth century was the gradual shift to producing a single play

Minnie Maddern Fiske in the title role of Ibsen's Hedda Gabler.
(Courtesy of KaiDib Films International, Glendale, Calif.)

and planning for it to run as long as possible. New York was by the 1880s the center of American theatrical production, and not only combination companies but duplicate companies—road companies for a current New York show—were common. In addition the situation for the individual actor had changed drastically from the early part of the nineteenth century. Not only had the sharing system been abandoned, but the traditional benefit performance had given way by 1880 to a straight salary system. New York's emergence as the theatrical hub required that actors use the city as their base for employment in the arts. The long running show meant that most actors were hired for a single play. By the beginning of the twentieth century, typecasting had replaced casting according to the traditional lines of business that had been in use for two hundred years. Because theatre was now big business, the position of the nonstar actor was none too secure. Consistent with the plight of workers in other areas of big business in the United States at that time, the actor's two-century predominance in theatre was closing. Henceforth, the producer-director and starmaker would be the preeminent and controlling figure on the American theatrical scene.

Poster for a melodrama of the period.
(Courtesy of KaiDib Films International, Glendale, Calif.)

DRAMA

Following the Civil War, American playwrights found their scripts were affected by three possible factors. First there was the continued presence of melodrama, which would continue to dominate American play writing for the balance of the century. The second influence, most notable after 1870, was the rising influence of dramatic realism and the tendency of playwrights to concentrate on the character and locality of the American scene. Third, American play writing was influenced by the broad diversity of American tastes themselves. The stage types of the Yankee, the frontiersman, and the Indian enjoyed a cross-fertilization with other aspects of the popular theatre of the nineteenth century, and this created a range of dramatic offerings unparalleled in the theatre. The cultural and economic boom that followed the Civil War created a need for every type of dramatic expression, from the old classic repertory to the wild west shows of Buffalo Bill Cody. But melodrama was king, and only as the twentieth century began did realism take center stage.

Playwrights

Important to the general development of American play writing was Bronson Howard (1842–1909). His immensely popular *Shenandoah* (1888), which dealt with an aspect of the Civil War, attracted audiences for many years. The story is highly intricate, and the characters and melodramatic intrigues are complex. In production it made great use of spectacle that dazzled the eye with its numerous realistic stage effects. Howard advanced the art of American play writing by the inventiveness of his stories, his ability to write clever dialogue, and his keen sense of proper theatrical effects. Howard's contribution to American play writing did not stop with his writing alone. He organized the American Dramatists Club (later known as the Society of American Dramatists and Composers), and he was instrumental in the strengthening of copyright laws.

Another contributor to the growing tide of realism was William Gillette (1855–1937). He was most active in melodrama, writing and acting in many plays that combined the exciting physical and emotional action of that type of play with a keenly defined sense of realistic detail. In his play *Secret Service* (1895), one act takes place in a telegraph office done in such authentic detail as to include the presence of a working telegraph key. In such details American technological innovation and drama were closely fused. Reviews of Gillette's acting indicate a realistic manner relatively free from the excesses of the romantic style, with great attention paid to understated detail.

Probably the most influential early disciple of dramatic realism in the United

William Gillette (right) in his stage adaptation of Sherlock Holmes *(1899). Gillette successfully played this role until 1931.*

(Courtesy of the Theatre Collection of the Museum of the City of New York)

States was James A. Herne (1839–1901). Herne switched from a writing career that had centered on melodrama to that of being a champion of realism. After receiving encouragement from David Belasco for his early works in realism, Herne made a major contribution to the development of realism on the American stage with *Margaret Flemming* (1890). Although the subject matter of the play caused most commercial theatre managers to reject the script (it dealt with infidelity and illegitimacy), it nonetheless was a great advance for American dramaturgy.

As the twentieth century began, Clyde Fitch (1865–1909) was considered the leading realistic dramatist of his day. Fitch was a prolific and popular writer, and at one time he had four of his plays running concurrently on Broadway. In order to ensure that the realistic elements in his plays were observed, Fitch assumed complete responsibility for every production detail, including casting and directing. His major plays are *The Girl and the Judge* (1901), *The Girl with the Green Eyes* (1902), *The Truth* (1906), and *The City* (1909).

William Vaughan Moody (1869–1910) appeared at the turn of the century as a dramatist of great promise. Unfortunately his untimely death at the age of

Clyde Fitch.
(Courtesy of KaiDib Films International, Glendale, Calif.)

Clyde Fitch's Captain Jinks of the Horse Marines *(1901), which provided the young Ethel Barrymore (*right*) with her first starring role.*
(Courtesy of the Theatre Collection of the Museum of the City of New York)

forty-one left only two major plays, *The Great Divide* (1906) and *The Faith Healer* (1909), for posterity to judge his talents. Dealing with starkly American situations and character types, Moody's plays were almost too intellectual and idealistic for mass popular taste. Yet his plays were significant in moving American drama out of its nineteenth-century stereotypes.

As the nineteenth century was coming to a close, dramatic realism began to replace melodrama in the mainstream of public taste, and more intellectual approaches to realistic play writing, such as in the works of Fitch and Moody, were beginning to bring audiences to the theatre.

VAUDEVILLE, BURLESQUE, AND THE BIRTH OF THE AMERICAN MUSICAL

As noted in the last chapter, theatre in the nineteenth-century United States was a broad form of popular entertainment. This theatre, which included such dramatic forms as vaudeville, burlesque, the minstrel show, the circus, and the wild west show, provided the mass entertainment of the period. Like film and television in our own time, it was a type of theatre that seemed to fit the sprawling expansionist character of the century. It was theatre that could cross all barriers created by taste and language, and it had a universal base in appealing to all classes of people.

Vaudeville

Vaudeville, or the variety show, was essentially a collection of individual acts emphasizing singing, comedy, dancing, mimicry, and other isolated speciality performances. These were loosely gathered together into a single show to form a full evening's entertainment. At the beginning of the nineteenth century, these speciality acts had already found an audience in the saloons and concert halls of America. By the conclusion of the Civil War, this popular entertainment was well established in virtually every sizable town in the United States, and it was to contribute to the establishment of the great vaudeville circuits that flourished before the Great Depression. Among the popular theatre forms discussed in the preceding chapter, the

Tony Pastor's Theatre in New York.
(Courtesy of the Theatre Collection of the Museum of the City of New York)

minstrel show contributed most significantly to the form and substance of vaudeville.

Vaudeville was originally considered too rowdy for women and children. It was through the efforts of one man, Tony Pastor (1837–1908), that vaudeville became accepted as family entertainment. Working in New York, Pastor put together a wholesome bill of variety entertainment and advertised it as acceptable for family consumption. The entertainments were quite mixed and varied, not unlike portions of the televised variety show of today. At first the public was quite skeptical of Pastor's efforts, but as he proved he could deliver what he advertised, public acceptability rose and vaudeville became a major entertainment form.

Burlesque

In its original form, burlesque was a parody or takeoff on some serious subject, either a play, person, or event. Following the Civil War, George L. Fox (1825–1877) was making a steady practice of providing parodies on famous Shakespearian heroes, and his burlesque pantomime *Humpty Dumpty* ran for an extended period from its introduction in 1868. It was not long, however, before burlesque began to diverge from its original purpose into what we expect from the genre today. Individual producers began introducing scantily clad women into burlesque in the early nineteenth century, but this practice was reestablished in 1866 with the opening of a spectacular extravaganza known as *The Black Crook*. This unlikely marriage of a melodrama and a stranded ballet company was tremendously popular; it ran for sixteen months and played in excess of two thousand performances. *The Black Crook* was the first attempt, however crude, to put ballet into a story-based musical format. Staging was quite elaborate, with extensive use of dance and a large ensemble of chorus girls.

Ixion, an English import of 1868, was the next significant contribution to the development of burlesque and the musical. In this play Lydia Thompson and her "British Blondes" provided New York with a mixture of songs, dances, and other variety-type activity. Although criticized for its lack of dramatic content, *Ixion* was sufficiently popular for Thompson and her blondes to tour the United States for ten years. The last thirty years of the nineteenth century saw the popularity of burlesque spread rapidly throughout America. Managers who did not mount full-fledged burlesque shows were certainly willing to add burlesque segments to their variety or minstrel shows. And the public was more than willing to pay for a fleeting glimpse of a lady in tights.

The Musical

The birth of the American musical had no magical starting date. Song and dance had been a part of the American stage since the middle of the eighteenth century. Certainly vaudeville and burlesque made heavy use of musical numbers, but not in the same manner as the blend of story and music that was first seen in the United States in William Dunlap's *The*

Archers (1796). *The Black Crook* further refined the basic elements of the musical show with its combination of story, singing, dancing, and spectacle. Added to this were elements borrowed from the operetta format, introduced by Gilbert and Sullivan when their *H.M.S. Pinafore* was done in New York in 1879. Operetta brought romance and glamour to the musical scene; it also brought heavy dependence upon European settings and models. Operetta writers such as Victor Herbert, Rudolph Friml, and Sigmund Romberg helped change the settings for operetta from Europe to the United States, yet the European influence was still significant.

A break from the European traditions was introduced by George M. Cohan (1878–1941). His plays were distinctly American. Working in what was essentially a star-system revue, Cohan brought the American colloquial idiom to the musical. His 1904 production of *Little Johnny Jones*, with its story and music somewhat integrated into a general dramatic theme, was a significant step foward for the developing American musical. Yet it would remain for Jerome Kern and Guy Bolton to create the first true musical in the years just before the First World War.

George M. Cohan in the title role of Little Johnny Jones *(1904).*

(Courtesy of Hoblitzelle Theatre Arts Library, Humanities Research Library, University of Texas at Austin)

COMMERCIALISM AND THE THEATRE: FROM ART TO BIG BUSINESS

As the nineteenth century began, the business of theatre in the United States was still in the hands of actors. By the end of the century, however, the seeds were already planted for the commercialism and trust-building extant in other segments of American business to enter the theatre. With New York the theatrical center for generating traveling road shows, significant booking problems emerged that often left local theatre managers with major holes in a season's schedule. Recognizing the problem, and how they might control it to their great financial advantage, a small group of men in Philadelphia and New York formed the Theatrical Syndicate in 1896. Chief among these men was Charles Frohman (1854–1915), since he was the only one of the group to be involved in the production details of the operation. The tactics of the Syndicate were quite simple. No attempt was made to gain direct control over all the country's theatres. The tactic was to concentrate on the large cities and the key touring routes between them. Theatres too far off the beaten path were not important enough for the Syndicate to deal with, and in time they would simply be unable to draw an audience. If the Syndicate could not gain outright control of the theatres it did want to own, it built rival houses and stocked them with superb productions at prices that undercut the competition. Simple economics soon forced the competing "target" theatres to go bankrupt, at which time they usually met the Syndicate's terms. Actors and producers who resisted the Syndicate were not used in its shows. Through these tactics, the Syndicate effectively controlled the American theatre by 1900. That accomplished, it was in a position to influence play choice significantly. The Syndicate would not produce and tour works that in Frohman's judgment would not appeal to a mass audience. Another of Frohman's tenets was that stars with large public followings were necessary to support Syndicate efforts. Consequently, actors such as Otis Skinner (1858–1942), Maude Adams (1872–1953), and Ethel Barrymore (1879–1959) were among those used in Syndicate productions. All of this reduced the American theatre to a business venture catering to mass public taste. Experimentation, so necessary for art to survive, enjoyed little support.

As in other areas of a free enterprise system, monopolistic control is difficult to maintain. Important in resisting Syndicate control were Minnie Maddern Fiske, Sarah Bernhardt (American tours 1880–1918), David Belasco, and the Shuberts (Sam, Lee, and Jacob). By the close of the first decade of the twentieth century, Belasco's work was sufficiently popular that the Syndicate had to accept his terms. This major concession to Belasco was the first important break in the Syndicate's control and was brought about, in part, by the rise of a rival booking agency under the control of the Shuberts. The clash between the Shuberts and the Syndicate began as early as 1905 when the Syndicate disallowed its theatres to show Shubert productions. The rival theatre chain that the Shuberts established at that time was embraced by many local theatre owners who were dissatisfied with the Syndicate's methods. By 1910 the Shuberts had established an effective rivalry with the Syndicate, and they took control of the American theatre following Charles Frohman's death in 1915. No better than the Syndicate in terms of dictatorial control, they continued to control the mainstream of American theatre well into the twentieth century, and only a government order in 1956 finally forced them to sell many of their road theatres.

CONCLUSION

Commercialization placed a heavy burden on the American theatre. There was virtually no risk taking or innovation, as the Theatrical Syndicate and the Shuberts guaranteed that what most Americans saw was calculated to mass appeal. It would be up to the theatre practitioner of the middle twentieth century to chart new directions and provide new forms for the American theatre.

RETROSPECT

The development of the American theatre was parallel to the development of the country itself. Originally a pioneer society concerned with the struggle to establish itself, the United States had unrefined cultural needs. Yet the early thirst for theatre was quenched by itinerant players and plays suited to the tastes and times. By the middle of the eighteenth century, the country was culturally stable enough to attract the first professional theatre efforts, and these were tremendously popular. When the eighteenth century ended, theatre organization in the United States centered on several repertory companies, each in a large city in the East and each touring productions to its immediate region.

As the nineteenth century began, playwrights in the United States captured the emerging egalitarianism, materialism, and anti-intellectualism of the nation by interjecting distinctly American characters and forms into the drama. The United States was beginning to discover its identity, and the drama reinforced the innate worth of the country and its people. By the middle of the century, theatre had expanded to the South and Midwest, following the general expansion into those areas and developing along a pattern similar to that which had been employed in the East. Yet fundamental changes in theatrical organization were beginning to occur following the public's changing and expanding tastes. The traveling star and combination company, for example, would alter theatre organization forever. The playhouse and its production machinery grew increasingly representational, reacting to the dictates of melodrama and the emerging realism desired by the public. By 1880 the West had been conquered and theatre had established itself among the people in that region. Production was aimed at mounting a single play and running as many consecutive performances as possible. At the close of the century, the resident repertory company was dead.

By 1900 theatres presented spectacular realism routinely through the use of the box setting and detailed exterior settings. The golden age of American acting was waning as the theatre, like the country, shifted to big business, with the producer-director as the major figure among the collective artists of theatre practice. As in other areas of business, theatrical trusts were established, then broken. By 1920 the rejuvenation needed in the American theatre was recognized by producers and public alike as they beheld a commercially successful yet artistically sterile product.

Date	U.S. History	U.S. Theatre History	World History	World Theatre History
800–1000	Viking exploration and settlement.		Norman invasion of England.	Quem quaeritis Easter trope.
1453			Fall of Eastern Roman Empire.	
1492–1504	Columbus's voyages to the Americas.			
1558			Elizabeth I begins reign.	
1580				Teatro Olimpico.
1588			Defeat of Spanish Armada.	
1606				Ben Jonson's *Volpone*.
1607	Establishment of Jamestown colony.			
1616			Richelieu becomes French minister of state.	Death of Shakespeare.
1620	Plymouth colony established.			
1626	Dutch buy Manhattan Island.			
1636				Corneille's *El Cid*.
1642				London theatres closed.
1649			Charles I of England beheaded.	
1665		*Ye Bare and Ye Cubb* performed.		
1666			Great London Fire.	
1670	Charleston established.			
1673				Molière's *The Imaginary Invalid*.
1674				Drury Lane Theatre opens.

Date	U.S. History	U.S. Theatre History	World History	World Theatre History
1670	Bacon's Rebellion.			
1680				Comédie Française founded.
1703		Anthony Aston, strolling player.		
1706	Ben Franklin born.			
1715			Death of Louis XIV.	
1716		First playhouse erected.		
1732	George Washington born.			
1737				Licensing Act.
1741				David Garrick's debut.
1752		Hallam family arrives in colonies.		
1756	French and Indian War begins.			
1765	Stamp Act. Founding of the Sons of Liberty.			
1766		John Street Theatre built. Godfrey's *Prince of Parthia*.		
1769			Birth of Napoleon.	
1770	Boston Massacre.			
1771				DeLoutherbourg engaged by Garrick.
1772				Royal Danish Theatre founded.
1773	Boston Tea Party.			
1775	Battle of Bunker Hill.	Old American Company leaves for Jamaica.		Goethe begins management of Weimar Court Theatre.

(Continued on page 506)

Date	U.S. History	U.S. Theatre History	World History	World Theatre History
1776	Declaration of Independence.			David Garrick retires from stage.
1776–1781	American Revolution.			
1782		Old American Company returns.		
1787		Royall Tyler's *The Contrast*.		
1789	President Washington's first term.		French Revolution.	
1798		Park Theatre opens.		Pixérécourt's *Victor*.
1800			Napoleon comes to power in France.	
1803		Dunlap's *The Glory of Columbia*.		
1810		George Frederick Cooke's first U.S. tour.		
1812–	War of 1812.			Birth of Wagner.
1815			Battle of Waterloo.	
1820		Edmund Kean's first U.S. tour.		
1823				Charles Kemble's *King John*.
1829	President Jackson's first term.	Edwin Forrest first appears in *Metamora*.		
1830				*Hernani* riot at Comédie Française.
1831		Chapman's first showboat.		
1834		St. Charles Theatre opens.		
1836	Republic of Texas established.			

Date	U.S. History	U.S. Theatre History	World History	World Theatre History
1837			Queen Victoria begins reign.	
1844				Charles Fechter's debut.
1846–1848	War with Mexico.			
1848	Gold discovered in California.			
1849		Astor Place riot.		Birth of Strindberg.
1853			Crimean War begins.	
1856		Edwin Booth's N.Y. debut.		
1857	Dred Scott decision. John Brown's raid on Harper's Ferry.			
1861–1865	Civil War.		Serfs emancipated in Russia. (1861)	Sarah Bernhardt's debut. (1862)
1865	Lincoln assassinated by actor in Ford's Theatre.			Constanin Stanislavsky born.
1866	President Grant's first term. Completion of transcontinental railroad.	*The Black Crook.* Booth's Theatre opens.		
1870			Franco-Prussian War.	
1874				Meiningen Players' first tour.
1876	Telephone invented by Bell.			Festspielhaus opens at Bayreuth.
1877	End of Reconstruction era in South.			
1879		Daly's Theatre opens.		Ibsen's *A Doll House.*
1883		Henry Irving's first U.S. tour.		
1887			Queen Victoria's Golden Jubilee.	Antoine's Théâtre Libre opens.

(Continued on page 508)

Date	U.S. History	U.S. Theatre History	World History	World Theatre History
1888		Eugene O'Neill born.		
1895				H. Irving knighted.
1896		Theatrical Syndicate established.	Tsar Nicholas II begins reign.	
1898	Spanish-American War.			Moscow Art Theatre established.
1900		Belasco's *Madame Butterfly* staged.	Boxer Rebellion in China.	
1901	President McKinley assassinated. T. Roosevelt becomes President.		Death of Queen Victoria.	Chekhov's *Three Sisters*.
1903	Wright brothers' first flight.	Porter's film *The Great Train Robbery*.		
1904		Cohan's *Little Johnny Jones*.		Abbey Theatre opens.
1905				E. G. Craig publishes *Art of Theatre*.
1906	San Francisco earthquake.			
1907		Ziegfeld Follies begin.		
1913	President Wilson begins first term.	Shubert brothers break Theatrical Syndicate.		Théâtre du Vieux Colombier established.
1914	Panama Canal opens.		World War I begins.	
1915		Provincetown Players founded. J. Kern's *Very Good Eddie*.		
1917	U.S. enters World War I.		October Revolution in Russia.	Apollinaire's *The Breasts of Tiresias* produced.

Date	U.S. History	U.S. Theatre History	World History	World Theatre History
1918	World War I ends.	Theatre Guild established.		
1919	Volstead Act (Prohibition) passed by Congress.	Actors Equity strike closes down Broadway.	First aircraft crossing of Atlantic.	Jessner's *Richard III* at Berlin State Theatre.

SELECTED READINGS

Coad, Oral S., and Edwin Mims, Jr. *The American Stage*. Vol. 14 of *The Pageant of America*. New Haven: Yale University Press, 1929.
    A detailed pictorial and narrative account of the early history of the American theatre.

Dunlap, William. *History of the American Theatre*. New York: Burt Franklin, 1963.
    A reprint of the first history of the American stage, originally published in 1797, written by one of the major contributors to the development of theatre in the U.S.

Graham, Philip. *Showboats: The History of an American Institution*. Austin: University of Texas Press, 1976.
    The best available account of the rise and decline of this form of American theatre.

Hewitt, Barnard. *Theatre U.S.A., 1668–1957*. New York: McGraw-Hill, 1959.
    A detailed examination of the development of American theatre to the mid–twentieth century. Extensive quotations from other sources document this work.

Ludlow, Noah M. *Dramatic Life As I Found It*. New York: Benjamin Blom, 1966.
    First published in 1880, this is a fascinating firsthand account of an actor's life in the early years of the nineteenth century.

Meserve, Walter J. *An Emerging Entertainment: The Drama of the American People to 1828*. Bloomington: Indiana University Press, 1977.
    A highly informative study of the drama and theatre of the early republic.

Moody, Richard. *America Takes the Stage: Romanticism in American Drama and Theatre, 1750–1900*. Bloomington: Indiana University Press, 1955.
    A fine thematic treatment of the nineteenth-century stage, with particular attention paid to native themes and characters.

_____. *Edwin Forrest: First Star of the American Stage*. New York: Alfred A. Knopf, 1960.
    The best of the biographies of the first major American actor.

Poggi, Jack. *Theatre in America: The Impact of Economic Forces, 1870–1967*. Ithaca: Cornell University Press, 1968.
    An interesting study of the business of show business. Important for an understanding of the understructure of the modern American stage.

Quinn, Arthur H. *A History of the American Drama from the Beginning to the Civil War*. New York: Appleton-Century-Crofts, 1923.

_____. *A History of the American Drama from the Civil War to the Present Day*. New York: Appleton-Century-Crofts, 1927.
    Dated but still highly useful volumes on the history of American play writing.

Rankin, Hugh F. *The Theatre in Colonial America*. Chapel Hill: University of North Carolina Press, 1960.
    This work is the major study of the American stage before the Revolutionary War.

Toll, Robert C. *Blacking Up: The Minstrel Show in Nineteenth-Century America*. New York: Oxford University Press, 1974.

The most complete history available of this uniquely American contribution to world theatre.

_____. *On With the Show: The First Century of Show Business in America*. New York: Oxford University Press, 1976.

This wonderful book contains chapters on P. T. Barnum, the circus, minstrel shows, vaudeville, Flo Ziegfeld, and the early forms of the musical. Contains many illustrations.

Wilson, Garff B. *A History of American Acting*. Bloomington: Indiana University Press, 1966.

This excellent history traces the development of American acting from the 1820s to the middle of the twentieth century.

_____. *Three Hundred Years of American Drama and Theatre*. Englewood Cliffs, N.J.: Prentice-Hall, 1973.

A highly readable account of the evolution of theatre in the United States, this work is the best one-volume treatment of the subject now available.

NEW YORK

●MOSCOW

PART XII

Distortions in the Mirror:
TWENTIETH-CENTURY
THEATRE TO 1950

The first half of the twentieth century witnessed unprecedented advances in science and technology that transformed the outlook and habits of civilization. It also marked the most violent and self-destructive era in human history. This paradoxical situation, a world that holds both the promise of Utopia and the terror of Armageddon, has created a human consciousness that is unique to the twentieth century.

Rapid mass communication has compounded the problematic nature of this situation, for at no previous time in history have so many of the world's problems been presented to so many of the world's people. The vastness of it all has led many to feelings of despair, inadequacy, and intellectual paralysis. The fragmentation of the theatre in this century is a direct result of this new consciousness.

The early part of the century saw increasing levels of dissatisfaction with the tenets of realism by certain segments of the theatrical world. The symbolists and expressionists sought to add new meaning to productions by going beyond surface reality. The surrealists, dadaists, and futurists totally repudiated the traditional theatre and strove to create new art forms. Mainstream theatre continued to work in the realistic manner. The period of the First World War was conservative in theatrical matters, and the twenties may be considered nearly reactionary. Only in revolutionary Russia were theatrical innovations actively encouraged. The economic problems of the 1930s resulted in an increasing emphasis on social issues onstage and increasing competition for the theatre from other mass entertainment forms. The post–World War II era would find the theatre being relegated to a lesser position as a social mirror, and in future decades its very vitality as a living art form would be seriously questioned.

24

THE REVOLT AGAINST REALISM

It has been suggested that the one constant of the human species is change. We are at once a paradox: while we need the surety of routine, we constantly seek change in the status quo to keep life interesting and avoid boredom. This is the life pattern of modern Western humanity. It is a pattern in our aesthetic lives as well, spilling into every artistic choice we make. The mind-set for making these choices was established in the early decades of the twentieth century. Whether we embrace the specific artistic styles discussed in this chapter or not, they have conditioned us, and we respond accordingly.

Background: The Mainstream Modified

As the twentieth century dawned, the dominant aesthetic in the theatre continued to be realism. Although this chapter deals with the departures from this aesthetic, it clearly remained the mainstream throughout the first half of the century, and, in fact, continued to grow and prosper. A case in point is the development of realism in Ireland, seen primarily in the workings of the Abbey Theatre. The Abbey Theatre developed along similar lines as the Independent Theatre Movement theatres in that a few people felt the need for a strong artistic, national drama and a place for its presentation. Dublin was a natural site for such a venture, and in 1904 the theatre opened with William Butler Yeats's *On Baile's Strand* and Lady Augusta Gregory's *Spreading the News*.

During the next half-dozen years, the Abbey increased in stature, presenting realistic pieces and Irish poetic drama. A turn toward greater realism was taken in 1910 under the management of Lennox Robinson, who established a major touring program, including tours to the United States. Throughout its early years, the Abbey Theatre sponsored a number of playwrights whose work contributed to the development of world drama. Among these were J. M. Synge's *Riders to the Sea* (1904) and *The Playboy of the Western World* (1907), Shaw's *The Shewing-Up of Blanco Posnet* (1909), and O'Casey's *Juno and the Paycock* (1924). In 1924 the Abbey became the first English-speaking state-supported theatre when it received a government grant from Eire. Thereafter its financial success was assured, and it gradually turned toward more Irish poetic drama, which required its actors to be fluent in Gaelic. By midcentury it had clearly established itself as the preeminent theatre in Ireland and as one of the major theatre centers in the Western world. As the Abbey entered the decades after 1950, it successfully operated within the constraints of realism, but it also managed to handle some of the antirealistic forms as well.

Not all theatre operations were as successful in walking between forms. In fact, most operated with one dominant style as the hallmark of the producing organization or, in a few cases, the producer. The styles to be considered in this chapter all had such exponents, and all functioned as pure examples of the philosophies they represented, at least in their initial, active phase. A revolt from realism must, after all, be initially a revolt.

General Aesthetic Considerations

The reasons for the general revolt were many and varied. They fall, however, into two distinct types: artistic and philosophical. Artistically, those advocating a departure from realism believed that art had a higher calling than just the representation of objective life on the stage; that the theatre had a responsibility to create a truly theatrical environment for its audience. Thus most of the departures from realism argued for the restoration of theatricality to dramatic literature and production. This theatricality took several forms. Theme replaced story as the major dramatic element, and the stage was viewed as a platform for the actor's use. The actor was responsible for evoking the audience's imagination and heightening its willingness to participate in a frankly make-believe situation. Often the plane of the proscenium arch was broken as actor and audience reunited in a celebration of a shared theatre experience, much like the Greek, medieval, Elizabethan, and *commedia dell'arte* theatre experiences. The illusion created might well continue to be representational, but clearly all of it was taking place in the theatre. This heightened theatricality had its own paradoxes: the actor was simultaneously an actor and a character; setting details were at once representative of objective life and symbolic of it. A dual level of audience consciousness was required—a separate and simultaneous awareness of reality and theatricality present in the same production.

Philosophically, the revolt's movements from realism were rooted in a high concern for humanity and in a growing belief that scientism, positivism, and technology could not, in and of themselves, make things better for the world. Social scientists, under the influence of Darwin and Comte, had not been able to solve humanity's problems, and technology had served to further dehumanize the species. Materialism and the ugliness of the world were philosophically rejected as the revolt movements alternately took mystical flights into the rather ideal world of higher truth and beauty, one reminiscent of the universal truths of German romanticism in the late eighteenth century. Whatever specific forms the revolts from realism took, they were filled with the subjectivism and humanitarianism thought missing from that "lower" art of the theatre, realism.

In all cases truth in the theatre was sought, but the concept of truth was seen as larger than the objective perceptions of the eye. For a time the eye of the soul became more important.

The revolts from realism were accepted selectively. A significant portion of the theatregoing public never totally accepted the concepts. The essential problem here was one of the universality of the symbols employed in creating the notion of the ideal. As long as objective reality was the goal of theatrical endeavor, practitioners and audience alike had a standard against which to judge theatrical activity. In departing from that goal, some practitioners and many audience members no longer had a sufficiently common standard against which to judge a work of theatrical art, owing to the subjective nature of the work. Thus questions like "How do I know this is good?" were difficult to answer. With the universality of objective artistic standards gone, the chance for charlatans increased exponentially, potentially leading the public into accepting bad artistic work passed off as good. The twentieth-century alienation of artists from a large segment of the general public stems from this chicanery, but enough good practitioners established standards of excellence, if not of common understanding, so that this alienation was not total. But it remained true that for the vast majority of theatre consumers in the early twentieth century, realism was the primary product.

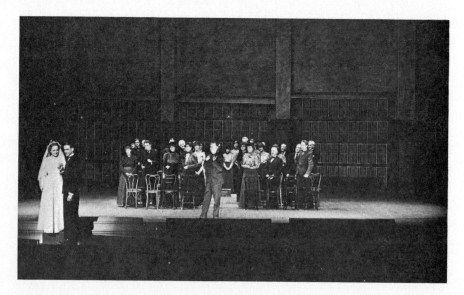

A scene from the original New York production of Thornton Wilder's Our Town *(1938), which rejected the scenic conventions of realism.*

(Courtesy of the Theatre Collection of the Museum of the City of New York)

SYMBOLISM

The revolt against realism known as symbolism was briefly introduced in the discussion of the New Stagecraft in Chapter 21. But the movement was considerably larger than the scope of that introduction.

Philosophy

As its basic philosophical aim, symbolism attempted to dramatize fleeting impressions and vague, chaotic feelings about visions and dreams. The goal was to produce the illusion of subjective reality through verisimilitude. The play, then, became a metaphor, and allegory occupied an important place in the playwright's lexicon of values. With symbolism, the return of the poet to the theatre occurred in the works of such playwrights as Leonid Andreyev, Maurice Maeterlinck, Edmond Rostand, T. S. Eliot, and W. B. Yeats. These and other playwrights brought symbolism into their works by using concrete images to express a larger abstract idea or emotion. The images were generally employed in some combination of two types: particular objects were used in highly personal and private ways by the playwright, and concrete images were used to suggest an ideal world apart from objective reality. In the latter case, playwrights deliberately obscured objective reality so that the images of the idealized world became clearer for the audience.

If symbolism had a definitive manifesto, or statement of intentions, it probably first appeared in 1886 in the newspaper *Le Figaro*. There Jean Moreas pronounced realism dead and declared that symbolic poetry was the ideal to be cherished from that point on. As in most of the revolts from realism, symbolism started not in the theatre but in the literary world. Theatre remains a reflective art to the society in which it exists and rarely takes the lead in new artistic movements. Yet once a new movement appears, it is often the theatre that gives it its first broadbased exposure. So it was with the various revolts against realism.

Production Practices

Symbolist theatre in practice was very consistent with the philosophical aims of the movement. The emphasis of all production aspects supported the creation of the illusion of the reality of the spirit by using symbols to suggest that reality. In scenery simplification was the key, as the works of Appia and Craig attest. The aim was to achieve great beauty in the theatre through movement, and the New Stagecraft experiments nobly served that aim. Appia led the way in lighting by creating concepts that allowed light to be the unifier of the total atmosphere of mood or tone in the play. In the United States the work of Robert Edmond Jones made practical the ideas of Appia and Craig, and with his works symbolist design moved further into mainstream theatre. Acting and directing were also modified to suit the

*Robert Edmond Jones, one of America's leading symbolist designers, created this set for
the New York production of Eugene O'Neill's* Mourning Becomes Electra.
(Courtesy of KaiDib Films International, Glendale, Calif.)

symbolist movement. While both remained essentially representational, objective reality was emphasized less than other concerns. Exaggerated yet truncated movement suggested larger patterns of reality, with each move economically planned to represent the whole. Occasionally the proscenium plane was
broken. Dialogue was similarly truncated, and it was often delivered with more
staccato than in ordinary speech. In some ways, the art of the theatre had come
full circle here. The symbolists, perhaps unwittingly, were borrowing heavily
from the Greeks and the Middle Ages.

An Innovator and Several Playwrights

Although Paul Fort was the first to produce symbolist
plays, the movement's clear champion was Aurelien-Marie Lugné-Poë (1869–
1940). Lugné-Poë had worked at the Théâtre Libre and became manager of the
Théâtre d'Art after 1892. He renamed it the Théâtre de l'Oeuvre, and he was a
major force in its affairs from the opening production in 1893 until his
retirement in 1929. From the outset, Lugné-Poë concentrated on the works of
contemporary playwrights, and he specialized in French symbolists until 1897.
His production style during the early years of the Théâtre de l'Oeuvre was
characterized by simplified settings using little furniture and properties, clearly
and colorfully painted backdrops, and costuming essentially devoid of historical accuracy. In his later years, he included the works of some realistic writers
in his repertory, notably Ibsen, but the theatre generally continued its focus on

nonrealistic plays and techniques. During his career he assisted emerging playwrights, made the French theatre more aware of itself and the contemporary theatre of other countries, and contributed significantly not only to symbolism but to the other revolts through his dramatic and critical work.

Among the many playwrights who were produced at the Théâtre de l'Oeuvre, two stand out for special contributions to the symbolist cause, Maurice Maeterlinck (1862–1949) and Alfred Jarry (1873–1907). Maeterlinck's *Pélleas et Mélisande* (1892) was the opening production at the Théâtre de l'Oeuvre, and it was typical of the playwright's style. Essentially a theatrical poem, the play features characters that are moved by hidden forces around them, seen as emanating from the ethereal environment in which they live. Symbols laden with special meaning saturate the play: bloodstains that do not disappear and the dropping of wedding rings into a fountain, for example. Maeterlinck believed that only in silent times can humanity truly find itself, and these abound in his plays. Like Lugné-Poë, he modified his style in later years to reflect more of the dramatic mainstream, but his work continued to be rooted in symbolism. Of his later plays, the allegorical *L'Oiseau bleu* (The Blue Bird, 1909) serves as the best example of his use of symbolism.

Jarry's reputation as a symbolist—and a precursor to a later style, surrealism—was made primarily through one play, *Ubu Roi* (King Ubu, 1896). The

This 1967 set by Josef Svoboda illustrates the use of symbolism in a modern production of Wagner's Tristan and Isolde.

(Courtesy of KaiDib Films International, Glendale, Calif.)

play attacks the realistic theatre in its use of symbols of reality juxtaposed in bizarre ways, and through its main character, Ubu, who criticizes contemporary middle-class society for its lack of humanitarianism, its ugliness, its materialism, and its irrationality. Ubu epitomizes all this as he makes himself King of Poland through his vanity, stupidity, total lack of conventional morality, cruelty, and pomposity. The play, and its author, presented a gross picture of humanity that foreshadowed late surrealists and absurdists. Primarily for this contribution, Jarry is remembered and honored.

EXPRESSIONISM

The term "expressionism" emerged at the turn of the century and was first applied to the art of Julien Hervé and other French painters (as opposed to the impressionism of Manet), but for theatrical purposes it refers to a dramatic movement that grew out of Germany and Austria around the time of World War I. The time is important here, because expressionism essentially sprang from the dissatisfaction with authoritarianism and materialism that so occupied the consciousness of Germany during the first two decades of the twentieth century. As with the other revolts from realism, expressionism in its pure form flourished briefly but brilliantly, dominated the theatre in the early 1920s, then slipped into the theatrical backwaters. The economic and social chaos after World War I also contributed to the ascendancy of the movement and to its subjectivity and humanitarianism. But whereas the symbolists had sought refuge from the insanity of the real world by creating an ideal world of their own, the expressionists sought to attack that real world through satire and sarcasm. In the expressionistic art of painters like Kokoschka and Kandinsky can be found the violent colors and twisted forms that create expressions of their emotional state rather than comment on the outside world. By the late 1920s expressionism had run its course as a pure style, but it continued to influence a number of playwrights in the United States and Europe. Among them were Eugene O'Neill, Elmer Rice, Sean O'Casey, Thornton Wilder, Samuel Beckett, and Eugene Ionesco.

Philosophy

The philosophical purpose of expressionism was to reveal and project to an audience the inner feelings and experiences of the characters rather than the outer reality in which they exist. The focus was on the protagonist and the journeys of his or her soul through a montage of seemingly unrelated events. Thus there was an effort to displace the unities of time, place, and action by varying the direction and the speed of the thoughts articulated. In fact, expressionist plays show little interest in adhering to the restrictions of other writing epochs and styles. Thus the selection, order, and arrangement of the events of expressionist plays are done for heightened theatricality, not for logical consequence. There is an absolute rejection of the representation of the actual and factual in favor of exaggeration and distortion so as to point up thoughts on particular social, political, and psychological issues.

In all this the influence of Sigmund Freud (1856–1939) cannot be minimized. Freudian psychology played a major role in developing expressionist thought, for it gave the movement a somewhat scientific justification to look within humanity for the reasons for actions, rather than seek these justifications in the external environment advocated by the realistic school. In justifying actions internally, the movement had the impetus it needed to rationalize on the stage previously irrational thought and to argue, through the quasi-scientific method of the Freudians, that its approach was indeed truth in the theatre.

Production Practices

Much of the focus of expressionist drama is on acting and direction. The dramatic truth to be presented is that of the hero, and all other characters (and the other production aspects generally) are exaggerated, distorted, and emotionally driven. Movement is highly stylized and symbolic; much use of patterns to represent a larger whole is common. Dialogue is exaggerated, distorted, and highly emotional in order to convey the desired theme. Neither movement nor speech operate within the confines of the objective world; logical thought and action patterns are not important here. Where group movement is required, it is usually highly mechanized and forced into a pattern that is regimented yet broken. The directing style of expressionist plays is highly pictorial, with much attention paid to composition. Many areas are utilized, as are multiple levels. Balance about the stage is presented formally, albeit asymmetrically, and directorial focus is quite direct. Subtlety and innuendo are not greatly used elements in the expressionist directorial style. In the staging of these plays, there is an emphasis on downstage action and actor placement, and the entire rhythm of the production is abrupt, shocking, and staccato.

In physical production, the scenery, lighting, sound, and costumes are quite active and highly intensified to dramatize the subjective. To the objective observer, these production elements seem highly arbitrary and lacking in motivation. But the audience must remember that in expressionist production it is the mind of the protagonist that is being explored, and that mind determines the reality of the objects presented.

Playwrights

A number of playwrights experimented with expressionism either as a phase of their writing or as a technique to incorporate into other styles, but the leading exponent in terms of developing the pure style was George Kaiser (1878–1945). Kaiser was less concerned with a literary drama than with dramatizing a dramatic argument. His plays do not center on character creation, but rather explore contemporary consciousness. The early plays sought to attack earlier dramatic forms, and they stressed with alarm humanity's dependence on environmental concerns. In his *Von Morgens bis Mitternachts* (From Morn to Midnight, 1916), an Everyman figure searches for life's inner meaning but succumbs to the evils of external society. In *Gas II* (1920), Kaiser illustrates the fall of humanity to the evils of industrialization. August Strindberg has already been discussed generally, but some of his later plays contributed significantly to the development of expressionism. Strindberg was well qualified for this contribution. After a period of severe depression and a flight from the "sane" world in the 1890, and heavily influenced by Maeterlinck, he was personally and professionally ready for his foray into this new dramatic genre. His "dream plays" were written during this period, the most famous of which are *Till Damaskus* (To Damascus, a trilogy written in 1898 and 1904), *Ett drömspel* (The Dream Play, 1902), and *Spöksonaten* (The Ghost Sonata, 1907). In these plays Strindberg explored facets of his own subjective consciousness as reality. Logical order was abandoned and replaced with whatever the dream state found plausible. Likely because of his own experiences with mental illness, Strindberg treated the alienation of humanity with great compassion and caring as the species tried to reconcile life in the early twentieth century. As an early experimenter of the subconscious as reality and the psychological state of modern humanity, he greatly influenced later playwrights, among them Eugene O'Neill.

Ernest Toller (1893–1939) represents a more mature phase of expressionist writing. His first play, *Wandlung* (Transfiguration, 1918), follows the progress of a young soldier from naive patriotism to bitter antiwar pacifism and, in essence, pleads for tolerance of the pacifistic point of view. Clearly his most famous and important play was *Masse-Mensch* (Man and the Masses, 1921), a careful study of the clash between social idealism and political realism, and the latter's unfortunate triumph over humanitarianism. Revenge of a sort was achieved in his next play, *Die Maschinensturmer* (The Machine Wreckers, 1922). Here the protagonist, Jim Cobbett, labors to bring about the final organization of workers into a caring and harmonious society. Such peace was not to be for Toller himself. He left Germany for the United States as the events leading to World War II unfolded, and, unable to reconcile himself to these, committed suicide in 1939.

From the First World War until the Great Depression, expressionism was an active production style as well as a tool of the playwright. Many of the contributions were developed in Germany and seemed quite in character with the events that were happening there. Among the most significant contributions were those made by Leopold Jessner (1878–1948). Jessner became director of the Berlin State Theatre in 1919 and was soon internationally famous for his implementation of New Stagecraft principles applied to the staging of the classics. Steps (known as *Jessnertreppen*) and platforms became his stock in trade, and his expressionistic use of composition highlighted the emotional and symbolic elements within the plays. Another director, Jürgen Fehling (1890–1968), achieved similar results in the staging of expressionist dramas at the Volksbühne, beginning in 1921. His productions employed light and sound in highly expressionistic ways, always aimed at evoking emotional responses from the audience. During the Nazi era, Fehling served as director of the Berlin State Theatre, where he continued expressionistically oriented productions.

FUTURISM

The revolt from realism called futurism was initially a literary movement, although it rapidly expanded in the arts in the second decade of the twentieth century. The movement was seen in its purest form in Italy and to a lesser extent in Russia. An Italian poet, Filippo Tommaso Marinetti (1876–1944), first articulated the principles of the style in 1909. Futurism, which sought to amalgamate all the arts, declined rapidly in the 1930s. No major plays or playwrights in the style emerged, but as a production tool and a general aesthetic that influenced others, it remains important. It greatly affected the early Italian and Russian filmmakers.

Philosophy

Futurism was a fairly militant movement that sought to reconcile art with the machine age of the early twentieth century. As applied to drama and production, the movement sought to compress time and space and to show multiple unrelated scenes simultaneously in one dramatic setting. That setting had to be as far from the traditional setting for theatre as was possible, purposefully confronting the audience with the production. Thus, traditional theatres were rejected in favor of circuses, music halls, or any place that would break the traditional space separation of the proscenium arch theatre. The style specialized in being against traditional staging ideas and forms. Futuristic plays are compressions of a series of dramatic events employing a variety of art forms to jolt the audience into an appreciation for and realization of multimedia events. The movement embodied the worship of technology and a glorification of the speed of modern living in a technocratic age. Psychological introspection and development were of no consequence here.

Production Practices

The entire production of the futurists was confrontational. Nontraditional performance forms, such as acting in the auditorium, were combined with a performance mix of forms often operating in conjunction with other happenings. A single audience focus on a singular point or event was not readily possible. Readings, visual events, dances, traditionally acted stories, and dazzling displays of light and sound were sequentially or concurrently presented. Indeed, the atmosphere of the circus was appropriate for the totality of a futurist presentation, and the audience reaction was no doubt similar.

Although chaotic, futurism did provide a lasting impact on theatrical presentation in the twentieth century. The breaking of the barrier of the proscenium arch by mixing actor and audience, the use of simultaneous performance, the mixing of all art forms, and the glorification of technology in staging and special effects all have a common origin in futurist performance. From this origin, such productions as *Hair* (1967) were possible.

DADAISM

Of all the revolts from realism, dadaism was the most nihilistic. Emerging in Switzerland at the conclusion of World War I, it was espoused by a group of refugee artists and writers who were disillusioned with and disenchanted by a society that could allow a world war. Its leading spokesman was the Rumanian poet Tristan Tzara (1896–1963), who wrote several manifestos for the movement between 1916 and 1920. By the early 1920s the movement had disbanded, but its elements would resurface during the 1960s in America in the antiwar movement and in the push for minority civil rights.

Philosophy and Production Practices

Dadaist theatre rejected all conventions of the proscenium arch space and the types of performances associated with it. Logical order was replaced by disharmony in all things. The world, after all, was mad and chaotic, and the stage must reflect this perceived reality. Language was reduced to nonsense, story to simple cause and effect, music to noise, and chronological events to mere chance happenings. The byword of the dadaists was "nothing"—no order, no logic, no meaning, no optimism. By and large, dadaist theatre was little more than an illogical arrangement of dramatic events and stagings of unrelated objects and words. Like futurism, dadaism produced no significant plays or playwrights, but it did provide the basis for theatrical happenings to emerge in the 1960s and served as a worthy precursor to other revolts from realism.

SURREALISM

The revolt from realism known as surrealism—literally "superrealism"—grew out of several other revolts, most notably from the symbolists under Jarry, the dadaists, and the French expressionists. First articulated by Guillaume Apollinaire (1880–1918) through his play *Les Mamelles de Tiresias* (The Breasts of Tiresias, written 1903, produced 1917), this artistic revolt rejects normal logic and order and substitutes a mixture of art forms to create a new realism, or surrealism. Following the death of Apollinaire in World War I, André Bréton (1896–1966) picked up the mantle of surrealism in a published manifesto in 1924. Bréton argued for a new reality based on

A production of Guillaume Apollinaire's The Breasts of Tiresias *(1903) at Pomona College.*

(*Courtesy of KaiDib Films International, Glendale, Calif.*)

artistic truth defined as the subconscious dream state of the mind. The movement was far more important in the visual arts than in theatre and did not decline until the late 1930s.

Philosophy and Production Practices

According to Bréton, surrealism was "pure psychic automatism, intended to express, verbally, in writing, or by other means, the real process of thought." This thought was to be free from societal conventions, such as commonly defined morality and commonly held notions of aesthetic correctness. It is primarily in the positioning of events that this new reality emerges; taken individually, the specific events can take on a strange logic if not applied to the succeeding event. Thus dramatic production takes on a superreality not unlike that of the futurists in the mixing of theatrical and nontheatrical entertainment forms. Comedy mixes with tragedy, the presentational with the representational, the world of the circus with that of legitimate theatre. The resultant new order of the surrealists was advanced as the true state of reality in the twentieth century.

Cocteau

The single most important surrealist practitioner in the theatre was Jean Cocteau (1892–1963). Already well known as a poet and artist, Cocteau attracted attention as a dramatist with *Orphee* (Orpheus), produced at the Théâtre d'Art in 1926, and with a new production of *Antigone* in 1922. In *La Machine infernale* (The Infernal Machine, 1934), Cocteau's reworking of the Oedipus myth, the skillful juxtaposition of fact with fantasy clearly illustrates the surrealist elements in his work. Cocteau was largely responsible for reactivating the French theatre in the period between the world wars. In addition to his surrealist contributions, his experiments with a whole variety of forms were typical of the emerging late-twentieth-century aesthetic of letting the individual style suit the particular production.

CONCLUSION

In many ways, the surrealists provided a fitting finale to the active development of initial revolts from realism. They believed there was a significant new knowledge to be gained in the depths of subconscious thought. The psychic forces that had been stifled by society and the war effort could be reawakened through the study of dreams, hallucinations, and the moments of that semiconscious state between sleeping and waking. In this way surrealism and the other revolts from realism went beyond Freud. In so doing, they set up the exploration of twentieth-century humanity as it tried to

This contemporary setting shows a blend of most of the departures from realism.
(Courtesy of KaiDib Films International, Glendale, Calif.)

reconcile events after the Second World War. All the revolts from realism experimented with varying levels of what is essentially a stream-of-consciousness technique, and they paved the way for the theatre of the absurd. The modern theatre continues to be more interested in the essence of human life, even within the bounds of contemporary realism, and this current mainstream is a reflection of the best from each of these revolts. The modern theatre owes them a great debt indeed.

25

THE RISE OF THE RUSSIAN THEATRE

The development of theatre and drama came late to Russia. Dominated for centuries by strong Oriental influences, it was only in the seventeenth century that a new ruling dynasty in Russia, the Romanovs, decidedly turned toward the culture of western Europe. With Tsar Peter the Great (1672–1725), the push for westernization became an imperial shove and the country joined the cultural and intellectual family of European nations. By the late nineteenth century the Russian theatre had produced a number of talented performers, Anton Chekhov, and the Moscow Art Theatre. During the first three decades of the twentieth century it became the leader of Western theatre in acting theory, directing, and nonrealistic stage presentations.

RUSSIAN THEATRE BEFORE 1900

Aristocratic Theatre

The second tsar of the Romanov dynasty, Alexis Mikhailovich, had German actors brought to Moscow in the 1670s to perform for the court and to develop an acting school for Russian performers. During the reign of Alexis' son, Peter the Great, the first public theatre in Russia was built and a company of German actors established in it. When the tsar moved his capital to the new city of Saint Petersburg in the early 1700s, one of the first buildings to be constructed was the Saint Petersburg Theatre. During this period foreign actors dominated the Russian stage: first Germans, then Italians, and finally the French. Neoclassical theatre was introduced into Russia by Caroline Neuber when her company of German actors replaced an Italian *commedia dell'arte* troupe at court. The Germans were in turn replaced by a French company. The French remained the favorites of the Russian court for fifteen years and helped establish French as the fashionable language of the Russian nobility.

During the reign of the empress Elizabeth (1741–1762) there appeared the first significant native playwright, Alexei Petrovich Sumarokov, and actor-manager, Feodor Grigoryevich Volkov. *Khorev*, the first play by Sumarokov (1718–1777), was produced in 1749 and was written in the neoclassical style, as were the playwright's eight additional plays. Sumarokov worked hard to establish a true Russian theatre freed from foreign elements, and in 1756 he was appointed head of the Russian language theatre in Saint Petersburg. He was also instrumental in the development of the first professional Russian acting company. This group was formed from members of an amateur company started by Feodor Volkov (1729–1763), who had established Russia's first provincial theatre in the early 1750s. Through the attention of the empress and the influence of Sumarokov, Volkov and other members of his company received formal training as actors. In 1755 a professional company was organized by Sumarokov, with Volkov as the principal actor. This company firmly established a truly national theatre and removed the dominance of foreign companies from the Russian stage.

One other aspect of the early Russian theatre, the serf theatre, deserves brief mention. Near the end of the eighteenth century many Russian nobles formed acting companies on their vast country estates. These acting companies were generally composed of serfs from the estates. These enslaved peasants were trained to provide theatrical entertainments for the amusement of their master and his guests. Although despicable because of its participation in slavery, the serf theatre did provide an opportunity for peasants to gain the elements of an education and unearthed a considerable amount of talent for the Russian stage. One of the first great actors of the Russian theatre, Mikhail Semyonovich

Mikhail Shchepkin.

(*From V. Komissarzhevsky,* Moscow Theatres*)*

Shchepkin (1788–1863), was a serf actor. He did not gain his freedom until 1822, when he was thirty-four and well known to Russian theatregoers. The serf theatre died out after the emancipation of the serfs in 1861.

Theatre of the Middle Class

With the exception of the serf theatres, the playhouses of Russia were under state control until the middle of the nineteenth century. At that time a number of private theatres began to appear in Moscow and Saint Petersburg. They were the preserves in which wealthy amateurs indulged their theatrical interests. These amateurs were from the lesser nobility, merchant class, and intelligentsia, and they were interested in the new trends in European drama, particularly the works of the early realists.

The first Russian realist playwright was Alexander Nikolaivich Ostrovsky (1823–1886), who was founder of the Society of Russian playwrights and closely associated with the Maly Theatre in Moscow. His plays are remarkable for their close portrayal of contemporary Russian society. Because of their high degree of local color and use of idiomatic speech, few of Ostrovsky's over fifty plays have been translated into English. Best known of these are *The Storm* (1859), *Diary of a Scoundrel* (1868), and *Bankrupt* (1849). Through his efforts the monopoly of the state theatres was removed, and this opened the way in the early 1880s for the first private, commercial theatres.

Two of the early private, commercial theatres in Moscow were started by Anna Brenko and F. A. Korsch. Brenko started her Pushkin Theatre in 1881, a year before the abolition of the state theatre monopoly. This theatre for the general public was served by a company of actors who lived and worked together, who spent more than the normal time in rehearsing a production, and who placed the emphasis on ensemble rather than individual work. Although the Pushkin Theatre remained open for only a year, its founder remained active in the theatre and later opened the first free acting school for amateurs from the working classes. Korsch formed his commercial theatre around a strong group of actors, several of whom he hired away from state theatres. Yet with Korsch an early concern with artistic standards soon gave way to an emphasis on box office receipts. The new commercial freedom of the Russian theatre did not produce a noticeable improvement in the Russian stage. This was to come in the late nineties with the founding of the Moscow Art Theatre.

MOSCOW ART THEATRE

In June 1897 a historic meeting took place in a Moscow restaurant on Nikolskaya Street. There Constantin Sergeivich Alexeiev and Vladimir Ivanovich Nemirovich-Danchenko agreed to join together to create a new theatre company that would set as its task the reformation of the Russian theatre. This new theatre company, which would eventually be called the Moscow Art Theatre (MAT), would do more than reform the Russian stage.

It would set new artistic standards for the entire theatre of western Europe and the United States.

Constantin Stanislavsky

Constantin Sergeivich Alexeiev (1863–1938), who is best known under his stage name, Stanislavsky, was the son of a wealthy merchant. Possessing a passion for the theatre from his early childhood, Stanislavsky developed into a highly skilled amateur actor by his midtwenties. As both actor and director in productions by the Moscow Society for Art and Literature, which he helped found in 1888, he gained considerable fame in Moscow's theatrical circles by the early 1890s. The visits to Moscow by the Meiningen Company had a great influence on Stanislavsky's early views on production, particularly in the areas of historical accuracy and ensemble acting. Already, in these years just before the founding of the MAT, Stanislavsky was exploring new ways to approach roles, to discover the inner stresses and desires of the character to be played. By the late 1890s, Stanislavsky was committed to moving the actor in new directions away from the clichés of the nineteenth century.

Constantin Stanislavsky.

(From V. Komissarzhevsky, Moscow Theatres*)*

Vladimir Nemirovich-Danchenko

In 1897 Nemirovich-Danchenko (1858–1943) was well known as a critic, playwright, and teacher of acting. With his students Danchenko stressed the need to understand the character to be played, and he urged them to reflect on the life of the character before and after the time portrayed on the stage. He tried to get the Maly Theatre, where his own plays were staged and where he was a member of the repertory committee, to break away from the traditional routines that were causing the stagnation of professional theatre in Russia. His suggestions included longer periods of preparation before a production was presented, attention to historical detail, and new costumes and sets for each production. In 1891 he was placed in charge of the acting classes of the Moscow Philharmonic Society, and there he trained many of the young actors who were to form the core of the MAT.

Impressed with the work of Stanislavsky, Danchenko made arrangements to meet with him in June 1897. During a conversation of over fifteen hours, the two discovered their remarkable like-mindedness on theatrical reforms. After

Vladimir Nemirovich-Danchenko.

(From V. Komissarzhevsky, Moscow Theatres)

agreeing to establish a new theatre company to accomplish these reforms, Stanislavsky and Danchenko drew up a list of actors, mainly from the Philharmonic Society and the Society of Art and Literature, who would be the first members of the MAT. The two also agreed to divide their responsibilities in the new venture: Danchenko would serve as theatre manager, literary adviser, and director, while Stanislavsky would concentrate on directing and actor training. Agreements made, the would-be reformers proceeded to find the money to finance their plans.

Early Years of the MAT

Having raised the necessary money and rented a theatre, the MAT began rehearsal in June 1898 of its first production, *Tsar Fyodor*. Rehearsals ran from 11:00 A.M. to 5:00 P.M. and then from 7:00 to 11:00 P.M. The work on *Tsar Fyodor* and other plays in the repertory continued for five months. The opening performance, on October 14, 1898, was a critical and popular success. Yet the next five offerings by the new company met with failure. With the total collapse of the company becoming a near certainty, Danchenko managed to persuade a friend to allow the MAT to stage a play of his that had met with an earlier failure. With the production of Anton

Anton Chekhov.

(From V. Komissarzhevsky, Moscow Theatres*)*

Chekhov's *The Sea Gull*, the MAT found solid success, a playwright, and a type of drama exactly fitted to the theatrical goals of its founders.

Not only were the audiences at *The Sea Gull* impressed with the reality of the acting and its inner strengths, they were amazed with the technical details of the production. Attempts were made to approximate the lighting suggested by the time of day in the script, and the sounds of the environment—bird songs, the clatter of dishes, harness bells—were floated over the audience. Never before had Russian theatregoers been faced with such artistic totality. The production firmly established realism in the Russian theatre and the MAT as its principal exponent. The work on the production gave Stanislavsky new insights in his quest to understand the actor's art. Later in his career he wrote, "Chekhov gave that inner truth to the art of the stage which served as the foundation for what was later called the Stanislavsky system."

In 1901 the MAT opened a formal acting school. Those accepted spent a one-year probationary period attending rehearsals, playing in crowd scenes, and being closely observed by Danchenko and Stanislavsky. After the successful completion of an examination at the end of the probationary year, the students were admitted to the acting school. In these early years of the MAT, the basis for actor training was experimental since Stanislavsky was still in the process of formulating his unique approach to acting. In the summer of 1906, following a highly successful tour of the MAT to Germany, Poland, and Austria, Stanislavsky vacationed in Finland and began to give serious consideration to a formal system of actor training. The first written ideas on the Stanislavsky System appeared in 1909 in a short manuscript available for the members of

A scene from act 1 of the Moscow Art Theatre production of Chekhov's Three Sisters.
(From V. Komissarzhevsky, Moscow Theatres*)*

the MAT. Two years later the MAT officially adopted Stanislavsky's acting methods, but it was still vague to both its creator and the members of the company. During the next two decades Stanislavsky would observe, experiment, and refine the elements of his System. While this work was going on, the success of the MAT and the dispersal of former MAT actors spread an interest in and an imperfect understanding of the System to the rest of Europe and the United States.

The Stanislavsky System

The system of actor training developed by Stanislavsky was strongly grounded in late-nineteenth-century psychology. Particularly influential was the work of Theodule Ribot, whose *Psychologie des sentiments* (Psychology of Feeling, 1897) was published in Russian translation the year the MAT was founded. Stanislavsky gained from Ribot the important concept of emotional memory, which was to be a key element in his effort to move his performers away from traditional acting clichés. In his System, Stanislavsky stressed the importance of the actor's awareness and recollection of personal psychological reactions and the reactions of others. Other important elements in the System were the magic if, given circumstances, imagination, relaxation, and communication.

In the early version of the System used at the MAT, the actor's tasks were broken down into progressive units of (1) *desiring* to understand the role, (2) *exploring* the available emotional material on personal and observer levels, (3) *creating* the inner and outer realities of the character, and (4) *presenting* the completed character in such a manner as to bring the audience into its reality. A driving force behind the entire creative process was the collective effort of the cast to discover the principal want or desire of the play and the interaction of the actors' individual character wants and desires with this central concept. The result was a highly complex presentation of emotional exchanges carefully orchestrated by the director into a single artistic entity. The System gave the MAT a combination of superior ensemble and individual acting unknown in Europe, and made it into the most important dramatic company in the Western world in the early decades of the twentieth century.

The Studios

The studios of the MAT were created by Stanislavsky to serve as laboratories for training young actors in the System. The First Studio of the Moscow Art Theatre was opened in 1912 under the direction of Stanslavsky and his assistant, Leopold Antonovich Sulerzhitsky. Housed in a former motion picture theatre, the First Studio was a small, intimate performance place where the aim was, according to Stanislavsky, "to give practical and conscious methods for the awakening of superconscious creativeness." The first production offered by the First Studio was *The Good Hope* by the Dutch playwright Herman Heijerman. The play was directed by Richard Boleslavsky, and members of the cast included Eugene Vakhtangov and

Michael Chekhov. Boleslavsky and Chekhov, nephew of the playwright, were later to be instrumental in spreading the System in the United States, and Vakhtangov was to become one of the most brilliant directors in Russia.

This initial production of the First Studio was well received, and Stanislavsky noted that following its opening actors, critics, and the general public "began to pay a great deal of attention to what I said about the new methods of acting." It was at the First Studio that improvisation was introduced as a teaching method in actor training, and it became an established part of the System. In 1924, with the permission of the new Soviet government and the MAT, the First Studio became an independent theatrical organization called the Second Moscow Art Theatre. Although independent, the Second MAT worked closely with its parent organization. During the politically troubled 1930s, the Second MAT was dissolved by the government and its actors were assigned to other theatre companies.

Stanislavsky's experimental ventures were not limited to the First Studio. In 1916 a third generation of young actors was formed into the Second Studio. This studio, unlike the first, did not develop into a regular production company. Rather it remained as a training school with a three-year course of study. Actors graduating from this demanding program were used to fill the ranks of the MAT as older members of the company began to retire. The Third Studio opened in 1920 and was under the control of Vakhtangov. The brief directorship of the Third Studio by Vakhtangov, who died in 1922, is considered one of the artistic high points of the postrevolutionary Russian theatre. The Fourth Studio was started in 1921 and was limited to the presentation of classic plays of the world theatre. Following a request by the Bolshoi Opera to assist in improving the acting abilities of their singers, Stanislavsky, in 1918, set up an Opera Studio. A student's notes from Stanislavsky's lectures at this studio from 1918 to 1922 have been translated and published under the title *Stanislavsky on the Art of the Stage*. Important books written by Stanislavsky are *My Life in Art*, *An Actor Prepares*, *Building a Character*, and *Creating a Role*. These books and the work of Stanslavsky's students have made the System one of the major contemporary approaches to acting.

RUSSIAN THEATRE AFTER THE REVOLUTION

Following the victory of the Communists in the October Revolution of 1917, all aspects of Russian society and culture were subjected to radical changes. The Russian theatre was quickly utilized by the new Soviet regime as a means to spread the ideas of the Revolution and to keep the Russian people, a majority of whom were illiterate, informed of new developments. The Soviets intended a complete break with the past and a repudiation of former traditions and standards. In this massive task the theatre was to play an important role. All the theatres of the U.S.S.R. were nationalized and placed under the control of a Central Theatre Committee. Under the guidance of the People's Commissar of Enlightenment, the Central Theatre Committee was given the task of creating "a new theatre connected with the rebuilding of the state and society upon the principles of socialism."

Theatre of the People

In the first decade after the Revolution, theatre blossomed throughout the U.S.S.R. During a period filled with hunger, deprivation, and civil war, tens of thousands of amateur acting companies were founded. Theatre became a kind of refuge as the masses of the nation crowded into unheated playhouses and makeshift playing areas across the land. Before the Revolution, theatre had been a pastime for the wealthy and the city dweller. Now the magic of the stage was available to all. Trained actors were in great demand as the government attempted to meet the calls for assistance. Actors became the shock troops of the new Soviet regime, instructing the nation in the small villages, the factories, and the army barracks. Typical of this form of theatrical activity were the Sinyaya Bluza (Blue Blouse) companies, which performed *agitkas*, or propaganda skits, based on current issues. These "living newspapers" were given in factories during work breaks and at workers' clubs. In the mid-1920s over five thousand Blue Blouse companies were performing throughout Russia.

Monumental productions were also offered by the new government to both instill pride in the Revolution and provide theatrics for the people. The most famous of these massive efforts was *The Seizure of the Winter Palace*, which was staged in Petrograd (Saint Petersburg) in 1920. The action occurred in front of the Winter Palace, the site of the original event in 1917, and involved eight thousand participants, trucks, canons, and the battle cruiser *Aurora*. The audience for this spectacle filled the square and streets in front of the palace and numbered over sixty thousand. An even grander production, entitled *The Struggle and Victory of the Soviet*, was planned for the following year. It would involve several thousand army troops, airplanes, armored trains, tanks, bands, and choirs. The scale of the venture proved too large even for its highly visionary director, Vsevolod Emilievich Meyerhold.

Vsevolod Meyerhold

The MAT was primarily an actors' theatre, but the First and Third Studios and several of the theatre companies established by former MAT members tended to reflect the individual artistic goals of a single director. The most individualistic of the new directors in the Russian theatre was Vsevolod Emilievich Meyerhold (1874–1940). A student of Danchenko at the Moscow Philharmonic Society, Meyerhold was one of the members of the original company of the MAT. He left the MAT in 1902 to direct in the provinces, but returned in 1905 to direct two productions. Stanislavsky did not approve these shows to go beyond the dress rehearsal stage. Embittered by his treatment by Stanislavsky, Meyerhold completely broke with the MAT and remained hostile toward it for the rest of his life.

A scene from Meyerhold's production of Gogol's The Inspector General *(1836).*
(From V. Komissarzhevsky, Moscow Theatres)

Between 1906 and 1917, Meyerhold directed at several major theatres, traveled in Europe, and established his own acting studio. With the Revolution of 1917, he became actively involved in the theatrical activities of the Communists. A firm believer in the Revolution and, after 1918, a Communist party member, Meyerhold was placed by the Commissar of Enlightenment in charge of the Theatre Division of Moscow. In the early 1920s he organized directing courses at his Moscow workshop, began to develop his theory of biomechanics for actors, and experimented with constructivism. In 1923 he established, with strong government support, his own Meyerhold Theatre. In the 1930s Meyerhold's experimental approaches to production began to come under strong criticism from the government of Joseph Stalin. In 1938 the government ordered the Meyerhold Theatre closed, in 1939 Meyerhold was arrested, and in February 1940 he was executed in a Moscow prison.

Meyerhold's work represented a radical break with the realistic traditions of the MAT. He became the champion of anti-illusionistic theatre in the Soviet Union, but his pursuit of the grotesque as a reflection of the human condition placed him at odds with official Soviet views on theatre. It eventually cost him his life. Governmental disapproval kept Meyerhold's ideas on the theatre from fully developing in Russia, but many of his production concepts were incorporated by other European directors. Two of his key ideas, constructivism and biomechanics, were best utilized in his 1922 production of Fernand Crommelynck's *Le Cocu magnifique* (The Magnificent Cuckold).

Biomechanics for Meyerhold was the theatre's equivalent of time-and-motion study, the skills of the actor governed by the principles of technology. The actor was reduced to a mechanism and acting to a formula: "$N = A_1 + A_2$ (where N = the actor; A_1 = the artist who conceives the idea and issues the instructions necessary for its execution; A_2 = the executant who executes the conception of A_1." The actor should be prepared to execute the wishes of the director instantaneously and in a prescribed manner. The actor prepared through a series of individual and group exercises that could be incorporated into a production. Meyerhold derived the exercises from earlier work with mime and *commedia dell'arte*. At the heart of biomechanics was physical training for the actor, and as an indirect result of Meyerhold's work, physical training is now a required part of actor training in the Soviet Union.

Constructivism was a Russian art movement that made constructions out of modern industrial materials. Meyerhold, who had seen an exhibition by five young constructivists in 1921, invited one of the artists, Lyubov Popova, to join the staff of his theatre workshop. The nondecorative and highly utilitarian aspect of constructivism appealed to Meyerhold as having possibilities for a multipurpose stage setting. On a completely bare stage, with an exposed backwall, Popova constructed a series of platforms, catwalk, and steps around two large wheels and the vestige of a windmill's sail. This was the set for the production of *Le Cocu magnifique*. Within this playing space, Meyerhold created a parable on jealousy with his actors, all in loose-fitting overalls, using many of their biomechanical exercises to support their roles. The production has been considered by many of Meyerhold's contemporaries as the greatest work of his career.

Alexander Tairov

The most enduring of the antirealistic Russian directors was Alexander Yakovlevich Tairov (1885–1950), whose Kamerny Theatre was founded in 1914. Strongly influenced by Meyerhold, Tairov disagreed with Stanislavsky's aims in actor training and the productions of the MAT. He found the work of Stanislavsky lacking in essential form: "By concentrating on experience exclusively, by depriving the actor of the means to express himself, by subordinating his work to truth of life with all its haphazardness, the naturalistic theatre has annihilated the form of the stage."

In his work at the Kamerny Theatre, Tairov attempted to achieve a form of production he called synthetic theatre. This was a blending of the theatrical arts into an artistic whole, with an emphasis on the magical, mystic aspects of staging. Rhythm, music, and color were key elements in Tairov's production with text and language being minor considerations. Against the stage reality of the MAT and the machine-age pictures of the Meyerhold Theatre, the presentations at the Kamerny were exotic refuges of color and movement that pleased the eye and did not trouble the mind. On three tours to western Europe

(1923, 1925, 1930), the Kamerny Theatre excited audiences with its theatre of musical color and movement, and, in turn, enriched Russian theatre by bringing back and producing many new European plays, including the first productions in the Soviet Union of the plays of Eugene O'Neill. In 1934 Tairov fell into disfavor with the government, which believed he was out of touch with the Russian people, and the Kamerny Theatre was taken from his control and placed under a committee. He continued to work at his theatre, under the supervision of the committee, until his death in 1950.

Eugene V. Vakhtangov

Perhaps the most brilliant of Stanislavsky's students at the MAT was Eugene V. Vakhtangov (1883–1922). Unlike Meyerhold and Tairov, Vakhtangov was able to synthesize the System and realism with anti-illusionistic experimentation to create a style of production uniquely his own. Placed in charge of the Third Studio of the MAT in 1920, he strove to establish a center for theatrical realism as opposed to the realism that was an imitation of life. To him theatrical realism was "the tendency in the theatre arts that aspired

Eugene V. Vakhtangov.
(From V. Komissarzhevsky, Moscow Theatres*)*

A scene from Vakhtangov's production of Turandot.

(From V. Komissarzhevsky, Moscow Theatres)

creatively to establish a special and theatrical life on the stage, a life that would strike the audience as a new reality. This theatrical life could be called life precisely because it would be presented with the conviction of real life."

Vakhtangov's 1922 production of Carlo Gozzi's *Turandot* at the Third Studio, which was later named after him, is considered his greatest achievement as a director. The presentation was a combination of elegance, *commedia dell'arte*, and charades. The actors, dressed in contemporary evening clothes, created their costumes out of a few pieces of colored cloth and performed on a set arranged in sight of the audience. There was no standard theatrical illusion as to time, place, and characters, and yet it was pure theatricality with all the magic of "Let's pretend." Vakhtangov did not live to see the production, but it continues to be a part of the repertory of the Vakhtangov Theatre.

CONCLUSION

Increasing efforts of the Soviet government in the late 1930s to control the plays in its theatres resulted in a stifling of directorial innovations. With the emphasis on socialist realism by the government, the play rather than the production became the focal point on the Russian stage. Socialist realism stressed the themes of the Communist party and the concerns of "the class struggle of the working class against its exploiters, the Civil War, socialist industrialization, the collectivization of agriculture, and the role of the intellectuals in the revolution." The resulting standardization of the Russian stage brought an end to a highly creative era in Western theatre.

26
MAJOR TWENTIETH-CENTURY PLAYWRIGHTS TO 1950

Realism, the depiction of "real life" on the stage, was possible because of a shared belief in social stability in the nineteenth century. This belief began to fragment in the twentieth century under the stress of scientific discoveries, philosophical relativism, decline in religious beliefs, increased social mobility, and the inhumanity of total warfare as witnessed in World War I. It increasingly became clear that things were not as they seemed, that appearances were highly illusionistic, and the realism of the nineteenth century an artistic sham.

The playwrights selected for brief discussion in this chapter reflect the state of confused concern that is symptomatic of this century. For the most part, their works were created and originally performed in the period from 1920 to 1950. Bertolt Brecht, a major playwright who wrote during this period but whose influence on world theatre appears after World War II, will be discussed in a later chapter along with the playwrights of absurdism and existentialism. The concern and despair of these playwrights was a continuation of the anguish that began to appear after 1918. The first major playwright to explore the near-paralytic condition of modern humanity was Pirandello.

Luigi Pirandello

Born into a wealthy Sicilian family, Luigi Pirandello (1867–1936) was educated at the University of Rome and the University of Bonn, where in 1891 he received a doctorate in philology. He returned to Rome in 1892, and six years later assumed a teaching position in Italian literature at a school for women. In 1904 his father's mining operations were destroyed, causing bankruptcy, and Pirandello's wife suffered a nervous breakdown. With these reverses in fortune, he turned to writing to earn additional money for his family. Pirandello was nearly fifty years old before he began to write seriously for the stage. Yet before his first theatrical production, he had established a solid literary reputation by writing essays, poems, over two hundred short stories, and seven novels. From 1917 on, he was totally devoted to the theatre and wrote forty-six plays, many of which were staged by his own theatre company, the Teatro d'Arte di Roma. In the 1920s Pirandello was one of the most produced playwrights in Europe, and in 1934, two years before his death, he was awarded the Nobel Prize for Literature.

An important key to the understanding of the plays of Pirandello is his book-length essay *L'Umorismo* (On Humor, 1908, revised 1920), which deals with the conflict between surface appearances and deeper realities. In Pirandello's view, we are all many personalities. Different roles or masks are brought into play to deal with the various aspects of our lives, yet we attempt a sense of personal unity that is in itself yet another role. Occasionally we catch a glimpse of ourselves in the mirror of the mind as we play one of our many roles. In this mirror we briefly see ourselves as we imagine others see us, and we are embarrassed by our role playing. Yet further introspection reveals that there is nothing but role play, there is no reality to reality, and all the world is a stage, a place of make-believe. Under these conditions, the theatre contains more reality than life itself. Such a view is at the heart of Pirandello's most famous play, *Sei personaggi in cerca d'autore* (Six Characters in Search of an Author, 1921).

Shortly after it premiered in Rome, *Six Characters* was being produced throughout Italy and Europe, and by 1925 it had been translated into twenty-five languages. The invasion of a play rehearsal by six characters, who insist that their play be enacted to its conclusion since their author abandoned the project, created a sensation by its challenge to accepted concepts of reality and the creative act. It was nearly a form of theatrical self-destruction as it ran through and rejected all the existing approaches to theatre as incapable of conveying the "truth" of the six characters. Then the play purposely failed to resolve, in a conventional manner, the issues raised, leaving the audience faced with the "reality" of the remaining characters onstage. Small wonder the first audience in Rome threatened violence to the playwright. In their eyes, Pirandello had managed to undermine the entire foundation of Western theatre. *Six Characters* called into question the nature of role playing, both on and off the stage, and the existence of the reality of appearances. It started an entire generation of playwrights questioning the role of the theatre and is one of the most important and influential dramas written in this century.

The theatre as setting was also used in two other well-known plays by Pirandello, *Questa sera si recita a soggetto* (Tonight We Improvise, 1929) and *Ciascuno a suo modo* (Each in His Own Way, 1924). In *Tonight We Improvise*, the destruction of a theatrical production is shown by the intrusion of various levels of reality on the improvising actors. With *Each in His Own Way*, the playwright adds an additional level to the two used in *Six Characters*. The complete play encompasses the actual audience, a stage audience, a double set of actors, and an "actual" event that is incorporated into the play within a play. The entire affair is an elaborate set of theatrical mirrors, arranged to show that each of us sees the world in our own way.

Enrico IV (Henry IV, 1922) is considered by many to be Pirandello's masterpiece. The focus of this play is on the theatricality of life, but it does not use the stage and actors as its setting. Called by one critic the "*Hamlet* of the twentieth century," *Henry IV* is a study in madness, pretense, and indecision. It centers on a modern man trapped in the masquerade of being an eleventh-century emperor, and it is an excellent embodiment of Pirandello's view that we are all ultimately trapped in the roles we play.

Pirandello was one of the greatest theatrical innovators of this century and one of the most successful. He worked within the conventional theatre of realism, yet used its very conventions to point out its weaknesses and the unreality it was attempting to portray. He was the first major playwright to confront audiences with the confusion, fragmentation, and alienation of modern life, and he did it by forcing them to see themselves in the mirror of the stage.

Eugene O'Neill

In 1916 a recently formed theatre company, the Provincetown Players, performed a one-act play written by one of the company. This first production of *Bound East for Cardiff* launched the play writing career of Eugene O'Neill (1888–1953), a career that would bring international attention to the American theatre. During the next thirty years,

Eugene O'Neill.

(Photograph by Carl Van Vechten, courtesy of the National Portrait Gallery, Smithsonian Institution, Washington, D.C.)

O'Neill would have over fifty plays produced, win the Nobel Prize for Literature, be called the founder of the American drama, and at the same time be labeled undisciplined, unskilled, and a bad writer. The stormy professional life of O'Neill, who worked in near-total contempt for the commercial theatre, was as troubled as his private life. As with Strindberg, a dramatist greatly admired by O'Neill, private life provided the dramatic anguish for the professional playwright.

The third son of the popular nineteenth-century actor James O'Neill, Eugene O'Neill dropped out of Princeton University in his first year. After three years of wandering, he returned to his family, recovered from tuberculosis, and began to be interested in writing for the stage. Four years after the first production by the Provincetown Players, O'Neill's first full-length play, *Beyond the Horizon* (1920), was produced on Broadway. This play won him a Pulitzer Prize, the first of four, and instant fame. During the next ten years he had seventeen plays produced in New York. During the decade after he won the Nobel Prize in 1936, O'Neill offered no plays for production. During this period, when many thought he was finished as a playwright, O'Neill pursued his private demons and wrote his greatest plays. Of these only *The Iceman Cometh* (1946) and *A Moon for the Misbegotten* (1947) were staged before O'Neill's death in 1953.

The historic importance of O'Neill in the American theatre is generally unchallenged. He was the first major playwright to emerge from the United States and the only one to date who has achieved and maintained an international reputation. Yet the aspects of O'Neill's greatness as a playwright are contestable. It must, of course, reside in the plays, but even there are encountered major obstacles, the results of O'Neill's continual search for the ultimate dramatic form.

Of the early plays, the most notable are *The Emperor Jones* (1920) and *Desire under the Elms* (1924). *The Emperor Jones* brought expressionism to the New York stage and provided the opportunity for Charles Gilpin, in the title role, to become the first black actor to star in a Broadway play. *Desire under the Elms* has been called the first important tragedy to be written in America, and reflected O'Neill's interest in working with Americanized elements of classical mythology. The subject matter was highly controversial in 1924: the play was banned in Boston and Great Britain, and the entire cast was arrested on obscenity charges in Los Angeles. Such troubles attracted the wrong type of audience, according to O'Neill, who was not particularly interested in the popular success of his plays. In fact, he attacked the strong materialistic aspect of modern society in two plays produced after *Desire*, *The Great God Brown* (1926) and *Marco Millions* (1928).

Two plays from O'Neill's middle period, *Mourning Becomes Electra* (1929-1931) and *Ah, Wilderness!* (1932) stand out from the rest in both scope and variation. *Ah, Wilderness!*, the best of O'Neill's two attempts at comedy, is a joyful look at coming of age in New England in the years before World War I. The first of O'Neill's autobiographical plays, it is the only one not touched by the O'Neill death wish. *Mourning Becomes Electra*, a massive work that requires over five hours to perform, consists of three plays, *The Homecoming*,

A scene from the original New York production of Desire Under the Elms. *Set by Robert Edmund Jones.*
(Courtesy of the Theatre Collection of the Museum of the City of New York)

The Hunted, and *The Haunted*. Based on Aeschylus's *Oresteia*, the trilogy relates the destruction of a New England family in the post–Civil War era. This work, which was written within the traditions of realism, was O'Neill's most ambitious project to be realized on the stage.

Unlike the work of most modern playwrights, the final plays of Eugene O'Neill are his greatest. For all of their problems, *The Iceman Cometh, A Moon for the Misbegotten*, and *Long Day's Journey into Night* (1956) are masterpieces of world theatre. All three are autobiographical, but the most haunting is *Long Day's Journey*, which covers eighteen hours of an August day, 1912, in the Tyrone (O'Neill) home. In *Long Day's Journey* and *A Moon for the Misbegotten* the private torments of O'Neill are finally laid to rest.

O'Neill wrote too much, tried too much, and failed to totally master the

A scene from the Theatre Guild's 1931 production of Mourning Becomes Electra.
(Courtesy of the Theatre Collection of the Museum of the City of New York)

skills of a professional playwright. Yet his raw power, spiritual anguish, and sheer theatricality make him one of the world's greatest dramatists. His best plays transcend their American environment and take on a universality identifiable with few playwrights. Their appeal is to a world audience.

Federico García Lorca

The theatrical career of Federico García Lorca (1898–1936) was brief, but during a period of less than a decade he wrote several noteworthy plays and attempted to reform the Spanish theatre. García Lorca, the eldest child of a wealthy landowner, began writing in his teens and completed his first play and a volume of poetry before he was twenty-four. In the early 1930s he became involved in the affairs of the government and was placed in charge of a national company of actors, La Barraca. This group toured Spain and presented the plays of the Golden Age. By 1933 García Lorca had achieved a significant reputation in Spain and South America as a poet and playwright. In 1936, at the start of the Spanish Civil War, García Lorca was assassinated because of his political associations.

García Lorca wrote thirteen plays, but he is chiefly remembered for three: *Bodas de sangre* (Blood Wedding, 1933), *Yerma* (1934), and *La casa de*

A scene from García Lorca's The House of Bernarda Alba.
(Courtesy of KaiDib Films International, Glendale, Calif.)

Bernarda Alba (The House of Bernarda Alba, 1936). *Blood Wedding* has been Lorca's most-produced play in Spanish and non-Spanish-speaking countries. A highly sensual play that uses the honor theme from the Golden Age, it both upholds and attacks traditional Spanish attitudes. *Yerma* also uses the honor theme, but in this play, García Lorca's most creatively ambitious, the poetic symbolism is in conflict with the psychological development of the characters. *The House of Bernarda Alba* centers on sexual repression in a family of females. The play illustrates García Lorca's movement away from poetic symbolism toward a form of social drama. García Lorca's attempts to reform the Spanish theatre and move it in a new direction away from middle-class drama were cut short by his assassination. Spain and the world lost a highly promising playwright.

Sean O'Casey

Born in the slums of Dublin and raised in abject poverty, Sean O'Casey (1880–1964) was forty-three years old before his first play was produced. During those first four decades of his life, he taught himself to read and write, worked as a common laborer, helped organize a labor union, and actively participated in the Irish rebellion against England. In 1919 he began to submit plays to the Abbey Theatre, where his efforts were encouraged by William Butler Yeats and Lady Augusta Gregory. With the production of *The Shadow of a Gunman* in 1923, O'Casey began his career as a playwright. Following the riots at the performance of *The Plough and the Stars* (1926), he left Ireland to live in London. He remained in England until his death.

The first three of O'Casey's twenty-two plays were written in a realistic style that brought to the Dublin stage the sounds and characters of the tenements. *The Shadow of a Gunman* was well received, as was his next play, *Juno and the Paycock* (1924). In this tragicomedy, O'Casey depicted people he knew in showing the strutting peacock of a man, "Captain" Jack Boyle, and his long-suffering wife, Juno. In this and several other O'Casey plays, the strength and courage of the Irish are seen only in the women. *The Plough and the Stars*, regarded by many as O'Casey's finest play, caused riots in the theatre and very heated debates in Dublin's pubs because of its unflattering picture of the Irish freedom fighters of 1916.

After *The Plough and the Stars*, O'Casey turned away from realism. His expressionistic *The Silver Tassie* (1929) was the cause of his break with the Abbey Theatre when Yeats rejected it. *The Silver Tassie* also marked the period in O'Casey's career when he began to move to broader themes than contemporary Dublin. Yet he retained an avid interest in things Irish, and the best of his later plays, such as *Red Roses for Me* (1943) and *The Bishop's Bonfire* (1955), continued his battles with the Irish character. "Like [James] Joyce," O'Casey noted, "it is only through an Irish scene that my imagination can weave a way, within the Irish shadows or out in the Irish sunshine." His fame now rests on his early Dublin plays, but productions of his later experimental works may yet establish O'Casey as a major innovator of the modern drama.

Thornton Wilder and Maxwell Anderson

Although he wrote nearly forty plays, the fame of Thornton Wilder (1897–1975) for originality in the theatre rests with two plays, *Our Town* (1938) and *The Skin of Our Teeth* (1942). The son of a newspaper editor, Wilder earned degrees from Yale and Princeton before his second novel, *The Bridge of San Luis Rey*, became a best-seller and won him his first Pulitzer Prize in 1928.

In *Our Town*, Wilder attempts to break through the vicarious aspects of realism to unite the audience with the spiritual and universal truths being presented to them. Specific events that happen in Grover's Corners, New Hampshire, between 1901 and 1913 make up the action of the play, but Wilder was not trying to draw a realistic picture of New Hampshire life. It was an attempt, according to the playwright, "to find a value above all price for the smallest events of our daily life." In presenting this picture of the priceless value of even the smallest elements in human life, Wilder's tone is tragic because everyone is unaware of these valuable, irretrievable moments. The play, presented to the audience by the stage manager in a direct, conversational manner, with no scenery and few props, is starkly theatrical and highly effective.

The tone of *The Skin of Our Teeth* is more comic and hopeful than that of *Our Town*. Based on material in James Joyce's novel *Finnegans Wake* and several of Wilder's earlier plays, *The Skin of Our Teeth* is a highly experimental work depicting the survival of humanity in the family of George Antrobus. The several allegorical levels in the play, its use of paired ideas, and the general chaos of the production were overwhelming to many audience members. It was by far the most theatrical production mounted on the American stage in the first half of the twentieth century, and it remains a great expression of faith in the indomitable will of humanity.

One of the most notable attempts to revive verse drama in the American commercial theatre is found in the work of Maxwell Anderson (1888–1959), a native of Pennsylvania who was educated at the University of North Dakota and Stanford University. His first play, *White Desert*, was produced in 1923,

In this 1948 production of The Skin of Our Teeth, *the playwright performs the role of Antrobus, the modern Everyman.*

(Photograph by Fred Fehl, Hoblitzelle Theatre Arts Library, Humanities Research Center, University of Texas at Austin)

A scene from Mary of Scotland *with Helen Hayes (*left*) in the title role.*
(Courtesy of the Theatre Collection of the Museum of the City of New York)

but he achieved a major success in the following year with *What Price Glory?*, which he wrote with Laurence Stallings. Broadway's most realistic picture to date of soldiers in combat conditions, it introduced genteel audiences to a new and strong vocabulary. *What Price Glory?* was a strong antiwar statement, but it was far from Anderson's dream of returning the language of the theatre to the grandeur of the Elizabethan era. Between 1930 and 1940 he made a determined effort to do just that.

With *Elizabeth the Queen* (1930), *Mary of Scotland* (1933), *Winterset* (1935), *High Tor* (1937), and *Key Largo* (1939), the American theatre had a brief, nostalgic romance with poetic drama. The first two contain strong echoes of Shakespeare in addition to their Elizabethan setting, but with *Winterset* Anderson moved to contemporary New York to tell his story of star-crossed lovers. *High Tor* combines prose and poetry in a fantasy comedy involving ghosts, lovers, land development, and idealism. *Key Largo* comments on aspects of fascism and the need to take action against evil. Anderson's poetic gifts were not equal to his aspirations, so he did not succeed in creating a renaissance for verse drama. He did, however, establish the fact that audiences were still interested in poetic language on the stage.

A scene from the conclusion of High Tor. *The set is by Jo Mielziner.*

(Courtesy of the Theatre Collection of the Museum of the City of New York).

Jean Giraudoux and Jean Anouilh

Jean Giraudoux (1882–1944) was the most important and successful playwright in France in the period between the two world wars, a success due in equal part to his talents and his close working relationship with actor-director Louis Jouvet. With his great verbal skills and ability to create connections between disparate things, Giraudoux was a perfect playwright to pair with a gifted director. A professional diplomat who had published essays and novels, Giraudoux's first play, *Siegfried*, was presented by Jouvet in 1928, after he had made the playwright revise it seven times. At age forty-six, Giraudoux became a popular playwright. His next play, *Amphitryon 38* (1929), established the dramatic form he was to follow for the rest of his theatrical career.

In such plays as *Amphitryon 38, Intermezzo* (The Enchanted, 1933), *Ondine* (1939), *L'Apollon de Bellac* (The Apollo of Bellac, 1942), and *La Folle de Chaillot* (The Madwoman of Chaillot, 1945), Giraudoux displayed a witticism, whimsicality, and preciosity matched only by Molière or Marivaux. In his more serious plays—*Judith* (1931), *Electre* (Electra, 1937), *Sodome et Gomorrhe* (Sodom and Gomorrah, 1943), and *Le Guerre de Troie n'aura pas lieu* (Tiger at the Gates, 1935)—the playwright demonstrated a great concern with humanity's struggle against fate.

Tiger at the Gates *in a production at the University of Utah.*
(Courtesy of KaiDib Films International, Glendale, Calif.)

Since the 1950s and the rise of the absurdists in the French theatre, the works of Giraudoux have lost some of their popularity. Yet their richness and fanciful complexities still command respect. His ability to transcend the ordinary levels of reality to reach a new and better reality gives hope to audiences who would like to believe, along with the heroine of *The Madwoman of Chaillot*, that "nothing is ever so wrong in this world that a sensible woman can't set it right in the course of an afternoon."

Jean Anouilh (1910–) is the most technically accomplished playwright France has produced in this century. He started writing plays when he was twelve and witnessed the first professional production of one of his plays before he was twenty-two. By 1936 he was established as a professional playwright whose darkly cynical plays were studded with brilliant comic moments. The author of over forty plays, Anouilh is best known outside France for *Le Bal des voleurs* (Thieves' Carnival, 1932), *L'Invitation au château* (Ring 'Round the Moon, 1947), *La Valse des toreadors* (The Waltz of the Toreadors, 1952), and *Becket, ou L'Honneur de Dieu* (Becket, or The Honor of God, 1959).

Anouilh's work was, in its early stage, strongly influenced by Molière, *commedia dell'arte,* Giraudoux, and Pirandello. By midcareer his own themes of impurity, social class irreconcilability, absurd duty, and death were influencing other French playwrights. A pessimistic writer, Anouilh views the world as void of true solutions and condemned to unhappiness. Decisions are pointless

*Helen Hayes
in a 1957 New York production of Anouilh's* Time Remembered.

*(Photograph by Fred Fehl, Hoblitzelle
Theatre Arts Library, Humanities
Research Center, University of Texas
at Austin)*

but must be made, and only individual integrity has meaning. His work shares much in common with the later French existentialists.

J. B. Priestley and T. S. Eliot

The major playwright of the British stage in the thirties, J. B. Priestley (1894–   ) has written plays that were both popular and innovative. A prolific novelist, essayist, and critic, Priestley's first theatrical venture was a stage version of his international best-seller, *The Good Companions* (1931). He went on to write nearly forty additional plays.

Although Priestley had a number of commercial successes with standard realistic plays, such as *Dangerous Corner* (1932), *Eden End* (1934), and *The Linden Tree* (1948), he was most interested in working with new material and ideas for the stage. A particular fascination for Priestley was the concept of time, the seeming reality of a sequence of temporal events. This interest resulted in a number of time plays: *Time and the Conways* (1937), *I Have Been Here Before* (1937), *Music at Night* (1938), and *Johnson Over Jordan* (1939). In these plays he worked at both the problem of time and the illusional aspects of past, present, and future, and the difficulties of presenting a multidimensional play form. They were some of the most experimental productions presented in England before World War II. His most popular play has been *An Inspector Calls* (1946), a mystery play with a message. It is a message found throughout the plays of Priestley, that life without tolerance and understanding is no life at all.

Another significant British innovator of the 1930s was T. S. Eliot (1888–1965), who stimulated theatregoers with the possibilities of verse drama. Eliot, American-born and educated at Harvard, Oxford, and the Sorbonne, had emerged, with the publication in 1917 of *Prufrock and Other Observations*, as an important new poetic talent in England. Although his major poems of the 1920s, *The Hollow Men* and *The Waste Land*, were filled with despair and disillusionment, Eliot underwent a conversion to Anglo-Catholicism in the late twenties. As a result, all of his subsequent poetic work, including his plays, reflected a strong Christian undercurrent.

After writing a well-received pageant play, *The Rock* (1934), Eliot accepted an invitation to write a play for the Canterbury Festival of 1935. The result was *Murder in the Cathedral* (1935), considered by many to be one of the greatest religious plays ever written. His next play, *The Family Reunion* (1939), demonstrated a desire not to repeat himself by writing another historical or religious play and to work in a contemporary setting so as to develop a verse form that approximated modern speech. The play, based on Aeschylus's *Eumenides*, concerns Harry, Lord Monchensey, and a family curse. Chekhovian in tone, it contains the best use of Eliot's poetic gifts in a theatrical form.

Eliot's last three plays, *The Cocktail Party* (1949), *The Confidential Clerk* (1953), and *The Elder Statesman* (1958), revealed his continued experimentation with form in his attempt to write a modern poetic drama. Each effort

A scene from Eliot's The Cocktail Party.
(Courtesy of KaiDib Films International, Glendale, Calif.)

resulted in his carving away at his poetry to make the text more accessible, to put the poetry "on a very thin diet," as he remarked. Such a diet was a disservice to the plays and the attempted revival of poetic drama. Although Eliot believed that the craving for poetic drama was permanent in human nature, few gifted dramatic poets have appeared in this century. In the postmodern theatre, with its stress on the bankruptcy of language and the inability of humans to communicate, the poetic drama has found few champions.

Arthur Miller and Tennessee Williams

In 1947 Broadway audiences were excited by new plays by two young dramatists who were obviously talents to be reckoned with, Arthur Miller (1915–   ) and Tennessee Williams (1911–1983). Although they gained fame at the same time and were jointly hailed as the new forces in American drama, their styles and themes were nearly opposite. Miller is primarily a social playwright whose thesis plays are strongly indebted to Scribe and Ibsen. His first play on Broadway, *The Man Who Had All the Luck* (1944), ran for only four performances. His next script, *All My Sons* (1947), was highly successful and established Miller in the American theatre. Miller's international

In the original New York publication of Death of a Salesman, *Lee J. Cobb (seated) created the role of Willy Loman.*

(*Photograph by Fred Fehl, Hoblitzelle Theatre Arts Library, Humanities Research Center, University of Texas at Austin*)

reputation rests on his third play, *Death of a Salesman* (1949). In this Pulitzer Prize winner, Miller introduced his view of the common man, Willy Loman, who is so blinded by his own distorted dream of life that he is unable to deal with reality.

Miller considers it a tragic situation when a character is forced to sacrifice his life, if need be, to secure his sense of personal dignity. By this definition Loman is a tragic figure, and such figures are central in Miller's only significant plays from the fifties, *The Crucible* (1953) and *A View from the Bridge* (1955, revised 1957). Following his marriage to film star Marilyn Monroe, Miller left the theatre for several years to work on screenplays. His return in 1964 with *After the Fall* and *Incident at Vichy*, revealed a change in direction in Miller's views, from social to polemic drama, and a deterioration of his play writing skills.

Tennessee Williams, acknowledged by many as second only to Eugene O'Neill among America's best playwrights, had his first Broadway production and success with *The Glass Menagerie* (1944). This was followed by a brilliant period of creativity that produced such major works as *Summer and Smoke* (1947), *A Streetcar Named Desire* (1947), *The Rose Tattoo* (1951), *Camino Real* (1953), and *Cat on a Hot Tin Roof* (1955).

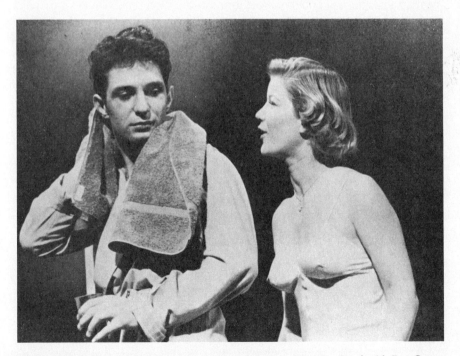

Barbara Bel Geddes was the original Maggie in Cat on a Hot Tin Roof *with Ben Gazzara as Brick.*

(*Photograph by Fred Fehl, Hoblitzelle Theatre Arts Library, Humanities Research Center, University of Texas at Austin*)

Williams viewed life as a kind of hell, undignified, lonely, corrupt, and obscene. Although sensitivity, purity, and beauty are admired, they are doomed to destruction by all that is crass and brutal in the world. Williams felt great compassion for the plight of humanity, but he offered little hope. Escape from this sorry state was a major theme in the plays, escape in the form of sex, drugs, fantasies, madness, or death.

After *The Night of the Iguana* (1961), the remainder of the sixties saw Williams at the lowest point in his career. During the last decade of his life he continued to write and to experiment with various dramatic forms. Although nothing of this period equaled his greatest plays, there were several noteworthy pieces, such as *Small Craft Warnings* (1972) and the poignant *A Lovely Sunday at Creve Coeur* (1979). His last play, *A House Not Meant to Stand*, opened in Chicago in 1982. The power and dramatic complexity of Williams's work has assured his permanent place in the history of the American theatre.

CONCLUSION

During the first half of the twentieth century, the theatre began to lose the vast audience it had commanded in the previous century to such rival entertainment forms as the music hall, vaudeville, radio, and film. Competition and economics reduced the number of available commercial playhouses in Europe and the United States, and the remaining playhouses offered limited opportunities for serious playwrights. Ironically, there was at the same time a blossoming of dramatic talent throughout the Western theatre. The plays offered by these writers differed from the scripts of the previous century. Rather than reflect the surface reality of contemporary society in the realistic manner, these plays were more introspective. The unprecedented human slaughter of World War I was a cause of great anguish and despair. This great concern for the state of humanity in the face of such organized destruction is apparent in many plays of the period that examine the human condition, probe the nature of reality, and question the validity of life itself. Hope, joy, and contentment became rare elements in the drama of the twentieth century.

27
THE AMERICAN MUSICAL COMES OF AGE

The musical is the most internationally known aspect of the American theatre. Evolving from elements of the English ballad opera, American minstrel show, European light opera, and French vaudeville, the American musical still lacked a clear form and structure as the nation entered the twentieth century. Victor Herbert, with his operettas of a Viennese flavor, and George M. Cohan, with his vaudeville-inspired music plays, were pulling the developing musical in opposite directions in the first decade of the century. Then, in the years just before the United States entered World War I, the musical was molded into a definite theatrical form in a small Broadway theatre.

DEVELOPMENT OF THE BOOK MUSICAL

The term "book musical" means a production in which the story, song lyrics, and music support and develop one another when they are integrated into an artistic totality. Such totality, often involving the work of many individuals in the key roles of playwright, lyricist, and composer, is not easily achieved. The playwright provides the book, the story frame, for the production; the lyricist attempts to make the words of the songs a natural extension of the playwright's dialogue; and the composer's music sets the songs and provides the show's emotional frame. The book musical's overall unity was not strongly present in its early stages. The process, from *Nobody Home* to *Gypsy*, took nearly a half century.

The Princess Musicals

A small 299-seat theatre located at the bottom of the New York theatre district, the Princess Theatre had not been a successful business venture for its owners, the Shubert brothers and F. Ray Comstock, during its first two years of operation. In 1915, in an attempt to improve business, Comstock engaged a rising young composer named Jerome Kern (1885–1945) and a novice librettist named Guy Bolton (1883–1979) to create the "smartest musical offering of the New York season." The small size of the house and Comstock's budget placed certain limitations on Bolton and Kern: a modern story, a cast of thirty or less, limited costume changes, an eleven-piece orchestra, and only two sets. The result was *Nobody Home* (1915), the first of the Princess musicals.

Between 1915 and 1918, Kern, Bolton and, later, P. G. Wodehouse created the book musical. Their shows at the Princess offered New Yorkers something different: they featured everyday people and events, they were adult yet simple, and they were funny and tuneful. Their success was not an accident since Kern knew what made them different from other shows on Broadway. "It is my opinion," he remarked in 1917, "that the musical numbers should carry on the action of the play, and should be representative of the personalities of the characters who sing them. In other words, songs must be suited to the action and the mood of the play." In this integration of music and story, the book musical found its structural form.

The shows associated with the Princess Theatre are six: *Nobody Home* (1915), *Very Good Eddie* (1915), *Go to It* (1916), *Oh, Boy!* (1917), *Leave It to Jane* (1917), and *Oh, Lady! Lady!* (1918). *Nobody Home* was somewhat feeble and caused some skeptical comments on the proposed reform of the musical stage. *Very Good Eddie* established the new form, had a long run, and was very profitable for its road companies. *Go to It*, the only one of the shows not done by Bolton and Kern, was a flop because Comstock attempted to alter the new

A scene from the original production of **Very Good Eddie** *at the Princess Theatre, 1915.*
(*Courtesy of the Theatre Collection of the Museum of the City of New York*)

form. *Oh, Boy!*, the first of the shows to include lyrics by Wodehouse, was the most successful of the shows. With *Oh, Boy!* still running at the Princess, *Leave It to Jane* opened at a larger Broadway theatre. The first musical about football and the American college, the show has had several revivals since 1917. *Oh, Lady! Lady!*, the last of the Princess shows, was acclaimed by the *New York Times* as "virtually flawless." The Princess team broke up in 1918, but in the previous three years they had produced four landmarks in the development of the American musical theatre.

Jerome Kern

There is little question that Jerome Kern is the most significant composer in the development of the American musical. Called by composer Arthur Schwartz "the daddy of modern musical comedy music," Kern's presence was a constant in the early decades of the history of the musical. In 1914 his classic "They Didn't Believe Me" established the basic pattern for the modern show tune. Between 1915 and 1918 he helped create the book musical at the Princess Theatre, and with *Show Boat* (1927) Kern and Oscar Hammerstein II introduced the serious musical.

A native of New York City, Kern got his first songwriting job in London, where he went after studying theory and composition in Europe. He returned to New York in 1904 and had his first hit song the following year. During the next decade he wrote a large number of songs for an equally large number of Broadway shows. The great success of "They Didn't Believe Me," which Kern supplied for the English show *The Girl from Utah* (1914), firmly established him as a major talent and prompted F. Ray Comstock to ask him to compose for the proposed new musicals at the Princess Theatre.

Although the Princess shows had been highly praised, Kern discovered that Broadway producers were more interested in hit songs than book musicals. It was not until his work with Oscar Hammerstein II (1895–1960) on *Show Boat* that Kern got another opportunity to make a notable contribution to the American stage. Of his many musicals, *Show Boat* is his most impressive work. Kern wrote his first film music before 1918, but in the 1930s he moved to California to work on film scores. In 1945 he returned to New York to work on a musical to be called *Annie Oakley*. Shortly after his return, he had a cerebral hemorrhage and died on November 5, 1945. The musical he had returned to work on later opened as *Annie Get Your Gun* (1946), with music and lyrics by Irving Berlin (1888–   ).

MUSICAL THEATRE OF THE TWENTIES AND THIRTIES

The Twenties

The hit of the first Broadway season after World War I was the musical *Irene* (1919), whose 670 performances made it Broadway's longest running musical until the middle of the 1930s. A Cinderella story about a poor seamstress, its book and music were in the tradition of the Princess musicals. Two of the Princess team, Kern and Bolton, were reunited in 1920 to create *Sally*, a show business musical produced by Flo Ziegfeld. The show was similar to *Irene* and was designed as a vehicle for *Follies* star Marilynn Miller. For the next few years the development of the book musical languished on Broadway. The early 1920s witnessed the last big fling at large-scale revues in New York. Yearly editions of the *Ziegfeld Follies, George White's Scandals, Music Box Revue,* and *Greenwich Village Follies* filled the stages of theatres with mindless sketches, hummable tunes, and young women in elaborate forms of undress.

Operetta   At this low point in the early history of the book musical, the American operetta had a major burst of creativity. In 1921 Sigmund Romberg (1887–1951) gave the Shubert brothers a great moneymaker with *Blossom Time*, which toured the backroads of the United States for the next quarter of a century. Road companies of this appalling musical biography of Franz Schubert became an artistic purgatory for actors of the 1930s. Romberg composed better shows later in the 1920s, notably *The Student Prince* (1924) and *The Desert Song* (1926).

Rudolf Friml (1879–1972), Romberg's chief rival in the creation of romantic operettas, gave Broadway two big hits in the 1920s, *Rose-Marie* (1924) and *The Vagabond King* (1925). With a book and lyrics by Oscar Hammerstein II, *Rose-Marie* became the biggest financial success of the twenties and thirties. Hammerstein claimed at the time that there was a close integration of story and music in *Rose-Marie* and that the show represented a "revolution in musical comedy." The show was far from being revolutionary and was not that much of an advance from Victor Herbert's *The Red Mill* (1906). Hammerstein's claims for advancing the musical would later come true with *Show Boat*.

From the mid-1920s on, composers and lyricists gained more control over the shows on which they worked. This resulted in increased musical integrity in the developing book musical and removed from the stage the musical play with songs from several sources. During this period the thirty-two-bar song in the AABA pattern became the standard form. The AABA made for easy reception and quick assimilation by the audience. This musical form consists of four lines of lyric, each containing eight measures of music (hence the thirty-two bars). The lines follow a general formula: A—the first line makes a statement; A—the second line is a variation or repetition of the first to the same melody; B—is a different melody and thought in relation to A (this is often called the release or bridge); A—back to the original melody and statement to complete the song. An example of a song of this type is "I Could Have Danced All Night" from *My Fair Lady*.

Show Boat   A best-seller in 1926, Edna Ferber's novel *Show Boat* covered the lives of many characters over a fifty-year period, from the 1870s to the 1920s. Jerome Kern thought the book had "a million-dollar title," and he and Oscar Hammerstein II obtained permission from the author to turn her novel into a musical. On December 27, 1927, when *Show Boat* opened at the New Ziegfeld Theatre, Kern gave the American theatre his greatest achievement as a composer, and the American theatre recorded a major step forward in the development of the book musical.

Avoiding the extremes of the typical 1920s musical comedy or operetta, *Show Boat* offered the theatregoer a serious story with well-integrated music. Kern's score, which used a great deal of incidental music to underscore the action and to foreshadow events, was praised by serious musicians for its technical advances. Hammerstein's book deftly handled the fifty-year time span of the novel without undue strain, and it presented the first musical to deal with miscegenation and race relations. Most audience members at the time were not aware they were seeing a historic event in the musical theatre, but they loved the story and the beautiful score, which contained such songs as "Make Believe," "Ol' Man River," "Can't Help Lovin' Dat Man," and "Bill."

Show Boat, for all its success, was to have no immediate successors. Shortly after the show concluded its original run of 572 performances, the stock market collapsed and the stress of the Depression began to change the character of the American theatre. The type of musical theatre that *Show Boat* was meant to usher in was interrupted by a rush to light, escapist entertainment and then a movement to social criticism. *Show Boat* remained a unique creation in the American theatre until the arrival of *Oklahoma!* in 1943. It is a classic of the American stage.

A scene from the original production of Show Boat *at the Ziegfeld Theatre in 1927.*
(Courtesy of the Billy Rose Theatre Collection, New York Public Library)

The Thirties

During the 1920s a new group of highly talented composers and lyricists began to work on Broadway. These men, who included Richard Rodgers, Lorenz Hart, George and Ira Gershwin, Oscar Hammerstein II, and Cole Porter, began to create a distinctive type of musical that reflected the impudent and independent aspect of the urban character during the Prohibition era. During the 1930s their work matured and took on a cynical edge. Most of the revues of the thirties were of the small, literate variety, a fashion started by *The Garrick Gaieties* (1925). Satire became popular in both revues and book musicals. During the early thirties, the film musical began to give serious competition to the stage as Hollywood offered up such elaborately mounted productions as *42nd Street* and *Gold Diggers of 1933*. Ironically, the subject of films of this type was often the Broadway musical. From this period until the 1960s, Hollywood would be a constant drain on Broadway as it offered greater financial rewards and national fame to the talents of the musical stage.

Musical Satire *Strike Up the Band* (1930), with music by George Gershwin (1898–1937) and lyrics by Ira Gershwin (1896–1983), concerned a future war between the United States and Switzerland over

A scene from the political musical Of Thee I Sing.
(Courtesy of the Theatre Collection of the Museum of the City of New York)

chocolate. This show started a trend for satirical musicals that lasted most of the decade. Presidental politics took a musical drubbing in *Of Thee I Sing* (1931), the next hit by the Gershwins. Campaign slogans, diplomacy, Congress, the vice-presidency, and the Supreme Court were some of the targets for the broad humor of this show. In addition to its satire on major American institutions, *Of Thee I Sing* was a major advance in form for the musical. There was almost continuous use of music in the show, either for songs, underscoring, or entire scenes. The music and story for *Of Thee I Sing* were the most closely integrated of any Broadway show up to its time, and it was the first musical to win the Pulitzer Prize for Drama.

In 1932 the Gershwins wrote *Let 'Em Eat Cake*, a sequel to *Of Thee I Sing*, but the show lacked the charm of the original and had a run of fewer than one hundred performances. Its lack of success did not signify a decline in the satiric or political musical during the thirties. Irving Berlin and Moss Hart's *Face the Music* (1932) centered on the career of New York's colorful playboy mayor Jimmy Walker, and they followed it with *As Thousands Cheer* (1933), which stuck satiric barbs into many contemporary events. The most serious political musical of the decade was the antiwar *Johnny Johnson* (1936), presented by the Group Theatre, with lyrics and book by Paul Green and music by Kurt Weill. The bitterness in the book and the advanced harmonies of the score failed to

Adele and Fred Astaire perform the number "White Heat" in The Band Wagon *(1931).*
(Courtesy of the Theatre Collection of the Museum of the City of New York)

find an appreciative audience, and it closed after fewer than seventy performances.

Labor-related plays became fashionable in the late 1930s, and the musical stage was not an exception. Marc Blitzstein's *The Cradle Will Rock* (1937) was originally planned as a production of the WPA's Federal Theatre Project, but because of the antibusiness attitude of the script, federal support was withdrawn the day before the opening. The show's intrepid producer and director, John Houseman and Orson Welles, rented a theatre and presented their show for nineteen performances. The following year it had a regular run, but its strident tone did not appeal to the regular musical theatre audience. Such was not the case with *Pins and Needles* (1937), a revue presented by members of the International Ladies' Garment Workers Union. With lyrics and music by Harold Rome, this prolabor show ran for over eleven hundred performances as it presented songs with "social significance."

The Rise of Dance   Most of the more than 150 book musicals and revues of the thirties were not concerned with serious satire, politics, or labor issues. They were bright entertainments intended to lighten the spirits of a nation in the midst of the worst economic depression in its history. Yet a few of these shows made significant contributions to the advancement of the American musical theatre. During this period dance began to gain importance in relation to character and story development. The new

Rodgers and Hart's The Boys from Syracuse *featured the choreography of George Balanchine.*
(Courtesy of the Theatre Collection of the Museum of the City of New York)

role for dance appeared in the work of Richard Rodgers (1902–1979) and Lorenz Hart (1895–1943), whose dozen shows between 1930 and 1940 are remarkable for their great music and lyrics. For Rodgers and Hart's *On Your Toes* (1936), George Balanchine (1904–1983) created a masterpiece of modern dance for the show's final number, "Slaughter on Tenth Avenue." As danced by the show's star, Ray Bolger, it became one of Broadway's magical moments. The following year Balanchine, who has been called the Mozart of choreographers, created musical theatre's first dream ballet for Rodgers and Hart's *Babes in Arms*. The idea of a completely danced fantasy was used again by Balanchine in *I Married an Angel* (1938), also by Rodgers and Hart. By the end of the 1930s, dance was beginning to be considered as more than just an incidental of the book musical.

Pal Joey   Rodgers and Hart collaborated on twenty-eight shows, but their greatest achievement, and a major advancement for the musical theatre, was *Pal Joey* (1940). Based on a series of short stories by John O'Hara, this musical featured a self-serving gigolo as its antihero and was set in the world of nightclubs. The show's cynical and adult subject matter upset some, but most agreed with the judgment of the *Herald Tribune*: "brilliant, sardonic and strikingly original."

The characters in the show are either unlikable or stupid, and they are

Gene Kelly's first major role was Joey Evans in the original production of Pal Joey.
(Photograph by Fred Fehl, Hoblitzelle Theatre Arts Library, Humanities Research Center, University of Texas at Austin)

different from characters previously encountered on the musical stage. Here boy meets girl, drops girl for older woman, is in turn dropped by both woman and girl, and goes, no wiser for his experiences, to meet another girl. Even the show's only love song, "I Could Write a Book," is an expression of the insincerity of the play's protagonist.

The unsentimental and cynical story of Joey's conquests and failures is greatly assisted by a score that gives the principal actors songs that both advance and strengthen their characterizations. The nightclub numbers gave Hart and choreographer Robert Alton an opportunity to satirize the general inanity of such production numbers. Although there is a theatre myth that this highly innovative musical was a flop in 1940, it had a respectable run of 374 performances and was both a financial and an artistic success. When its revival opened on Broadway in 1952 for a run of over a year, the show was hailed as a masterpiece of the American theatre.

MUSICAL THEATRE OF THE FORTIES AND FIFTIES

The Forties

The swing or big-band era in popular music, which began in the midthirties, reached its peak in the first years of the forties. Like the rock music of the 1960s and 1970s, swing was a less theatrical idiom than ragtime and had difficulty finding creative outlets on the musical stage. This highly popular expression of musical taste was largely ignored by Broadway, with the result that, for the first time in the century, show music and popular music began to appeal to different listeners. This became significant with the growing importance of record sales, which in the 1940s replaced sheet music as the principal form of transmission of popular music.

The forties was the era that witnessed the beginning of the long-running musical, shows that ran for more than a thousand performances. This was a result of a number of factors other than a show's popularity. Principal business reasons were the rising cost of musicals, less competition on Broadway, few road companies, and the challenges from film, radio, and the new wonder, television. The long-running musical, like the long-running play, gave security to a few, but reduced the opportunities for performer, composer, and lyricist. This, in turn, would have a detrimental effect on the musical theatre as these individuals looked for other sources of employment.

During the first half of the decade the United States was engaged in World War II, and the conflict sent Broadway in search of material that would provide a brief respite from the stress and horror of war. Optimism became a hallmark of the musical stage in the 1940s, and during this period a wistful and nostalgic eye was turned toward the past. With Broadway's younger talents either in Hollywood or the armed forces, Irving Berlin, Richard Rodgers, and Cole Porter took the lead in settling a sentimental mood on the American musical. The supreme example of the musical of this era is *Oklahoma!*.

Oklahoma! The prospects of creating a success-
ful musical out of Lynn Riggs's play *Green Grow the Lilacs* were rather bleak in
1942. The venture had a number of elements against it: the play had been
unsuccessful when it was presented in the 1930s; Richard Rodgers had never
before worked with Oscar Hammerstein II; the chorus girls didn't come on
until the middle of the first act and then in long dresses; and, as Rodgers
remarked, "Could anyone give a damn about a story whose burning issue was
who takes whom to a box social?" After March 31, 1943, it appeared that a
great many people cared. *Oklahoma!* went on to run for over five years and to
break all box office records up to that time. The first show by the new team of
Rodgers and Hammerstein turned out to be very special indeed.

Part of the success of *Oklahoma!* came from the fact that it was the right
musical at the right time. There was little on Broadway to compete with it in
1943, and its optimism and pure joy were nearly electrifying at a very dark
point in the war. When the curtain opened and the audience saw a lone
woman sitting on a porch churning butter and heard a man begin to sing,
offstage, "Oh, What a Beautiful Mornin'," they knew that right would triumph
in the world. But in addition to the circumstances of its opening, *Oklahoma!* is
an outstanding piece of musical theatre.

There is excellent integration of book, lyrics, music, and dance in *Oklahoma!*, and all the parts reflect the folk idiom of the play. The choreography of
Agnes de Mille, built upon the pioneer work done by Balanchine in the 1930s,
makes the dream ballet at the end of the first act one of the classic moments of

Original cast of Oklahoma!.

(Courtesy of KaiDib Films International, Glendale, Calif.)

the musical stage. It also started a rash of imitations that plagued musicals into the 1970s. The simple vocabulary and uncomplicated rhymes of Hammerstein's lyrics were perfectly fitted to the characters. Rodgers's score moves away from his sound of the previous decade to a lyrical freshness that captures the rhythms and newness of the American frontier. The book is the weakest section of the show, but the music, dance, and lyrics nicely cover its problems. Through its frequent revivals, *Oklahoma!* remains a major influence on the American musical.

Rodgers and Hammerstein Richard Rodgers said the effect of *Oklahoma!* on the musical was to make everyone "integration-conscious, as if the idea of welding together song, story and dance had never been thought of before." What it did was send producers in search of composers and lyricists who could write in the manner of Rodgers and Hammerstein. Although there were many attempts, Rodgers and Hammerstein had the market cornered. They would dominate the Broadway musical for the next sixteen years. *Carousel* came in 1945, followed by *Allegro* (1947), *South Pacific* (1949), *The King and I* (1951), *Me and Juliet* (1953), *Pipe Dream* (1955), *Flower Drum Song* (1958), and *The Sound of Music* (1959).

With their first show, Rodgers and Hammerstein announced to the theatre world that they were willing to give musical treatment to unconventional material. This attitude and the success of *Oklahoma!* set new standards and resulted in attempts by others to introduce new subjects and approaches to the

Richard Rodgers and Oscar Hammerstein II.
(Courtesy of the National Portrait Gallery, Smithsonian Institution, Washington, D.C.)

musical. The level of seriousness in story and theme of a Rodgers and Hammerstein show, and the masterful use of near-total integration of elements, have made Rodgers and Hammerstein pivotal as creative forces in the history of the American musical. The very importance of Rodgers and Hammerstein has caused some harsh criticism to be leveled against their work. The cynicism of the post-1960s led to a reaction against the optimism and wholesomeness of the shows. The air of innocence that permeates the attitudes of the characters strikes a false note with audience members born after 1960. Yet those who criticize are forced to admit that Rodgers and Hammerstein gave new energy and purpose to the book musical.

Musicals after World War II   Rodgers and Hammerstein occupy such a sizable section of the development of the musical in the 1940s that other noteworthy efforts, either innovative or traditional, are often

The *"No Business Like Show Business"* number from the 1946 production of Annie Get Your Gun.

(Photograph by Fred Fehl, Hoblitzelle Theatre Arts Collection, Humanities Research Center, University of Texas at Austin)

Mary Martin sings "I'm Gonna Wash That Man Right Outa My Hair" in the original production of South Pacific.

(Photograph by Fred Fehl, Hoblitzelle Theatre Arts Library, Humanities Research Center, University of Texas at Austin)

overshadowed. Fantasy was the principal ingredient in E. Y. Harburg and Burton Lane's *Finian's Rainbow* (1947) and *Brigadoon* (1947), the first hit for the new team of Frederick Loewe (1904–   ) and Alan Jay Lerner (1918–   ). *Annie Get Your Gun* (1946), with a book by Herbert and Dorothy Fields and music and lyrics by Irving Berlin, had a run of over eleven hundred performances and gave American theatre its unofficial anthem, "There's No Business Like Show Business." George Abbott and Frank Loesser (1910–1969) gave Broadway a bit of old-fashioned fun with *Where's Charley?* (1948), and Cole Porter (1891–1964) brushed up his Shakespeare to delight audiences with *Kiss Me, Kate* (1948), which proved to be his most successful musical. The tremendous success of *South Pacific* (1949) brought the forties to a heady close for the musical. The next decade would witness the perfection of the book musical and the first signs of its collapse.

Alfred Drake starred in
Kiss Me, Kate, *Cole Porter's most successful musical.*

(Photograph by Fred Fehl, Hoblitzelle Theatre Arts Library, Humanities Research Center, University of Texas)

The Fifties

In the fifties the book musical reached its final stage of development and achieved near-perfect form in two musicals, *Guys and Dolls* (1950) and *Gypsy* (1959). During this time a period of artistic stagnation set in as book musicals began to appear as if written to formula. What was needed in the musical theatre was a new direction away from the book show, yet innovations during the decade were either not followed up or poorly received. The major creative block of the 1950s was the attempt by so many people to write a Rodgers and Hammerstein show. This problem even beset Rodgers and Hammerstein. Yet there were three highly noteworthy attempts during the fifties to move the musical in new directions.

Candide (1956) is the most intellectually challenging show yet written for the American musical stage. This brilliant work, with book by Lillian Hellman, lyrics by Richard Wilber, and music by Leonard Bernstein (1918–   ), retained the satiric flare of Voltaire's eighteenth-century novel, but failed to find an audience in the mid–twentieth century. Although it closed after a mere

A duet from the highly original Candide.

(Photograph by Fred Fehl, Hoblitzelle Theatre Arts Library, Humanities Research Center, University of Texas at Austin)

seventy-three performances, the influence of this sophisticated show on the musicals of the 1970s, and particularly on the work of Stephen Sondheim, should not be overlooked.

Frank Loesser's *The Most Happy Fella* (1956) was the most completely musical show written during the decade, and it attempted to move the musical into a more operatic form. The story, based on a successful play of the 1920s, was told through the use of over thirty separate musical numbers. This type of production, with the emphasis on music and lyrics with little or no conventional dialogue, would achieve popularity nearly three decades later in such shows as *Evita* and *Sweeney Todd*.

Dance was the focal point in *West Side Story* (1957), which was directed and choreographed by Jerome Robbins (1918–   ). This contemporary version of Shakespeare's *Romeo and Juliet* set the dynamic dance numbers of Robbins to music by Leonard Bernstein and lyrics by Stephen Sondheim (1930–   ). The importance of dance as an intrinsic part of the structure of the book musical had been slowly developing since the late thirties, but *West Side Story* was the first musical conceived as a dance show. *West Side Story* clearly illustrated that dance could be the central element in a show and that the choreographer was

The dance-at-the-gym number from West Side Story.
(Photograph by Fred Fehl, Hoblitzelle Theatre Arts Library, Humanities Research Center, University of Texas at Austin)

capable of giving a musical its artistic shape. Two decades later choreographers would move into a major position on Broadway and produce such hits as *A Chorus Line, Dancin'*, and *Cats*.

Perfection of the Book Musical Although *West Side Story* and *Most Happy Fella* were successful, additional shows of their type did not appear again on Broadway until the 1970s. The bulk of the 110 musicals produced in the 1950s were in the tradition of the book musical. Notable among them were *The King and I* (1951), *My Fair Lady* (1956), and *The Music Man* (1957). *The Boy Friend* (1954), a popular British import, was a travesty of the Princess musicals. When travesties and parodies begin to appear, it is a sure sign of artistic stagnation of a particular art form. Yet before the book musical began to collapse in the 1960s, two shows were created that stand as the finest examples of the fully integrated book show.

Guys and Dolls (1950) was based on short stories by Damon Runyon, and it brought to the stage the colorful characters of contemporary Times Square. With music and lyrics by Frank Loesser and book by Abe Burrows, *Guys and Dolls* illustrated a concern for the integration of book and music without trying to follow the pattern of Rodgers and Hammerstein. There is a delightful mix of sentiment and farce in the comedy, and the songs develop the characters and give a necessary atmosphere to the show. The nightclub parody numbers are a bit too reminiscent of *Pal Joey*, but they did produce a hit song in "A Bushel and a Peck." The show ran for twelve hundred performances and provided, in the words of one chronicler, "a tonal and structural cohesion rare in the annals of the American Musical Theatre."

Gypsy (1959) is the most carefully integrated of the book musicals, a remarkable achievement considering the time span covered by its story. The book, by Arthur Laurents, is based on the autobiography of burlesque queen Gypsy Rose Lee, but the central character is not Gypsy but her terror of a stage mother, Rose. The music by Jule Styne and lyrics by Stephen Sondheim greatly assisted in holding the story together. The use of "Let Me Entertain You" as a sort of motif for the show is an example of their expert skills. The psychological levels in the show, particularly in the character of Rose, far exceeded anything that had previously been attempted on the musical stage. Perhaps the greatest accomplishment of *Gypsy* was that all of its outstanding elements were carefully enclosed in what appeared to be a loud, rambunctious, old-fashioned musical comedy. It is a great contribution to the American theatre.

Ethel Merman and Jack Klugman perform "You'll Never Get Away from Me" from Gypsy.

(Photograph by Fred Fehl, Hoblitzelle Theatre Arts Library, Humanities Research Center, University of Texas at Austin)

CONCLUSION

Gypsy brought a close and a beginning to an era of the American stage. Ethel Merman, who had been a musical star since 1930, created her last role when she played Rose. Stephen Sondheim would become a central figure in the creation of a new type of musical in the seventies. The book musical, a particularly American theatrical form, had grown into maturity along with the nation in the twentieth century. Now, as the nation entered a new decade that would be one of the most internally disruptive and disillusioning in its history, the book musical was an exhausted artistic form without any apparent theatrical heir. In a state of creative bankruptcy, the American musical stage faced the sixties and the onslaught of rock.

28

TWENTIETH-CENTURY THEATRE ARCHITECTURE AND PRODUCTION PRACTICES

Realism's coexistence with the various revolts against it was reflected in the theatre architecture and production practices of the first half of the twentieth century. This dual reality in the theatre, so expertly explored by Pirandello, provided a significant aesthetic among twentieth-century theatres and productions. This was the eclectic approach to truth in the theatre, or the freedom to choose among the various aesthetics of the distant and immediate past. These were blended into a production unity that embraced elements of them all. Realistic acting could be presented before symbolic scenery, and the eclectic aesthetic thus created was an accepted convention in theatrical staging by the 1950s.

In the twentieth century there was a concurrent return to older forms of production practices and architectural modes as valid expressions of aesthetic truth. With the reexamination of verisimilitude as the only goal of theatrical art, theatre practitioners found appealing presentational forms of staging, and they rediscovered the old pre-seventeenth-century relationship between the production and its audience. Greek, Roman, medieval, and Elizabethan staging forms were mixed with selected notions of modern theatre practice as the current general aesthetic of the theatre emerged. This general aesthetic is prevalent in every aspect of the modern practice of theatre and its architecture.

PLAYHOUSE AND STAGE ALTERATIONS

The Auditorium

Theatre architecture at the beginning of the twentieth century was still under the influence of Wagner's Festspielhaus at Bayreuth. Consistent with that design, most early-twentieth-century theatres were built with a steeply raked main auditorium with few balconies. Proscenium and balcony boxes became passé and were used only for ornamentation. The center aisle fell into disuse in the early decades of the 1900s, replaced by either continental seating or two aisles that divided the main seating section into thirds or into a one-quarter, one-half, one-quarter relationship. Aisles at the extreme sides of the auditorium were retained. In all cases, interest continued in improving the audibility and visibility of the production, and in ensuring the audience's safety during an emergency.

The architectural mainstream of the period still required playhouses to be palaces of culture fully equipped to handle the preponderance of stage machinery that full realism demanded. These large halls continued to emphasize the proscenium as a focal point, and they continued to grow toward the Renaissance ideal of a perfect theatre space. In the early twentieth century, these theatres often occupied an entire city block. They were built with elaborate foyers and other public spaces, including shops, restaurants, and, occasionally, hotels. Behind the proscenium, fly and offstage spaces increased to accommodate the needs of handling full illusionistic scenery. Most of the mainstream professional theatres throughout Europe and America were of this type.

In auditorium decor, a fundamental change occurred during the first few

Proscenium of the Embassy Theatre, Fort Wayne, Ind., with nonfunctional proscenium boxes that were included in the architectural concept.

(Photograph by Gabriel R. DeLobbe)

decades of the twentieth century. As the nineteenth century ended, most auditoriums and proscenium arches were highly ornamented, with elaborate plasterwork done by skilled craftsmen. By midcentury, however, lack of skilled craftsmen and high costs made this type of ornamentation prohibitive. The rising tide of movie theatre architecture, with its harsh rectangularity and sterility, greatly influenced the aesthetic and construction practices of legitimate theatres.

Economics played a major part in theatre architecture. Where balconies were used, they were located at the back of the house and were quite steep and deep to accommodate the patrons that had formerly occupied the forsaken side balconies. The graceful interiors of pre-Depression theatres were replaced by sharp angles and a seating pattern that required concentration on the picture behind the proscenium arch. The entire structure became more utilitarian, concentrating on a graceless supplying of patron needs, both in the auditorium and in the auxiliary areas.

Examples of auditorium alterations illustrating the above abound. Max Littman (1862–1931), for example, designed the Kunstlertheatre (1908) for the Munich Art Theatre under the direction of Georg Fuchs (1868–1949). Fuchs had long argued for an increase in the pure theatrical nature of the theatre and for a concurrent decline in pictorial reality, and Littmann's design happily obliged. He retained the raked auditorium but abandoned the wedge-shaped

Interior of the Embassy Theatre, Fort Wayne, Ind. Opened in 1928, this auditorium illustrates the large rear balcony common in most early-twentieth-century theatres.

(Courtesy of the Embassy Theatre Foundation)

581

Twentieth-Century Theatre Architecture and Production Practices

Interior of the Community Center for the Performing Arts, Fort Wayne, Ind. This Louis Kahn–designed theatre features an unadored, rectangular auditorium, a concept introduced in the early twentieth century.

(*Photograph by Gabriel R. DeLobbe*)

seating of Bayreuth. Instead, the seating was arranged within a rectangle, a pattern that greatly improved sight lines and was much copied by midcentury. Stage ornamentation was plain, and no fly space existed. Stage space behind the proscenium was minimal, with most of the space for acting clearly in front of the arch. This theatre was widely copied throughout Europe for "art" theatre spaces and in the United States in both regional and educational settings.

The Stage

In many ways, the stage underwent more far-reaching and fundamental alterations during the first half of the twentieth century than the auditorium. While Wagner's theatre had greatly influenced the house, it had reaffirmed the glory of the proscenium arch, a notion that the antirealists found repugnant. Consistent with the tenets of the revolts from realism, interest increased in breaking the proscenium barrier and in reconnecting the action with the audience in one theatrical setting. Thus in state-of-the-art theatres in the early decades of the twentieth century, extended apron stages emerged so that the acting could occur in front of the proscenium or no proscenium arches

*The lobby of the Embassy Theatre, Fort Wayne, Ind., which reflects the concerns in the
early twentieth century for more spacious public areas in theatres.*
(Courtesy of the Embassy Theatre Foundation)

were included in these structures at all. All innovations were aimed at returning
the theatre to a single aesthetic and artistic space for production and audience
alike. Two theatres, both built in 1919, serve as outstanding examples of this
trend, the Théâtre du Vieux Colombier in Paris, and the Grosses Schauspielhaus in Berlin.

The Vieux Colombier was the creation of Jacques Copeau (1878–1949), a
French actor and producer. Its importance to Western theatre was in the fact
that the converted warehouse had no proscenium arch and that its stage had a
permanent setting used for all plays. The set decor consisted only of a few
steps, door openings, and playing levels, with a single step replacing the
proscenium arch and dividing the production and audience spaces. The
machinery for production, such as the lighting instruments, was openly
displayed. The audience was clearly in a theatre, and the old pre-Renaissance
aesthetic of a shared theatrical space was reaffirmed. Although Copeau's
theatre was of tremendous importance in breaking the proscenium notion in
theatre architecture, contemporary reviews suggest that after a time audiences
found the single setting concept boring. A blend of aesthetic concepts, it would
seem, was the answer.

The answer came in part with the Grosses Schauspielhaus of Max Reinhardt
(1873–1943). Reinhardt remodeled an indoor circus building into a huge
theatre, with the major acting area thrust well into the 3,500-seat auditorium.

This forestage was U-shaped and surrounded on three sides by a steeply raked auditorium. The forestage could be lowered and used as part of the auditorium. Behind the forestage was a large, inconspicuous proscenium, and behind that existed more conventional stage trappings. Although the theatre was not to succeed because of its huge size and poor acoustics, conceptually it was of extreme importance. By blending the concepts of the extended forestage and the proscenium arch, Reinhardt foreshadowed the eclecticism in theatre architecture that was to prevail by midcentury. A theatre that was sufficiently flexible to present all types and forms of plays was to be consistent with the late-twentieth-century aesthetic. The Grosses Schauspielhaus served as a worthy precursor for this aesthetic.

The same could be said for Reinhardt himself. Working primarily in Germany and, after 1933, in the United States, he readily adapted his production style to the aims, needs, and objectives of the specific production upon which he was working. No one style dominated his concept of theatre, and in this flexibility he demonstrated a fluidity in production style that would be the hallmark of the late-twentieth-century producer. As the concept of ''form follows function'' came to dominate architecture, so was it applied to Reinhardt and the example he provided to the half century that has followed him.

From the experiments of Reinhardt, Copeau, and others, it was only a short aesthetic step to experiments with full arena stages with audience seating around all sides of the performance space. The full story of this development happened outside the purview of this chapter, but with it theatre architecture came full circle—back to the pre-*skene* era of the Greeks. Thus has theatre architecture attained the maximum freedom and flexibility it enjoys today.

PRODUCTION PRACTICES

With the early-twentieth-century realization of the styles of realism and its departures, there was general acceptance of the notion that all production elements must integrate to harmoniously present the playwright's intent and the director's interpretation of the mood and form of the

Two 1909 photographs of the stage bridges of the Drury Lane Theatre at different levels.

play. It became increasingly difficult to separate these elements from the production style for detailed analysis and discussion. All were oriented, nonetheless, to fulfilling their support role in revealing the playwright's intent, mood, and style. In the first half of the twentieth century, the accurate depiction of the script's intent and scope was the goal of the collaborative arts in the theatre.

The Producer

Among the various artists in the collective art of the theatre active today, only one was left to emerge in the first half of the twentieth century. The notion of a single person being responsible for the overall production of the play was not a new idea, since managers had existed for centuries. But to have such a person serve in what was becoming a distinct profession was unique. The role of producer in the modern theatre concerns itself with the management of the production rather than with the artistic side of the production elements. The producer is responsible for securing the right to produce the play, with finding a space in which the production will be housed, hiring the director and star actors, finding the financial backing for the production, if the producer cannot finance it alone, and for the general receipts and disbursements in connection with the presentation of the play. In England and on the Continent the role of producer does touch the artistic side of the production, but this function varies depending upon whether the production is commercially oriented.

The position of producer probably emerged in response to the increasing need for detached supervision of the artistic product and to partially ensure the control necessary for financial success. Actor-managers and "star" actors were not suited to serve as the disinterested parties that the rising tide of production unity and ensemble harmony demanded. All early-twentieth-century producers had extensive experience in the theatre in other roles—director, designer, actor—that served well as apprenticeships to the function of producer. And, as one critic has suggested, these roles probably gave them insights into the most important skill needed by a producer—the proper handling of people to get the job done.

Scene Design and Construction

As in the other production arts of the theatre, scenery reflected the general philosophical and aesthetic divergence of early-twentieth-century theatre practice. True to the growing spirit of eclecticism, designers were not limited simply to embracing one of the major aesthetics; freedom to choose selective elements from a variety of styles and forms existed. For the most part, a designer's selection could range from the detailed photographic realism of a Belasco to the abstract theatrical constructivism of a Meyerhold. Most mainstream designers followed the lead of Reinhardt in selecting those elements that best suited the production, once the collective judgment about that was agreed upon.

Although three-dimensional settings remained the norm in the first half of

An example of early-twentieth-century scene painting. The center of this wing and drop setting illustrates the blend of painterly and practical scenery during this period.

the twentieth century, the painter's art, scorned with the advent of the three-dimensional set at the end of the nineteenth century, resurfaced as a viable adjunct to scene design. Painted cycloramas and backdrops, whether realistic or stylized, were standard upstage additions in exterior settings and were mainstays in ballet, opera, and musical productions. In addition to the return of painted scenery to the designer's aesthetic, painters themselves found their way into the art of scene design. Salvador Dali designed a number of ballet sets, as did Picasso and Léger. The full return of scene painting to the art of modern scene design would come after the Second World War, but its presence was felt in those years between the wars.

This cross-fertilization of the visual arts and the theatre undoubtedly was encouraged as a twentieth-century phenomenon by the ideas and work of Walter Gropius (1883–1969) at the Staatliches Bauhaus. Established in Germany in 1919 as a School of Fine Arts and Crafts, the Bauhaus experiment sought to fully integrate the visual artist and the crafts artist into a single artistic enterprise. When the Nazis came to power, the Bauhaus moved to the University of Chicago, where it continued to influence architecture for another twenty years.

Designers

Only a few of the significant designers can be mentioned here, partially because of their number and partially because of their integration with other roles in the theatre. In the United States most designers were of the symbolist school, although New Stagecraft is the term applied most commonly to their collective aesthetic. Robert Edmond Jones (1887–1954), the dean of American scene design, used skewed cardboard arches to suggest the turns of fortune for Macbeth in a 1921 production. Norman Bel Geddes (1893–1958) sought to stage Dante's *Divine Comedy* in Madison Square Garden, using a gigantic flight of stairs and *mansions* to suggest the stations between heaven and hell. Perhaps mercifully, this production remained in the planning stage. England remained largely committed to the box set and realism, but one designer, Claud Lovat Fraser (1890–1921), deserves mention for his imaginative staging of Gay's *The Beggar's Opera* in 1920. The design utilized a permanent setting of steps and levels, requiring only the shift of two scenic panels to alter the scene, much in the vein of Copeau.

In France the distinction between designer, director, and producer was the most blurred, but a few names can be mentioned because of their primary fascination with decor. Louis Jouvet (1887–1951), the noted actor and producer, took up the mantle of Copeau and championed nonillusionistic simplicity in all his productions. Charles Dullin (1885–1949) borrowed the idea of moving screens from Craig for his version of constructivism. Gaston Baty (1885–1952) followed Jouvet at the Comédie des Champs-Elysées and brought an attention for detail to the simplicity of his scenes, both as a designer and as a director. From Russia came actor Georges Pitoëff (1896–1939), whose constructivist style included a fascination with medieval *mansions* and their application to the three-dimensional stage.

From these examples a common aesthetic emerged: selected real and nonreal elements mixed on the stage for the proper suggestion of the essence of the playwright's intent. This aesthetic would dominate the world of scene design after midcentury.

Acting Styles

Acting styles followed general production styles quite closely in the decades before the Second World War. Thus style varied from production to production depending upon their representational/presentational form, the relative proximity to or from realism, and the general aesthetic of the country in which the production was performed. Acting, then, varied from the realistic, motivated from the psychological base advocated by Stanislavsky, to the highly nonrealistic styles advocated by the antirealists.

The differences between the styles of Stanislavsky and Brecht demand significantly different approaches for the actor. Stanislavsky has already been examined, and Brecht will be discussed in the next chapter. Most actors chose some sense of the middle path, employing stylistic techniques when the production so required, yet motivating these according to some modification of psychological reality.

In other sections on acting throughout the book, specific actors were cited to illustrate the styles examined. That approach is not valid here, for the first half of the twentieth century did not produce an exponent of any style that was so clearly associated with that style to warrant such a discussion. As suggested above, most of the successful actors were sufficiently flexible to generate the appropriate style required for the production in which they were employed at the time, and to vary that to another style as another production, and acting opportunity, demanded. A case in point is that of Laurence Olivier (1907–   ). Certainly one of the great actors of our time, Olivier prides himself on the versatility he brings to his craft and for not getting locked into a single style, thereby limiting him to only a few specific types of parts. His performances in *Hamlet*, in Osborne's *The Entertainer*, in *King Lear*, and in a number of Strindberg's plays demanded widely different styles and approaches to acting. He and others like him practice their craft readily in the Western world; those without that flexibility do not.

Directors

The variations in directing style have been fully explored in other chapters in this part of the book, but a few directors will be examined here to illustrate the range of directorial style in the decades before the Second World War. Most of these directors had picked up the mantle of eclecticism from Reinhardt and, foreshadowing late-twentieth-century directors, applied it to their individual productions.

Italy was concerned before World War II primarily with the futurists, but Anton Bragaglia (1890–1960), director at the Teatro degli Independenti in Rome, staged the works of most of the major antirealistic playwrights. His directorial style varied from production to production, but in all cases it was decidedly nonrealistic. His stage was small, and he brought much imagination to the use of scenic elements (always minimal) and to his groupings of actors.

Spain's Alejandro Casona (1903–1966) was both a playwright and a director. He directed a major government touring company that played the provinces with primarily light, entertaining short plays. The plays he wrote and staged became his hallmark—masterful blends of realism and stylization that suggested an optimistic future for the human race. His staging was similarly optimistic and positive, was highly theatrical, and always avoided the acting and directing techniques of the darker revolts from realism.

The French producer-director Louis Jouvet has already been mentioned, but his directorial contributions deserve some focus here. As a director, Jouvet made a lasting impression in presenting the works of Jean Giraudoux (1882–1944). Giraudoux's style was to blend realism and fantasy, and Jouvet's imaginative staging brought out the best in his plays. Above all, Jouvet insisted upon careful textual analysis. The actors were carefully rehearsed in a detailed way based on that analysis, and Jouvet's staging always reflected the intent and the precise dictates of the language of the play. In addition to Jouvet, Dullin, Baty, and Pitoëff also directed, blending imaginative theatrical staging with fairly realistically motivated acting.

In England two companies emerged in the early twentieth century as supreme—Sadler's Wells and the Old Vic. At the Old Vic, director Tyrone

Guthrie (1900–1971) played a leading role among English directors. He was known for his unique blend of relatively realistic acting and his use of historically accurate costuming with highly theatrical scenery and staging, particularly in the presentation of standard works. His blocking and movement requirements were noted for their excitement and their ability to bring out special nuances in the texts.

From these examples a view of early-twentieth-century directing can be seen. It was an eclectic approach to the playwright's intent and meaning, often staged with a blend of real and nonreal elements. The various production elements did not have to agree absolutely, but all were aimed, through the mind of the director, toward a common organic unity and aesthetic whole. This trend would be further refined in the period after the Second World War.

Stage Lighting

By the end of the first decade of the twentieth century, most of the lighting theories and practices used today were established. Most of these were codified in Georg Fuchs's single work, *Stage Lighting* (1929). It was left to the early twentieth century to supply technology and scientific principles to the theories of three-dimensionality in stage lighting provided by Appia, Craig, Fuchs, Belasco, and others. To produce the form-revealing light that the increased interest in three-dimensionality had kindled, spotlights replaced

The switchboard of the Drury Lane Theatre in 1909.

floodlighting as the major source of stage illumination. Spotlights became practical with the invention of scientifically designed reflectors and lenses, thus allowing light to be efficiently channeled to the stage. Depending upon the location of the spotlight, instruments were used from the anteproscenium (in the house) position and from battens or pipes upstage from the proscenium. In thrust or arena productions, the instruments were hung in a grid suspended above the acting area.

To achieve Appia's goal of shadow-producing light, a system emerged that required at least two spotlights to be aimed onto a single acting area so that shadow and three-dimensionality were created. Background surfaces, such as backdrops and cycloramas, were still lit with floodlights since these surfaces needed an even wash of light. Special projectors and instruments, such as the Linnebach lantern, were developed to create the nonrealistic effects needed or to simulate natural special effects such as sun- and moonlight. Elaborate dimmer boards were developed to control the stage and auditorium lighting. By midcentury these boards had entered the beginnings of the electronic age, and by the late 1960s the computer was making inroads into the control center of dimmer boards. In many ways, the area of stage lighting shows the clearest marriage of twentieth-century technology and artistic expression in the theatre.

Costume

Costuming lagged behind the other production arts in embracing the revolt from realism for a number of reasons. First, the path toward realizing full historical accuracy in costuming had been long and hard, and practitioners were not all that ready to give it up. Besides, historically accurate costumes served a number of production styles well, and no need was felt for wholesale changes. Second, many costume designers were scene designers as well, and the state of the art was concerned more with changes in scenery. Thus costuming was sometimes an artistic appendage to the aesthetic cutting edge of the production. Norman Bel Geddes's costumes for his *Lysistrata*, for example, were less avant-garde than the set. Third, much of the New Stagecraft and constructivist techniques were applied to new productions of the classics, where, once again, historical accuracy served the costuming better than any other production aspect. Finally, costuming most directly affected the actor in that it must be worn, actively used, and freely moved about in. Costumes that were too stylized often impeded the actor's movement, and that, in turn, had an adverse effect on the production. Thus some resistance from the actors themselves may well have slowed the full revolt from realistic costuming in the early twentieth century.

Reforms did come, however. Germany's Ernst Stern (1876–1954), designing in the vein of his producer, Max Reinhardt, created some superlative costumes that were noted for their slightly stylized and simplified realism. In this regard, Stern set the tone for exploration in costuming by going as far as he could in abstracting his designs, yet providing the actor with something that could easily be used. In England, Charles Ricketts (1866–1931) set the tone for costume designs during the first two decades of the twentieth century. A staunch believer that simple historical accuracy and realism were not enough, Ricketts brought a light-hearted, easy stylization to his costumes for *Saint Joan* (1924). Other designers made similar contributions, but the general tone was set—a balance between embracing the revolt from realism and acknowledging that the actor was a real being who had to live and work in the product of the design.

THE IMPACT OF FILM, RADIO, AND TELEVISION

During the first two decades of the twentieth century, live, or legitimate, theatre began to experience a decline in total attendance. Some of this decline was due to other forms of performance entertainment that were emerging from the technological revolution of the late nineteenth century. Primary among these was film.

Film

The advent of film as a mass entertainment medium had been only a minor irritant to the legitimate stage during the early years of the 1900s. This new medium had to be taken seriously when film pioneer D. W. Griffith produced *The Birth of a Nation* in 1915. Not only was the film feature-length, giving the audience a full evening of a single experience rather than the short pieces they had been seeing, but the film outdid Belasco in creating detailed realism. Stage realism, no matter how well contrived, always had a conventionality about it that film could easily transcend. And for the mainstream audience member, the spectacular illusionistic melodrama film created was easily, quickly, and enthusiastically embraced.

By the late 1910s, film used multiple camera locations so that the audience was treated to close-ups and differing angles and views of the performance space. This provided the film audience with an artistic invasion of the performance space that the live theatre could not duplicate, particularly in the area of presenting the details of psychological realism. Through the close-up, audiences could see the developing and realized emotions of the characters; the best stage realism could do was bring the characters downstage or thrust them into the audience, a poor second to what the close-up could accomplish.

The final steps in the triumph of the motion picture came in 1919 with the German expressionistic film *The Cabinet of Dr. Caligari*, which proved that the revolts from realism could be handled at least as well through film as in the live theatre. In the late 1920s the addition of sound to motion pictures added the aspect of heard dialogue and music to the medium. These, coupled with the significantly lower ticket prices of the movies and the impact of the Great Depression on the live theatre, were forces against which the stage had no defenses. In New York the number of Broadway productions stopped growing

A battle scene from D. W. Griffith's The Birth of a Nation *(1915). The realism of such film scenes far exceeded the possibilities of the stage.*

after the 1927–28 season, and the number of productions on the road shrank drastically. By the 1930s film was the most popular public performing art, a position from which it has never retreated.

Radio

No one imagined the performance possibilities of radio when, in 1895, Guglielmo Marconi became the first person to send telegraph signals through the air. But the possibilities began to be realized when radio stations KDKA in Pittsburgh and WWJ in Detroit started their first regular commercial broadcasts in 1920. Network broadcasting started in 1922, and the golden age of radio was ushered in. From 1925 to midcentury, radio was one of the major sources of family entertainment. During this period, entire families would gather around the radio to listen to afternoon adventures, soap-company-sponsored daytime dramas (known as soap operas), and evening comedies, dramas, and music. Sports and news programming also received wide attention.

Performance programming was king. The *Amos 'n' Andy* show, aired weekdays at 7:00 P.M. EST through the 1930s, was so popular that for the fifteen minutes it was broadcast, many movie theatres shut down their projectors and turned on radios so that their audiences would not miss the program. In 1938 one of Orson Welles's *Mercury Theater on the Air* programs, H. G. Wells's novel *The War of the Worlds*, was broadcast as a newscast. Even though the announcer advised listeners that the program was drama, widespread panic throughout New Jersey and New York ensued. Many people left their homes or called local authorities for instructions, and some had to be treated for shock at local hospitals.

Radio's impact on the theatre was not as direct as that of the film. It did not provide the full performance experience of sight and sound, but instead, through its adventures and dramas, allowed active visualizations to be self-generated in the mind from the sound images presented. It did, however, bring performance into the home, thus enabling masses of people to enjoy professional entertainment at little effort or financial cost. Although radio continued to grow in the 1950s, it changed to a music, news, weather, and sports orientation as its former performance function shifted to television.

Television

Television, unlike radio, had a major impact on theatre. Although the first practical television system had been demonstrated in the 1920s, it was not until 1936 that RCA, through the NBC network, installed its first system in 150 New York City area homes, thus establishing the medium as home-oriented performance entertainment from the outset. The Second World War suspended the development of television, but the postwar boom more than made up for that hiatus. Television rapidly shifted from experimental shows to a full range of home entertainments, including performances. Particularly in America, the television boom exploded. The purchase of television sets increased tenfold from 1950 to 1960. The public was quick to see the advantages of low-cost, stay-at-home, quality sight-and-sound performance opportunities.

Television's attempt to compete with the theatre was direct. On an experimental basis, the first play to be telecast was J. Hartley Manners's *The Queen's Messenger* in 1928. Even before the Second World War, interest arose among television producers in concurrent telecasts of Broadway productions. The first of these was J. B. Priestley's *When We Were Married* in 1940. This experiment did not fare well, however, and the idea never fully matured. During the 1950s television mounted a number of "theatres" of its own, and these, by and large, were successful. The most noteworthy was *Playhouse 90*. Some interest continued in presenting full stage shows. These attempts had the advantages of color telecasting, and the first production so telecast, J. M. Barrie's *Peter Pan*, utilized a Broadway cast including Mary Martin. It was aired in 1955, less than a year after the production had opened at the Winter Garden. By the late 1970s cable franchises were common, offering a wider range of programming, including full stage plays and productions. With the exception of the aspect of "live" theatre, modern television has it all, including camera work that allows the emotional excitement of the close-up and the presentation of actual productions. Thus for the foreseeable future, television will hold a considerable advantage over the theatre in attracting the mass audience.

CONCLUSION

The era in Western theatre that lasted through the Second World War was marked by profound changes in the structure of the playhouse and in production practices. Although realism continued to dominate the mainstream of theatrical practice, many practitioners sought to break the proscenium barrier and reunite the audience and the production in a single artistic space. Playing spaces were thrust into the previously sacred space inhabited by the audience as the theatre sought to reestablish itself against the onslaught of film, radio, and television. In all the production arts—acting, direction, and the technical aspects of theatre—a growing understanding that the art needed to be uniquely theatrical rather than only a copy of objective reality permeated the artists' consciousness. After midcentury, it was ready to ascend to the artistic eclecticism needed to achieve this end, and to become the diverse, multifaceted aesthetic enterprise it is today.

Penthouse Theatre, University of Washington. This academic theatre was an early departure from traditional playhouse forms.

(Courtesy of KaiDab Films International, Glendale, Calif.)

RETROSPECT

Throughout most of the nineteenth century, theatre had enjoyed a preeminent place as the most popular public performing art in the Western world. The century had witnessed a clear progression toward the goal of verisimilitude in the theatre, culminating in the Independent Theatre Movement of the 1880s and 1890s. The antirealists active in the late nineteenth century were little more than minor irritants to the mainstream, and it appeared that theatre's popular place in society was assured.

The first decade of the twentieth century changed all that. The dominance of live theatre began to decline. There were many reasons for this decline, with no single one more significant than the others. The commercialism of Western theatre had gradually increased prices to a point where the mass audience looked elsewhere for entertainment that it could readily afford. Film, radio, and television greatly affected the decline in theatre's popularity by combining low prices with significant other features, most notably the ability to achieve verisimilitude better than the stage. Practitioners concerned about this decline realized that the theatre needed to reassert its unique nature as a performing art, and not compete as a form devoted to the commercialization of realism.

Had that reassertion been able to find a common focus, the theatre of today might be quite different, but it was not to be. The revolts from realism were as varied as the new view of the nature of humanity was, each arguing that it was the new "truth" in the theatre. Much of the basis for these new "truths" was rooted in the psychological devastation of World War I of the belief in the possibility of an ideal, ordered world. Thus, with the exception of the musical theatre, there was little joy in dramatic literature. Theatre architects and scenographers sought ways to reveal this joyless aesthetic to theatre's shrinking audience.

If the state of the theatre at midcentury were to be succinctly expressed, it would be that no succinct statement is possible. What can be said is that Western theatre by the 1950s was simply too diverse in play writing, theatre architecture, and productions practices to categorize, too eclectic to suggest a dominant production style as the style of the age. If any practice appeared common, it was that a variety of practices and performance forms was available to the theatre artist and that that variety, that eclecticism, was the "style" of the midcentury theatre. Although some variation of realism was most common in terms of total theatrical activity, a general philosophy of "anything goes" prevailed. True to the notion that various facets of humanity were too diverse to form a single collective consciousness, the theatre, in reflecting that notion, was equally diverse.

The horrors of the Second World War confirmed to some playwrights and theatre practitioners that humanity was confused and life was as meaningless as World War I had suggested. With this view, elements of prewar "isms" seemed to merge in the works of Brecht and Artaud, and in the last major style to emerge in this century, absurdism. Absurdism stressed the relative meaninglessness of daily life and the inability of ordinary people to champion causes larger than themselves. While surface order was the presumed reality, underneath that surface was an empty existence of desperate loneliness and an inability to connect with other people, whether through actions or words. This was the principal dramatic philosophy with which the theatre had to deal after midcentury.

Date	World History	Theatre History
1914	World War I begins. Battle of the Marne saves Paris and France. U.S. Marines occupy Vera Cruz, Mexico.	Tairov opens Kamerny Theatre.
1915	German and English naval blockades begin. German airships bomb London.	Washington Square and Provincetown Players organized. Kern and Bolton's *Very Good Eddie*.
1916	Battle of the Somme; over one million killed. Battle of Verdun; over half a million killed. Easter uprising in Dublin, Ireland.	O'Neill's *Bound East for Cardiff*. Kaiser's *From Morn to Midnight*.
1917	Russian Revolution. Tsar abdicates; Russia withdraws from WWI. French troops mutiny at front lines.	Apollinaire's *The Breasts of Tiresias* produced.
1918	End of WWI; over 10 million killed and 20 million wounded. The new state of U.S.S.R. proclaimed. Civil war begins in Russia. Influenza pandemic begins; will kill over 20 million by 1922. Weimar Republic established in Germany.	Kern, Bolton, and Wodehouse's *Oh, Lady! Lady!*
1919	First nonstop airplane flight across the Atlantic. IRA and Black and Tans battle in Ireland.	Actors' strike shuts down Broadway. Theatre Guild founded. Grosses Schauspielhaus opens in Berlin.
1920	League of Nations established. End of Russian civil war. First radio station goes on the air in U.S.A. Prohibition begins in U.S.A.	Kaiser's *Gas*. O'Neill's *Beyond the Horizon*. Third Studio of MAT opens.
1921		Pirandello's *Six Characters in Search of an Author*.
1922	Mussolini's fascists take Rome. Turkey declared a republic.	Vakhtangov's production of *Turandot*. Pirandello's *Henry IV*.
1924	Lenin dies; power struggle begins in Russia. Civil war begins in China.	Shaw's *Saint Joan*. O'Neill's *Desire under the Elms*. Romberg's *Student Prince*. Friml's *Rose-Marie*.
1925	Hitler reorganizes the Nazi party and publishes *Mein Kampf*. Fascists declared the only political party in Italy.	
1926	General strike in England. Kingdom of Saudi Arabia established.	O'Casey's *The Plough and the Stars*.
1927	Lindbergh's solo flight from N.Y.C. to Paris. Sound films introduced in U.S.A.	Kern and Hammerstein's *Show Boat*.

Date	World History	Theatre History
1928	Kellog-Briand Pact to outlaw war signed by sixty-five nations.	Weill and Brecht's *Threepenny Opera*.
1929	Stock market collapse in U.S.A.; beginning of Great Depression. Vatican State created.	Giraudoux's *Amphitryon 38*.
1930	Mass executions in Russia over farm collectivism.	Anderson's *Elizabeth the Queen*.
1931	Banks fail in Germany. Republic established in Spain.	O'Neill's *Mourning Becomes Electra*. Gershwins' *Of Thee I Sing*.
1932	Franklin Roosevelt elected U.S. president; 12 million unemployed in U.S.A.	O'Neill's *Ah, Wilderness!*. Anouilh's *Thieves' Carnival*. Priestley's *Dangerous Corners*.
1933	Japan invades China. Hitler becomes German chancellor; Nazis take control. Famine in Russia.	García Lorca's *Blood Wedding*.
1934	Purge trials begin in Russia. Italy begins war in Ethiopia.	Cocteau's *The Infernal Machine*.
1935		Eliot's *Murder in the Cathedral*.
1936	Civil war begins in Spain. Germany reoccupies Rhineland.	Rodgers and Hart's *On Your Toes*.
1937	Jet engine invented.	*Pins and Needles*. Blitzstein's *The Cradle Will Rock*.
1938	Germany occupies Austria. Munich agreement; Germany occupies the Sudetenland.	Wilder's *Our Town*. Rodgers and Hart's *The Boys from Syracuse*.
1939	Germany invades Poland; beginning of World War II.	Giraudoux's *Ondine*. Eliot's *The Family Reunion*.
1940	France surrenders to Germany. Nazis occupy most of Europe. Battle of Britain.	Rodgers and Hart's *Pal Joey*.
1941	Germany invades Russia. Japanese bomb Pearl Harbor. U.S.A. enters war.	Weill's *Lady in the Dark*. Hellman's *Watch on the Rhine*.
1942	Battles of Coral Sea and Midway. Siege of Stalingrad. Japanese invade Alaska. First electronic computer built in U.S.A. Nuclear reactor invented.	Wilder's *The Skin of Our Teeth*.
1943	Mussolini overthrown; Germans occupy northern Italy.	Rodgers and Hammerstein's *Oklahoma!*.

(Continued on page 598)

Date	World History	Theatre History
1944	Normandy landing by Allied armies. Germans use rockets to bomb England.	Williams's *The Glass Menagerie.*
1945	First atomic bomb exploded. End of WWII; over 30 million killed since 1939. United Nations established.	Giraudoux's *The Madwoman of Chaillot.*
1946	Greek civil war. Riots in India.	O'Neill's *The Iceman Cometh.* Priestley's *An Inspector Calls.*
1947	Marshall Plan for European recovery. Independence for India. First supersonic flight by aircraft.	Williams's *A Streetcar Named Desire.* Anouilh's *Ring 'Round the Moon.* Lerner and Loewe's *Brigadoon.*
1948	State of Israel proclaimed by U.N.; First Arab-Israeli war. Berlin airlift.	Porter's *Kiss Me, Kate.*
1949	German Democratic Republic established. Communists take control of China.	Rodgers and Hammerstein's *South Pacific.* Miller's *Death of a Salesman.*
1950	Korean War begins.	Loesser's *Guys and Dolls.* McCuller's *The Member of the Wedding.*

SELECTED READINGS

Balakian, Anne E. *Surrealism*. New York: Farrar, Straus & Giroux, 1959.
An examination of surrealism in the visual arts and dramatic literature, stressing the playwright's use of it.

Bordman, Gerald. *American Musical Theatre: A Chronicle*. New York: Oxford University Press, 1978.
With coverage from the 1700s to 1978, this is the most comprehensive account of the musical yet published.

Braun, Edward. *The Theatre of Meyerhold: Revolution on the Modern Stage*. New York: Drama Book Specialists, 1979.
A fine, comprehensive biography of an important director.

Carpenter, Frederic I. *Eugene O'Neill*. Boston: Twayne Publishers, 1979.
A good introduction to O'Neill's life and works.

Carter, Huntly. *The Theatre of Max Reinhardt*. New York: Benjamin Blom, 1964.
A superlative overview of the influence and contributions of Reinhardt to the modern theatre.

Chiari, Joseph. *The Contemporary French Theatre: The Flight from Naturalism*. New York: Gordian Press, 1970.
A good review of the French theatre, with an emphasis on the drama of the first half of this century.

Cornell, Kenneth. *The Symbolist Movement*. New Haven: Yale University Press, 1951.
A survey of the role of symbolism in art, with a particular focus on theatre.

Edwards, Christine. *The Stanislavsky Heritage: Its Contribution to the Russian and American Theatre*. New York University Press, 1965.
A good concise account of the development of the MAT, the System, and its spread in the U.S.

Fowlie, Wallace. *Age of Surrealism*. Bloomington: Indiana University Press, 1960.
A philosophical examination of the tie between symbolism and surrealism, stressing the role of subconscious thought.

Fuerst, Walter R., and Samuel J. Hume. *Twentieth Century Stage Decoration*. 2 vols. New York: Alfred A. Knopf, 1928.
A pictorial summary with notations in vol. 1 on the stage design revolts from realism after 1910.

Fulop-Miller, René, and Joseph Gregor. *The Russian Theatre*. Paul England, trans. New York: Benjamin Blom, 1969.
Although first published in 1930, this work is still very useful for an understanding of the Russian theatre before and after the Revolution.

Gorchakov, Nikolai A. *The Theatre in Soviet Russia*. Edgar Lehrman, trans. New York: Columbia University Press, 1957.

Although the author's hostility to the Communists colors his views, this is an excellent work on the Russian theatre from the late 1800s to the early 1950s.

Green, Stanley. *The World of Musical Comedy*. New York: A. S. Barnes, 1974.
An very readable account of the development of the musical related in terms of the careers of the major composers and lyricists. Numerous illustrations.

Hainaux, René, ed. *Stage Design throughout the World Since 1935*. New York: Theatre Arts Books, 1956.
A superior collection of stage and costume designs from the first half of the twentieth century.

Jones, Robert Edmond. *The Dramatic Imagination*. New York: Theatre Arts Books, 1941.
An enjoyable manifesto of symbolist theatrical design by the leading U.S. exponent of that style.

Kirby, Michael. *Futurist Performance*. New York: E. P. Dutton, 1971.
A detailed examination of the philosophy and production practices in theatre, film, and music of the Italian futurists.

Lehmann, Andrew. *The Symbolist Aesthetic in France, 1885–1895* 2nd ed. New York: Barnes & Noble, 1968.
A general survey of the movement during its peak in Europe, focusing on France.

Melzer, Annabelle. *Latest Rage the Big Drum: Dada and Surrealist Performance*. Ann Arbor: UMI Research Press, 1980.
A detailed examination of the theory and performance practices of the Swiss and French dadaists. Less emphasis on surrealism.

Oliver, Roger W. *Dreams of Passion: The Theatre of Luigi Pirandello*. New York: New York University Press, 1979.
An excellent introduction to Pirandello's plays and theories, including detailed discussions of six of his major plays.

Rodgers, Richard. *Musical Stage: An Autobiography*. New York: Random House, 1975.
A highly informative autobiography by one of the most important people involved in the development of the musical.

Segel, Harold B. *Twentieth-Century Russian Drama: From Gorky to the Present*. New York: Columbia University Press, 1979.
An excellent account of the trends and troubles in twentieth-century Russian drama. Since it is outside the scope of the book, little is said about the production of these plays.

Smith, Cecil, and Glenn Litton. *Musical Comedy in America*. New York: Theatre Arts Books, 1981.
Although not nearly as comprehensive as Bordman, this very readable paperback belongs in the library of anyone interested in the musical.

Southern, Richard. *The Open Stage*. New York: Theatre Arts Books, 1959.
An examination of the rediscovery of open and thrust stages in the first half of the twentieth century.

Toll, Robert C. *The Entertainment Machine: American Show Business in the Twentieth Century*. New York: Oxford University Press, 1982.
An excellent brief account of the impact of radio, film, and television on the American theatre and culture.

Willet, John. *Expressionism*. New York: McGraw-Hill, 1970.
An overview of theatrical expressionism as seen through a detailed examination of expressionist plays.

LONDON

EAST BERLIN

PARIS

NEW YORK

PART XIII

The Broken Mirror:
THEATRE SINCE 1950

The modern theatre came into existence at the end of the nineteenth century, and its foundation was composed of the conventional rules of society and a shared sense of reality. The supposed solidity of this foundation made realism in the theatre possible and provided the intellectual framework for revolts against these conventions. In the period after 1945 the agreed-upon rules of Western society began to appear increasingly artificial and the very nature of reality itself was questioned. Out of this intellectual and emotional ferment emerged the postmodern theatre.

The postmodern theatre exists at present alongside the modern theatre, but it is not yet another in a long line of theatrical revolts. In its most extreme forms, the postmodern theatre is more than a challenge to the previously agreed-upon conventions of the stage. It considers those conventions null and void. The theatre can only exist where there is a shared sense of reality, yet in the postmodern era this sense of reality has been fragmented into many realities or denials of reality. The mirror of the theatre has been shattered, and the pieces reflect the fragmentation of modern culture. In this culture there is little agreement upon anything, including what is theatre.

29
NEW DIRECTIONS IN THE POSTMODERN THEATRE

The nearly unbelievable destruction and death from 1939 to 1945 called into question the conventional rules of Western civilization. How could so-called civilized, cultured societies bring forth such madness into the world? The spread of nuclear weapons to a number of hostile nations during the postwar years raised the specter of an even greater level of destruction in a future war, one that might end human life on earth. Out of this intellectual and emotional climate emerged the postmodern theatre. It is a theatre that holds two major theorists and a group of playwrights whose dramas reflect the fears of a society that has lost its sense of social cohesion.

BERTOLT BRECHT

Born in Augsburg, in the Kingdom of Bavaria, Bertolt Brecht (1898–1956) had poems published while he was still in high school. He began to study medicine at the University of Munich in 1917, but his studies were interrupted the following year when he was drafted into the army, where he served four months as a medical orderly in his native city. Before he was drafted Brecht wrote his first play, *Baal* (1918), shortly to be followed by *Trommeln in der Nacht* (Drums in the Night, 1918). The successful 1922 production of *Drums* in Munich was followed by productions all over Germany and the awarding of the prestigious Kleist Prize to the young playwright.

In 1924 Brecht moved to Berlin to become assistant director to Max Reinhardt. During the next nine years in Berlin he wrote and worked with other innovative directors. Important among these was Erwin Piscator (1893–1966), the originator of epic drama. This type of theatrical production, which made use of film, constructivism, and high political rhetoric, made a lasting impression on Brecht. His first international success came in 1928 with *Die Dreigroschenoper* (The Threepenny Opera), a modernization of John Gay's *The Beggar's Opera* (1728) with music by Kurt Weill. Brecht's poetry, plays,

A scene from a production of The Threepenny Opera *in Zurich in 1972.*
(Courtesy of KaiDib Films International, Glendale, Calif.)

and Communist party affiliation had placed him high on the liquidation list of the Nazi party. When Hitler came into power in 1933, Brecht went into exile for fifteen years.

During these years, as he and his family moved from country to country, Brecht wrote his major plays. In 1947 he left the United States, where he had lived since 1941, to return to Germany. The East German government provided him with a theatre in East Berlin and state support. Here Brecht developed the Berliner Ensemble, one of the finest acting companies in the world and the foremost interpreter of Brechtian drama.

Major Plays

The exile plays, written between 1938 and 1944, represent the highest levels of Brecht's considerable dramatic talents. Foremost of these are *Leben des Galilei* (Galileo, 1938), *Mutter Courage und ihre Kinder* (Mother Courage and Her Children, 1939), *Der Güte Mensch von Sezuan* (The Good Person of Setzuan, 1941), and *Der Kaukasische Kreiderkreis* (The Caucasian Chalk Circle, 1944). In exile, away from the time demands of daily theatrical and political activities, he was able to write his masterpieces.

Mother Courage and Her Children follows the canteen wagon of Anna Fierling through twelve scenes as she accompanies the armies during the Thirty Years' War (1618–1648). Although determined to keep her three children out

A scene from the first section of Mother Courage and Her Children *as performed by the Berliner Ensemble.*
(*Courtesy of KaiDib Films International, Glendale, Calif.*)

of the conflict, Mother Courage is a hard businesswoman whose livelihood depends on war. In the end, all her children fall victims to the forces of war. Old, weary, nearly destroyed by grief, she hitches herself to her wagon and goes back to business. Tennessee Williams considered Mother Courage the greatest play of the twentieth century, and there are many who agree with his assessment. The role of Mother Courage is certainly one of the finest ever written for an actress.

How to be good and yet live: that is the problem Brecht poses in *The Good Person of Setzuan*. A parable play, *Good Person* presents the ethical dilemma faced by the "good" Shen Te, who must invent the "evil" Shui Ta to survive in a vicious capitalistic society. Human indifference is a major theme in this play, indifference in the face of human exploitation. The playwright offers no direct solution to the problems in the play, but the challenge he presents to the audience is that the world can and must be changed. In *The Caucasian Chalk Circle*, Brecht's most cheerful play, the tone is more hopeful. This work is his most structurally complex play and makes the greatest use of the techniques of epic theatre. Here the idea of the changeability of the world is shown through a double narrative. The entire play is charmingly poetic and contains, in the persons of Grusha and Azdak, two of the most memorable characters in modern drama.

Brechtian Production

Bertolt Brecht had a strong dislike of the traditional theatre, particularly the traditional theatre as represented by the somewhat pretentious German stage of the nineteenth century. His revolt was against the illusionistic theatre that drew the audience into its stories and characters and offered a means of escape from the realities of the world. To Brecht this was morally and intellectually unacceptable because it just increased the difficulties of trying to understand the world outside the theatre. The neglect of the traditional theatre in supplying the audience with a critical frame of mind led Brecht to consider the possibilities available in the epic theatre.

"To expound the principles of the epic theatre in a few catch phrases," Brecht wrote in 1927, "is not possible. The essential point of the epic theatre is perhaps that it appeals less to the feelings than to the spectator's reason. Instead of sharing an experience the spectator must come to grips with things." He believed the production methods associated with the epic theatre helped break the magic of illusionistic staging, awakened the audience, and forced it to think critically about what it was viewing. Devices used to break the stage illusion

A view from backstage at the theatre of the Berliner Ensemble, East Berlin.
(Courtesy of KaiDib Films International, Glendale, Calif.)

included songs, film clips, projected slides, signs, and the visibility of the technical aspects of the production.

By the late 1920s, Brecht had arrived at his important dramatic concept of *Verfremdung*, or alienation (literally, "making strange"). *Verfremdung* is made possible in a play by the *Verfremdungeffekt* or V-effect: the means whereby an effect of estrangement is accomplished onstage. The object of the V-effect is to show things in a new and unfamiliar manner so the audience will critically consider something that had heretofore been taken for granted. "To see one's mother," notes Brecht, "as a man's wife one needs a V-effect; this is provided, for example, when one acquires a stepfather." The V-effect is a question of detachment, of reorientation, and it is a key structural device in the plays and production techniques of Brecht.

Brecht worked on his dramatic theories for nearly thirty years, including them in notes and prefaces to the plays and expounding them in brief essays. In 1948 he published his major theoretical work on the theatre, *Kleines Organon für das Theater* (A Short Organum for the Theatre). This beautifully conceived study, modeled on the *Poetics* of Aristotle, was written shortly before he returned to Germany. Stressing the need for a new style of presentation in the theatre, the *Short Organum* discusses what this new style will mean to the people of the theatre. It is an important aid in understanding the intellectual foundations of Brecht's plays.

Brechtian Acting

Much of the burden of making a success of Brechtian production methods falls on the actor, and for the actor Brecht proposed a new, anti-Stanislavskian approach. At the center of Brechtian acting is the principle of *der Zeigende gezeigt wird*—the showing itself must be shown. The actor is not to express feeling but to *gestus*, to show attitudes. Brechtian acting is acting in quotation marks. The actor narrates the actions of a character rather than trying to impersonate the character. The character shown and the actor showing remain differentiated, and the actor retains the right to comment on the actions of the character being shown.

Since Brecht was in conflict with the illusionistic stage and did not want the audience to identify with the characters onstage, he was strongly opposed to an actor's identifying with a role during performance. The actor must not only understand the character but also suggest to the audience that the character's action was not the only course possible. "The actor must be able," comments Brecht, "to suggest at suitable moments apart from what he does, something else, what he does not do, i.e., he acts in such a manner that one can see the alternative course of action, so that any given action can be seen as only one among a number of variants." The Stanislavskian actor is introverted, the Brechtian extroverted. In the Brechtian approach the investigation of human nature is replaced by studies in human relations.

The basic attitudes in human relations are expressed in the *gestus*, and the *gestus* implies all the outward signs of social relationships. Brecht shifted the

A scene from a 1957 production by the Berliner Ensemble of The Good Person of Setzuan.
(Courtesy of KaiDib Films International, Glendale, Calif.)

emphasis in his plays away from the inner lives of his characters to the way they interact with each other. He wrote dialogues that contain what he considered the proper *gestus*, and through this means he nearly forces his actors to assume his concept of the production. Because of its importance in the composition of the script, the *gestus* governs the work of both actor and director. While this approach is the very heart of a Brecht play, it offers exciting possibilities in all types of theatre. The Brechtian style of acting has not yet made a significant impact in Western theatre, but it should not be lightly dismissed. It may yet become the major approach in the postmodern theatre.

ANTONIN ARTAUD

It is not easy to understand the importance of Antonin Artaud (1896–1948) on the contemporary stage. He was not particularly successful as a poet or playwright, and he spent nearly a third of his life in asylums for the mentally ill. Yet since his death, his influence has continued to grow, and there are many, particularly in Europe, who consider him one of the most important forces in twentieth-century theatre. Artaud left over a million words in his collected works, and it is from these writings that the influence spread to various fields: theatre, literary criticism, psychology, the drug cult, and philosophy. He is one of the true mysteries of contemporary theatre and thought.

Artaud was born in Marseilles in 1896 and had his first serious illness when he was five. At the age of fifteen he started a literary magazine, and in 1915 he began his lifelong drug habit. Invalided out of the French army because of his mental problems, he spent the next four years in mental clinics. He began his acting career in 1920, working with such directors as Lugné-Poë and Charles Dullin. In 1924 he joined the surrealist movement and began acting in films. Two years later he founded the Théâtre Alfred Jarry with Roger Vitrac. During the 1930s he continued to act, direct, and write. His first manifesto on the theatre of cruelty appeared in 1932, and six years later his most famous work on the theatre, *Le Théâtre et son double* (The Theatre and Its Double), was published. That same year he was committed to an asylum for the incurably insane, and he spent the next nine years in various mental institutions. Released in 1946 through the efforts of his friends and admirers, he won a major literary prize the following year for an essay on Van Gogh and gave a disastrous solo performance at the Théâtre du Vieux Colombier. He died of cancer in 1948.

Artaud's theories about the theatre underwent considerable change during his career, but one constant was his belief in the mission of the theatre, in its power to change society. He despised the traditional theatre and wanted to

A photograph of Artaud by his fellow surrealist, the American artist Man Ray.

(Copyright Juliet Man Ray, Man Ray Archives, Paris.)

change it into a religious force. For him the theatre was the double, the representative, "of that great magic active force of which the theatre through its form is the figuration until the time when it becomes its transfiguration." Artaud's theatre would make manifest the cosmic forces through physical means, and these would touch the subconscious energies of the audience. This manifestation of cosmic forces was central to his concept of the theatre of cruelty. As he observed: "We are not free. The heavens can still fall upon our heads. And the theatre exists, in the first place, to teach us that."

The theatre, as discussed in *The Theatre and Its Double*, is essentially a self-defining religious ritual, an assembly of people attempting to establish contact with their own inner being. By reaching these deep emotional forces within, the theatre could change people's basic attitudes and thus transform society. The central artistic element in the Artaudian theatre is the director, who will shape the performance without undue concern about a written script. The actors are to be totally under the control of the director, without individual initiative, and will rely heavily upon gesture and expression. The performance space will not be the traditional theatre. Instead the audience will be seated in the center of a large space and the action will take place on several levels all around them. No scenery will be used, but new, explosive light systems will be created that will, in combination with music, engulf the audience in intense tonal and visual waves.

The influence of Artaud on Western culture has been significant and widespread. "The course of all recent serious theatre in Europe and the Americas," according to critic-philosopher Susan Sontag, "can be said to divide into two periods—before Artaud and after Artaud." Artaud's work has thrown into question the nature of theatre, and no one working the contemporary theatre is untouched by his ideas. Major theatrical artists who are strongly influenced by Artaud's ideas include Jean-Louis Barrault, Roger Blin, Peter Brook, Charles Marowitz, Jerzy Grotowski, Julian Beck, Joseph Chaikin, and Richard Schechner. Outside the theatre, his impact has been acknowledged in music, psychology, and film. Bertolt Brecht is the century's only other theatrical theorist whose importance and profundity rival Artaud's.

EXISTENTIALISM AND ABSURDISM

The Philosophy of Existentialism

Existentialism is concerned with the problems of human existence. Aspects of what was to become the philosophical position known as existentialism appear in the writings of Saint Augustine, Descartes, and Pascal, but the major point of origin was in the work of the Danish philosopher Søren Kierkegaard (1813–1855). He introduced new ideas in relation to the concepts of existence, the role of the individual, decision and choice, fear, and despair. Many of his ideas became pivotal in the thinking of such contemporary existentialists as Martin Buber, Karl Jaspers, Martin Heidegger, Paul Tillich, and Jean-Paul Sartre.

Existentialists are especially intrigued by the question of how one exists as a true human being. Because of an intense interest in personal freedom, there is a strong distrust among these thinkers for philosophical systems that deal in abstract and universal rules. Freedom is ultimately an act of individual will and, as such, is not governed by the collective notions of universal rules. This interest in the problems of individual freedom explains why so much existential writing is in the form of the drama, novel, or short story. These literary forms allow a close analysis of a unique human situation. In these works, individual consciousness, choice, and freedom are central themes.

The existential person is committed to life and aware of the burdensome responsibility of freedom. Philosopher-playwright Sartre sees each individual as the arbitrator of all values, responsible for being the supreme legislator for his or her total destiny. Yet closely linked to the ideas of freedom and responsibility are the notions of abandonment, anguish, and fear. Our freedom has also cut us off from the rest of humanity. Thus existence is viewed as a state filled with anxiety and frustration, a lonely journey to the nothingness of the grave. With this point of view, it is easy to see why existentialist writers are attracted to the absurdity of life. This interest in absurdity is a common element in the work of such playwrights as Genet, Beckett, Pinter, Albee, and Ionesco.

Appearing as it did after the incredible human slaughter and destruction of the Second World War, there is little joy in existentialistic literature. Many critics consider existentialism an unbalanced view of human existence. The protests of the existentialists appear too extreme and too willing to deny any relevance to abstract truths concerning humanity. Their emphasis on inwardness, subjectivity, and absolute individual freedom has made the concept of social life philosophically indefensible. Since the theatre has always relied on the depiction of some aspect of social life, the existentialistic approach taken by leading playwrights has had a major impact on Western theatre.

Absurdism

The term "theatre of the absurd" was coined by critic Martin Esslin for the title of a book he wrote in 1961. He used the term as a working hypothesis "to make certain fundamental traits, which seem to be present in the works of a number of dramatists, accessible to discussion by tracing the features they have in common. That and no more." It should be understood that there is no organized movement or school of playwrights called the theatre of the absurd. Such a school would imply a common philosophical or artistic foundation among these playwrights and no such foundation exists. All the playwrights considered absurdists have been influenced in a direct or indirect fashion by existentialism, but it cannot be claimed that they share a common philosophical approach. Their most obvious common link is a belief in nonconventional theatre and an intrinsic understanding of theatre's roots.

The plays of the absurdists are highly subjective and not concerned with conveying information or telling a story. Situations rather than sequential events are important, and the language of the plays tends to be based on patterns of images rather than discussions. Characters talk at each other but not to each other since no one really listens. These plays are not dramatic in the conventional sense since the traditional types of conflicts are absent, but they do weave complex image patterns that, like a musical composition, make a total impression in the viewer's mind.

The influence of film comedy and the human delight in verbal nonsense are important elements in the plays of the absurdists. There is a nightmarish quality in early film comedy that is reflected in these plays, for both depict worlds in constant but purposeless motion. Eugène Ionesco once remarked that the French surrealists had "nourished" him but that the three greatest influences on his work had been Chico, Harpo, and Groucho Marx. Sigmund Freud has noted that our delight in nonsense has its roots in the freedom we enjoy when we abandon the straitjacket of logic. The verbal nonsense in an absurdist play helps destroy the primary role language holds in the conventional theatre. With the logic of language called into question, the absurdists are free to build a world where the rules are constantly changing, a world of free associations, inverted logic, and feigned or real madness. A world, they would maintain, in which we truly exist.

MAJOR PLAYWRIGHTS

Jean-Paul Sartre and Albert Camus

As one of the major existential philosophers in Europe, Jean-Paul Sartre (1905–1980) was expected to imbue his plays with strong philosophical statements. What surprised many critics was that they were also strong dramas. Although he wrote less than a dozen works for the stage, Sartre's stature as a philosopher, novelist, essayist, and critic assured his plays of serious and widespread attention. They represented the first exposure for many audience members to existentialism's dark and lonely message.

Sartre received his formal education in the finest schools in France and obtained his first academic appointment in 1928 as a professor of philosophy. His first philosophical and literary works were published in the late 1930s. During the German occupation of France in World War II, he was active in the Resistance and published an underground newspaper. His first plays, *Les Mouches* (The Flies, 1943) and *Huis clos* (No Exit, 1944), were produced in German-controlled Paris. During the next fifteen years he achieved his greatest popularity as a literary figure and wrote the rest of his plays. In 1964 Sartre was awarded the Nobel Prize for Literature, which he refused on the grounds that such awards transformed a writer into an institution.

In addition to *The Flies* and *No Exit*, Sartre's other major plays are *Les Mains sales* (Dirty Hands, 1948), *Le Diable et le bon dieu* (The Devil and the Good Lord, 1951), and *Les Séquestres d'Altona* (The Condemned of Altona, 1959). Three Sartrean themes link these plays: human solitude in the world, the freedom of will that governs this solitude, and the destroying responsibility of this freedom. The tension between the solitude or alienation of the individual and the individual's responsibilities in the world creates the anguish or absurdity that is at the center of these plays. Sartre's plays hold up for examination the excuses and routines we use to attempt to remove our alienated state and to avoid our personal responsibilities of will. Variations of these existential themes reappear in the plays of Sartre's sometimes friend and colleague, Albert Camus.

Born in French Algeria, Albert Camus (1913–1960) began his involvement with the stage in 1934 when he organized an amateur theatre group. In 1935 he received his degree in philosophy from the University of Algiers, and two years later he was working as an actor and director in Algeria. In occupied Paris he was a member of the Resistance. During the war his second play, *Le Malentendu* (The Misunderstanding, 1944), was produced. His first play, and perhaps his best, *Caligula*, was written in 1938 but not produced until 1945. After the war Camus's novels and essays made him, along with Sartre, the leading literary exponent of existentialism. Between the end of the war and his death in an automobile accident in 1960, Camus wrote seven additional plays. In 1957 he was awarded the Nobel Prize for Literature.

Camus is known primarily as a novelist and philosopher, and his theatrical work is often considered a marginal activity in his career. Yet he was an actor, director, and playwright who was devoted to the theatre. At the time of his death, he was on his way to assume control of a new state-supported experimental theatre. Camus was devoted to the theatre because he believed it to be the highest form of artistic expression. His goal was to re-create a tragic theatre in France after an absence of nearly three hundred years, a contemporary tragic theatre that would capture the anguish of modern humanity. His four major plays, *Caligula*, *Le Malentendu*, *L'Etat de siege* (The State of Siege, 1948) and *Les Justes* (The Just Assassins, 1950), attempt such a tragic theatre. That he failed should not obscure the fact that his efforts were influential on an entire generation of playwrights.

Samuel Beckett

The numerous productions in the mid-1950s of *En attendant Godot* (Waiting for Godot, 1953) brought major critical and popular attention to its author, Samuel Beckett (1906–) and the absurdist theatre. In the over thirty years and twenty plays since *Godot*, Beckett continues to confuse, outrage, amuse, and intrigue critics and audiences alike. He persists at striving at increased miniaturization (*Breath* takes only thirty-five seconds to perform), and he holds in contempt the massive amount of comment on his plays. "My work," Beckett has remarked, "is a matter of fundamental sounds made as fully as possible, and I accept responsibility for nothing else. If people want to have headaches among the overtones, let them."

Born near Dublin, Ireland, in 1906, Beckett received his B.A. and M.A. degrees from Trinity College. While living in Paris in the late 1920s Beckett became the friend and secretary to his fellow Irish expatriate, James Joyce, whose experiments with language strongly influenced him. His first volume of short stories was published in 1934 and his first novel in 1938. After the war Beckett wrote a trio of novels that established his international reputation. He had begun to experiment with dramatic pieces in the early 1930s, but his first play to be produced and published was *Waiting for Godot*. Since that time Beckett has continued to experiment with plays for stage, radio, and television. Some of these plays are without words or onstage actors. In 1969 Beckett was awarded the Nobel Prize for Literature.

The Beckett plays that have received the most productions and attention are his three longer plays: *Waiting for Godot, Fin de partie* (Endgame, 1957), and *Oh les beaux jours* (Happy Days, 1961). *Waiting for Godot* has been called a play in which nothing happens, twice. The setting is a country road and a tree. The script has lines for five characters during two acts. Amid action that is reminiscent of vaudeville, Beckett explores questions of life, death, and existence. The two principal characters endeavor to pass the time as they wait, their activities essentially meaningless, without form, reflective of the formless wait for death that we call life. *Endgame* is a darker play than *Godot*, more "inhuman" according to Beckett. Again there are two principal characters, but here the anguish is not in waiting but in going. It is a painful play about the dying of the last humans. Yet the structure of the play is circular, so the dying is never finished, the endgame never concluded. In *Happy Days* the heroine is

A scene from a production of Waiting for Godot *at the State Theatre, Salzburg.*
(Courtesy of KaiDib Films International, Glendale, Calif.)

buried up to her waist in the first act and then up to her neck in the second. Cheerfully she waits as she returns to the dust, refusing to be dismayed, displaying great courage in the face of the approaching nothingness.

Beckett reduces the theatre to bare essentials and presents enormous challenges to actors and audiences alike. His plays, particularly those written in the last twenty years, form a bridge between staged theatrical and nontheatrical events. As he proceeds to reduce the theatrical to its most basic level or less, such as removing actors from the stage, he creates a new type of theatre. Resolution in this theatre is not on the stage but in the expanded imagination of the audience member. Beckett's theatre may be the ultimate revolt against the conventional theatre, a new theatre filled with silence.

Eugène Ionesco

The originality of the plays of Eugène Ionesco (1912–) rests in their theatricality, in the visualized ideas created by the playwright. The most prolific and produced of the dramatists who are intellectually engaged by the absurdity of life, Ionesco gives his plays comic, even farcical, elements that are absent from the work of most of his contemporaries. Yet the human anguish over death is never far beneath the surface in Ionesco's work. He has said that humans think they should be immortal, thus they are afraid to die. This unwillingness to accept the human condition creates considerable tension in his plays.

Ionesco was born in Romania but spent his youth in France. He returned to his homeland to attend the University of Bucharest, then returned to France in 1938, where he has lived since. While reading a language phrase book he conceived the idea for his first play, *La Cantatrice chauve* (The Bald Soprano, 1950). He considers this work an antiplay, "a criticism of the commonplace, a parody of the old-fashioned theatre." Since 1950 Ionesco has written over thirty plays and established an international reputation as a creator of the unusual.

Ionesco's most creative period was from 1948 to 1960. During this time he wrote his best-known plays: *The Bald Soprano*, *La Leçon* (The Lesson, 1951), *Les Chaises* (The Chairs, 1952), *Tuer sans gages* (The Killer, 1958), *Rhinocéros* (Rhinoceros, 1959) and *Le Roi se meurt* (Exit the King, 1962). All these plays reveal the playwright's desire for the "dislocation and disarticulation of language," and his belief that theatre is an "extreme exaggeration of feelings that disjoints the real." Ionesco's plays are among the best of the postmodern dramas at expressing the lost sense of historical dimension in human endeavors, the missing awareness of progress. Throughout his plays there is the impression that existence is an absurd pattern of eternal repetition.

Jean Genet

The most atypical playwright among this group of dramatists who focus on the absurdity of existence is Jean Genet (1910–). A reformed thief turned author, Genet's world is that of the condemned, the betrayer, the guilty. His plays move the viewer into a hypnotic, sensual atmosphere filled with hatred and violence that is perversely beatific.

An illegitimate child, Genet was placed in a foster home after he was abandoned by his mother. He began to steal at age seven and was sent to a reformatory before his teens. For the next twenty-five years he lived in prison or as a member of the criminal world of Europe. While in prison in the early forties he began to write, and by 1948 he was the author of three published novels, two plays, and a book of poetry. He gained reprieve from a life sentence for larceny through the intervention of some of the most prominent writers in France. He was granted a pardon by the president of France in 1948.

To date Genet's work for the stage consists of five plays: *Haute surveillance* (Deathwatch, 1947), *Les Bonnes* (The Maids, 1947), *Le Balcon* (The Balcony, 1956), *Les Negres* (The Blacks, 1959), and *Les Paravants* (The Screens, 1961). They are all, like the bordello location of the *The Balcony*, houses of illusion. Here the boundaries between reality and fantasy blur or fade, and life is shown to be "an architecture of emptiness and words." Genet's theatre is a ritualistic theatre in the Artaudian sense, yet it is a ritual of darkness, a salvation through hate. This is possible by reflecting on his negative views. These views are like Genet's comments on lies: "Discover the truth in them. Discover what I want to hide."

Harold Pinter and Edward Albee

The complexity of the plays of Harold Pinter (1930–   ), the foremost of the English existentialist playwrights, has resulted in a cottage industry of Pinter criticism, near-frantic attempts to find out what these plays are *really* about. The author of over twenty works for the stage, Pinter has been called one of the most exciting and original dramatists to have emerged since World War II, and his major plays represent perhaps the best example of the postmodern theatre's ability to combine the old and the new.

Born in the East End of London, Pinter entered the Royal Academy of Dramatic Art under a government grant in 1948 but dropped out after two terms. He began his professional acting career in 1950 with various touring companies. Pinter's first play, *The Room*, was produced at Bristol University in 1957. Its entry in a drama festival attracted the attention of a London producer, who took an option on his next play. *The Birthday Party* (1958) received less than enthusiastic reviews from the London critics ("It will be best enjoyed by those who believe that obscurity is its own reward," wrote one reviewer), but Pinter's career as a playwright was launched. Since then he has been active as a playwright, screenwriter, and director.

Of his many plays, Pinter's most familiar are *The Birthday Party*, *The Caretaker* (1960), *The Homecoming* (1965), and *Old Times* (1971). Underlying all of his plays is the question of dominance and subservience and a tone of menace. His plays appear to be in the realistic tradition, but the forces that control the action and dialogue are not far from Beckett or Ionesco. Pinter's plays contain contact with the world the audience believes to be real, and it is this contact that gives them their power. Pinter manages to carefully orchestrate the terrors of the mundane and the emptiness of daily human contact. This dramatic talent he shares to a certain extent with his contemporary, the American playwright Edward Albee.

Edward Albee (1928–   ) grew up in a very affluent family and attended a number of schools before he graduated from Choate. After he was dismissed from Trinity College in Connecticut during his sophomore year, Albee moved to New York in 1950 to pursue a career as a writer. For the next ten years he lived off a trust fund from his grandmother and the income from various odd jobs. His first play, *Zoo Story*, was produced in 1959, and it was soon followed by productions of *The Sandbox* (1960) and *The American Dream* (1961). *Who's Afraid of Virginia Woolf* (1962) won a number of awards, including a Tony and the New York Drama Critics Award. In 1966 he won a Pulitzer Prize for Drama for *A Delicate Balance*, an honor he again received in 1975 for *Seascape*. Albee has written nineteen plays to date; the latest, *Finding the Sun*, was produced in 1983.

During the sixties and seventies, Albee was considered the leading absurdist playwright in the United States. The world depicted in his plays lacks

A scene from the production of Who's Afraid of Virginia Woolf *at the Enchanted Hills Playhouse, Syracuse, Ind.*

(Photograph by Gabriel R. DeLobbe)

compassion; it is a place where cruelty is a form of communication between desperate individuals. The disillusionment that is a major element in existential thought was a late arrival in the United States. But in the second decade after World War II, the materialism and social conventions of the United States began to be questioned. Albee's plays clearly reflect the early stages of a review of the nature of the American myth, and his work has brought the postmodern theatre to the mainstream American stage.

CONCLUSION

The playwrights working under the influence of the existentialistic point of view are attempting to deal with a world they consider absurd and pointless. Their plays reflect a search for a reason for existence in a world of lifeless conventionality. Some of the plays expose or ridicule the artificialities of modern life, and others delve into the loneliness of existence. They are cries for help, sobs of despair, and defiant shouts into the silence. Western civilization has always used the theatre to mirror its hopes, follies, fears, and dreams, but civilization has changed. These dramatists reflect a world that has behind it mass destruction on a scale previously unknown and in front of it nuclear extinction. The universal certainties of past generations are destroyed or in disarray. The traditional mirror of the theatre is broken, and in its frame is nothingness. It is truly a world of the absurd.

30
POSTMODERN THEATRE PRACTICE

It is difficult to define Western theatre style after midcentury. Each decade went through such significant changes that they all almost stand alone as minicultures, with their own theatrical thrusts and reflections, making mainstream trends virtually impossible to chart. Theatre practice throughout these decades reflected the divergent cultural patterns emerging in each of them.

The 1950s saw little experimentation until the very end of the decade. The theatrical consciousness-raising of Artaud, however, fostered a great deal of experimentation in the theatre after 1960. This experimentation took many forms as the varying moods of the postmodern theatrical era evolved: some

This production of Chekhov's Three Sisters *at the Guthrie Theatre, Minn., illustrates a realistic play done in a nontraditional setting.*
(Courtesy of KaiDib Films International, Glendale, Calif.)

passive, some violent, some self-serving, a few selfless. In all cases, however, two trends were clear about the theatre after 1950. One was the virtual explosion of theatrical activity across the Western world, and the other was the artistic eclecticism that explosion fostered.

During this period theatre became decentralized and, to a degree, internationalized. Professional theatre activities expanded to whatever portion of the population could support it, and they became equally diverse in the types of forms presented. The diversification of place and performance types led to greater abstraction and experimentation throughout the period. Yet this artistic explosion has not presented a single, significant new mainstream style. The fragmentation and individualism of the second half of the twentieth century has not been conducive to this type of cohesion.

What did occur was an intensification of the eclecticism of the immediate past and the variations on old themes. If a mainstream still exists, it is a modified form of realism that is less centered on story than on the display of theme and character, which are revealed through psychological introspection. Even in the musical there has been a de-emphasis on story since 1960. The theatre of today is primarily concerned with the production values of the particular piece being presented and in focusing current freedom of artistic choices on that production. It is a theatre that is eclectic and artistically diversified.

THEATRE ARCHITECTURE AND PRODUCTION PRACTICES

Playhouse Forms

The major playhouse form to emerge after midcentury was the full arena. This form was a logical extension of the breaking of the proscenium barrier and the thrust stage, and it simply extended the audience around the back of the production. The common use of this innovation was foreshadowed by Walter Gropius in his 1927 Totaltheatre project for Erwin Piscator. In this theatre Gropius attempted to blend the proscenium, thrust, and arena concepts of staging and audience seating. The primary acting area and the front seating area were mounted on a large revolve so that the relationship between the revolving seating and the permanent seating could change. By rotating the acting area 180 degrees from its thrust position, a full arena with audience seating surrounding the acting area on all sides was created. This theatre was never built, and most extant arena theatres do not have the flexibility Gropius proposed, but the concept did provide an impetus to the full arena form. This form was given a healthy embrace by educational and regional theatres after midcentury. The theatre at the University of Miami (1950) and Arena Stage in Washington, D.C. (1961), serve as good examples of the arena form.

With this development the playhouse of the modern theatre became as eclectic and diverse as the productions it housed. All presentation styles were

The Arena Stage in Washington, D.C., is an example of the postmodern full arena theatre.
(Courtesy of KaiDib Films International, Glendale, Calif.)

possible: proscenium and nonproscenium, thrust, and arena. Some playhouses were flexible enough to accommodate more than one production style, and they, too, were dispersed throughout the Western world. In the United States the off-Broadway and off-off-Broadway movements have spawned a series of small "black box" theatres, essentially open black rooms that are eminently

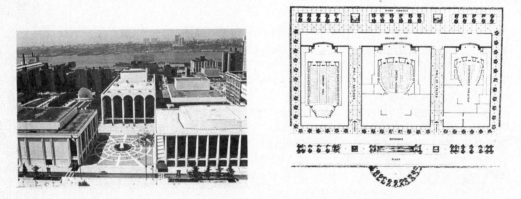

Lincoln Center, New York, and the John F. Kennedy Center for the Performing Arts, Washington, D.C., fully illustrate the postmodern concept of an integrated arts structure.
(Courtesy of KaiDib Films International, Glendale, Calif.)

adaptable to a variety of production styles. After midcentury the larger mainstream theatres generally consisted of a steeply raked auditorium floor and a similar rake to whatever balconies or galleries existed. Some sense of apron or thrust stage is present in these theatres, thereby allowing closer contact between audience and the actor. A fairly unadorned proscenium exists, as well as a general lack of auditorium decor. Considerable space is devoted to the offstage areas—dressing rooms, production storage, and work areas—and front-of-the-house areas for audience comfort and traffic flow.

Scenery

By 1950 the period of basic innovation in most of the production arts was over. What changes occurred were experiments in new combinations of elements and in new methods of implementation. This was certainly true with scenery. Scene painting, generally scorned as the century began, was commonly used with three-dimensional elements in both realistic and nonrealistic settings by the 1960s. In the 1970s plastics were a common material for use in set construction, props, and costumes. Today modern technology has blended with design eclecticism to provide a scenic art that is exciting in concept and implementation.

If there is any general direction to scene design, it is toward the creation of

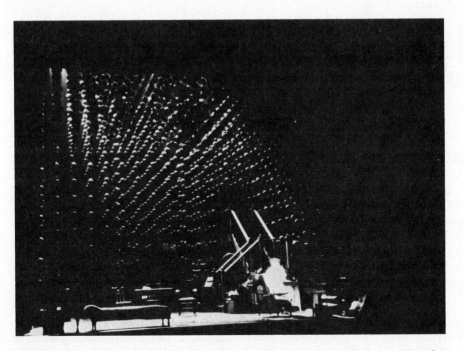

This Josef Svoboda setting illustrates the eclecticism of postmodern scene design. Note the realistic furniture against the nonrealistic scenic elements above.

(Courtesy of KaiDib Films International, Glendale, Calif.)

playing spaces, locales for action, rather than in the creation of environmental reality. To be sure, realistic sets still dominate scenic practice, but the trend is toward simplified or suggested realism for the staging of realistic plays. In today's theatrical eclecticism, realistic plays are often done in front of nonrealistic settings.

An excellent example of the state-of-the-art in scene design is the work of Czechoslovakian architect-designer Josef Svoboda (1920–   ). Svoboda's settings are essentially nonrealistic, yet they possess an active pragmatism that achieves a dynamic and organic unity for the production. They are a combination of light, sound, and sight that blend the honest and obvious use of materials with an intense desire neither to create an illusionistic setting nor engage in Brechtian alienation. His own statements best capture his design aesthetic, and, in turn, the primary aesthetic of the age: "I don't want a static picture, but something that evolves, that has movement, not necessarily physical movement, of course, but a setting that is dynamic, capable of expressing changing relationships, feelings, moods, perhaps only by light, during the course of the action." For most scene designers in the last half of the twentieth century, this credo stands.

Costume

The trend in costuming, as in scene design, has been toward the more theatrical with a simpler and cleaner line than was in common usage at midcentury. Where realistic costuming is necessary, it is fully accurate for the period in which the production is set. Antirealistic costuming adopted an approach involving a mix-and-match of coordinated separates, typical of standard Western dress of the 1970s. Current productions of the avant-garde are usually costumed in whatever suits the production values: rehearsal clothing, leotards, jumpsuits, selected realistic dress, or highly abstracted pieces of cloth that serve as little more than drapes. The choices are unlimited and can go as far as the designer's imagination can carry them.

Acting

Since 1950 acting has followed the dual path of that advocated by Brecht on the one hand and by Stanislavsky on the other. More plays and productions from the 1960s on, however, are demanding more from the actor in terms of physical primacy than in the detailed building of a role in the classic sense. The actor's responsibility in recent years has centered more on the accomplishment of tasks than the emotional and intellectual playing of a role. Improvisation and physicality play a major part in current acting, and for the modern actor versatility between the opposites of the physical and the psychological is a must. Total knowledge of the character is necessary, yet presenting the character to the audience requires a keen technical awareness of the inherent physical and visual values of the production. In many ways the principal artist in the current theatre is, as in the distant past, the actor, who is primarily responsible for delivering the textual and production values to the audience.

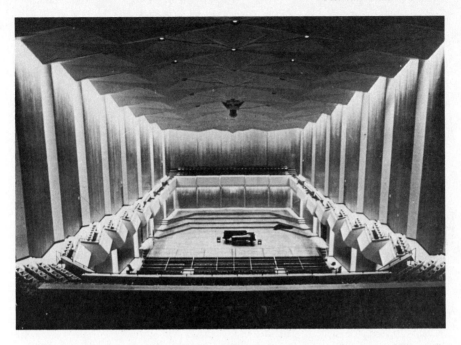

The balcony boxes in the Great Hall of the Krannert Center at the University of Illinois illustrate the blending of traditional elements in postmodern theatre architecture.
(Courtesy of KaiDib Films International, Glendale, Calif.)

Acting today, although generally avoiding a uniform style, is of a high quality. Public expectations have risen to the point where a concept and standard of good acting, largely spread through film, is common. What is expected is precisely that—good acting rather than star actors. The modern theatre audience is in tune with a sense of ensemble that precludes the acceptance of a good actor or two against a sea of mediocrity. Nineteenth-century-type star actors do not, in general, survive on the current stage. This has allowed a concentration on the totality of the theatrical piece and on a gradual maturation of audience expectation in acting. This trend has served the profession well.

THE EXPERIMENTAL THEATRE

Without doubt the most notable and most consistent trend since the 1950s has been the emergence and development of the multitude of theatrical activity known broadly as experimental theatre. This trend is deeply rooted in the changing social consciousness of each decade and reflects a wide variety of production values and styles. These experiments refined the major antirealistic styles and used them in new ways and combinations to express the specific social, political, and aesthetic views of the decades after midcentury. Although more diverse and eclectic than any general movement of its time, the experimental theatre has captured the hopes and frustrations of the human condition in modern times and has influenced the realistic mainstream in profound and significant ways.

Tradition versus Experimentation

Philosophically and aesthetically, the best overview of experimental theatre can be seen when juxtaposed against the tenets of the traditional theatre. The major difference is in the approach to the play script and the form taken for its presentation. Thus a variety of styles is possible within the experimental theatre, while a common production form seems to emerge.

Much of what can be said about the form of the traditional theatre has been explored in earlier chapters. Traditional theatre works from a text or script in creating an organic system of relationships concerning story, character, and place. It involves a series of understandable changes in outlook and situation, all presented within a contained space. It attempts, through whatever style it embraces, the depiction of actual rhythms and patterns of living.

The experimental theatre rejects most of the tenets of the traditional theatre. The script is generally rejected in favor of a scenario or free-form outline of the actions to be undertaken. Thus the emphasis is not on textual analysis and the presentation of a story, but on the presentation of images and events that are activity-oriented and open-ended in terms of the results to be achieved. The actors achieve these results through the accomplishment of tasks rather than the creation of roles, and the scenario is presented to an audience that is expected to participate, not just watch. This participation is assured because most experimental theatre is presented in playhouses that consist of one single space for production and audience alike—sometimes so intertwined that the audience, as a distinct entity, does not exist. Unlike the theme or thesis play, no meaning is preset for the audience and the production. Thus the focus of the production is not single-directed but multifocused on a variety of occurrences. The emphasis in this type of production is on process more than product. How things occur is as important as what occurs.

The tenets of the traditional and experimental theatre present polar opposites. In practice most productions in the second half of the twentieth century lie somewhere in between in terms of the values they present. Actual performances tend toward one direction or the other, and eclectic choice is still the governing principle.

Experimental Theatre Beginnings

The modern experimental theatre has its roots in the works and philosophy of Artaud and the dada and surrealistic experiments of the 1920s. In terms of organized experimental theatre, however, the genre most likely traces its origin to the Living Theatre, founded in 1951 under the direction of Julian Beck (1925–   ) and Judith Malina (1926–   ). The history of the Living Theatre presents a microcosm of the development of the entire spectrum of experimental theatre.

From the outset the Living Theatre exposed the views of its anarchist-pacifist founder, Julian Beck. He was searching for a theatrical form that would "so shake people up, so move them, so cause feeling to be felt," Beck later recalled, "that the steel world of law and order which civilization had forged to protect itself from barbarism would melt." For him the so-called rational world of law and order had been the chief destroyer of human feeling. Beck designed the productions of the Living Theatre not only to entertain but to jar the audience into a new consciousness. The actuality used in these productions would not allow the spectator to separate art from life. Living and acting were one in the same, with the theatre being an active, rather than a reactive, force. Through confrontation the audience was to be affected so deeply that a positive catharsis and direct social action would result.

By the late 1960s there was no separation between life and art for the Living Theatre. Earlier in the decade the company had left the United States for income tax–related reasons, and as its political activism grew (particularly in regard to the Vietnam War), it became even more confrontational in its productions and the personal life-styles of its members. The group's productions led to arrests in several countries during the 1970s. The Living Theatre still performs, but its influence has diminished beside the rising tide of the experimental theatre groups it helped to foster.

Happenings

In 1959 another experimental form emerged that was destined to heavily influence theatrical art and culture during the 1960s. The happening, or multimedia event, came into being when Allan Kaprow, an American artist, coined the term in connection with an exhibition of his that year. The notion of letting art just occur, or happen, was not entirely new, for Artaud had touched on that element in theatre in his writings some twenty years earlier. A happening is a nonstructured, usually mixed-media artistic event that does just what its name implies—it happens without extensive planning and preparation as in the traditional theatre. Highly improvised, often occurring only once, these theatrical events reject the notion that there is a particular place for theatre—it could happen anywhere. Elements of it are close to the *commedia dell'arte*, and it often uses visual and audio elements in addition to the traditional elements of acting and scenery.

As this form of experimental theatre evolved in the 1960s, it moved, according to experimental director Richard Schechner, into three forms. The first of these is the technological happening, essentially an electronic event. In its most sophisticated form, the technological happening combines electronic music and art in an environmental, or natural, setting. The modern theatrical rock concert is a prime example of this type of happening, particularly when held outdoors. There are those who suggest that this form of happening is the ultimate in Artaudian thought and philosophy. The second form of the happening is the free-for-all. This type of happening is roughly sketched out by the author. A group of people (actors) is assembled and given instructions. Another group (audience) is invited to watch and, if it wishes, to participate.

The planned portion of the happening, the scenario, consists primarily of tasks, some timed as in the case of John Cage's *Theatre Piece*. Thus, disassociated images and activities are brought together in one place for a specific duration. Whatever happens, happens. The third type, which Schechner calls a ceremony, combines elements of the first two. In the ceremony there is no audience as such. The participants are simply given a set of instructions and told not to improvise but to do. Kaprow's *Arrivals*, for example, contains the following directions: unused airstrip, tarring cracks on airstrip, painting guidelines on airstrip, cutting grass at airstrip's edge, placing mirrors on airstrip, watching for reflections of planes.

The place of the happening in theatre art is hotly debated. Some argue that the form is not theatre at all, while others contend that it is pure Artaudian theatre and, as such, reflects the state of the late-twentieth-century Western world better than any other theatrical form. This may be decided in another century. For all its shortcomings, the happening has had a decisive influence on all the arts, and on the theatre of the 1960s and 1970s in particular. Certainly the development of environmental theatre owes a great debt to the happening.

Environmental Theatre in the United States

The leading exponent of the experimental form known as environmental theatre is American director-teacher Richard Schechner (1934–   ). In 1968 he sought to codify the form in a *Tulane Drama Review* article that set forth six "axioms" for environmental theatre. This type of theatre makes no distinction between performance space and audience space. Old performance barriers, like the proscenium arch, are seen as artificial. A second general tenet of environmental theatre is that text is less important than production values, and it can be reworked at will to achieve the desired dramatic aims. Schechner's theatre exists, in his view, on a continuum with actual life on one end and art on the other. Placed along this continuum from life to art are public events and demonstrations, happenings, environmental theatre, and traditional theatre. These are seen as "competing independent systems within the same aesthetic frame." The text only matters in the last two, and the closer the form is to the middle of the continuuum, the more legitimate it is for textual alteration. Environmental theatre is a series of related transactions, the primary ones being the interaction among performers, among members of the audience, and between performers and audience members. Secondary interactions have to do with the interface between and among the production elements and the performers and audience. The final interaction takes place between the entire production and the space, either created or "found," in which the production takes place. The single focus of the traditional theatre is expanded to include multifocus, such as in a three-ring circus, and localfocus, where only a few members of the audience can witness the event at a time. These additional reality planes contribute significantly to the environmental nature of this form of theatre.

The main vehicle for the practice of environmental theatre was the Performance Group, which Schechner established in 1967. Its early productions remain its most famous, for it was through these that the hallmark of the group was established: *Dionysus in 69* (1968), *Makbeth* (1969), and *Commune* (1970). The group continues as the Wooster Group, but Schechner is no longer associated with it. Located on Wooster Street in New York City, the group continues to experiment with what can be done with an empty space, no theatrical preconceptions, and a general disregard for convention.

Schechner's group was not the only one to practice environmental theatre. In 1963, German sculptor Peter Schumann (1934–) established the Bread and Puppet Theater in New York, where he engaged in the practice of sharing bread with the audience, thus part of the name. The other part of the name came from the use of giant puppets, some as tall as fifteen feet, with more conventional masked actors. Schumann's theatre does not have the Living Theatre's flavor of political protest, but he attacks naturalism and the dehumanization that contemporary urban life imposes upon people. The performances are quite simple, almost childlike. Performances vary in time from minutes to hours, and are local or multifocused. Visual production elements are dominant over any textual considerations, and the audience members are more participants, if somewhat passive, than mere watchers. Above all, Schumann wants the audience to respond emotionally to forces that uplift the human spirit and

Characters from the Bread and Puppet Theater.

(Photograph by Don Whipple, used courtesy of the Bread and Puppet Theater, Glover, Vt.)

to strike down those that are dehumanizing. Since 1970, the theatre has been based in Glover, Vermont, where large open-air performances are most commonly done, and the Bread and Puppet Museum has been established.

European Experiments

Europe also had its experimental counterparts. The first environmental theatre group to gain wide recognition was the Polish Laboratory Theater, established by Jerzy Grotowski (1933–). Of all the experiments in environmental theatre, this group enjoyed the widest reputation outside the United States. Originally founded in Opole in 1959, the Laboratory Theater was concerned primarily with two artistic objectives. Grotowski believed that most of the production elements of theatre, the scenery, lights, and so on, were unnecessary intrusions into the life of the theatre, and that live theatre had borrowed too heavily from other media, particularly film and television. All these elements had to be eliminated so that an essential or "poor" theatre could be created. The second of Grotowski's concerns was the theatrical relationship between the actor and the audience, which he believed was the essence of theatrical art. For Grotowski this relationship had to be open and honest. Every measure to integrate the audience, physically and emotionally, with the actors was taken. A single space for the performance and

A scene from Apocalypsis cum Figuris *at Grotowski's Actor's Institute/Laboratory Theatre.*

(Courtesy of KaiDib Films International, Glendale, Calif.)

audience is established for each production, much along the lines of the "black box" concept. In this space Grotowski's actors work and interact with the audience. The actors are actors, not characters, for Grotowski believes that the actor must create all. Consequently actors do not change costume or use external trappings to alter character mood or change characters, since this is all technically generated by the actor. Acting style is based on external control, much in the vein of Meyerhold, an emphasis on body and voice control being paramount. Texts are cut and rearranged at will to suit the performance aims and to get at the essential actor-audience relationship and interaction.

The Polish Laboratory Theater moved in 1965 to Wroclaw, where it continued operation until 1970. At that time Grotowski realized that his initial experiment had run its course and that a new direction had to be charted. That new direction took on an educational theatre aspect in that Grotowski stopped active production and concentrated more on researching and discussing the origins of theatre. His work continues.

There are many theatrical experiments throughout Europe, but the one that seems to have had the most impact in terms of Western theatre direction is that of the Théâtre National Populaire in France and the work of Roger Planchon (1931–   ). Planchon's work consists primarily of theatrical collages that make a great use of film. These collages, Planchon claims, make the productions successful for the broadest spectrum of people. Planchon is heavily influenced by Brecht's concepts and implementations. Through the use of projections and

Jerzy Grotowski (left) and Peter Brook, two major artists of the postmodern theatre.
(Courtesy of KaiDib Films International, Glendale, Calif.)

many of the scenic qualities of the environmental theatre, Planchon has brought this fresh approach to classic as well as contemporary works. All his work has had a strong orientation toward the mass audience. He and the other directors at the Théâtre National Populaire have been greatly aided in their aims by the director of scenography, Jacques Le Marquet (1927–). His designs have been in the general style of Svoboda, although distinctly his own, and his blendings of realistic elements with abstract stylization have been most successful.

In England, the most widely recognized and successful experimentalist has been Peter Brook (1925–). The genius of Brook, and his lesson for other late-twentieth-century practitioners, is in the eclectic use of experimental elements rather than in innovation. Brook has alternately worked with contemporary and classic productions done in a variety of techniques, including Artaud's theatre of cruelty, Meyerhold's biomechanics, Grotowski's poor theatre, Brecht's alienation effect, and selected elements from the major departures from realism. The magic of Brook is in the creative blend of these elements while giving full due to the text. For *A Midsummer Night's Dream* (1970), for example, he blended many elements to give the text more immediacy through a completely white performance space with a circus atmosphere created by costuming and set pieces. Because of this unique eclecticism, Brook remains one of the most respected directors of our time. He published his theories of the theatre in a single work, *The Empty Space* (1968), and since the early 1970s has continued his eclectic experiments in Paris at the International Center for Theater Research.

A scene from Peter Brook's 1970 landmark production of A Midsummer Night's Dream.
(Courtesy of KaiDib Films International, Glendale, Calif.)

Musical Theatre Experiments

After the early 1960s, the musical was affected by some of the same forces that had been so active in the experimental theatre. Broadly speaking, these forces contributed to the gradual shift of the musical from the tightly integrated story-oriented format to an emphasis on visual production values and technical effects. The "concept" musical has replaced the book musical as the state-of-the-art in that genre, meaning that the idea for the production has transcended the story as the primary motivating force. This radical change did not happen overnight.

Glimmers of the change in the musical began to surface with Richard Rodgers's *No Strings* (1962). Although it still possessed a story emphasis and developed characters, the scenery was minimal and abstract, and the orchestra, without strings, was located onstage and interacted with the production. At one point, the trombone player loses his slide, it glides into the acting area, is picked by one of the characters and returned to him, all without skipping a beat in the production rhythm. By the late 1960s more theatrical experimentation had entered the musical format. *Hair* (1968), *Jesus Christ Superstar* (1971), and *Pippin* (1972) brought overtly rock elements to the musical, but that trend failed to enter the mainstream after the rock musical craze ended. The 1970s saw increased experimentation with a variety of mixed forms in the musical theatre, including elements of the revue, a new emphasis on dance as a production element, a number of Brechtian and Artaudian influences, and an active borrowing of elements of the past. None of these has created a new mainstream, but all contributed to the continued development of the musical toward the concept approach. In such shows as *Company* (1970), *A Chorus Line* (1975), *Dancin'* (1978), and *Cats* (1982), the elements of the revue, emphasis on dance, and the increased use of production aspects can be seen. The blending of past theatre forms with the concepts of Brecht and Artaud are best realized in *Sweeney Todd* (1979). Combining elements of opera with nineteenth-century melodrama, epic theatre staging, and audience confrontation, the musical presents flashes of developed characters within a well-designed story. More than any other recent musical, it shows the eclecticism that may be necessary in establishing a new musical mainstream.

CONCLUSION: THE DIVERSIFICATION OF THE POSTMODERN THEATRE

The practice of theatre today is tremendously diverse, not only in production style and form, but in its spread throughout the Western world. No one country or location within a country can claim a monopoly on theatre practice, although the organization of such practice varies radically from country to country. That variance has a lot to do with the relative amount of commercialization versus state support that any country's theatrical activity receives.

The United States

Of all theatrical activity in the Western world, the American theatre is the most commercially oriented. This stems from a long tradition of artistic self-sufficiency and a general belief that the arts are subject to the same free enterprise system as business. Unfortunately, this attitude generates little fundamental experimentation since playing to popular taste often involves other considerations. Broadway, for example, caters to relatively safe revivals, musicals, British imports, and well-established popular playwrights, such as Neil Simon (1927–   ).

By midcentury theatre practitioners, sufficiently concerned that the commercial orientation was stifling serious experimentation, created the theatrical area called off-Broadway. Dedicated to producing shows that were more experimental and less commercially oriented, the off-Broadway theatres fostered new playwrights, such as Edward Albee and Lanford Wilson (1934–   ), and provided a showcase for new acting talent. Unlike Broadway, whose theatres are generally pre-1927 proscenium structures, the off-Broadway theatres seat fewer than three hundred people and are generally of the thrust or arena stage type. Off-Broadway is a fully professional endeavor, however, and as production costs rise, experimentation declines. These theatres are still far more experimental than Broadway, but the mantle of major experimentation has passed to its successor, off-off-Broadway.

The off-off-Broadway movement dates from the 1960s and remains the place where the most experimental work is done in New York theatre. Primarily dedicated to introducing new talent to the American theatre, the movement got its start from producer Ellen Stewart, who established the Cafe LaMama in 1961. The Cafe LaMama organization was of tremendous importance because its tours spread the gospel of American experimental theatre throughout Europe, and because it showcased new playwrights in the United States, such as John Guare, Sam Shepard, and Tom O'Horgan. Of these playwrights, Sam

These two scenes from productions of Garcia Lorca's Yerma *and Sam Shepard's* Operation Sidewinder *at the Vivian Beaumont Theatre, New York, are typical of the eclectic approaches of the postmodern era of theatre.*

(Courtesy of KaiDib Films International, Glendale, Calif.)

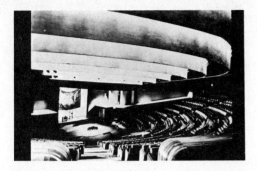 

The Alley Theatre, Houston, Tex., and the Mark Taper Forum, Los Angeles, Calif., are two of the finer examples of the modern, open-stage professional theatre.
(Courtesy of KaiDib Films International, Glendale, Calif.)

Shepard (1943–) has continued to realize his initial promise, winning the Pulitzer Prize in 1979 with his *Buried Child*. Other than Broadway's Harold Prince and David Merrick, the most influential producer in New York City is an inhabitant of off-off-Broadway, Joseph Papp (1921–). In the 1950s Papp presented free Shakespeare to mass audiences in Central Park and in the early 1960s toured other productions around New York's various neighborhoods. In 1967 he acquired the Astor Library and converted it into the New York Shakespeare Festival Public Theatre. There with government support he continues to work.

The regional professional theatres, chiefly the LORT (League of Resident Theatres) group, have brought high-quality theatre to the major population centers across America. Here experimentation is freely mixed with tradition, and in many ways these theatres are broadly representative of the mainstream in public theatrical taste. Emerging in the late 1940s, they rapidly expanded in the 1960s and took the place of the dying road business. Among the major regional theatres are the Arena Stage in Washington, D.C., the Tyrone Guthrie Theatre in Minneapolis, Playhouse-in-the-Park in Cincinnati, the Actors Theater of Louisville, the American Conservatory Theatre in San Francisco, and the Mark Taper Forum in Los Angeles. These theatres have been a major outlet for today's theatre practitioners.

The proliferation of theatre in the United States has extended to amateur groups as well as professional ones. Today most colleges and universities offer course and production work in theatre. Schools with major programs provide the training in all areas of the performing arts needed for a professional career. College and university theatres offer the most viable apprenticeship, for those who need it, that the American professional theatre has.

Contemporary European Theatre

The theatre in Europe is as varied and diverse as in the United States, yet there is one major difference—the attitude toward subsidy and the place of theatre within the cultural fabric of society. Government funding for libraries, museums, and theatres in Europe is high in comparison with that of the United States. Both West and East Germany have over two hundred state-supported theatres, for example, while England and France maintain a few each. England's National Theatre and the Royal Shakespeare Company are subsidized organizations, as are France's traditional Comédie Française and experimental Théâtre National Populaire. While running the risk of state interference, these theatres are freer to experiment because the pressures of the box office are less than for those that are commercially oriented.

Commercially oriented theatre does exist in Europe. London has its equivalents to Broadway, off-Broadway, and regional theatre in the theatres of the West End, elsewhere in the city, and in the provinces. In France, where Paris remains the cultural capital of the country, the theatres of the boulevards provide the closest Broadway equivalent. Eastern-bloc countries have no close comparisons to Western commercial theatre owing to a high level of state support.

Whether commercial or state-supported, the theatre in Western Europe and the United States is multifaceted and diverse. It presents a range of eclecticism that is unparalleled in the history of the theatre, delivered through a range of playhouse forms and locations equally unparalleled. While no significant new mainstream has emerged in this portion of the century, the theatre that is practiced has a vitality through its style and physical diversity that makes it one of the most exciting in the history of the stage.

A scene from a postmodern street theatre production in New York.
(Courtesy of KaiDib Films International, Glendale, Calif.)

RETROSPECT

In no period of history has it been more difficult to chart mainstream theatrical directions than that of the last thirty-five years. Much of this has to do with the various directions the decades took in seeking cultural and aesthetic values. Most of the 1950s were characterized by a complacency that favored structured organizational values and stressed behavior according to societal, rather than individual, dictates. Indeed, that decade was the last one in this half of the twentieth century where there was an agreed-upon set of social standards.

The 1960s generally saw individual values as the primary motivation for action. In the early 1960s this individualism was centered on a passive humanitarianism and a rather naive belief that society could, and readily would, change. By the late 1960s this naiveté had given way to social and political change through violence. This attitude in the United States alone fostered political assassinations, civic protest, and strong antiwar feelings.

The humanitarianism of the 1960s turned into a certain degree of narcissism in the 1970s as organized societal values were continually rejected and individual values turned increasingly toward a satisfying of self. Distrust in societal values remained high, and by the late 1970s it appeared that the absurdists were right in their assessment of humanity.

The 1980s in many ways have been the most complex years to evaluate since midcentury. So far the decade has a multiple value consciousness: in some basic areas a replay of the 1950s can be observed; in others, a new humanitarianism transcending self seems to be emerging. The conservatism that swept several countries in the early 1980s was primarily fiscal, and that conservatism has been far less successful in retrenching moral, social, and cultural values. It remains, however, too early to clearly define the cultural patterns of the 1980s.

Besides these trends, several other factors have affected the theatre after midcentury. From the late 1960s to the present there has been a rising distrust of things noble. Genuine heroes are rare today, in life and in drama, and there are those who question the existence of the type at all. When one is encountered, motives are instantly suspect. This role-model deprivation has added to continued skepticism in the 1980s. Since the 1950s Western nations have known prosperity as never before. Despite economic fluctuations, most people today have a material well-being far in excess of their forebears. This has led to an "instant gratification" syndrome, in which few are content to wait for the positive results of some tangible or psychic investment. The return must be immediate and guaranteed. This lack of patience has infected the dramatic literature of today as well as theatre practice.

In the practice of theatre the same forces are present. The age has fostered meteoric rises and declines among playwrights, directors, actors, and, to a lesser extent, technical theatre practitioners. The notion of a detailed apprenticeship leading to long-term success is relatively rare. Today there are many playwrights rather than a few major ones, and the success of most of these has been made from a very small body of work. Many playwrights who showed great promise after their first success have failed to live up to that promise.

For these reasons, and those explored in the preceding two chapters, the theatre of today is truly diverse and eclectic. The experimental theatre that has emerged since 1950 has fundamentally changed the direction of the art through textual restructuring and environmental staging, while providing no basic new single direction. The postmodern theatre is thus fragmented: the mirror by which the past was judged has been broken, and each fragment now represents a separate view of the art. And the mirror did not fragment simply into smaller pieces of the whole. These fragments are as many and varied as the objects in the postmodern age they reflect. Like other competing aspects of society, each claims to be *the* way, creating a situation of equal aesthetics vying for attention. From this confusion a multidirectional theatre has emerged.

If the theatre is generally multidirectional, then just how vital can it possibly remain? In response: one given does not necessarily assure the other. Among the various theatrical performing arts—radio, film, television, and legitimate theatre—the theatre is the only one that utilizes the complete feedback loop of performer to audience and back to performer again. This continues to make for a vitality in the "live" theatre that the others do not possess. That vitality, that special magic of the theatre, shall ensure its continuation, however diffused and eclectic the form of that continuance becomes. Multidirectional? At present, yes. Eclectic? Certainly. Vital? Always.

Date	World History	Theatre History
1950	U.S. begins construction of hydrogen bomb. Chinese troops enter North Korea and U.S. placed in charge of U.N. troops in Korea.	Camus's *Just Assassins*.
1951		Beck and Malina establish Living Theatre group. Sartre's *Devil and the Good Lord*. Ionesco's *The Bald Soprano*.
1952	Queen Elizabeth II assumes English throne.	Ionesco's *The Chairs*.
1953	Death of Stalin; power shift in U.S.S.R.	Beckett's *Waiting for Godot*. Miller's *The Crucible*.
1954	Civil war begins in Algeria. French defeated in Vietnam.	
1955	Republic of South Vietnam established. Polio vaccine invented. Hungarian uprising against Soviet Union control.	Williams's *Cat on a Hot Tin Roof*.
1956		Death of Brecht. Genet's *The Balcony*.
1957	Federal troops enforce integration at Little Rock, Ark., high school. U.S.S.R. places first earth satellite in space.	Camus awarded Noble Prize. Beckett's *Endgame*. Bernstein and Sondheim's *West Side Story*.
1958	De Gaulle becomes president of Fifth French Republic. U.S. troops sent to Lebanon.	Pinter's *The Birthday Party*. Cafe Cino opens; beginning of off-off Broadway.
1959	Castro seizes control of Cuba. St. Lawrence Seaway opened.	Grotowski's Laboratory Theatre established. Ionesco's *Rhinoceros*. Albee's *Zoo Story*. Genet's *The Blacks*.
1960	Lasers invented. Kennedy elected president.	Camus killed in auto accident. Pinter's *The Caretaker*.
1961	Berlin Wall erected. Bay of Pigs invasion of Cuba fails. U.S.S.R. major is first person to orbit the earth.	Albee's *The American Dream*. Beckett's *Happy Days*. Bread and Puppet Theatre established. Cafe LaMama opens.
1962	War between China and India. U.S. naval blockade of Cuba and confrontation with U.S.S.R. Second Vatican Council begins in Rome.	Albee's *Who's Afraid of Virginia Woolf*.
1963	President Kennedy assassinated.	England's National Theatre opens. Guthrie Theatre opens.
1964	North Vietnam attacks U.S. ships in Tonkin Bay. Race riots in several U.S. cities. U.S. bombs North Vietnam.	Weiss's *Marat/Sade*. Shaffer's *Royal Hunt of the Sun*.

(Continued on page 640)

Date	World History	Theatre History
1965	U.S. spacecraft lands on moon. Demonstrations in U.S. against involvement in Vietnam.	Pinter's *The Homecoming.*
1966		Albee's *A Delicate Balance.*
1967	Six-Day War between Israel and Arab nations. Race riots in several U.S. cities.	Performance Group established. Stoppard's *Rosencrantz and Guildenstern Are Dead.*
1968	Uprising in Czechoslavokia. Martin Luther King and Robert Kennedy assassinated. Period of violence begins in Northern Ireland.	Censorship of plays ends in England after 200 years. *Hair.* Kopit's *Indians.* C. Marowitz establishes Open Space.
1969	U.S. astronaut walks on moon.	Beckett awarded Noble Prize.
1970	General strike in France. Student riots in U.S.	Sondheim's *Company.* P. Brook's production of *Midsummer Night's Dream.*
1971	Large-scale bombing of North Vietnam by U.S. U.S.S.R. lands space capsule on Mars.	
1972	Watergate scandal begins. Palestinian guerrillas kill members of Israeli Olympic team.	Schwartz's *Pippin.*
1973	U.S. troops leave Vietnam. Yom Kippur War between Israel and Arab nations. Arab oil embargo against U.S. and Japan.	Sondheim's *A Little Night Music.* S. Shepard's *The Tooth of Crime.* P. Shaffer's *Equus.*
1974	President Nixon resigns over Watergate scandal.	
1975	U.S. and U.S.S.R. spacecrafts link up in space.	M. Bennett's *A Chorus Line.* B. Fosse's *Chicago.* Albee's *Seascape.*

SELECTED READINGS

Barnard, G. C. *Samuel Beckett: A New Approach*. New York: Dodd, Mead, 1979.
A reasonable introduction to Beckett, but a bit inclined to complete answers to puzzling works.

Biber, Pierre. *The Living Theatre*. 2nd ed. New York: Horizon Press, 1972.
A tracing of the philosophy and production methodology of this important experimental theatre.

Brook, Peter. *The Empty Space*. New York: Athenaeum, 1968.
An outstanding contemporary director's views on all facets of the experimental theatre.

Brooks, Peter and Joseph Halpern. *Genet: A Collection of Critical Essays*. Englewood Cliffs, N.J.: Prentice-Hall, 1979.
A fine collection of essays that will introduce Genet and the controversy that surrounds his work.

Cohn, Ruby. *Back to Beckett*. Princeton: Princeton University Press, 1973.
A challenging but rewarding examination of Beckett's novels and plays.

Esslin, Martin. *Antonin Artaud*. New York: Penguin Books, 1977.
A fine and highly readable introduction to Artaud.

——————. *The Theatre of the Absurd*. Rev. ed. Harmondsworth: Penguin Books, 1968.
Although challenged by many other critics, Esslin's observations on the absurdists are still useful to those who are beginning a review of this area of contemporary theatre.

Gale, Steven H. *Butter's Going Up: A Critical Analysis of Harold Pinter's Work*. Durham, N.C.: Duke University Press, 1977.
A fine discussion of Pinter's work up to *Old Times*.

Grotowski, Jerzy. *Toward a Poor Theatre*. New York: Simon & Schuster, 1968.
Grotowski explains the philosophy and aesthetics of his theatre.

Hayman, Ronald. *Eugene Ionesco*. New York: Frederick Ungar, 1976.
A useful examination of a majority of Ionesco's plays.

Hill, Claude. *Bertolt Brecht*. Boston: Twayne Publishers, 1975.
An excellent introductory look at the theatre of Brecht.

Kirby, Michael. *Happenings*. New York: E. P. Dutton, 1965.
An introductory look at this experimental form with production pictures and scenarios.

Leavitt, Dinah Luise. *Feminist Theatre Groups*. Jefferson, N.C.: McFarland and Co., 1980.
A study of U.S. feminist theatre as seen through the history of several Minneapolis groups and four theatres that served as their precursors.

Lesnick, Henry. *Guerilla Street Theatre*. New York: Avon Books, 1973.
This work surveys the specific form of experimental theatre that focuses on the street dweller and rural worker.

Morley, Michael. *Brecht: A Study*. London: Heinemann, 1977.
This work provides the beginning student of Brecht with a useful analysis of the major plays and Brecht's dramatic theories.

Pasolli, Robert. *A Book on the Open Theatre*. Indianapolis: Bobbs-Merrill, 1970.
A survey of the initial development of the Open Theatre through a discussion of the plays it presented.

Schechner, Richard. *Environmental Theatre*. New York: Hawthorn Books, 1973.
A detailed work on the philosophy and production practices of this major form of experimental theatre by its founder.

Sellin, Eric. *The Dramatic Concepts of Antonin Artaud*. Chicago: University of Chicago Press, 1968.
An exciting and detailed study of Artaud's idea on the theatre.

Shank, Theodore. *American Alternative Theatre*. New York: Grove Press, 1982.
A detailed study of the developments and philosophies of experimental theatres in the United States.

Temkine, Raymond. *Grotowski*. New York: Avon Books, 1972.
An interesting look at the initial work of Grotowski and the Polish Laboratory Theater.

Trewin, J. C. *Peter Brook*. London: Macdonald and Co., 1971.
A superlative review of the contributions of this outstanding director to the postmodern theatre.

INDEX